Visit the Student Site for

Understanding World Societies

bedfordstmartins.com/mckayworldunderstanding

FREE Online Study Guide

Get instant feedback on your progress with

- Chapter self-tests
- Key terms review
- Map quizzes
- Timeline activities
- Note-taking outlines
- Chapter study guide steps

FREE History Research and Writing Help

Refine your research skills and find plenty of good sources with

- A database of useful images, maps, documents, and more at *Make History*
- A guide to online sources for history
- Help with writing history papers
- A tool for building a bibliography
- Tips on avoiding plagiarism

Understanding World Societies

A BRIEF HISTORY

Understanding World Societies

A BRIEF HISTORY

VOLUME 1 To 1600

John P. McKay
University of Illinois at Urbana-Champaign

Bennett D. Hill
Late of Georgetown University

John Buckler
Late of University of Illinois at Urbana-Champaign

Patricia Buckley Ebrey
University of Washington

Roger B. Beck
Eastern Illinois University

Clare Haru Crowston
University of Illinois at Urbana-Champaign

Merry E. Wiesner-Hanks
University of Wisconsin–Milwaukee

BEDFORD/ST. MARTIN'S
Boston • New York

FOR BEDFORD/ST. MARTIN'S

Publisher for History: Mary Dougherty
Executive Editor for History: Traci M. Crowell
Director of Development for History: Jane Knetzger
Senior Developmental Editor: Laura Arcari
Production Editor: Katherine Caruana
Senior Production Supervisor: Dennis J. Conroy
Executive Marketing Manager: Jenna Bookin Barry
Editorial Assistant: Victoria Royal
Production Assistant: Elise Keller
Copyeditor: Susan Moore
Indexer: Leoni Z. McVey
Cartography: Mapping Specialists, Ltd.
Photo Researchers: Carole Frohlich and Elisa Gallagher, The Visual Connection Image Research, Inc.
Permissions Manager: Kalina K. Ingham
Senior Art Director: Anna Palchik
Text Designer: Boynton Hue Studio
Cover Designer: Donna Lee Dennison
Cover Art: Serving boy, from the country feast fresco, Persian Palace of Chihil Soutoun (Pavilion of 40 Columns), 16th century, Isfahan, Iran. The Art Archive at Art Resource, NY.
Composition: Jouve
Printing and Binding: RR Donnelley and Sons

President, Bedford/St. Martin's: Denise B. Wydra
Presidents, Macmillan Higher Education: Joan E. Feinberg and Tom Scotty
Director of Marketing: Karen R. Soeltz
Production Director: Susan W. Brown
Associate Production Director: Elise S. Kaiser
Managing Editor: Elizabeth M. Schaaf

Library of Congress Control Number: 2012932453

Manufactured in the United States of America.

7 6 5 4 3 2
f e d c b a

For information, write: Bedford/St. Martin's, 75 Arlington Street, Boston, MA 02116 (617-399-4000)

ISBN 978-1-4576-1867-3 (Combined edition)
ISBN 978-1-4576-1873-4 (Volume 1)
ISBN 978-1-4576-1874-1 (Volume 2)

Preface

Understanding World Societies grew out of many conversations about the teaching, study, and learning of history in the last decade. This book sets out to solve a number of problems that students and instructors face. First, we knew that many instructors wanted a world history text that introduced students to overarching trends and developments but that also re-created the lives of ordinary men and women in appealing human terms. We also recognized that instructors wanted a text that presented cutting-edge scholarship while simultaneously showing that history is a discipline based on interpretation and debate. At the same time, we understood that despite the fact that many students dutifully read their survey texts, they came away overwhelmed and confused about what was most important. We knew too that convenience was important to students, and that having digital choices and cost-saving format options was valuable to today's students. We also came to realize that a growing number of instructors thought that their students needed a brief text, either because instructors were assigning more supplemental reading or because they thought their students would be better able to grasp key concepts given less detail. Finally, many instructors wanted a text that would help students focus as they read, that would keep their interest in the material, and that would encourage students to learn historical thinking skills.

With these issues in mind, we took a hard look at the course from a number of different directions. We reflected on the changes in our own classrooms, reviewed state-of-the-art scholarship on effective teaching, consulted learning experts and instructional designers, and talked to students and instructors about their needs. We looked at how many people are teaching online, and listened to instructors' wish lists for time-saving support materials. The product of these efforts is a textbook designed to address all of these concerns: *Understanding World Societies: A Brief History*. With this book, we offer something new—an abridged world history that focuses on important developments, combined with an innovative design and pedagogy orchestrated to work together to foster students' comprehension and historical thinking. This brief narrative with distinctive pedagogy will help your students grasp important developments and begin to think like historians.

Narrative

We believe the study of world history in a broad and comparative context is an exciting, important, and highly practical pursuit. It is our conviction, based on considerable experience in introducing large numbers of students to world history, that a book reflecting current trends in scholarship can fascinate readers and inspire an enduring interest in the long human experience. Our approach has been twofold.

First, we have made social and cultural history the core elements of our narrative. We seek to re-create the lives of ordinary people in appealing human terms, and also highlight the interplay between men's and women's lived experiences and the ways that men and women reflect on these to create meaning. Second, we have made every effort to strike an effective global and regional balance. Thus we have adopted a comprehensive regional organization with a global perspective that is clear and manageable for students. So for example, students are introduced in depth to East Asia in Chapter 7, while at the same time the chapter highlights the cultural connections that occurred via the Silk Road and the spread of Buddhism. We study all geographical areas while stressing the links among cultures, political units, and economic systems, for it is these connections that have made the world what it is today. We make comparisons and connections across time as well as space, for understanding the unfolding of the human story in time is the central task of history.

In response to the calls for a briefer, less detailed text, in developing *Understanding World Societies*, we shortened the narrative of the parent text, *A History of World Societies*, by 25 percent. We condensed and combined thematically related sections and aimed throughout the text to tighten our exposition while working hard to retain topical balance, up-to-date scholarship, and lively, accessible writing. The result is a brief edition that preserves the narrative flow, balance, and power of the full-length work, and that allows students to better discern overarching trends and connect these with the individuals who animate the past. And in response to the changing needs of instructors and students, we offer a variety of e-book options—including some that make it easy for instructors to customize the book for their unique classroom needs.

Pedagogy and Features

In trying to create a text that would help students grasp key concepts, maintain their interest in reading, and help them develop historical-thinking skills, we then joined this brief narrative with an innovative design and unique pedagogy. *Understanding World Societies'* chapter architecture supports students' reading, helps them to identify key themes and ideas, and shows them how to think like historians. All chapters open with a succinct statement about the main themes and events of the chapter, designed to establish clear learning outcomes. Chapters are organized into three to six main sections, with **section headings crafted as questions** to facilitate active reading and to emphasize that history is an inquiry-based discipline. **Quick review questions** at the end of each major section prompt students to check their comprehension and reflect on what they've read. **Chapter-opening chronologies** underscore the sequence of events, and definitions in the margins highlight **key terms**, providing on-the-page reinforcement and a handy tool for review. **Chapter locators** across the bottom of each two-page spread keep students focused on where they are in the chapter and helps them see how the material they are reading connects to what they have already reviewed and to what is coming next.

We also reconsidered the traditional review that comes at the end of the chapter. Each chapter includes a **"Connections"** conclusion that provides an insightful synthesis of the chapter's main developments and draws connections and comparisons between countries and regions that explain how events relate to larger global processes such as the influence of the Silk Road, the effects of the transatlantic slave trade, and the ramifications of colonialism. Each chapter ends with a three-step **Chapter Study Guide** that encourages students to move beyond a basic knowledge of what happened and moves them toward a deeper synthesis of how events relate to each other. In essence, the chapter-review sections provide the tools to help students develop the skills of historical analysis and interpretation while also helping them to read and think critically. Students can also test their mastery of the reading using the Online Study Guide and via Learning Curve, a game-like interface that helps students test their historical knowledge at their own pace.

We hope that this combination of design and pedagogy will help students to grasp meaning as they read and also model how historians think, how they pose questions, and how they answer those questions with evidence and interpretation.

Other features of the book further reinforce historical thinking, expand upon the narrative, and offer opportunities for classroom discussion and assignments. In our years of teaching world history, we have often noted that students really come alive when they encounter stories about real people in the past. Thus, each chapter includes an **"Individuals in Society"** biographical essay that offers a brief study of an individual or group, informing students about the societies in which they lived. The spotlighting of individuals, both famous and obscure, underscores the book's attention to cultural and intellectual developments and highlights human agency. Biographical essays in *Understanding World Societies* include features on Lord Mengchang, who in the third century B.C.E. rose to rule the Chinese state of Qi; Hürrem of the Ottoman State, a slave concubine and imperial wife who lived in the sixteenth century; and Henry Meiggs, a nineteenth-century speculator who built and lost fortunes in South America.

Each chapter also includes a primary source feature, **"Listening to the Past,"** chosen to extend and illuminate a major historical issue considered in each chapter through the presentation of a single original source or several voices on the subject. Each opens with an introduction and closes with "Questions for Analysis" that invite students to evaluate the evidence as historians would. Selected for their interest and importance, and carefully fitted into their historical context, these sources allow students to observe how history has been shaped by individuals. Documents include sixth-century biographies of Buddhist nuns; Katib Chelebi on the spread and practice of smoking tobacco in the Ottoman Empire; and the Burmese opposition politician Aung San Suu Kyi's 1991 "Freedom from Fear" speech.

Rounding out the book's feature program is the **"Global Trade"** feature, essays that focus on a particular commodity, exploring the world trade, social and economic impact, and cultural influence of that commodity. Each essay is accompanied by a detailed map showing the trade routes of the commodity. Topics range from pottery to slaves, and from oil to arms.

We are particularly proud of the illustrative component of our work—the art and map program. Although this is a brief book, over 300 illustrations, all contemporaneous with the subject matter, reveal to today's visually attuned students how the past speaks in pictures as well as in words. Recognizing students' difficulties with geography, we also offer 100 full-size, full-color maps and 79 spot maps. Each chapter includes a **"Mapping the Past"** activity that helps improve students' geographical literacy and a **"Picturing the Past"** visual activity that gives students valuable skills in reading and interpreting images.

The new directions in format and pedagogy that are the hallmark of *Understanding World Societies* have not changed the central mission of the book since it first appeared in its original format, which is to introduce students to the broad sweep of world history in a fresh yet balanced manner. As we have made changes, large and small, we have always sought to give students and teachers an integrated perspective so that they could pursue—on their own or in the classroom—those historical questions that they find particularly exciting and significant. We hope students would then take the habits of thinking developed in the history classroom with them, for understanding the changes of the past might help them to handle the ever-faster pace of change in today's world.

Acknowledgments

It is a pleasure to thank the many editors who have assisted us over the years, first at Houghton-Mifflin and now at Bedford/St. Martin's. At Bedford/St. Martin's, these include: development editor Laura Arcari; associate editor Robin Soule; editorial assistant Victoria Royal; executive editor Traci Crowell; director of development Jane Knetzger; publisher for history Mary Dougherty; photo researcher Carole Frohlich; text permissions editor Heather Salus; Katherine Caruana, production editor, with the assistance of Elise Keller and the guidance of managing editor Elizabeth Schaaf and assistant managing editor John Amburg. Other key contributors were designer Cia Boynton, copyeditor Susan Moore, proofreaders Anne True and Angela Morrison, indexer Leoni McVey, and cover designer Donna Dennison. We would also like to thank president Denise Wydra and co-president of Macmillan Higher Education Joan E. Feinberg.

Many of our colleagues at the University of Illinois, the University of Washington, the University of Wisconsin-Milwaukee, and Eastern Illinois University continue to provide information and stimulation, often without even knowing it. We thank them for it. The authors also thank the many students they have taught over the years. Their reactions and opinions helped shape this book. Merry Wiesner-Hanks would, as always, also like to thank her husband Neil, without whom work on this project would not be possible. Clare Haru Crowston thanks her husband Ali, and her children Lili, Reza, and Kian, who are a joyous reminder of the vitality of life that we try to showcase in this book. Roger Beck is thankful to Ann for keeping the home fires burning while he was busy writing and to the World History Association for all past, present, and future contributions to his understanding of world history.

Each of us has benefited from the criticism of his or her co-authors, although each of us assumes responsibility for what he or she has written. We'd like to especially thank the founding authors, John P. McKay, Bennett D. Hill, and John Buckler, for their enduring contributions and for their faith in each of us to carry on their legacy.

Brief Contents

Contents

3 The Foundation of Indian Society

4 China's Classical Age

5 The Greek Experience

6 The World of Rome

7 East Asia and the Spread of Buddhism

8 Continuity and Change in Europe and Western Asia

9 The Islamic World
600–1400 208

10 African Societies and Kingdoms
1000 B.C.E.–1500 C.E. 236

11 The Americas

2500 B.C.E.–1500 C.E. 264

12 Cultural Exchange in Central and Southern Asia

to 1400 290

13 States and Cultures in East Asia

14 Europe in the Middle Ages

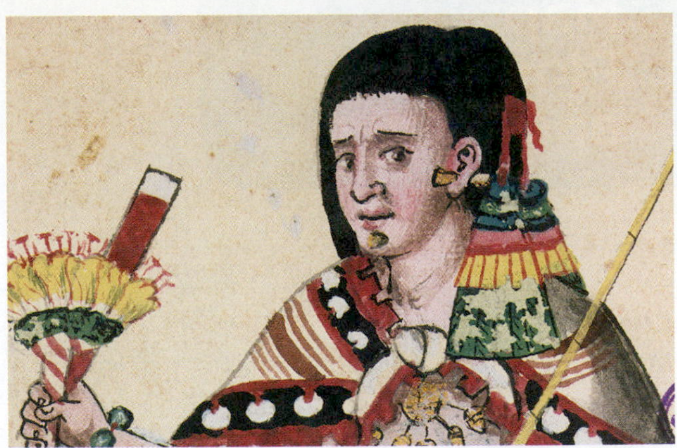

Maps, Figures, and Tables

Maps

Figures and Tables

Special Features

Listening to the Past

Individuals in Society

Global Trade

Versions and Supplements

Adopters of *Understanding World Societies: A Brief History* and their students have access to abundant extra resources, including documents, presentation and testing materials, the acclaimed Bedford Series in History and Culture volumes, and much much more. See below for more information, visit the book's catalog site at **bedfordstmartins.com/mckayworldunderstanding/catalog**, or contact your local Bedford/St. Martin's sales representative.

Get the Right Version for Your Class

To accommodate different course lengths and course budgets, *Understanding World Societies: A Brief History* is available in several different versions and e-book formats, which are available at a substantial discount.

- Combined edition (Chapters 1–34) — available in paperback and e-book formats
- Volume 1: To 1600 (Chapters 1–16) — available in paperback and e-book formats
- Volume 2: Since 1450 (Chapters 16–34) — available in paperback and e-book formats

The online, interactive **Bedford e-Book** can be examined or purchased at a discount at **bedfordstmartins.com/ebooks**. Your students can also purchase *Understanding World Societies* in other popular e-book formats for computers, tablets, and e-readers.

Online Extras for Students

The book's companion site at **bedfordstmartins.com/mckayworldunderstanding** gives students a way to read, write, and study by providing plentiful quizzes and activities, study aids, and history research and writing help.

FREE ***Online Study Guide***. Available at the companion site, this popular resource provides students with quizzes and activities for each chapter, including multiple-choice self-tests that focus on important concepts; flashcards that test students' knowledge of key terms; timeline activities that emphasize causal relationships; and map quizzes intended to strengthen students' geography skills. Instructors can monitor students' progress through an online Quiz Gradebook or receive e-mail updates.

FREE ***Research, Writing, and Anti-plagiarism Advice***. Available at the companion site, Bedford's **History Research and Writing Help** includes the textbook authors' **Suggested Reading** organized by chapter; **History Research and Reference Sources**, with links to history-related databases, indexes, and journals; **More Sources and How to Format a History Paper**, with clear advice on how to integrate primary and secondary sources into research papers and how to cite and format sources correctly; **Build a Bibliography**, a Web-based tool known as The Bedford Bibliographer that generates bibliographies in four commonly used documentation styles; and **Tips on Avoiding Plagiarism**, an online tutorial that reviews the consequences of plagiarism and features exercises to help students practice integrating sources and recognize acceptable summaries.

Resources for Instructors

Bedford/St. Martin's has developed a rich array of teaching resources for this book and for this course. They range from lecture and presentation materials and assessment tools to course management options. Most can be downloaded or ordered at **bedfordstmartins.com/mckayworldunderstanding/catalog**.

HistoryClass for Understanding World Societies, now with LearningCurve. HistoryClass, a Bedford/St. Martin's Online Course Space, puts the online resources available with this textbook in one convenient and completely customizable course space. There you and your students can access an interactive e-book and primary source reader; maps, images, documents, and links; chapter review quizzes, including **LearningCurve**, a game-like adaptive quizzing system that provides students with immediate feedback; interactive multimedia exercises; and research and writing help. In HistoryClass you can get all of our premium content and tools and assign, rearrange, and mix them with your own resources. For more information, visit **yourhistoryclass.com**.

Bedford Coursepack for Blackboard, WebCT, Desire2Learn, Angel, Sakai, or Moodle. We have free content to help you integrate our rich materials into your course management system. Registered instructors can download coursepacks easily and with no strings attached. The coursepack for *Understanding World Societies: A Brief History* includes book-specific content as well as our most popular free resources. Visit **bedfordstmartins.com/coursepacks** to see a demo, find your version, or download your coursepack.

Instructor's Resource Manual. The instructor's manual offers both experienced and first-time instructors tools for preparing lectures and running discussions. It includes chapter review material, teaching strategies, and a guide to chapter-specific supplements available for the text.

Computerized Test Bank. The test bank includes a mix of fresh, carefully crafted multiple-choice, matching, short-answer, and essay questions for each chapter. It also contains the Review, Visual Activity, Map Activity, Individuals in Society, and Listening to the Past questions from the textbook and model answers for each. The questions appear in Microsoft Word format and in easy-to-use test bank software that allows instructors to easily add, edit, re-sequence, and print questions and answers. Instructors can also export questions into a variety of formats, including WebCT and Blackboard.

The Bedford Lecture Kit:* PowerPoint Maps, Images, Lecture Outlines, and i>clicker Content.** Look good and save time with ***The Bedford Lecture Kit. These presentation materials are downloadable individually from the Instructor Resources tab at **bedfordstmartins.com/mckayworldunderstanding/catalog** and are available on ***The Bedford Lecture Kit* Instructor's Resource CD-ROM**. They provide ready-made and fully customizable PowerPoint multimedia presentations that include lecture outlines with embedded maps, figures, and selected images from the textbook and extra background for instructors. Also available are maps and selected images in JPEG and PowerPoint formats; content for i>clicker, a classroom response system, in Microsoft Word and PowerPoint formats; the Instructor's Resource Manual in Microsoft Word format; and outline maps in PDF format for quizzing or handing out. All files are suitable for copying onto transparency acetates.

***Make History*—Free Documents, Maps, Images, and Web Sites.** *Make History* combines the best Web resources with hundreds of maps and images, to make it simple to find the source material you need. Browse the collection of thousands of resources by course or by topic, date, and type. Each item has been carefully chosen and helpfully annotated to make it easy to find exactly what you need. Available at **bedfordstmartins.com/makehistory**.

Videos and Multimedia. A wide assortment of videos and multimedia CD-ROMs on various topics in world history is available to qualified adopters through your Bedford/St. Martin's sales representative.

Package and Save Your Students Money

For information on free packages and discounts up to 50%, visit **bedfordstmartins.com/mckayworldunderstanding/catalog**, or contact your local Bedford/St. Martin's sales representative.

Bedford e-Book. The e-book for this title can be packaged with the print text at a discount.

***Sources of World Societies,* Second Edition.** This two-volume primary source collection provides a rich selection of sources to accompany *Understanding World Societies: A Brief History*. Each chapter features five to six written and visual sources that present history from well-known figures and ordinary individuals alike. A Viewpoints feature highlights two or three sources that address the same topic from different perspectives. Document headnotes and reading and discussion questions promote student understanding. Available free when packaged with the print text.

Sources of World Societies e-Book. The reader is also available as an e-book. When packaged with the print or electronic version of the textbook, it is available for free.

The Bedford Series in History and Culture. More than one hundred titles in this highly praised series combine first-rate scholarship, historical narrative, and important primary documents for undergraduate courses. Each book is brief, inexpensive, and focused on a specific topic or period. For a complete list of titles, visit **bedfordstmartins.com/history/series**. Package discounts are available.

Rand McNally Historical Atlas of the World. This collection of over seventy full-color maps illustrates the eras and civilizations of world history from the emergence of human societies to the present. Available for $3.00 when packaged with the print text.

The Bedford Glossary for World History. This handy supplement for the survey course gives students historically contextualized definitions for hundreds of terms—from *abolitionism* to *Zoroastrianism*—that they will encounter in lectures, reading, and exams. Available free when packaged with the print text.

World History Matters: A Student Guide to World History Online. Based on the popular "World History Matters" Web site produced by the Center for History and New Media, this unique resource, edited by Kristin Lehner (The Johns Hopkins University), Kelly Schrum (George Mason University), and T. Mills Kelly (George Mason University), combines reviews of 150 of the most useful and reliable world history Web sites with an introduction that guides students in locating, evaluating, and correctly citing online sources. Available free when packaged with the print text.

Trade Books. Titles published by sister companies Hill and Wang; Farrar, Straus and Giroux; Henry Holt and Company; St. Martin's Press; Picador; and Palgrave Macmillan are available at a 50% discount when packaged with Bedford/St. Martin's textbooks. For more information, visit **bedfordstmartins.com/tradeup**.

A Pocket Guide to Writing in History. This portable and affordable reference tool by Mary Lynn Rampolla, now also available as a searchable e-book, provides reading, writing, and research advice useful to students in all history courses. Concise yet comprehensive advice on approaching typical history assignments, developing critical reading skills, writing effective history papers, conducting research, using and documenting sources, and avoiding plagiarism—enhanced with practical tips and examples throughout—have made this slim reference a bestseller. Package discounts are available.

A Student's Guide to History. This complete guide to success in any history course provides the practical help students need to be effective. Author Jules Benjamin introduces students to the nature of the discipline, teaches a wide range of skills from preparing for exams to approaching common writing assignments, and explains the research and documentation process with plentiful examples. Package discounts are available.

How to use this book to figure out what's really important.

The **chapter title** tells you the subject of the chapter and identifies the time span that will be covered.

The **chapter introduction** identifies the most important themes, events, and people that will be explored in the chapter.

16

The Acceleration of Global Contact

1450–1600

Before 1500 Europeans were relatively marginal players in a centuries-old trading system that linked Africa, Asia, and Europe. Elite classes everywhere prized Chinese porcelains and silks, while wealthy Chinese wanted ivory and black slaves from East Africa and exotic goods and peacocks from India. African people wanted textiles from India and cowrie shells from the Maldives. Europeans craved spices and silks, but they had few desirable goods to offer their trading partners.

The Indian Ocean was the locus of these desires and commercial exchanges, which sparked competition among Arab, Persian, Turkish, Indian, African, Chinese, and European merchants and adventurers. They fought each other for the trade that brought great wealth. They also jostled with Muslim scholars, Buddhist teachers, and Christian missionaries, who competed for the religious adherence of the peoples of Sumatra, Java, Borneo, and the Philippine Islands.

The European search for better access to Asian trade goods led to a new overseas empire in the Indian Ocean and the accidental discovery of the Western Hemisphere. With this discovery South and North America soon joined an international network of trade centers and political empires, which Europeans came to dominate. The era of globalization had begun, creating new forms of cultural exchange, assimilation, conversion, and resistance. Europeans sought to impose their cultural values on the peoples they encountered while struggling to comprehend them and their societies. The Age of Discovery from 1450 to 1650, as the time of these encounters is known, laid the foundations for the modern world as we know it today.

Mexica Noble This image from the early-seventeenth-century indigenous *Codex Ixtlilxochitl* shows a Mexica noble holding flowers and a tube of tobacco in his right hand. His jewelry and decorated cape emphasize his wealth and social standing. (Codex Ixtlilxochitl, Facsimile edition by ADEVA, Graz, Austria)

406

Memorizing facts and dates for a history class won't get you very far. That's because history isn't just about "facts." It's also about understanding cause and effect and the significance of people, places, and events from the past that still have relevance to your world today. This textbook is designed to help you focus on what's truly significant in the history of world societies and to give you practice in thinking like a historian.

Chapter Preview

- How did trade link the peoples of Africa, Asia, and Europe prior to 1492?
- How and why did Europeans undertake voyages of expansion?
- What was the impact of conquest?
- How did expansion shape values and beliefs in Europe and the Americas?

The **Chapter Preview** lists the questions that open each new section of the chapter and will be addressed in turn on the following pages. You should think about answers to these as you read.

Each section has tools that help you focus on what's important.

The **question in red** asks about the specific topics being discussed in this section. Think about answers to these as you read, and then pause to answer the **quick review question** at the end of each main section.

How did trade link the peoples of Africa, Asia, and Europe prior to 1492?

Historians now recognize that a type of world economy, known as the Afroeurasian trade world, linked the products and people of Europe, Asia, and Africa in the fifteenth century. Prior to 1492, the West was not the dominant player in world trade. Nevertheless, wealthy Europeans were eager consumers of luxury goods from the East, which they received through Venetian and Genoese middlemen.

The Trade World of the Indian Ocean

The Indian Ocean was the center of the Afroeurasian trade world, serving as a crossroads for commercial and cultural exchanges between China, India, the Middle East, Africa, and Europe (Map 16.1). From the seventh through the fourteenth centuries, the volume of this trade steadily increased, declining only during the years of the Black Death.

Merchants congregated in a series of multicultural, cosmopolitan port cities strung around the Indian Ocean. Most of these cities had some form of autonomous self-government, and mutual self-interest had largely limited violence and attempts to monopolize trade. The most developed area of this commercial web was made up of the ports surrounding the South China Sea. In the fifteenth century the port of Malacca became a great commercial entrepôt (AHN-truh-poh), a trading post to which goods were shipped for storage while awaiting redistribution to other places.

The Mongol emperors opened the doors of China to the West, encouraging Europeans to do business there. After the Mongols fell to the Ming Dynasty in 1368, China entered a period of agricultural and commercial expansion, population growth, and urbanization. Historians agree that China had the most advanced economy in the world until at least the start of the eighteenth century.

China also took the lead in exploration, sending Admiral Zheng He's fleet as far west as Egypt. (See "Individuals in Society: Zheng He," page 410.) From 1405 to 1433, each of his seven expeditions involved hundreds of ships and tens of thousands of men. The purpose of the voyages was primarily diplomatic, to enhance China's prestige and seek tribute-paying alliances. The voyages came to a sudden halt after the deaths of Zheng and the emperor who initiated his voyages, probably due to court opposition to their high cost and contact with foreign peoples.

By ending large-scale exploration on China's part, this decision marked a turning point in history. Nonetheless, Zheng He's voyages left a legacy of increased Chinese trading in the South China Sea and Indian Ocean. Following Zheng He's voyages, tens of thousands of Chinese emigrated to the Philippines, where they acquired commercial dominance of the island of Luzon by 1600.

Another center of Indian Ocean trade was India, the crucial link between the Persian Gulf and the Southeast Asian and East Asian trade networks. Trade among ports bordering the Indian Ocean was revived in the Middle Ages by Arab merchants who circumnavigated India on their way to trade in the South China Sea. The need for stopovers led to the establishment of trading posts at Gujarat and on the Malabar coast, where the cities of Calicut and Quilon became thriving commercial centers.

The inhabitants of India's Coromandel coast traditionally looked to Southeast Asia, where they had ancient trading and cultural ties. Hinduism and Buddhism arrived in Southeast Asia from India during the Middle Ages, and a brisk trade between Southeast Asian and Coromandel port cities persisted from that time until the arrival of the Portuguese in the sixteenth century. India i

The **chapter locator** at the bottom of the page puts this section in the context of the chapter as a whole, so you can see how this section relates to what's coming next.

408 **Chapter 16** The Acceleration of Global Contact • 1450–1600

system. Most of the world's pepper was grown in India, and Indian cotton and silk textiles were also highly prized.

Peoples and Cultures of the Indian Ocean

Indian Ocean trade connected peoples from the Malay Peninsula (the southern extremity of the Asian continent), India, China, and East Africa, among whom there was an enormous variety of languages, cultures, and religions. In spite of this diversity, certain sociocultural similarities linked these peoples, especially in Southeast Asia.

For example, by the fifteenth century, inhabitants of what we call Indonesia, Malaysia, the Philippines, and the many islands in between all spoke languages of the Austronesian family, reflecting continuing interactions among them. A common environment led to a diet based on rice, fish, palms, and palm wine. In comparison to India, China, or even Europe after the Black Death, Southeast Asia was sparsely populated. People were concentrated in port cities and in areas of intense rice cultivation.

Another difference between Southeast Asia and India, China, and Europe was the higher status of women in the region. Women took the primary role in planting and harvesting rice, giving them authority and economic power. At marriage, which typically occurred around age twenty, the groom paid the bride (or sometimes her family) a sum of money called **bride wealth**, which remained under her control. This practice was in sharp contrast to the Chinese, Indian, and European dowry, which came under the husband's control. Property was administered jointly, in contrast to the Chinese principle and Indian practice that wives had no say in the disposal of family property. All children, regardless of gender, inherited equally.

Respect for women carried over to the commercial sphere. Women participated in business as partners and independent entrepreneurs, even undertaking long commercial sea voyages. When Portuguese and Dutch men settled in the region and married local women, their wives continued to play important roles in trade and commerce.

In contrast to most parts of the world other than Africa, Southeast Asian peoples had an accepting attitude toward premarital sexual activity, and no premium was placed on virginity at marriage. Divorce carried no social stigma, and it was easy if a pair proved incompatible. Either the woman or the man could initiate a divorce, and common property and children were divided.

Chapter Chronology

1450–1650	Age of Discovery
1492	Columbus lands on San Salvador
1494	Treaty of Tordesillas ratified
1518	Atlantic slave trade begins
1519–1521	Spanish conquest of Aztec capital of Tenochtitlán
1533	Pizarro conquers Inca Empire
1571	Spanish found port of Manila in the Philippines
1580	Michel de Montaigne's *Essays* published
1602	Dutch East India Company established

The **Chapter Chronology** shows the sequence of events and underlying developments in the chapter.

bride wealth In early modern Southeast Asia, a sum of money the groom paid the bride or her family at the time of marriage, in contrast to the husband's control of dowry in China, India, and Europe.

Key terms in the margins give you background on important people, ideas, and events. Use these for reference while you read, but also think about which are emphasized and why they matter.

Trade with Africa and the Middle East

On the east coast of Africa, Swahili-speaking city-states engaged in the Indian Ocean trade, exchanging ivory, rhinoceros horn, tortoise shells, copra (dried coconut), and slaves for textiles, spices, cowrie shells, porcelain, and other goods. Peopled by confident and urbane merchants, East African cities were known for their prosperity and culture.

Mansa Musa This detail from the Catalan Atlas of 1375 depicts a king of Mali, Mansa Musa, who was legendary for his wealth in gold. European desires for direct access to the trade in sub-Saharan gold helped inspire Portuguese exploration of the west coast of Africa in the fifteenth century. (Bridgeman-Giraudon/Art Resource, NY)

The Chapter Study Guide provides a process that will build your understanding and your historical skills.

Visit the FREE Online Study Guide to do these steps online and to check how much you've learned.

Chapter 16 **Study Guide**

To do these exercises online, go to bedfordstmartins.com/mckayworldunderstanding.

STEP 1
Identify the key terms and explain their significance.

Step 1

GETTING STARTED

Below are basic terms about this period in global history. Can you identify each term below and explain why it matters?

TERMS	WHO (OR WHAT) AND WHEN	WHY IT MATTERS
bride wealth, p. 409		
caravel, p. 414		
Ptolemy's *Geography*, p. 414		
Treaty of Tordesillas, p. 418		
conquistador, p. 420		
Mexica Empire, p. 420		
Inca Empire, p. 422		
viceroyalties, p. 423		
encomienda system, p. 423		
Columbian exchange, p. 424		

STEP 2
Analyze differences and similarities among ideas, events, people, or societies discussed in the chapter.

Step 2

MOVING BEYOND THE BASICS

The exercise below requires a more advanced understanding of the chapter material. Examine the nature and impact of Spanish exploration and conquest in the Americas by filling in the chart below with descriptions of the motives behind Spanish expansion across the Atlantic. Next, identify key Spanish conquests and discoveries and the institutions of Spanish rule in the Americas. Finally, describe the impact of Spanish conquest in the New World and Europe. When you are finished, consider the following questions: How do the motives you listed help explain the course of Spanish expansion in the New World? Were the ambitions of the men who carried out Spain's conquests always consistent with those of the crown? What intended and unintended consequences resulted from Spanish expansion?

MOTIVES	CONQUESTS AND DISCOVERIES	INSTITUTIONS OF SPANISH RULE	IMPACT IN THE NEW WORLD AND EUROPE

432

Online Study Guide at bedfordstmartins.com/mckayworldunderstanding

Step 3

PUTTING IT ALL TOGETHER

Now that you've reviewed key elements of the chapter, take a step back and try to see the big picture. Remember to use specific examples from the chapter in your answers.

STEP 3
Answer the big-picture questions using specific examples or evidence from the chapter.

THE AFROEURASIAN TRADE WORLD BEFORE COLUMBUS

- Which states were at the center of global trade prior to 1492? Why?
- Why were Europeans at a trading disadvantage prior to 1492? How did geography limit European participation in world trade? What role did Europe's economy and material culture play in this context?

DISCOVERY AND CONQUEST

- In your opinion, what was the most important motive behind European expansion? What evidence can you provide to support your position?

- What was the Columbian exchange? How did it transform both Europe and the Americas?

CHANGING VALUES AND BELIEFS

- How did European expansion give rise to new ideas about race?
- How did expansion complicate Europeans' understanding of themselves and their place in the world?

LOOKING BACK, LOOKING AHEAD

- If Europe was at the periphery of the global trading system prior to 1492, where was it situated by the middle of the sixteenth century? What had changed? What had not?
- What connections can you make between our own experience of globalization in the twenty-first century and the experience of globalization in the sixteenth century? In what ways are the experiences similar? In what ways do they differ?

In Your Own Words Imagine that you must explain Chapter 16 to someone who hasn't read it. What would be the most important points to include and why?

ACTIVE RECITATION
Explain the important points in your own words to make sure you have a firm grasp of the chapter material.

433

Understanding World Societies

A BRIEF HISTORY

1

The Earliest Human Societies

to 2500 B.C.E.

When does history begin? Previous generations of historians generally answered that question with "when writing begins." Thus they started their histories with the earliest known invention of writing, which happened about 3000 B.C.E. in the Tigris and Euphrates River Valleys of Mesopotamia, in what is now Iraq. Anything before that was "prehistory." That focus on only the last five thousand years leaves out most of the human story, however, and today historians no longer see writing as such a sharp dividing line. They explore all eras of the human past with many different types of sources, and some push the beginning of history back to the formation of the universe, when time itself began. This very new conceptualization of "big history" is actually similar in scope to the world's oldest histories, because for thousands and perhaps tens of thousands of years many peoples have narrated histories of their origins that also begin with the creation of the universe.

West African Man Humans began to portray themselves on the surfaces of places where they lived and traveled as early as 50,000 B.C.E. This rock painting from the region of Niger in Africa shows a person, perhaps a shaman, wearing a large headdress. (© David Coulson/Robert Estall Agency UK)

Exploring the entire human past means beginning in Africa, where millions of years ago humans evolved from a primate ancestor. They migrated out of Africa in several waves, eventually spreading across much of the earth. Their tools were initially multipurpose sharpened stones and sticks, but gradually they invented more specialized tools that enabled them to obtain food more easily, make clothing, build shelters, and decorate their surroundings. Environmental changes, such as the advance and retreat of the glaciers, shaped life dramatically and may have led to the most significant change in all of human history, the domestication of plants and animals.

Chapter Preview

- How did humans evolve, and where did they migrate?
- What were the key features of Paleolithic society?
- How did plant and animal domestication transform human society?
- How did Neolithic societies change over time?

How did humans evolve, and where did they migrate?

Drawing on a variety of techniques and disciplines, scholars have examined early human evolution, traced the expansion of the human brain, and studied migration out of Africa and across the planet. Combined with spoken language, that larger brain enabled humans to adapt to many different environments and to be flexible in their responses to new challenges.

Understanding the Early Human Past

In their natural state, members of a species resemble one another, but over time they can become increasingly dissimilar. (Think of Chihuahuas and Great Danes, both members of the same species.) Ever since humans began shaping the world around them, this process has often been the result of human action. But in the long era before humans, the increasing dissimilarity resulted, in the opinion of most scientists, from the process of natural selection. Small variations within individuals in one species allowed them to acquire more food and better living conditions and made them more successful in breeding, thus passing their genetic material to the next generation. When a number of individuals within a species became distinct enough that they could no longer interbreed successfully with others, they became a new species. Species also become extinct, particularly during periods of mass extinctions such as the one that killed the dinosaurs about 65 million years ago.

Scientists have associated humans with Primates since the eighteenth century, the period in which the biological classification system based on kingdom, order, family, genus, and species was developed. According to this system, humans were in the animal kingdom, the order of Primates, the family Hominidae, and the genus *Homo*. Like all classifications, this was originally based on externally visible phenomena: humans were placed in the Primates order because, like other primates, they have hands that can grasp, eyes facing forward to allow better depth perception, and relatively large brains; they were placed in the **hominid** family along with chimpanzees, gorillas, and orangutans because they shared even more features with these great apes. More recently, these classifications (along with many others) have been supported by genetic evidence, particularly that provided by DNA, the basic building block of life. Over 98 percent of human DNA is the same as that of chimpanzees, which indicates to most scientists that humans and chimpanzees share a common ancestor. That common ancestor probably lived between 5 million and 7 million years ago.

hominids Members of the family Hominidae that contains humans, chimpanzees, gorillas, and orangutans.

Physical remains were the earliest type of evidence studied to learn about the distant human past, and scholars used them to develop another system of classification, one that distinguished between periods of time rather than types of living creatures. They gave labels to eras according to the primary materials out of which tools that survived were made. Thus the earliest human era became the Stone Age, the next era the Bronze Age, and the next the Iron Age. They further divided the Stone Age into the Old Stone Age, or **Paleolithic era**, during which people used stone, bone, and other natural products to make tools and gained food largely by **foraging**—that is, by gathering plant products, trapping or catching small animals and birds, and hunting larger prey. This was followed by the New Stone Age, or **Neolithic era**, which saw the beginning of agricultural and animal domestication. People around the world adopted agriculture at various times, though some never did, but the transition between the Paleolithic and the Neolithic is usually set at about 9000 B.C.E., the point at which agriculture was first developed.

Paleolithic era Period during which humans used tools of stone, bone, and wood and obtained food by gathering and hunting. Roughly 250,000–9,000 B.C.E.

foraging A style of life in which people gain food by gathering plant products, trapping or catching small animals and birds, and hunting larger prey.

Neolithic era Period beginning in 9000 B.C.E. during which humans obtained food by raising crops and animals and continued to use tools primarily of stone, bone, and wood.

Geologists refer to the last twelve thousand years as the Holocene epoch. The entire history of the human species fits within the Holocene and the previous geologic epoch, the Pleistocene (PLIGH-stuh-seen), which began about 2.5 million years ago. The Pleistocene was marked by repeated advances in glaciers and continental ice sheets. Glaciers tied up huge quantities of the earth's water, leading to lower sea levels, making it possible for animals and eventually humans to walk between places that were separated by oceans during interglacial times. Animals and humans were also prevented from migrating to other places by the ice sheets themselves, however, and the colder climate made large areas unfit to live in. Climate thus dramatically shaped human cultures.

Genetic analysis can indicate many things about the human family, and physical remains can provide some evidence about how people lived in the distant past, but the evidence is often difficult to interpret. By themselves, tools and other objects generally do not reveal who made or used them, nor do they indicate what the objects meant to their creators or users. Thus to learn about the early human past, scholars often also study groups of people from more recent times whose technology and way of life offers parallels with those of people in the distant past. They read written reports of conquerors, government officials, and missionaries who encountered groups that lived by foraging, and they directly observe the few remaining groups that maintain a foraging lifestyle today. Such evidence is also problematic, however. Outsiders had their own perspectives, generally regarded those who lived by foraging as inferior, and often misinterpreted what they were seeing. Contemporary foragers are not fully cut off from the modern world, nor is it correct to assume that their way of living has not changed for thousands of years. Thus evidence from more recent groups must be used carefully, but it can provide valuable clues.

Chapter Chronology

ca. 2.5–4 million years ago	*Australopithecus* evolve in Africa
ca. 500,000–2 million years ago	*Homo erectus* evolve and spread out of Africa
ca. 250,000–9000 B.C.E.	Paleolithic era
ca. 250,000 years ago	*Homo sapiens* evolve in Africa
ca. 30,000–150,000 years ago	Neanderthals flourish in Europe and western Asia
ca. 120,000 years ago	*Homo sapiens* migrate out of Africa to Eurasia
ca. 50,000 years ago	Human migration to Australia
ca. 20,000–30,000 years ago	Possible human migration from Asia to the Americas
ca. 25,000 B.C.E.	Earliest evidence of woven cloth and baskets
ca. 15,000 B.C.E.	Earliest evidence of bows and atlatls
ca. 15,000–10,000 B.C.E.	Final retreat of glaciers; humans cross the Bering Strait land bridge to the Americas; megafaunal extinctions
ca. 9000 B.C.E.	Beginning of the Neolithic; horticulture; domestication of sheep and goats
ca. 7000 B.C.E.	Domestication of cattle; plow agriculture
ca. 5500 B.C.E.	Smelting of copper
ca. 4000 B.C.E.	Wheel adapted for use with carts
ca. 3000 B.C.E.	Earliest known invention of writing
ca. 2500 B.C.E.	Bronze technology spreads; beginning of the Bronze Age

A note on dates: This book generally uses **B.C.E.** (Before the Common Era) and **C.E.** (Common Era) when giving dates, a system of chronology based on the Christian calendar and now used widely around the world. Scholars who study the very earliest periods of hominid and human history usually use the phrase "years ago" to date their subjects, as do astrophysicists and geologists; this is often abbreviated as **B.P.** (Before the Present). Because the scale of time covered in Chapter 1 is so vast, a mere 2,000 years does not make much difference, and so **B.C.E.** and "years ago" have similar meaning.

Hominid Evolution

Using many different pieces of evidence from all over the world, archaeologists, paleontologists, and other scholars have developed a view of human evolution whose basic outline is widely shared, though there are disagreements about details. Most primates, including other hominids such as chimpanzees and gorillas, have lived primarily in trees, but at some point a group of hominids in East Africa began to spend more time on the ground, and between 5 million and 7 million years ago they began to walk upright at least some of the time.

Over many generations the skeletal and muscular structure of some hominids evolved to make upright walking easier, and they gradually became fully bipedal. The earliest fully bipedal hominids, whom paleontologists place in the genus *Australopithecus*, lived

Archaeologists at a Dig These researchers at a Native American site in the Boise National Forest in Idaho follow careful procedures to remove objects from the soil and note their location. The soil itself may also yield clues, such as seeds or pollen, about what was growing in the area, allowing better understanding of the people who once lived at the site. (David R. Frazier/Photo Researcher, Inc.)

in southern and eastern Africa between 2.5 million and 4 million years ago. Here they left bones, particularly in the Great Rift Valley that stretches from Ethiopia to Tanzania. Walking upright allowed australopithecines to carry and use tools, which allowed them to survive better and may have also spurred brain development.

Sometime around 2.5 million years ago, one group of australopithecines in East Africa began to make simple tools as well as use them, evolving into a different type of hominid that later paleontologists judged to be the first in the genus *Homo*. Called *Homo habilis* ("handy human"), they made sharpened stone pieces and used them for various tasks. This suggests greater intelligence, and the skeletal remains support this, for *Homo habilis* had a larger brain than did the australopithecines.

About 2 million years ago another species, called *Homo erectus* ("upright human") by most paleontologists, evolved in East Africa. *Homo erectus* had still larger brains—about two-thirds the size of modern human brains—and made tools that were slightly specialized for various tasks, such as handheld axes, cleavers, and scrapers. Archaeological remains indicate that *Homo erectus* lived in larger groups than had earlier hominids and engaged in cooperative gathering, hunting, and food preparation. The evidence also suggests that they were able to make a wider range of sounds than were earlier hominids, so they may have relied more on vocal sounds than on gestures to communicate ideas to one another.

Gradually small groups of *Homo erectus* migrated out of East Africa onto the open plains of central Africa, and from there into northern Africa (Map 1.1). From 1 million to 2 million years ago the earth's climate was in a warming phase, and these hominids ranged still farther, moving into western Asia by as early as 1.8 million years ago, and to China and the island of Java in Indonesia by about 1.5 million years ago. (Sea levels were lower than they are today, and Java could be reached by walking.) *Homo erectus* also walked north, reaching what is now Spain by at least 800,000 years ago and what is now Germany by 500,000 years ago. In each of these places, *Homo erectus* adapted gathering and hunting techniques to the local environment, learning about new sources of plant food and how to best catch local animals. Although the climate was warmer than it is today, central Europe was not balmy, and these hominids may have used fire to provide light

The Great Rift Valley

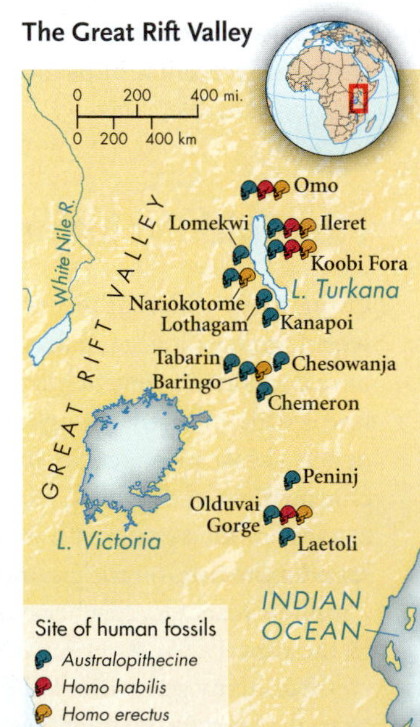

and heat, cook food, and keep away predators. Many lived in the open or in caves, but some built simple shelters, another indication of increasing flexibility and problem solving.

Homo Sapiens, "Thinking Humans"

Homo erectus was remarkably adaptable, but another hominid proved still more so: *Homo sapiens* ("thinking humans"). A few scientists think that *Homo sapiens* evolved from *Homo erectus* in a number of places in Afroeurasia, but the majority think that, like hominid evolution from earlier primates, this occurred only in East Africa beginning 250,000 years ago.

Although there is some debate about where and when *Homo sapiens* emerged, there is little debate about what distinguished these humans from earlier hominids: a bigger brain, in particular a bigger forebrain, the site of conscious thought. The ability to think reflectively allowed for the creation of symbolic language, that is, for language that follows certain rules and that can refer to things or states of being that are not necessarily present. Greater intelligence allowed *Homo sapiens* to better understand and manipulate the world around them, and symbolic language allowed this understanding to be communicated within a group and passed from one generation to the next. Through spoken language *Homo sapiens* began to develop collective explanations for the world around them that we would now call religion, science, and philosophy. Spoken language also enabled *Homo sapiens* to organize socially into larger groups, thus further enhancing their ability to affect the natural world.

The question of why hominids developed ever-larger brains might best be answered by looking at how paleontologists think it happened. As *Homo habilis*, *Homo erectus*, and *Homo sapiens* made and used tools, the individuals whose mental and physical abilities allowed them to do so best were able to obtain more food and were more likely to mate and have children who survived. This created what biologists term selective pressure that favored better tool users, which meant individuals with bigger brains. Thus bigger brains led to better tools, but the challenges of using and inventing better tools also created selective pressure that led to bigger brains.

The same thing may have happened with symbolic language and thought. A slightly bigger brain, or a brain that kept developing rapidly after birth and was capable of learning more, allowed for more complex thought and better language skills. These thinking and speaking skills enabled individuals to better attract mates and fend off rivals, which meant a greater likelihood of passing on the enhanced brain to the next generation. As we know from contemporary research on the brain, learning language promotes the development of specific areas of the brain.

The growth in brain size and complexity may also have been linked to social organization. Individuals who had better social skills were more likely to mate than those who did not, and thus to pass on their genetic material. Social skills were particularly important for females, because the combination of bipedalism and growing brain size led to selective pressure for hominid infants to be born at an even earlier stage in their development than other primate infants. Thus the period when human infants are dependent on others is very long, and mothers with good social networks to assist them were more likely to have infants who survived. Humans are unique in the duration and complexity of their care for children, and cooperative child rearing, along with the development of social skills and the adaptability this encouraged, may have been an impetus to brain growth.

All these factors operated together in processes that promoted bigger and better brains. In the Paleolithic period, *Homo sapiens'* brains invented highly specialized tools made out of a variety of materials. By 25,000 years ago, and perhaps earlier, humans in some parts of the world were weaving cloth and baskets, and by 15,000 years ago they were using

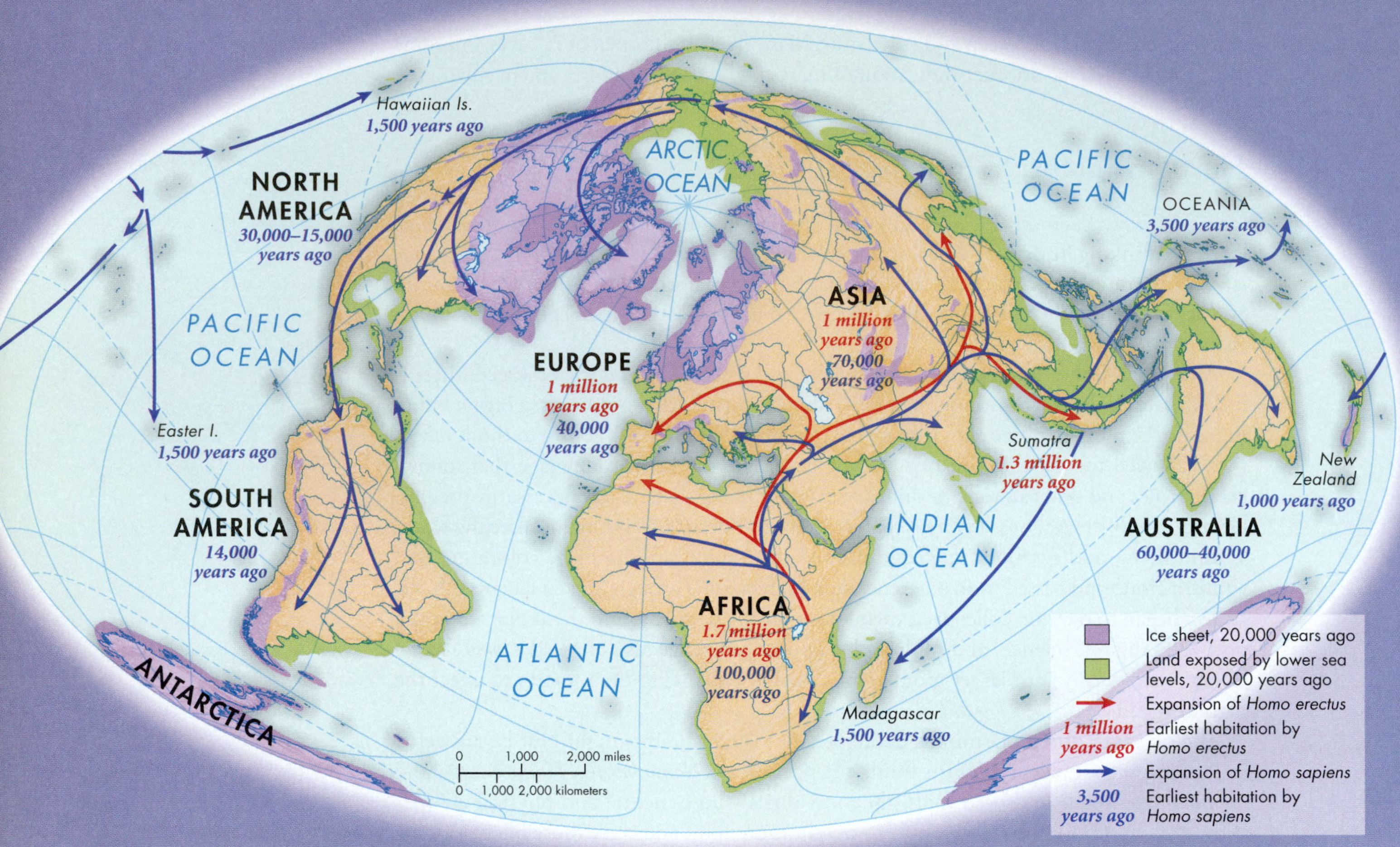

Mapping the Past

Map 1.1 Human Migration in the Paleolithic and Neolithic Eras

ANALYZING THE MAP What were the major similarities with and differences between the migrations of *Homo erectus* and those of *Homo sapiens*? How did environmental factors shape human migration?

CONNECTIONS What types of technology were required for the migration patterns seen here? What do these migration patterns suggest about the social organization of early people?

bows and atlatls (AHT-lah-tuhlz)—notched throwing sticks made of bone, wood, or antler—to launch arrows and barbs with flint points bound to wooden shafts. The archaeological evidence for increasingly sophisticated language and social organization is less direct than that for tool use, but it is hard to imagine how humans could have made the tools they did—or would have chosen to decorate so many of them—without both of these.

Migration and Differentiation

Like *Homo erectus* had earlier, groups of *Homo sapiens* moved. By 200,000 years ago they had begun to spread across Africa, and by 120,000 years ago they had begun to migrate out of Africa to Eurasia (see Map 1.1). They most likely walked along the coasts of India and Southeast Asia, and then migrated inland. At the same time, further small evolutionary changes led to our own subspecies of anatomically modern humans, *Homo sapiens sapiens*. *Homo sapiens sapiens* moved into areas where there were already *Homo erectus* populations, eventually replacing them.

The best-known example of interaction between *Homo erectus* and *Homo sapiens sapiens* is that between Neanderthals and a group of anatomically modern humans called Cro-Magnons. **Neanderthals** lived throughout Europe and western Asia beginning about 150,000 years ago, had brains as large as those of modern humans, and used tools that enabled them to survive in the cold climate of Ice Age central Europe and Russia. They built freestanding houses and decorated objects and themselves. They sometimes buried their dead carefully with tools, animal bones, and perhaps flowers, which suggests that they understood death to have a symbolic meaning. These characteristics led them to be originally categorized as a branch of *Homo sapiens*, but DNA evidence from Neanderthal bones now indicates that they were a separate branch of highly developed *Homo erectus.*

Neanderthals Group of *Homo erectus* with brains as large as those of modern humans that flourished in Europe and western Asia between 150,000 and 30,000 years ago.

Cro-Magnon peoples moved into parts of western Asia where Neanderthals lived by about 70,000 years ago, and into Europe by about 45,000 years ago. The two peoples appear to have lived side by side for millennia, hunting the same types of animals and gathering the same types of plants. In 2010 DNA evidence demonstrated that they also had sex with one another, for between 1 and 4 percent of the DNA in modern humans living outside of Africa likely came from Neanderthals. The last evidence of Neanderthals as a separate species comes from about 30,000 years ago, but it is not clear exactly how they died out. They may have been killed by Cro-Magnon peoples, or they simply may have lost the competition for food as the climate worsened around 30,000 years ago and the glaciers expanded.

Homo erectus migrated great distances, but *Homo sapiens sapiens* made use of greater intelligence and better tool-making capabilities to migrate still farther. They used simple rafts to reach Australia by at least 50,000 years ago and perhaps earlier, and by 35,000 years ago had reached New Guinea. By at least 20,000 years ago humans had walked across the land bridges then linking Siberia and North America at the Bering Strait and had crossed into the Americas. Because by 14,000 years ago humans were already in southern South America, ten thousand miles from the land bridges, many scholars now think that people came to the Americas much earlier. (See Chapter 11 for a longer discussion of this issue.)

Land Bridge Across the Bering Strait, ca. 15,000 B.C.E.

With the melting of glaciers sea levels rose, and parts of the world that had been linked by land bridges, including North America and Asia as well as many parts of Southeast Asia, became separated by water. This cut off migratory paths, but also spurred innovation. Humans designed and built ever more sophisticated boats and learned how to navigate at sea. They sailed to increasingly remote islands, including those in the Pacific, the last parts of the globe to be settled. The western Pacific islands were inhabited by about 2000 B.C.E., Hawai'i by about 500 C.E., and New Zealand by about 1000 C.E. (For more on the settlement of the Pacific islands, see Chapter 12.)

Once humans spread out over much of the globe, groups often became isolated from one another, and people mated only with other members of their own group or those who lived nearby, a practice anthropologists call endogamy. Thus, over thousands of generations, although humans remained one species, *Homo sapiens sapiens* came to develop differences in physical features, including skin and hair color, eye and body shape, and amount of body hair. Language also changed over generations, so that thousands of different languages were eventually spoken. Groups created widely varying cultures and passed them on to their children, further increasing diversity among humans.

Beginning in the eighteenth century, European natural scientists sought to develop a system that would explain human differences at the largest scale. They divided people into very large groups by skin color and other physical characteristics and termed these groups "races," a word that had originally meant lineage. They first differentiated these races by

Quick Review
How did *Homo sapiens* differ from earlier hominids, and why were these differences significant?

continent of origin—Americanus, Europaeus, Asiaticus, and Africanus—and then by somewhat different geographic areas. This meaning of *race* has had a long life, though biologists and anthropologists today do not use it, as it has no scientific meaning or explanatory value. All humans are one species that has less genetic variety than chimpanzees.

What were the key features of Paleolithic society?

Eventually human cultures became widely diverse, but in the Paleolithic period people throughout the world lived in ways that were similar to one another. Archaeological evidence and studies of modern foragers suggest that people lived in small groups of related individuals and moved throughout the landscape in search of food. Although in areas where food resources were especially rich—such as along seacoasts, they built structures and lived more permanently in one place. In the later Paleolithic, people in many parts of the world created art and music, and they developed religious ideas that linked the natural world to a world beyond.

Foraging for Food

Paleolithic peoples have often been called hunter-gatherers. However, most scholars now call them foragers, since most of what they ate were plants, and much of the animal protein in their diet came from foods gathered or scavenged rather than hunted directly: insects, shellfish, small animals and fish caught in traps and nets, and animals killed by other predators. Gathering and hunting probably varied in importance from year to year depending on environmental factors and the decisions of the group.

Paleolithic peoples did hunt large game. Groups working together forced animals over cliffs, threw spears, and, beginning about 15,000 B.C.E., used bows and atlatls to shoot projectiles so that they could stand farther away from their prey while hunting. The final retreat of the glaciers also occurred between 15,000 and 10,000 years ago, and the warming climate was less favorable to the very large mammals that had roamed the open spaces of many parts of the world. Wooly mammoths, mastodons, and wooly rhinos all died out in Eurasia in this **megafaunal extinction**, as did camels, horses, and sloths in the Americas and giant kangaroos and wombats in Australia. In many places, these extinctions occurred just about the time that modern humans appeared, and increasing numbers of scientists think that they were at least in part caused by human hunting.

megafaunal extinction Die-off of large animals in many parts of the world about 15,000–10,000 B.C.E., caused by climate change and perhaps human hunting.

division of labor Differentiation of tasks by gender, age, training, status, or other social distinction.

Most foraging societies that exist today, or did so until recently, have some type of **division of labor** by sex and also by age. Men are more often responsible for hunting, through which they gained prestige as well as meat, and women for gathering plant and animal products. This has led scholars to assume that in Paleolithic society men were also responsible for hunting, and women for gathering. Such a division of labor is not universal, however: in some of the world's foraging cultures, such as the Agta of the Philippines, women hunt large game, and in numerous others women are involved in certain types of hunting. The division of labor during the Paleolithic period may have been somewhat flexible, particularly during periods of scarcity.

Obtaining food was a constant preoccupation, but it was not a constant job. Studies of recent foragers indicate that, other than in times of environmental disasters such as prolonged droughts, people need only about ten to twenty hours a week to gather food and carry out the other tasks needed to survive. Moreover, the diet of foragers is varied and nutritious. Despite the slow pace of life and healthy diet, Paleolithic people often died at young ages from injuries, infections, animal attacks, and interpersonal violence. Mothers and infants died in childbirth, and many children died before they reached adulthood.

Total human population thus grew very slowly during the Paleolithic. Scholars can make rough estimates only, but one of them proposes that there were perhaps 500,000 humans in the world about 30,000 years ago. By about 10,000 years ago this number had grown to 5 million — ten times as many people. This was a significant increase, but it took twenty thousand years. The low population density meant that human impact on the environment was relatively small, although still significant.

Family and Kinship Relationships

Small bands of humans — twenty or thirty people was a standard size for foragers in harsh environments — were scattered across broad areas, but this did not mean that each group lived in isolation. Their travels in search of food brought them into contact with one another, not simply for talking and celebrating, but also for providing opportunities for the exchange of sexual partners, which was essential to group survival. Today we understand that having sexual relations with close relatives is disadvantageous because it creates greater risk of genetic disorders. Earlier societies did not have knowledge of genetics, but most of them developed rules against sexual relations among immediate family members. Thus people needed to seek mates outside their own group, and the bands living in large areas became linked by bonds of kinship. Mating arrangements varied in their permanence, but many groups seem to have developed a somewhat permanent arrangement whereby a man or woman left his or her original group and joined the group of his or her mate — what would later be termed marriage.

Within each band, and within the larger kin groups, individuals had a variety of identities; they were simultaneously fathers, sons, husbands, and brothers, or mothers, daughters, wives, and sisters. Each of these identities was relational (parent to child, sibling to sibling, spouse to spouse), and some of them, especially parent to child, gave one power over others. In many areas, kin groups remained significant power structures for millennia, and in some areas they still have influence over major aspects of life. Paleolithic people were not differentiated by wealth, for in a foraging society accumulating material goods was not advantageous. But they were differentiated by such factors as age, gender, and position in a family, and no doubt by personal qualities such as intelligence, courage, and charisma.

Stereotypical representations of Paleolithic people often portray a society dominated by male hunters. Studies of the relative importance of gathering to hunting, women's participation in hunting, and gender relations among contemporary foraging peoples have led some analysts to turn this stereotype on its head. They see Paleolithic bands as egalitarian groups in which the contributions of men and women to survival were recognized and valued, and in which both men and women had equal access to the limited amount of resources held by the group. Other scholars argue that this is also a stereotype, overly romanticizing Paleolithic society. They note that although social relations among foragers were not as hierarchical as they were in other types of societies, many foraging groups had one person who held more power than others, and that person was almost always a man. This debate about gender relations is often part of larger discussions about whether Paleolithic society — and by implication, "human nature" — was primarily peaceful and nurturing or violent and brutal, and whether these qualities are gender-related. Like much else about the Paleolithic, sources about gender and about violence are fragmentary and difficult to interpret; there may simply have been a diversity of patterns, as there is among more modern foragers.

Cultural Creations and Spirituality

Early human societies are often described in terms of their tools, but this misses a large part of the story. Beginning in the Paleolithic, human beings have expressed themselves through what we would now term the arts or culture: painting and decorating walls and objects, making music, telling stories, dancing alone or in groups. Evidence from the Paleolithic, particularly from after about 50,000 years ago, includes flutes, carvings, jewelry, and paintings done on cave walls and rock outcroppings that depict animals, people, and symbols.

Some cultural creations were created to honor and praise ancestors or leaders, help people remember events and traditions, or promote good hunting or safe childbirth. Some were easy to do, and everyone in a culture was expected to participate in some way: to dance in order to bring rain or give thanks, to listen when stories were told, to take part in ceremonies. Others of these creations required particular talents or training and were probably undertaken only by specialists.

At the same time that people marked and depicted the world around them, they also developed ideas about supernatural forces that controlled some aspects of the natural world and the place of humans in it, what we now term spirituality or religion. Paleo-

Finger Marks from Rouffignac Cave in France, 18,000–9000 B.C.E., and Handprints from Cueva de las Manos (Cave of the Hands) in Argentina, ca. 8000 B.C.E. Paleolithic hand markings have been found in many parts of the world. The finger marks of a young girl (right) are among those made by a group of adults and children who each left such finger flutings in the wet surfaces of the cave, far from the entrance, indicating that they would have used torches to see as they decorated the walls and ceiling. The handprints below, made by blowing colored clay around the hand through a bone pipe, are from different individuals. All are slightly smaller than adult hands, which suggests that this might have been some sort of ceremony involving adolescents. Most are left hands, which indicates that even in the Paleolithic, most people were right-handed, since they would have held the pipe for blowing in the hand they normally used for tasks. (finger marks: © Leslie Van Gelder; handprints: Hubert Stadler/Corbis)

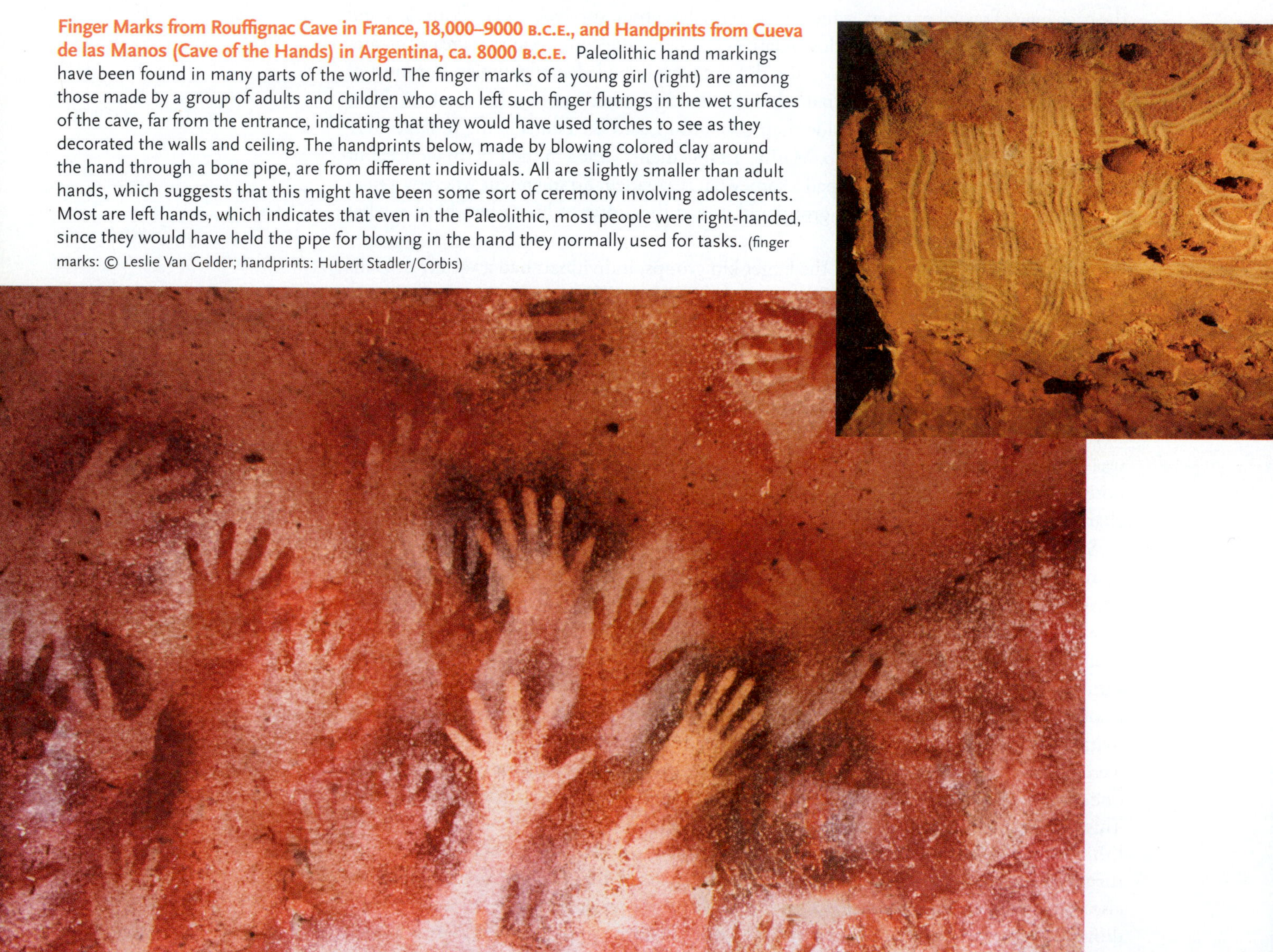

Picturing the Past

Cave Paintings of Horses and a Horned Auroch from Lascaux Cave, Southern France, ca. 15,000 B.C.E.

The artist who made these amazing animals in charcoal and red ochre first smoothed the surface, just as a contemporary artist might. This cave includes paintings of hundreds of animals, including predators such as lions, as well as abstract symbols. (JM Labat/Photo Researchers, Inc.)

ANALYZING THE IMAGE The artist painted the animals so close together that they overlap. What might this arrangement have been trying to depict or convey?

CONNECTIONS Why might Paleolithic people have made cave paintings? What do these paintings suggest about Stone Age culture and society?

lithic burials, paintings, and objects indicate that people thought of their world as extending beyond the visible. People, animals, plants, natural occurrences, and other things around them had spirits, an idea called **animism**.

animism Idea that animals, plants, natural occurrences, and other parts of the physical world have spirits.

Death took people from the realm of the living, but for Paleolithic groups people continued to inhabit an unseen world, along with spirits and deities, after death; thus kin groups included deceased as well as living members of a family. The unseen world regularly intervened in the visible world, for good and ill, and the actions of dead ancestors, spirits, and gods could be shaped by living people. Concepts of the supernatural pervaded all aspects of life; hunting, birth, death, and natural occurrences such as eclipses, comets, and rainbows all had religious meaning. Supernatural forces were understood to determine the basic rules for human existence, and upsetting these rules could lead to chaos.

Ordinary people learned about the unseen world through dreams and portents, and messages and revelations were also sent more regularly to **shamans**, spiritually adept men and women who communicated with the unseen world. Shamans created complex rituals through which they sought to ensure the health and prosperity of an individual, family, or group. Objects understood to have special power, such as carvings or masks in the form of an animal or person, could give additional protection, as could certain plants or mixtures eaten, sniffed, or rubbed on the skin. (See "Listening to the Past: Paleolithic Venus Figures,"

shamans Spiritually adept men and women who communicated with the unseen world.

LISTENING TO THE PAST

Paleolithic Venus Figures

Written sources provide evidence about the human past only after the development of writing, allowing us to listen to the voices of people long dead. For most of human history, however, there were no written sources, so we "listen" to the past through objects. Interpreting written documents is difficult, and interpreting archaeological evidence about the earliest human belief systems is even more difficult and often contentious. For example, small stone statues of women with enlarged breasts and buttocks dating from the later Paleolithic period (roughly 33,000–9,000 B.C.E.) have been found in many parts of Europe. These were dubbed "Venus figures" by nineteenth-century archaeologists, who thought they represented Paleolithic standards of female beauty just as the goddess Venus represented classical standards. A reproduction of one of these statues is shown here. Venus figures provoke more questions than answers: Are they fertility goddesses, evidence of people's beliefs in a powerful female deity? Or are they aids to fertility, carried around by women hoping to have children — or perhaps hoping not to have more — and then discarded in the household debris where they have been most commonly found? Or are they sexualized images of women carried around by men, a sort of Paleolithic version of the centerfold in a men's magazine? Might they have represented different things to different people? Like so much Paleolithic evidence, Venus figurines provide tantalizing evidence about early human cultures, but evidence that is not easy to interpret.

The Venus of Lespugue from France, made from tusk ivory around 25,000 years ago. (Ronald Sheridan/Ancient Art & Architecture Ltd.)

QUESTIONS FOR ANALYSIS

1. Some scholars see Venus figures as evidence that Paleolithic society was egalitarian or female-dominated, but others point out that images of female deities or holy figures are often found in religions that deny women official authority. Can you think of examples of the latter? Which point of view seems most persuasive to you?
2. As you look at this statue, does it seem to link more closely with fertility or with sexuality? How might your own situation as a twenty-first-century person shape your answer to this question?

above.) Shamans thus also operated as healers, with cures that included what we would term natural medicines and religious healing. Because their spiritual and the material worlds appear to have been closely intertwined, Paleolithic people most likely did not make a distinction between natural and spiritual cures.

The rituals and medicines through which shamans and healers operated were often closely guarded secrets, but they were passed orally from one spiritually adept individual to another, so that gradually a body of knowledge about the medicinal properties of local plants and other natural materials was built up. By observing natural phenomena and testing materials for their usable qualities, Paleolithic people began to invent what would later be called science.

Quick Review
How did the demands of the forager lifestyle shape Paleolithic society and culture?

How did plant and animal domestication transform human society?

Foraging remained the basic way of life for most of human history, and for groups living in extreme environments, such as tundras or deserts, it was the only possible way to survive. In a few especially fertile areas, however, the natural environment provided enough food that people could become more settled. As they remained in one place, they began to plant seeds as well as gather wild crops, to raise certain animals instead of hunting, and to selectively breed both plants and animals to make them more useful to humans. This seemingly small alteration was the most important change in human history; because of its impact it is often termed the **Agricultural Revolution**. Plant and animal domestication marked the transition from the Paleolithic to the Neolithic. It allowed the human population to grow far more quickly than did foraging, but it also required more labor, which became increasingly specialized.

Agricultural Revolution Dramatic transformation in human history resulting from the change from foraging to raising crops and animals.

The Development of Horticulture

Areas of the world differed in the food resources available to foragers. In some, acquiring enough food to sustain a group was difficult, and groups had to move constantly. In others, moderate temperatures and abundant rainfall allowed for verdant plant growth; or seas, rivers, and lakes provided substantial amounts of fish and shellfish. Groups in such areas were able to become more settled. About 15,000 years ago, the earth's climate entered a warming phase, and the glaciers began to retreat. As it became warmer, the climate became wetter, and more parts of the world were able to support sedentary or semi-sedentary groups of foragers.

In several of these places, foragers began planting seeds in the ground along with gathering wild grains, roots, and other foodstuffs. By observation, they learned the optimum times and places for planting. They removed unwanted plants through weeding and selected the seeds they planted in order to get crops that had favorable characteristics, such as larger edible parts. Through this human intervention, certain crops became **domesticated**, that is, modified by selective breeding so as to serve human needs.

domesticated Plants and animals modified by selective breeding so as to serve human needs; domesticated animals behave in specific ways and breed in captivity.

This early crop-planting was done by individuals using hoes and digging sticks, and it is often termed **horticulture** to distinguish it from the later agriculture using plows. Intentional crop-planting developed first about 9000 B.C.E. in the area archaeologists call the Fertile Crescent, which runs from present-day Lebanon, Israel, and Jordan north to Turkey and then south to the Iran-Iraq border (Map 1.2). Over the next two millennia, intentional crop-planting emerged in the Nile River Valley, western Africa, China, Papua New Guinea, and Mesoamerica. In each of these places, the development of horticulture occurred independently, and it may have happened in other parts of the world as well. Archaeological evidence does not survive well in tropical areas like Southeast Asia and the Amazon Basin, which may have been additional sites of plant domestication.

horticulture Crop-raising done with hand tools and human power.

The Fertile Crescent

Why, after living successfully as foragers for tens of thousands of years, did humans in so many parts of the world all begin raising crops at about the same time? The

answer to this question is not clear, but crop-raising may have resulted from population pressures in those parts of the world where the warming climate provided more food. More food meant lower child mortality and longer life spans, which allowed population to grow. People then had a choice: they could move to a new area—the solution that foragers had relied on when faced with the same problem—or they could develop ways to increase the food supply to keep up with population growth, a solution that the warming climate was making possible. They chose the latter and began to plant more intensively, beginning cycles of expanding population and intensification of land use that have continued to today.

In the Fertile Crescent, parts of China, and the Nile Valley, within several centuries of initial crop-planting, people were relying on domesticated food products alone. They built permanent houses near one another in villages with fields around them, and they invented new ways of storing foods, such as in pottery made from clay. Villages were closer together than were the camps of foragers, so population density as well as total population grew.

A field of planted and weeded crops yields ten to one hundred times as much food—measured in calories—as the same area of naturally occurring plants. It also requires much

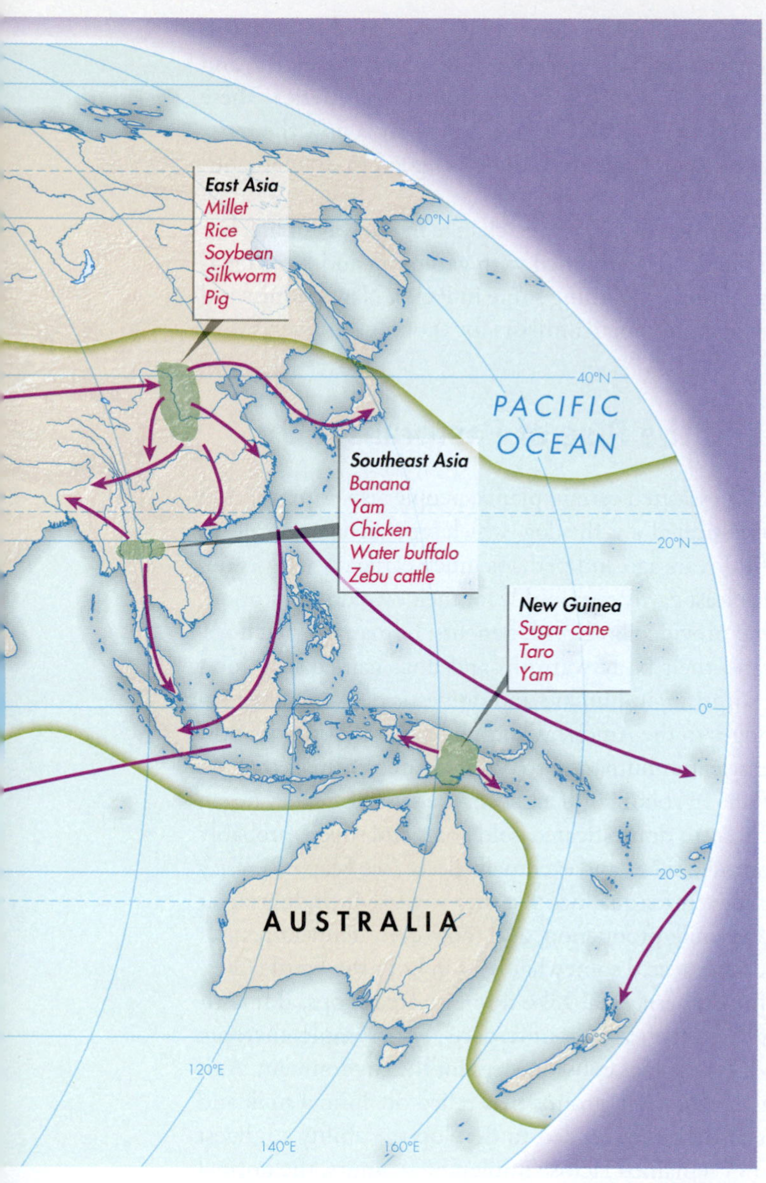

Map 1.2 The Spread of Agriculture and Pastoralism Local plants and animals were domesticated in many different places. Agriculturalists and pastoralists spread the knowledge of how to raise them, and spread the plants and animals themselves, through migration, trade, and conquest.

more labor, however, which was provided both by the greater number of people in the community and by those people working longer hours. In contrast to the twenty hours a week foragers spent on obtaining food, farming peoples were often in the fields from dawn to dusk, particularly during planting and harvest time, but also during the rest of the growing year because weeding was a constant task.

Foragers who lived at the edge of horticultural communities appear to have recognized the negative aspects of crop-raising, for they did not immediately adopt this new way of life. Instead farming spread when a village became too large and some residents moved to a new area, cleared land, planted seeds, and built a new village, sometimes intermarrying with the local people. Because the population of farming communities grew so much faster than that of foragers, however, horticulture quickly spread into fertile areas. Thus, crop-raising spread out from the areas in which it was first developed. Slowly larger and larger parts of Europe, China, South and Southeast Asia, and Africa were home to horticultural villages.

People adapted crops to their local environments, choosing seeds that had qualities that were beneficial, such as drought resistance. They also domesticated new kinds of crops.

In the Americas, for example, by about 3000 B.C.E. corn was domesticated in southern Mexico, and potatoes and quinoa were grown in the Andes region of South America, and by about 2500 B.C.E. squash and beans were domesticated in eastern North America. These crops then spread, so that by about 1000 B.C.E. people in much of what is now the western United States were raising corn, beans, and squash. Crop-raising led to dramatic human alteration of the environment.

In some parts of the world horticulture led to a dramatic change in the way of life, but in others it did not. Horticulture can be easily combined with gathering and hunting as plots of land are usually small; many cultures, including some in Papua New Guinea and North America, remained mixed foragers and horticulturists for thousands of years.

Animal Domestication and the Rise of Pastoralism

At roughly the same time that they domesticated certain plants, people also domesticated animals. The earliest animal to be domesticated was the dog, which separated genetically as a subspecies from wolves at least 15,000 years ago and perhaps much earlier. Scientists debate whether wolves themselves were at least partly responsible for their own domestication. However it happened, the relationship provided both with benefits: humans gained dogs' better senses of smell and hearing and their body warmth, and dogs gained new food sources and safer surroundings. Not surprisingly, humans and domestic dogs migrated together, including across the land bridges to the Americas and on boats to Pacific islands.

Dogs fit easily into a foraging lifestyle, but humans also domesticated animals that led them to completely alter their way of life. In about 9000 B.C.E., at the same time they began to raise crops, people in the Fertile Crescent domesticated wild goats and sheep, probably using them first for meat, and then for milk, skins, and eventually fleece (see Map 1.2). They began to breed the goats and sheep selectively for qualities that they wanted, including larger size, greater strength, better coats, more milk production, and more even temperaments.

After goats and sheep, pigs were domesticated somewhat later in both the Fertile Crescent and China, as were chickens in southern Asia. Like domesticated crops, domesticated animals eventually far outnumbered their wild counterparts. For example, there are more than a billion and half cattle, with enormous consequences for the environment. Animal domestication also shaped human evolution; groups that relied on animal milk and milk products for a significant part of their diet tended to develop the ability to digest milk as adults, while those that did not remained lactose intolerant as adults, the normal condition for mammals.

pastoralism An economic system based on herding flocks of goats, sheep, cattle, or other animals.

Sheep and goats allow themselves to be herded, and people developed a new form of living, **pastoralism**, based on herding and raising livestock, sometimes training dogs to assist them. In areas with sufficient rainfall and fertile soil, pastoralism can be relatively sedentary, and thus easily combined with horticulture; people built pens for animals, or in colder climates constructed special buildings or took them into their houses. They learned that animal manure increases crop yields, so they gathered the manure from enclosures and used it as fertilizer.

Increased contact with animals and their feces also increased human contact with various sorts of disease-causing pathogens. This was particularly the case where humans and animals lived in tight quarters, for diseases spread fastest in crowded environments. Thus pastoralists and agriculturalists developed illnesses that had not plagued foragers, and the diseases became endemic, that is, widely found within a region without being deadly. Ultimately people who lived with animals developed resistance to some of these illnesses, but foragers' lack of resistance to many illnesses meant that they died more readily after coming into contact with new endemic diseases, as was the case when Europeans brought smallpox to the Americas in the sixteenth century.

In drier areas, flocks need to travel long distances from season to season to obtain enough food, so some pastoralists became nomadic. Nomadic pastoralists often gather wild plant foods as well, but they tend to rely primarily on their flocks of animals for food. Pastoralism was well-suited to areas where the terrain or climate made crop-planting difficult, such as mountains, deserts, dry grasslands, and tundras. Eventually other grazing animals, including cattle, camels, horses, yak, and reindeer, also became the basis of pastoral economies in central and western Asia, many parts of Africa, and far northern Europe.

Plow Agriculture

Horticulture and pastoralism brought significant changes to human ways of life, but the domestication of certain large animals had an even bigger impact. Cattle and water buffalo were domesticated in some parts of Asia and North Africa in which they occurred naturally by at least 7000 B.C.E., and horses, donkeys, and camels by about 4000 B.C.E. All these animals consent to carry people or burdens on their backs and pull against loads dragged behind them, two qualities that are rare among the world's animal species. The domestication of large animals dramatically increased the power available to humans to carry out their tasks, which had both an immediate effect in the societies in which this happened and a long-term effect when they later encountered societies in which human labor remained the only source of power.

The pulling power of animals came to matter most, because it could be applied to food production. Sometime in the seventh millennium B.C.E., people attached wooden sticks to frames that animals dragged through the soil, thus breaking it up and allowing seeds to sprout more easily. These simple scratch plows were pulled first by cattle and water buffalo, and later by horses. Over millennia, moldboards—angled pieces that turned the soil over, bringing fresh soil to the top—were added, which reduced the time needed to plow and allowed each person to work more land.

Using plows, Neolithic people produced a significant amount of surplus food, so that some people in the community could spend their days doing other things, increasing the division of labor. Surplus food had to be stored, and some began to specialize in making products for storage, such as pots, baskets, bags, bins, and other kinds of containers. Others specialized in making tools, houses, and other things needed in village life, or in producing specific types of food. Families and households became increasingly interdependent, trading food for other commodities or services. In the same way that foragers had continually improved their tools and methods, people improved the processes through which they made things.

Sometime in the fifth millennium B.C.E. pot-makers in Mesopotamia invented the potter's wheel, which by a millennium later had been adapted for use on carts and plows pulled by animals. Wheeled vehicles led to road-building, and wheels and roads together made it possible for people and goods to travel long distances more easily, whether for settlement, trade, or conquest.

Neolithic Pot, from China, ca. 2600–2300 B.C.E. This two-handled pot, made in the Yellow River Valley of baked ceramics, is painted in a swirling red and black geometric design. Neolithic agricultural communities produced a wide array of storage containers for keeping food and other commodities from one season to the next. (Palace Museum, Beijing)

Stored food was also valuable and could become a source of conflict, as could other issues in villages where people lived close together. Villagers needed more complex rules about how food was to be distributed and how different types of work were to be valued than did foragers. Certain individuals began to specialize in the determination and enforcement of these rules, and informal structures of power gradually became more formalized as elites developed. These elites then distributed resources to their own advantage, often using force to attain and maintain their power.

Quick Review
How did the development of horticulture, pastoralism, and agriculture change the relationship between human beings and the natural world?

How did Neolithic societies change over time?

social hierarchies Divisions between rich and poor, elites and common people that have been a central feature of human society since the Neolithic era.

The division of labor that plow agriculture allowed led to the creation of **social hierarchies**, the divisions between rich and poor, elites and common people that have been a central feature of human society since the Neolithic era. Plow agriculture also strengthened differentiation based on gender, with men becoming more associated with the world beyond the household and women with the domestic realm. Social hierarchies were reinforced over generations as children inherited goods and status from their parents. People increasingly communicated ideas within local and regional networks of exchange, just as they traded foodstuffs, tools, and other products.

Social Hierarchies and Slavery

Archaeological finds from Neolithic villages, particularly burials, show signs of growing social differentiation. Some people were buried with significant amounts of material goods, while others were buried with very little. How were some people able to attain such power over their neighbors that they could even take valuable commodities with them to the grave? This is one of the key questions in all of human history. Written sources do not provide a clear answer because social hierarchies were already firmly in place by the time writing was invented around 3000 B.C.E. in Mesopotamia. As a result, scholars have largely relied on archaeological sources. (See "Individuals in Society: The Iceman," page 21.)

Within foraging groups, some individuals already had more authority because of their links with the world of gods and spirits, positions as heads of kin groups, or personal characteristics. These three factors gave individuals advantages in agricultural societies, and the advantages became more significant over time as there were more resources to control. Priests and shamans developed more elaborate rituals and became full-time religious specialists. In many communities, religious specialists were the first to work out formal rules of conduct that later become oral and written codes of law. The codes threatened divine punishment for those who broke them, and they often required people to accord deference to priests as the representatives of the gods, so that they became an elite group with special privileges.

Individuals who were the heads of large families or kin groups had control over the labor of others, which became more significant when that labor brought material goods that could be stored. Material goods—plows, sheep, cattle, sheds, pots, carts—gave one the ability to amass still more material goods, and the gap between those who had them and those who did not widened. Storage also allowed wealth to be retained over long periods of time, so that over generations small differences in wealth grew larger. The ability to

INDIVIDUALS IN SOCIETY

The Iceman

IN 1991, TWO GERMAN VACATIONERS CLIMBING in the Italian Alps came upon a corpse lying facedown and covered in ice. Scientists determined that the Iceman, as the corpse is generally known, dates to the Neolithic period, having died 5,300 years ago. He was between twenty-five and thirty-five years old at the time of his death, and he stood about five feet two inches tall. An autopsy revealed much about the man and his culture. The bluish tinge of his teeth showed a diet of milled grain, which proves that he came from an environment where crops were grown. The Iceman hunted as well as farmed: he was found with a bow and arrows and shoes of straw, and he wore a furry cap and a robe of animal skins that he had stitched together with thread that he had made from grass.

The equipment discovered with the Iceman demonstrates his mastery of several technologies. He carried a hefty copper ax, indicating a knowledge of metallurgy. He relied chiefly on archery to kill game. In his quiver were numerous wooden arrow shafts and two finished arrows. The arrows had flint heads, a sign of stoneworking, and feathers were attached to the ends of the shafts with resin-like glue. He knew the value of feathers to direct the arrows; thus he had mastered the basics of ballistics. His bow was made of yew, a relatively rare wood in central Europe that is among the best for archers.

Yet a mystery still surrounds the Iceman. When his body was first discovered, scholars assumed that he was a hapless traveler overtaken in a fierce snowstorm. But the autopsy found an arrowhead lodged under his left shoulder. The Iceman was not alone on his last day. Someone was with him, and that someone had shot him from below and behind. The Iceman is the victim in the first murder mystery of Western civilization, and the case will never be solved.

QUESTIONS FOR ANALYSIS

1. What do these images demonstrate about the Iceman's knowledge of his environment?
2. What does the Iceman reveal about the society in which he lived?

The artifacts found with the body tell scientists much about how the Iceman lived. The Iceman's shoes, made with a twine framework stuffed with straw and covered with skin, indicate that he used all parts of the animals he hunted. (discovery: Courtesy, Roger Teissl; shoes: South Tyrol Museum of Archaeology, http://www.iceman.it)

control the labor of others could also come from physical strength, a charismatic personality, or leadership talents, and this also led to greater wealth.

Wealth itself could command labor, as individuals or families could buy the services of others to work for them or impose their wishes through force, hiring soldiers to threaten or carry out violence. Eventually some individuals bought others outright. Like animals, slaves were a source of physical power for their owners, providing them an opportunity to amass still more wealth and influence. In the long era before the invention of fossil fuel technology, the ability to exploit animal and human labor was the most important mark of distinction between elites and the rest of the population.

Gender Hierarchies and Inheritance

patriarchy Social system in which men have more power and access to resources than women and some men are dominant over other men.

Along with hierarchies based on wealth and power, the development of agriculture was intertwined with a hierarchy based on gender. The system in which men have more power and access to resources than women and some men are dominant over other men is called **patriarchy**, and is found in every society in the world with written records. Plow agriculture heightened patriarchy. Although farming with a hoe was often done by women, plow agriculture came to be a male task, perhaps because of men's upper-body strength or because plow agriculture was more difficult to combine with care for infants and small children than was horticulture. At the same time that cattle began to be raised for pulling plows and carts rather than for meat, sheep began to be raised primarily for wool. Spinning thread and weaving cloth became primarily women's work; the earliest Egyptian hieroglyph for weaving is, in fact, a seated woman with a shuttle, and a Confucian moral saying from ancient China asserts that "men plow and women weave." Spinning and weaving were generally done indoors and involved simpler and cheaper tools than plowing; they could also be taken up and put down easily, and so could be done at the same time as other tasks.

Though in some ways this arrangement seems complementary, with each sex doing some of the necessary labor, plow agriculture increased gender hierarchy. Men's responsibility for plowing and other agricultural tasks took them outside the household more often than women, enlarging their opportunities for leadership. It also led to their being favored as inheritors of family land and the right to farm communally held land when inheritance systems were established to pass land and other goods on to the next generation. Thus over generations, women's independent access to resources decreased, and it became increasingly difficult for women to survive without male support.

As inherited wealth became more important, men wanted to make sure that their sons were theirs, so they restricted their wives' movements and activities. This was especially the case among elite families. Among foragers and horticulturalists, women needed to be mobile for the group to survive; their labor outdoors was essential. Among agriculturalists, the labor of animals, slaves, and hired workers could substitute for that of women in families that could afford them. Thus in some Neolithic societies, there is evidence that women spent more and more of their time within the household. Social norms and ideals gradually reinforced this pattern, so that by the time written laws and other records emerged in the second millennium B.C.E., elite women were expected to work at tasks that would not take them beyond the household or away from male supervision. Non-elite women also tended to do work that could be done within or close by the household, such as cooking, cloth production, and the care of children, the elderly, and small animals.

Social and gender hierarchies were enhanced over generations as wealth was passed down unequally, and they were also enhanced by rules and norms that shaped sexual relationships, particularly heterosexual ones. However their power originated, elites began to think of themselves as a group apart from the rest with something that made them

Egyptian Couple Planting Grain, ca. 1500–1300 B.C.E. In this wall painting from the tomb of an official, a man guides a wooden ox-drawn plow through the soil, while the woman walking behind throws seed in the furrow. The painting was not designed to show real peasants working, but to depict the well-to-do man buried in the tomb doing work viewed as worthy of an afterlife. Nevertheless, the gender division of labor and the plow itself are probably accurate. (Erich Lessing/Art Resource, NY)

distinctive—such as connections with a deity, military prowess, and natural superiority. They increasingly understood this distinctive quality to be hereditary and developed traditions—later codified as written laws—that stipulated which heterosexual relationships would pass this quality on, along with passing on wealth. Relationships between men and women from elite families were formalized as marriage and generally passed down both status and wealth. Relationships between elite men and non-elite women generally did not do so, or did so to a lesser degree; the women were defined as concubines or mistresses, or simply as sexual outlets for powerful men. Relations between an elite woman and a non-elite man generally brought shame and dishonor to the woman's family and sometimes death to the man.

Thus along with the distinctions among human groups that resulted from migration and were enhanced by endogamy, distinctions developed within groups that were reinforced by social endogamy, what we might think of as the selective breeding of people. Elite men tended to marry elite women, which in some cases resulted in actual physical differences over generations, as elites had more access to food and were able to become taller and stronger. By 1800 C.E., for example, men in the highest level of the English aristocracy were five inches taller than the average height of all English people.

No elite can be completely closed to newcomers, however, because the accidents of life and death, along with the genetic problems caused by repeated close intermarriage, make it difficult for any small group to survive over generations. Thus mechanisms were developed in many cultures to adopt boys into elite families, to legitimate the children of concubines and slave women, or to allow elite girls to marry men lower on the social hierarchy. All systems of inheritance also need some flexibility. The inheritance patterns in some cultures favored male heirs exclusively, but in others close relatives were favored over those more distant, even if this meant allowing daughters to inherit. The drive to keep wealth and property within a family or kin group often resulted in women inheriting, owning, and in some cases managing significant amounts of wealth, a pattern that continues today. Hierarchies of wealth and power thus intersected with hierarchies of gender in complex ways, and in many cultures age and marital status also played roles. In many European and African cultures, for example, widows were largely able to control their own property, while unmarried sons were often under their father's control even if they were adults.

Trade and Cross-Cultural Connections

The increase in food production brought by the development of plow agriculture allowed Neolithic villages to grow ever larger. By 7000 B.C.E. or so, some villages in the Fertile Crescent may have had as many as ten thousand residents. One of the best known of these, Çatal Hüyük in what is now modern Turkey, shows evidence of trade as well as of the specialization of labor. Çatal Hüyük's residents lived in mud-brick houses whose walls were covered in white plaster. The men and women of the town grew wheat, barley, peas, and almonds and raised sheep and perhaps cattle, though they also seem to have hunted. They made textiles, pots, figurines, baskets, carpets, copper and lead beads, and other goods, and decorated their houses with murals showing animal and human figures. They gathered, sharpened, and polished obsidian, a volcanic rock that could be used for knives, blades, and mirrors, and then traded it with neighboring towns, obtaining seashells and flint. From here the obsidian was exchanged still farther away, for Neolithic societies slowly developed local and then regional networks of exchange and communication.

Among the goods traded in some parts of the world was copper. Pure copper occurs naturally close to the surface in some areas, and people, including those at Çatal Hüyük, hammered it into shapes for jewelry and tools. Like most metals, copper occurs more often mixed with other materials in a type of rock called ore, and by about 5500 B.C.E. people in the Balkans had learned that copper could be extracted from ore by heating it in a smelting process. Smelted copper was poured into molds and made into spear points, axes, chisels, beads, and other objects. Smelting techniques were discovered independently in many places around the world, including China, Southeast Asia, West Africa, and the Andes region. Pure copper is soft, but through experimentation artisans learned that it would become harder if they mixed it with other metals such as arsenic, zinc, or tin during heating, creating an alloy called bronze.

Because it was stronger than copper, bronze had a far wider range of uses, so much so that later historians decided that its adoption marked the beginning of a new period in human history, the Bronze Age. Like all new technologies, bronze arrived at different times in different places, but by about 2500 B.C.E. it was making a difference in many places around the world. Techniques of copper and bronze metallurgy were later applied to precious metals such as gold and silver, and then to iron, which had an even greater impact than bronze. (See "Global Trade: Iron," page 46.) It is important to remember that all metals were expensive and hard to obtain, however, so that stone, wood, and bone remained the primary materials for tools and weapons long into the Bronze Age.

Objects were not the only things traded increasingly long distances during the Neolithic period, for people also carried ideas as they traveled on foot, boats, or camels, and in wagons or carts. Knowledge about the seasons and the weather was vitally important for those who depended on crop-raising, and agricultural peoples in many parts of the world began to calculate recurring patterns in the world around them, slowly developing calendars. Scholars have demonstrated that people built circular structures of mounded earth or huge upright stones to help them predict the movements of the sun and stars, including Nabta Playa, erected about 4500 B.C.E. in the desert west of the Nile Valley in Egypt, and Stonehenge, erected about 2500 B.C.E. in southern England.

The rhythms of the agricultural cycle and patterns of exchange also shaped religious beliefs and practices. Among foragers, human fertility is a mixed blessing, as too many children can overtax food supplies, but among crop-raisers and pastoralists, fertility of the land, animals, and people is essential. Shamans and priests developed ever more elaborate rituals designed to assure fertility, in which the gods were often given something from a community's goods in exchange for their favor. In many places gods came to be associated with patterns of birth, growth, death, and regeneration. Like humans, the gods came to have a division of labor and a social hierarchy. Thus there were rain gods and sun gods, sky goddesses and moon goddesses, gods that assured the health of cattle or the growth of corn, goddesses of the hearth and home. Powerful father and mother gods sometimes presided, but they were challenged and overthrown by virile young male gods, often in epic battles. Thus as human society was becoming more complex, so was the unseen world.

Quick Review
Why did social, gender, and economic inequality tend to increase as Neolithic societies grew more complex?

Connections

THE HUMAN STORY is often told as a narrative of unstoppable progress toward greater complexity: the simple stone hand axes of the Paleolithic were replaced by the specialized tools of the Neolithic and then by bronze, iron, steel, plastic, and silicon; the small kin groups of the Paleolithic gave way to Neolithic villages that grew ever larger until they became cities and eventually today's megalopolises; egalitarian foragers became stratified by divisions of wealth and power that were formalized as aristocracies, castes, and social classes; oral rituals of worship, healing, and celebration in which everyone participated grew into a dizzying array of religions, philosophies, and branches of knowledge presided over by specialists including priests, scholars, scientists, doctors, generals, and entertainers. The rest of this book traces this story and explores the changes over time that are the central thread of history.

As you examine what—particularly in world history—can seem to be a staggering number of developments, it is also important to remember that many things were slow to change and that some aspects of human life in the Neolithic, or even the Paleolithic, continued. Foraging, horticulture, pastoralism, and agriculture have been the primary economic activities of most people throughout the entire history of the world. Though today there are only a few foraging groups in very isolated areas, there are significant numbers of horticulturalists and pastoralists, and their numbers were much greater just a century ago. At that point the vast majority of the world's people still made their living directly through agriculture. The social patterns set in early agricultural societies—with most of the population farming the land, and a small number of elite who lived off their labor—lasted for millennia. You have no doubt recognized other similarities between the early peoples discussed in this chapter and the people you see around you, and it is important to keep these continuities in mind as you embark on your examination of human history.

- **For a list of suggested readings for this chapter, visit** *bedfordstmartins.com/mckayworldunderstanding*.
- **For primary sources from this period, see** *Sources of World Societies*, Second Edition.
- **For Web sites, images, and documents related to topics in this chapter, see Make History at** *bedfordstmartins.com/mckayworldunderstanding*.

Chapter 1 **Study Guide**

To do these exercises online, go to bedfordstmartins.com/mckayworldunderstanding.

Step **1**

GETTING STARTED

Below are basic terms about this period in global history. Can you identify each term below and explain why it matters?

TERMS	WHO (OR WHAT) AND WHEN	WHY IT MATTERS
hominids, p. 4		
Paleolithic era, p. 4		
foraging, p. 4		
Neolithic era, p. 4		
Neanderthals, p. 9		
megafaunal extinction, p. 10		
division of labor, p. 10		
animism, p. 13		
shamans, p. 13		
Agricultural Revolution, p. 15		
domesticated, p. 15		
horticulture, p. 15		
pastoralism, p. 18		
social hierarchies, p. 20		
patriarchy, p. 22		

Step **2**

MOVING BEYOND THE BASICS

The exercise below requires a more advanced understanding of the chapter material. Compare and contrast Paleolithic and Neolithic society by filling in the chart below with descriptions of each society in four key areas: social organization and hierarchy, gender relations, technology and trade, and religion and spirituality. When you are finished, consider the following questions: How did the shift to settled agriculture contribute to the differences you note in each area? In what ways were Paleolithic and Neolithic societies the most similar? How would you explain these instances of continuity?

	SOCIAL ORGANIZATION AND HIERARCHY	GENDER RELATIONS	TECHNOLOGY AND TRADE	RELIGION AND SPIRITUALITY
Paleolithic Society				
Neolithic Society				

Step 3

PUTTING IT ALL TOGETHER

Now that you've reviewed key elements of the chapter, take a step back and try to see the big picture. Remember to use specific examples from the chapter in your answers.

HUMAN EVOLUTION AND MIGRATION

- What explains the evolution of ever larger brains in successive hominid species?
- How did geography and climate shape the migration and distribution of early human communities?

PALEOLITHIC SOCIETY

- What role did family, kinship, and gender relations play in Paleolithic society?
- What do we know about the culture and spirituality of Paleolithic peoples? How do we know it?

THE AGRICULTURAL REVOLUTION AND THE DEVELOPMENT OF NEOLITHIC SOCIETY

- Why did some human communities make the transition from foraging to settled agriculture while others did not?
- How did agriculture contribute to the development of new social, political, and economic institutions in Neolithic communities?

LOOKING BACK, LOOKING AHEAD

- In your opinion, at what point did human history begin? With the first bipedal hominids? Later? Why did you choose the point in the past you did?
- Argue for or against the following statement. "The Agricultural Revolution should be considered the fundamental turning point in human history, the moment when the foundations of all future social, economic, and political institutions were laid down."

In Your Own Words Imagine that you must explain Chapter 1 to someone who hasn't read it. What would be the most important points to include and why?

2

The Rise of the State in Southwest Asia and the Nile Valley

3200–500 B.C.E.

Five thousand years ago, humans were living in most parts of the planet. They had designed technologies to meet the challenges presented by deep forests and jungles, steep mountains, and blistering deserts. As the climate changed, they adapted, building boats to cross channels created by melting glaciers and finding new sources of food when old sources were no longer plentiful. In some places domesticated plants and animals allowed people to live in much closer proximity to one another than they had as foragers.

That proximity created opportunities, as larger groups of people pooled their knowledge to deal with life's challenges, but it also created problems. Human history from that point on can be seen as a response to these opportunities, challenges, and conflicts. As small villages grew into cities, people continued to develop technologies and systems to handle new issues. They created structures of governance to control their more complex societies, along with military forces and taxation systems to support the structures of governance. In some places they invented writing to record taxes, inventories, and payments, and they later put writing to other uses, including the preservation of stories, traditions, and history. These new technologies and systems were first introduced in the Tigris and Euphrates River Valleys of southwest Asia and the Nile Valley of northeast Africa, areas whose history became linked through trade connections, military conquests, and migrations.

Egyptian Lyre Player
Ancient Egyptians hoped that life after death would be a pleasant continuation of life on this earth, and their tombs reflected this. This mural from the tomb of an official who died about 1400 B.C.E. shows a female musician—for a good afterlife would surely include music. (Werner Forman/ Art Resource, NY)

Chapter Preview

- How is the invention of writing connected to the rise of cities and states?
- What kinds of states and societies emerged in ancient Mesopotamia?
- What were the characteristics of Egyptian civilization?
- What was unique about Hebrew civilization?
- How did the Assyrians and Persians build and maintain their empires?

How is the invention of writing connected to the rise of cities and states?

Archaeological remains provide our only evidence of how people lived during most of the human past. Beginning about five thousand years ago, however, people in some parts of the world developed a new technology, writing, the surviving examples of which have provided a much wider range of information. Writing was developed to meet the needs of complex urban societies, and particularly to meet the needs of the state, a new political form that developed during the time covered in this chapter.

Written Sources and the Human Past

Historians who study human societies that developed systems of writing continue to use many of the same types of physical evidence as do those who study societies without writing. For other cultures the writing or record-keeping systems have not yet been deciphered, so our knowledge of these people also depends largely on physical evidence. Scholars can read the writing of a great many societies, however, adding greatly to what we can learn about them.

Clay Letter Written in Cuneiform and Its Envelope, ca. 1850 B.C.E. In this letter from a city in what is now southern Turkey, a merchant complains to his brother that life is hard, and comments on the trade in silver, gold, tin, and textiles. Letters were often enclosed in envelopes and sealed with a piece of soft clay that was stamped, just as you might use a stamped wax seal today. Here the sender's seal shows people approaching a king. (Courtesy of the Trustees of the British Museum)

Much ancient writing survives only because it was copied and recopied, sometimes years after the writing was first produced. The survival of a work means that someone from a later period — and often a long chain of someones — judged it worthy of the time, effort, and resources needed to produce copies. Not surprisingly, the works considered worthy of copying tend to be those that refer to political and military events involving major powers, that record religious traditions, or that come from authors who were later regarded as important. By contrast, written sources dealing with the daily life of ordinary men and women were few to begin with and were rarely saved or copied because they were not seen as significant.

Some early written texts survive in their original form because people inscribed them in stone, shells, bone, or other hard materials, intending them to be permanent. Stones with inscriptions were often erected in the open in public places for all to see, so they include things that leaders felt had enduring importance, such as laws, religious proclamations, decrees, and treaties. Sometimes this permanence was accidental: in ancient Mesopotamia (in the area of modern Iraq), all writing was initially made up of indentations on soft clay tablets, which then hardened. Thousands of these tablets have survived, allowing historians to learn about many aspects of everyday life, including taxes and wages. By contrast, writing in Egypt at the same time was often done in ink on papyrus sheets, made from a plant that grows abundantly in Egypt. Some of these papyrus sheets have survived, but papyrus is a much more fragile material than hardened clay, so most have disintegrated. In China, the oldest surviving writing is on bones and turtle shells from about 1200 B.C.E., but it is clear that writing was done much earlier on less permanent materials such as silk and bamboo. (For more on the origins of Chinese writing, see page 84.)

However they have survived and however limited they are, written records often become scholars' most important original sources for investigating the past. Thus the discovery of a new piece of written evidence from the ancient past is always a major event. But reconstructing and deciphering what are often crumbling documents can take decades, and disputes about how these records affect our understanding of the past can go on forever.

Chapter Chronology

ca. 7000–3000 B.C.E.	Villages slowly grow into cities in Sumer
ca. 3200 B.C.E.	Invention of cuneiform writing
ca. 3000–2600 B.C.E.	Establishment of city-states with hereditary kingship in Sumer
2660–2180 B.C.E.	Period of the Old Kingdom in Egypt
2331 B.C.E.	Sargon conquers Sumer and establishes an empire
ca. 1790 B.C.E.	Hammurabi's law code
ca. 1600 B.C.E.	Hittites expand their empire into Mesopotamia
ca. 1550–1070 B.C.E.	Period of the New Kingdom in Egypt
ca. 1100–700 B.C.E.	Phoenicians play a dominant role in international trade
ca. 1020–930 B.C.E.	Period of united monarchy in the Hebrew Kingdom
ca. 800–612 B.C.E.	Assyrian Empire
720 B.C.E.	Assyrian conquest of northern Hebrew kingdom of Israel
727–653 B.C.E.	Kushite rule in Egypt
ca. 600–500 B.C.E.	Spread of Zoroastrianism
587 B.C.E.	Conquest of southern Hebrew kingdom of Judah by the Babylonians
550 B.C.E.	Creation of Persian Empire
538 B.C.E.	Persian king Cyrus's conquest of Babylonia; Jewish exiles begin return to Jerusalem

Cities and the Idea of Civilization

Along with writing, the growth of cities has often been a way that scholars have marked the increasing complexity of human societies. In the ancient world, residents of cities generally viewed themselves as more advanced and sophisticated than rural folk. They saw themselves as more "civilized," a word that comes from the Latin adjective *civilis*, which refers to a citizen, either a citizen of a town or of a larger political unit such as an empire.

This depiction of people as either civilized or uncivilized was gradually extended to whole societies. Beginning in the eighteenth century European scholars described those societies in which political, economic, and social organizations operated on a large scale, not primarily through families and kin groups, as "civilizations." Civilizations had cities; laws that governed human relationships; codes of manners and social conduct that regulated how people were to behave; and scientific, philosophical, and theological ideas that explained the larger world. Generally only societies that used writing were judged to be civilizations, for writing allowed laws, norms, ideas, and traditions to become more complex.

Until the middle of the twentieth century, historians often referred to the earliest places where writing and cities developed as the "cradles of civilization," proposing a model of development for all humanity patterned on that of an individual person. However, the idea that all human societies developed (or should develop) in a uniform process from a "cradle" to a "mature" civilization has now been largely discredited, and some world historians choose not to use the word *civilization* at all because its meaning is so value-laden. But they have not rejected the idea that about 5,000 years ago a new form of human society appeared, first in the valley formed by the Tigris and Euphrates Rivers — an area the Greeks later called Mesopotamia — and then in other places around the world, often in river valleys. These societies all had cities with tens of thousands of people.

The Rise of States, Laws, and Social Hierarchies

Cities concentrated people and power, and they required more elaborate mechanisms to make them work than had small agricultural villages and foraging groups. These mechanisms were part of what political scientists call "the state," an organization distinct from a tribe or kinship group in which a small share of the population is able to coerce resources out of everyone else in order to gain and then maintain power. In a state, the interest that gains power might be one particular family, a set of religious leaders, or even a charismatic or talented individual.

However they are established, states coerce people through violence, or the threat of violence, and develop permanent armies for this purpose. Using armed force every time they need food or other resources is not very efficient, however, so states also establish bureaucracies and systems of taxation. States also need to keep track of people and goods, so they develop systems of recording information and accounting, usually through writing, though not always. For example, in the Inca Empire, a large state established in the Andes, information about money, goods, and people was recorded on collections of colored knotted strings called *khipus* (see page 269). Systems of recording information allow the creation of more elaborate rules of behavior, often written down in the form of law codes or in the form of religious traditions.

Written laws and traditions generally create more elaborate social hierarchies, in which divisions between elite groups and common people are established more firmly. They also generally heighten gender hierarchies. Those who gain power in states are most often men, so they tend to establish laws and norms that favor males.

Whether we choose to call the process "the birth of civilization" or "the growth of the state," beginning about 3200 B.C.E. some human societies began to develop into a new form. Neolithic agricultural villages expanded into cities, where most people did not raise their own food but depended on that produced by the surrounding countryside and instead carried out other tasks. The organization of this more complex division of labor was undertaken by an elite group, which enforced its will by armed force, along with laws, taxes, and bureaucracies backed up by the threat of force. Social and gender hierarchies became more complex and rigid. All this happened first in Mesopotamia, then in Egypt, and then in India and China.

Quick Review
How did the development of writing serve the interests of the rulers of cities and states?

What kinds of states and societies emerged in ancient Mesopotamia?

States first developed in Mesopotamia, where sustained agriculture reliant on irrigation from the Euphrates and Tigris Rivers resulted in larger populations, a division of labor, and the growth of cities. Priests and rulers developed ways to control and organize these complex societies, including armies. Conquerors from the north unified Mesopotamian city-states into larger empires and spread Mesopotamian culture over a large area.

Environmental Challenges, Irrigation, and Religion

Mesopotamia was part of the Fertile Crescent, where settled agriculture first developed (see pages 15–18). Beginning around 7000 B.C.E., more and more villages were built in the part of southern Mesopotamia known as Sumer, where the Tigris and Euphrates Rivers brought fresh soil when they flooded each spring. The area did not have enough rainfall for farming the ever-expanding fields, so villagers began to build and maintain irrigation ditches that took water from the rivers, allowing more food to be grown and the population to expand. By about 3000 B.C.E., some villages, including Ur and Uruk, had grown into true cities with populations of 40,000 to 50,000. Because they ruled the surrounding countryside, they were really city-states, and the irrigation system they depended on required cooperation and at least some level of social and political cohesion.

The authority to run this system was initially assumed by Sumerian priests. We cannot know for certain how the priests assumed power, as this happened before the invention of writing, but it appears that the uncertainties of life in Sumerian cities convinced people that humans needed to please and obey the gods in order to bring rain, prevent floods, and ensure good harvests. They saw the cosmos as a struggle between order and disorder; to ensure order, people believed they needed to serve the gods by obeying the rules set by religious leaders. Citizens of each city worshipped a number of gods but often focused primarily on one who controlled the economic basis of the city. Encouraged and directed by the priesthood, people erected a large temple in the center of each city, often in the form of a step-pyramid or **ziggurat** (ZIH-guh-rat).

ziggurat Temple in the form of a step-pyramid built in the center of a Mesopotamian city to honor the gods.

The best way to honor the gods was to make the temple as grand and as impressive as possible. Thus, temples grew into elaborate complexes of buildings with storage space for grain and other products and housing for animals. To support these construction efforts, and to support themselves, temple officials developed taxation systems in which people paid a portion of their harvest to the temple or worked a certain number of days per year on land owned directly by the temple.

Sumerian Politics and Society

During times of emergencies, such as floods or invasions by other cities, a chief priest or sometimes a military leader assumed what was supposed to be temporary authority over a city. Temporary power gradually became permanent kingship, and sometime before 2600 B.C.E. kings in some Sumerian city-states began to establish hereditary dynasties in which power was handed down through the male line. The symbol of royal status was the palace, which came to rival the temple in its grandeur. Kings made alliances with other powerful individuals, often through marriage, and a hereditary aristocracy of nobles developed. Acting together, priests, nobles, and kings in Sumerian cities used force, persuasion, and

Ziggurat The ziggurat is a stepped pyramid-shaped temple that dominated the landscape of the Sumerian city. Surrounded by a walled enclosure, it stood as a monument to the gods. Religious ceremonies for the welfare of the community were often performed on the top, and grain, animals, and equipment stores were within the outer enclosure. (Charles & Josette Lemars/Corbis)

threats of higher taxes to maintain order, keep the irrigation systems working, and keep food and other goods flowing.

The king and the nobles held extensive tracts of land that were, like the estates of the temple, worked by others—specifically, clients and slaves. Slaves were prisoners of war, convicts, and debtors. While they were subject to their owners' will, they could engage in trade, make profits, and even buy their freedom. Clients were free people who were dependent on the nobility. In return for their labor, they received small plots of land to work for themselves, although the land they worked remained the possession of the nobility or the temple. Some individuals and families owned land outright and paid their taxes in the form of agricultural products or things they had made. The city-states that developed later throughout Mesopotamia had similar social categories.

Sumerian society made clear distinctions based on gender. All Mesopotamian city-states were patriarchal—that is, most power was held by older adult men. Because other hierarchies such as those of hereditary aristocracy gave privilege to women connected to powerful or wealthy men, however, women saw themselves as either privileged or not, rather than as members of a single lower-ranking group. Therefore, they tended not to object to institutions and intellectual structures that subordinated them, or perhaps their objections were not recorded.

The Invention of Writing and Other Intellectual Advances

In the villages of Sumer, people used small clay objects made into different forms to represent various types of goods that they owned. By 3200 B.C.E. in the growing Sumerian cities, these objects had been replaced by tablets marked with wedge-shaped symbols standing for the goods. This style of writing is known as **cuneiform** (kyoo-NEE-uh-form), from the Latin term for "wedge-shaped." Initially cuneiform writing was pictographic, showing pictures of the objects, but gradually scribes simplified the system, creating stylized symbols called ideograms. These were used to represent actual objects but also came to represent ideas that were difficult to depict. Thus the sign for star (see line A in Figure 2.1) could also be used to indicate heaven, sky, or even god. Signs were also combined. For example, because many slaves in Sumer came from mountainous regions far from cities, the sign for mountain was combined with the sign for woman to indicate "slave woman" (see lines B, C, and D).

Around 2700 B.C.E. scribes in some cities began to use signs to represent sounds rather than concepts. For instance, scribes drew two parallel wavy lines to indicate the word *a* or "water" (see line E in Figure 2.1). Besides water, the word *a* in Sumerian also meant "in." Instead of trying to invent a sign to mean "in," some clever scribe used the sign for water because the two words sounded alike. This phonetic use of signs made possible the combining of signs to convey abstract ideas.

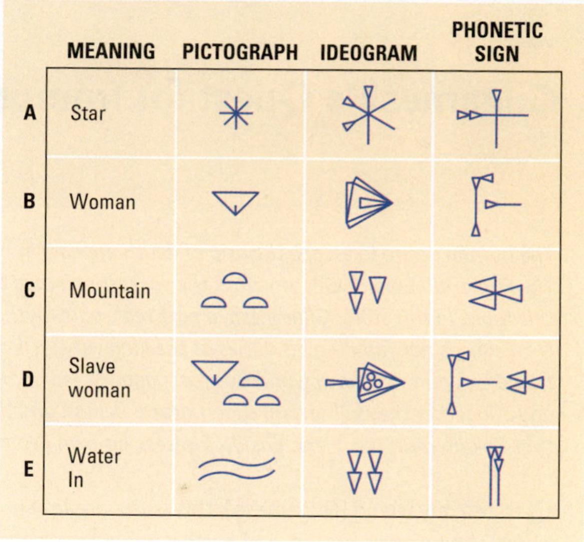

	MEANING	PICTOGRAPH	IDEOGRAM	PHONETIC SIGN
A	Star			
B	Woman			
C	Mountain			
D	Slave woman			
E	Water In			

Figure 2.1 Sumerian Writing (**Source:** Excerpted from S. N. Kramer, *The Sumerians: Their History, Culture, and Character*. Copyright © 1963 by the University of Chicago Press. Used by permission of The University of Chicago Press.)

Over time, the Sumerian system of writing became so complicated that only professional scribes mastered it after many years of study. By 2500 B.C.E. scribal schools flourished throughout Sumer. Most students came from wealthy families, and all were male. Each school had a master, a teacher, and monitors. Discipline was strict, and students were caned for sloppy work and misbehavior.

cuneiform The wedge-shaped writing system that developed in Sumer, the first writing system in the world.

Scribal schools were primarily intended to produce individuals who could keep records of the property and wealth of temple officials, kings, and nobles. Thus writing first developed as a way to enhance the growing power of elites, not to record speech, although it came to be used for that purpose.

Writing also came to be used to record religious traditions and stories of great heroes. These stories often took the form of **epic poems**, narrations of the lives of heroes that embody a people's or a nation's conception of its own past. Historians can use epic poems to learn about various aspects of a society, particularly its ideals. The Sumerians produced the first epic poem, the *Epic of Gilgamesh*, which recounts the wanderings of Gilgamesh, the part real–part mythological king of the Sumerian city of Uruk. The oldest surviving cuneiform tablets that record stories of Gilgamesh date from about 2100 B.C.E., but these tales were certainly told and probably first written down much earlier. (See "Listening to the Past: Gilgamesh's Quest for Immortality," page 36.)

epic poems Narrations of the achievements and sometimes the failures of heroes that embody a people's or a nation's conception of its own past. This type of writing first developed in ancient Sumer.

Myths are the earliest known attempts to answer the question "How did it all begin?" and the story of Gilgamesh incorporates many of the myths of the Sumerians, including those about the creation of the universe. According to one myth (echoed in Genesis, the first book of the Hebrew Bible), only the primeval sea existed at first. The sea produced Heaven and earth, which were united. Heaven and earth gave birth to the god Enlil, who separated them and made possible the creation of the other gods.

The Sumerians did not spend all their time speculating about the origins of the universe. The building of cities, palaces, temples, and irrigation canals demanded practical knowledge of geometry and trigonometry. The Sumerians and later Mesopotamians made significant advances in mathematics using a numerical system based on units of sixty, ten, and six, from which we derive our division of hours into sixty minutes and minutes into sixty seconds. They also developed the concept of place value—that the value of a number depends on where it stands in relation to other numbers.

LISTENING TO THE PAST

Gilgamesh's Quest for Immortality

The human desire to escape the grip of death appears in many cultures. The Sumerian Epic of Gilgamesh *is the earliest recorded treatment of this topic. In this story, Gilgamesh, a part real–part mythological king of Uruk who is not fulfilling his duties as the king very well, sets out with his friend Enkidu to perform wondrous feats against fearsome agents of the gods. Together they kill several supernatural beings, and the gods decide that Enkidu must die. Here, Enkidu foresees his own death in a dream.*

" Listen, my friend [Gilgamesh], this is the dream I dreamed last night. The heavens roared, and earth rumbled back an answer; between them I stood before an awful being, the somber-faced man-bird; he had directed on me his purpose. His was a vampire face, his foot was a lion's foot, his hand was an eagle's talon. He fell on me and his claws were in my hair, he held me fast and I smothered; then he transformed me so that my arms became wings covered with feathers. He turned his stare towards me, and he led me away to the palace of Irkalla, the Queen of Darkness [the goddess of the underworld; in other words, an agent of death], to the house from which none who enters ever returns, down the road from which there is no coming back. "

After Enkidu sickens and dies, a distraught Gilgamesh determines to become immortal. He decides to journey to Utnapishtim and his wife, the only mortals whom the gods had granted eternal life in a beautiful paradise. Gilgamesh's journey involves the effort not only to escape from death but also to reach an understanding of the meaning of life. During his travels he meets with Siduri, the wise and good-natured goddess of wine, who gives him the following advice.

" Gilgamesh, where are you hurrying to? You will never find that life for which you are looking. When the gods created man they allotted to him death, but life they retained in their own keeping. As for you, Gilgamesh, fill your belly with good things; day and night, night and day, dance and be merry, feast and rejoice. Let your clothes be fresh, bathe yourself in water, cherish the little child that holds your hand, and make your wife happy in your embrace; for this too is the lot of man. "

Ignoring Siduri's advice, Gilgamesh continues his journey until he finds Utnapishtim and puts to him the question that is the reason for his quest.

" Oh, father Utnapishtim, you who have entered the assembly of the gods, I wish to question you concerning the living and the dead, how shall I find the life for which I am searching?

Utnapishtim said, "There is no permanence. Do we build a house to stand forever, do we seal a contract to hold for all time? Do brothers divide an inheritance to keep forever, does the flood-time of rivers endure? . . . From the days of old there is no permanence. . . . What is there between the master and the servant when both have fulfilled their doom? When the Anunnaki [the gods of the underworld], the judges, and Mammetun [the goddess of fate] the mother of destinies, come together, they decree the fates of men. Life and death they allot but the day of death they do not disclose."

Then Gilgamesh said to Utnapishtim the Faraway, "I look at you now, Utnapishtim, and your appearance is no different from mine; there is nothing strange in your features. I thought I should find you like a hero prepared for battle, but you lie here taking your ease on your back. Tell me truly, how was it that you came to enter the company of the gods and to possess everlasting life?" Utnapishtim said to Gilgamesh, "I shall reveal to you a mystery, I shall tell you a secret of the gods. . . . In those days the world teemed, the

The Triumph of Babylon and the Spread of Mesopotamian Civilization

Judging by the fact that they had walls and other fortifications, the city-states of Sumer regularly fought one another. Their battles were sometimes sparked by disputes over water, as irrigation in one area reduced or altered the flow of the rivers into other areas. During the third millennium B.C.E., the climate also became warmer and drier, which further heightened conflicts.

The wealth of Sumerian cities also attracted conquerors from the north. In 2331 B.C.E. Sargon, the chieftain of a group of loosely organized villages to the north of Sumer, conquered a number of Sumerian cities with what was probably the world's first permanent army. He tore down their defensive walls and appointed his own sons as rulers, creating

people multiplied, the world bellowed like wild bull, and the great god [Enlil, the warrior god] was aroused by the clamor . . . so the gods agreed to exterminate mankind." ”

Utnapishtim continues, telling Gilgamesh that one of the gods, Ea, had taken an oath to protect humanity, so he warned Utnapishtim to build a boat big enough to hold his family, various artisans, and all animals in order to survive the flood that was to come. The great flood killed all who were not on the boat. Although Enlil was initially infuriated by the Sumerians' survival, he ended up blessing Utnapishtim and his wife with eternal life. Gilgamesh wants this as well, but he fails two opportunities Utnapishtim provides for him to achieve it and returns to Uruk. The last part of the epic notes a different kind of immortality.

Gilgamesh, from decorative panel of a lyre unearthed at Ur. (Courtesy of the Penn Museum, Image #150108)

“ The destiny was fulfilled which the father of the gods, Enlil of the mountain, had decreed for Gilgamesh: "In nether-earth the darkness will show him a light: of mankind, all that are known, none will leave a monument for generations to compare with his. The heroes, the wise men, like the new moon have their waxing and waning. Men will say, 'Who has ever ruled with might and power like him?' As in the dark month, the month of shadows, so without him there is no light. O Gilgamesh, this was the meaning of your dream [of immortality]. You were given the kingship, such was your destiny, everlasting life was not your destiny. Because of this do not be sad at heart, do not be grieved or oppressed; he [Enlil] has given you power to bind and to loose, to be the darkness and the light of mankind. He has given you unexampled supremacy over the people, victory in battle from which no fugitive returns, in forays and assaults from which there is no going back. But do not abuse this power, deal justly with your servants in the palace, deal justly before the face of the Sun." ”

Source: *The Epic of Gilgamesh*, translated with an introduction by N. K. Sanders. Penguin Classics 1960, Third edition, 1972, pp. 89–116. Copyright © N. K. Sanders, 1960, 1964, 1972. Used with permission of Penguin Books Ltd.

QUESTIONS FOR ANALYSIS

1. What does the *Epic of Gilgamesh* reveal about Sumerian attitudes toward the gods and human beings?
2. What does the epic tell us about Sumerian views of the nature of human life? Where do human beings fit into the cosmic world?
3. At the end of his quest, did Gilgamesh achieve immortality? If so, what was the nature of that immortality?

a new form of government, a state made up of several city-states, what we might think of as a small empire. Sargon led his armies to the Mediterranean Sea, spreading Mesopotamian culture throughout the Fertile Crescent, and encouraged trading networks that brought in goods from as far away as the Nile (Map 2.1) and the Indus River in modern Pakistan.

Sargon's empire lasted about two hundred years and was then absorbed into the empire centered on the city of Babylon. Babylon was in an excellent position to dominate trade on both the Tigris and Euphrates, and it was fortunate in having a very able ruler in Hammurabi (hahm-moo-RAH-bee; r. 1792–1750 B.C.E.). He unified Mesopotamia using military force, strategic alliances with the rulers of smaller territories, and religious ideas. Under Hammurabi, Babylonian ideas and beliefs traveled throughout Mesopotamia and beyond, with Babylonian traders spreading them farther as they reached the shores of the Mediterranean Sea and the Harappan cities of the Indus River Valley (see page 58).

Map 2.1 **Spread of Cultures in the Ancient Near East, ca. 3000–1640 B.C.E.** This map illustrates the spread of the Mesopotamian and Egyptian cultures through a semicircular stretch of land often called the Fertile Crescent. From this area, the knowledge and use of agriculture spread throughout western Asia.

Hammurabi's Code and Its Social Consequences

Hammurabi's most memorable achievement was the code, introduced around 1790 B.C.E., that established the law of the land. Hammurabi claimed that divine authority stood behind the laws that promoted the welfare of the people. Laws regulating behavior and punishments set for crimes differed according to social status and gender. Hammurabi's code provides a wealth of information about daily life in Mesopotamia. Because of farming's fundamental importance, the code dealt extensively with agriculture. It governed, for example, the duties and rights of tenant farmers, who were expected to cultivate the land carefully and to keep canals and ditches in good repair.

Hammurabi gave careful attention to marriage and the family. The fathers of the prospective bride and groom legally arranged the marriage, with her father giving the bride a dowry that remained hers for the rest of her life. The groom's father gave a bridal gift to the bride's father. The wife was expected to be rigorously faithful, and a woman found guilty of adultery could be put to death. (Sex between a married man and a woman who was not his wife was not defined as adultery and carried no penalty.)

Law Code of Hammurabi Hammurabi ordered his code to be inscribed on stone pillars and set up in public throughout the Babylonian empire. At the top of the pillar Hammurabi is depicted receiving the scepter of authority from the god Shamash. (Réunion des Musées Nationaux/Art Resource, NY)

The husband technically had absolute power over his household. He could, for example, sell his wife and children into slavery, although the law made it very difficult for him to go to such extremes. Evidence other than the law code indicates that family life was not so grim. Wills and testaments show that husbands habitually left their estates to their wives, who in turn willed the property to their children. And though marriage was primarily an arrangement between families, a few poems speak of romantic love.

Quick Review
What political and religious institutions and ideas did the Mesopotamians develop, and how did their culture spread beyond the borders of Mesopotamian states?

What were the characteristics of Egyptian civilization?

At about the same time that Sumerian city-states developed in the Tigris and Euphrates Valleys, a more cohesive state under a single ruler grew in the valley of the Nile River in North Africa. This was Egypt, which for long stretches of history was prosperous and secure. At various times groups migrated into Egypt seeking better lives or invaded and conquered Egypt. Often these newcomers adopted aspects of Egyptian culture, and Egyptians also carried their traditions with them when they established an empire and engaged in trade.

The Nile and the God-King

No other single geographical factor had such a fundamental and profound impact on the shaping of Egyptian life, society, and history as the Nile River (see Map 2.2). The Nile flooded once a year, bringing fertile soil and moisture for farming. In contrast to the violent and destructive floods of the Tigris and Euphrates, Nile floods were relatively gentle, and Egyptians praised the Nile primarily as a creative and comforting force:

Hail to thee, O Nile, that issues from the earth and comes to keep Egypt alive! . . .
He that waters the meadows which Ra created,
He that makes to drink the desert . . .
He who makes barley and brings emmer [wheat] into being . . .
He who brings grass into being for the cattle . . .
He who makes every beloved tree to grow . . .
O Nile, verdant art thou, who makest man and cattle to live[1]

The regular flooding of the Nile brought life back to the fields, which may have been why the Egyptians developed strong ideas about life after death. They saw both life on this earth and life after death as pleasant, not as the bleak struggle that the Mesopotamians envisioned. The Nile also unified Egypt, serving as a highway that promoted easy communication.

The political power structures that developed in Egypt came to be linked with the Nile. Somehow the idea developed that a single individual, a living god-king whom the Egyptians called the **pharaoh**, controlled the rise and fall of the Nile. The Egyptians divided their history into dynasties, or families, of pharaohs. Modern historians have combined the many dynasties into periods with distinctive characteristics (see page 41). The political unification of Egypt ushered in the period known as the Old Kingdom (2660–2180 B.C.E.), an era remarkable for prosperity, artistic flowering, and the evolution of religious beliefs. The focal point of religious and political life in the Old Kingdom was the pharaoh, who commanded the wealth, resources, and people of Egypt.

pharaoh The leader of religious and political life in the Old Kingdom, he commanded the wealth, the resources, and the people of Egypt.

Egyptian Gods and Goddesses
Amon (AH-muhn): the sky-god, who created the universe by his thoughts
Ra (rah): the sun-god, who brought life to the land and its people and commanded the sky, the earth, and the underworld
Amon-Ra: a later god who combined the attributes of Amon and Ra
Osiris (oh-SIGH-ruhs): king of the dead
Isis (EYE-suhs): sister and wife of Osiris
Horus: son of Isis and Osiris

The pharaoh was only one of the many gods honored by the Egyptians, whose **polytheistic** religious ideas evolved over thousands of years. Egyptians often adopted new deities that they learned about through trade or conquest, or combined the powers and features of these with existing deities.

During the Old Kingdom, the pharaoh was widely understood to be the power who achieved the integration between gods and human beings, and this integration was seen to represent the gods' pledge to care for their people (strikingly unlike the gods of Mesopotamia). The pharaoh's surroundings had to be worthy of a god, and only a magnificent palace was suitable for his home. Just as the pharaoh occupied a great house in life, so he reposed in a great pyramid after death, and the massive tomb contained everything he needed in his afterlife. To this day the great pyramids at Giza near Cairo bear silent but magnificent testimony to the god-kings of Egypt.

polytheism Belief in many deities.

The pharaoh was not the only one with an afterlife. For all Egyptians, life after death depended both on how one had lived one's life on earth and on the conduct of proper funeral rituals, in which mummification of the physical body was essential. Egyptian beliefs about death and the afterlife are detailed in the ***Book of the Dead***, written to help guide the dead through difficulties they would encounter on the way to the underworld. This book explained that, after making the journey safely, the soul and the body became part of the divine.

Book of the Dead A book that preserved Egyptians' ideas about death and the afterlife.

To ancient Egyptians the pharaoh embodied justice and order. If the pharaoh was weak or allowed anyone to challenge his unique position, he opened the way to chaos. Twice in Egyptian history the pharaoh failed to maintain centralized power. During those two eras, known as the First and Second Intermediate Periods, Egypt suffered invasions and internal strife. Yet the monarchy survived, and in each period a strong pharaoh arose to crush the rebels or expel the invaders and restore order.

Social Divisions and Work in Ancient Egypt

Egyptian society reflected the pyramids that it built. At the top stood the pharaoh, who relied on a circle of nobles, officials, and priests to administer the kingdom. All of them were assisted by scribes, who wrote with a brush on papyrus sheets or on walls in characters called **hieroglyphs** (HIGH-ruh-glifs). Like cuneiform, Egyptian hieroglyphs include both ideograms and symbols used phonetically. Aside from scribes, the cities of the Nile Valley were home to artisans of all types, along with merchants and other tradespeople. The wealthier lived in spacious homes with gardens, walls for privacy, and specialized rooms for eating, sleeping, and entertaining.

hieroglyphs Egyptian letters, including both ideograms and phonetic signs, written with a brush on papyrus sheets or on walls.

Most people in Egypt were farmers. The regularity of the climate meant that the agricultural year was routine and dependable, so farmers seldom suffered from foul weather and damaged crops. Farmers grew a wide variety of crops, tended cattle and poultry, and when time permitted they hunted and fished in the marshlands of the Nile. Their houses were small, which suggests that they lived in small family groups, not as large extended families. Marriage was arranged by the couple's families and seems to have taken place at a young age. Once couples were married, having children, especially sons, was a high priority. In terms of property rights within marriages, women in Egypt owned and controlled property more than they did in Mesopotamia, and they were especially active in doing so when they were widows.

As in Mesopotamia, common people paid their obligations to their superiors in products and in labor, and many may not have been able to easily leave the land of their own

Picturing the Past

Egyptian Home Life

This grave painting depicts an intimate moment in the life of an aristocratic family, with the father and mother in the center and their children around them. Often found in Egyptian tombs are statuettes of cats (inset), family pets and the symbol of the goddess Bastet.

(family: The Art Archive at Art Resource, NY; cat: Courtesy of the Trustees of the British Museum)

ANALYZING THE IMAGE What evidence do you find in the painting that Egyptian artists based the size of figures on people's status in the household?

CONNECTIONS Based on your reading, how might an image of a poor family differ from this depiction?

free will. True slavery, however, did not become widespread until the New Kingdom (1570–1070 B.C.E.; see page 42). Young men were drafted into the pharaoh's army, which served both as a fighting force and as a labor corps.

Migrations and Political Revivals

While Egypt flourished, momentous changes were taking place around it that would leave their mark even on this rich, insular civilization. These changes involved vast movements of peoples throughout the Fertile Crescent, as various groups migrated and then accommodated themselves to local cultures.

One of these groups was made up of speakers of a Semitic language whom the Egyptians called Hyksos (HIK-sahs). Looking for good land, bands of Hyksos entered the eastern Nile Delta about 1600 B.C.E. (Map 2.2). The migration of the Hyksos, combined with a series of famines and internal struggles for power, led Egypt to fragment politically in what later came to be known as the Second Intermediate Period. During this time the

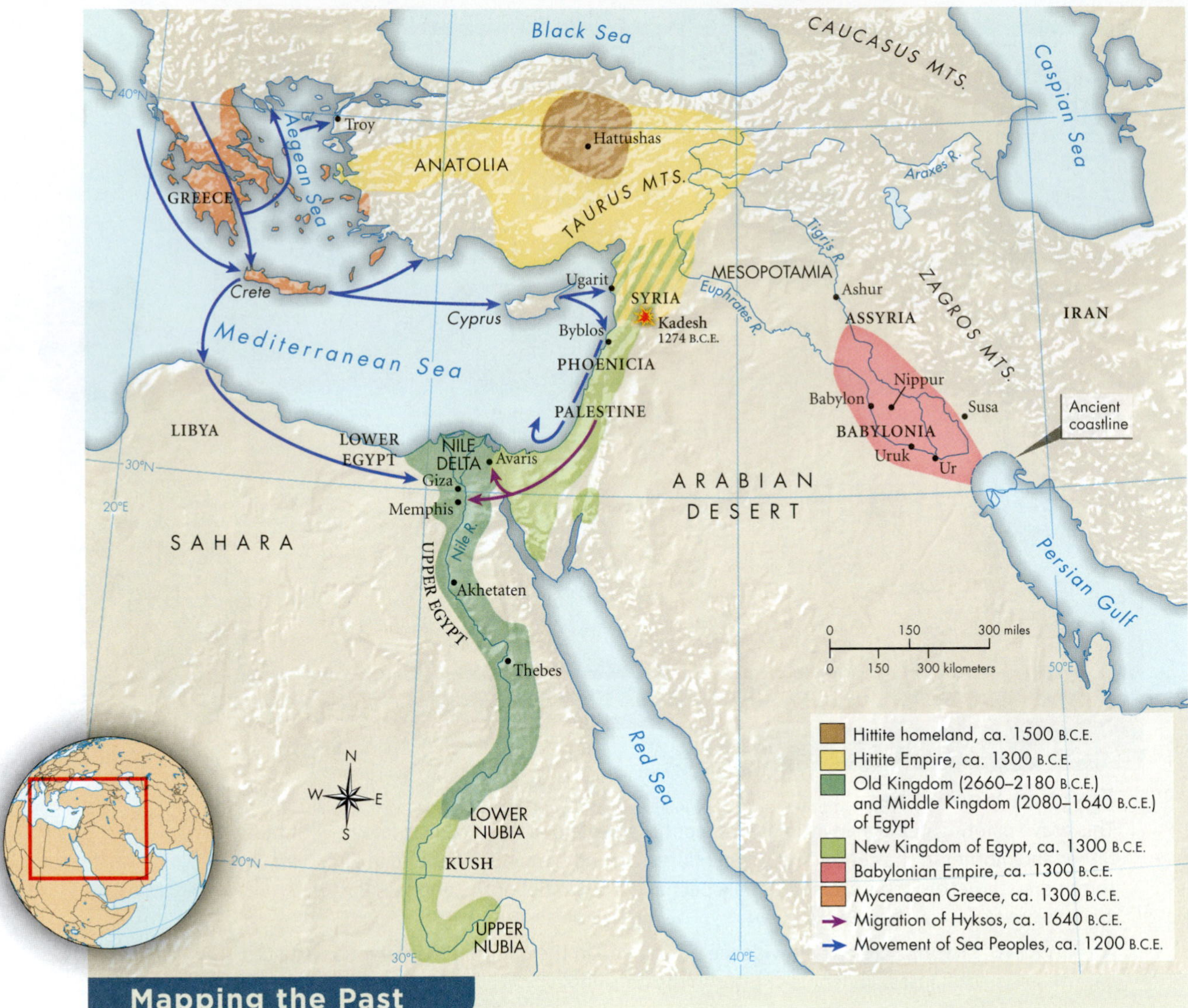

Mapping the Past

Map 2.2 Empires and Migrations in the Eastern Mediterranean
The rise and fall of empires in the eastern Mediterranean were shaped by internal developments, military conflicts, and the migration of peoples to new areas.

ANALYZING THE MAP At what point was the Egyptian empire at its largest? The Hittite Empire? What were the other major powers in the eastern Mediterranean at this time?

CONNECTIONS What were the major effects of the migrations of the Hyksos? Of the Sea Peoples? What clues does the map provide as to why the Sea Peoples had a more powerful impact than did the Hyksos?

Egyptians adopted bronze technology and new forms of weaponry from the Hyksos, while the newcomers began to worship Egyptian deities and modeled their political structures on those of the Egyptians.

About 1570 B.C.E. a new dynasty of pharaohs seeking to unite Egypt sent armies against the Hyksos, pushing them out of the Nile Delta and inaugurating what scholars refer to as the New Kingdom. During this period the pharaohs expanded Egyptian power beyond the Nile Valley and created the first Egyptian empire, which they celebrated with monuments on a scale unparalleled since the pyramids of the Old Kingdom. Also during this period, probably for the first time, widespread slavery became a feature of Egyptian life.

The pharaoh's armies returned home from conquests leading hordes of slaves who constituted a new labor force for imperial building projects.

One of the most extraordinary of this unusual line of pharaohs was Akhenaten (ah-keh-NAH-tuhn; r. 1367–1350 B.C.E.), who was more concerned with religion than with conquest. Nefertiti (nef-uhr-TEE-tee), his wife and queen, encouraged his religious bent. (See "Individuals in Society: Hatshepsut and Nefertiti," page 44.) Although the precise nature of Akhenaten's religious beliefs remain debatable, most historians agree that the royal pair were monotheists: they believed in only one god, Aton, a newer version of the sun-god. However, Akhenaten's monotheism, imposed from above, failed to find a place among the people, and his religion died with him.

Indo-European language family A large family of languages that includes English, most of the languages of modern Europe, Greek, Latin, Persian, Hindi, Bengali, and Sanskrit, the sacred tongue of ancient India.

At about the same time that the Hyksos migrated into the Nile Delta, another group, the Hittites, established an empire in the eastern Mediterranean that would eventually also confront Egyptian power. The Hittites had long been settled in Anatolia (modern Turkey), and beginning about 1600 B.C.E. they expanded their empire east and south into Mesopotamia (see Map 2.2).

The Hittites were different from other peoples in the region in two significant ways. First, they spoke a language that scholars have identified as belonging to the **Indo-European language family**, a large family of languages that includes English, most of the languages of modern Europe, Greek, Latin, Persian, Hindi, Bengali, and Sanskrit, the sacred tongue of ancient India. (For more on Sanskrit, see page 60.) This suggests that their ancestors originated in central Asia, which historians of language see as the homeland of the Indo-European languages.

Second, by the end of their period of expansion the Hittites used iron weapons to some degree. Techniques for smelting iron appear to have been invented first in Mesopotamia or Anatolia. (They were independently invented in other places as well, including India and West Africa; see "Global Trade: Iron," page 46.) Iron swords and spear tips are much stronger than bronze ones, and by 1000 B.C.E. iron weapons were the deciding factors in battles in southwest Asia and the eastern Mediterranean.

Around 1300 B.C.E. the Hittites and the Egyptians confronted each other, but decided to make an alliance, which eventually included the Babylonians as well. The alliance facilitated the exchange of ideas throughout western Asia, and the Hittite kings and Egyptian pharaohs used the peace to promote prosperity and concentrate their incomes. Peace was short-lived, however. Beginning about 1200 B.C.E. waves of foreign invaders, the most famous of whom the Egyptians called the Sea Peoples, broke the Hittite Empire apart and drove the Egyptians back to the Nile Valley for a long period of political fragmentation and conquest by outsiders that scholars of Egypt refer to as the Third Intermediate Period (ca. 1100–653 B.C.E.).

New Political and Economic Powers

The decline of Egypt allowed new powers to emerge. South of Egypt along the Nile was a region called Nubia (NOO-bee-uh), which as early as 2000 B.C.E. served as a conduit of trade through which ivory, gold, ebony, and other products flowed north from sub-Saharan Africa. Small kingdoms arose in this area, with large buildings and rich tombs. As Egypt expanded during the New Kingdom, it took over northern Nubia, incorporating

Nubian Cylinder Sheath This small silver sheath made about 520 B.C.E., perhaps for a dagger, shows a winged goddess and the Egyptian god Amon-Ra. It was found in the tombs of the king of Kush and suggests ways that Egyptian artistic styles and religious ideas influenced cultures farther up the Nile. (Nubian, Napatan Period, reign of King Amani-natakelebte, 538–519 B.C.E. Findspot: Sudan, Nubia, Nuri, Pyramid 10. Gilded silver, colored paste inclusions. Height x diameter: 12 x 3.1 cm [4¾ x 1¼ in.]. Museum of Fine Arts, Boston. Harvard University–Museum of Fine Arts Expedition, 20.275)

INDIVIDUALS IN SOCIETY

Hatshepsut and Nefertiti

Granite head of Hatshepsut. (Bildarchiv Preussischer Kulturbesitz/Art Resource, NY)

EGYPTIANS UNDERSTOOD THE PHARAOH TO BE the living embodiment of the god Horus, the source of law and morality, and the mediator between gods and humans. His connection with the divine stretched to members of his family, so that his siblings and children were also viewed as in some ways divine. Because of this, a pharaoh often took his sister or half-sister as one of his wives. This concentrated divine blood set the pharaonic family apart from other Egyptians (who did not marry close relatives) and allowed the pharaohs to imitate the gods, who in Egyptian mythology often married their siblings. A pharaoh chose one of his wives to be the "Great Royal Wife," or principal queen. Often this was a relative, though sometimes it was one of the foreign princesses who married pharaohs to establish political alliances.

The familial connection with the divine allowed a handful of women to rule in their own right in Egypt's long history. We know the names of four female pharaohs, of whom the most famous was Hatshepsut (r. 1479–1458 B.C.E.). She was the sister and wife of Thutmose II and, after he died, served as regent — as adviser and co-ruler — for her young stepson Thutmose III, who was the son of another woman. Hatshepsut sent trading expeditions and sponsored artists and architects, ushering in a period of artistic creativity and economic prosperity. She built one of the world's great buildings, an elaborate terraced temple at Deir el Bahri, which eventually served as her tomb. Hatshepsut's status as a powerful female ruler was difficult for Egyptians to conceptualize, and she is often depicted in male dress or with a false beard, thus looking more like the male rulers who were the norm. After her death, Thutmose III tried to destroy all evidence that she had ever ruled, smashing statues and scratching her name off inscriptions, perhaps because of personal animosity and perhaps because he wanted to erase the fact that a woman had once been pharaoh. Only within recent decades have historians and archaeologists begun to (literally) piece together her story.

Though female pharaohs were very rare, many royal women had power through their position as Great Royal Wives. The most famous was Nefertiti (ca. 1370–1330 B.C.E.), the wife of Akhenaten. Her name means "the perfect (or beautiful) woman has come," and inscriptions give her many other titles.

Nefertiti used her position to spread the new religion of the sun-god Aton. Together she and Akhenaten built a new palace at Akhetaten, the present-day Amarna, away from the old centers of power. There they developed the cult of Aton to the exclusion of the traditional deities. Nearly the only literary survivor of their religious belief is the "Hymn to Aton," which declares Aton to be the only god. It describes Nefertiti as "the great royal consort whom he! Akhenaten! Loves, the mistress of the Two Lands! Upper and Lower Egypt!"

Nefertiti is often shown as being the same size as her husband, and in some inscriptions she is performing religious rituals that would normally have been carried out only by the pharaoh. The exact details of her power are hard to determine, however. An older theory held that her husband removed her from power, though there is also speculation that she may have ruled secretly in her own right after his death. Her tomb has long since disappeared, though some scholars believe that an unidentified mummy discovered in 2003 in Egypt's Valley of the Kings may be Nefertiti's.

QUESTIONS FOR ANALYSIS

1. Why might it have been difficult for Egyptians to accept a female ruler?
2. What opportunities do hereditary monarchies such as that of ancient Egypt provide for women? How does this fit with gender hierarchies in which men are understood as superior?

Painted limestone bust of Nefertiti. (Bildarchiv Preussischer Kulturbesitz/Art Resource, NY)

it into the growing Egyptian empire. The Nubians adopted many features of Egyptian culture, including Egyptian gods, the use of hieroglyphs, and the building of pyramids. Many Nubians became officials in the Egyptian bureaucracy and officers in the army, and there was significant intermarriage between the two groups.

With the contraction of the Egyptian empire, an independent kingdom, Kush, rose to power in Nubia, with its capital at Napata in what is now Sudan. The Kushites conquered southern Egypt, and in 727 B.C.E. the Kushite king Piye swept through the entire Nile Valley to the delta in the north. United once again, Egypt enjoyed a brief period of peace during which the Egyptian culture continued to influence that of its conquerors. In the seventh century B.C.E. invading Assyrians (see page 50) pushed the Kushites out of Egypt, and the Kushite rulers moved their capital farther up the Nile to Meroë. Meroë became a center of iron production, and iron products from Meroë were traded to much of Africa and across the Red Sea and the Indian Ocean to India.

Phoenician Settlements in the Mediterranean

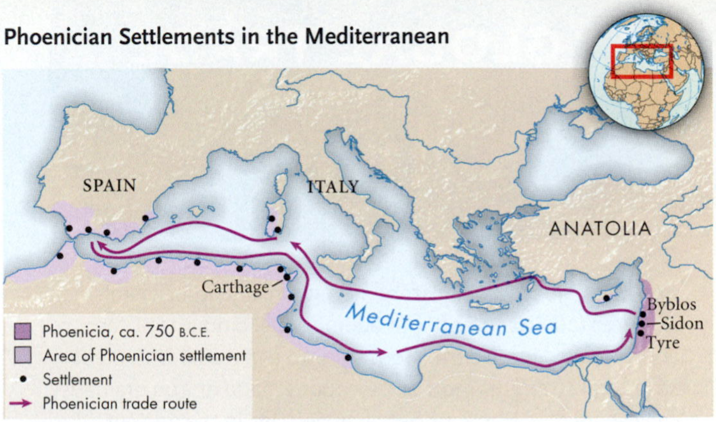

While Kush expanded in the southern Nile Valley, another group rose to prominence along the Mediterranean. These were the **Phoenicians** (fih-NEE-shuhnz), a Semitic-speaking people who had long inhabited several cities along the coast of modern Lebanon and who took to the sea to become explorers and merchants. Phoenician culture was urban, based on the prosperous commercial city-states of Tyre, Sidon, and Byblos, each ruled by a separate king and council of nobles. Especially from about 1100 to 700 B.C.E., the Phoenicians played a predominant role in international trade.

Phoenicians People of the prosperous city-states in what is now Lebanon who dominated trade throughout the Mediterranean and spread the letter alphabet.

The variety and quality of the Phoenicians' trade goods generally made them welcome visitors. They established colonies and trading posts throughout the Mediterranean and as

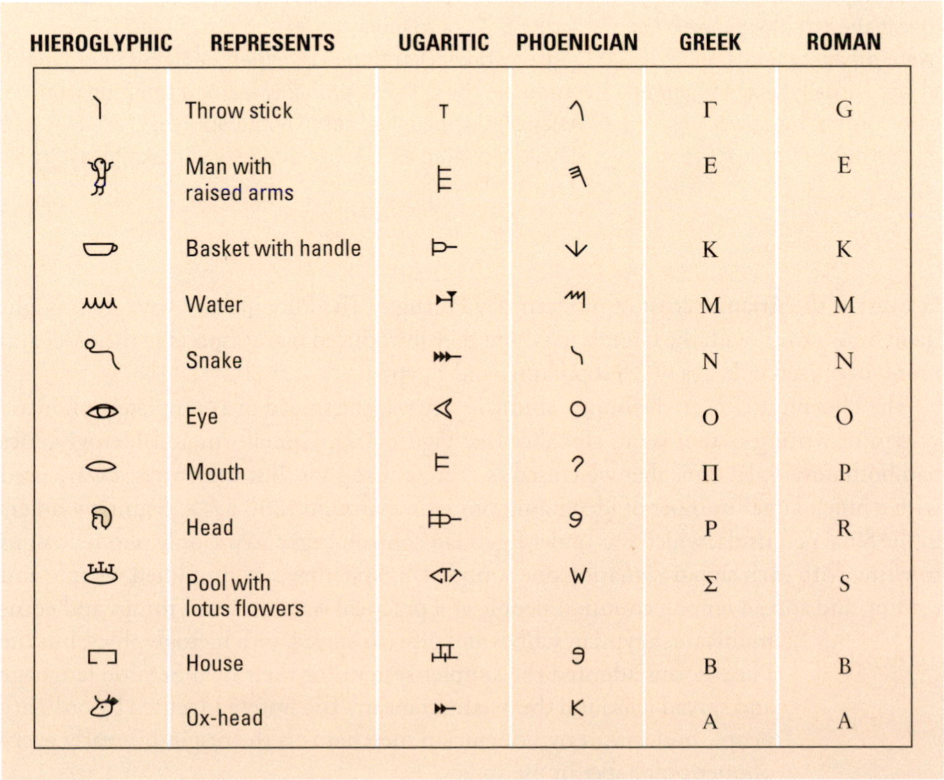

HIEROGLYPHIC	REPRESENTS	UGARITIC	PHOENICIAN	GREEK	ROMAN
	Throw stick			Γ	G
	Man with raised arms			E	E
	Basket with handle			K	K
	Water			M	M
	Snake			N	N
	Eye			O	O
	Mouth			Π	P
	Head			P	R
	Pool with lotus flowers			Σ	S
	House			B	B
	Ox-head			A	A

Figure 2.2
Origins of the Alphabet
List of hieroglyphic, Ugaritic, Phoenician, Greek, and Roman sign forms. (**Source:** A. B. Knapp, *The History and Culture of Ancient Western Asia and Egypt*. © 1988 Wadsworth, a division of Cengage Learning, Inc. Reproduced by permission, www.cengage.com/permissions.)

GLOBAL TRADE

Iron

Iron has shaped world history more than any other metal. In its pure state iron is soft, but adding small amounts of carbon and various minerals transforms it into a material with great structural strength. Tools and weapons made of iron dramatically shaped interactions between peoples in the ancient world, and machines made of iron and steel literally created the modern world.

Human use of iron began during the Paleolithic era, when people living in what is now Egypt used small pieces of hematite, a type of iron oxide, as part of their tools, along with stone, bone, and wood. Beginning around 4000 B.C.E. people in several parts of the world began to pick up iron-nickel meteorites and pound them into shapes. Such meteorites were rare, and the jewelry, weapons, and other objects produced from them were luxury goods, not things for everyday use. Found in China, Africa, and North and South America, these objects were traded very long distances, including thousands of miles around the Arctic, where indigenous peoples traded sharpened pieces from a gigantic iron meteorite that fell in Greenland for use as harpoon tips and knife blades.

Iron is the most common element in the earth, but most iron on or near the earth's surface occurs in the form of ore, which must be smelted to extract the metal. This is also true of copper and tin, but these can be smelted at much lower temperatures than iron, so they were the first metals to be produced to any great extent, and were usually mixed together to form bronze. As artisans perfected bronze metalworking techniques, they developed a long and difficult process to smelt iron, using burning charcoal and a bellows (which raised the temperature further) to extract the iron from the ore. This was done in an enclosed furnace, and the process was repeated a number of times as the ore was transformed into wrought iron, which could be formed into shapes.

Exactly where and when the first smelted iron was produced is a matter of debate, but it was somewhere in Mesopotamia or Anatolia (modern-day Turkey) and occurred perhaps as early as 2500 B.C.E. The Hittites became a powerful empire in the eastern Mediterranean in part through their skills in making and using iron weaponry, and by 1200 B.C.E. or so iron objects were traded throughout the Mediterranean and beyond. Knowledge of smelting traveled as well. By 1700 B.C.E. artisans in northern India were making and trading iron implements. By 1200 B.C.E. iron was being produced and sold in southern India, though scholars debate whether smelting was discovered independently there or learned through contact with iron-making cultures to the north. Iron objects were traded from Anatolia north into Greece, central Europe, and western Asia, and by 500 B.C.E. knowledge of smelting had traveled these routes as well.

Smelting was discovered independently in what is now Nigeria in western Africa about 1500 B.C.E. by a group of people who spoke Bantu languages. They carried iron hoes, axes, shovels, and weapons, and the knowledge of how to make them, as they migrated south and east over many centuries, which gave them a distinct advantage over foraging peoples. In East Africa, the Kushite people learned the advantages of iron weaponry when the iron-using Assyrians drove them out of Egypt, and they then established a major center of iron production at Meroë, and traded down the African coast and across the sea to India.

Ironworkers continued to experiment and improve their products. The Chinese probably learned smelting from central Asian steppe peoples, but in about 500 B.C.E. artisans in China developed more efficient techniques of making cast iron using

far west as the Atlantic coast of modern-day Portugal. The Phoenicians' voyages brought them into contact with the Greeks, to whom they introduced many aspects of the older and more urbanized cultures of Mesopotamia and Egypt.

The Phoenicians' overwhelming cultural legacy was the spread of a completely phonetic system of writing—that is, an alphabet (see Figure 2.2). Cuneiform and hieroglyphics had both developed signs that were used to represent sounds, but these were always used with a much larger number of ideograms. Sometime around 1800 B.C.E. Semitic workers in the Sinai peninsula, which was under Egyptian control, began to use only phonetic signs to write, with each sign designating one sound. This system vastly simplified writing and reading and spread among common people as a practical way to record things and communicate. Egyptian scribes and officials stayed with hieroglyphics, but the Phoenicians adopted the simpler system for their own Semitic language and spread it around the Mediterranean. The system invented by ordinary people and spread by Phoenician merchants is the origin of nearly every phonetic alphabet in use today.

Quick Review
What explains ancient Egypt's remarkable stability and prosperity?

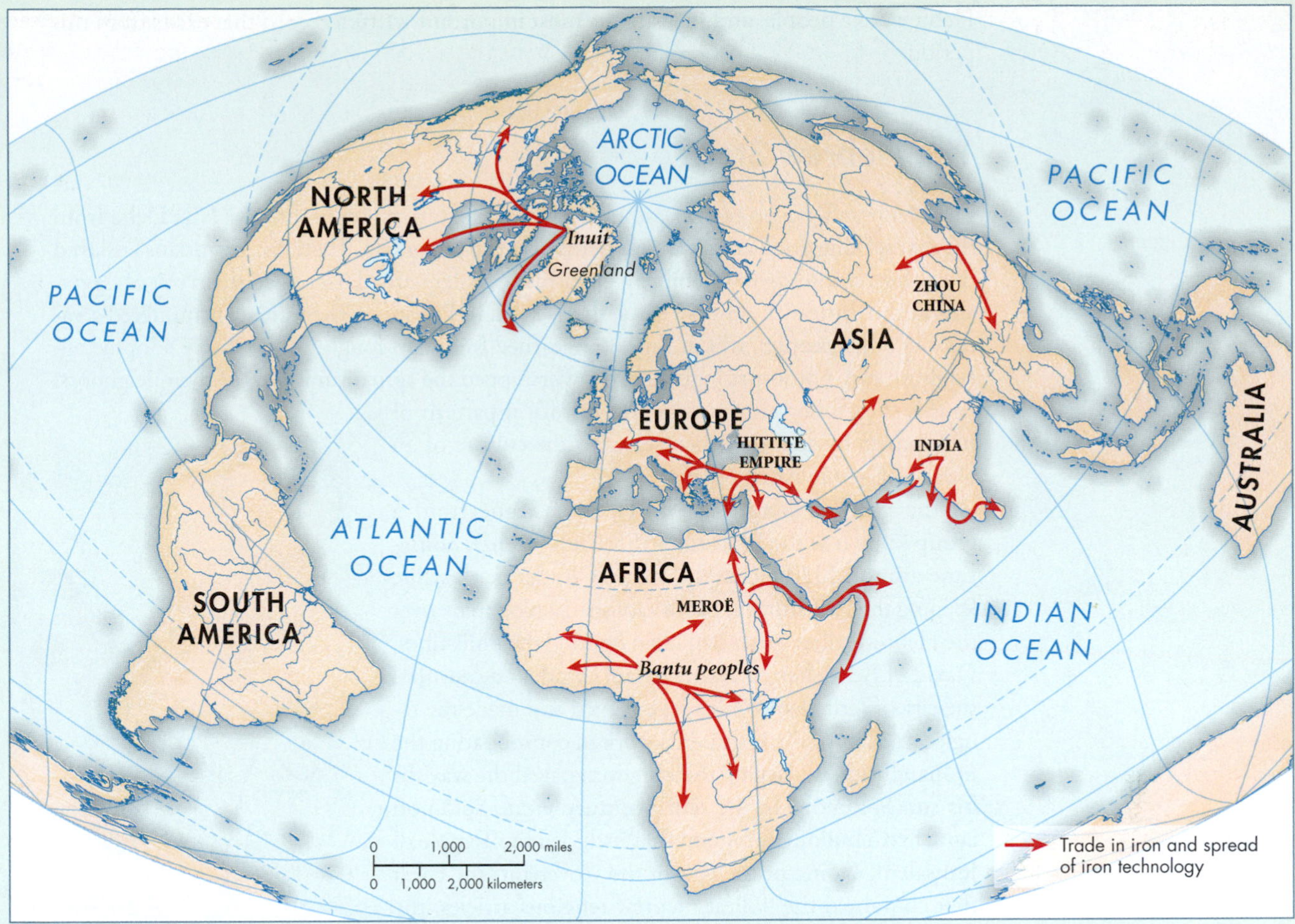

Map 2.3 Trade in Iron and Iron Technology, to 500 B.C.E.

molds. In the Near East ironworkers discovered that if the relatively brittle wrought iron objects were placed on a bed of burning charcoal and then cooled quickly, the outer layer would form into a layer of a much harder material, steel. Goods made of cast iron were usually traded locally because they were heavy, but fine sword and knife blades of steel traveled long distances, and the knowledge of how to make them followed.

What was unique about Hebrew civilization?

Another people took advantage of Egypt's collapse to found an independent state, and their legacy has been even more far-reaching than that of the Phoenicians. For several centuries, a Semitic people known as the Hebrews or the Israelites controlled a small state on the western end of the Fertile Crescent. Politically unimportant when compared with the Egyptian or Babylonian empires, the Hebrews created a new form of religious belief, a monotheism based on the worship of an all-powerful god they called **Yahweh** (YAH-way, Anglicized as Jehovah). They began to write down their religious ideas, traditions, laws, advice literature, prayers, hymns, history, and prophecies in a series of books. These were gathered together to form the Hebrew Bible. These writings are what came to define the

Yahweh All-powerful god of the Hebrew people and the basis for the enduring religious traditions of Judaism.

Hebrews as a people, and they are the most important written record that exists from this period.

The Hebrew State

The Hebrews were nomadic pastoralists who probably migrated into the Nile Delta from the east seeking good land for their herds of sheep and goats. There the Egyptians enslaved them, but, according to the Bible, a charismatic leader named Moses led them out of Egypt, and in the thirteenth century B.C.E. they settled in Palestine. There they encountered a variety of other peoples, whom they both learned from and fought. They slowly adopted agriculture and, not surprisingly, at times worshipped the agricultural gods of their neighbors. In this they followed the common historical pattern of newcomers by adapting themselves to the culture of an older, well-established people.

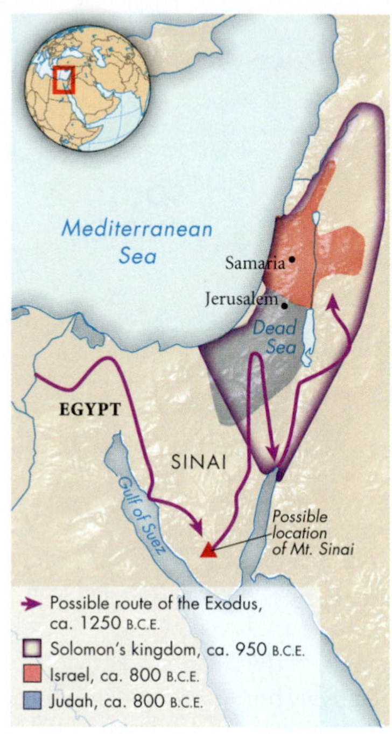

The Hebrew Exodus and State, ca. 1250–800 B.C.E.

The greatest danger to the Hebrews came from a group known as the Philistines (FIH-luh-steenz). Sometime around 1020 B.C.E. the Hebrew leader Saul, while keeping the Philistines at bay, established a monarchy over the Hebrew tribes. After Saul died fighting the Philistines, David of Bethlehem continued Saul's work and captured the city of Jerusalem, which he enlarged and made the religious center of the realm. His work in consolidating the monarchy and enlarging the kingdom paved the way for his son Solomon. In the tenth century B.C.E. Solomon launched a building program that included the Temple of Jerusalem. Home of the Ark of the Covenant, the chest that contained the holiest Hebrew religious articles, the Temple of Jerusalem was intended to be the religious heart of the kingdom, a symbol of Hebrew unity and of Yahweh's approval of the state built by Saul, David, and Solomon.

The unified Hebrew state did not last long. Upon Solomon's death his kingdom broke into political halves. The northern part became Israel, with its capital at Samaria, and the southern half was Judah, with Jerusalem remaining its center. War broke out between the northern and southern halves, and the Assyrians wiped out the northern kingdom of Israel in 720 B.C.E. Judah survived numerous invasions until the Babylonians crushed it in 587 B.C.E. The survivors were sent into exile in Babylonia, a period commonly known as the Babylonian Captivity. In 538 B.C.E. the Persian king Cyrus the Great conquered the Babylonians and permitted some forty thousand exiles to return to Jerusalem (see page 51).

The Jewish Religion

During and especially after the Babylonian Captivity, the most important Hebrew texts of history, law, and ethics were edited and brought together in the Torah, the first five books of the Hebrew Bible. The exiles redefined their beliefs and practices, thereby establishing what they believed to be the law of Yahweh. Those who lived by these precepts came to be called Jews and their religion Judaism.

Fundamental to an understanding of the Jewish religion is the concept of the Covenant, a formal agreement between Yahweh and the Hebrew people. According to the Bible,

The Golden Calf According to the Bible, Moses descended from Mount Sinai, where he had received the Ten Commandments, to find the Hebrews worshipping a golden calf, which was against Yahweh's laws. In July 1990 an American archaeological team found this model of a gilded calf inside a pot. The figurine, which dates to about 1550 B.C.E., is strong evidence for the existence of the cult represented by the calf in Palestine. (Harvard Semitic Museum, Ashkelon Excavations)

Yahweh appeared to Moses while he was leading the Hebrews out of Egypt and made the Covenant with the Hebrews: if they worshipped Yahweh as their only god, he would consider them his chosen people and protect them from their enemies. That worship was embodied in a series of rules of behavior, the Ten Commandments, which Yahweh gave to Moses. From the Ten Commandments a complex system of rules of conduct was created and later written down as Hebrew law.

The monotheistic Jewish religion contrasted sharply with the polytheism of most peoples of the surrounding area. Mesopotamian and Egyptian deities were powerful and often immortal, but they were otherwise just like humans, with good and bad personal qualities. They demanded ceremonies in their honor but were relatively unconcerned with how people behaved toward one another. The Hebrews, however, could please their god only by living up to high moral standards as well as by worshipping him. In polytheistic systems, people could easily add new gods or goddesses to the group of deities they honored. Yahweh, by contrast, demanded that the Hebrews worship him alone. Like Mesopotamian deities, Yahweh punished people, but the Hebrews also believed he would protect them all, not simply kings and powerful priests, and make them prosper if they obeyed his commandments.

Because Yahweh is a single god, not surrounded by lesser gods and goddesses, there is no female divinity in Judaism. Occasionally, however, aspects of God are described in feminine terms, such as Sophia, the wisdom of God. Religious leaders were important in Judaism, but not as important as the written texts they interpreted; these texts came to be regarded as the word of Yahweh and thus had status that other writings did not.

The Family and Jewish Life

Although the Hebrews originally were nomadic, they adopted settled agriculture in Palestine, and some lived in cities. These shifts affected more than just how people fed themselves. Communal use of land gave way to family or private ownership, and tribal identity was replaced by loyalty to a state and then to the traditions of Judaism.

Marriage and the family were fundamentally important in Jewish life. As in Mesopotamia and Egypt, marriage was a family matter, too important to be left solely to the whims of young people. Although sexual relations were seen as a source of impurity, sex itself was viewed as part of Yahweh's creation and the bearing of children was in some ways a religious function. A firstborn son became the head of the household upon his father's death. Mothers oversaw the early education of the children, but as boys grew older, their fathers provided more of their education.

The development of urban life among Jews created new economic opportunities, especially in crafts and trade, but the most important task for observant Jews was studying religious texts, especially after the return from Babylon. Until the twentieth century this activity was limited to men. For their part, women were obliged to provide for men's physical needs while they were studying. This meant that Jewish women were often more active economically than their contemporaries of other religions, trading goods the household produced.

Quick Review
How did the Hebrew religious tradition differ from that of most other peoples of their region?

How did the Assyrians and Persians build and maintain their empires?

Small kingdoms like those of the Phoenicians and the Jews could exist only in the absence of a major power. In the ninth century B.C.E. one major power arose in the form of the Assyrians, who starting in northern Mesopotamia created an empire through often brutal military conquest. And from a base in what is now southern Iran, the Persians established an even larger empire, developing effective institutions of government, building roads, and allowing a variety of customs, religions, and traditions to flourish.

Assyria, the Military Monarchy

Assyria rose at the beginning of the ninth century B.C.E. and came to dominate northern Mesopotamia from its chief capital at Nineveh on the Tigris River. The Assyrians were a Semitic people heavily influenced by the Babylonian culture to the south. They were also one of the most warlike people in history, carving out an empire that stretched from east and north of the Tigris River to central Egypt.

Those who stood up to Assyrian might were often systematically tortured and slaughtered, but Assyria's success was also due to sophisticated, farsighted, and effective military tactics, technical skills, and organization. For example, the Assyrians developed a wide variety of siege machinery and techniques, including excavations to undermine city walls and battering rams to knock down walls and gates. The Assyrians also knew how to coordinate their efforts both in open battle and in siege warfare. They divided their armies into different organizational units of infantry who fought with iron swords and spears, others who fought with slings or bows and arrows, and a third group who used chariots.

Not only did the Assyrians know how to win battles, but they also knew how to take advantage of their victories. As early as the eighth century B.C.E. the Assyrian kings began to organize their conquered territories into an empire. The lands closest to Assyria became provinces governed directly by Assyrian officials. In more distant parts of the empire, Assyrian kings chose local rulers whom they favored, and required them to pay tribute.

In the seventh century B.C.E. Assyrian power seemed firmly established. Yet the downfall of Assyria was swift and complete. Babylon won its independence in 626 B.C.E. and joined forces with a new group, the Medes, an Indo-European-speaking people from Persia. Together the Babylonians and the Medes destroyed the Assyrian Empire in 612 B.C.E., paving the way for the rise of the Persians.

The Rise and Expansion of the Persian Empire

As we have seen, Assyria rose to power from a base in the Tigris and Euphrates River Valleys of Mesopotamia, which had been home to many earlier empires. The Assyrians were defeated by a coalition that included a Mesopotamian power—Babylon—but also a people with a base of power in a part of the world that had not been the site of earlier urbanized states: Persia (modern-day Iran), a land of mountains and deserts with a broad central plateau in the heart of the country (Map 2.4).

Iran's geographical position and topography explain its traditional role as the highway between western and eastern Asia. Nomadic peoples migrating south from the broad steppes (grasslands) of Russia and Central Asia have streamed into Iran throughout much of history. (For an in-depth discussion of these groups, see Chapter 12.) Confronting the uncrossable salt deserts, most have turned either westward or eastward, moving on until

Map 2.4 The Assyrian and Persian Empires, ca. 1000–500 B.C.E. The Assyrian Empire at its height in ca. 650 B.C.E. included almost all of the old centers of power in the ancient Near East. By 513 B.C.E., however, the Persian Empire not only included more of that area but also extended as far east as western India.

they reached the urban centers of Mesopotamia and India. Cities did emerge along these routes, however, and Iran became the area where nomads met urban dwellers.

Among these nomads were various Indo-European-speaking peoples who migrated into this area about 1000 B.C.E. with their flocks and herds. They were also horse breeders, and the horse gave them a decisive military advantage over those who already lived in the area. One of the Indo-European groups was the Medes, who settled in northern Iran. With the rise of the Medes, marked by their union under one king and their defeat of the Assyrian Empire with the help of the Babylonians, the balance of power in western Asia shifted east of Mesopotamia for the first time.

The Persians were another Indo-European group, and they settled in southern Iran. In 550 B.C.E. Cyrus the Great (r. 559–530 B.C.E.), king of the Persians, conquered the Medes. The conquest resulted not in slavery and slaughter but in the union of the two peoples. Having united Iran, Cyrus set out to achieve two goals. First, he wanted to win control of the west and thus of the terminal ports of the great trade routes that crossed Iran and Anatolia (modern western Turkey). Second, he strove to secure eastern Iran from the threats of nomadic invasions. In a series of major campaigns Cyrus achieved both goals. He conquered the various kingdoms of the Tigris and Euphrates Valleys and swept into Anatolia, easily overthrowing the young kingdom of Lydia. His generals subdued the Greek cities along the coast of Anatolia and the Phoenician cities south of these, thus gaining him flourishing ports on the Mediterranean. Finally, Cyrus conquered the regions of Parthia and Bactria in central Asia, though he ultimately died on the battlefield there.

With these victories Cyrus demonstrated to the world his benevolence as well as his military might. He spared the life of the conquered king of Lydia, Croesus, who came to be Cyrus's friend and adviser. He also allowed the Greeks to live according to their customs, making possible the spread of Greek culture farther east. Cyrus's humanity likewise extended to the Jews, whom he allowed to return from Babylon to Jerusalem, where he paid for the rebuilding of their temple.

Cyrus's successors continued the Persian conquests, creating the largest empire the world had yet seen (see Map 2.4). In 525 B.C.E. his son Cambyses (r. 530–522 B.C.E.) subdued the Egyptians and the Nubians. Upon Cambyses's death, Darius (r. 521–486 B.C.E.) took over the throne and conquered Scythia in central Asia, along with much of Thrace and Macedonia, areas north of the Aegean Sea. By 510 the Persians also ruled the western coast of Anatolia and many of the islands of the Aegean. Thus, within forty years the Persians had transformed themselves from a subject people to the rulers of a vast empire that included all of the oldest kingdoms and peoples of the region, as well as many outlying areas (see Map 2.4) Although invasions of Greece by Darius and his son Xerxes were unsuccessful, the Persian Empire lasted another two hundred years, until it became part of the empire of Alexander the Great (see page 117).

The Persians also knew how to preserve the peace they had won on the battlefield. They created an efficient administrative system to govern the empire based in their newly built capital city of Persepolis, near modern Schiras, Iran. Under Darius, they divided the empire into districts and appointed either Persian or local nobles as administrators called satraps to head each one. The satrap controlled local government, collected taxes, heard legal cases, and maintained order. He was assisted by a council and also by officials and army leaders sent from Persepolis who made sure that he knew the will of the king and that the king knew what was going on in the provinces. This system was in line with the Persians' usual practice of respecting their subjects and allowing them to practice their native customs and religions, giving the Near East both political unity and cultural diversity. It also lessened opposition to Persian rule by making local elites part of the system of government, although sometimes satraps used their authority to build up independent power.

Persian Saddle-Cloth This elaborately painted piece of leather, dating from the fourth or third century B.C.E., shows running goats with huge curved horns. The fact that it survived suggests that it was not actually used, but served a ceremonial function. (© The State Hermitage Museum, St. Petersburg. Photo by Vladimir Terebenin)

Throughout the Persian Empire communication and trade were eased by a sophisticated system of roads. The main highway, the famous Royal Road, spanned some 1,677 miles (see Map 2.4). Other roads branched out from this main route to link all parts of the empire. These highways meant that the king was usually in close touch with officials and subjects, and they simplified the defense of the empire by making it easier to move Persian armies. The roads also aided the flow of trade, which Persian rulers further encouraged by building canals, including one that linked the Red Sea and the Nile.

The Religion of Zoroaster

Originally Persian religion was polytheistic, with many deities under a chief god Ahuramazda (ah-HOOR-uh-MAZ-duh), the creator of all living creatures. Around 600 B.C.E., however, the alternative views of one prophet, Zoroaster (zo-roh-ASS-tuhr), became more prominent. A thinker and preacher whose birth and death dates are uncertain, Zoroaster is regarded as the author of key religious texts, later collected as a collection of sacred texts called the *Avesta*. He introduced new spiritual concepts to the Persian people, stressing devotion to Ahuramazda alone and emphasizing the individual's responsibility to choose between the forces of creation, truth, and order and those of nothingness, chaos, falsehood, and disorder. He taught that people possessed the free will to decide between these and that they must rely on their own consciences to guide them through an active life in which they focused on "good thoughts, good words, and good deeds." Their decisions were crucial, Zoroaster warned, for there would come a time of reckoning. At the end of time the forces of order would win, and Ahuramazda would preside over a last judgment to determine each person's eternal fate.

King Darius became a follower of **Zoroastrianism**, and in many inscriptions proclaimed that he was divinely chosen by Ahuramazda. Continuing the common Persian pattern of toleration, Darius did not impose his religious beliefs on others, but under the protection of the Persian kings, Zoroastrianism won converts throughout Iran and the rest of the Persian Empire and spread into central China. It became the official religion of the later Persian Empire ruled by the Sassanid dynasty, and much later Zoroastrians migrated to western India, where they became known as Parsis and still live today. The religion survived the fall of the Persian Empire to influence Judaism, Christianity, Islam, and Buddhism, and its key tenets are shared by many religions: good behavior in the world, even though it might be unrecognized during one's life, will be amply rewarded in the hereafter. Evil, no matter how powerful in life, will be punished after death.

Zoroastrianism The religion based on the teachings of Zoroaster, who emphasized the individual's responsibility to choose between good and evil.

Quick Review
What were the most important differences between the Assyrian and Persian Empires?

Connections

"HISTORY IS WRITTEN by the victors," goes a common saying often incorrectly attributed to Sir Winston Churchill. This is not always true; people who have been vanquished in wars or devastated by oppression have certainly made their stories known. But in other ways it is always true, for writing created records and therefore was the origin of what many people understand as history. Writing was invented to serve the needs of people who lived close to one another in cities and states, and almost everyone who could write lived in states. Because most history, including this book, concentrates on areas with states, the next two chapters examine the states that were developing in India and China during the period discussed in this chapter. In Chapter 5 we pick up on developments in the Mediterranean that link to those in Mesopotamia, Egypt, and Persia discussed in this chapter.

It is important to remember that, as was the spread of agriculture, the growth of the state was a slow process. States became the most powerful and most densely populated forms of human society, and today almost everyone on the planet is at least hypothetically a citizen of a state (or sometimes of more than one, if he or she has dual citizenship). Just three hundred years ago, however, only about a third of the world was governed by states; in the rest of the world, people lived in bands of foragers, villages led by kin leaders, family groups of pastoralists, chiefdoms, confederations of tribes, or other forms of social organization. In 500 B.C.E. perhaps only a little over 5 percent of the world's population lived in states. Thus, in their attempts to provide a balanced account of all the world's peoples, historians today are looking beyond written sources. Those sources invariably present only part of the story, as Winston Churchill—a historian as well as a political leader—noted in something he actually *did* say: "History will bear me out, particularly as I shall write that history myself."

- **For a list of suggested readings for this chapter, visit** *bedfordstmartins.com/mckayworldunderstanding*.
- **For primary sources from this period, see** *Sources of World Societies*, Second Edition.
- **For Web sites, images, and documents related to topics in this chapter, see Make History at** *bedfordstmartins.com/mckayworldunderstanding*.

Chapter 2 **Study Guide**

To do these exercises online, go to bedfordstmartins.com/mckayworldunderstanding.

Step 1

GETTING STARTED

Below are basic terms about this period in global history. Can you identify each term below and explain why it matters?

TERMS	WHO (OR WHAT) AND WHEN	WHY IT MATTERS
ziggurat, p. 33		
cuneiform, p. 35		
epic poems, p. 35		
pharaoh, p. 39		
polytheism, p. 40		
Book of the Dead, p. 40		
hieroglyphs, p. 40		
Indo-European language family, p. 43		
Phoenicians , p. 45		
Yahweh, p. 47		
Zoroastrianism, p. 53		

Step 2

MOVING BEYOND THE BASICS

The exercise below requires a more advanced understanding of the chapter material. Examine the development of regional powers in Mesopotamia, Egypt, Assyria, and Persia by filling in the chart below with descriptions of the four key factors contributing to the emergence of a powerful state in each region: government, methods of expansion, role of religion, and role of trade. When you are finished, consider the following questions: What techniques did ruling elites use to justify and perpetuate their power? How would you characterize the relationship between each state and the other cultures and societies that came under its control?

	GOVERNMENT	METHODS OF EXPANSION	ROLE OF RELIGION	ROLE OF TRADE
Mesopotamia				
Egypt				
Assyria				
Persia				

Step 3

PUTTING IT ALL TOGETHER

Now that you've reviewed key elements of the chapter, take a step back and try to see the big picture. Remember to use specific examples from the chapter in your answers.

GOVERNMENT AND SOCIETY IN ANCIENT MESOPOTAMIA AND EGYPT

- What role did religion play in legitimizing the power of Mesopotamian and Egyptian rulers?
- What similarities and differences do you note in the structure of Mesopotamian and Egyptian society? How would you explain these similarities and differences?

HEBREW RELIGION AND SOCIETY

- How did the experience of subjugation and exile shape Hebrew religion and culture?
- How did the Hebrew's relationship with Yahweh differ from that of their neighbors' relationships with their deities?

IMPERIAL POWERS: ASSYRIA AND PERSIA

- How did the brutality of Assyrian rule contribute both to the rise and fall of their empire?
- How did the Persians build and maintain their empire? What explains its long-term stability?

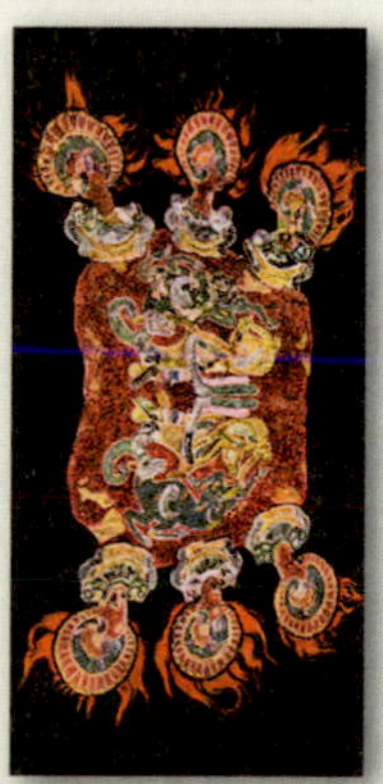

LOOKING BACK, LOOKING AHEAD

- How did the states of Mesopotamia, Egypt, Assyria, and the Persian Empire differ from earlier forms of social and political organization?
- How would you explain the fact that, over time, the state became the dominant form of political organization in societies around the world?

In Your Own Words Imagine that you must explain Chapter 2 to someone who hasn't read it. What would be the most important points to include and why?

3

The Foundation of Indian Society

to 300 C.E.

During the centuries when the peoples of ancient Mesopotamia and Egypt were developing urban civilizations, people in India were wrestling with the same challenges—food production, the building of cities, political administration, and questions about human life and the cosmos. Like the civilizations of the Near East, the earliest Indian civilization centered on a great river, the Indus. From about 2800 to 1800 B.C.E. the Indus Valley, or Harappan (huh-RAH-puhn), culture thrived and expanded over a huge area.

A very different Indian society emerged after the decline of this civilization. It was dominated by the Aryans, warriors who spoke an early version of Sanskrit. The Indian caste system and the Hindu religion, key features of Indian society into modern times, had their origins in early Aryan society. By the middle of the first millennium B.C.E. the Aryans had set up numerous small kingdoms throughout north India. This was the great age of Indian religious creativity, when Buddhism and Jainism were founded and the early Brahmanic religion of the Aryans developed into Hinduism.

Female Spirit from an Indian Stupa Royal patronage aided the spread of Buddhism in India. This head of a female spirit (called a *yakshini*) is from the stupa that King Ashoka had built at Bharhut in central India. (India Museum, Calcutta, India/Giraudon/The Bridgeman Art Library)

The first major Indian empire, the Mauryan (MAWR-ee-uhn) Dynasty, emerged in the wake of the Greek invasion of north India in 326 B.C.E. In less than two centuries, however, the empire broke up, and for several centuries India was politically divided. Although India never had a single language and only periodically had a centralized government, cultural elements dating back to the ancient period—the core ideas of Brahmanism, the caste system, and the early epics—spread through trade and other contact, even when the subcontinent was divided into hostile kingdoms.

Chapter Preview

- What were the key characteristics of India's first civilization?
- What kind of society and culture did the Indo-European Aryans create?
- What new religious beliefs emerged to challenge Brahmanism?
- How was the Mauryan Empire created and what were its achievements?
- How did political disunity shape Indian life after 185 B.C.E.?

What were the key characteristics of India's first civilization?

The subcontinent of India juts southward into the warm waters of the Indian Ocean. In India, as elsewhere, the possibilities for both agriculture and communication have always been strongly shaped by geography. Some regions of the subcontinent are among the wettest on earth; others are arid deserts and scrubland. Most areas in India are warm all year. Monsoon rains sweep northward from the Indian Ocean each summer. The lower reaches of the Himalaya Mountains in the northeast are covered by dense forests that are sustained by heavy rainfall. Immediately to the south are the fertile valleys of the Indus and Ganges Rivers, the centers of India's great empires. To their west are the deserts of Rajasthan and southeastern Pakistan, historically important in part because their flat terrain enabled invaders to sweep into India from the northwest. South of the great river valleys rise the jungle-clad Vindhya Mountains and the dry, hilly Deccan Plateau. India's long coastlines and predictable winds fostered maritime trade with other countries bordering the Indian Ocean.

Neolithic settlement of the Indian subcontinent occurred somewhat later than in the Near East, but agriculture followed a similar pattern of development and was well established by about 7000 B.C.E. Wheat and barley were the early crops, probably having spread in their domesticated form from the Middle East. Farmers also domesticated cattle, sheep, and goats and learned to make pottery.

Harappan The first Indian civilization; also known as the Indus Valley civilization.

The first civilization in India is known today as the Indus Valley or the **Harappan** civilization. Archaeologists have discovered some three hundred Harappan cities and many more towns and villages in both Pakistan and India (Map 3.1). It was a literate civilization, like those of Egypt and Mesopotamia, but no one has been able to decipher the more than four hundred symbols inscribed on stone seals and copper tablets. The civilization's most flourishing period was from 2800 to 1800 B.C.E.

Map 3.1 Harappan Civilization, ca. 2500 B.C.E. The earliest civilization in India developed in the Indus River Valley in the west of the subcontinent.

The Harappan civilization extended over nearly five hundred thousand square miles, making it more than twice as large as ancient Egypt or Sumer. Yet Harappan civilization was marked by a striking uniformity. Throughout the region, for instance, even in small villages, bricks were made to the same standard proportion (4:2:1). Figurines of pregnant women have been found throughout the area, suggesting common religious ideas and practices.

Like Mesopotamian cities, Harappan cities were centers for crafts and trade, and they were surrounded by extensive farmland. The Harappans were the earliest known manufacturers of cotton cloth, and this cloth was so abundant that goods were wrapped in it for shipment. Trade was extensive. As early as the reign of Sargon of Akkad in the third millennium B.C.E. (see page 36), trade between India and Mesopotamia carried goods and ideas between the two cultures, probably by way of the Persian Gulf.

The cities of Mohenjo-daro in southern Pakistan, and Harappa, some 400 miles to the north, were huge for this period, more than 3 miles in circumference, with populations estimated at 35,000 to 40,000. Both were defended by great citadels that towered 40 to 50 feet above the surrounding plain. The cities had obviously been planned and built before being settled. Large granaries stored food. Streets were straight and varied from

9 to 34 feet in width. The houses were substantial, many two stories tall, some perhaps three. The focal point of a house was a central courtyard onto which the rooms opened, much like many houses today in both rural and urban India.

Perhaps the most surprising aspect of the elaborate planning of these cities was their complex system of drainage, which is well preserved at Mohenjo-daro. Each house had a bathroom with a drain connected to brick-lined sewers located under the major streets. Openings allowed the refuse to be collected, probably to be used as fertilizer on nearby fields. No other ancient city had such an advanced sanitation system.

The prosperity of the Indus civilization depended on constant and intensive cultivation of the rich river valley. Although rainfall seems to have been greater then than in recent times, the Indus, like the Nile, flowed through a

Chapter Chronology

2800–1800 B.C.E.	Height of Harappan civilization
ca. 1500–500 B.C.E.	Vedic Age; flourishing of Aryan civilization; *Rigveda*
ca. 1000 B.C.E.	Introduction of iron
750–500 B.C.E.	*Upanishads*
ca. 513 B.C.E.	Persians conquer the Indus Valley and Kashmir
ca. 500 B.C.E.	Founding of Buddhism and Jainism
ca. 400 B.C.E.–200 C.E.	Gradual evolution of the Brahman religion into Hinduism
326 B.C.E.	Alexander the Great enters Indus Valley
ca. 322–185 B.C.E.	Mauryan Empire
ca. 300 B.C.E.	Jain religion splits into two sects
ca. 269–232 B.C.E.	Reign of Ashoka
ca. 200 B.C.E.–200 C.E.	Classical period of Tamil culture
ca. 100 C.E.	More inclusive Mahayana form of Buddhism emerges
ca. 200 C.E.	Code of Manu

Mohenjo-daro The Harappan city of Mohenjo-daro was a planned city built of fired mud brick. Its streets were straight, and covered drainpipes were installed to carry away waste. From sites like this, we know that the early Indian political elite had the power and technical expertise to organize large, coordinated building projects. Found in Mohenjo-daro, this small ceramic figurine (inset) shows a woman adorned with six necklaces. (site: J. M. Kenoyer/Courtesy, Department of Archaeology and Museums, Government of Pakistan; figurine: Angelo Hornak/Alamy)

relatively dry region made fertile by annual floods and irrigation. And as in Egypt, agriculture was aided by a long, hot growing season and near constant sunshine.

Because the written language of the Harappan people has not been deciphered, their political, intellectual, and religious life is largely unknown. There clearly was a political structure with the authority to organize city planning and facilitate trade, but we do not even know whether there were hereditary kings. There are clear connections between Harappan and Sumerian civilization, but just as clear differences. For instance, the Harappan script, like the Sumerian, was incised on clay tablets and seals, but it has no connection to Sumerian cuneiform, and the artistic style of the Harappan seals also is distinct.

Soon after 2000 B.C.E. the Harappan civilization mysteriously declined. Many cities were abandoned and others housed only a fraction of their earlier populations. Scholars have offered many explanations for Harappan decline. The decline cannot be attributed to the arrival of powerful invaders, as was once thought. Rather it was internally generated. Environmental theories include an earthquake that led to a shift in the course of the river, or a severe drought. Perhaps the long-term practice of irrigation led to the buildup of salts and alkaline in the soil until they reached levels toxic to plants. Some scholars speculate that long-distance commerce collapsed, leading to an economic depression. Others theorize that the population fell prey to diseases, such as malaria, that caused people to flee the cities.

Quick Review
What can we infer about Harappan civilization from the available archaeological evidence? What questions will likely remain unanswered?

What kind of society and culture did the Indo-European Aryans create?

Aryans The dominant people in north India after the decline of the Indus Valley civilization; they spoke an early form of Sanskrit.

After the decline of the Harappan civilization, a people who called themselves **Aryans** became dominant in north India. They were speakers of an early form of Sanskrit, an Indo-European language closely related to ancient Persian. The Aryans flourished during the Vedic Age (ca. 1500–500 B.C.E.). Named for the Vedas, a large and significant body of ancient sacred works written in Sanskrit, this period witnessed the Indo-Aryan development of the caste system and Brahman religion and the writing of the great epics that represent the earliest form of Indian literature.

Aryan Dominance in North India

Until relatively recently, the dominant theory was that the Aryans came into India from outside, perhaps as part of the same movements of people that led to the Hittites occupying parts of Anatolia, the Achaeans entering Greece, and the Kassites conquering Sumer—all in the period from about 1900 to 1750 B.C.E. Some scholars, however, have proposed that the Indo-European languages spread to this area much earlier; to them it seems possible that the Harappan people were speakers of an early Indo-European language. If that was the case, the Aryans would be one of the groups descended from this early population.

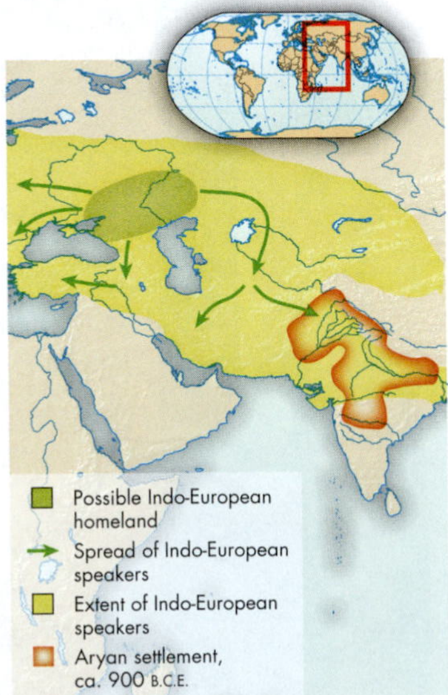

Indo-European Migrations and the Vedic Age

The central source of information on the early Aryans is the **Rigveda**, the earliest of the Vedas, an originally oral collection of hymns, ritual texts, and philosophical treatises composed in Sanskrit between 1500 and 500 B.C.E. Like Homer's epics in Greece, written in this same period, these texts were transmitted orally and are in verse. The *Rigveda* portrays the Aryans as warrior tribes who glorified military skill and heroism. The Aryans did not sweep across India in a quick campaign, nor were they a disciplined army led by one conqueror. Rather they were a collection of tribes that frequently fought with each other and only over the course of several centuries came to dominate north India.

Rigveda The earliest collection of Indian hymns, ritual texts, and philosophical treatises; it is the central source of information on early Aryans.

The key to the Aryans' success probably lay in their superior military technology, including two-wheeled chariots, horses, and bronze swords and spears. Their epics present the struggle for north India in religious terms, describing their chiefs as godlike heroes and their opponents as irreligious savages who did not perform the proper sacrifices. In time, however, the Aryans clearly absorbed much from those they conquered, such as agricultural techniques and foods.

At the head of each Aryan tribe was a chief, or raja (RAH-juh). The warriors in the tribe elected the chief for his military skills. Next in importance to the chief was the priest. In time, priests evolved into a distinct class, rather like the priest classes in ancient Egypt, Mesopotamia, and Persia. Below them in the pecking order was a warrior nobility who rode into battle in chariots and perhaps on horseback. The warrior class met at assemblies to reach decisions and advise the raja. The common tribesmen tended herds and worked the land. It is difficult to define precisely the social status of the conquered non-Aryans. Though probably not slaves, they were certainly subordinate to the Aryans and worked for them in return for protection.

Bronze Sword This bronze sword, with a rib in the middle of the blade for strength, is a striking example of the quality of Aryan arms. Superior weapons gave the Aryans military advantage. (Courtesy of the Trustees of the British Museum)

Over the course of several centuries, the Aryans pushed farther east into the valley of the Ganges River, at that time a land of thick jungle. The tremendous challenge of clearing the jungle was made somewhat easier by the introduction of iron around 1000 B.C.E., probably by diffusion from Mesopotamia. (See "Global Trade: Iron," page 46.) Iron made it possible to produce strong axes and knives relatively cheaply.

The Aryans did not gain dominance over the entire Indian subcontinent. South of the Vindhya range, people speaking Dravidian languages maintained their control. In the great Aryan epics the *Ramayana* and *Mahabharata*, the people of the south and Sri Lanka are spoken of as dark-skinned savages and demons who resisted the Aryans' conquests. Along with the *Rigveda*, these epics would become part of the common cultural heritage of all of India.

As Aryan rulers came to dominate large settled populations, the style of political organization changed from tribal chieftainship to territorial kingship. In other words, the ruler now controlled an area with people living in permanent settlements, not a nomadic tribe that moved as a group. The priests, or **Brahmins**, supported the growth of royal power in return for royal confirmation of their own power and status. The Brahmins also served as advisers to the kings. In the face of this royal-priestly alliance, the old tribal assemblies of warriors withered away, and kings were no longer elected. By the time Persian armies reached the Indus around 513 B.C.E., there were sixteen major Aryan kingdoms in north India.

Brahmins Priests of the Aryans; they supported the growth of royal power in return for royal confirmation of their own religious rights, power, and status.

Life in Early India

Caste was central to the social life of these north Indian kingdoms. Early Aryan society had distinguished among the warrior elite, the priests, ordinary tribesmen, and conquered subjects. These distinctions gradually evolved into the **caste system**, which divided society into four hereditary hierarchical strata whose members did not eat with or marry each other. These strata, or varna, were Brahmin (priests), Kshatriya (warriors and officials), Vaishya

caste system The Indian system of dividing society into hereditary groups whose members interacted primarily within the group, and especially married within the group.

LISTENING TO THE PAST

Conversations Between Rama and Sita from the *Ramayana*

The Ramayana, *an epic poem of about fifty thousand verses, is attributed to the third-century* B.C.E. *poet Valmiki. Its main character, Rama, the oldest son of a king, is an incarnation of the great god Vishnu. As a young man, he wins the princess Sita as his wife when he alone among her suitors proves strong enough to bend a huge bow. Rama and Sita love each other deeply, but court intrigue disturbs their happy life. After the king announces that he will retire and consecrate Rama as his heir, the king's beautiful junior wife, wishing to advance her own son, reminds the king that he has promised her a favor of her choice. She then asks to have him appoint her son heir and to have Rama sent into the wilderness for fourteen years. The king is forced to consent, and Rama obeys his father.*

The passage below gives the conversations between Rama and Sita after Rama learns he must leave. In subsequent parts of the very long epic, the lovers undergo many other tribulations, including Sita's abduction by the lord of the demons, the ten-headed Ravana, and her eventual recovery by Rama with the aid of monkeys.

The Ramayana *eventually appeared in numerous versions in all the major languages of India. Hearing it recited was said to bring religious merit. Sita, passionate in her devotion to her husband, has remained the favorite Indian heroine. Rama, Sita, and the monkey Hanuman are cult figures in Hinduism, with temples devoted to their worship.*

"For fourteen years I must live in Dandaka, while my father will appoint Bharata prince regent. I have come to see you before I leave for the desolate forest. You are never to boast of me in the presence of Bharata. Men in power cannot bear to hear others praised, and so you must never boast of my virtues in front of Bharata. . . . When I have gone to the forest where sages make their home, my precious, blameless wife, you must earnestly undertake vows and fasts. You must rise early and worship the gods according to custom and then pay homage to my father Dasaratha, lord of men. And my aged mother Kausalya, who is tormented by misery, deserves your respect as well, for she has subordinated all to righteousness. The rest of my mothers, too, must always receive your homage. . . . My beloved, I am going to the great forest, and you must stay here. You must do as I tell you, my lovely, and not give offense to anyone."

So Rama spoke, and Sita, who always spoke kindly to her husband and deserved kindness from him, grew angry just because she loved him, and said, "My lord, a man's father, his mother, brother, son, or daughter-in-law all experience the effects of their own past deeds and suffer an individual fate. But a wife, and she alone, bull among men, must share her husband's fate. Therefore I, too, have been ordered to live in the forest. It is not her father or mother, not her son or friends or herself, but her husband, and he alone, who gives a woman permanent refuge in this world and after death. If you must leave this very day for the trackless forest, Rama, I will go in front of you, softening the thorns and sharp *kusa* grass. Cast out your anger and resentment, like so much water left after drinking one's fill. Do not be reluctant to take me, my mighty husband. There is no evil in me. The shadow of a husband's feet in any circumstances surpasses the finest mansions, an aerial chariot, or even flying through the sky. . . . O Rama, bestower of honor, you have the power to protect any other person in the forest. Why then not me? . . .

"If I were to be offered a place to live in heaven itself, Rama, tiger among men, I would refuse it if you were not there. I will go to the trackless forest teeming with deer, monkeys, and elephants, and live there as in my father's house, clinging to your feet alone, in strict self-discipline. I love no one else; my heart is so attached to you that were we to be parted I am resolved to die. Take me, oh please grant my request. I shall not be a burden to you." . . .

When Sita finished speaking, the righteous prince, who knew what was right and cherished it, attempted to dissuade her. . . .

"Sita, give up this notion of living in the forest. The name 'forest' is given only to wild regions where hardships abound. . . . There are lions that live in mountain caves; their roars are redoubled by mountain torrents and are a painful thing to hear — the forest is a place of pain. At night worn with fatigue, one must sleep upon the ground on a bed of leaves, broken off of themselves — the forest is a place of utter pain. And one has to fast, Sita, to the limit of one's endurance, wear clothes of barkcloth and bear the burden

(merchants), and Shudra (peasants and laborers). The three upper varnas probably accounted for no more than 30 percent of the population. The caste system thus allowed the numerically outnumbered Aryans to maintain dominance over their subjects and not be culturally absorbed by them.

Those without places in the four varna — that is, newly conquered peoples and those who had lost their caste status through violations of ritual — were outcastes. That simply meant that they belonged to no caste. In time, some of them became "untouchables" be-of matted hair. . . . There are many creeping creatures, of every size and shape, my lovely, ranging aggressively over the ground. . . . Moths, scorpions, worms, gnats, and flies continually harass one, my frail Sita — the forest is wholly a place of pain. . . ."

Sita was overcome with sorrow when she heard what Rama said. With tears trickling down her face, she answered him in a faint voice. . . . "If from feelings of love I follow you, my pure-hearted husband, I shall have no sin to answer for, because my husband is my deity. My union with you is sacred and shall last even beyond death. . . . If you refuse to take me to the forest despite the sorrow that I feel, I shall have no recourse but to end my life by poison, fire, or water."

Though she pleaded with him in this and every other way to be allowed to go, great-armed Rama would not consent to taking her to the desolate forest. And when he told her as much, Sita fell to brooding, and drenched the ground, it seemed, with the hot tears that fell from her eyes. . . . She was nearly insensible with sorrow when Rama took her in his arms and comforted her. . . . "Without knowing your true feelings, my lovely, I could not consent to your living in the wilderness, though I am perfectly capable of protecting you. Since you are determined to live with me in the forest, Sita, I could no sooner abandon you than a self-respecting man his reputation. . . . My father keeps to the path of righteousness and truth, and I wish to act just as he instructs me. That is the eternal way of righteousness. Follow me, my timid one, be my companion in righteousness. Go now and bestow precious objects on the brahmins, give food to the mendicants and all who ask for it. Hurry, there is no time to waste."

Finding that her husband had acquiesced in her going, the lady was elated and set out at once to make the donations. ”

Source: *The Ramayana of Valmiki: An Epic of India*, vol. 2: *Ayodhyakanda*, trans. Sheldon I. Pollock, ed. Robert P. Goldman (Princeton, N.J.: Princeton University Press, 1986), pp. 134–142, modified slightly.

Rama and Sita in the forest, from a set of miniature paintings done in about 1600. (National Museum, New Delhi)

QUESTIONS FOR ANALYSIS

1. What can you infer about early Indian family life and social relations from this story?
2. What do Sita's words and actions indicate about women's roles in Indian society of the time?
3. What do you think accounts for the continuing popularity of the story of Rama throughout Indian history?

cause they were "impure." They were scorned because they earned their living by performing such "polluting" jobs as slaughtering animals and dressing skins.

Slavery was a feature of early social life in India, as it was in Egypt, Mesopotamia, and elsewhere in antiquity. People captured in battle often became slaves. Later, slavery was less connected with warfare and became more of an economic and social institution. As in ancient Mesopotamia, a free man might sell himself and his family into slavery because he could not pay his debts. And, as in Hammurabi's Mesopotamia, he could, if clever, hard-working, or fortunate, buy his and his family's way out of slavery. At birth, slave children automatically became the slaves of their parents' masters. Indian slaves could be bought, used as collateral, or given away.

Women's lives in early India varied according to their social status, much as men's did. Like most nomadic tribes, the Aryans were patrilineal and patriarchal (tracing descent through males and placing power in the senior men of the family). Thus the roles of women in Aryan society probably were more subordinate than were the roles of women in local Dravidian groups, many of which were matrilineal (tracing descent through females). But even in Aryan society women were treated somewhat more favorably than in later Indian society. They were not yet given in child-marriage, and widows had the right to remarry. In epics such as the *Ramayana*, women are often portrayed as forceful personalities. (See "Listening to the Past: Conversations Between Rama and Sita from the *Ramayana*," page 62.)

Brahmanism

The Aryans' religious beliefs recognized a multitude of gods. These gods shared some features with the gods of other early Indo-European societies such as the Persians and Greeks. Some of them were great brawling figures, such as Agni, the god of fire and, as in ancient Persia, a particularly important god; Indra, wielder of the thunderbolt and god of war; and Rudra, the divine archer who spread disaster and disease by firing his arrows at people. Others were shadowy figures, such as Dyaus, the father of the gods, related to the Greek Zeus. Varuna, the god of order in the universe, was a hard god, quick to punish those who sinned and thus upset the balance of nature. Ushas, the goddess of dawn, was a gentle deity who welcomed the birds, gave delight to human beings, and warded off evil spirits.

Ordinary people dealt with these gods through priests who made animal sacrifices to them. Gradually, under the priestly monopoly of the Brahmins, correct sacrifice and proper ritual became so important that most Brahmins believed that a properly performed ritual would force a god to grant a worshipper's wish. Ordinary people could watch a ceremony, such as a fire ritual, which was often held outdoors, but could not perform the key steps in the ritual.

The *Upanishads* (oo-PAH-nih-shadz), composed between 750 and 500 B.C.E., record speculations about the mystical meaning of sacrificial rites and about cosmological questions of man's relationship to the universe. They document a gradual shift from the mythical worldview of the early Vedic age to a deeply philosophical one. Associated with this shift was a movement toward asceticism (uh-SEH-tuh-siz-uhm)—severe self-discipline and self-denial. Always male, ascetics believed that disciplined meditation on the ritual sacrifice could produce the same results as the physical ritual itself. Thus they reinterpreted ritual sacrifices as symbolic gestures with mystical meanings.

Ancient Indian cosmology (theories of the universe) focused not on a creator who made the universe out of nothing, but rather on endlessly repeating cycles. Key ideas were **samsara**, the reincarnation of souls by a continual process of rebirth, and **karma**, the tally of good and bad deeds that determined the status of an individual's next life. Good deeds led to better future lives, evil deeds to worse future lives.

samsara The transmigration of souls by a continual process of rebirth.

karma The tally of good and bad deeds that determines the status of an individual's next life.

To most people, especially those on the low end of the economic and social scale, these ideas were attractive. By living righteously and doing good deeds, people could improve their lot in the next life. Yet for some, these ideas gave rise to a yearning for release from the relentless cycle of birth and death. One solution offered in the *Upanishads* was moksha, or release from the wheel of life. Brahmanic mystics claimed that life in the world was actually an illusion and that the only way to escape the wheel of life was to realize that ultimate reality was unchanging.

The unchanging ultimate reality was called **brahman**. Brahman was contrasted to the multitude of fleeting phenomena that people consider important in their daily lives. The individual soul or self was ultimately the same substance as the universal brahman, in the same way that each spark is in substance the same as a large fire.

brahman The unchanging ultimate reality, according to the *Upanishads*.

The *Upanishads* gave the Brahmins a high status to which the poor and lowly could aspire in a future life. Consequently, the Brahmins greeted the concepts presented in these works and those who taught them with tolerance and understanding and made a place for them in traditional religious practice. The rulers of Indian society also encouraged the new trends, since the doctrines of samsara and karma encouraged the poor and oppressed to labor peacefully and dutifully. In other words, although the new doctrines were intellectually revolutionary, in social and political terms they supported the existing power structure.

Quick Review
In what ways did the Aryans create the foundations for later Indian political and religious institutions and ideas?

What new religious beliefs emerged to challenge Brahmanism?

By the sixth and fifth centuries B.C.E., cities once again dotted India, merchants and trade were thriving, and written language had reappeared. This was a period of intellectual ferment throughout Eurasia—the period of the early Greek philosophers, the Hebrew prophets, Zoroaster in Persia, and Confucius and the early Daoists in China. In India it led to numerous sects that rejected various elements of Brahmanic teachings. (See "Individuals in Society: Gosala," page 66.) The two most influential were Jainism and Buddhism. Hinduism emerged in response to these new religions but at the same time was the most direct descendant of the old Brahmanic religion.

Jainism

The key figure of Jainism, Vardhamana Mahavira (fl. ca. 520 B.C.E.), was the son of the chief of a small state and a member of the warrior class. Like many ascetics of the period, he left home to become a wandering holy man. For twelve years, he traveled through the Ganges Valley until he found enlightenment and became a "completed soul." Mahavira taught his doctrines for about thirty years, founding an order of monks and gaining the support of many lay followers, male and female.

Mahavira accepted the Brahman doctrines of karma and rebirth but developed these ideas in new directions, founding a new religion referred to as Jainism. He argued that human beings, animals, plants, and even inanimate objects all have living souls enmeshed in matter, accumulated through the workings of karma. The ascetic, who willingly undertakes suffering, can dissipate some of the accumulated karma and make progress toward liberation. If a soul at last escapes from all the matter weighing it down, it floats to the top of the universe, where it remains forever in inactive bliss.

Mahavira's followers pursued such liberation by living ascetic lives and avoiding evil thoughts and actions. The Jains considered all life sacred and tried to live without destroying other life. Some early Jains went to the extreme of starving themselves to death, since it is impossible to eat without destroying at least plants, but most took the less extreme step of distinguishing between different levels of life. The most sacred life-forms were human beings, followed by animals, plants, and inanimate objects. A Jain who wished to avoid violence to life became a vegetarian and took pains not to kill any creature, even tiny insects in the air and soil. The Jains' radical nonviolence was motivated by a desire to escape

INDIVIDUALS IN SOCIETY

Gosala

TEXTS THAT SURVIVE FROM EARLY INDIA ARE RICH in religious and philosophical speculation and in tales of gods and heroes, but not in history of the sort written by the early Chinese and Greeks. Because Indian writers and thinkers of antiquity had little interest in recording the actions of rulers or accounting for the rise and decline of different states, few people's lives are known in any detail.

Religious literature, however, does sometimes include details of the lives of followers and adversaries. The life of Gosala, for instance, is known primarily from early Buddhist and Jain scriptures. He was a contemporary of both Mahavira, the founder of the Jains, and Gautama, the Buddha, and both of them saw him as one of their most pernicious rivals.

According to the Jain account, Gosala was born in the north Indian kingdom of Magadha, the son of a professional beggar. The name Gosala, which means "cowshed," alluded to the fact that he was born in a cowshed where his parents had taken refuge during the rainy season. The Buddhist account adds that he became a naked wandering ascetic when he fled from his enraged master after breaking an oil jar. As a mendicant he soon fell in with Mahavira, who had recently commenced his life as an ascetic. After accompanying Mahavira on his travels for at least six years, Gosala came to feel that he was spiritually more advanced than his master and left to undertake the practice of austerities on his own. According to the Jain account, after he gained magical powers, he challenged his master and gathered his own disciples.

Both Jain and Buddhist sources agree that Gosala taught a form of fatalism that they saw as dangerously wrong. A Buddhist source says that he taught that people are good or bad not because of their own efforts but because of fate. "Just as a ball of string when it is cast forth will spread out just as far and no farther than it can unwind so both fools and wise alike wandering in transmigration exactly for the allotted term shall then and only then make an end of pain."* Some people reach perfection not by their own efforts, but rather through the course of numerous rebirths over hundreds of thousands of years until they rid themselves of bad karma.

The Jains claimed that Gosala violated the celibacy expected of ascetics by living with a potter woman and, moreover, that he taught that sexual relations were not sinful. The followers of Gosala, a Buddhist source stated, wore no clothing and were particular about the food they accepted, refusing food specially prepared for them, food in a cooking pan, and food from couples or women with children. Like other ascetics, Gosala's followers owned no property, carrying the principle further than the Jains, who allowed the possession of a food bowl. They made a bowl from the palms of their hands, giving them the name "hand lickers."

Jain sources report that after sixteen years of separation, Mahavira happened to come to the town where Gosala lived. When Gosala heard that Mahavira spoke contemptuously of him, he and his followers went to Mahavira's lodgings, and the two sides came to blows. Soon thereafter, Gosala became unhinged, gave up all ascetic restraint, and, after six months of singing, dancing, drinking, and other riotous living, died, though not before telling his disciples, the Jains report, that Mahavira was right. Doubt is cast on this version of his end by the fact that for centuries to come, Gosala's followers, called the Ajivikas, were an important sect in several parts of India. The Mauryan ruler Ashoka honored them among other sects and dedicated some caves to them.

*A. F. R. Hoernle, "Ajivikas," in *Encyclopedia of Religion and Ethics*, vol. 1, ed. James Hastings (Edinburgh: T. & T. Clark, 1908), p. 262.

QUESTIONS FOR ANALYSIS

1. How would Gosala's own followers have described his life? What sorts of distortions are likely in a life known primarily from the writings of rivals?
2. How would the early Indian economy have been affected by the presence of ascetic beggars?

For several years before setting off on his own, Gosala followed Mahavira, depicted here at a Jain cave temple. (Dinodia Picture Agency)

the karmic consequences of causing harm to a life. In other words, violence had to be avoided above all because it harms the person who commits it.

For the first century after Mahavira's death, the Jains were a comparatively small and unimportant sect. Jainism began to flourish under the Mauryan Dynasty (ca. 322–185 B.C.E.; see pages 71–72), and Jain tradition claims the Mauryan Empire's founder, Chandragupta, as a major patron. About 300 B.C.E. the Jain scriptures were recorded. Over the next few centuries Jain monks were particularly important in spreading northern culture into the Deccan and Tamil regions of south India.

Although Jainism never took hold as widely as Hinduism and Buddhism (discussed below), it has been an influential strand in Indian thought and has several million adherents in India today. Fasting and nonviolence as spiritual practices in India owe much to Jain teachings. In the twentieth century Mohandas Gandhi, leader of the Indian independence movement, was influenced by these ideas through his mother, and the American civil rights leader Dr. Martin Luther King, Jr., was influenced by Gandhi.

Siddhartha Gautama and Buddhism

Siddhartha Gautama (fl. ca. 500 B.C.E.) is best known as the Buddha ("enlightened one"). Born the son of a chief of one of the tribes in the Himalayan foothills in what is now Nepal, he left home at age twenty-nine to become a wandering ascetic. He traveled south to the kingdom of Magadha, where he took up extreme asceticism. According to tradition, while meditating under a bo tree at Bodh Gaya, he reached enlightenment—that is, perfect insight into the processes of the universe. After several weeks of meditation, he preached his first sermon, urging a "middle way" between asceticism and worldly life. For the next forty-five years, the Buddha traveled through the Ganges Valley, propounding his ideas. To reach as wide an audience as possible, the Buddha preached in the local language, Magadhi, rather than in Sanskrit, which was already becoming a priestly language. Probably because he refused to recognize the divine authority of the Vedas and dismissed sacrifices, he attracted followers mostly from among merchants, artisans, and farmers, rather than Brahmins.

In his first sermon the Buddha outlined his main message, summed up in the **Four Noble Truths** and the **Eightfold Path**. The Four Noble Truths are as follows: (1) pain and suffering, frustration, and anxiety are ugly but inescapable parts of human life; (2) suffering and anxiety are caused by human desires and attachments; (3) people can understand these weaknesses and triumph over them; and (4) this triumph is made possible by following a simple code of conduct, the Eightfold Path. The basic insight of Buddhism is thus psychological. The deepest human longings can never be satisfied, and even those things that seem to give pleasure cause anxiety because we are afraid of losing them. Attachment to people and things causes sorrow at their loss.

Four Noble Truths The Buddha's message that pain and suffering are inescapable parts of life; suffering and anxiety are caused by human desires and attachments; people can understand and triumph over these weaknesses; and the triumph is made possible by following a simple code of conduct.

Eightfold Path The code of conduct set forth by the Buddha in his first sermon, beginning with "right conduct" and ending with "right contemplation."

The Buddha offered an optimistic message in that all people can set out on the Eightfold Path toward liberation. All they have to do is take a series of steps, beginning with recognizing the universality of suffering ("right knowledge"), deciding to free themselves from it ("right purpose"), and then choosing "right conduct" (including abstaining from taking life), "right speech," "right livelihood," and "right endeavor." The seventh step is "right awareness," constant contemplation of one's deeds and words, giving full thought to their importance and whether they lead to enlightenment. "Right contemplation," the last step, entails deep meditation on the impermanence of everything in the world. Those who achieve liberation are freed from the cycle of birth and death and enter the state called **nirvana**, a kind of blissful nothingness and freedom from reincarnation.

nirvana A state of blissful nothingness and freedom from reincarnation.

Buddhism differed from Brahmanism and later Hinduism in that it ignored the caste system. Everyone, noble and peasant, educated and ignorant, male and female, could follow the Eightfold Path. Moreover, the Buddha was extraordinarily undogmatic. Convinced that each person must achieve enlightenment on his or her own, he emphasized that the

Picturing the Past

Gandharan Frieze Depicting the Buddha

This carved stone from ca. 200 C.E. is one in a series portraying scenes from the life of the Buddha. From the Gandharan kingdom (located in modern Pakistan), this frieze depicts the Buddha seated below the bo tree, where he was first enlightened. (Freer Gallery of Art, Smithsonian Institution, Washington, D.C., Purchase, F1949.9b)

ANALYZING THE IMAGE What are the people around the Buddha doing? What animals are portrayed?

CONNECTIONS Does this frieze effectively convey any Buddhist principles? If so, which ones?

path was important only because it led the traveler to enlightenment, not for its own sake. Thus, there was no harm in honoring local gods or observing traditional ceremonies, as long as one remembered the goal of enlightenment and did not let sacrifices become snares or attachments. The willingness of Buddhists to tolerate a wide variety of practices aided the spread of the religion.

sutras The written teachings of the Buddha, first transcribed in the second or first century B.C.E.

Like Mahavira, the Buddha formed a circle of disciples, primarily men but including some women as well. The Buddha's followers transmitted his teachings orally until they were written down in the second or first century B.C.E. These scriptures are called **sutras**. Within a few centuries Buddhist monks began to set up permanent monasteries, generally on land donated by kings or other patrons. Orders of nuns also appeared, giving women the opportunity to seek truth in ways men had traditionally used. The main ritual that monks and nuns performed in their monastic establishments was the communal recitation of the sutras. Lay Buddhists could aid the spread of the Buddhist teachings by providing food for monks and support for their monasteries, and they could pursue their own spiritual progress by adopting practices such as abstaining from meat and alcohol.

Because Buddhism had no central ecclesiastical authority like the Christian papacy, early Buddhist communities developed several divergent traditions and came to stress different sutras. One of the most important of these, associated with the monk-philosopher Nagarjuna (fl. ca. 100 C.E.), is called **Mahayana**, or "Great Vehicle," because it was a more inclusive form of the religion. It drew on a set of discourses allegedly given by the Buddha and kept hidden by his followers for centuries. One branch of Mahayana taught that reality is empty (that is, nothing exists independently of itself). Another branch held that ultimate reality is consciousness, that everything is produced by the mind.

Mahayana The "Great Vehicle," a tradition of Buddhism that aspires to be more inclusive.

Just as important as the metaphysical literature of Mahayana Buddhism was its devotional side, influenced by the religions then prevalent in Central Asia, such as Zoroastrianism (see page 53). The Buddha became deified and was placed at the head of an expanding pantheon of other Buddhas and **bodhisattvas** (boh-dih-SUHT-vuhz). Bodhisattvas were Buddhas-to-be who had stayed in the world after enlightenment to help others on the path to salvation. The Buddhas and bodhisattvas became objects of veneration, especially the Buddha of Infinite Light, Amitabha and the bodhisattva of infinite compassion and mercy, Avalokitesvara (uh-vuh-lohk-ih-TEYSH-veh-ruh). With the growth of Mahayana, Buddhism attracted more and more laypeople.

bodhisattvas Buddhas-to-be who stayed in the world after enlightenment to help others on the path to salvation.

Buddhism remained an important religion in India until about 1200 C.E. By that time it had spread widely through East, Central, and Southeast Asia. After 1200 Buddhism declined in India, losing out to both Hinduism and Islam, and the number of Buddhists in India today is small. Buddhism never lost its hold in Sri Lanka and Nepal, however, and today it is also a major religion in Southeast Asia, Tibet, China, Korea, and Japan.

Hinduism

Both Buddhism and Jainism were direct challenges to the old Brahmanic religion. Both rejected animal sacrifice, which by then was a central element in the rituals performed by Brahmin priests. Even more important, both religions tacitly rejected the caste system, accepting people of any caste into their ranks. Over the next several centuries (ca. 400 B.C.E.–200 C.E.), in response to this challenge, the Brahmanic religion evolved in a more devotional direction, developing into the religion commonly called Hinduism. In Hinduism Brahmins retained their high social status, but it became possible for individual worshippers to have more direct contact with the gods, showing their devotion without using priests as intermediaries.

The bedrock of Hinduism is the belief that the Vedas are sacred revelations and that a specific caste system is implicitly prescribed in them. Hinduism is a guide to life, the goal of which is to reach union with brahman, the unchanging ultimate reality. There are four steps in this search, progressing from study of the Vedas in youth to complete asceticism in old age. In their quest for brahman, people are to observe **dharma** (DAHR-muh), the moral law. Dharma stipulates the legitimate pursuits of Hindus: material gain, as long as it is honestly and honorably achieved; pleasure and love for the perpetuation of the family; and moksha, release from the wheel of life and unity with brahman.

dharma The Sanskrit word for moral law, central both to Buddhist and Hindu teachings.

Hinduism assumes that there are innumerable legitimate ways of worshipping brahman, including devotion to personal gods. After the third century B.C.E. Hinduism began to emphasize the roles and personalities of thousands of powerful gods. Brahma, the creator; Shiva, the cosmic dancer who both creates and destroys; and Vishnu, the preserver and sustainer of creation were three of the main male deities. Important female deities included Lakshmi, goddess of wealth, and Saraswati, goddess of learning and music. These gods were usually represented by images, either small ones in homes or larger ones in temples. People could show devotion to their personal gods by reciting hymns or scriptures and by making offerings of food or flowers before these images. Hinduism's

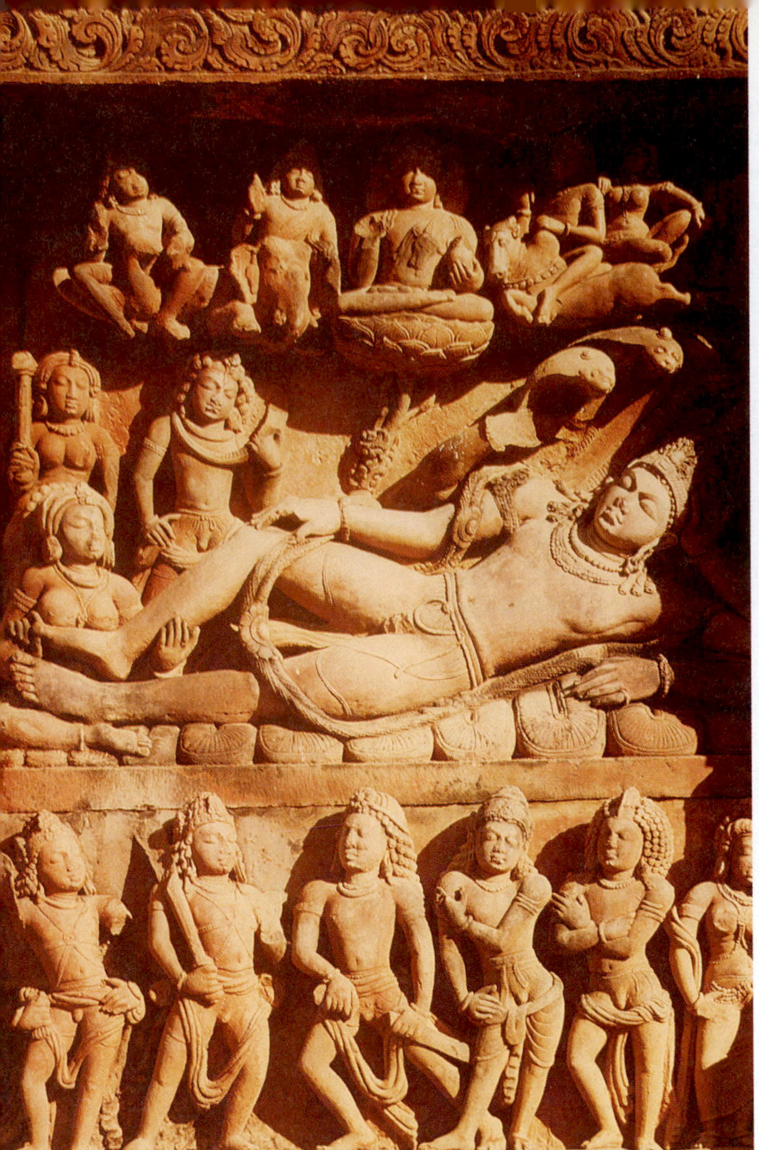

The God Vishnu Vishnu reclining on his protector, the serpent Shesha, is the subject of this stone relief from the Temple of Vishnu in central India at Deogarh, which dates from the Gupta period, ca. 500 C.E. (Deogarh, Uttar Pradesh, India/Giraudon/The Bridgeman Art Library)

embrace of a large pantheon of gods enabled it to incorporate new sects, doctrines, beliefs, rites, and deities.

A central ethical text of Hinduism is the *Bhagavad Gita* (BAH-guh-vahd GEE-tuh), a part of the world's longest ancient epic, the *Mahabharata*. The *Bhagavad Gita* offers guidance on the most serious problem facing a Hindu — how to live in the world and yet honor dharma and thus achieve release from the wheel of life. The heart of the *Bhagavad Gita* is the spiritual conflict confronting Arjuna, a human hero about to ride into battle against his kinsmen. As he surveys the battlefield, struggling with the grim notion of killing his relatives, Arjuna voices his doubts to his charioteer, none other than the god Krishna. When at last Arjuna refuses to spill his family's blood, Krishna instructs him on the true meaning of Hinduism, clarifying the relationship between human reality and the eternal spirit. He explains compassionately to Arjuna the duty to act — to live in the world and carry out his duties as a warrior. Indeed, the *Bhagavad Gita* emphasizes the necessity of action, which is essential for the welfare of the world. For Arjuna the warrior's duty is to wage war in compliance with his dharma. Only those who live within the divine law without complaint will be released from rebirth. One person's dharma may be different from another's, but both individuals must follow their own dharmas.

Hinduism provided a complex and sophisticated philosophy of life and a religion of enormous emotional appeal that was attractive to ordinary Indians. Over time it grew to be the most common religion in India. Hinduism also inspired the preservation of literary masterpieces in Sanskrit and the major regional languages of India. Among these are the *Puranas*, which are stories of the gods and great warrior clans, and the *Mahabharata* and *Ramayana*, which are verse epics of India's early kings. Hinduism validated the caste system, adding to the stability of everyday village life, since people all knew where they stood in society.

Quick Review
What was the appeal of Jainism and Buddhism, and how did the Brahmanic religion evolve in response to the challenges presented by these new faiths?

How was the Mauryan Empire created and what were its achievements?

In the late sixth century B.C.E., with the creation of the Persian Empire that stretched from the west coast of Anatolia to the Indus River (see pages 50–52), west India was swept up in events that were changing the face of the ancient Near East. A couple of centuries later, by 322 B.C.E., the Greeks had supplanted the Persians in northwest India. Chandragupta saw this as an opportunity to expand his territories, and he successfully unified all of north India. The Mauryan Empire that he founded flourished under the reign of his grandson, Ashoka, but after Ashoka's death the empire declined.

Encounters with the West

India became involved in the turmoil of the sixth century B.C.E. when the Persian emperor Darius conquered the Indus Valley and Kashmir about 513 B.C.E. Persian control did not reach eastward beyond the Punjab, but even so it fostered increased contact between India and the Near East and led to the introduction of new ideas, techniques, and materials into India. From Persian administrators Indians learned more about how to rule large tracts of land and huge numbers of people. They also learned the technique of minting silver coins, and they adopted the Persian monetary standard to facilitate trade with other parts of the empire. Even states in the Ganges Valley, which were never part of the Persian Empire, adopted the use of coinage.

The Persian Empire in turn succumbed to Alexander the Great, and in 326 B.C.E. Alexander led his Macedonian and Greek troops through the Khyber Pass into the Indus Valley (discussed in Chapter 5 on page 118). The India that Alexander encountered was composed of many rival states. He defeated some of these states in the northwest and heard reports of others.

The Greeks were intrigued by the Indian culture they encountered. Alexander had heard of the sophistication of Indian philosophers and summoned some to instruct him or debate with him. The Greeks were also impressed with Indian cities, most notably Taxila, a major center of trade in the Punjab. From Taxila, Alexander followed the Indus River south, hoping to find the end of the world. His men, however, mutinied and refused to continue. When Alexander turned back, he left his general Seleucus (suh-LOO-kuhs) in charge of his easternmost region.

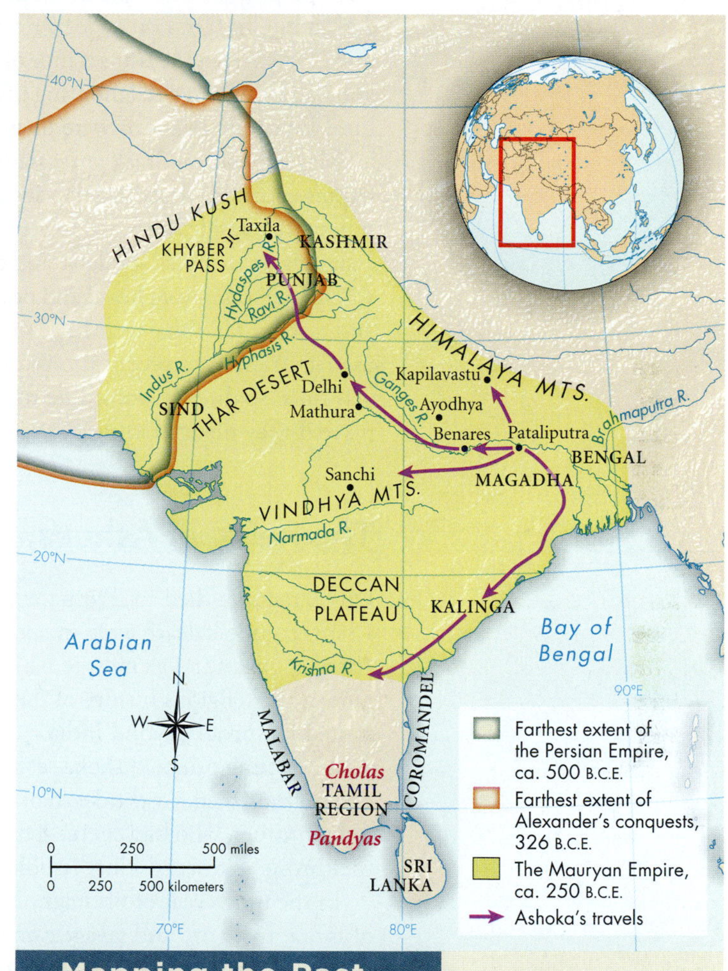

Mapping the Past

Map 3.2 The Mauryan Empire, ca. 250 B.C.E.
The Ganges River Valley was the heart of the Mauryan Empire. Although India is protected from the cold by mountains in the north, mountain passes in the northwest allowed both migration and invasion.

ANALYZING THE MAP Where are the major rivers of India? How close are they to mountains?

CONNECTIONS Can you think of any reasons that the Persian Empire and Alexander's conquests both reached into the same region of northwest India?

Chandragupta and the Founding of the Mauryan Empire

The one to benefit most from Alexander's invasion was Chandragupta, the ruler of a growing state in the Ganges Valley. He took advantage of the crisis caused by Alexander's invasion to expand his territories, and by 322 B.C.E. he had made himself sole master of north India (Map 3.2). In 304 B.C.E. he defeated the forces of Seleucus.

Chandragupta applied the lessons learned from Persian rule. He adopted the Persian practice of dividing the area into provinces. Each province was assigned a governor, usually drawn from Chandragupta's own family. He established a complex bureaucracy to see to the operation of the state and a bureaucratic taxation system that financed public services through taxes on agriculture. He also built a regular army, complete with departments for everything from naval matters to the collection of supplies.

For the first time in Indian history, one man governed most of the subcontinent, exercising control through delegated power. From his capital at Pataliputra in the Ganges Valley (now Patna in Bihar), Chandragupta sent agents to the provinces to oversee the workings of government and to keep him informed of conditions in his realm. In designing his bureaucratic system, Chandragupta was assisted by his minister Kautilya, who wrote a treatise on royal power, rather like the Legalist treatises produced in China later that century (discussed in Chapter 4 on page 97). Kautilya urged the king to use propaganda to gain support. He stressed the importance of seeking the enemies of his enemies, who would make good allies. When a neighboring prince was in trouble, that was the perfect time to attack him. Interstate relations were likened to the law of the fish: the large swallow the small.

Megasthenes, a Greek ambassador sent by Seleucus, spent fourteen years in Chandragupta's court. He described the city as square and surrounded by wooden walls, twenty-two miles on each side, with 570 towers and 64 gates. It had a university, a library, and magnificent palaces, temples, gardens, and parks. The king personally presided over court sessions where legal cases were heard and petitions received. The king claimed for the state all mines and forests, and there were large state farms, granaries, shipyards, and spinning and weaving factories. Even prostitution was controlled by the state. Only a portion of the empire was ruled so directly, according to Megasthenes. In outlying areas, local kings were left in place if they pledged loyalty.

The Reign of Ashoka, ca. 269–232 B.C.E.

Chandragupta died in 298 B.C.E., leaving behind a powerful kingdom. The years after Chandragupta's death were an epoch of political greatness, thanks largely to his grandson Ashoka, one of India's most remarkable figures. The era of Ashoka was enormously important in the religious history of the world, because Ashoka embraced Buddhism and promoted its spread beyond India.

As a young prince, Ashoka served as governor of two prosperous provinces where Buddhism flourished. At the death of his father about 274 B.C.E., Ashoka rebelled against his older brother, who had succeeded as king, and after four years of fighting won his bid for the throne. Crowned king, Ashoka ruled intelligently and energetically.

In the ninth year of his reign, 261 B.C.E., Ashoka conquered Kalinga, on the east coast of India. In a grim and savage campaign, Ashoka reduced Kalinga by wholesale slaughter. Instead of exulting like a conqueror, however, Ashoka was consumed with remorse and revulsion at the horror of war. He embraced Buddhism and used the machinery of his empire to spread Buddhist teachings throughout India. Two years after his conversion, he undertook a 256-day pilgrimage to all the holy sites of Buddhism, and on his return he sent missionaries to all known countries. Buddhist tradition also credits him with erecting 84,000 stupas (structures containing Buddhist relics) throughout India, among which the ashes or other bodily remains of the Buddha were distributed, beginning the association of Buddhism with monumental art and architecture.

Ashoka's remarkable crisis of conscience, like the later conversion to Christianity of the Roman emperor Constantine, affected the way he ruled. He emphasized compassion, nonviolence, and adherence to dharma. He appointed officials to oversee the moral welfare of the realm and required local officials to govern humanely. He may have perceived dharma as a kind of civic virtue, a universal ethical model capable of uniting the diverse peoples of his extensive empire. Ashoka erected stone pillars, on the Persian model, with inscriptions to inform the people of his policies. He also had long inscriptions carved into large rock surfaces near trade routes. In his last important inscription he spoke of his efforts to encourage his people toward the path of righteousness:

> *I have had banyan trees planted on the roads to give shade to man and beast; I have planted mango groves, and I have had ponds dug and shelters erected along the roads at every eight kos. Everywhere I have had wells dug for the benefit of man and beast. But his benefit is but small, for in many ways the kings of olden time have worked for the welfare of the world; but what I have done has been done that men may conform to righteousness.*[1]

Ashoka felt the need to protect his new religion and to keep it pure. He warned Buddhist monks that he would not tolerate schism—divisions based on differences of opinion about doctrine or ritual. According to Buddhist tradition, a great council of Buddhist monks was held at Pataliputra, where the earliest canon of Buddhist texts was codified. At the same time, Ashoka honored India's other religions, even building shrines for Hindu and Jain worshippers. In one edict he banned rowdy popular fairs, allowing only religious gatherings.

The North Gate at Sanchi This is one of four ornately carved gates guarding the stupa at Sanchi in the state of Madhya Pradesh in India. Containing the relics of the Buddha, this Buddhist memorial shrine from the second century B.C.E. was commissioned by Ashoka. (Jean-Louis Nou/La Collection, Paris)

Despite his devotion to Buddhism, Ashoka never neglected his duties as emperor. He tightened the central government of the empire and kept a close check on local officials. He built roads and rest spots to improve communication within the realm. These measures also facilitated the march of armies and the armed enforcement of Ashoka's authority.

Ashoka directly administered the central part of the empire, focusing on Magadha. Beyond it were four large provinces under princes who served as viceroys, each with its own sets of smaller districts and officials. The interior of south India was described as inhabited by undefeated forest tribes. Farther south, along the coasts, were peoples that Ashoka maintained friendly relations with but did not rule, such as the Cholas and Pandyas. Relations with Sri Lanka were especially close under Ashoka, and the king sent a branch of the tree under which the Buddha gained enlightenment to the Sri Lankan king. According to Buddhist legend, Ashoka's son Mahinda traveled to Sri Lanka to convert the people there.

Ashoka ruled for thirty-seven years. After he died in about 232 B.C.E. the Mauryan Dynasty went into decline, and India broke up into smaller units, much like those in existence before Alexander's invasion. Even though Chandragupta had instituted bureaucratic methods of centralized political control and Ashoka had vigorously pursued the political and cultural integration of the empire, the institutions they created were not entrenched enough to survive periods with weaker kings.

Quick Review
How did contact with other cultures shape the policies and administration of the Mauryan Empire?

How did political disunity shape Indian life after 185 B.C.E.?

After the Mauryan Dynasty collapsed in 185 B.C.E., and for much of subsequent Indian history, political unity would be the exception rather than the rule. By this time, however, key elements of Indian culture — the caste system; the religious traditions of Hinduism, Buddhism, and Jainism; and the great epics and legends — had given India a cultural unity strong enough to endure even without political unity.

In the years after the fall of the Mauryan Dynasty, a series of foreign powers dominated the Indus Valley and adjoining regions. The first were hybrid Indo-Greek states ruled by the inheritors of Alexander's defunct empire stationed in what is now Afghanistan. The city of Taxila became a major center of trade, culture, and education, fusing elements of Greek and Indian culture.

The great, slow movement of nomadic peoples out of East Asia that brought the Scythians to the Near East brought the Shakas to northwest India. They controlled the region from about 94 to 20 B.C.E., when they were displaced by a new nomadic invader, the Kushans, who ruled the region of today's Afghanistan, Pakistan, and west India as far south as Gujarat. Buddhist sources refer to their king Kanishka (r. ca. 78–ca. 103 C.E.) as not only a powerful ruler but also a major patron of Buddhism. Some of the coins he issued had a picture of him on one side and of the Buddha on the other. The famous silk trade from China to Rome (see "Global Trade: Silk," page 164) passed through his territory.

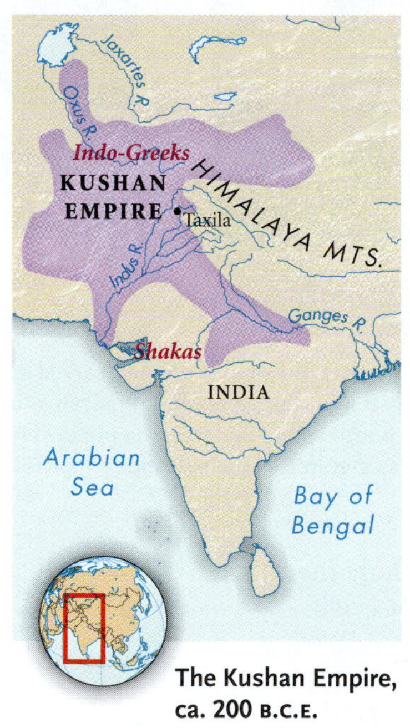

The Kushan Empire, ca. 200 B.C.E.

During the Kushan period, Greek culture had a considerable impact on Indian art. Indo-Greek artists and sculptors working in India adorned Buddhist shrines, modeling the earliest representation of the Buddha on Hellenistic statues of Apollo. Another contribution from the Indo-Greek states was coin cast with images of the king, which came to be widely adopted by Indian rulers, aiding commerce and adding evidence of rulers' names and sequence to the historical record. Places where coins are found also show patterns of trade.

Cultural exchange also went in the other direction. Old Indian animal folktales were translated into Syriac and Greek and from that source eventually made their way to Europe. South India in this period was also the center of active seaborne trade, with networks reaching all the way to Rome. Indian sailing technology was highly advanced, and much of this trade was in the hands of Indian merchants. Roman traders based in Egypt followed the routes already used by Arab traders to sail to the west coast of India. In the first century C.E. a Greek merchant involved in this trade reported that the traders sold coins, topaz, coral, crude glass, copper, tin, and lead and bought pearls, ivory, silk (probably originally from China), jewels of many sorts (probably many from Southeast Asia), and above all cinnamon and pepper. More Roman gold coins of the first and second centuries C.E. have been found near the southern tip of India than in any other area.

Even after the fall of Rome, many of the traders on the southwest coast of India remained. These scattered communities of Christians and Jews lived in the coastal cities into modern times. When Vasco da Gama, the Portuguese explorer, reached Calicut in 1498, he found a local Jewish merchant who was able to interpret for him.

Code of Manu The codification of early Indian law that lays down family, caste, and commercial law.

During these centuries there were significant advances in science, mathematics, and philosophy. Indian astronomers charted the movements of stars and planets and recognized that the earth was spherical. In the realm of physics, Indian scientists, like their Greek counterparts, conceived of matter in terms of five elements: earth, air, fire, water, and ether. This was also the period when Indian law was codified. The **Code of Manu**,

Kushan Gold Coin Kanishka I had coins made depicting a standing Buddha with his left hand raised in a gesture of renunciation (right). The reverse side (far right) shows the king performing a sacrifice, the legend reading "Kanishka the Kushan, king of kings." (Courtesy of the Trustees of the British Museum)

which lays down family, caste, and commercial law, was compiled in the second or third century C.E., drawing on older texts.

Regional cultures tend to flourish when there is no dominant unifying state, and the Tamils of south India were one of the major beneficiaries of the collapse of the Mauryan Dynasty. The third century B.C.E. to the third century C.E. is considered the classical period of Tamil culture, when many great works of literature were written under the patronage of the regional kings. Some of the poems at this time provide evidence of lively commerce, mentioning bulging warehouses, ships from many lands, and complex import-export procedures. From contact of this sort, the south came to absorb many cultural elements from the north, but also retained differences. Castes were present in the south before contact with the Sanskrit north, but took distinct forms, as the Kshatriya (warrior) and Vaishya (merchant) varna were hardly known in the far south.

Quick Review
How did cultural exchange affect Indians and the outside invaders who came in waves after 185 B.C.E.?

Connections

INDIA WAS A VERY DIFFERENT PLACE in the third century C.E. than it had been in the early phase of Harappan civilization more than two thousand years earlier. The region was still divided into many different polities, but people living there in 300 shared much more in the way of ideas and traditions. The great epics such as the *Mahabharata* and the *Ramayana* provided a cultural vocabulary for groups that spoke different languages and had rival rulers. New religions had emerged, notably Buddhism and Jainism, and Hinduism was much more a devotional religion. Contact with ancient Mesopotamia, Persia, Greece, and Rome had brought new ideas, practices, and products.

During this same time period, civilization in China underwent similar expansion and diversification. China was farther away than India from other Eurasian centers of civilization, and its developments were consequently not as closely linked. Logographic writing appeared with the Bronze-Age Shang civilization and was preserved into modern times, in striking contrast to India and lands to its west, which developed written languages that represented sounds. Still, some developments affected both India and China, such as the appearance of chariots and horseback riding. The next chapter takes up the story of these developments in early China. In Chapter 12, after considering early developments in Europe, Asia, Africa, and the Americas, we return to the story of India.

- **For a list of suggested readings for this chapter, visit** *bedfordstmartins.com/mckayworldunderstanding*.
- **For primary sources from this period, see** *Sources of World Societies*, Second Edition.
- **For Web sites, images, and documents related to topics in this chapter, see Make History at** *bedfordstmartins.com/mckayworldunderstanding*.

Chapter 3 **Study Guide**

To do these exercises online, go to bedfordstmartins.com/mckayworldunderstanding.

Step 1

GETTING STARTED

Below are basic terms about this period in global history. Can you identify each term below and explain why it matters?

TERMS	WHO (OR WHAT) AND WHEN	WHY IT MATTERS
Harappan, p. 58		
Aryans, p. 60		
Rigveda, p. 61		
Brahmins, p. 61		
caste system, p. 61		
samsara, p. 64		
karma, p. 64		
brahman, p. 65		
Four Noble Truths, p. 67		
Eightfold Path , p. 67		
nirvana, p. 67		
sutras, p. 68		
Mahayana, p. 69		
bodhisattvas, p. 69		
dharma, p. 69		
Code of Manu , p. 74		

Step 2

MOVING BEYOND THE BASICS

The exercise below requires a more advanced understanding of the chapter material. Compare and contrast India's great indigenous religious traditions by filling in the chart below with descriptions of three key aspects of these religions: core beliefs, social and ethical implications, appeal and spread. When you are finished, consider the following questions: What aspects of Brahmanic belief and practice did Jainism and Buddhism reject? What core Brahmanic beliefs remained a part of Hinduism?

	CORE BELIEFS	SOCIAL AND ETHICAL IMPLICATIONS	APPEAL AND SPREAD
Jainism			
Buddhism			
Hinduism			

Step 3

PUTTING IT ALL TOGETHER

Now that you've reviewed key elements of the chapter, take a step back and try to see the big picture. Remember to use specific examples from the chapter in your answers.

EARLY INDIAN CIVILIZATIONS

- What similarities were there between Harappan civilization and the civilizations of Mesopotamia and Egypt?
- How did Brahmanism shape early Indian society and politics?

INDIA'S GREAT RELIGIONS

- What beliefs do Jainism, Buddhism, and Hinduism have in common?
- How would you explain the fact that Hinduism eventually grew to be the most common religion in India?

THE RISE AND FALL OF THE MAURYAN EMPIRE

- What were the keys to Mauryan political success?

- How did encounters with outsiders contribute to both the rise of the Mauryan Empire and to Indian development in the centuries after the empire's fall?

LOOKING BACK, LOOKING AHEAD

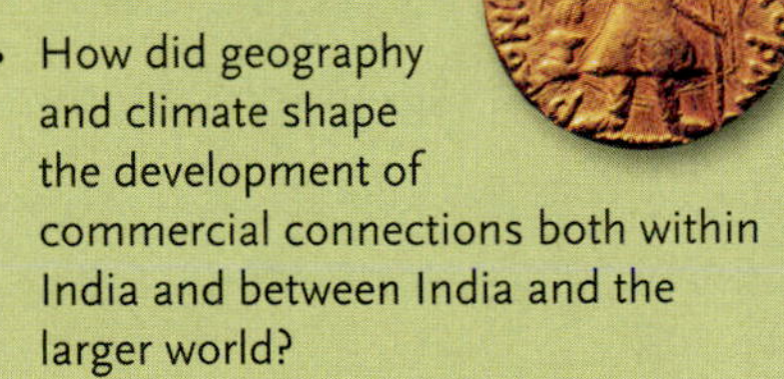

- How did geography and climate shape the development of commercial connections both within India and between India and the larger world?
- How would you explain the fact that, up until the establishment of the Mughal Empire in the sixteenth century, periods of political unification of the Indian subcontinent have been the exception and not the rule? What light does the early history of India shed on this question?

In Your Own Words Imagine that you must explain Chapter 3 to someone who hasn't read it. What would be the most important points to include and why?

4

China's Classical Age

to 221 B.C.E.

In comparison to India and the ancient Middle East, China developed in relative isolation. Communication with West and South Asia was very difficult, impeded by high mountains and vast deserts. Though there was some trade, the distances were so great that it did not allow the kind of cross-fertilization that occurred in western Eurasia. Moreover, there were no cultural breaks comparable to the rise of the Aryans in India or the Assyrians in Mesopotamia to introduce new peoples and languages. The impact of early China's relative isolation is found in many distinctive features of its culture. Perhaps the most important is its writing system; unlike the other major societies of Eurasia, China retained a logographic writing system with a symbol for each word. This writing system shaped not only Chinese literature and thought but also key social and political processes, such as the nature of the ruling class and interactions with non-Chinese.

Bronze Head from China Archaeological discoveries continue to expand our knowledge of early China. This 20-inch-tall bronze head was found among a large set of sacrificial offerings in the modern province of Sichuan. (Sanxingdui Museum, Guanghan, Sichuan Province, © Cultural Relics Press)

Chinese history is commonly discussed in terms of a succession of dynasties. The Shang Dynasty (ca. 1500–1050 B.C.E.) was the first to have writing, metalworking, cities, and chariots. The Shang were overthrown by one of their vassal states, which founded the Zhou Dynasty (ca. 1050–256 B.C.E.). The Zhou rulers set up a decentralized feudal governmental structure that evolved over centuries into a multistate system. As warfare between the states intensified in the sixth century B.C.E., social and cultural change quickened, and China entered one of its most creative periods, when the philosophies of Confucianism, Daoism, and Legalism were developed.

Chapter Preview

- How did geography shape the development of Chinese societies?
- What were the most important developments in Shang China?
- What was China like during the Zhou Dynasty?
- How did new technologies contribute to the rise of independent states?
- What ideas did Confucius teach, and how were they spread after his death?
- How did Daoism, Legalism, and other philosophies differ from Confucianism?

How did geography shape the development of Chinese societies?

The historical China, also called China proper, was smaller than present-day China. The contemporary People's Republic of China includes Tibet, Inner Mongolia, Turkestan, Manchuria, and other territories that in premodern times were neither inhabited by Chinese nor ruled directly by Chinese states. The geography of the region in which Chinese civilization developed has had an impact on its historical development to the present.

The Impact of Geography

China proper, about a thousand miles north to south and east to west, occupies much of the temperate zone of East Asia (Map 4.1). The northern part, drained by the Yellow River, is colder, flatter, and more arid than the south, and it is well suited to crops like wheat

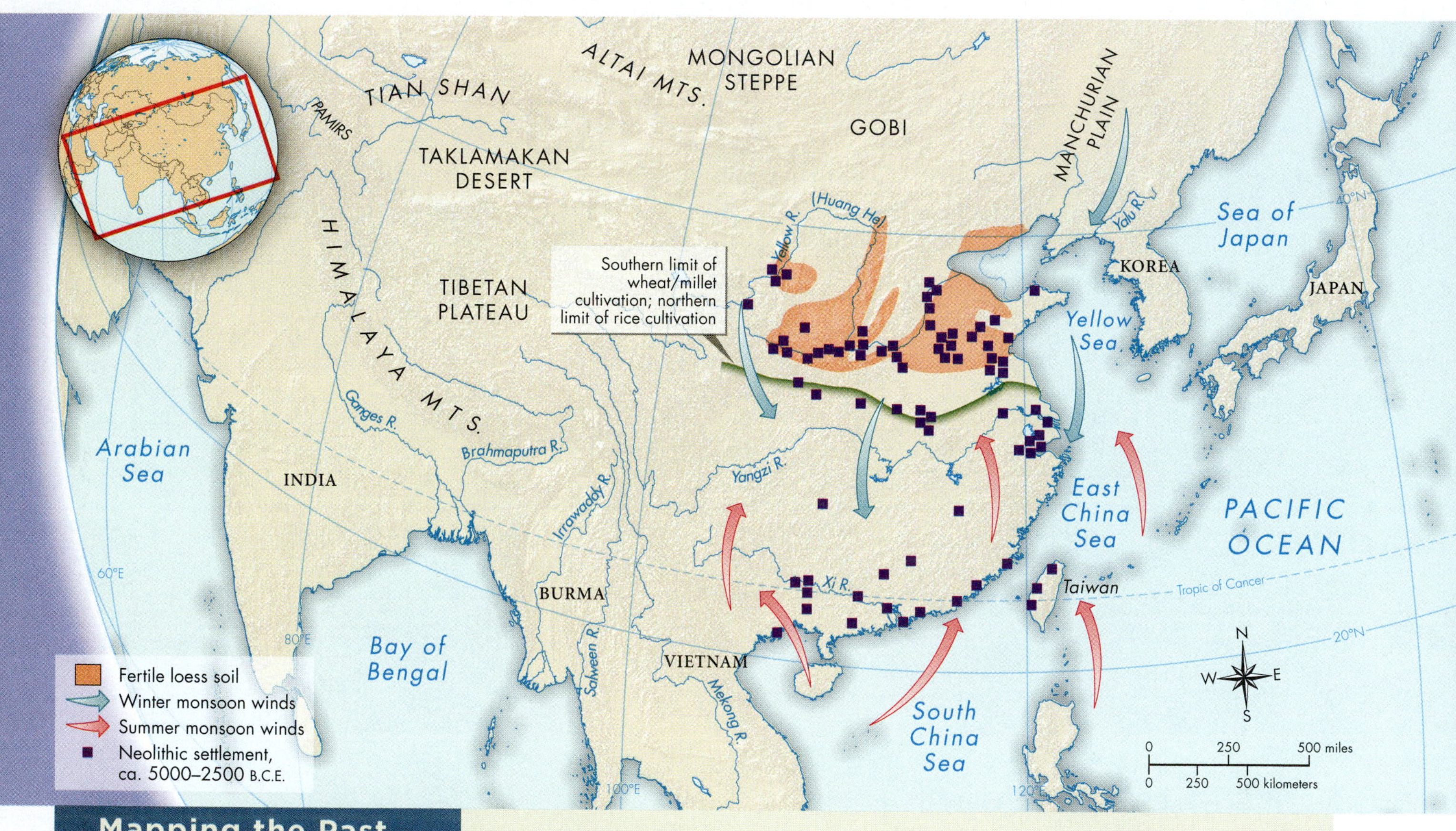

Mapping the Past

Map 4.1 The Geography of Historical China

Chinese civilization developed in the temperate regions drained by the Yellow and Yangzi Rivers.

ANALYZING THE MAP Trace the routes of the Yellow and Yangzi Rivers. Where are the areas of loess soil? Where are the Neolithic sites concentrated?

CONNECTIONS Does China's geography explain much about its history? (See also Map 4.2.) What geographical features had the greatest impact in the Neolithic Age? How might the fact that the Yellow and Yangzi Rivers flow west to east, rather than north to south, have influenced the development of Chinese society?

and millet. The dominant soil is **loess**—fine wind-driven earth that is fertile and easy to work even with simple tools. Because so much of the loess ends up as silt in the Yellow River, the riverbed rises and easily floods unless diked. Drought is another perennial problem for farmers in the north. The Yangzi (YANG-zuh) River is the dominant feature of the warmer, wetter, and more lush south, a region well suited to rice cultivation. The Yangzi and its many tributaries are navigable, so boats were traditionally the preferred means of transportation in the south.

Mountains, deserts, and grasslands separated China proper from other early civilizations. Between China and India lay Tibet, with its vast mountain ranges and high plateaus. North of Tibet are great expanses of desert, and north of the desert grasslands stretch from Ukraine to eastern Siberia. Chinese civilization did not spread into any of these Inner Asian regions, above all because they were not suited to growing crops. Inner Asia, where raising animals is a more productive use of land than planting crops, became the heartland of China's traditional enemies, such as the nomadic tribes of the Xiongnu (SHUHNG-noo) and Mongols.

Chapter Chronology

ca. 5000 B.C.E.	Emergence of regional Neolithic settlements
ca. 1500–1050 B.C.E.	Shang Dynasty
ca. 1200 B.C.E.	Evidence of writing found in royal tombs; chariots come into use
ca. 1050–256 B.C.E.	Zhou Dynasty
ca. 900	*Book of Songs*, *Book of Changes*, *Book of Documents*
551–479 B.C.E.	Confucius
ca. 500 B.C.E.	Iron technology in wide use; cities spread across the central Zhou states
500–200 B.C.E.	Golden age of Chinese philosophy
453–403 B.C.E.	*The Art of War*
403-221 B.C.E.	Period of the Warring States; decline of the Zhou Dynasty
ca. 370–300 B.C.E.	Mencius
ca. 350 B.C.E.	Infantry armed with crossbows
ca. 310–215 B.C.E.	Xunzi
ca. 300–200 B.C.E.	Early Daoist teachings outlined in *Laozi* and the *Zhuangzi*

Early Agricultural Societies of the Neolithic Age

From about 10,000 B.C.E. agriculture was practiced in China. It apparently originated independently, but it was perhaps influenced by developments in Southeast Asia, where rice was also cultivated very early. By 5000 B.C.E. there were Neolithic village settlements in several regions of China. The primary Neolithic crops were millet, grown in the loess soils of the north, and rice, grown in the wetlands of the lower reaches of the Yangzi River, where inhabitants supplemented their diet with fish. In both areas pigs, dogs, and cattle were domesticated, and by 3000 B.C.E. sheep had become important in the north and water buffalo in the south. Silk production can also be traced back to this period.

loess Soil deposited by wind; it is fertile and easy to work.

Over the course of the fifth to third millennia B.C.E. many distinct regional Neolithic cultures emerged. These Neolithic societies left no written records, but

Neolithic Jade Plaque This small plaque (2.5 inches by 3.25 inches), dating from about 2000 B.C.E., is similar to others of the Liangzhu area near modern Shanghai. It is incised to depict a human figure who merges into a monster mask. The lower part could be interpreted as his arms and legs but at the same time resembles a monster mask with bulging eyes, prominent nostrils, and a large mouth. (Zheijiang Provincial Institute of Archaeology/© Cultural Relics Press)

we know from the material record that over time they came to share more and more social and cultural practices. Many practices related to treatment of the dead spread to other groups from their original area, including use of coffins, ramped chambers, large numbers of grave goods, and divination aimed at communicating with ancestors or gods based on interpreting cracks in cattle bones. Fortified walls made of rammed earth came to be built around settlements in many areas, suggesting not only increased contact between Neolithic societies but also increased conflict. (For more on life in Neolithic societies, see Chapter 1.)

Quick Review
How did the differences between southern and northern China shape the two regions' development?

What were the most important developments in Shang China?

After 2000 B.C.E. a Bronze Age civilization appeared in north China that shared traits with Bronze Age civilizations elsewhere in Eurasia, such as Mesopotamia, Egypt, and Greece. These traits included writing, metalworking, domestication of the horse, class stratification, and cult centers. These archaeological findings can be linked to the Shang Dynasty, long known from early texts.

Shang Society

Anyang One of the Shang Dynasty capitals from which the Shang kings ruled for more than two centuries.

Shang civilization was not as densely urban as Mesopotamia, but Shang kings ruled from large settlements (Map 4.2). The best excavated is **Anyang**, from which the Shang kings ruled for more than two centuries. At the center of Anyang were large palaces, temples, and altars. These buildings were constructed on rammed-earth foundations (a feature of Chinese building practice that would last for centuries). Outside the central core were industrial areas where bronzeworkers, potters, stone carvers, and other artisans lived and worked. Many homes were built partly below ground level, probably as a way to conserve heat. Beyond these urban settlements were farming areas and large forests. Deer, bears, tigers, wild boars, elephants, and rhinoceros were still plentiful in north China in this era.

Texts found in the Shang royal tombs at Anyang show that Shang kings were military chieftains. The king regularly sent out armies of three thousand to five thousand men on campaigns. They fought rebellious vassals and foreign tribes, but the situation constantly changed as vassals became enemies and enemies accepted offers of alliance. War booty was an important source of the king's revenue, especially the war captives who could be made into slaves. Captives not needed as slaves might end up as sacrificial victims.

Bronze-tipped weapons were widely used by Shang warriors, giving them an advantage over less technologically advanced groups. Bronze was also used for the fittings of the chariots that came into use around 1200 B.C.E. Chariot technology apparently spread by diffusion across Asia, passing from one society to the next. The chariot provided commanders with mobile stations from which they could supervise their troops; it also gave archers and soldiers armed with long halberds increased mobility.

Shang power did not rest solely on military supremacy. The Shang king was also the high priest, the one best qualified to offer sacrifices to the royal ancestors and the high god Di. Royal ancestors were viewed as able to intervene with Di, and the king divined his ancestors' wishes by interpreting the cracks made in heated cattle bones or tortoise shells prepared for him by professional diviners.

The Shang royal family and aristocracy lived in large houses built on huge platforms of rammed earth similar to those used in the Neolithic period. Shang palaces were constructed of perishable material like wood, and nothing of them remains today, unlike the stone buildings and monuments so characteristic of the ancient West. What has survived are the lavish underground tombs built for Shang kings and their consorts.

The one royal tomb not robbed before it was excavated was for Lady Hao, one of the many wives of the king Wu Ding (ca. 1200 B.C.E.). The tomb was filled with almost 500 bronze vessels and weapons, over 700 jade and ivory ornaments, and sixteen people who would tend to Lady Hao in the afterlife. Some of those buried with kings were not sacrificial victims but followers or servants. The bodies of people who voluntarily followed their ruler to the grave were generally buried with their own ornaments and grave goods such as weapons.

Shang society was marked by sharp status distinctions. The king and other noble families had family and clan names transmitted along patrilineal lines, from father to son. Kingship similarly passed along patrilineal lines, from elder to younger brother and father to son, but never to or through sisters or daughters. The kings and the aristocrats owned slaves, many of whom had been captured in war. In the urban centers there were substantial numbers of craftsmen who worked in stone, bone, and bronze.

Shang farmers were essentially serfs of the aristocrats. Their lives were not that different from the lives of their Neolithic ancestors, and they worked the fields with similar stone tools. They usually lived in small, compact villages surrounded by fields. Some new crops became common in Shang times, most notably wheat, which had spread from West Asia. Farmers probably also raised silkworms, from whose cocoons fine silk garments could be made for the ruling elite.

Map 4.2 The Shang and Early Zhou Dynasties, ca. 1500–400 B.C.E. The early Zhou government controlled larger areas than the Shang did, but the independent states of the Warring States Period were more aggressive about pushing out their frontiers, greatly extending the geographical boundaries of Chinese civilization.

Bronze Metalworking

As in Egypt, Mesopotamia, and India, the development of more complex forms of social organization in Shang China coincided with the mastery of metalworking, specifically bronze. The bronze industry required the coordination of a large labor force and skilled artisans. Bronze was used more for ritual than for war in Shang times. Most surviving Shang bronze objects are vessels that would have originally been used during sacrificial ceremonies. They were beautifully formed in a great variety of shapes and sizes.

The decoration on Shang bronzes seems to say something interesting about Shang culture, but scholars do not agree about what that is. In the art of ancient Egypt, Assyria, and Babylonia, representations of agriculture and of social hierarchy are very common, matching our understandings of the social, political, and economic development of those societies. In Shang China, by contrast, images of wild animals predominate. The most common image, the stylized animal face called the **taotie** (taow-tyeh), epitomizes the difficulty of scholarly interpretation. To some it is a monster — a fearsome image that would scare away evil forces. Others imagine a dragon — an animal whose vast powers had more positive associations. Some hypothesize that it reflects masks used in rituals. Others associate it with animal sacrifices, totemism, or shamanism. Still others see these images as hardly more than designs. Without new evidence, scholars can only speculate.

taotie A stylized animal face commonly seen in Chinese bronzes.

Bronze Vessels The Shang Dynasty bronze vessel on the left, dating to the twelfth century B.C.E. and about 10 inches tall, is covered with symmetrical animal imagery, including stylized taotie masks. The early Zhou Dynasty inscribed bronze pan (below), dating to before 900 B.C.E., was one of 103 vessels discovered in 1975 by farmers clearing a field. The inscription tells the story of the first six Zhou kings and of the family of scribes who served them. (pan: Zhou Yuan Administrative Office of Cultural Relics, Fufeng, Shaanxi Province, © Cultural Relics Press; taotie vessel: © Image Copyright Metropolitan Museum of Art/Art Resource, NY)

The Development of Writing

The survival of divination texts inscribed on bones from Shang tombs demonstrates that writing was already a major element in Chinese culture by 1200 B.C.E. Writing must have been developed earlier, but the early stages cannot be traced, probably because writing was done on wood, bamboo, silk, or other perishable materials.

The invention of writing had profound effects on China's culture and government. A written language made possible a bureaucracy capable of keeping records and corresponding with commanders and governors far from the palace. Hence literacy became the ally of royal rule, facilitating communication with and effective control over the realm. Literacy also preserved the learning, lore, and experience of early Chinese society and facilitated the development of abstract thought.

logographic A system of writing in which each word is represented by a single symbol, such as the Chinese script.

Like ancient Egyptian and Sumerian, the Chinese script was **logographic**: each word was represented by a single symbol. In the Chinese case, some of the symbols were pictures, but for the names of abstract concepts other methods were adopted. Sometimes the symbol for a different word was borrowed because the two words were pronounced alike. Sometimes two different symbols were combined; for instance, to represent different types of trees, the symbol for *tree* could be combined with another symbol borrowed for its pronunciation (Figure 4.1).

In western Eurasia logographic scripts were eventually modified or replaced by phonetic scripts, but that never happened in China. Because China retained its logographic writing system, many years were required to gain full mastery of reading and writing, which added to the prestige of education.

Why did China retain a logographic writing system even after encounters with phonetic ones? Although phonetic systems have many real advantages, especially with respect to ease of learning to read, there are some costs to dropping a logographic system. People who learned to read Chinese could communicate with a wider range of people than can people who read scripts based on speech. Since characters did not change when the pronunciation changed, educated Chinese could read texts written centuries earlier without the need for them to be translated. Moreover, as the Chinese language developed regional vari-

WORD	ox	goat, sheep	tree	moon	earth	water	to show, declare	then (men and bowl)	heaven	to pray
SHANG SYMBOL										
MODERN CHARACTER	牛	羊	木	月	土	水	示	就	天	祝

Figure 4.1 The Origins of Chinese Writing The modern Chinese writing system (bottom row) evolved from the script employed by diviners in the Shang period (upper row). (**Source:** Adapted from Patricia Buckley Ebrey, *The Cambridge Illustrated History of China* [Cambridge: Cambridge University Press, 1996], p. 26. Reprinted by permission of Cambridge University Press.)

ants, readers of Chinese could read books and letters by contemporaries whose oral language they could not comprehend. Thus the Chinese script played a large role in holding China together and fostering a sense of connection with the past. In addition, many of China's neighbors (Japan, Korea, and Vietnam, in particular) adopted the Chinese script, allowing communication through writing between people whose languages were totally unrelated. In this regard, the Chinese language was like Arabic numerals, which have the same meaning however they are pronounced.

Quick Review
What role did bronze metalworking and writing play in shaping life in Shang China?

What was China like during the Zhou Dynasty?

The Shang campaigned constantly against enemies in all directions. To the west of the Shang were the fierce Qiang (chyang), considered barbarian tribesmen by the Shang. Between the Shang capital and the Qiang were the Zhou (joe), who seem to have both inherited cultural traditions from the Neolithic cultures of the northwest and absorbed most of the material culture of the Shang. In about 1050 B.C.E. the Zhou rose against the Shang and defeated them in battle. The cultural and political advances that the Shang rulers had introduced were maintained by their successors.

Zhou Politics

The early Zhou period is the first one for which transmitted texts exist in some abundance. The ***Book of Documents*** (ca. 900 B.C.E.) describes the Zhou conquest of the Shang as the victory of just and noble warriors over decadent courtiers led by an irresponsible and sadistic king. These documents also show that the Zhou recognized the Shang as occupying the center of the known world, were eager to succeed them in that role, and saw the writing of history as a major way to legitimate power. The three early Zhou rulers who are given the most praise are King Wen (the "cultured" or "literate" king), who expanded the Zhou domain; his son King Wu (the "martial" king), who conquered the Shang; and Wu's brother, the Duke of Zhou, who consolidated the conquest and served as loyal regent for Wu's heir.

Book of Documents One of the earliest Chinese books, containing documents, speeches, and historical accounts about early Zhou rule.

Like the Shang kings, the Zhou kings sacrificed to their ancestors, but they also sacrificed to Heaven. The *Book of Documents* assumes a close relationship between Heaven and the king, who was called the Son of Heaven. According to the documents, Heaven gives the king a mandate to rule only as long as he rules in the interests of the people. Because the last king of the Shang had been decadent and cruel, Heaven took the mandate away from him and entrusted it to the virtuous Zhou kings. Because this theory of the **Mandate of Heaven** does not seem to have had any place in Shang cosmology, it may have been elaborated by the early Zhou rulers as a kind of propaganda to win over the conquered subjects of the Shang. Whatever its origins, it remained a central feature of Chinese political ideology from the early Zhou period on.

Mandate of Heaven The theory that Heaven gives the king a mandate to rule only as long as he rules in the interests of the people.

Rather than attempt to rule all their territories directly, the early Zhou rulers set up a decentralized feudal system. They sent relatives and trusted subordinates with troops to establish walled garrisons in the conquered territories. Such a vassal was generally able to pass his position on to a son, so that in time the domains became hereditary fiefs ruled by lords. Each lord appointed officers to serve him in ritual, administrative, or military capacities. These posts and their associated titles tended to become hereditary as well.

As generations passed and ties of loyalty and kinship grew more distant, regional lords became so powerful that the king could no longer control them. In 771 B.C.E. the Zhou king was killed by an alliance of non-Chinese tribesmen and Zhou vassals. One of his sons was put on the throne, and then for safety's sake the capital was moved east out of the Wei River Valley to modern Luoyang, just south of the Yellow River in the heart of the central plains (see Map 4.2).

The revived Zhou Dynasty never fully regained control over its vassals, and China entered a prolonged period without a strong central authority. For a couple of centuries a code of conduct still regulated warfare between the states: one state would not attack another that was in mourning for its ruler; during battles one side would not attack before the other side had time to line up; ruling houses were not wiped out, so that successors could continue to sacrifice to their ancestors; and so on. Thereafter, however, such niceties were abandoned, and China entered a period of nearly constant conflict.

Life During the Zhou Dynasty

During the early Zhou period, aristocratic attitudes and privileges were strong. Inherited ranks placed people in a hierarchy ranging downward from the king to the rulers of states with titles like duke and marquis, the hereditary great officials of the states, the lower ranks of the aristocracy—men who could serve in either military or civil capacities, known as **shi**—and finally to the ordinary people (farmers, craftsmen, and traders). Patrilineal family ties were very important in this society, and at the upper reaches, at least, sacrifices to ancestors were one of the key rituals used to forge social ties.

shi The lower ranks of Chinese aristocracy; these men could serve in either military or civil capacities.

Glimpses of what life was like at various social levels in the early Zhou Dynasty can be found in the ***Book of Songs*** (ca. 900 B.C.E.), which contains the earliest Chinese poetry. Some of the songs are hymns used in court religious ceremonies. Others clearly had their origins in folk songs.

Book of Songs The earliest collection of Chinese poetry; it provides glimpses of what life was like in the early Zhou Dynasty.

Many of the folk songs are love songs that depict a more informal pattern of courtship than prevailed in later China. One stanza reads:

Please, Zhongzi,
Do not leap over our wall,
Do not break our mulberry trees.
It's not that I begrudge the mulberries,
But I fear my brothers.

You I would embrace,
But my brothers' words—those I dread.[1]

There were also songs of complaint, such as this one in which the ancestors are rebuked for failing to aid their descendants:

The drought has become so severe
That it cannot be stopped.
Glowing and burning, We have no place.
The great mandate is about at an end.
Nothing to look forward to or back upon.
The host of dukes and past rulers
Does not help us.
As for father and mother and the ancestors,
How can they bear to treat us so?[2]

Other songs in this collection are court odes that reveal attitudes of the aristocrats. One such ode expresses a deep distrust of women's involvement in politics:

Clever men build cities,
Clever women topple them.
Beautiful, these clever women may be
But they are owls and kites.
Women have long tongues
That lead to ruin.
Disorder does not come down from heaven;
It is produced by women.[3]

Part of the reason for distrust of women in politics was the practice of concubinage. Rulers regularly demonstrated their power and wealth by accumulating large numbers of concubines (legal spouses who ranked lower than the wife) and thus would have children by several women. This led to much scheming for favor among the various sons and their mothers and the common perception that women were incapable of taking a disinterested view of the larger good.

Social and economic change quickened after 500 B.C.E. Cities began appearing all over north China. Thick earthen walls were built around the palaces and ancestral temples of the ruler and other aristocrats, and often an outer wall was added to protect the artisans, merchants, and farmers who lived outside the inner wall. Accounts of sieges launched against these walled citadels are central to descriptions of military confrontations in this period.

The development of iron technology in the early Zhou Dynasty promoted economic expansion and allowed some people to become very rich. By the fifth century B.C.E. iron was being widely used for both farm tools and weapons. In the early Zhou inherited status and political favor had been the main reasons some people had more power than others. Beginning in the fifth century wealth alone also was an important basis for social inequality. Late Zhou texts frequently mention trade across state borders, and people who grew wealthy from trade or industry began to rival rulers for influence. Rulers who wanted trade to bring prosperity to their states welcomed traders and began casting coins to facilitate trade.

Social mobility increased over the course of the Zhou period. Rulers often sent out their own officials rather than delegating authority to hereditary lesser lords. This trend toward

INDIVIDUALS IN SOCIETY

Lord Mengchang

DURING THE WARRING STATES PERIOD, MEN often rose to high rank on the basis of political talent. Lord Mengchang rose on the basis of his people skills: he treated his retainers so well that he attracted thousands of talented men to his service, enabling him to rise to prime minister of his native state of Qi (chee) in the early third century B.C.E.

Lord Mengchang's beginnings were not promising. His father, a member of the Qi royal family, already had more than forty sons when Mengchang was born, and he ordered the mother, one of his many concubines, to leave the baby to die. However, she secretly reared him, and while still a child, he was able to win his father's approval through his cleverness.

At his father's death Mengchang succeeded him. Because Mengchang would provide room and board to men who sought to serve him, he soon attracted a few thousand retainers, many of humble background, some fleeing justice. Every night, we are told, he ate with them all in his hall, treating them equally no matter what their social origins.

Most of the stories about Mengchang revolve around retainers who solved his problems in clever ways. Once, when Mengchang had been sent as an envoy to Qin, the king of Qin was persuaded not to let so talented a minister return to help Qi. Under house arrest, Mengchang was able to ask one of the king's consorts to help him, but in exchange she wanted a fur coat kept in the king's treasury. A former thief among Mengchang's retainers stole it for him, and Mengchang was soon on his way. By the time he reached the barrier gate, Qin soldiers were pursuing him, and he knew that he had to get through quickly. One of his retainers imitated the crowing of a cock, which got the other cocks to crow, making the guards think it was dawn, so they opened the gates and let his party through.

When Mengchang served as prime minister of Qi, his retainers came up with many clever strategems that convinced the nearby states of Wei and Han to join Qi in resisting Qin. Several times, one of his retainers of modest origins, Feng Xuan (schwan), helped Mengchang withstand the political vicissitudes of the day. When sent to collect debts owed to Mengchang in his fief of Xue, Feng Xuan instead forgave all the debts of those too poor to repay their loans. Later, when Lord Mengchang lost his post at court and returned to his fief, most of his retainers deserted him, but he found himself well loved by the local residents, all because of Feng Xuan's generosity in his name. After Mengchang reattained his court post and was traveling back to Qi, he complained to Feng Xuan about those who had deserted him. Feng Xuan, we are told, got down from the carriage and bowed to Lord Mengchang, and when pressed said that the lord should accept the retainers' departures as part of the natural order of things:

*Wealth and honor attract while poverty and lowliness repel; such is the nature of things. Think of it like the market. In the morning it is crowded and in the evening it is deserted. This is not because people prefer the morning to the evening, but rather because what they want can not be found there [in the evening]. Do not let the fact that your retainers left when you lost your position lead you to bar them from returning. I hope that you will treat them just the way you did before.**

**Shi ji* 75.2362. Translated by Patricia Ebrey.

QUESTIONS FOR ANALYSIS

1. How did Mengchang attract his many retainers, and how did their service benefit him?
2. Who in this story benefited from hereditary privilege and who advanced because of ability? What does this suggest about social mobility during the Warring States Period?
3. Many of the stories about Mengchang are included in *Intrigues of the Warring States*, a book that Confucians disapproved of. What do you think they found objectionable?

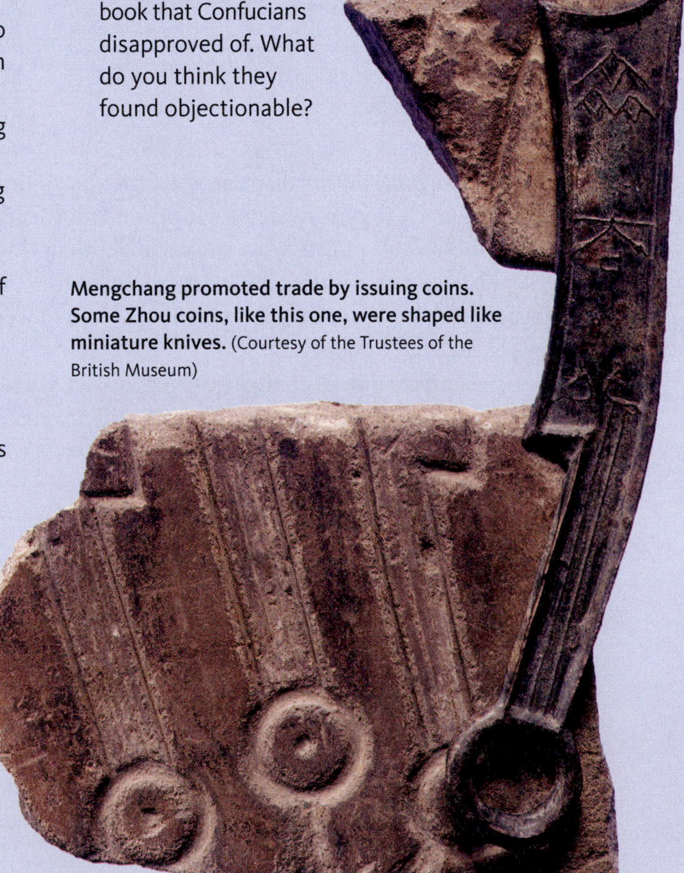

Mengchang promoted trade by issuing coins. Some Zhou coins, like this one, were shaped like miniature knives. (Courtesy of the Trustees of the British Museum)

centralized bureaucratic control created opportunities for social advancement for the shi on the lower end of the old aristocracy. Competition among such men guaranteed rulers a ready supply of able and willing subordinates, and competition among rulers for talent meant that ambitious men could be selective in deciding where to offer their services. (See "Individuals in Society: Lord Mengchang," page 88.)

Religion in Zhou times was not simply a continuation of Shang practices. The practice of burying the living with the dead—so prominent in the royal tombs of the Shang—steadily declined in the middle Zhou period. New deities and cults also appeared, especially in the southern state of Chu, where areas that had earlier been considered barbarian were being incorporated into China's cultural sphere. The state of Chu expanded rapidly in the Yangzi Valley, defeating and absorbing fifty or more small states as it extended its reach north and east. By the late Zhou period Chu was on the forefront of cultural innovation and produced the greatest literary masterpiece of the era, the *Songs of Chu*, a collection of fantastical poems full of images of elusive deities and shamans who can fly through the spirit world. Images found in Chu tombs, painted on coffins or pieces of silk, show both fearsome deities and spirit journeys.

Quick Review
What sort of society developed during the Zhou Dynasty?

How did new technologies contribute to the rise of independent states?

By 400 B.C.E. advances in military technology were undermining the old aristocratic social structure of the Zhou. Large, well-drilled infantry armies able to withstand and defeat chariot-led forces became potent military forces in the **Warring States Period**, which lasted from 403 to 221 B.C.E. Fueled by the development of new weaponry and war tactics, the Chinese states destroyed each other one by one until only one state was left standing—the state of Qin (chin).

Warring States Period The period of Chinese history between 403 and 221 B.C.E. when states fought each other and one state after another was destroyed.

The Warring States, 403–221 B.C.E.

New Technologies for War

By 300 B.C.E. states were sending out armies of a few hundred thousand drafted foot soldiers, usually accompanied by horsemen. Adding to their effectiveness was the development of the **crossbow** around 350 B.C.E. The intricate bronze trigger of the crossbow allowed a foot soldier to shoot farther than could a horseman carrying a light bow. To defend against crossbows soldiers began wearing armor and helmets. Most of the armor was made of leader strips tied with cords. Helmets were sometimes made of iron.

crossbow A powerful mechanical bow developed during the Warring States Period.

The introduction of cavalry in this period further reduced the need for a chariot-riding aristocracy. Shooting bows and arrows from horseback was first perfected by non-Chinese peoples to the north of China proper who at that time were making the transition to a nomadic pastoral economy. The northern state of Jin developed its own cavalry armies to defend itself from the attacks of these horsemen. Once it started using cavalry against other Chinese states, they too had to master the new technology. From this time on, acquiring and pasturing horses was a key component of military preparedness.

Mounted Swordsman This depiction of a warrior fighting a leopard decorates a bronze mirror inlaid with gold and silver dating from the Warring States Period. (From *Gugong wenwu yuekan*, 91/National Palace Museum, Taipei, Taiwan © Cultural Relics Press)

Because these developments made commoners and craftsmen central to military success, rulers tried to find ways to increase their populations. To increase agricultural output, they brought new land into cultivation, drained marshes, and dug irrigation channels. Rulers began surveying their land and taxing farmers. They wanted to undermine the power of lords over their subjects in order to get direct access to the peasants' labor power. Serfdom thus gradually declined. Registering populations led to the extension of family names to commoners at an earlier date than anywhere else in the world.

The development of infantry armies also created the need for a new type of general, and rulers became less willing to let men lead troops merely because of aristocratic birth. Treatises on the art of war described the ideal general as a master of maneuver, illusion, and deception. In *The Art of War* (453–403 B.C.E.) Sun Wu argued that heroism is a useless virtue that leads to needless deaths. But discipline is essential, and he insisted that the entire army had to be trained to follow the orders of its commanders without questioning them. He also explicitly called for the use of deceit:

> *War is the Way of deceit. Thus one who is competent pretends to be incompetent; one who uses [his army] pretends not to use it; one who draws near pretends to be distant; one who is distant pretends to draw near. If [the enemy] is enraged, irritate him [further]. If he is humble, make him haughty. If he is rested, make him toil. If he is intimate [with his ranks], separate them. Attack where he does not expect it and go where he has not imagined. This is how military experts are victorious.*[4]

The Victorious States

During the Warring States Period states on the periphery of the Zhou realm had more room to expand than states in the center. With access to more resources, they were able to pick off their neighbors, one after the other. Still, for a couple of centuries the final outcome was far from clear, as alliances among states were regularly made and nearly as regularly broken.

By the third century B.C.E. there were only seven important states remaining. These states were much more centralized than their early Zhou predecessors. Their kings had eliminated indirect control through vassals and in its place dispatched royal officials to remote cities, controlling them from a distance through the transmission of documents and dismissing them at will. By the end of the third century one state, Qin, would have conquered all of the others, a development discussed in Chapter 7.

Quick Review
What resulted from changes in the nature of warfare?

What ideas did Confucius teach, and how were they spread after his death?

The Warring States Period was the golden age of Chinese philosophy, the era when the "Hundred Schools of Thought" contended. During the same period in which Indian sages and mystics were developing religious speculation about karma, souls, and eons of time (see Chapter 3), Chinese thinkers were arguing about the ideal forms of social and political organization and man's connections to nature.

Confucius

Confucius (traditional dates: 551–479 B.C.E.) was one of the first men of ideas. As a young man, he had served in the court of his home state of Lu without gaining much influence. After leaving Lu, he set out with a small band of students and wandered through neighboring states in search of a ruler who would take his advice.

Confucius's ideas are known to us primarily through the sayings recorded by his disciples in the *Analects*. The thrust of his thought was ethical rather than theoretical or metaphysical. He talked repeatedly of an ideal age when everyone was devoted to fulfilling his or her role: superiors looked after those dependent on them; inferiors devoted themselves to the service of their superiors; parents and children, husbands and wives all wholeheartedly embraced what was expected of them.

Confucius considered the family the basic unit of society. He extolled **filial piety**, which to him meant more than just reverent obedience of children to their parents:

filial piety Reverent attitude of children to their parents extolled by Confucius.

Serving Parents with Filial Piety This twelfth-century C.E. illustration of a passage in the *Classic of Filial Piety* shows how commoners should serve their parents: by working hard at productive jobs such as farming and tending to their parents' daily needs. The married son and daughter-in-law offer food or drink to the older couple as their own children look on, thus learning how they should treat their own parents after they become aged. (National Palace Museum, Taipei, Taiwan © Cultural Relics Press)

LISTENING TO THE PAST

The Book of Mencius

The book that records the teachings of Mencius (ca. 370–300 B.C.E.) was modeled on the Analects *of Confucius. It presents, in no particular order, conversations between Mencius and several rulers, philosophers, and disciples. Unlike the* Analects*, however, the Book of Mencius includes extended discussions of particular points, suggesting that Mencius had a hand in recording the conversations.*

Mencius had an audience with King Hui of Liang. The king said, "Sir, you did not consider a thousand *li* too far to come. You must have some ideas about how to benefit my state."

Mencius replied, "Why must Your Majesty use the word 'benefit'? All I am concerned with are the benevolent and the right. If Your Majesty says, 'How can I benefit my state?' your officials will say, 'How can I benefit my family,' and officers and common people will say, 'How can I benefit myself?' Once superiors and inferiors are competing for benefit, the state will be in danger.

"When the head of a state of ten thousand chariots is murdered, the assassin is invariably a noble with a fief of a thousand chariots. When the head of a fief of a thousand chariots is murdered, the assassin is invariably head of a subfief of a hundred chariots. Those with a thousand out of ten thousand, or a hundred out of a thousand, had quite a bit. But when benefit is put before what is right, they are not satisfied without snatching it all. By contrast, there has never been a benevolent person who neglected his parents or a righteous person who put his lord last. Your Majesty perhaps will now also say, 'All I am concerned with are the benevolent and the right.' Why mention 'benefit'?"

After seeing King Xiang (SHEE-ang) of Liang, Mencius said to someone, "When I saw him from a distance, he did not look like a ruler, and when I got closer, I saw nothing to command respect. But he asked, 'How can the realm be settled?'

"I answered, 'It can be settled through unity.'

"'Who can unify it?' he asked.

"I answered, 'Someone not fond of killing people.'

"'Who could give it to him?'

"I answered, 'Everyone in the world will give it to him. Your Majesty knows what rice plants are? If there is a drought in the seventh and eighth months, the plants wither, but if moisture collects in the sky and forms clouds and rain falls in torrents, the plants suddenly revive. This is the way it is; no one can stop the process. In the world today there are no rulers disinclined toward killing. If there were a ruler who did not like to kill people, everyone in the world would crane their necks to catch sight of him. This is really true. The people would flow toward him the way water flows down. No one would be able to repress them.'"

After an incident between Zou and Lu, Duke Mu asked, "Thirty-three of my officials died but no common people died. I could punish them, but I could not punish them all. I could refrain from punishing them, but they did angrily watch their superiors die without

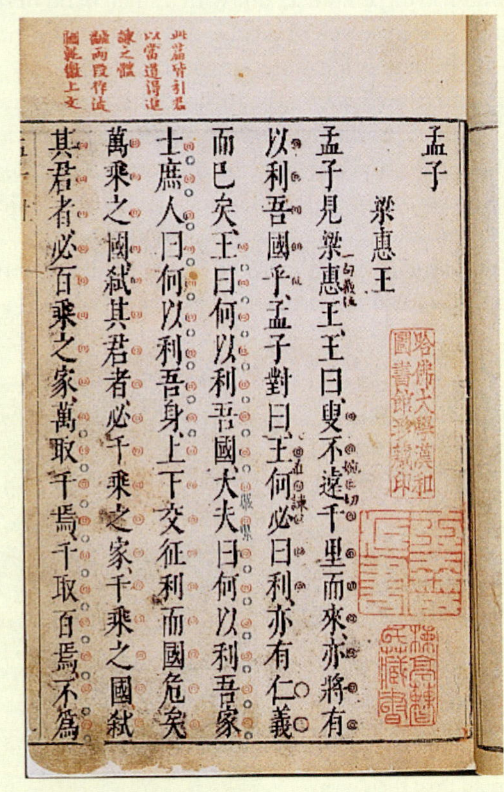
孟子
梁惠王
孟子見梁惠王王曰叟不遠千里而來亦將有
以利吾國乎孟子對曰王何必曰利亦有仁義
而已矣王曰何以利吾國大夫曰何以利吾家
士庶人曰何以利吾身上下交征利而國危矣
萬乘之國弑其君者必千乘之家千乘之國弑
其君者必百乘之家萬取千焉千取百焉不為

Opening page of a 1617 edition of the Book of Mencius. (From *Mengzi* [Book of Mencius]. Image courtesy, Harvard-Yenching Library)

The Master said, "You can be of service to your father and mother by remonstrating with them tactfully. If you perceive that they do not wish to follow your advice, then continue to be reverent toward them without offending or disobeying them; work hard and do not murmur against them."[5]

The relationship between father and son was one of the five cardinal relationships stressed by Confucius. The others were between ruler and subject, husband and wife, elder and

saving them. What would be the best course for me to follow?"

Mencius answered, "When the harvest failed, even though your granaries were full, nearly a thousand of your subjects were lost — the old and weak among them dying in the gutters, the able-bodied scattering in all directions. Your officials never reported the situation, a case of superiors callously inflicting suffering on their subordinates. Zengzi said, 'Watch out, watch out! What you do will be done to you.' This was the first chance the people had to pay them back. You should not resent them. If Your Highness practices benevolent government, the common people will love their superiors and die for those in charge of them."

King Xuan of Qi asked, "Is it true that Tang banished Jie and King Wu took up arms against Zhou?"

Mencius replied, "That is what the records say."

"Then is it permissible for a subject to assassinate his lord?"

Mencius said, "Someone who does violence to the good we call a villain; someone who does violence to the right we call a criminal. A person who is both a villain and a criminal we call a scoundrel. I have heard that the scoundrel Zhou was killed, but have not heard that a lord was killed."

King Xuan of Qi asked about ministers.

Mencius said, "What sort of ministers does Your Majesty mean?"

The king said, "Are there different kinds of ministers?"

"There are. There are noble ministers related to the ruler and ministers of other surnames."

The king said, "I'd like to hear about noble ministers."

Mencius replied, "When the ruler makes a major error, they point it out. If he does not listen to their repeated remonstrations, then they put someone else on the throne."

The king blanched. Mencius continued, "Your Majesty should not be surprised at this. Since you asked me, I had to tell you truthfully."

After the king regained his composure, he asked about unrelated ministers. Mencius said, "When the king makes an error, they point it out. If he does not heed their repeated remonstrations, they quit their posts."

Bo Gui said, "I'd like a tax of one part in twenty. What do you think?"

Mencius said, "Your way is that of the northern tribes. Is one potter enough for a state with ten thousand households?"

"No, there would not be enough wares."

"The northern tribes do not grow all the five grains, only millet. They have no cities or houses, no ritual sacrifices. They do not provide gifts or banquets for feudal lords, and do not have a full array of officials. Therefore, for them, one part in twenty is enough. But we live in the central states. How could we abolish social roles and do without gentlemen? If a state cannot do without potters, how much less can it do without gentlemen.

"Those who want to make government lighter than it was under Yao and Shun are to some degree barbarians. Those who wish to make government heavier than it was under Yao and Shun are to some degree [tyrants like] Jie."

Gaozi said, "Human nature is like whirling water. When an outlet is opened to the east, it flows east; when an outlet is opened to the west, it flows west. Human nature is no more inclined to good or bad than water is inclined to east or west."

Mencius responded, "Water, it is true, is not inclined to either east or west, but does it have no preference for high or low? Goodness is to human nature like flowing downward is to water. There are no people who are not good and no water that does not flow down. Still, water, if splashed, can go higher than your head; if forced, it can be brought up a hill. This isn't the nature of water; it is the specific circumstances. Although people can be made to be bad, their natures are not changed." ”

Source: Reprinted and edited with the permission of The Free Press, a Division of Simon & Schuster Adult Publishing Group, from *Chinese Civilization: A Sourcebook*, Second Edition, revised and expanded by Patricia Buckley Ebrey.

QUESTIONS FOR ANALYSIS

1. Does Mencius give consistent advice to the kings he talks to?
2. Do you see a link between Mencius's views on human nature and his views on the true king?
3. What role does Mencius see for ministers?

younger brother, and friend and friend. Mutual obligations of a hierarchical sort underlay the first four of these relationships: the senior leads and protects; the junior supports and obeys. The exception was the relationship between friends, which was conceived in terms of mutual obligations between equals.

A man of moderation, Confucius was an earnest advocate of gentlemanly conduct. He redefined the term *gentleman* (*junzi*) to mean a man of moral cultivation rather than a man of noble birth. He repeatedly urged his followers to aspire to be gentlemen rather than petty men intent on personal gain. Confucius did not advocate social equality, but his teachings minimized the importance of class distinctions and opened the way for intelligent and talented people to rise in the social scale. The Confucian gentleman found his calling in service to the ruler. Loyal advisers should encourage their rulers to govern through ritual, virtue, and concern for the welfare of their subjects, and much of the *Analects* concerns the way to govern well.

ren The ultimate Confucian virtue; it is translated as perfect goodness, benevolence, humanity, human-heartedness, and nobility.

To Confucius the ultimate virtue was **ren** (humanity). A person of humanity cares about others and acts accordingly:

> *[The disciple] Zhonggong asked about humanity. The Master said, "When you go out, treat everyone as if you were welcoming a great guest. Employ people as though you were conducting a great sacrifice. Do not do unto others what you would not have them do unto you."*[6]

In the Confucian tradition, studying texts came to be valued over speculation, meditation, and mystical identification with deities. Confucius encouraged the men who came to study with him to master the poetry, rituals, and historical traditions that we know today as Confucian classics. Many passages in the *Analects* reveal Confucius's confidence in the power of study:

> *The Master said, "I am not someone who was born wise. I am someone who loves the ancients and tries to learn from them."*
>
> *The Master said, "I once spent a whole day without eating and a whole night without sleeping in order to think. It was of no use. It is better to study."*[7]

The Spread of Confucian Ideas

The eventual success of Confucian ideas owes much to Confucius's followers in the three centuries following his death. The most important of them were Mencius (ca. 370–300 B.C.E.) and Xunzi (ca. 310–215 B.C.E.).

Mencius, like Confucius, traveled around offering advice to rulers of various states. (See "Listening to the Past: The Book of Mencius," page 92.) In his view, the ruler able to win over the people through benevolent government would succeed in unifying "all under Heaven." Mencius proposed concrete political and financial measures to ease tax burdens and otherwise improve the people's lot. Men willing to serve an unworthy ruler earned his contempt, especially when they worked hard to fill the ruler's coffers or expand his territory. With his disciples and fellow philosophers, Mencius also discussed other issues in moral philosophy, arguing strongly, for instance, that human nature is fundamentally good.

Xunzi, a half century later, took the opposite view of human nature, arguing that people are born selfish and that only through education and ritual do they learn to put moral principle above their own interest. Much of what is desirable is not inborn but must be taught:

> *When a son yields to his father, or a younger brother yields to his elder brother, or when a son takes on the work for his father or a younger brother for his elder brother, their actions go against their natures and run counter to their feelings. And yet these are the way of the filial son and the principles of ritual and morality.*[8]

Neither Confucius nor Mencius had had much actual political or administrative experience, but Xunzi had worked for many years in the court of his home state. Not surprisingly, he showed more consideration than either Confucius or Mencius for the difficulties a ruler might face in trying to rule through ritual and virtue. Xunzi was also a more rigorous thinker than his predecessors and developed the philosophical foundations of many ideas merely outlined by Confucius and Mencius. Confucius, for instance, had declined to discuss gods, portents, and anomalies. Xunzi went further and explicitly argued that Heaven does not intervene in human affairs.

Still, Xunzi did not propose abandoning traditional rituals. In contrast to Daoists (discussed below), who saw rituals as unnatural or extravagant, Xunzi saw them as an efficient way to attain order in society. Rulers and educated men should continue traditional ritual practices such as complex funeral protocols because the rites themselves have positive effects on performers and observers. Not only do they let people express feelings and satisfy desires in an orderly way, but because they specify graduated ways to perform the rites according to social rank, ritual traditions sustain the social hierarchy.

The Confucian vision of personal ethics and public service found a small but ardent following in the Warring States Period. In later centuries rulers came to see men educated in Confucian virtues as ideal advisers and officials. Neither revolutionaries nor flatterers, Confucian scholar-officials opposed bad government and upheld the best ideals of statecraft. Confucian political ideals shaped Chinese society into the twentieth century.

The Confucian vision also provided the moral basis for the Chinese family into modern times. Repaying parents and ancestors came to be seen as a sacred duty. Because people owe their very existence to their parents, they should reciprocate by respecting their parents, making efforts to please them, honoring their memories, and placing the interests of the family line above personal preferences. Since the family line is a patrilineal line from father to son to grandson, placing great importance on it has had the effect of devaluing women.

Quick Review
What were Confucius's ideas about the family and how did these views shape his philosophy as a whole?

How did Daoism, Legalism, and other philosophies differ from Confucianism?

During the Warring States Period, rulers took advantage of the destruction of states to recruit newly unemployed men to serve as their advisers and court assistants. Lively debate often resulted as these strategists proposed policies and defended their ideas against challengers. Followers took to recording their teachers' ideas, and the circulation of these "books" (rolls of silk, or strips of wood or bamboo tied together) served further to stimulate debate.

Many of these schools of thought directly opposed the ideas of Confucius and his followers. Most notable were the Daoists, who believed that the act of striving to improve something only made it worse, and the Legalists, who argued that a strong government rested not just on moral leadership but also on effective laws and procedures.

Daoism

Confucius and his followers believed in moral effort and statecraft. They thought men of virtue should devote themselves to making the government work to the benefit of the people. Those who came to be labeled Daoists disagreed. They thought striving to make things better generally made them worse. Daoists defended private life and wanted the rulers to leave the people alone. They sought to go beyond everyday concerns and to let their minds wander freely. Rather than making human beings and human actions the center of concern, they focused on the larger scheme of things, the whole natural order identified as the Way, or **Dao**.

Dao The Way, the whole natural order in Daoist philosophy. In Confucianism it means the moral order.

Picturing the Past

Inscribed Bamboo Slips

In 1993 Chinese archaeologists discovered a late-fourth-century B.C.E. tomb in Hubei province that contained 804 bamboo slips bearing some 12,000 Chinese characters. Scholars have been able to reconstruct more than a dozen books from them, many of them previously unknown. (Jingmen City Museum, © Cultural Relics Press)

ANALYZING THE IMAGE Can you spot any repeated characters? Can you see any very simple characters? Look in particular at the strip that is at far right. Do you see the name of the deity Taiyi (Great One) twice? Hint: *One* is a single horizontal line.

CONNECTIONS What were the consequences of recording texts on bamboo or wooden strips? How might doing so have shaped reading and writing in Zhou times? For modern archaeologists who discover these texts in tombs, would the medium used pose any challenges?

Early Daoist teachings are known from two surviving books, the *Laozi* and the *Zhuangzi*, both dating to the third century B.C.E. A recurrent theme in the *Laozi*, a brief, aphoristic text is the mystical superiority of yielding over assertion and of silence over words: "The Way that can be discussed is not the constant Way."[9] The highest good is like water: "Water benefits all creatures but does not compete. It occupies the places people disdain and thus comes near to the Way."[10]

Because purposeful action is counterproductive, the ruler should let people return to a natural state of ignorance and contentment:

A sage governs this way:
He empties people's minds and fills their bellies.
He weakens their wills and strengthens their bones.
Keep the people always without knowledge and without desires,
For then the clever will not dare act.
Engage in no action and order will prevail.[11]

In the philosophy of the *Laozi*, the people would be better off if they knew less, gave up tools, renounced writing, stopped envying their neighbors, and lost their desire to travel or engage in war.

Zhuangzi (369–286 B.C.E.), the author of the book of the same name, shared many of the central ideas of the *Laozi*, including an avowed disinterest in politics. The *Zhuangzi* is filled with parables, flights of fancy, and fictional encounters between historical figures, including Confucius and his disciples. A more serious strain of Zhuangzi's thought concerned death. He questioned whether we can be sure life is better than death. People fear what they do not know, the same way a captive girl will be terrified when she learns she is to become the king's concubine. Perhaps people will discover that death has as many delights as life in the palace.

Zhuangzi was similarly iconoclastic in his political ideas. In one parable a wheelwright insolently tells a duke that books are useless because all they contain are the dregs of men long dead. The duke, insulted, threatens to execute the wheelwright if he cannot give an adequate explanation of his remark. The wheelwright replies:

> *I see things in terms of my own work. When I chisel at a wheel, if I go slow, the chisel slides and does not stay put; if I hurry, it jams and doesn't move properly. When it is neither too slow nor too fast, I can feel it in my hand and respond to it from my heart. My mouth cannot describe it in words, but there is something there. I cannot teach it to my son, and my son cannot learn it from me. So I have gone on for seventy years, growing old chiseling wheels. The men of old died in possession of what they could not transmit. So it follows that what you are reading are their dregs.*[12]

To put this another way, truly skilled craftsmen respond to situations spontaneously; they do not analyze or reason or even keep in mind the rules they have mastered. This strain of Daoist thought denies the validity of verbal reasoning and the sorts of knowledge conveyed through words.

Daoism can be seen as a response to Confucianism, a rejection of many of its basic premises. Nevertheless, over the course of Chinese history, many people felt the pull of both Confucian and Daoist ideas and studied the writings of both schools. Even Confucian scholars who had devoted much of their lives to public service might find that the teachings of the *Laozi* or *Zhuangzi* helped to put their frustrations in perspective. Whereas Confucianism often seems sternly masculine, Daoism is more accepting of feminine principles and even celebrates passivity and yielding. Those drawn to the arts were also often drawn to Daoism, with its validation of spontaneity and freedom. Rulers, too, were drawn to the Daoist notion of the ruler who can have great power simply by being himself without instituting anything.

Legalism

Over the course of the fourth and third centuries B.C.E. one small state after another was conquered, and the number of surviving states dwindled. Rulers fearful that their states might be next were ready to listen to political theorists who claimed expertise in the accumulation of power. These theorists, labeled **Legalists** because of their emphasis on the need for rigorous laws, argued that strong government depended not on the moral qualities of the ruler and his officials, as Confucians claimed, but on establishing effective laws and procedures. Legalism, though eventually discredited, laid the basis for China's later bureaucratic government.

Legalists Political theorists who emphasized the need for rigorous laws and laid the basis for China's later bureaucratic government.

In the fourth century B.C.E. the state of Qin radically reformed itself. The king of Qin, under the guidance of Lord Shang (d. 338 B.C.E.), his chief minister, adopted many Legalist policies. He abolished the aristocracy. Social distinctions were to be based on military ranks determined by the objective criterion of the number of enemy heads cut off in battle. In place of the old fiefs, the Qin king created counties and appointed officials to govern them according to the laws he decreed at court. To increase the population, Qin recruited migrants from other states with offers of land and houses. To encourage farmers to work hard and improve their land, they were allowed to buy and sell it. Ordinary farmers were thus freed from serf-like obligations to the local nobility, but direct control by the state could be even more onerous. Taxes and labor service obligations were heavy. Travel required a permit, and vagrants could be forced into penal labor service. All families were grouped into mutual responsibility groups of five and ten families; whenever anyone in the group committed a crime, all the others were equally liable unless they reported it.

In the century after Lord Shang, Legalism found its greatest exponent in Han Feizi (ca. 280?–233 B.C.E.). Han Feizi had little interest in Confucian values of goodness or ritual. In his writings he warned rulers of the political pitfalls awaiting them. They had to be careful where they placed their trust, for "when the ruler trusts someone, he falls under that person's control."[13] Given subordinates' propensities to pursue their own selfish interests, the ruler should keep them ignorant of his intentions and control them by manipulating competition among them. Warmth, affection, or candor should have no place in his relationships with others.

Han Feizi saw the Confucian notion that government could be based on virtue as naive:

> *Think of parents' relations to their children. They congratulate each other when a son is born, but complain to each other when a daughter is born. Why do parents have these divergent responses when both are equally their offspring? It is because they calculate their long-term advantage. Since even parents deal with their children in this calculating way, what can one expect where there is no parent-child bond? When present-day scholars counsel rulers, they all tell them to rid themselves of thoughts of profit and follow the path of mutual love. This is expecting rulers to go further than parents.*[14]

If rulers would make the laws and prohibitions clear and the rewards and punishments automatic, then the officials and common people would be easy to govern. Uniform laws get people to do things they would not otherwise be inclined to do, such as work hard and fight wars, essential to the goal of establishing hegemony over all the other states.

The laws of the Legalists were designed as much to constrain officials as to regulate the common people. The third-century B.C.E. tomb of a Qin official has yielded statutes detailing the rules for keeping accounts, supervising subordinates, managing penal labor, conducting investigations, and many other responsibilities of officials. Infractions were generally punishable through the imposition of fines.

Legalism saw no value in intellectual debate or private opinion. Divergent views of right and wrong lead to weakness and disorder. The ruler should not allow others to undermine his laws by questioning them. In Legalism, there were no laws above or independent of the wishes of the rulers, no laws that might set limits on rulers' actions in the way that natural or divine laws did in Greek thought.

Rulers of several states adopted some Legalist ideas, but only the state of Qin systematically followed them. The extraordinary but brief success Qin had with these policies is discussed in Chapter 7.

Yin and Yang

Confucians, Daoists, and Legalists had the greatest long-term impact on Chinese civilization, but the Hundred Schools of Thought also included everyone from logicians, hedonists, and utopians to agriculturalists who argued that no one should eat who does not farm, and hermits who justified withdrawal from social life. Natural philosophy was one of the most important of these alternative schools of early Chinese thought.

yin and yang A concept of complementary poles, one of which represents the feminine, dark, and receptive, and the other the masculine, bright, and assertive.

One such philosophy was the cosmological concept of **yin and yang**, first described in the divination manual called the *Book of Changes* (ca. 900 B.C.E.), and developed into much more elaborate theories by late Zhou theorists. Yin is the feminine, dark, receptive, yielding, negative, and weak; yang is the masculine, bright, assertive, creative, positive, and strong. Yin and yang are complementary poles rather than distinct entities or opposing forces. These models based on observation of nature were extended to explain not only phenomena we might classify as natural, such as illness, storms, and earthquakes, but also social phenomena, such as the rise and fall of states and conflict in families. In all these realms, unwanted things happen when the balance between yin and yang gets disturbed.

In recent decades archaeologists have further complicated our understanding of early Chinese thought by unearthing records of the popular religion of the time—astrological manuals, handbooks of lucky and unlucky days, medical prescriptions, exercises, and ghost stories. The tomb of an official who died in 316 B.C.E., for example, has records of divinations showing that illness was seen as the result of unsatisfied spirits or malevolent demons, best dealt with through exorcisms or offering sacrifices to the astral god Taiyi (Grand One).

Quick Review
What aspects of life during the Warring States Period help explain the appeal of Daoism and Legalism?

Connections

CHINA'S TRANSITION from Neolithic farming villages to a much more advanced civilization with writing, metalworking, iron coinage, crossbows, philosophical speculation, and competing states occurred centuries later than in Mesopotamia or India, but by the Warring States Period China was at much the same stage of development as other advanced societies in Eurasia. Although many elements of China's civilization were clearly invented in China—such as its writing system, its method of casting bronze, and its Confucian philosophy—it also adopted elements that diffused across Asia, such as the cultivation of wheat, the horse-driven chariot, and riding horseback.

Greece, the subject of the next chapter, is located very close to the ancient Near Eastern civilizations, so its trajectory was quite different from China's. It was also much smaller than China, yet in time had enormous impact on the wider world. With India and China in mind, the originality of the political forms and ideas of early Greece will stand out more clearly. We return to China's history in Chapter 7, after looking at Greece and Rome.

- **For a list of suggested readings for this chapter, visit** *bedfordstmartins.com/mckayworldunderstanding*.
- **For primary sources from this period, see** *Sources of World Societies*, Second Edition.
- **For Web sites, images, and documents related to topics in this chapter, see Make History at** *bedfordstmartins.com/mckayworldunderstanding*.

Chapter 4 Study Guide

To do these exercises online, go to bedfordstmartins.com/mckayworldunderstanding.

Step 1

GETTING STARTED

Below are basic terms about this period in global history. Can you identify each term below and explain why it matters?

TERMS	WHO (OR WHAT) AND WHEN	WHY IT MATTERS
loess, p. 81		
Anyang, p. 82		
taotie, p. 83		
logographic, p. 84		
Book of Documents, p. 85		
Mandate of Heaven, p. 86		
shi, p. 86		
Book of Songs, p. 86		
Warring States Period, p. 89		
crossbow, p. 89		
filial piety, p. 91		
ren, p. 94		
Dao, p. 95		
Legalists, p. 97		
yin and yang, p. 98		

Step 2

MOVING BEYOND THE BASICS

The exercise below requires a more advanced understanding of the chapter material. Compare and contrast the three philosophical traditions that originated during China's Classical Age by filling in the chart below with descriptions of three key aspects of these philosophies: core beliefs, social and ethical teachings, and vision of politics and public life. When you are finished, consider the following questions: What problems and tensions in Chinese society did each of these philosophies attempt to remedy? How would adherents of each of these philosophies have described the ideal ruler? How did adherents of each of these philosophies imagine such a ruler would solve China's problems?

	CORE BELIEFS	SOCIAL AND ETHICAL TEACHINGS	VISION OF POLITICS AND PUBLIC LIFE
Confucianism			
Daoism			
Legalism			

Step 3 PUTTING IT ALL TOGETHER

Now that you've reviewed key elements of the chapter, take a step back and try to see the big picture. Remember to use specific examples from the chapter in your answers.

DEVELOPMENT OF EARLY CHINESE SOCIETY

- How did geography shape the way Chinese culture spread and developed?
- What role did the Shang king play in Shang society? What was the source of his power and legitimacy?

ZHOU DYNASTY AND THE WARRING STATES PERIOD

- What innovations did the Zhou introduce into Chinese society and politics? What were their consequences?
- What were the social and cultural consequences of political decentralization during the Warring States Period?

CHINESE PHILOSOPHY IN THE CLASSICAL AGE

- What role do hierarchical relationships play in Confucians' philosophy? What light does this shed on Chinese beliefs and values in the Classical Age?
- How would you explain the fact that the Warring States Period, a time of unrest and conflict, was also the golden age of Chinese philosophy?

LOOKING BACK, LOOKING AHEAD

- What similarities and differences do you see between Chinese society and government under the Shang and society and government in the early kingdoms of Mesopotamia? How would you explain the similarities and differences you note?
- How would you explain the long-term influence of Confucianism on Chinese society and culture? What elements of Confucianism might explain its enduring appeal?

In Your Own Words Imagine that you must explain Chapter 4 to someone who hasn't read it. What would be the most important points to include and why?

5

The Greek Experience

3500–100 B.C.E.

The people of ancient Greece developed a culture that fundamentally shaped the civilization of the western part of Eurasia much as the Chinese culture shaped the civilization of the eastern part. The Greeks were the first in the Mediterranean and neighboring areas to explore most of the philosophical questions that still concern thinkers today. Going beyond mythmaking, the Greeks strove to understand the world in logical, rational terms. The result was the birth of philosophy and science, subjects as important to many Greeks as religion. Drawing on their day-by-day experiences, the Greeks also developed the concept of politics, and their contributions to literature still fertilize intellectual life today.

The history of the Greeks is divided into two broad periods: the Hellenic, roughly the time between the founding of the first complex societies in the area that is now the Greek islands and mainland, about 3500 B.C.E., and the rise of the kingdom of Macedonia in the north of Greece in 338 B.C.E.; and the Hellenistic, the years from the reign of Alexander the Great (336–323 B.C.E.) through the spread of Greek culture from Spain to India (ca. 100 B.C.E.; see Chapter 3). During the Hellenic period Greeks developed a distinctive form of city-state known as the polis and made lasting cultural and intellectual achievements. During the Hellenistic period Macedonian and Greek armies defeated the Persian Empire and built new cities and kingdoms. During their conquests they blended their ideas and traditions with those of the societies they encountered, creating a vibrant culture.

Greek Boy with Goose
In the Hellenistic culture that developed after Alexander the Great's conquests, wealthy residents wanted art that showed real people rather than gods. This statue of a little boy wrestling a goose, originally carved about 200 B.C.E., no doubt found an eager buyer. (Vanni/Art Resource, NY)

Chapter Preview

- How did geography shape the early history of the Greeks?
- How did Greek society and government develop during the Archaic age?
- What were the lasting achievements of the classical period?
- What were the social and political consequences of Alexander's conquests?
- How did the mixing of cultures shape Hellenistic thought?

How did geography shape the early history of the Greeks?

Geography acted as an enormously divisive force in Greek life; mountains divide the land, and, although there are good harbors on the sea, there are no navigable rivers (Map 5.1). The geographical fragmentation of Greece encouraged political fragmentation, and communications between settlements were poor. Early in Greek history several kingdoms did emerge, which later became known as the Minoan (muh-NOH-uhn) and Mycenaean (migh-suh-NEE-uhn), but the rugged terrain prohibited the growth of a great empire like those of Mesopotamia or Egypt. Instead the independent city-state, known as the polis, became the most common form of government.

The Minoans and Mycenaeans

The first humans to arrive in Greece were hunter-gatherers, but techniques of agriculture and animal domestication had spread into Greece from Turkey by about 6500 B.C.E., after which small farming communities worked much of the land. Early Greek settlers brought

Map 5.1 Classical Greece, ca. 450 B.C.E. In antiquity the home of the Greeks included the islands of the Aegean and the western shore of Turkey as well as the Greek peninsula itself. Crete, the home of Minoan civilization, is the large island at the bottom of the map. The Peloponnesian peninsula, where Sparta is located, is connected to the rest of mainland Greece by a very narrow isthmus at Corinth.

skills in making bronze weapons and tools, which had become more common about 3500 B.C.E.

On the large island of Crete, farmers and fishermen began to trade their surpluses with their neighbors, and cities grew, housing artisans and merchants. Beginning about 2000 B.C.E. Cretan traders voyaged throughout the eastern Mediterranean and the Aegean. Social hierarchies developed, and in many cities certain individuals came to hold power, although exactly how this happened is not clear. The Cretans began to use writing about 1900 B.C.E., in a form later scholars called Linear A, but this has not been deciphered. At about the same time that writing began, rulers in several cities of Crete began to build large structures with hundreds of interconnected rooms. The largest of these, at Knossos (NO-suhs), has over a thousand rooms along with pipes for bringing in drinking water and sewers to get rid of waste. The archaeologists who discovered these huge structures called them palaces, and they named the flourishing and vibrant culture of this era Minoan, after the mythical king of Crete, Minos.

Minoan society was wealthy and, to judge by the absence of fortifications on the island, relatively peaceful. Few specifics are known about Minoan political life except that a king and a group of nobles stood at its head. In terms of their religious life, Minoans appear to have worshipped goddesses far more than gods. Whether this translated into more egalitarian gender roles is unclear, but surviving Minoan art shows women as well as men leading religious activities, watching entertainment, and engaging in athletic competitions, such as leaping over bulls.

As Minoan culture was flourishing on Crete, a different type of society developed on the mainland. This society was founded by groups who had migrated in during the period after 2000 B.C.E., and its members spoke an early form of Greek. By about 1650 B.C.E. one group of these immigrants had founded a powerful kingdom at Mycenae, from which later scholars gave the culture its name, Mycenaean. Early Mycenaean Greeks raised palaces and established cities at Thebes, Athens, and elsewhere. As in Crete, the political unit was the kingdom, and the king and his warrior aristocracy stood at the top of society. The seat and symbol of the king's power was his palace, which was also the economic center of the kingdom.

Palace scribes kept records with a script known as Linear B, which has been deciphered so that information on Mycenaean culture comes through inscriptions and other forms of written records as well as buildings and other objects. All of these point to a society in which war was common. Mycenaean cities were all fortified by thick stone walls, and graves contain spears, javelins, swords, helmets, and the first examples of metal armor known in the world.

Contacts between the Minoans and Mycenaeans were originally peaceful, and Minoan culture and trade goods flooded the Greek mainland. But around 1450 B.C.E., possibly in the wake of an earthquake that left Crete vulnerable, the Mycenaeans attacked Crete, destroying many towns and occupying Knossos. For about the next fifty years, the Mycenaeans ruled much of the island. The palaces at Knossos and other cities of the Aegean became grander as wealth gained through trade and tribute flowed into the treasuries of various Mycenaean kings. Prosperity, however, did not bring peace, and between 1300 and 1000 B.C.E. various kingdoms in and beyond Greece ravaged one another in a savage series of wars that destroyed both the Minoan and Mycenaean civilizations.

Chapter Chronology

ca. 3500–338 B.C.E.	Hellenic period
ca. 2000–ca. 1000 B.C.E.	Minoan and Mycenaean civilizations
ca. 1100–800 B.C.E.	Greece's Dark Age; evolution of the polis
ca. 800–500 B.C.E.	Archaic age; rise of Sparta and Athens
776 B.C.E.	Founding of the ancient Olympic games
ca. 750–550 B.C.E.	Spread of Greek population in the Mediterranean
ca. 525–322 B.C.E.	Birth and development of tragic drama, historical writing, and philosophy
499–404 B.C.E.	Persian and Peloponnesian wars
ca. 470–322 B.C.E.	Rise of the philosophies of Socrates, Plato, and Aristotle
340–250 B.C.E.	Rise of Epicurean and Stoic philosophies
336–323 B.C.E.	Reign of Alexander the Great
336–100 B.C.E.	Hellenistic period

The fall of the Minoans and Mycenaeans was part of what some scholars see as a general collapse of Bronze Age civilizations in the eastern Mediterranean, including the end of the Egyptian New Kingdom and the fall of the Hittite Empire (see Chapter 2). This collapse appears to have had a number of causes: invasions and migrations by outsiders, including groups the Egyptians called the Sea Peoples and later Greeks called the Dorians; changes in warfare and weaponry, which made foot soldiers the most important factor in battles and reduced the power of kings and wealthy nobles fighting from chariots; and natural disasters, which contributed to famines.

polis Generally translated as "city-state," it was the basic political and institutional unit of ancient Greece.

In Greece these factors worked together to usher in a period of poverty and disruption that historians have traditionally called the "Dark Age" of Greece (ca. 1100–800 B.C.E.). Even writing, which was not widespread in any case, was a casualty of the chaos. Traditions and stories continued to circulate orally, however. These included tales of the heroic deeds of legendary heroes similar to the epic poems of Mesopotamia. Sometime in the eighth or seventh century many of these were gathered together in two long epic poems, the *Iliad*, which tells of a war similar to those fought by Mycenaean kings, and the *Odyssey*, which records the adventures of one of the heroes of that war. These poems were recited orally, and once writing was reintroduced to Greece, they were written down and attributed to an author named Homer. The two poems present human and divine characters who are larger than life but also petty, vindictive, pouting, and deceitful, flaws that drive the action forward, usually with tragic results.

Spartan Hoplite This bronze figurine portrays an armed foot soldier about to strike an enemy. His massive helmet with its full crest gives his head nearly complete protection, while a metal corselet covers his chest and back, and greaves (similar to today's shin guards) protect his shins. In his right hand he carries a thrusting spear (now broken off), and in his left a large round shield. (Bildarchiv Preussischer Kulturbesitz/Art Resource, NY)

The Development of the Polis

Greece's Dark Age actually saw two developments that would be central to later Greek history and to Greek influence on the world. The first of these was the migration of Greek-speaking peoples around the Aegean, spreading their culture to the islands and to the shores of Anatolia. The second, and more important, development was the **polis** (plural *poleis*), which is generally translated as "city-state." The earliest states in Sumer were also city-states, as were many of the small Mycenaean kingdoms. What differentiated this new Greek form from the older models is the fact that the polis was more than a political institution; it was a community of citizens with their own customs and laws. The physical, religious, and political form of the polis varied from place to place, but everywhere it was relatively small, reflecting the fragmented geography of Greece. The very smallness of the polis enabled Greeks to see how they fit individually into the overall system—and in this way, how the individual parts made up the social whole. This notion of community was fundamental to the polis and was the very badge of Greekness.

The polis included a city and its surrounding countryside. The people of the polis typically lived in a compact group of houses within the city, which by the fifth century B.C.E. was generally surrounded by a wall. Another feature was a usually elevated area called the acropolis, where the people erected temples, altars, and public monuments. The polis also contained a public square or marketplace, the agora. Originally the place where the warrior assembly met, the agora became the political center of the polis.

The *chora* (KOHR-uh), which included the surrounding countryside of the polis, was typically the community's source of wealth. Farmers left the city each morning to work their fields or tend their flocks of sheep and goats, and they returned at night. On the lands not suitable for farming or grazing, people often quarried stone or mined for precious metals. Thus the polis was the scene of both urban and agrarian life.

The average polis did not have a standing army. For protection it instead relied on its citizens. Very rich citizens often served as cavalry, which was, however, never as important as the heavily armed infantrymen known as **hoplites**, who were the backbone of the army.

Greek poleis had several different types of government, of which the most common were democracy and oligarchy. In practice, Greek **democracy** meant the rule of citizens, not the people as a whole, and citizenship was limited to free adult men who had lived in the polis a long time. The remaining free men, resident foreigners, slaves, and all women were not citizens and had no political voice. In other words, none of the Greek democracies reflected the modern concept that all people are created equal.

Oligarchy, which literally means "the rule of the few," was government by a small group of wealthy citizens. Although oligarchy was the government of the prosperous, it left the door open to political and social advancement. If members of the polis could meet property or money qualifications, they could enter the governing circle. Moreover, oligarchs generally listened to the concerns of the people, a major factor in the long success of this form of government.

Sporadic periods of violent political and social upheaval often led to a third type of government—tyranny. **Tyranny** was rule by one man who had seized power by unconstitutional means, generally by using his wealth to win a political following that toppled the existing legal government. Tyrants were not always oppressive rulers, however, and sometimes used their power to benefit average citizens.

hoplites Heavily armed citizens who served as infantrymen and fought to defend the polis.

democracy A type of Greek government in which all citizens administered the workings of government.

oligarchy A type of Greek government in which a small group of wealthy citizens, not necessarily of aristocratic birth, ruled.

tyranny Rule by one man who took over an existing government, generally by using his wealth to gain a political following.

Quick Review
What factors contributed to the rise of the city-state as the dominant form of government in ancient Greece?

How did Greek society and government develop during the Archaic age?

The maturation of the polis coincided with an era, later termed the Archaic age, that saw two developments of lasting importance. The first was the even wider geographical reach of the Greeks, who now ventured as far east as the Black Sea and as far west as the Atlantic Ocean. The next was the rise to prominence of two particular poleis, Sparta and Athens, each with a distinctive system of government.

Greece's Overseas Expansion

With stability and prosperity, the Greek world grew in wealth and numbers, which brought new problems. The increase in population created more demand for food than the land could supply. The resulting social and political tensions drove many people to seek new homes outside of Greece (Map 5.2).

From about 750 to 550 B.C.E. Greeks poured onto the coasts of the northern Aegean and the Black Sea, southward along the North African coast, and then westward to Sicily, southern Italy, and beyond to Spain and the Atlantic. In all these places the Greeks established flourishing cities that created a much larger market for agricultural and manufactured goods. A later wave of colonization from 500 to 400 B.C.E. spread Greeks throughout the northern coast of the Black Sea as far east as southern Russia. Colonization on this scale meant that the future culture of this entire area would be Greek.

Around the time of these territorial expansions, important changes were taking place within Greece, in Sparta and Athens. These included the formation of new social and political structures.

The Growth of Sparta

During the Archaic period, one of the poleis on the Peloponnesian peninsula, Sparta, also faced problems of overpopulation and shortages of fertile land. The Spartans solved both by conquering the agriculturally rich region of Messenia to the west of Sparta in 715 B.C.E. (see Map 5.2), making the Messenians helots, state slaves. The helots soon rose in a revolt that took the Spartans thirty years to crush. Afterward, non-nobles who had shared in the fighting appear to have demanded rights equal to those of the nobility and a voice in the government.

Under intense pressure the aristocrats agreed to remodel the state into a new system, called the Lycurgan regimen. Under this system all Spartan citizens were given equal political rights. Two kings, who were primarily military leaders, and a council of nobles shared executive power with five ephors (EH-fuhrs), overseers elected by the citizens. Economi-

Map 5.2 Greek Colonization, ca. 750–550 B.C.E. The Greeks established colonies along the shores of the Mediterranean and the Black Seas, spreading Greek culture and creating a large trading network.

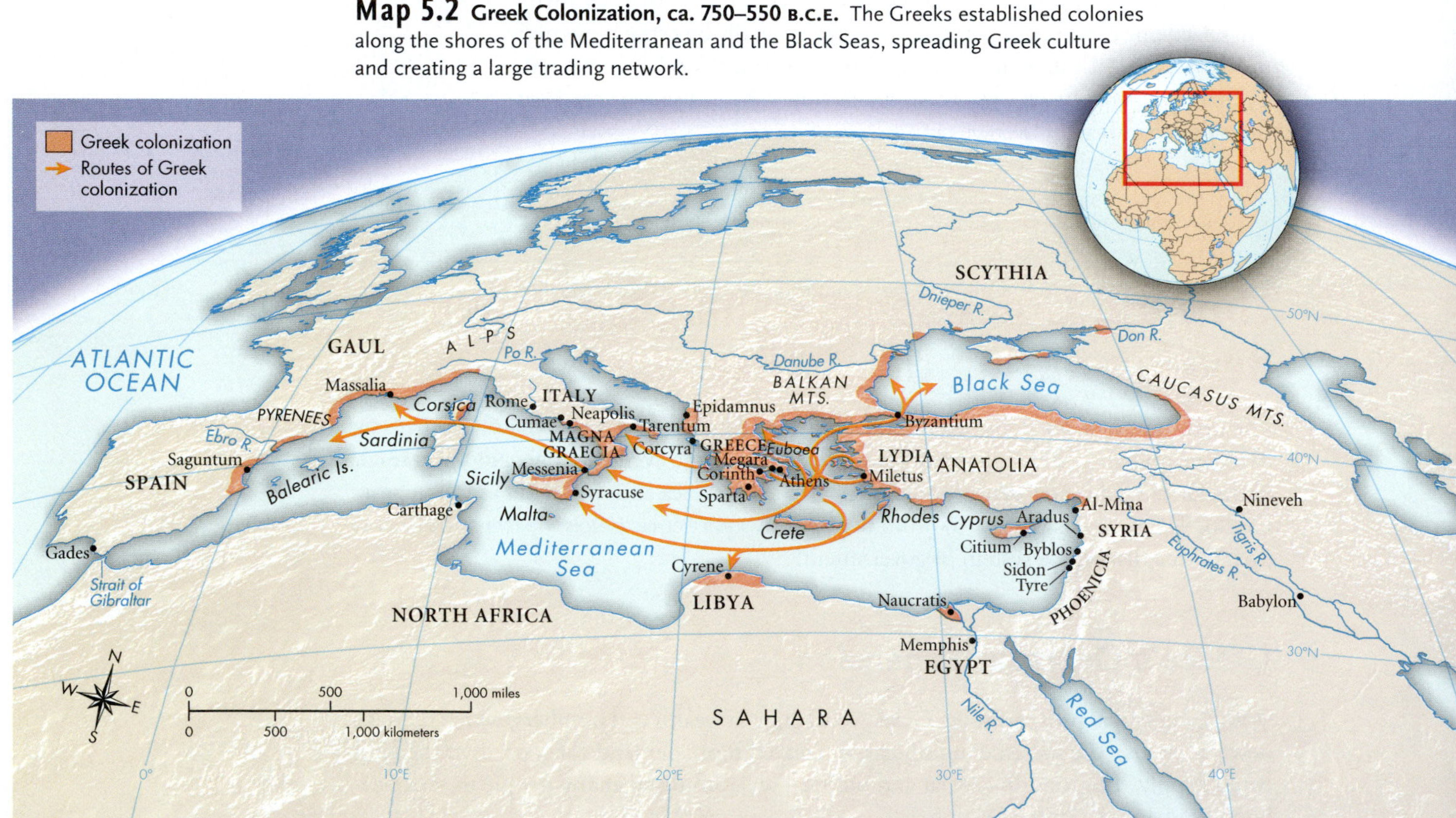

cally, the helots did all the work, while Spartan citizens devoted their time to military training, and Sparta became extremely powerful.

In the Lycurgan system every citizen owed primary allegiance to Sparta, and individuals placed the defense of Sparta over their own needs. Even family life was sacrificed. After long, hard military training that began at age seven, citizens became lifelong soldiers. In battle Spartans were supposed to stand and die rather than retreat. Spartan men were expected to train vigorously, do with little, and like it, qualities reflected even today in the word *spartan*.

Similar rigorous physical training was applied to Spartan women, who were unique in all Greek society. With men in military service much of their lives, women in citizen families ran the estates and owned land in their own right, and they were not physically restricted or secluded. But Spartans expected them to be good wives and strict mothers of future soldiers. Because men often did not see their wives or other women for long periods not only in times of war but also in peace, their most meaningful relations were same-sex ones. The Spartan military leaders viewed such relationships as advantageous because they believed that men would fight even more fiercely for lovers and comrades. Close links among men thus contributed to Spartan civic life, which was admired throughout the Greek world.

The Evolution of Athens

Like Sparta, Athens faced pressing social and economic problems during the Archaic period. The late seventh century B.C.E. was for Athens a time of turmoil because aristocrats, many of them wealthy from trade, had begun to seize the holdings of smaller landowners. In 621 B.C.E. the aristocrat Draco (DRAY-koh), under pressure from small landholders and with the consent of the nobles, published the first law code of the Athenian polis. His code was harsh, but it embodied the ideal that the law belonged to all citizens. Yet the aristocracy still governed Athens oppressively, and despite Draco's code, noble landholders continued to force small farmers and artisans into economic dependence. Many families were sold into slavery as settlement for debts, while others were exiled and their land mortgaged to the rich. Solon (SOH-luhn), an aristocrat and a poet, railed against these injustices. Solon's sincerity and good sense convinced other aristocrats that he was no crazed revolutionary. Moreover, he gained the trust of the common people, whose problems provoked them to demand access to political life, much as commoners in Sparta had. Around 594 B.C.E. the nobles elected him *archon* (AHR-kahn), chief magistrate of the polis, and gave him extraordinary power to reform the state.

Solon allowed nobles to keep their land, but he immediately freed all people enslaved for debt, recalled all exiles, canceled all debts on land, and made enslavement for debt illegal. Also, he allowed commoners into the old aristocratic assembly, where they could vote in the election of magistrates. Later sixth-century leaders further broadened the opportunities for commoners to take part in government, transforming Athens into a democracy.

The democracy functioned on the ideal that all full citizens should play a role in government, yet not all citizens could take time from work to do this. They therefore delegated their power to other citizens by creating various offices to run the democracy. The most prestigious of these offices was the board of ten archons, whose members, elected for one year, handled legal and military affairs.

Making laws was the responsibility of two bodies, the boule (BOO-lee), or council, composed of five hundred members, and the ecclesia (ee-KLEE-zhee-uh), the assembly of all citizens. The boule was perhaps the major institution of the democracy. By supervising the various committees of government and proposing bills to the assembly, it guided Athenian political life. However, the ecclesia, by a simple majority vote, had the final word. Like all democracies in ancient Greece, the one in Athens was limited. Women, slaves, and outsiders could not be citizens, and their opinions were neither recorded nor legally binding.

Quick Review
What were the most important differences between Spartan and Athenian society?

What were the lasting achievements of the classical period?

Between 500 and 338 B.C.E. Greek civilization reached its highest peak in politics, thought, and art, even as it engaged in violent conflicts. First, the Greeks beat back the armies of the Persian Empire. Then, turning against one another, they destroyed their own political system in a century of warfare that began with the Peloponnesian War. This era also saw the flowering of philosophy as thinkers pondered the meaning of the universe and human nature. In other achievements of this time, the Greeks invented drama and reached their artistic zenith in architecture. Because of these various intellectual and artistic accomplishments, this age is called the classical period.

The Deadly Conflicts, 499–404 B.C.E.

Warfare marked most of the classical period. In 499 B.C.E. the Greeks who lived in Ionia unsuccessfully rebelled against the Persian Empire, which had ruled the area for fifty years (see Chapter 2). The Athenians provided feeble help to the Ionians, and in retaliation the Persians struck at Athens, only to be defeated by the Athenian hoplites at the battle of Marathon. In 480 B.C.E. the Persian king Xerxes (ZUHRK-seez) personally led a massive invasion of Greece. Under the leadership of Sparta by land and Athens by sea, many Greeks united to fight the Persians, and they engaged in major battles at the pass of Thermopylae and in the waters off Artemisium. The larger Persian army was victorious and occupied Athens, but only a month or so later the Greeks defeated the Persian navy in the decisive battle of Salamis, and in 479 B.C.E. they overwhelmed the Persian army at Plataea.

Areas of Persian control
Greek states at war with Persia
Neutral Greek states
Thermopylae 480 B.C.E.
Artemisium 480 B.C.E.
Plataea 479 B.C.E.
Marathon 490 B.C.E.
Salamis 480 B.C.E.
Crete

The Persian Wars, 499–479 B.C.E.

Delian League A grand naval alliance created by the Athenians aimed at liberating Ionia from Persian rule.

The victorious Athenians and their allies then formed the **Delian League**, a grand naval alliance intended to liberate Ionia from Persian rule. While driving the Persians out of Asia Minor, the Athenians also turned the league into an Athenian Empire. They often collected tribute from other cities by force and took control of their economic resources. Athenian ideas of freedom and democracy did not extend to conquered peoples, and cities that objected to or revolted over Athenian actions were put down. Under Pericles (PEHR-uh-kleez; ca. 494–429 B.C.E.) the Athenians grew so powerful and aggressive that they alarmed Sparta and its allies. In 431 B.C.E. Athenian imperialism finally drove Sparta into a generation long conflict known as the Peloponnesian War (431–404 B.C.E.). Athens launched an attack on the island of Sicily, which ended in disaster. The Spartans encouraged revolts in cities that were subject to Athens and defeated the Athenian fleet in naval battles. In 404 B.C.E. the Athenians finally surrendered; Sparta stripped it of its empire, but did not destroy the city itself.

The Delian League, ca. 478–431 B.C.E.

Writers at the time described and analyzed these wars, seeking to understand their causes and consequences. Herodotus (ca. 484–425 B.C.E.) traveled the Greek world to piece together the course of the Persian wars. Thucydides (ca. 460–ca. 399 B.C.E.) was an Athenian general in the Peloponnesian War but was banished early in the conflict because of a defeat. His account of the war saw human greed and desire for power as the root of the conflict, and he viewed the war itself as a disaster.

Athenian Arts in the Age of Pericles

While Athens eventually lost to Sparta on the battlefield, the period leading up to the Peloponnesian War was one of Athenian cultural and intellectual achievement. In the last half of the fifth century B.C.E. Pericles turned Athens into the showplace of Greece by making the Acropolis a wonder for all time. He appropriated Delian League money to fund a huge building program for the Acropolis. Workers erected temples and other buildings housing statues and carvings showing the gods in human form and celebrating the Athenian

Picturing the Past

The Acropolis of Athens

The natural rock formation of the Acropolis probably had a palace on top as early as the Mycenaean period, when it was also surrounded by a defensive wall. Temples were constructed beginning in the sixth century B.C.E., and after the Persian War Pericles ordered the reconstruction and expansion of many of these, as well as the building of new and more magnificent temples and an extension of the defensive walls. The largest building is the Parthenon, a temple dedicated to the goddess Athena, which originally housed a 40-foot-tall statue of Athena made of ivory and gold sheets attached to a wooden frame. Much of the Parthenon was damaged when it was shelled during a war between Venice and the Ottoman Empire in the seventeenth century, and air pollution continues to eat away at the marble. (Courtesy, Sotiris Toumbis Editions)

ANALYZING THE IMAGE Imagine yourself as an Athenian walking up the hill toward the Parthenon. What impression would the setting and the building itself convey?

CONNECTIONS What were the various functions of the Acropolis?

victory over the Persians. The Acropolis was crowned by the Parthenon, a temple that celebrated the greatness of Athens and its patron goddess Athena, who was represented by a huge ivory and gold statue.

Other aspects of Athenian culture, including the development of drama, were also rooted in the life of the polis. The polis sponsored plays as part of the city's religious festivals and required wealthy citizens to pay the expenses of their production. Although many plays were highly controversial, they were neither suppressed nor censored. Not surprisingly, given the incessant warfare, conflict was a constant element in Athenian drama, and playwrights used their art in attempts to portray, understand, and resolve life's basic conflicts.

Aeschylus (EHS-kuh-luhs; 525–456 B.C.E.) was the first dramatist to explore such basic questions as the rights of the individual, the conflict between the individual and society, and the nature of good and evil. In his trilogy of plays, *The Oresteia*, he treats the themes of betrayal, murder, and reconciliation, urging the use of reason and justice to reconcile fundamental conflicts.

The plays of Sophocles (SAH-fuh-kleez; 496–406 B.C.E.) also deal with matters personal, political, and divine. In *Antigone*—which tells of how a king's mistakes in judgment lead to the suicides of his son, his son's fiancée, and his wife—Sophocles emphasizes the precedence of divine law over political law and family custom. In *Oedipus the King* Sophocles tells the story of a good man doomed by the gods to kill his father and marry his mother. When Oedipus fails to avoid his fate, he blinds himself in despair and flees into exile. In *Oedipus at Colonus* Sophocles treats the last days of the broken man, whose patient suffering and uncomplaining piety ultimately win the blessings and honor of the gods.

Euripides (you-RIH-puh-deez; ca. 480–406 B.C.E.) likewise explored the theme of personal conflict within the polis and sounded the depths of the individual. With Euripides drama entered a new and more personal phase. To him the gods mattered far less than people.

Aeschylus, Sophocles, and Euripides are considered writers of tragedies. Athens also produced writers of comic dramas, which used humor as political commentary in an effort to suggest and support the best policies for the polis. Best known of the comedians is Aristophanes (eh-ruh-STAH-fuh-neez; ca. 445–386 B.C.E.), a merciless critic of cranks, quacks, and fools. He used his art of sarcasm to dramatize his ideas on the right conduct of the citizen and his leaders for the good of the polis.

Daily Life and Social Conditions in Athens

The Athenians, like other Greeks, lived with comparatively few material possessions in houses that were rather simple. A typical Athenian house consisted of a series of rooms opening onto a central courtyard that contained a well, an altar, and a washbasin. Meals consisted primarily of various grains, as well as lentils, olives, figs, grapes, fish, and a little meat.

In the city a man might support himself as a craftsman, or he could contract with the polis to work on public buildings. Certain crafts, including spinning and weaving, were generally done by women. Men and women without skills worked as paid laborers. Slavery was commonplace in Greece, as it was throughout the ancient world. Slaves, who were paid for their work, were usually foreigners.

In ancient Athens the main function of women from citizen families was to bear and raise children. They ideally lived secluded lives in which the only men they usually saw were relatives and tradesmen. How far this ideal was actually a reality is impossible to say, but women in citizen families probably spent most of their time at home, leaving the house only to attend religious festivals, and perhaps occasionally plays, although this is debated. In their quarters of the house they oversaw domestic slaves and hired labor, and together with servants and friends worked wool into cloth. Women from noncitizen families lived freer lives, although they worked harder and had fewer material comforts. They performed

Hetaera and Young Man In this scene painted on the inside of a drinking cup, a hetaera holds the head of a young man who has clearly had too much to drink. Sexual and comic scenes were common on Greek pottery, particularly on objects that would have been used at a private dinner party hosted by a citizen, known as a symposium. Wives did not attend symposia, but hetaerae and entertainers were often hired to perform for the male guests. (Martin von Wagner Museum der Universität Wurzburg. Photo: Karl Oehrlein)

manual labor in the fields or sold goods in the agora. Prostitution was legal in Athens, and sophisticated courtesans known as hetaerae added intellectual accomplishments to physical beauty. Hetaerae accompanied men in public settings where their wives would not have been welcome.

Same-sex relations were generally accepted in all of ancient Greece, not simply in Sparta. In classical Athens part of a male adolescent citizen's training was supposed to entail a hierarchical sexual and tutorial relationship with an older man, who most likely was married and may have had female sexual partners as well. These relationships between adolescents and men were often celebrated in literature and art, in part because Athenians regarded perfection as possible only in the male.

Same-sex relations did not mean that people did not marry, for Athenians saw the continuation of the family line as essential. Sexual desire and procreation were both important aspects of life, but ancient Greeks did not necessarily link them.

Greek Religion in the Classical Period

Like most peoples of the ancient world, the Greeks were polytheists, worshipping a variety of gods and goddesses who were immortal but otherwise acted just like people. Migration, invasion, and colonization brought the Greeks into contact with other peoples and caused their religious beliefs to evolve. But by the classical era these beliefs centered on a group of gods understood to live on Mount Olympus, the highest mountain in Greece.

Besides these Olympian gods, each polis had its own minor deities, each with his or her own local group of worshippers. The polis administered the cults and religious festivals, and everyone was expected to participate in these civic rituals, which were more like today's patriotic parades or ceremonies than expressions of belief. Individual families also honored various deities in their homes, and some people turned to what later became known as "mystery religions" (see page 122).

The Greeks had no sacred books such as the Bible, nor did religion impose an ethical code of conduct. In contrast to Mesopotamia, Egypt, and Vedic India, priests held little power in Greece; their purpose was to care for temples and sacred property and to conduct the proper rituals, but not to make religious or political rules or doctrines, much less to enforce them.

Though much of Greek religion was local and domestic, the Greeks also shared some Pan-Hellenic festivals, the chief of which were held at Olympia to honor Zeus and at Delphi to

Greek Gods and Goddesses
Zeus: king of the gods and the most powerful of them
Hera: Zeus's wife and sister; goddess of marriage
Ares: god of war and physical bravery
Apollo: god of music, poetry, light, and the sun
Athena: goddess of wisdom, military strategy, and justice; patron goddess of Athens

LISTENING TO THE PAST

Aristotle, On the Family and On Slavery, from *The Politics*

The Athenian philosopher Aristotle sought to understand everything in the world around him, including human society as well as the physical world. In The Politics, *one of his most important works, he examines the development of government, which he sees as originating in the family. Thus before discussing relations of power within the city, he discusses them within the household, which requires him to confront the issue of slavery and the very unequal relations between men and women.*

"The city belongs among the things that exist by nature, and man is by nature a political animal. . . .

He who thus considers things in their first growth and origin, whether a state or anything else, will obtain the clearest view of them. . . . Out of these two relationships between man and woman, master and slave, the first thing to arise is the family, and Hesiod is right when he says,

> First house and wife and an ox for the plough,

for the ox is the poor man's slave. The family is the association established by nature for the supply of men's everyday wants.

Seeing then that the state is made up of households, before speaking of the state we must speak of the management of the household. The parts of household management correspond to the persons who compose the household, and a complete household consists of slaves and freemen. . . .

Property is a part of the household, and the art of acquiring property is a part of the art of managing the household; for no man can live well, or indeed live at all, unless he be provided with necessaries. And as in the arts which have a definite sphere the workers must have their own proper instruments for the accomplishment of their work, so it is in the management of a household. Now instruments are of various sorts; some are living, others lifeless; in the rudder, the pilot of a ship has a lifeless, in the look-out man, a living instrument; for in the arts the servant is a kind of instrument. Thus, too, a possession is an instrument for maintaining life. And so, in the arrangement of the family, a slave is a living possession. . . .

It is clear that the rule of the soul over the body, and of the mind and the rational element over the passionate, is natural and expedient; whereas the equality of the two or the rule of the inferior is always hurtful. The same holds good of animals in relation to men; for tame animals have a better nature than wild, and all tame animals are better off when they are ruled by man; for then they are preserved. Again, the male is by nature superior, and the female inferior; and the one rules, and the other is ruled; this principle, of necessity, extends to all mankind.

Where then there is such a difference as that between soul and body, or between men and animals (as in the case of those whose business is to use their body, and who can do nothing better), the lower sort are by nature slaves, and it is better for them as for all inferiors that they should be under the rule of a master. For he who can be, and therefore is, another's and he who participates in the rational principle enough to apprehend, but not to have, such a principle, is a slave by nature. Whereas the lower animals cannot even apprehend a principle; they obey their instincts. And indeed the use made of slaves and of tame animals is not very different; for both with their bodies minister to the needs of life. . . .

A question may indeed be raised, whether there is any excellence at all in a slave beyond and higher than merely instrumental and ministerial qualities — whether he can have the virtues of temperance, courage, justice, and the like; or whether slaves possess only bodily and ministerial qualities. And, whichever way we answer the question, a difficulty arises; for, if they have virtue, in what will they differ from freemen? On the other hand, since they are men and share in rational principle, it seems absurd to say that they have no virtue. A similar question may be raised about women and children, whether they too have virtues: ought a woman to be temperate and brave and just, and is a child to be called temperate, and intemperate, or not. . . . Here the very constitution of the soul has shown us the way; in it one part naturally rules, and the other is subject, and the virtue of the ruler we

honor Apollo. The festivities at Olympia included the famous athletic contests that inspired the modern Olympic games. Held every four years after they started in 776 B.C.E., the contests were unifying factors in Greek life and lasted well into Christian times.

The Flowering of Philosophy

Just as the Greeks developed rituals to honor gods, they spun myths and epics to explain the origin of the universe. Over time, however, as Greeks encountered other peoples with different beliefs, some of them began to question their old gods and myths, and they sought

In this painting from the side of a vase made in the fifth century B.C.E., a well-to-do young woman sits on an elegant chair inside a house, spinning and weaving. The bed piled high with coverlets on the left was a symbol of marriage in Greek art. The young woman's body language and facial expression suggest that she was not particularly happy with her situation. (Erich Lessing/Art Resource, NY)

maintain to be different from that of the subject; the one being the virtue of the rational, and the other of the irrational part. Now, it is obvious that the same principle applies generally, and therefore almost all things rule and are ruled according to nature. But the kind of rule differs; the freeman rules over the slave after another manner from that in which the male rules over the female, or the man over the child; although the parts of the soul are present in any of them, they are present in different degrees. For the slave has no deliberative faculty at all; the woman has, but it is without authority, and the child has, but it is immature. So it must necessarily be supposed to be with the moral virtues also; all should partake of them, but only in such manner and degree as is required by each for the fulfillment of his duty. . . . Clearly, then, moral virtue belongs to all of them; but the temperance of a man and of a woman, or the courage and justice of a man and of a woman, are not, as Socrates maintained, the same; the courage of a man is shown in commanding, of a woman in obeying. . . .

All classes must be deemed to have their special attributes; as the poet says of women,

> Silence is a woman's glory,

but this is not equally the glory of man. The child is imperfect, and therefore obviously his virtue is not relative to himself alone, but to the perfect man and to his teacher, and in like manner the virtue of the slave is relative to a master. Now we determined that a slave is useful for the wants of life, and therefore he will obviously require only so much virtue as will prevent him from failing in his duty through cowardice or lack of self-control. ”

Source: Aristotle, *Politics*, Book One, translated by Benjamin Jowett, at: http://classics.mit.edu/Aristotle/politics.1.one.html.

QUESTIONS FOR ANALYSIS

1. What does Aristotle see as the purpose of the family, and why does he begin his discussion of politics with relations within the family?
2. How does Aristotle explain and justify slavery? Given what you have read about Athenian slavery, does this argument make sense to you?
3. How does Aristotle explain and justify the differences between men and women?

rational rather than supernatural explanations for natural phenomena. These Greek thinkers, based in Ionia, are called the Pre-Socratics because their rational efforts preceded those of Socrates. Taking individual facts, they wove them into general theories that led them to conclude that, despite appearances, the universe is actually simple and subject to natural laws. The Pre-Socratics began an intellectual revolution that still flourishes today, creating what we now call philosophy and science.

Drawing on their observations, the Pre-Socratics speculated about the basic building blocks of the universe, and most decided that all things were made of four simple substances: fire, air, earth, and water. Democritus (dih-MAH-kruh-tuhs; ca. 460 B.C.E.) broke this down further and created the atomic theory that the universe is made up of invisible, indestructible

Procession to a Temple This detail from a vase shows Greek men and women approaching a temple, where a priestess, bough in hand, greets them. In this type of Greek pottery, men are shown with dark skin and women with white, reflecting the ideal that men's lives took place largely outside in the sun-filled public squares, and women's in the shaded interiors of homes. (Image copyright © The Metropolitan Museum of Art/Art Resource, NY)

particles. The stream of thought started by the Pre-Socratics branched into several directions. Hippocrates (hih-PAH-kruh-teez; ca. 470–400 B.C.E.) sought natural explanations for diseases and natural means to treat them. Illness was not caused by evil spirits, he asserted, but by physical problems in the body, particularly by imbalances in what he saw as four basic bodily fluids, called humors: blood, phlegm, black bile, and yellow bile.

The Sophists (SOF-ists), a group of thinkers in fifth century B.C.E. Athens, applied philosophical speculation to politics and language, questioning the beliefs and laws of the polis to understand their origin. They believed that excellence in both politics and language could be taught, and they provided lessons for the young men of Athens who wished to learn how to persuade others. Their later opponents criticized them for charging fees and also accused them of using rhetoric to deceive people instead of presenting the truth.

Socrates (ca. 470–399 B.C.E.), whose ideas are known only through the works of others, also applied philosophy to politics and to people. His approach when exploring ethical issues and defining concepts was to start with a general topic or problem and to narrow the matter to its essentials. He did so by continuously questioning participants in a discussion or argument rather than lecturing, a process known as the Socratic dialogue. Because he posed questions rather than giving answers, it is difficult to say exactly what Socrates thought about many things, although he does seem to have felt that through knowledge people could approach the supreme good and thus find happiness. He clearly thought that Athenian leaders were motivated more by greed and opportunism than by a desire for justice in the war with Sparta, and he criticized Athenian democracy openly. His views brought him into conflict with the government. The leaders of Athens tried him for corrupting the youth of the city, and in 399 B.C.E. they executed him.

Most of what we know about Socrates comes from his student Plato (427–347 B.C.E.). Plato developed the theory that there are two worlds: the impermanent, changing world that we know through our senses, and the eternal, unchanging realm of "forms" that constitute the essence of true reality. According to Plato, true knowledge and the possibility of living a virtuous life come from contemplating ideal forms, not from observing the visible world. Thus if you want to understand justice, asserted Plato, you should think about what would make perfect justice, not study the imperfect examples of justice around you.

Plato's student Aristotle (384–322 B.C.E.) also thought that true knowledge was possible, but he believed that such knowledge came from observation of the world, analysis of natural phenomena, and logical reasoning, not contemplation. Aristotle thought that everything had a purpose, so that to know something, one also had to know its function. (See "Listening to the Past: Aristotle, On the Family and On Slavery, from *The Politics*," page 114.) Aristotle's interests embraced logic, ethics, natural science, physics, politics, poetry, and art. He studied the heavens as well as earth and judged the earth to be the center of the universe, with the stars and planets revolving around it. Plato's idealism profoundly shaped Western philosophy, but Aristotle came to have an even wider influence; for many centuries in Europe, the authority of his ideas was second only to the Bible's.

Quick Review
How did the Athenians use drama and philosophy to explore and critique their own society?

What were the social and political consequences of Alexander's conquests?

The Greek city-states wore themselves out fighting one another, and Philip II, the ruler of Macedonia, a kingdom in the north of Greece, gradually conquered one after another and took over their lands. He then turned against the Persian Empire but was killed by an assassin, and his son Alexander continued the fight. A brilliant military leader, Alexander conquered the entire Persian Empire, along with many territories to the east of Persia. He also founded new cities in which Greek and local populations mixed. Although he, too, died prematurely, his successors continued to build cities and colonies, which became powerful instruments in the spread of Greek culture and in the blending of Greek traditions and ideas with those of other peoples. This era of cultural blending, that began with the start of Alexander's reign in 336 B.C.E. and continued for the following two centuries, has come to be known as the Hellenistic period.

From Polis to Monarchy, 404–200 B.C.E.

Immediately after the Peloponnesian War, Sparta began striving for empire over all of the Greeks, but could not maintain its hold. In 371 B.C.E. an army from the polis of Thebes destroyed the Spartan army, but the Thebans were unable to bring peace to Greece. Philip II, ruler of the kingdom of Macedonia on the northern border of Greece (r. 359–336 B.C.E.), turned the situation to his advantage. By clever use of his wealth and superb army, Philip won control of the northern Aegean, and in 338 B.C.E. he defeated a combined Theban-Athenian army, conquering Greece. Because the Greek city-states could not put aside their quarrels with one another, they fell to an invader.

After his victory, Philip united the Greek states with his Macedonian kingdom and got the states to cooperate in a crusade to liberate the Ionian Greeks from Persian rule. Before he could launch his crusade, Philip fell to an assassin's dagger in 336 B.C.E. His young son Alexander vowed to carry on Philip's mission and led an army of Macedonians and Greeks into western Asia. He won major battles against the Persians and seized Egypt from them without a fight. He ordered the building of a new city, Alexandria, where the Nile meets the Mediterranean. Within a century, Alexandria would be the largest city in the world. After honoring the priestly class, Alexander was proclaimed pharaoh, the legitimate ruler of Egypt. He also took the principal Persian capital of Persepolis and performed a symbolic act of retribution by burning the buildings of Xerxes, the invader of Greece during the Persian War 150 years earlier.

By 330 B.C.E. the Persian Empire had fallen, but Alexander had no intention of stopping, and he set out to conquer the rest of Asia. He plunged deeper into the East, and after four years of fighting his soldiers crossed the Indus River into India. Finally, at the Hyphasis River, the exhausted troops refused to go farther. Alexander reluctantly turned south to the Arabian Sea and then back west (Map 5.3). He never saw Macedonia again, however, as he died in Babylon in 323 B.C.E. from fever, wounds, and excessive drinking. In just thirteen years he had created an empire that stretched from his homeland of Macedonia to India. Alexander was instrumental in changing the face of politics in the eastern Mediterranean. His campaign swept away the Persian Empire, which had ruled the East for over two hundred years. In its place he established a Macedonian monarchy, although this fell apart with his death.

Several of the chief Macedonian generals aspired to become sole ruler, which led to a civil war lasting forty-three years that tore Alexander's empire apart. By the end of this conflict, the most successful generals had carved out their own smaller monarchies. Ptolemy (TAH-luh-mee) seized Egypt, and his descendants, the Ptolemies, assumed the powers and position of pharaohs. Antigonus (an-TIH-guh-nuhs) and his descendants, the Antigonids,

Mapping the Past

Map 5.3 Alexander's Conquests, 336–324 B.C.E.

Alexander's campaign of conquest was extensive and speedy. More important than the great success of his military campaigns was his founding of Hellenistic cities.

ANALYZING THE MAP Where are most of the cities founded by Alexander located in relation to Greece? What does this suggest about his aims?

CONNECTIONS Compare this map with Map 5.2, which shows Greek colonization in the Hellenic period (page 108). What are the major differences between the two processes of expansion?

maintained control of the Macedonian kingdom in Europe. Seleucus (suh-LOO-kuhs) won the bulk of Alexander's empire, his monarchy extending from western Asia to India (see below), but this Seleucid (si-LOO-sid) kingdom gradually broke into smaller states.

To encourage obedience Hellenistic kings often created ruler cults that linked the king's authority with that of the gods, or they adopted ruler cults that already existed, as Alexander did in Egypt. This created a symbol of unity within kingdoms ruling different peoples who at first had little in common; however, kingdoms never won the deep emotional loyalty that Greeks had once felt for the polis. Kings sometimes gave the cities in their territory all the external trappings of a polis, such as a council or an assembly of citizens, but these had no power. The city was not autonomous, as the polis had been, but had to follow royal orders. Hellenistic rulers generally relied on paid professionals to staff their bureaucracies, and on trained, paid, full-time soldiers rather than citizen hoplites to fight their wars.

Building a Shared Society

Alexander's most important legacy was the spread of Greek ideas and traditions across a wide area. As he moved farther eastward, Alexander founded new cities and military colonies, and he settled Greek and Macedonian troops and veterans in them. This practice continued after his death, with more than 250 new cities founded in North Africa, West and Central Asia, and southeastern Europe. These cities and colonies became powerful instruments in the spread of Hellenism and in the blending of Greek and other cultures. No comparable spread and sharing of cultures had occurred in this area since the days of the Mesopotamians.

Wherever it was established, the Hellenistic city resembled a modern city, serving as both a cultural and economic center. The ruling dynasties of the Hellenistic world were Macedonian in origin, and Greeks and Macedonians initially filled all important political, military, and diplomatic positions. The prevailing institutions and laws were Greek, and Greek became the common spoken language of the entire eastern Mediterranean. Also, a new Greek dialect called the koine (kaw-NAY), which means common, became the spoken language of the royal court, bureaucracy, and army. Everyone, Greek or easterner, who wanted to find an official position or compete in business had to learn it. Those who did gained an avenue of social mobility, and as early as the third century B.C.E. local people in some Greek cities began to rise in power and prominence. Cities granted citizenship to Hellenized natives, although the political benefits of citizenship were less than they had been in the classical period. The benefits natives gave to Hellenistic society were considerable, however. Their traditions mingled with Greek traditions to create an energetic and dynamic culture.

Although cultures blended in the Hellenistic world, the kingdoms were never entirely unified in language, customs, and thought. Greek culture generally did not extend far beyond the reaches of the cities. Many urban residents adopted the aspects of Hellenism that they found useful, but people in the countryside generally did not embrace it wholly. This meant that the spread of Greek culture was wider than it was deep, a very common pattern all over the world in eras of cultural change.

The spread of Greek culture was also shaped by the actions of rulers. The Seleucid kings built a shared society through extensive colonization. Their military settlements and cities spread from western Asia Minor along the banks of the Tigris and Euphrates Rivers and farther east to India. Although the Seleucids had no elaborate plan for Hellenizing the native population, they nevertheless introduced a large and vigorous Greek population to these lands.

In the eastern part of the large Seleucid kingdom, several Greek leaders defeated the Seleucids and established the independent kingdoms of Parthia and Bactria in today's Afghanistan and Turkmenistan (see Map 5.3). Bactria became an outpost of Hellenism, from which the Han Dynasty of China (Chapter 7) and the Mauryan Empire of India

(Chapter 3) learned of sophisticated societies other than their own. The Bactrian city of Ay Khanoum on the Oxus River, on the modern border of Russia and Afghanistan not far from China, is a good example of a far-flung city where cultures met. It had Greek temples and administration buildings, and on a public square was a long inscription carved in stone in Greek verse relating Greek ideals:

In childhood, learn good manners
In youth, control your passions
In middle age, practice justice
In old age, be of good counsel
In death, have no regrets.[1]

The city also had temples to local deities and artwork that blended Greek and local styles (for an example, see the metal plate at left). Also, some Greeks in Bactria, including several rulers, converted to Buddhism. In the second century B.C.E., after the collapse of the Mauryan Empire, Bactrian armies conquered part of northern India, establishing several small Indo-Greek states where the mixing of religious and artistic traditions was particularly pronounced (see page 71).

In Alexandria, the Ptolemies generally promoted Greek culture over that of the local Egyptians. Ptolemaic kings established what became the largest library in the ancient world, where scholars copied works loaned from many places onto papyrus scrolls, translating them into Greek if they were in other languages. They also studied the newest discoveries in science and mathematics. Alexandria was home to the largest Jewish community in the ancient world, and here Jewish scholars translated the Hebrew Bible into Greek for the first time.

Metal Plate from Ay Khanoum
This spectacular metal plate, made in the Bactrian city of Ay Khanoum in the second century B.C.E., probably depicts the goddess Cybele being pulled in a chariot by lions with the sun god above. Worship of Cybele, an earth-mother goddess, spread into Greece from Turkey, and was then spread by Greek followers as they traveled and migrated. (National Museum, Kabul/Ministry of Information and Culture, Islamic Republic of Afghanistan)

The Growth of Trade and Commerce

Alexander's conquests not only changed the political face of the ancient world but also merged it into one broad economic sphere. The period did not see a dramatic change in the way most people lived and worked; they continued to raise crops and animals using traditional methods, paying rents to their landlords and taxes to the state. By contrast, trade grew significantly as the spread of Greeks eastward created new markets. The economic unity of the Hellenistic world, like its cultural bonds, later proved valuable to the Romans, allowing them to trade products and ideas more easily over a broad area.

When Alexander conquered the Persian Empire, he found the royal treasury filled to the brim. The victors used this wealth to finance the building of roads, the development of harbors, and, as noted earlier, especially the founding of new cities. These cities opened whole new markets to all merchants, who eagerly took advantage of the unforeseen opportunities. Whenever possible, merchants sent their goods by water, but overland trade also became more prominent in the Hellenistic era. Overland trade with India was conducted by caravans that were largely in the hands of easterners. Once goods reached the Hellenistic monarchies, Greek merchants took a hand in the trade. Commerce from the east arrived at Egypt and the harbors of Palestine, Phoenicia, and Syria. From these ports goods flowed to Greece, Italy, and Spain. This period also saw the development of standardized business customs, so that merchants of different nationalities communicated in a way understandable to them all. Trade was further facilitated by the coining of money, which provided merchants with a standard way to value goods as well as a convenient method of payment.

The increased volume of trade helped create prosperity that made luxury goods affordable to more people. As a result, overland traders brought easily transportable luxuries such as gold, silver, and precious stones to market. They extended their networks into China in order to obtain silk, which became the most valuable overland commodity and gave the major route the name the Silk Road. (See "Global Trade: Silk," page 164.) In return the peoples of the eastern Mediterranean sent east manufactured or extracted goods, especially metal weapons, cloth, wine, and olive oil. (For more on the Silk Road in East Asia, see Chapter 7.)

More economically important than trade in exotic goods were commercial dealings in essential commodities like raw materials (such as wood), grain, and industrial products. The Hellenistic monarchies usually raised enough grain for their own needs as well as a surplus for export. For the cities of the Aegean the trade in grain was essential, because many of them could not grow enough in their mountainous terrain. Fortunately for them, abundant wheat supplies were available nearby in Egypt and in the Crimea in southern Russia.

The Greek cities paid for their grain by exporting olive oil, wine, honey, dried fruit, nuts, and vegetables. Another significant commodity supplied by the Greeks was fish, which for export was salted, pickled, or dried. This trade was doubly important because fish provided poor people with an essential element of their diet.

Throughout the Hellenistic world slave traders almost always found a ready market. Only the Ptolemies discouraged both the trade and slavery itself, but they did so for purely economic reasons. Their system had no room for slaves, who only would have competed with inexpensive labor provided by free people. Otherwise slave laborers could be found in cities and temples, in factories and fields, and in the homes of wealthier people.

While demand for goods increased during the Hellenistic period, few new techniques of production appeared. Manual labor far more than machinery continued to turn out agricultural produce, raw materials, and the few manufactured goods the Hellenistic world used. A typical form of manual labor was mining, in which slaves, criminals, or forced laborers dug the ore under frightful conditions. Besides gold and silver, used primarily for coins and jewelry, iron was the most important metal and saw the most varied use.

Quick Review

How did the Hellenistic city differ from the Hellenic polis, and how would you explain the differences you note?

How did the mixing of cultures shape Hellenistic thought?

The mixing of peoples in the Hellenistic era influenced religion, philosophy, and science. The Hellenistic kings promoted rituals and ceremonies like those in earlier Greek cities. But because many people found the rituals and ceremonies spiritually unsatisfying, they turned instead to mystery religions. In these religions, which blended Greek and non-Greek elements, followers gained secret knowledge in initiation rituals and were promised eternal life. Others turned away from religion to practical philosophies that provided advice on how to live a good life. In the scholarly realm, Hellenistic thinkers made advances in mathematics, astronomy, and mechanical design. Additionally, physicians used observation and dissection to better understand the way the human body works and to develop treatments for disease.

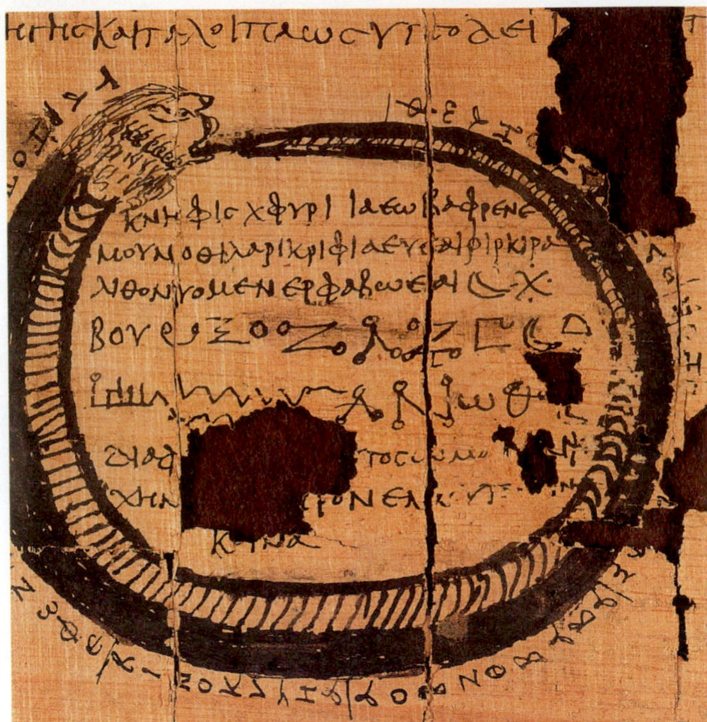

Hellenistic Magical Text This text, written in Greek and Egyptian on papyrus, presents a magical incantation surrounded by a lion-headed snake. Both Hellenic and Hellenistic Greeks sought to know the future through various means of divination and to control the future through rituals and formulas that called on spirits and gods. (© British Library Board, PAP. 121 fr 3)

Religion in the Hellenistic World

When Hellenistic kings founded cities, they also built temples, staffed by priests, for the old Olympian gods. In this way they spread Greek religious beliefs throughout the Near East. The transplanted religions, like those in Greece itself, sponsored literary, musical, and athletic contests, which were staged among splendid Greek-style buildings. On the whole, however, the civic religions were primarily concerned with ritual and did not embrace such matters as morality and redemption.

Consequently, people increasingly sought solace from other sources. Some relied on philosophy as a guide to life, while others turned to religion, magic, or astrology. Still others shrugged and spoke of Tyche (TIE-kee), which means "fate," "chance," or "doom"—a capricious and sometimes malevolent force.

Increasingly, many people were attracted to **mystery religions**, so called because they featured a body of rituals and beliefs not divulged to anyone not initiated into them. Early mystery religions in the Hellenic period were linked to specific gods in particular places, so that people who wished to become members had to travel; therefore, these religions never became very popular. But new mystery religions, like Hellenistic culture in general, were not tied to a particular place; instead they were spread throughout the Hellenistic world. In that sense the mystery religions came to the people, for temples of the new deities sprang up wherever Greeks lived.

mystery religions Religious systems in the Hellenistic world that incorporated aspects of both Greek and Eastern religions; they were characterized by secret doctrines, rituals of initiation, and the promise of an afterlife.

Mystery religions, which incorporated aspects of both Greek and Eastern religions, all claimed to save their adherents from the worst that fate could do and promised life for the soul after death. Most had a single concept in common: the belief that by the rites of initiation, in which the secrets of the religion were shared, devotees became united with a deity who had also died and risen from the dead. The sacrifice of the god and his victory over death saved the devotee from eternal death. Similarly, mystery religions demanded a period of preparation in which the converts strove to become holy, that is, to live by the religion's precepts. Once aspirants had prepared themselves, they went through the initiation, usually a ritual of great emotional intensity symbolizing the entry into a new life.

Philosophy and Its Guidance for Life

While some people turned to mystery religions to overcome Tyche and provide something permanent in a world that seemed unstable, others turned to philosophy. Several new schools of philosophical thought emerged, all of them teaching that people could be truly happy only when they had turned their backs on the world and focused full attention on one enduring thing. They differed chiefly on what that enduring thing was.

Epicureanism A Greek system of philosophy founded on the teachings of Epicurus that viewed a life of contentment, free from fear and suffering, as the greatest good.

Two significant philosophies caught the minds and hearts of many Greeks and easterners, as well as many later Romans. The first was **Epicureanism**. Epicurus (340–270 B.C.E.)

taught that the principal good of life is pleasure, which he defined as the absence of pain. He concluded that any violent emotion is undesirable. He advocated instead mild self-discipline and even considered poverty good so long as people had enough food, clothing, and shelter. Epicurus also taught that people can most easily attain peace and serenity by ignoring the outside world and looking instead into their personal feelings. His followers ignored politics because it led to tumult, which would disturb the soul.

Opposed to the passivity of the Epicureans, Zeno (335–262 B.C.E.) formed his own school of philosophy, **Stoicism**. To the Stoics the important matter was not whether they achieved anything but whether they lived virtuous lives. In that way they could triumph over Tyche, which could destroy their achievements but not the nobility of their lives. Stoicism became the most popular Hellenistic philosophy and later gained many followers among the Romans.

Stoicism The most popular of Hellenistic philosophies, it considered nature an expression of divine will and held that people can be happy only when living in accordance with nature.

Zeno and his fellow Stoics considered nature an expression of divine will, and they believed that people could be happy only when living in accordance with nature. They also stressed the brotherhood of man, the concept that all people were kindred who were obliged to help one another. The Stoics' most lasting practical achievement was the creation of the concept of natural law. They concluded that as all people were brothers, partook of divine reason, and were in harmony with the universe, one natural law governed them all.

Hellenistic Science and Medicine

Hellenistic culture achieved its greatest triumphs in science and medicine. In astronomy the most notable of the Hellenistic contributors to the field was Aristarchus of Samos (ca. 310–230 B.C.E.), who was educated at Aristotle's school. Aristarchus rightly concluded that the sun is far larger than the earth and that the stars are enormously distant from the earth. He also argued against Aristotle's view that the earth is the center of the universe, instead propounding the heliocentric theory—that the earth and planets revolve around the sun. Aristarchus's theories did not persuade the ancient world, and his heliocentric theory lay dormant until resurrected in the sixteenth century by the astronomer Nicolaus Copernicus.

In geometry Euclid (YOO-kluhd; ca. 300 B.C.E.), a mathematician living in Alexandria, compiled a valuable textbook of existing knowledge. His *The Elements of Geometry* became the standard introduction to the subject. Generations of students from antiquity to the present have learned the essentials of geometry from it.

The greatest thinker of the period was Archimedes (ah-kuh-MEE-deez; ca. 287–212 B.C.E.). A clever inventor, he devised new artillery for military purposes, a screw to draw water from a lower to a higher level, and the compound pulley to lift heavy weights. (See "Individuals in Society: Archimedes, Scientist and Inventor," page 124.) His chief interest, however, lay in pure mathematics. He founded the science of hydrostatics (the study of fluids at rest) and discovered the principle that the weight of a solid floating in a liquid is equal to the weight of the liquid displaced by the solid.

As the new artillery devised by Archimedes indicates, Hellenic science was used for purposes of war as well as peace. Theories of mechanics were applied to build machines that revolutionized warfare. The catapult shot large arrows and small stones against enemy targets. Engineers built wooden siege towers as artillery platforms. Generals added battering rams to bring down large portions of walls. If these new engines made warfare more efficient, they also added to the misery of the people. War came to embrace the whole population.

War and illness fed the need for medical advances, and the study of medicine flourished during the Hellenistic period, when physicians carried the work of Hippocrates

INDIVIDUALS IN SOCIETY

Archimedes, Scientist and Inventor

ARCHIMEDES (ca. 287–212 B.C.E.) WAS BORN IN the Greek city of Syracuse in Sicily, an intellectual center in which he pursued scientific interests. He was the most original thinker of his time and a practical inventor. In his book *On Plane Equilibriums* he dealt for the first time with the basic principles of mathematics, including the principle of the lever. He once said that if he were given a lever and a suitable place to stand, he could move the world. He also demonstrated how easily his compound pulley could move huge weights with little effort:

> *A three-masted merchant ship of the royal fleet had been hauled on land by hard work and many hands. Archimedes . . . sat far away from her; and without haste, but gently working a compound pulley with his hand, he drew her towards him smoothly and without faltering, just as though she were running on the surface.* (Plutarch, *Life of Marcellus*)

He likewise invented the Archimedian screw, a pump to bring subterranean water up to irrigate fields, which quickly came into common use. In his treatise *On Floating Bodies* Archimedes concluded that whenever a solid floats in a liquid, the weight of the solid equals the weight of the liquid displaced. This discovery and his reaction to it has become famous:

> *When he was devoting his attention to this problem, he happened to go to a public bath. When he climbed down into the bathtub there, he noticed that water in the tub equal to the bulk of his body flowed out. Thus, when he observed this method of solving the problem, he did not wait. Instead, moved with joy, he sprang out of the tub, and rushing home naked he kept indicating in a loud voice that he had indeed discovered what he was seeking. For while running he was shouting repeatedly in Greek, "Eureka, eureka" ("I have found it, I have found it").* (Vitruvius, *On Architecture*, 9 Preface, 10)

War between Rome and Syracuse unfortunately interrupted Archimedes's scientific life. In 213 B.C.E. during the Second Punic War, the Romans besieged the city. Hiero, its king and Archimedes's friend, asked the scientist for help in repulsing Roman attacks. Archimedes began to build remarkable devices that served as artillery. One shot missiles to break up infantry attacks. Others threw huge masses of stones that fell on the enemy with incredible speed and noise. They tore gaping holes in the Roman lines and broke up attacks. Against Roman warships he built a machine consisting of huge beams that projected over the targets. Then the artillerymen dropped great weights onto the ships, like bombs. Even more complicated was an apparatus with beams from which large claws dropped onto the hulls of enemy warships, hoisted them into the air, and dropped them back into the sea. In response, the Romans brought up an exceptionally large scaling ladder carried on ships. While the ships approached, Archimedes's artillery disabled the ladders by hitting them repeatedly with stones weighing 500 pounds. At last the Romans became so fearful that whenever they saw a bit of rope or a stick of timber projecting over one of the walls protecting Syracuse they shouted, "There it is. Archimedes is trying some engine on us" and fled. When the Romans finally breached the walls of Syracuse in 212 B.C.E., a Roman soldier came upon Archimedes in his study and killed him.

In the early twentieth century a scholar examining a thirteenth-century parchment manuscript realized that underneath the top text was another, partially scraped-off text, and that this was several works of Archimedes. He used a camera to help read the underlying text, but then the manuscript vanished. It turned up again in 1998 at a Christie's auction in New York, where it was purchased by an anonymous buyer and generously deposited at the Walters Art Museum in Baltimore. For ten years the manuscript was studied using ultraviolet and visible light and X-rays, which made the entire text visible. Contemporary science is enabling scholars of the classical world to read some of Archimedes's lost works.

QUESTIONS FOR ANALYSIS

1. What applications do you see in the world around you of the devices Archimedes improved or invented: the lever, the pulley, and artillery?
2. What effect did his weapons have on the Roman soldiers and their willingness to attack Syracuse?

Archimedes's treatises were found on a palimpsest, a manuscript that was scraped and washed so that another text could be written over it, thus reusing the expensive parchment. (Image by the Rochester Institute of Technology. Copyright resides with the owner of the Archimedes Palimpsest, but digital images of the entire manuscript can be found at: www.archimedespalimpsest.org)

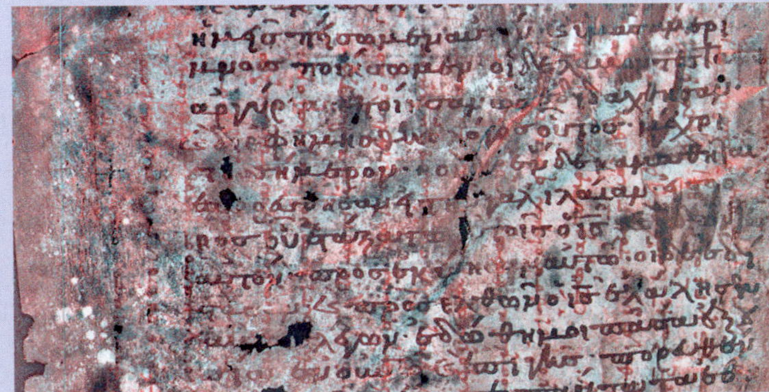

into new areas. Herophilus, who lived in the first half of the third century B.C.E., approached the study of medicine in a systematic, scientific fashion. He dissected corpses and measured what he observed, gaining new insights into the workings and construction of the human body. His students carried on his work, and they also discovered new means of treating disease and relieving pain, including opium.

Quick Review
What larger social and cultural trends were reflected in the increased popularity of mystery religions and philosophy during the Hellenistic period?

Connections

THE ANCIENT GREEKS built on the achievements of earlier societies in the eastern Mediterranean, but they also added new elements, including history, drama, philosophy, science, and realistic art. The Greek world was largely conquered by the Romans, as you will learn in the following chapter, and the various Hellenistic monarchies became part of the Roman Empire. In cultural terms the lines of conquest were reversed, with the Romans adopting and adapting many aspects of Greek culture, religion, and thought.

The influence of the ancient Greeks was not limited to the Romans, of course. As discussed in Chapter 3, art and thought in northern India was shaped by the blending of Greek and Buddhist traditions. And as you will see in Chapter 15, European thinkers and writers made conscious attempts to return to classical ideals in art, literature, and philosophy during the Renaissance. In America political leaders from the Revolutionary era on decided that important government buildings should be modeled on the Parthenon or other temples. In some ways, capitol buildings in the United States are good symbols of the legacy of Greece—gleaming ideals of harmony, freedom, democracy, and beauty that (as with all ideals) do not always correspond with realities.

- **For a list of suggested readings for this chapter, visit** *bedfordstmartins.com/mckayworldunderstanding*.
- **For primary sources from this period, see** *Sources of World Societies*, Second Edition.
- **For Web sites, images, and documents related to topics in this chapter, see Make History at** *bedfordstmartins.com/mckayworldunderstanding*.

Chapter 5 Study Guide

To do these exercises online, go to bedfordstmartins.com/mckayworldunderstanding.

Step 1

GETTING STARTED

Below are basic terms about this period in global history. Can you identify each term below and explain why it matters?

TERMS	WHO (OR WHAT) AND WHEN	WHY IT MATTERS
polis, p. 106		
hoplites, p. 107		
democracy, p. 107		
oligarchy, p. 107		
tyranny, p. 107		
Delian League, p. 110		
mystery religions, p. 122		
Epicureanism, p. 122		
Stoicism, p. 123		

Step 2

MOVING BEYOND THE BASICS

The exercise below requires a more advanced understanding of the chapter material. Examine Greek identity in the Hellenic and Hellenistic worlds by filling in the chart below with descriptions of key aspects of Hellenic Greece and the Hellenistic world. When you are finished, consider the following questions: How did the Greek sense of identity change after Alexander's conquests? How did the basis of political loyalty change? What about the role of religion in personal and public life?

	GOVERNMENT	ECONOMY	RELIGION AND PHILOSOPHY	CULTURAL DIVERSITY AND EXCHANGE
Hellenic Greece				
The Hellenistic World				

Step 3

PUTTING IT ALL TOGETHER

Now that you've reviewed key elements of the chapter, take a step back and try to see the big picture. Remember to use specific examples from the chapter in your answers.

THE ORIGINS AND EARLY DEVELOPMENT OF HELLENIC GREECE

- How did the polis embody key aspects of Greek society and culture? Is it fair to say that, in a sense, the polis was the essence of Greek civilization? Why or why not?
- Compare and contrast Sparta and Athens. To what extent do these two city-states represent different solutions to the same basic challenges?

THE CLASSICAL PERIOD

- What were the causes and consequences of the Peloponnesian War?
- How was the emergence of Athens as an imperial power reflected in Athenian thought and culture?

THE HELLENISTIC WORLD

- Why did Alexander's empire split apart shortly after his death? What impact did this political fragmentation have on the development of the Hellenistic world?
- What characterized the relationship between Greeks and Easterners in the Hellenistic period? To what extent were Easterners "Hellenized"?

LOOKING BACK, LOOKING AHEAD

- Classical Greece was a period of almost constant warfare. With this in mind, compare and contrast classical Greece with earlier periods of endemic warfare in the Near East. What factors seem to have been conducive to peace in the ancient world? What conditions tended to produce war?
- How would you explain the enduring influence of Greek ideas and ideals? What examples of the continuing influence of Greek culture can you identify in the contemporary world?

In Your Own Words Imagine that you must explain Chapter 5 to someone who hasn't read it. What would be the most important points to include and why?

6

The World of Rome

750 B.C.E.–400 C.E.

Like the Persians under Cyrus, the Mauryans under Chandragupta, and the Macedonians under Alexander, the Romans conquered vast territories. Their singular achievement lay in their ability to incorporate conquered peoples into the Roman system. Unlike the Greeks, who mostly refused to share citizenship, the Romans extended citizenship first to other peoples in Italy and later to inhabitants of Roman provinces. After a grim period of civil war that ended in 31 B.C.E., the emperor Augustus restored peace and expanded Roman power and law as far east as the Euphrates River, creating the institution that the modern world calls the "Roman Empire." Later emperors extended Roman authority farther still, so that at its largest the Roman Empire stretched from England to Egypt and from Portugal to Persia.

Roman history is usually divided into two periods. The first is the republic (509–27 B.C.E.), the age in which Rome grew from a small group of cities in Italy to a state that ruled much of the Mediterranean. To administer their growing territory, Romans established a republican form of government in which power was held by the senate whose members were primarily wealthy landowners. Social conflicts and wars of conquest led to serious political problems, and the republican constitution gave way to rule by a single individual, who took the title "emperor." Thus, the second period in Roman history is the empire (27 B.C.E.–476 C.E.), which saw further expansion, enormous building projects, and cultural flowering but also social upheavals and economic hardship. Rome's large territory eventually was split into eastern and western halves.

Woman from Pompeii
This fresco from Pompeii shows a young woman carrying a tray in a religious ritual. Pompeii was destroyed by a volcanic explosion in 79 C.E., and excavations have revealed life in what was a vacation spot for wealthy Romans. (Villa dei Misteri, Pompeii/The Bridgeman Art Library)

Chapter Preview

- What kind of society and government did the Romans develop in Italy?
- What were the causes and consequences of Roman expansion beyond Italy?
- How did Roman rule lead to a period of prosperity and relative peace?
- What was Christianity, and how did it affect life in the Roman Empire?
- How did rulers respond to the chaos of the third and fourth centuries?

What kind of society and government did the Romans develop in Italy?

The colonies established by Greek poleis (city-states) in the Hellenic era included a number along the coast of southern Italy and Sicily. So many Greek settlers came to this area that it later became known as Magna Graecia—Greater Greece. The Greek colonies of this region transmitted much of their culture to people who lived farther north in the Italian peninsula. These included the Etruscans (ih-TRUHS-kuhns), who built the first cities north of Magna Graecia, and then the Romans, who eventually came to dominate the peninsula. In addition to allying with conquered peoples and granting them citizenship, the Romans established a republic ruled by a senate. However, class conflicts over the rights to power eventually erupted and had to be resolved.

The Etruscans and Rome

The culture that is now called Etruscan developed from that of peoples who either were already living in north-central Italy or who spread into this area from unknown locations about 750 B.C.E. The Etruscans spoke a language that was not in the Indo-European language family (see page 43), so it is very different from Greek and Latin; however, they adopted the Greek alphabet to write their language.

The Etruscans established permanent settlements that evolved into cities resembling the Greek city-states in political organization (see page 106). From an early period the Etruscans began to trade natural products, especially iron, with their Greek neighbors to the south and with other peoples throughout the Mediterranean in exchange for luxury goods. The Etruscans thereby built a rich culture that became the foundation of civilization throughout Italy, and they began to take political control of a larger area.

The Etruscans, ca. 500 B.C.E.

In the process they encountered a small collection of villages subsequently called Rome. Located at an easy crossing point on the Tiber River, Rome stood astride the main avenue of communication between northern and southern Italy. Its seven hills provided safety from attackers and from the floods of the Tiber (Map 6.1).

Under Etruscan influence the Romans prospered. During the rule of Etruscan kings (ca. 750–509 B.C.E.) Rome enjoyed contacts with the larger Mediterranean world, while the city continued to grow. Temples and public buildings began to grace Rome, and the Forum (see Map 6.1) became a public meeting place similar to the Greek agora. In addition, trade in metalwork became common, and wealthier Romans began to import fine Greek vases. In cultural developments, the Romans adopted the Etruscan alphabet and even the Etruscan toga, the white woolen robe worn by citizens.

The Roman Conquest of Italy

Although it is certain that the Etruscans once ruled Rome, much else about early Roman history is an uneven mixture of fact and legend. The Romans have several different foundation myths. The most common of these centers on Romulus and Remus, twin brothers raised by a female wolf. When they were grown, they decided to build a city, but they quarreled over where it should be built. Romulus eventually prevailed, killed his brother, and named the city after himself. He also established a council of advisers later called the senate.

Later Roman historians continued the story by describing a series of kings after Romulus each elected by the senate. Because they had to fit this succession with the reality that, starting around 750 B.C.E., Rome was ruled by Etruscans, the historians described the last few of these kings as Etruscans. The kings apparently became more authoritarian, one possible reason they were overthrown. According to tradition, the Romans threw out the last Etruscan king in 509 B.C.E. and established a republic, led by the senate and two **consuls** elected for one-year terms.

Chapter Chronology

753 B.C.E.	Traditional founding of Rome
ca. 750–509 B.C.E.	Etruscan rule of an evolving Rome
ca. 500–265 B.C.E.	Roman conquest of Italy
509–27 B.C.E.	Roman republic
494–287 B.C.E.	Struggle of the Orders
264–146 B.C.E.	Punic Wars
53–31 B.C.E.	Civil wars among rival claimants to power
44 B.C.E.	Assassination of Julius Caesar
31 B.C.E.	Triumph of Augustus
27 B.C.E.–476 C.E.	Roman Empire
27 B.C.E.–68 C.E.	Rule of Julio-Claudian emperors
ca. 3 B.C.E.–29 C.E.	Life of Jesus
284–337 C.E.	Diocletian and Constantine reconstruct the empire, dividing it into western and eastern halves; construction of Constantinople
312 C.E.	Constantine legalizes Christianity
380 C.E.	Christianity made the official religion of the empire

In the following years the Romans fought numerous wars with their Italian neighbors, including the Etruscans. War also involved diplomacy, at which the Romans became masters. They very early learned the value of alliances with the towns in the province of Latium that surrounded Rome. These alliances involved the Romans in still other wars that took them farther afield in the Italian peninsula.

Around 390 B.C.E. the Romans suffered a major setback when a people new to the Italian peninsula, the Celts—or Gauls, as the Romans called them—swept down from the north and sacked Rome. In the century that followed the Romans rebuilt their city and recouped their losses. They brought Latium and their Latin allies fully under their control and conquered the Etruscans. In a series of bitter wars the Romans also subdued southern Italy, and then turned north. Their superior military institutions, organization, and manpower allowed them to conquer most of Italy by about 265 B.C.E. (see Map 6.1).

consuls Primary executives in the Roman republic, elected for one-year terms, who commanded the army in battle, administered state business, and supervised financial affairs; originally the office was limited to patricians.

As they expanded their territory, the Romans spread their religious traditions throughout Italy, blending them with local beliefs and practices. As the Romans conquered the cities of Magna Graecia, the Greek deities were absorbed into the Roman pantheon. As it was in Greece, religion was largely a matter of rites and ceremonies, not inner

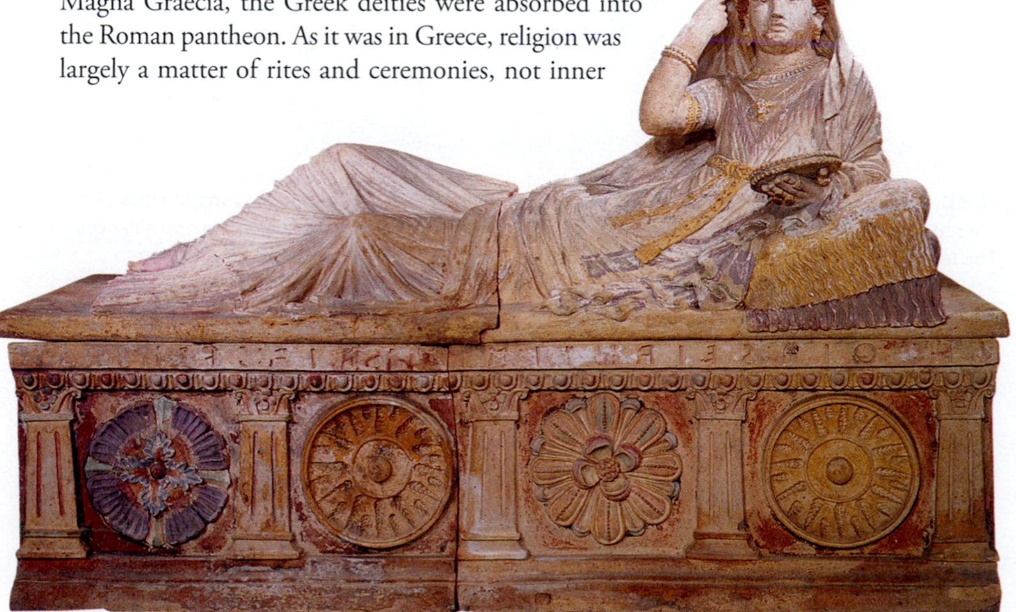

Sarcophagus of Lartie Seianti The woman portrayed on this lavish sarcophagus is the noble Etruscan Lartie Seianti. Although the sarcophagus is her place of burial, she is portrayed as in life, comfortable and at rest. The influence of Greek art on Etruscan is apparent in almost every feature of the sarcophagus. (Archaeological Museum, Florence/Nimatallah/Art Resource, NY)

Map 6.1 Roman Italy, ca. 265 B.C.E. As Rome expanded, it built roads linking major cities and offered various degrees of citizenship to the territories it conquered or with which it made alliances. The territories outlined in green were added by 218 B.C.E., largely as a result of the Punic Wars.

piety. Such rituals were an important way to express common values, however, which for Romans meant bravery, morality, family, and home.

Once they had conquered an area, the Romans did what the Persians had earlier done to help cement their new territory: they built roads. Roman roads facilitated the flow of communication, trade, and armies from the capital to outlying areas. They were the tangible sinews of unity, and many were marvels of engineering, as were the stone bridges the Romans built over Italy's many rivers.

In politics the Romans shared full Roman citizenship with many of their oldest allies, particularly the inhabitants of the cities of Latium. In other instances they granted citizen-

Picturing the Past

Battle Between the Romans and the Germans

Rome's wars with the barbarians of western Europe come to life in this relief from a Roman sarcophagus of 225 C.E. The Romans are wearing helmets, with the soldier at the far right even wearing iron or bronze chain mail, a technology they had most likely only recently picked up from the Germans. (Vanni/Art Resource, NY)

ANALYZING THE IMAGE How would you describe this depiction of war? How does the artist show Roman superiority over the barbarians through the placement, dress, and facial features of the soldiers?

CONNECTIONS How does this funeral sculpture reinforce or challenge what you have learned about Roman expansion and the Romans' treatment of the peoples they conquered?

ship without the franchise, that is, without the right to vote or hold Roman office. These allies were subject to Roman taxes and calls for military service but ran their own local affairs.

The Distribution of Power in the Roman Republic

In the early republic social divisions determined the shape of politics. Political power was in the hands of the aristocracy — the **patricians**, who were wealthy landowners. The common people of Rome, the **plebeians** (plih-BEE-uhns), were free citizens with a voice in politics, but they had few of the patricians' political and social advantages. They could not hold high office or marry into patrician families. While some plebeian merchants rivaled the patricians in wealth, most plebeians were poor artisans, small farmers, and landless urban dwellers.

The most important institution in the Roman government was the **senate**. During the republic the senate advised the consuls and other officials about military and political

patricians The Roman aristocracy; wealthy landowners who held political power.

plebeians The common people of Rome, who had few of the patricians' advantages.

senate The assembly that was the main institution of government in the Roman republic. It grew out of an earlier council of advisers to the king.

matters and handled government finances. Because the same senators sat year after year, while the consuls changed annually, the senate also provided stability. The senate could not technically pass legislation; it could only offer its advice. Yet increasingly, because of the senate's prestige, its advice came to have the force of law. The senate was also responsible for handling relations between Rome and other powers.

The primary executives in the republic were the two consuls, positions initially open only to patrician men. The consuls commanded the army in battle, administered state business, and supervised financial affairs. When the consuls were away from Rome, praetors (PREE-tuhrz) acted in their place. Otherwise, the praetors dealt primarily with the administration of justice. After the age of overseas conquest (see page 135), the Romans divided their lands in the Mediterranean into provinces governed by ex-consuls and ex-praetors. Other officials worked with the senate to oversee the public treasury, register citizens, and supervise the city of Rome.

A lasting achievement of the Romans was their development of law. Roman civil law, the *ius civile*, consisted of statutes, customs, and forms of procedure that regulated the lives of citizens. As the Romans came into more frequent contact with foreigners, the praetors applied a broader *ius gentium*, the "law of the peoples," to such matters as peace treaties, the treatment of prisoners of war, and the exchange of diplomats. In the ius gentium, all sides were to be treated the same regardless of their nationality. By the late republic Roman jurists had widened this still further into the concept of *ius naturale*, "natural law" based in part on Stoic beliefs (see page 123). Natural law, according to these thinkers, is made up of rules that govern human behavior that come from applying reason rather than customs or traditions, and so apply to all societies.

Social Conflict in Rome

Inequality between plebeians and patricians led to a conflict known as the Struggle of the Orders. In this conflict the plebeians sought to increase their power by taking advantage of the fact that Rome's survival depended on its army, which needed plebeians to fill the ranks of the infantry. According to tradition, in 494 B.C.E. the plebeians literally walked out of Rome and refused to serve in the army. Their general strike worked, and the patricians made important concessions. For one thing they allowed patricians and plebeians to marry one another. They also recognized the right of plebeians to elect their own officials, the tribunes, who could bring plebeian grievances to the senate for resolution and could also veto the decisions of the consuls. Thus, as in Archaic age Greece (see page 109), political rights were broadened because of military needs for foot soldiers.

The law itself was the plebeians' primary target. Only the patricians knew what the law was, and only they could argue cases in court. All too often they used the law for their own benefit. The plebeians wanted the law codified and published. In response, the patricians surrendered their legal monopoly, and they codified and published the Laws of the Twelve Tables. The patricians also made legal procedures public so that plebeians could argue cases in court.

After a ten-year battle, the Licinian-Sextian laws passed, giving wealthy plebeians access to all the offices of Rome, including the right to hold one of the two consulships. Once plebeians could hold the consulship, they could also sit in the senate and advise on policy. Though decisive, this victory did not automatically end the Struggle of the Orders. That happened only in 287 B.C.E. with the passage of the *lex Hortensia*, which gave the resolutions of the *concilium plebis*, the plebeian assembly, the force of law for patricians and plebeians alike. This compromise established a new elite of wealthy plebeians and patricians. Yet the Struggle of the Orders had made all citizens equal before the law, resulting in a Rome stronger and more united than before.

Quick Review

What social and political tensions accompanied Roman expansion in Italy, and how did the Romans resolve these tensions?

What were the causes and consequences of Roman expansion beyond Italy?

With their internal affairs settled, the Romans turned their attention abroad. In a series of wars they conquered lands all around the Mediterranean, creating an overseas empire that brought them unheard of power and wealth. As a result many Romans became more cosmopolitan and comfortable, and they were especially influenced by the culture of one conquered land: Greece. Yet social unrest also came in the wake of the wars, opening unprecedented opportunities for ambitious generals who wanted to rule Rome like an empire. Civil war ensued, which was quelled briefly by Julius Caesar. Only his grandnephew Octavian, better known to history as Augustus, finally restored peace and order to Rome.

Overseas Conquests and the Punic Wars, 264–133 B.C.E.

In 282 B.C.E., when the Romans reached southern Italy, they embarked upon a series of wars that left them the rulers of the Mediterranean world. They did not, however, have a grand strategy to conquer the world, as had Alexander the Great. Rather they responded to situations as they arose.

Their presence in southern Italy brought the Romans to the island of Sicily, where they confronted another great power in the western Mediterranean, Carthage (CAHR-thij). The city of Carthage had been founded by Phoenicians as a trading colony in the eighth century B.C.E. (see page 45). It commanded one of the best harbors on the northern African coast and was supported by a fertile inland. By the fourth century B.C.E. the Carthaginians began to expand their holdings. At the end of a long string of wars, the Carthaginians had created and defended a mercantile empire that stretched from western Sicily to beyond Gibraltar.

The conflicting ambitions of the Romans and Carthaginians led to the First Punic (PYOO-nik) War, which lasted from 264 to 241 B.C.E. During the course of the war, Rome built a navy and defeated Carthage in a series of sea battles. Sicily became Rome's first province, but despite a peace treaty the conflict was not over.

Carthaginian armies moved into Spain, where Rome was also claiming territory. The brilliant general Hannibal (ca. 247–183 B.C.E.) marched an army from Spain across what is now France and over the Alps into Italy, beginning the Second Punic War (218–201 B.C.E.). Hannibal won three major victories, including a devastating blow at Cannae in southeastern Italy in 216 B.C.E. He then spread devastation throughout Italy. Yet Hannibal was not able to win areas near Rome in central Italy. His allies, who included Philip V, the Antigonid king of Macedonia (see page 117), did not supply him with enough food and supplies to sustain his troops, and Rome fought back.

The Roman general Scipio Africanus (ca. 236–ca. 183 B.C.E.) copied Hannibal's methods of mobile warfare, streamlining the legions (army divisions) by making their components capable of independent action and using guerrilla tactics. He took Spain from the Carthaginians and then struck directly at Carthage itself, prompting the Carthaginians to recall Hannibal from Italy to defend the homeland. In 202 B.C.E., near the town of Zama, Scipio defeated Hannibal in one of the world's truly decisive battles. Scipio's victory meant that the world of the western Mediterranean would henceforth be Roman. Roman

The Carthaginian Empire and Roman Republic, 264 B.C.E.

language, law, and culture, fertilized by Greek influences, would in time permeate this entire region.

The Second Punic War contained the seeds of still other wars. Unabated fear of Carthage led to the Third Punic War, a needless, unjust, and savage conflict that ended in 146 B.C.E. when Scipio Aemilianus, grandson of Scipio Africanus, burned Carthage to the ground.

After the final defeat of Carthage, the Romans turned east. They remembered the alliance between Philip of Macedonia and Hannibal, and after provocation from the current king of Macedonia, Roman legions quickly conquered Macedonia and Greece. Then they moved farther east and defeated the Seleucid monarchy. In 133 B.C.E. the king of Pergamum in Asia Minor willed his kingdom to Rome when he died. The Ptolemies of Egypt retained formal control of their kingdom, but they obeyed Roman wishes in terms of trade policy. Declaring the Mediterranean *mare nostrum*, "our sea," the Romans began to create a political and administrative machinery to hold the Mediterranean together under a mutually shared cultural and political system of provinces ruled by governors sent from Rome.

New Influences and Old Values in Roman Culture

With the conquest of the Mediterranean world, Rome became a great city. The spoils of war went to build baths, theaters, and other places of amusement, and Romans and Italian townspeople began to spend more of their time in leisure pursuits. This new urban culture reflected Hellenistic influences. Romans developed a liking for Greek literature, and the Roman conquest of the Hellenistic East resulted in wholesale confiscation of Greek paintings and sculpture to grace Roman temples, public buildings, and private homes.

The baths were built in response to another Greek influence: a passion for bathing, which Romans came to share. The large buildings containing pools supplied by intricate systems of aqueducts were more than just places to bathe. Baths included gymnasia where men exercised, snack bars and halls where people chatted and read, and even libraries and lecture halls. Women had opportunities to bathe, generally in separate facilities or at separate times, and both women and men went to the baths to see and be seen. Conservative commentators objected to these new pastimes as a corruption of traditional Roman values, but they were widely adopted in the cities.

paterfamilias The oldest dominant male of the family, who held nearly absolute power over the lives of family members.

New customs did not change the core Roman social structures. The head of the family remained the **paterfamilias**, the oldest dominant male of the family. He held nearly absolute power over his wife and children. Until he died, his sons could not legally own property. To deal with important matters, he usually called a council of the family's adult males. The women of the family had no formal part in these councils, but they could inherit and own property. The Romans praised women who were virtuous and loyal to their husbands. They also accorded respect to women as mothers and thought that children should be raised by their mothers.

manumission The freeing of individual slaves by their masters.

Most Romans continued to work long days, but an influx of slaves from Rome's conquests provided labor for the fields and cities. To the Romans slavery was a misfortune that befell some people, but it was not based on racial theories. For loyal slaves the Romans always held out the possibility of freedom, and **manumission**, the freeing of individual slaves by their masters, became common. Nonetheless, slaves rebelled from time to time.

Religion played an important role in the lives of most Romans before and after the conquests. The Romans honored the cults of their gods, hoping for divine favor. For example, in the city of Rome the shrine of Vesta, the goddess of hearth and home, was tended by six "vestal virgins" chosen from patrician families. Roman military losses were sometimes blamed on inattention by the vestal virgins, another link between female honor and the Roman state. In addition to the great gods, the Romans believed in spirits who haunted fields and homes.

The Late Republic and the Rise of Augustus, 133–27 B.C.E.

The wars of conquest eventually created serious political problems for the Romans. When the legionaries (soldiers) returned home, they found their farms practically in ruins. Many were forced to sell their land to wealthy buyers, who combined their purchases into huge estates called latifundia. Now landless, veterans moved to the cities, especially Rome. These developments not only created unrest in the city but also threatened Rome's army by reducing its ranks. The Romans had always believed that only landowners should serve in the army, for only they had something to fight for. Landless men, even if they were Romans and lived in Rome, were forbidden to serve. The landless veterans were willing to follow any leader who promised help. The leader who answered their call was the aristocrat Tiberius Gracchus (163–133 B.C.E.). Elected tribune in 133 B.C.E., he proposed dividing public land among the poor. But a group of wealthy senators murdered him, launching a long era of political violence that would destroy the republic. Still, Tiberius's brother Gaius Gracchus (153–121 B.C.E.) passed a law providing the urban poor with cheap grain and urged practical reforms. Once again senators tried to stem the tide of reform by murdering him.

The next reformer, Gaius Marius (ca. 157–86 B.C.E.), recruited landless men into the army to put down a rebel king in Africa. He promised them land for their service. But after his victory, the senate refused to honor his promise. From then on, Roman soldiers looked to their commanders, not to the senate or the state, to protect their interests. The turmoil continued until 88 B.C.E., when the Roman general Sulla made himself dictator, an official office in the Roman republic given to a man who was granted absolute power temporarily to handle an emergency such as a war. Dictators were supposed to step down after six months, but Sulla held this position for nine years, and after that it was too late to restore the republican constitution. The senate and other institutions of the Roman state had failed to meet the needs of the people. As a result, the soldiers put their faith in generals rather than the state, and that doomed the republic.

The history of the late republic is the story of power struggles among many famous Roman figures, which led to a series of civil wars. Pompey (PAHM-pee), who had been one of Sulla's officers, used military success in Spain to force the senate to allow him to run for consul. In 59 B.C.E. he was joined in a political alliance called the First Triumvirate by Crassus, another ambitious politician, and by Julius Caesar (100–44 B.C.E.). Born of a noble family, Caesar, an able general, was also a brilliant politician. Recognizing that military success led to power, he led his troops to victory in Spain and Gaul, modern France. The First Triumvirate fell apart after Crassus was killed in battle in 53 B.C.E., leaving Caesar and Pompey in competition with each other for power. The result was civil war. The Ptolemaic rulers of Egypt became mixed up in this war, particularly Cleopatra VII, who allied herself with Caesar and had a son by him. (See "Individuals in Society: Queen Cleopatra," page 138.) Although the senate backed Pompey, Caesar was victorious.

Using his victory wisely, Caesar enacted basic reforms. He extended citizenship to many provincials outside Italy who had supported him. To relieve the pressure of Rome's huge population, he sent eighty thousand poor people to establish colonies in Gaul, Spain, and North Africa. These new communities—formed of Roman citizens, not subjects—helped spread Roman culture.

In 44 B.C.E. a group of conspirators assassinated Caesar and set off another round of civil war. (See "Listening to the Past: Cicero and the Plot to Kill Caesar," page 140.) His grandnephew and heir, the eighteen-year-old Octavian (63 B.C.E.–14 C.E.), joined with two of Caesar's followers, Marc Antony and Lepidus, in the Second Triumvirate. After defeating Caesar's murderers, they had a falling-out. Octavian forced Lepidus out of office and waged war against Antony, who had now also become allied with Cleopatra. In 31 B.C.E., Octavian defeated the combined forces of Antony and Cleopatra at the Battle of Actium in Greece.

INDIVIDUALS IN SOCIETY

Queen Cleopatra

CLEOPATRA VII (69–30 B.C.E.) WAS A MEMBER of the Ptolemy dynasty, the Hellenistic rulers of Egypt who had established power in the third century B.C.E. Although she was a Greek, she was passionately devoted to her Egyptian subjects and was the first in her dynasty who could speak Egyptian in addition to Greek. Just as ancient pharaohs had linked themselves with the gods, she had herself portrayed as the goddess Isis and may have seen herself as a reincarnation of Isis (see page 40).

At the time civil war was raging in the late Roman republic, Cleopatra and her brother Ptolemy XIII were in a dispute over who would be supreme ruler in Egypt. Julius Caesar captured the Egyptian capital of Alexandria, Cleopatra arranged to meet him, and the two became lovers, although Cleopatra was much younger and Caesar was married. The two apparently had a son, Caesarion, and Caesar's army defeated Ptolemy's army, ending the power struggle. Cleopatra came to Rome in 46 B.C.E., where Caesar put up a statue of her as Isis in one of the city's temples. The Romans hated her because they saw her as a decadent Eastern queen and a threat to what were considered traditional Roman values.

After Caesar's assassination, Cleopatra returned to Alexandria. There she witnessed the outbreak of another Roman civil war that pitted Octavian, Caesar's heir, against Marc Antony, who commanded the Roman army in the East. When Antony visited Alexandria in 41 B.C.E. he met Cleopatra, and though he was already married to Octavian's sister, he became her lover. He abandoned (and later divorced) his Roman wife, married Cleopatra in 37 B.C.E., and changed his will to favor his children by Cleopatra. Antony's wedding present to Cleopatra was a huge grant of territory, much of it Roman, that greatly increased her power and that of all her children, including Caesarion. Antony also declared Caesarion to be Julius Caesar's rightful heir.

Octavian used the wedding gift as the reason to declare Antony a traitor. He and other Roman leaders described Antony as a romantic fool captivated by the seductive Cleopatra. Roman troops turned against Antony and joined with Octavian, and at the battle of Actium in 31 B.C.E. Octavian defeated the army and navy of Antony and Cleopatra. Antony committed suicide, as did Cleopatra shortly afterward. Octavian ordered the teenage Caesarion killed, but the young children of Antony and Cleopatra were allowed to go back to Rome, where they were raised by Antony's widow. In another consequence of Octavian's victory, Egypt became a Roman province.

Roman sources are viciously hostile to Cleopatra, and she became the model of the femme fatale whose sexual attraction led men to their doom. Stories about her beauty, sophistication, allure, lavish spending, desire for power, and ruthlessness abounded and were retold for centuries. The most dramatic story was that she committed suicide through the bite of a poisonous snake, which may have been true and which has been the subject of countless paintings. Her tumultuous relationships with Caesar and Antony have been portrayed in plays, novels, movies, and television programs.

Bust of Cleopatra, probably from Alexandria. (Bildarchiv Preussischer Kulturbesitz/Art Resource, NY)

QUESTIONS FOR ANALYSIS

1. How did Cleopatra benefit from her relationships with Caesar and Antony? How did they benefit from their relationships with her?
2. How did ideas about gender and Roman suspicion of the more sophisticated Greek culture combine to shape Cleopatra's fate and the way she is remembered?
3. The "Individuals in Society" for Chapter 2 also focuses on leading female figures in Egypt, but they lived more than a thousand years before Cleopatra. How would you compare their situation with hers?

For his success, the senate in 27 B.C.E. gave Octavian the name Augustus, meaning "revered one." Tradition recognizes this date and Augustus's leadership as the start of the Roman Empire.

The Successes of Augustus

After Augustus ended the civil wars, he faced the monumental problems of reconstruction, and from 29–23 B.C.E. he toiled to heal Rome's wounds. He first had to rebuild the constitution and the organs of government. Next he had to demobilize much of the army and care for the welfare of the provinces. Then he had to address the danger of various groups on Rome's European frontiers.

Augustus claimed that in restoring the constitutional government he was also restoring the republic. Yet he had to modify republican forms and offices to meet the new circumstances. While expecting the senate to shoulder heavy administrative burdens, he failed to give it enough actual power to do the job. Many of the senate's prerogatives thus shifted to Augustus and his successors.

Augustus also had to fit his own position into the republican constitution. He did this not by creating a new office for himself but by gradually taking over many of the offices that traditionally had been held by separate people, consolidating power in his own hands in the process. The senate also gave him the honorary title *princeps civitatis*, "first citizen of the state." That title had no official powers attached to it, but the fact that it is the origin of the word *prince*, meaning sovereign ruler, is an indication of what Augustus actually did.

Ara Pacis In the middle years of Augustus's reign, the Roman senate ordered a huge altar, the Ara Pacis, built to honor him and the peace he had brought to the empire. This was decorated with life-size reliefs of Augustus and members of his family, prominent Romans, and other people and deities. One side shows a goddess figure, most likely the goddess Peace herself, with twin babies on her lap, surrounded by symbols of fertility and dominance, thus linking the imperial family with continued prosperity. (Scala/Art Resource, NY)

LISTENING TO THE PAST

Cicero and the Plot to Kill Caesar

Marcus Tullius Cicero was born in January 106 B.C.E. After an excellent education, he settled in Rome to practice law. His meteoric career took him to the consulship in 63 B.C.E. By the time of Caesar's death in 44 B.C.E., Cicero was sixty-two years old and a senior statesman. Like many others, he was fully caught up in the events leading to Caesar's assassination and the resulting revolution. Shortly before the plot was carried out on March 15, 44 B.C.E. — the Ides of March — Caesar wrote Cicero a flattering letter telling him that "your approval of my actions elates me beyond words. . . . As for yourself, I hope I shall see you at Rome so that I can avail myself as usual of your advice and resources in all things."[1] By then, however, Cicero knew of and supported the plot to assassinate Caesar and prudently decided not to meet him. The following letters and speeches offer a personal account of Cicero's involvement in the plot and its aftermath.

Trebonius, one of the assassins, wrote to Cicero describing the murder, and on February 2, 43 B.C.E., Cicero gave this frank opinion of the events:

" Would to heaven you had invited me to that noble feast that you made on the Ides of March: no remnants, most assuredly, should have been left behind. Whereas the part you unluckily spared gives us so much perplexity that we find something to regret, even in the godlike service that you and your illustrious associates have lately rendered to the republic. To say the truth, when I reflect that it was owing to the favor of so worthy a man as yourself that Antony now lives to be our general bane, I am sometimes inclined to be a little angry with you for taking him aside when Caesar fell as by this means you have occasioned more trouble to myself in particular than to all the rest of the whole community.[2] "

By the "part [of the feast] you unluckily spared" he meant Marc Antony, Caesar's firm supporter and a fierce enemy of the assassins. Another reason that Cicero was not entirely pleased with the results of the assassination was that it led to civil war. Two men led the cause for restoring the republic: Brutus, an aristocrat who favored traditional Roman values, and Cassius, an unpopular but influential senator. Still undecided about what to do after the assassination, Cassius wrote to Cicero asking for advice. Cicero responded:

" Where to advise you to begin to restore order I must acknowledge myself at a loss. To say the truth, it is the tyrant alone, and not the tyranny, from which we seem to be delivered: for although the man [Caesar] is destroyed, we still servilely maintain all his despotic ordinances. We do more: and under the pretence of carrying his designs into execution, we approve of measures which even he himself would never have pursued. . . . This outrageous man [Antony] represents me as the principal advisor and promoter of your glorious efforts. Would to heaven the charge were true! For had I been a party in your councils, I should have put it out of his power thus to bother and embarrass our plans. But this was a point that depended on yourselves to decide; and since the opportunity is now over, I can only wish that I were capable of giving you any effective advice. But the truth is that I am utterly at a loss in how to act myself. For what is the purpose of resisting where one cannot oppose force by force?[3] "

At this stage the young Octavian, the future Augustus and Caesar's heir, appeared to claim his inheritance. He too sought Cicero's advice, and in a series of letters to his close friend Atticus, Cicero discussed the situation:

" On the second or third of November 44 B.C.E. a letter arrived from Octavian. He has great schemes afoot. He has won the veterans at Casilinum and Calatia over to his views, and no wonder since he gives them 500 denarii apiece. He plans to make a round of the other colonies. His object is plain: war with Antony and himself as commander-in-chief. So it looks to me as though in a few days' time we shall be in arms. But whom are we to follow? Consider his name; consider his age. . . . In short, he proffers himself as our leader and expects me to back him up. For my part I have recommended him to go to Rome. I imagine he will have the city rabble behind him, and the honest men too if he convinces them of his sincerity. Ah Brutus, where are you? What a golden opportunity you are losing! I could not foretell *this*, but I thought something of the kind would happen.[4] "

Four days later Cicero records news of the following developments:

" Two letters for me from Octavian in one day! Now he wants me to return to Rome at once, says he wants to work through the senate. . . . In short, he presses and I play for time. I don't trust his age and I don't know what he's after. . . . I'm nervous of Antony's

Considering what had happened to Julius Caesar, Augustus wisely kept all this power in the background, and his period of rule is officially called the "principate." Although principate leaders were said to be "first among equals," Augustus's tenure clearly marked the end of the republic, and without specifically saying so, Augustus created the office of emperor. That word is derived from *imperator*, commander of the army, a link that reflects the fact that

Bust of Cicero. (Alinari/Art Resource, NY)

power and don't want to leave the coast. But I'm afraid of some star performance during my absence. Varro [an enemy of Antony] doesn't think much of the boy's [Octavian's, who was only eighteen] plan; I take a different view. He has a strong force at his back and *can* have Brutus. And he's going to work quite openly, forming companies at Capua and paying out bounties. War is evidently coming any minute now."[5] ❞

At last Cicero openly sided with Octavian. On April 21, 43 B.C.E., he denounced Antony in a speech to the senate. He reminded his fellow senators how they had earlier opposed Antony:

❝ Do you not remember, in the name of the immortal gods, what resolutions you have made against these men [Antony and his supporters]? You have repealed the acts of Antony. You have taken down his law. You have voted that they were carried by violence and with a disregard of the auspices. You have called out the troops throughout all Italy. You have pronounced that colleague and ally of all wickedness a public enemy. What peace can there be with this man? Even if he were a foreign enemy, still, after such actions as have taken place, it would be scarcely possible by any means whatever to have peace. Though seas and mountains and vast regions lay between you, still you would hate such a man without seeing him. But these men will stick to your eyes, and when they can to your very throats; for what fences will be strong enough for us to restrain savage beasts? Oh, but the result of war is uncertain. It is at all events in the power of brave men such as you ought to be to display your valor, for certainly brave men can do that, and not to fear the caprice of fortune.[6] ❞

When war broke out Cicero continued to speak out in the senate against Antony. Yet Cicero commanded no legions, and only legions commanded respect. At last Antony got his revenge when he had Cicero prosecuted as a public enemy. An ill and aging Cicero fled to the sea in a litter but was intercepted by Antony's men. With dignity Cicero stretched his head out of the window of the litter, and a centurion cut it off together with the hand that had written the speeches against Antony. Cicero's hands and head were displayed in the Roman Forum, showing the revenge taken on an enemy of the state. But years later Octavian, then the Roman emperor Augustus, said of Cicero: "A learned man, learned and a lover of his country."[7]

[1]*To Atticus* 9.16.2 in D. R. Shackleton-Bailey, *Cicero's Letters to Atticus*, vol. IV (Cambridge, U.K.: Cambridge University Press, 1968), pp. 203–205.

[2]*To Trebonius* in T. de Quincy, *Cicero: Offices, Essays, and Letters* (New York: E. P. Dutton, 1942), pp. 328–329.

[3]*To Cassius*, ibid., pp. 324–325.

[4]*To Atticus* 16.8.1–2 in D. R. Shackleton-Bailey, *Cicero's Letters to Atticus*, vol. VI (Cambridge, U.K.: Cambridge University Press, 1967), pp. 185–187.

[5]*To Atticus* 16.9, ibid., p. 189.

[6]*The Fourteenth Phillipic* in C. D. Yonge, *Cicero, Select Orations* (New York: Harper and Brothers, 1889), p. 499.

[7]Plutarch, *Cicero* 49.15.

QUESTIONS FOR ANALYSIS

1. What can you infer from these letters about how well prepared Brutus and Cassius were to take control of the government after Caesar's death?
2. What do these sources suggest about Cicero's importance?
3. What was Cicero's view of Octavian? Of Antony?

the main source of Augustus's power was his position as commander of the Roman army. The changes that Augustus made created a stable government, although the fact that the army was loyal to him as a person, not as the head of the Roman state, would lead to trouble later.

In other political reforms, Augustus made provincial administration more orderly and improved its functioning. He encouraged local self-government and the development of cities. Augustus encouraged the cult of *Roma et Augustus* (Rome and Augustus) as the guardian of the state. The cult spread rapidly and became a symbol of Roman unity. Augustus had himself portrayed on coins standing alongside the goddess Victory, and on celebratory stone arches built to commemorate military victories. In addition, he had temples, stadiums, marketplaces, and public buildings constructed in Rome and other cities.

In the social realm, Augustus promoted marriage and childbearing through legal changes that released free women and freedwomen (female slaves who had been freed) from male guardianship if they had given birth to a certain number of children. Men and women who were unmarried or had no children were restricted in the inheritance of property.

Mapping the Past

Map 6.2 Roman Expansion, 282 B.C.E.–138 B.C.E.

Rome expanded in all directions, eventually controlling every shore of the Mediterranean and vast amounts of land.

ANALYZING THE MAP How would you summarize the pattern of Roman expansion — that is, which areas were conquered first and which later? How long was Rome able to hold on to territories at the outermost boundaries of its empire?

CONNECTIONS Many of today's major cities in these areas were founded as Roman colonies. Why do you think so many of these cities were founded along the northern border of Roman territory?

Aside from addressing legal issues and matters of state, Augustus actively encouraged poets and writers. For this reason the period of his rule is known as the golden age of Latin literature. Roman poets and prose writers celebrated human accomplishments in works that were highly polished, elegant in style, and intellectual in conception.

Rome's greatest poet was Virgil (70–19 B.C.E.), whose masterpiece is the *Aeneid* (uh-NEE-id), an epic poem that is the Latin equivalent of the Greek *Iliad* and *Odyssey* (see page 106). Virgil's account of the founding of Rome and the early years of the city gave final form to the legend of Aeneas, the Trojan hero (and ancestor of Romulus and Remus; see page 130) who escaped to Italy at the fall of Troy. As Virgil told it, Aeneas became the lover of Dido (DIE-doh), the widowed queen of Carthage, but left her because his destiny called him to found Rome. In leaving Dido, an "Eastern" queen, Aeneas put the good of the state ahead of marriage or pleasure. The parallels between this story and the real events involving Antony and Cleopatra were not lost on Virgil's audience. Making the public aware of these parallels, and of Virgil's description of Aeneas as an ancestor of Julius Caesar, fit well with Augustus's aims. Therefore, he encouraged Virgil to write the *Aeneid* and made sure it was circulated widely immediately after Virgil died.

One of the most momentous aspects of Augustus's reign was Roman expansion into northern and western Europe (Map 6.2). Augustus completed the conquest of Spain, founded twelve new towns in Gaul, and saw that the Roman road system linked new settlements with one another and with Italy. After hard fighting, he made the Rhine River the Roman frontier in Germania (Germany). Meanwhile, generals conquered areas as far as the Danube River, and Roman legions penetrated the areas of modern Austria, southern Bavaria, and western Hungary. The regions of modern Serbia, Bulgaria, and Romania also fell. Within this area the legionaries built fortified camps. Roads linked these camps with one another, and settlements grew up around the camps, eventually becoming towns. Traders began to frequent the frontier and to do business with the native people who lived there; as a result, for the first time, central and northern Europe came into direct and continuous contact with Mediterranean culture.

Romans did not force their culture on native people in Roman territories. However, just as earlier ambitious people in the Hellenistic world knew that the surest path to political and social advancement lay in embracing Greek culture and learning to speak Greek (see page 119), those determined to get ahead now learned Latin and adopted aspects of Roman culture.

Quick Review
How did military success alter Roman society and contribute to the political unrest that culminated in the fall of the republic?

How did Roman rule lead to a period of prosperity and relative peace?

Augustus's success in creating solid political institutions was tested by the ineptness of some leaders who followed him, but later in the first century C.E., Rome entered a period of political stability, prosperity, and relative peace, which has come to be known as the ***pax Romana***, the Roman peace. During this time the growing city of Rome saw great improvements, and trade and production flourished in the provinces. Rome also expanded eastward and came into indirect contact with China.

pax Romana A period of Roman security, order, harmony, flourishing culture, and expanding economy during the first and second centuries C.E.

Political and Military Changes in the Empire

For fifty years after Augustus's death in 14 C.E. the dynasty that he established—known as the Julio-Claudians because all were members of the Julian and Claudian clans—provided the emperors of Rome. Some of the Julio-Claudians, such as Tiberius and Claudius, were sound rulers and created a bureaucracy of able administrators to help them govern. Others, including Caligula and Nero, were weak and frivolous.

In 68 C.E. Nero's inept rule led to military rebellion and widespread disruption. Yet only two years later Vespasian (r. 69–79 C.E.), who established the Flavian dynasty, restored order. He also turned Augustus's principate into a hereditary monarchy and expanded the emperor's powers. The Flavians (69–96 C.E.) repaired the damage of civil war to give the Roman world peace and paved the way for the Antonines (96–192 C.E.), a dynasty of emperors under whose leadership the Roman Empire experienced a long period of prosperity. In addition to the full-blown monarchy of the Flavians, other significant changes had occurred in Roman government since Augustus's day. Hadrian (HAY-dree-uhn), who became emperor in 117 C.E., made the imperial bureaucracy created by Claudius more organized, establishing imperial administrative departments and separating civil from military service. These innovations helped the empire run more efficiently while increasing the authority of the emperor, who was now the ruling power of the bureaucracy.

The Roman army also saw changes, transforming from a mobile unit to a defensive force. The frontiers became firmly fixed and defended by a system of forts and walls. Behind them the network of roads was expanded and improved both to supply the forts and to reinforce them in times of trouble. The Roman road system eventually grew to over fifty thousand miles, longer than the current interstate highway system in the United States.

The personnel of the legions were changing, too. Because Italy could no longer supply all the recruits needed for the army, increasingly only the officers came from Italy, while the soldiers were mostly drawn from the provinces. Among the provincial soldiers were barbarians who joined the army to gain Roman citizenship.

Life in Rome

The era of peace created great wealth, much of which flowed into Rome. The city, with a population of somewhere between 500,000 and 750,000, became the largest in the world at that time. Despite its great wealth, most Romans were poor, living in shoddily constructed houses and taking whatever work they could find.

Fire and crime were perennial problems even in Augustus's day, and sanitation was poor. In the second century urban planning and new construction greatly improved the situation. For example, engineers built an elaborate sewage collection system. They also built hundreds of miles of aqueducts, most of them underground, to bring fresh water into the city from the surrounding hills.

Rome grew so large that it became ever more difficult to feed. Emperors solved the problem by providing citizens with free bread, oil, and wine. By doing so, they also stayed in favor. They likewise entertained the people with gladiatorial contests in which participants fought to the death using swords and other weapons. Many gladiators were criminals, some the slaves of gladiatorial schools, and others prisoners of war. The Romans actually preferred chariot racing to gladiatorial contests. In these races, four permanent teams, each with its own color, competed against one other. Winning charioteers were idolized just as sports stars are today.

Prosperity in the Roman Provinces

Like Rome, the Roman provinces and frontiers saw extensive prosperity in the second century C.E. through the growth of agriculture, trade, and industry, among other factors. Peace and security opened Britain, Gaul, Germany, and the lands of the Danube to settlers from other parts of the Roman Empire. Many of these settlers became tenant farmers on small parcels of land, and eventually these farmers became the backbone of Roman agriculture.

Roman Architecture These two structures demonstrate the beauty and utility of Roman architecture. The Coliseum in Rome (left),a sports arena that could seat 50,000 spectators built between 70 and 80 C.E., was the site of gladiatorial games, animal spectacles, executions, and mock naval battles. The Pont du Gard at Nîmes in France (above) is a bridge over a river carrying an aqueduct that supplied millions of gallons of water per day to the Roman city of Nîmes in Gaul; the water flowed in a channel at the very top. Although this bridge was built largely without mortar or concrete, many Roman aqueducts and bridges relied on concrete for their strength. (Coliseum: Scala/Art Resource, NY; Pont du Gard: Vanni/Art Resource, NY)

In continental Europe the army was largely responsible for the new burst of expansion. The areas where legions were stationed became Romanized because legionaries, upon retirement, often settled where they had served, frequently marrying local women. Having learned a trade in the army, they brought essential skills to areas that badly needed trained men. The eastern part of the empire, including Greece, Anatolia, and Syria, shared in the boom in part by trading with other areas and in part because of local industries.

The expansion of trade during the pax Romana made the Roman Empire an economic as well as a political force. Britain and Belgium became prime grain producers, with much of their harvests going to the armies of the Rhine, and Britain's wool industry probably got its start under the Romans. Italy and southern Gaul produced huge quantities of wine. Roman colonists introduced the olive to southern Spain and northern Africa, which soon produced most of the oil consumed in the western part of the empire. In the East the olive oil production of Syrian farmers reached an all-time high, and Egypt produced tons of wheat that fed the Roman populace. Additionally, the Roman army in Mesopotamia

GLOBAL TRADE

Pottery

Pottery is used primarily for dishes today, but it served a surprisingly large number of purposes in the ancient world. Families used earthen pottery for cooking and tableware, for storing grains and liquids, and for lamps. On a larger scale pottery was used for the transportation and protection of goods traded overseas, much as today's metal storage containers are used.

The creation of pottery dates back to the Neolithic period. Few resources were required to make it, only abundant sources of good clay and wheels upon which potters could throw their vessels. Once made, the pots were baked in specially constructed kilns. Although the whole process was relatively simple, skilled potters formed groups that made utensils for entire communities. Later innovations occurred when the artisans learned to glaze their pots by applying a varnish before baking them in a kiln.

The earliest potters focused on coarse ware: plain plates, cups, and pots. One of the most popular pieces was the amphora, a large two-handled jar with a wide mouth, a round belly, and a base. It became the workhorse of maritime shipping because it protected contents from water and rodents, was easy and cheap to produce, and could be reused. Amphorae contained goods as varied as wine and oil, spices, dried fish, and pitch. The amphora's dependability and versatility kept it in use from the fourth century B.C.E. to the beginning of the Middle Ages.

In the Hellenistic and Roman periods amphorae became common throughout the Mediterranean and carried goods eastward to the Black Sea, Persian Gulf, and Red Sea. The Ptolemies of Egypt sent amphorae and their contents even farther, to Arabia, eastern Africa, and India.

By the eighth century B.C.E. Greek potters and artists began to decorate their wares by painting them with patterns and scenes from mythology, legend, and daily life. These images spread knowledge of Greek religion and culture. In the West, especially, the Etruscans in Italy and the Carthaginians in North Africa eagerly welcomed the pots, their decoration, and their ideas. The Hellenistic kings shipped these pots as far east as China. Pottery thus served as a means of cultural exchange among people scattered across huge portions of the globe.

The Romans took the manufacture of pottery to an advanced stage by introducing a wider range of vessels and by making some in industrial-scale kilns that were large enough to fire tens of thousands of pots at once. The most prized pottery was *terra sigillata*, reddish decorated tableware with a glossy surface. Methods for making terra sigillata spread from Italy northward into Europe, often brought by soldiers in the Roman army who had been trained in potterymaking in Italy. They set up facilities to make roof tiles, amphorae, and dishes for their units, and local potters began to copy their styles and methods of manufacturing. Terra sigillata often portrayed Greco-Roman gods and heroes, so that this pottery spread Mediterranean myths and stories. Local artisans added their own distinctive flourishes and sometimes stamped their names on the pots; these individual touches have allowed archaeologists to trace the pottery trade throughout the Roman Empire in great detail.

consumed a high percentage of the raw materials and manufactured products from Syria and Asia Minor. Provincial industry saw similar growth during this period. Aided by all this growth in trade and industry, Europe and western Asia were linked in ways they had not been before.

Eastward Expansion and Contacts Between Rome and China

The expansion of their empire took the Romans into West and Central Asia, which had two immediate effects. The first was a long military confrontation between the Romans and several western Asian empires. The second was a period of contact (often indirect) between the major ancient civilizations of the world, as Roman movement eastward coincided with Chinese expansion into the West (see page 164).

As the Romans drove farther eastward, they encountered the Parthians, who had established a kingdom in what is now Afghanistan and Iran in the Hellenistic period (see page 119). In the second century the Romans tried unsuccessfully to drive the Parthians out of Armenia and the Tigris and Euphrates Valleys. In 226 C.E. the Parthians fell to the

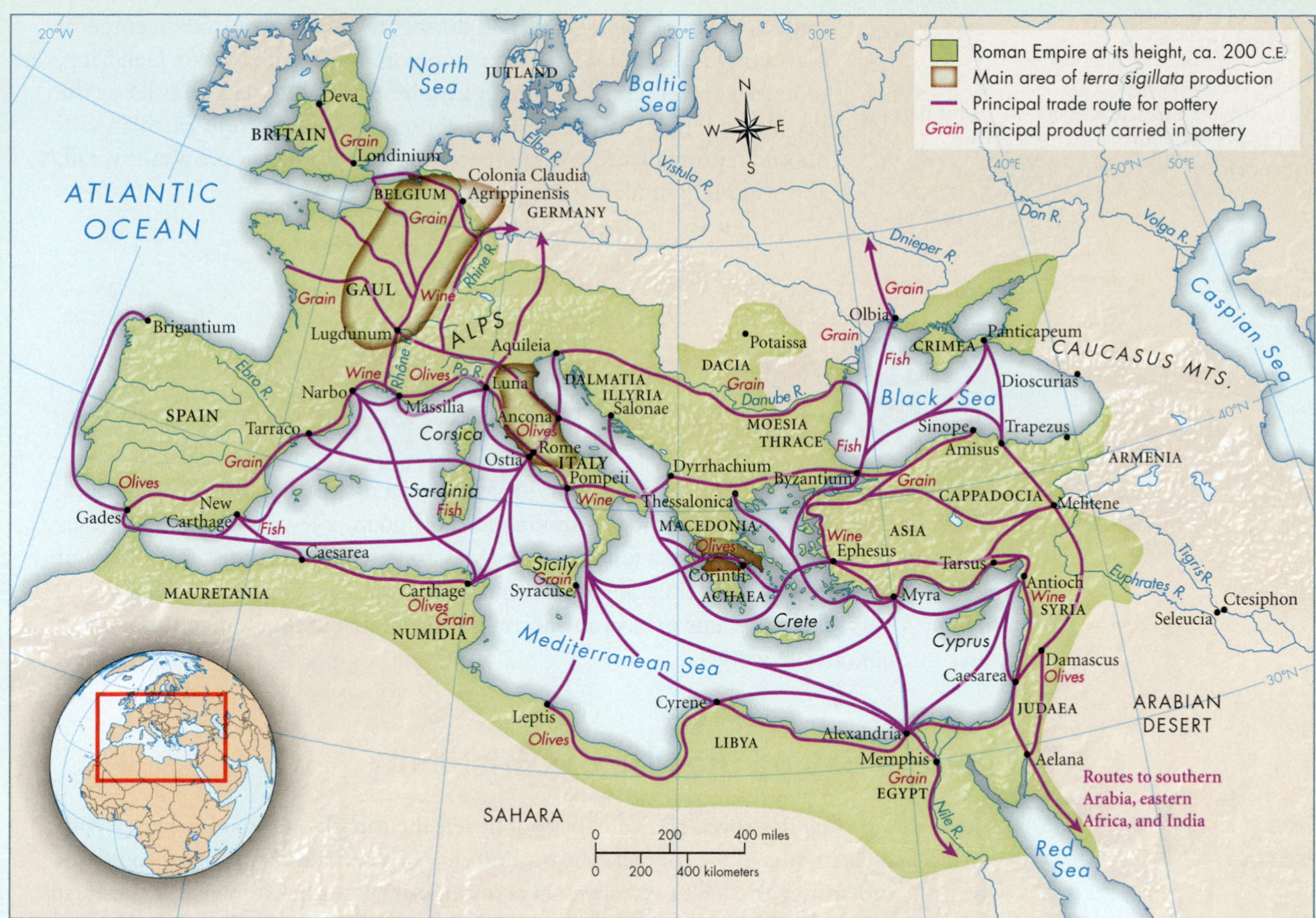

Map 6.3 The Roman Pottery Trade, ca. 200 C.E.

Sassanids, a new dynasty in the area (see page 185). When the Romans continued their attacks against this new enemy, the Sassanid king Shapur defeated the Romans, taking the emperor Valerian prisoner.

Although warfare disrupted parts of Asia, it did not stop trade that had prospered from Hellenistic times (see pages 120–121). Trade between the Chinese and Romans was indirect, with the Parthians acting as middlemen between them. Chinese merchants sold their wares to the Parthians. The Parthians then carried the goods overland to Mesopotamia or Egypt, from where they were shipped throughout the Roman Empire. Silk was still a major commodity from east to west, along with other luxury goods. In return the Romans traded glassware, precious gems, and slaves. The Parthians added exotic fruits, rare birds, and other products desired by the Chinese. (See "Global Trade: Pottery," page 146.)

The pax Romana was also an era of maritime trade, and Roman ships sailed from Egyptian ports to the mouth of the Indus River, where they traded local merchandise and wares imported by the Parthians. Roman mariners pushed into the Indian Ocean and beyond, reaching Malaya, Sumatra, and Java in Southeast Asia.

Maritime trade between Chinese and Roman ports began in the second century C.E., though no merchant traveled the entire distance. The period of this contact coincided with the era of Han greatness in China (see pages 159–164). The Han emperor Wu encouraged

Quick Review
How and why did trade and manufacturing increase throughout the Roman Empire during the pax Romana?

trade by sea as well as by land, and during the reign of the Roman emperor Nerva (r. 96–98 C.E.), a later Han emperor sent an ambassador, Gan Ying, to make contact with the Roman Empire. Gan Ying made it as far as the Persian Gulf ports, where he heard about the Romans from Parthian sailors and reported back to his emperor that the Romans were wealthy, tall, and strikingly similar to the Chinese.

What was Christianity, and how did it affect life in the Roman Empire?

During the reign of the emperor Tiberius (r. 14–37 C.E.), in the Roman province of Judaea, which had been created out of the Jewish kingdom of Judah, a Jewish man named Jesus of Nazareth preached, attracted a following, and was executed on the order of the Roman prefect Pontius Pilate. At the time this was a minor event, but Christianity, the religion created by Jesus's followers, came to have an enormous impact first in the Roman Empire and later throughout the world.

Factors Behind the Rise of Christianity

The civil wars that destroyed the Roman republic left their mark on Judaea, where Jewish leaders had taken sides in the conflict. The turmoil created a climate of violence throughout the area, and among the Jews two movements in opposition to the Romans spread. First were the Zealots (ZEH-luhts), who fought to rid Judaea of the Romans. The second movement was the growth of militant apocalypticism—the belief that the end of the world was near and that it would happen with the coming of a savior, or Messiah, who would destroy the Roman legions and inaugurate a period of happiness and plenty for Jews.

pagan From a Latin term meaning "of the country," used to describe non-Christian followers of Greco-Roman gods.

The pagan world also played its part in the story of early Christianity. The term **pagan** refers to all those who believed in the Greco-Roman gods. Roman paganism can be broadly divided into three spheres: the official state religion of Rome; the traditional Roman veneration of hearth, home, and countryside; and the new mystery religions that arose in the Hellenistic world (see page 122). Of these, only the mystery religions offered adherents spiritual satisfaction and the promise of eternal life, but they were exclusive. Therefore, many people's spiritual needs were unmet by these religious traditions, further paving the way for the rise of Christianity.

The Life and Teachings of Jesus

Into this climate of Messianic hope and Roman religious yearning came Jesus of Nazareth (ca. 3 B.C.E.–29 C.E.). According to Christian scripture, he was born to deeply religious Jewish parents and raised in Galilee. His ministry began when he was about thirty, and he taught by preaching and telling stories.

Like Socrates and the Buddha, Jesus left no writings. Accounts of his sayings and teachings first circulated orally among his followers and were later written down. The principal evidence for his life and deeds are the four Gospels of the Bible, books that are part of what Christians later termed the New Testament. These Gospels are records of Jesus's teachings, written sometime in the late first century. Their authors had probably heard many different people talk about what Jesus said and did, and there are discrepancies among the four ac-

Catacombs of Rome Christians favored burial of the dead rather than the more common Roman practice of cremation, and in the second century began to dig tunnels in the soft rock around Rome for burials. The bodies were placed in niches along the walls of these passageways and then sealed up. Memorial services for martyrs were sometimes held in or near catacombs, but they were not regular places of worship. Many catacombs contain some of the earliest examples of Christian art, and others, dug by Jews for their own dead, contain examples of Jewish art from this period. (Catacombe di Priscilla, Rome/Scala/Art Resource, NY)

counts. These differences indicate that early followers had a diversity of beliefs about Jesus's nature and purpose.

However, almost all the early sources agree on certain aspects of Jesus's teachings: he preached of a heavenly kingdom of eternal happiness in a life after death, and of the importance of devotion to God and love of others. His teachings were essentially Jewish, but Jesus deviated from orthodoxy in insisting that he taught in his own name, not in the name of Yahweh (the Hebrew name for God). Was he the Messiah — in the Greek translation of the Hebrew word *Messiah*, the Christ? A small band of followers thought so, and Jesus claimed that he was. Yet Jesus had his own conception of the Messiah. He would establish a spiritual kingdom, not an earthly one.

The prefect Pontius Pilate knew little about Jesus's teachings. He was concerned with maintaining peace and order. Crowds followed Jesus, and the prospect that these crowds would spark violence alarmed Pilate. Some Jews believed that Jesus was the long-awaited Messiah. Others hated and feared him because they thought him religiously dangerous. To avert riot and bloodshed, Pilate condemned Jesus to death, and his soldiers carried out the sentence. On the third day after Jesus's crucifixion, some of his followers claimed that he had risen from the dead. For his earliest followers and for generations to come, the resurrection of Jesus became a central element of faith.

The Spread of Christianity

The memory of Jesus and his teachings survived and flourished. Believers in his divinity met in small groups, often in one another's homes, to discuss the meaning of Jesus's message and to celebrate a ritual (later called the Eucharist or Lord's Supper) commemorating his last meal with his disciples before his arrest. Because they expected Jesus to return to the world very soon, they regarded earthly life and institutions as unimportant. Only later did these groups evolve into what came to be called the religion of Christianity, with a formal organization and set of beliefs.

The catalyst in the spread of Jesus's teachings and the formation of the Christian Church was Paul of Tarsus, a well-educated Hellenized Jew who was comfortable in both the Roman and the Jewish worlds. At first he persecuted members of the new sect, but on the road to the city of Damascus in Syria he was converted to belief in Jesus and became a vigorous promoter of Jesus's ideas. Paul traveled all over the Roman Empire and wrote letters of advice to many groups. These letters were copied and widely circulated, transforming Jesus's ideas into more specific moral teachings. As a result of his efforts Paul became the most important figure in changing Christianity from a Jewish sect into a separate religion.

The breadth of the Roman Empire was another factor behind the spread of Christianity. The Roman system of roads enabled early Christians easily to spread their faith throughout the known world, as Jesus had told his followers to do, thus making his teachings universal. The pagan Romans also considered their secular empire universal, and the early Christians combined the two concepts of universalism.

The earliest Christian converts included people from all social classes. These people were reached by missionaries and others who spread the Christian message through family contacts, friendships, and business networks. Many women were active in spreading Christianity. The growing Christian communities differed about the extent to which women should participate in the workings of the religion; some favored giving women a larger role in church affairs, while others were more restrictive.

People were attracted to Christian teachings for a variety of reasons. It was in many ways a mystery religion, offering its adherents special teachings that would give them immortality. But in contrast to traditional mystery religions, Christianity promised this immortality to all. Christianity also offered the possibility of forgiveness, for believers accepted that human nature is weak and that even the best Christians could fall into sin. Christianity was also attractive to many because it gave the Roman world a cause. By spreading the word of Christ, Christians played their part in God's plan for the triumph of Christianity on earth. They were not discouraged by temporary setbacks, believing Christianity to be invincible. Christianity likewise gave its devotees a sense of community, which was very welcome in the often highly mobile world of the Roman Empire. To stress the spiritual kinship of this new type of community, Christians often called one another brother and sister. Also, many Christians took Jesus's commandment to love one another as a guide and provided support for widows, orphans, and the poor, just as they would for family members.

The Growing Acceptance and Evolution of Christianity

At first many pagans in the Roman Empire misunderstood Christian practices and beliefs. For instance, they thought that the ritual of the Lord's Supper, at which Christians said that they ate and drank the body and blood of Jesus, was an act of cannibalism. Pagans also feared that the Greco-Roman gods would withdraw their favor from the Roman Empire because of the Christian insistence that the pagan gods either did not exist or were evil spirits. And many worried that Christians were trying to destroy the Roman family with their insistence on a new type of kinship.

Christians themselves were partly responsible for the religious misunderstandings. They exaggerated the degree of pagan hostility to them, and most of the gory stories about Christian martyrs are fictitious. Although there were some cases of pagan persecution of the Christians, with few exceptions they were local and sporadic in nature. As time went on, pagan hostility and suspicion decreased. Pagans realized that Christians were not working to overthrow the state and that Jesus was no rival of Caesar.

By the second century C.E. Christianity was also changing. The belief that Jesus was soon coming again gradually waned, and as the number of converts increased, permanent institutions were established. These included a hierarchy of officials often modeled on those of the Roman Empire. **Bishops**, officials with jurisdiction over a certain area, became especially important. They began to assert that they had the right to determine the correct interpretation of Christian teachings and to choose their successors. As the rise of the bishops shows, lines began to be drawn between what was considered correct teaching and what was considered incorrect, or **heresy**.

bishop A Christian Church official with jurisdiction over a certain area and the power to determine the correct interpretation of Christian teachings.

heresy A religious practice or belief judged unacceptable by church officials.

Christianity also began to attract more highly educated individuals who developed complex theological interpretations of issues that were not clear in scripture. Often drawing on Greek philosophy and Roman legal traditions, they worked out understandings of such issues as how Jesus could be both divine and human and how God could be both a father and a son (and later a spirit as well, a Christian doctrine known as the Trinity). Bishops and theologians often modified teachings that seemed upsetting to Romans, such as Jesus's harsh words about wealth. Given all these changes, Christianity became more formal in the second century, with power more centralized.

Quick Review
How did Christianity change as it gained both followers and acceptance within the Roman Empire?

How did rulers respond to the chaos of the third and fourth centuries?

The prosperity of the second century gave way to a period of chaos and stress in the Roman Empire. Trying to repair the damage was the major work of the emperors Diocletian and Constantine (r. 306–337 C.E.), both of whom rose to leadership through the ranks of the military. They enacted political and religious reforms that dramatically changed the empire.

Diocletian's Reforms

During the third century C.E. the Roman Empire was stunned by civil war, as different individuals claimed rights to leadership of the empire. Emperors often ruled for only a few years or even months. Army leaders in the provinces declared their loyalty to one faction or another, or they broke from the empire entirely. Barbarian groups invaded Roman-held territory along the Rhine and Danube, occasionally even crossing the Alps into Italy. In the East, Sassanid armies advanced all the way to the Mediterranean. By the time peace was restored, the empire's economy was shattered, cities had shrunk in size, and many farmers had left their lands.

The Division of the Roman World, 293

At the close of the third century C.E. the emperor Diocletian ended the period of chaos. Under Diocletian the princeps became *dominus*, "lord," reflecting the emperor's claim that he was "the elect of god," ruling because of divine favor. To underscore the emperor's exalted position, Diocletian and his successor, Constantine, adopted the court ceremonies and trappings of the Persian Empire.

Diocletian recognized that the empire had become too great for one man to handle and so divided it into a western and an eastern half. He assumed direct control of the eastern part, giving a colleague the rule of the western part along with the title *augustus*. Diocletian and his fellow augustus further delegated power by appointing two men to assist them. Although this system is known as the Tetrarchy (TEH-trahr-kee) because four men ruled the empire, Diocletian was clearly the senior partner and final source of authority.

Although the Tetrarchy soon failed, Diocletian's division of the empire into two parts became permanent. Throughout the fourth century C.E. the eastern and western sections drifted apart. In later centuries the western part witnessed the decline of Roman government and the rise of barbarian kingdoms, while the eastern half evolved into the Byzantine Empire.

Economic Hardship and Its Consequences

Major economic problems also confronted Diocletian and Constantine at a time when the empire was less capable of recovery than in previous eras. The emperors needed additional revenues to support the army and the imperial court, but the wars and invasions had harmed Roman agriculture, the primary source of tax revenues. In the cities markets, trade, and industry were disrupted, and travel between cities became dangerous. Moreover, the devastation of the countryside increased the difficulty of feeding and supplying the cities. Economic hardship had been met by cutting the silver content of coins until money was virtually worthless. The immediate result was crippling inflation throughout the empire.

In an attempt to curb inflation, Diocletian issued an edict that fixed maximum prices and wages throughout the empire. He and his successors dealt with the tax system just as strictly and inflexibly. Taxes became payable in kind, that is, in goods and services instead of money. All those involved in the growing, preparation, and transportation of food and other essentials were locked into their professions, as the emperors tried desperately to assure a steady supply of these goods. In this period of severe depression, many localities could not pay their taxes. In such cases local tax collectors had to make up the difference from their own funds. This system soon wiped out a whole class of moderately wealthy people.

During the third century C.E. many free tenant farmers and their families were killed in barbarian invasions. Others fled in advance of the invasions or after devastation from the fighting. Large tracts of land consequently lay deserted. Great landlords with ample resources began at once to claim as much of this land as they could. The huge estates that resulted, called villas, were self-sufficient. They became islands of stability in an unsettled world, and in return for the protection and security landlords could offer, many small landholders who remained in the countryside gave over their lands and their freedom. In this way, free people become what would later be called serfs.

Constantine, Christianity, and the Rise of Constantinople

The stress of the third century C.E. seemed to some emperors the punishment of the gods. Diocletian increased persecution of Christians, hoping that the gods would restore their blessing on Rome. Yet his persecutions were never very widespread or long-lived, and by the late third century most pagans accepted Christianity. Constantine made this toleration official, legalizing the practice of Christianity throughout the empire in 312 and later being baptized as a Christian. He supported the church throughout his reign, expecting in return the support of church officials in maintaining order. As a result of his partnership that gave it a favored position in the empire, Christianity slowly became the leading religion.

In time the Christian triumph would be complete. In 380 C.E. the emperor Theodosius (r. 379–395 C.E.) made Christianity the official religion of the Roman Empire. He allowed the church to establish its own courts and to use its own body of law, called "canon law." At that point Christians began to persecute the pagans for their religion.

Gold Solidus of Helena This gold coin, issued in the fourth century by the emperor Constantine and his mother Helena, shows Helena in profile, surrounded by her name and title. Every Roman emperor issued coins, which served as means of exchange and also as transmitters of political propaganda. The front showed a carefully chosen portrait, and the reverse often depicted a recent victory or an abstract quality such as health or peace. Helena's ability to issue her own coins indicates her status in the imperial household. (Morelli Collection, Lugano, Switzerland/Visual Connection Archive)

The acceptance of Christianity was not the only event that made Constantine's reign a turning point in Roman history. Constantine took the bold step of building a new capital for the empire. Constantinople, the New Rome, was constructed on the site of Byzantium, an old Greek city on the Bosporus, a strait on the boundary between Europe and Asia.

In his new capital Constantine built palaces, warehouses, public buildings, and even a hippodrome for horse racing. In addition, he built defensive works along the borders of the empire, trying hard to keep it together, as did his successors. Despite their efforts, the eastern and the western halves drifted apart throughout the fourth century.

Quick Review
What reforms did Diocletian and Constantine carry out, and why did their reforms fail to stabilize the empire?

Connections

THE ROMAN EMPIRE has long fascinated people. Politicians and historians have closely studied the reasons for its successes and have even more closely analyzed the weaknesses that led to its eventual collapse. By the fourteenth century European scholars were beginning to see the fall of the Roman Empire as one of the great turning points in Western history, the end of the classical era. That began the practice of dividing Western history into different periods—eventually, the ancient, medieval, and modern eras.

This three-part conceptualization also shapes the periodization of world history. As you saw in Chapter 4 and will see in Chapter 7, China is also understood to have had a classical age, and, as you will read in Chapter 11, the Maya of Mesoamerica did as well. The dates of these ages are different from those of the classical period in the Mediterranean, but there are striking similarities among all three places: successful large-scale administrative bureaucracies were established, trade flourished, cities grew, roads were built, and new cultural forms developed. In all three places—and in other countries described as having a classical era—this period was followed by an era of less prosperity and more warfare and destruction.

- **For a list of suggested readings for this chapter, visit** *bedfordstmartins.com/mckayworldunderstanding*.
- **For primary sources from this period, see** *Sources of World Societies*, Second Edition.
- **For Web sites, images, and documents related to topics in this chapter, see Make History at** *bedfordstmartins.com/mckayworldunderstanding*.

Chapter 6 Study Guide

To do these exercises online, go to bedfordstmartins.com/mckayworldunderstanding.

Step 1 GETTING STARTED

Below are basic terms about this period in global history. Can you identify each term below and explain why it matters?

TERMS	WHO (OR WHAT) AND WHEN	WHY IT MATTERS
consuls, p. 131		
patricians, p. 133		
plebeians, p. 133		
senate, p. 133		
paterfamilias, p. 136		
manumission, p. 136		
pax Romana, p. 143		
pagan, p. 148		
bishop, p. 151		
heresy, p. 151		

Step 2 MOVING BEYOND THE BASICS

The exercise below requires a more advanced understanding of the chapter material. Examine the impact of expansion on Roman identity by filling in the chart below with descriptions of the social, cultural, and political consequences of Roman expansion. When you are finished, consider the following questions: What steps did the Romans take to "Romanize" subject peoples? How was Roman life, in turn, altered by contact and connections with diverse peoples? How did the acquisition of an empire change what it meant to be a Roman citizen?

SOCIAL CONSEQUENCES OF ROMAN EXPANSION	POLITICAL CONSEQUENCES OF ROMAN EXPANSION	CULTURAL CONSEQUENCES OF ROMAN EXPANSION

Step 3

PUTTING IT ALL TOGETHER

Now that you've reviewed key elements of the chapter, take a step back and try to see the big picture. Remember to use specific examples from the chapter in your answers.

THE ORIGINS AND DEVELOPMENT OF THE ROMAN REPUBLIC

- How did the Romans integrate conquered Italian territories into their state? How did their policies in this regard create a foundation for further expansion?
- How did the evolution of Roman political institutions reflect the evolution of Roman society?

ROMAN IMPERIALISM AND ITS CONSEQUENCES

- What explains the instability that characterized Roman politics in the century following the Punic Wars? Why did republican institutions fail to produce the kinds of reforms and compromises that had resolved earlier political conflicts?
- How did Rome help connect greater Europe to the economic and cultural life of the Mediterranean world?

ROMAN DECLINE AND THE RISE OF CHRISTIANITY

- What factors facilitated the spread of Christianity throughout the Roman Empire? Why did many Romans initially fear Christianity? Why did such fears diminish over time?

- How and why did the political, cultural, and economic center of the Roman Empire shift from west to east starting in the third century C.E.?

LOOKING BACK, LOOKING AHEAD

- How was Roman society and culture shaped by Greek ideas and ideals? Why was Greek civilization so appealing to so many Romans?
- What are the implications of the claim that, together, Greek and Roman civilization represent the "classical era" in Western history? What does this claim suggest about the connections between these two civilizations and the contemporary Western world?

In Your Own Words Imagine that you must explain Chapter 6 to someone who hasn't read it. What would be the most important points to include and why?

7

East Asia and the Spread of Buddhism

221 B.C.E.–800 C.E.

East Asia was transformed over the millennium from 221 B.C.E. to 800 C.E. At the beginning of this era, China had just been unified into a single state upon the Qin defeat of all the rival states of the Warring States Period, but it still faced major military challenges with the confederation of the nomadic Xiongnu to its north. At the time China was the only place in East Asia with writing, iron technology, large cities, and complex state organizations. Over the next several centuries East Asia changed dramatically as new states emerged. War, trade, diplomacy, missionary activity, and the pursuit of learning led the Chinese to travel to distant lands and people from distant lands to go to China. Among the results were the spread of Buddhism from India and Central Asia to China and the adaptation of many elements of Chinese culture by near neighbors, especially Korea and Japan. Buddhism came to provide a common set of ideas and visual images to all of the cultures of East Asia, much the way Christianity linked societies in Europe.

Buddhist Monk Buddhism became the religion of much of Asia in the period from 200 to 800 C.E. This statue of a Buddhist monk is among the many that have survived in the cave temples of Dunhuang in northwest China. (Wang Lu/ChinaStock)

Increased communication stimulated state formation among China's neighbors: Tibet, Korea, Manchuria, Vietnam, and Japan. Written Chinese was increasingly used as an international language by the ruling elites of these countries, and the new states usually adopted political models from China as well. By 800 C.E. each of these regions was well on its way to developing a distinct political and cultural identity.

Chapter Preview

- How did political unification under the Qin and Han shape China?
- How and why did Buddhism spread throughout East Asia?
- What were the lasting accomplishments of the Sui and Tang Dynasties?
- How were elements of Chinese culture adapted throughout East Asia?

How did political unification under the Qin and Han shape China?

In much the same period in which Rome created a huge empire, the Qin and Han rulers in China created an empire on a similar scale. Like the Roman Empire (see Chapter 6), the Chinese empire was put together through force of arms and held in place by sophisticated centralized administrative machinery. The bureaucracies created by the Qin and Han Empires affected many facets of Chinese social, cultural, and intellectual life.

The Qin Unification, 221–206 B.C.E.

In 221 B.C.E., after decades of constant warfare, Qin (chin), the state that had adopted Legalist policies during the Warring States Period (see page 89), succeeded in defeating the last of its rivals, and China was unified for the first time in many centuries. Anticipating a long line of successors, the victorious king of Qin called himself the First Emperor (*Shihuangdi*). His state, however, did not long outlast him.

Great Wall A rammed-earth fortification built along the northern border of China during the reign of the First Emperor.

Army of the First Emperor The thousands of life-size ceramic soldiers buried in pits about a half mile from the First Emperor's tomb help us imagine the Qin military machine. It was the Qin emperor's concern with the afterlife that led him to construct such a lifelike guard. The soldiers were originally painted in bright colors, and they held real bronze weapons. (Robert Harding World Imagery)

Once Qin ruled all of China, the First Emperor and his Legalist minister Li Si embarked on a sweeping program of centralization. To cripple the nobility of the defunct states, the First Emperor ordered the nobles to leave their lands and move to the capital. The private possession of arms was outlawed to make it more difficult for subjects to rebel. The First Emperor dispatched officials to administer the territory that had been conquered. These officials owed their power and positions entirely to the favor of the emperor and had no hereditary rights to their offices.

To harness the enormous human resources of his people, the First Emperor ordered a census of the population. Census information helped the imperial bureaucracy to plan its activities: to estimate the cost of public works, the tax revenues needed to pay for them, and the labor force available for military service and building projects. To make it easier to administer all regions uniformly, Chinese script was standardized. This standardization would prove to be one of the most significant contributions of the Qin Dynasty. The First Emperor also standardized weights, measures, coinage, and even the axle lengths of carts.

To make it easier for Qin armies to move rapidly, thousands of miles of roads were built. These achievements indirectly facilitated trade. Most of the labor on the projects came from drafted farmers or convicts working out their sentences. Similarly, hundreds of thousands of subjects were drafted to build the **Great Wall** (ca. 230–208 B.C.E.), a rammed-earth fortification along the northern border between the Qin realm and the land controlled by the nomadic Xiongnu (SHE-OONG-noo). Like Ashoka in India a few decades earlier (see Chapter 3), the First Emperor erected many stone inscriptions to inform his subjects of his goals and accomplishments. After Li Si complained that scholars (especially Confucians) used records of the past to denigrate the emperor's achievements, the emperor had all writings other than useful manuals on topics such as agriculture, medicine, and divination collected and burned. As a result of this massive book burning, many ancient texts were lost.

After the First Emperor died in 210 B.C.E., the Qin state unraveled. The Legalist institutions designed to concentrate power in the hands of the ruler made the stability of the government dependent on his strength and character, and his heir proved ineffective. The heir was murdered by his younger brother, and uprisings soon followed.

Chapter Chronology

ca. 230–208 B.C.E.	Construction of Great Wall
221 B.C.E.	China unified under Qin Dynasty
206 B.C.E.–220 C.E.	Han Dynasty
145–ca. 85 B.C.E.	Sima Qian, Chinese historian
114 B.C.E.	Han government gains control over Silk Road trade routes across Central Asia
111 B.C.E.	Emperor Wu conquers Nam Viet
108 B.C.E.	Han government establishes colonies in Korea
105 C.E.	Chinese invention of paper
ca. 200 C.E.	Buddhism begins rapid growth in China
220–589 C.E.	Age of Division in China
313–668 C.E.	Three Kingdoms Period in Korea
372 C.E.	Buddhism introduced in Korea
538 C.E.	Buddhism introduced in Japan
581–618 C.E.	Sui Dynasty
604 C.E.	Prince Shōtoku introduces Chinese-style government in Japan
605 C.E.	Introduction of merit-based examination system for the selection of officials in China
618–907 C.E.	Tang Dynasty; great age of Chinese poetry
668 C.E.	First political unification of Korea under Silla
690 C.E.	Empress Wu declares herself emperor, becoming the only Chinese woman emperor
710 C.E.	Nara made the capital of Japan
735–737 C.E.	Smallpox epidemic in Japan
845 C.E.	Tang emperor begins persecution of Buddhism

The Han Dynasty, 206 B.C.E.–220 C.E.

The eventual victor in the struggle for power that ensued in the wake of the collapse of the Qin Dynasty was Liu Bang, known in history as Emperor Gaozu (r. 202–195 B.C.E.). Gaozu did not disband the centralized government created by the Qin, but he did remove its most unpopular features. Harsh laws were canceled, taxes were sharply reduced, and a policy of noninterference was adopted in an effort to promote economic recovery. With policies of this sort, relative peace, and the extension of China's frontiers, the Chinese population grew rapidly in the first two centuries of the Han Dynasty (Map 7.1). The census of 2 C.E. recorded a population of 58 million. Few other societies kept as good records, making comparisons difficult, but high-end estimates for the Roman Empire are in a similar range (50–70 million).

The Han government was largely supported by the taxes and forced labor demanded of farmers, but this revenue regularly fell short of the government's needs. To pay for his military campaigns, Emperor Wu, the "Martial Emperor" (r. 141–87 B.C.E.), took over the minting of coins, confiscated the land of nobles, sold offices and titles, and increased taxes on private businesses. A widespread suspicion of commerce as an unproductive exploitation of the true producers made it easy to levy especially heavy assessments on merchants. The worst blow to businessmen, however, was the government's decision to enter into market competition with them by selling the commodities that had been collected as taxes.

Han Intellectual and Cultural Life

In contrast to the Qin Dynasty, which favored Legalism, the Han came to promote Confucianism and recruit officials on the basis of their Confucian learning or Confucian moral qualities. The Han government's efforts to recruit men trained in the Confucian classics marked the beginning of the Confucian scholar-official system.

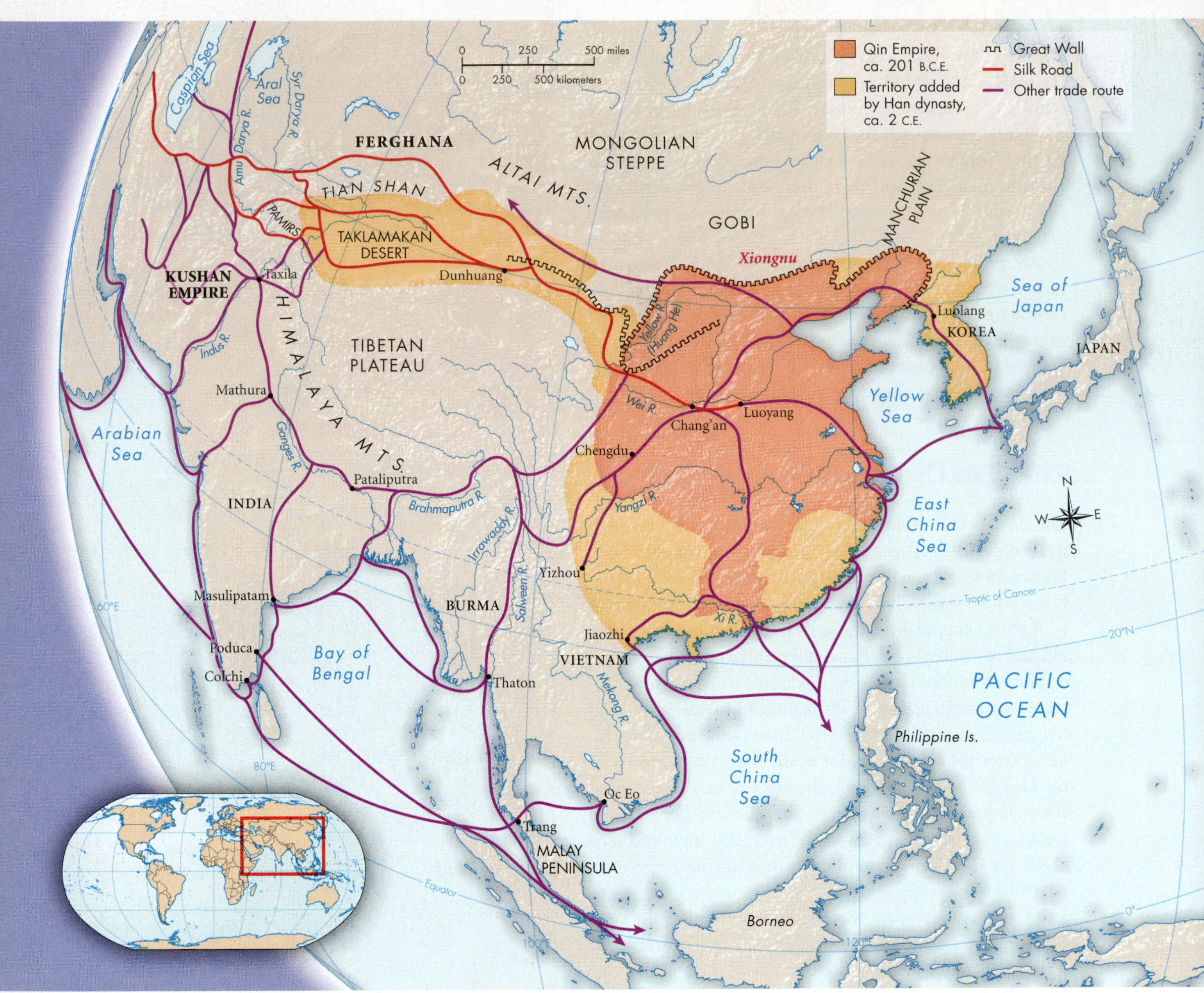

Map 7.1 The Han Empire, 206 B.C.E.–270 C.E. The Han Dynasty asserted sovereignty over vast regions from Korea in the east to Central Asia in the west and Vietnam in the south. Once garrisons were established, traders were quick to follow, leading to considerable spread of Chinese material culture in East Asia. Chinese goods, especially silk, were in demand far beyond East Asia, promoting long-distance trade across Eurasia.

Under the most activist of the Han emperors, Emperor Wu, Confucian scholars were given a privileged position. Confucian officials did not always please Emperor Wu and other emperors. Seeing criticism of the government as one of their duties, the officials tried to check abuse of power. Their willingness to stand up to the ruler also reflected the fact that most of the Confucian scholars selected to serve as officials came from landholding families, much like those who staffed the Roman government, which gave them some economic independence.

The Confucianism that made a comeback during the Han Dynasty was a changed Confucianism. Although Confucian texts had fed the First Emperor's bonfires, some dedicated scholars had hidden their books, and others had memorized whole works. The ancient books recovered in this way—called the **Confucian classics**—were revered as repositories of the wisdom of the past. Confucian scholars treated these classics with piety and attempted to make them more useful as sources of moral guidance by writing commentaries on them. Many Confucian scholars specialized in a single classic, and teachers passed on to their disciples their understanding of each sentence in the work. Other Han Confucians went to the opposite extreme, developing comprehensive cosmological theories that explained the world in terms of cyclical flows of yin and yang (see page 98) and the five phases (fire, water, earth, metal, and wood).

Confucian classics The ancient texts recovered during the Han Dynasty that Confucian scholars treated as sacred scriptures.

Han art and literature reveal a fascination with omens, portents, spirits, immortals, and occult forces. Much of this interest in immortality and communicating with the spirit world was absorbed into the emerging religion of Daoism, which also drew on the philosophical ideas of Laozi and Zhuangzi (see page 96).

A major intellectual accomplishment of the Han Dynasty was history writing. Sima Qian (145–ca. 85 B.C.E.) wrote a comprehensive history of China, dividing his account into a chronology recounting political events, biographies of key individuals, and treatises on subjects such as geography, taxation, and court rituals. Like the Greek historians Herodotus and Thucydides (see page 111), Sima Qian believed fervently in visiting the sites where history was made, examining artifacts, and questioning people about events. The result of his research, ten years or more in the making, was ***Records of the Grand Historian***, a massive work of literary and historical genius.

Records of the Grand Historian A comprehensive history of China written by Sima Qian.

For centuries to come, Sima Qian's work set the standard for Chinese historical writing, although most of the histories modeled after it covered only a single dynasty. The first of these was the work of three members of the Ban family in the first century C.E. (See "Individuals in Society: The Ban Family," page 166.)

The circulation of books like Sima Qian's was made easier by the invention of paper, which the Chinese traditionally date to 105 C.E. Scribes had previously written on strips of bamboo and wood or rolls of silk. Cai Lun, to whom the Chinese attribute the invention of paper, worked the fibers of rags, hemp, bark, and other scraps into sheets of paper. Paper, thus, was somewhat similar to the papyrus made from pounded reeds in ancient Egypt. Though much less durable than wood, paper was far cheaper than silk and became a convenient means of conveying the written word.

Inner Asia and the Silk Road

The difficulty of defending against the nomadic pastoral peoples to the north in the region known as Inner Asia is a major reason China came to favor a centralized bureaucratic form of government. Resources from the entire subcontinent were needed to maintain control of the northern border.

Beginning long before the Han Dynasty, China's contacts with its northern neighbors had involved both trade and military conflict. China's neighbors sought Chinese products such as silk and lacquer ware. When they did not have goods to trade or when trading relations were disrupted, raiding was considered an acceptable alternative in the tribal cultures of the region. Chinese sources speak of defending against raids of "barbarians" from Shang times (ca. 1500–ca. 1050 B.C.E.) on, but not until the rise of nomadism in the mid-Zhou period (fifth to fourth centuries B.C.E.) did the horsemen of the north become China's main military threat.

The economy of these nomads was based on raising sheep, goats, camels, and horses. Families lived in tents that could be taken down and moved north in summer and south in winter when groups of families moved in search of pasture. Herds were tended on horseback, and everyone learned to ride from a young age. The typical social structure of the steppe nomads was fluid, with family and clan units linked through loyalty to tribal chiefs

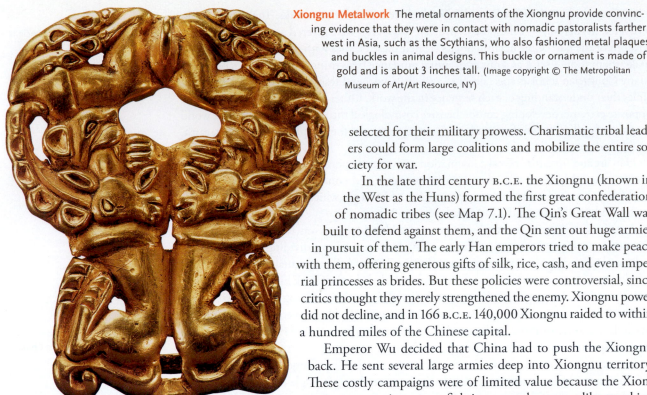

Xiongnu Metalwork The metal ornaments of the Xiongnu provide convincing evidence that they were in contact with nomadic pastoralists farther west in Asia, such as the Scythians, who also fashioned metal plaques and buckles in animal designs. This buckle or ornament is made of gold and is about 3 inches tall. (Image copyright © The Metropolitan Museum of Art/Art Resource, NY)

selected for their military prowess. Charismatic tribal leaders could form large coalitions and mobilize the entire society for war.

In the late third century B.C.E. the Xiongnu (known in the West as the Huns) formed the first great confederation of nomadic tribes (see Map 7.1). The Qin's Great Wall was built to defend against them, and the Qin sent out huge armies in pursuit of them. The early Han emperors tried to make peace with them, offering generous gifts of silk, rice, cash, and even imperial princesses as brides. But these policies were controversial, since critics thought they merely strengthened the enemy. Xiongnu power did not decline, and in 166 B.C.E. 140,000 Xiongnu raided to within a hundred miles of the Chinese capital.

Emperor Wu decided that China had to push the Xiongnu back. He sent several large armies deep into Xiongnu territory. These costly campaigns were of limited value because the Xiongnu were a moving target: fighting nomads was not like attacking walled cities. To try to find allies and horses, Emperor Wu turned his attention west, toward Central Asia. From the envoy he sent into Bactria, Parthia, and Ferghana in 139 B.C.E., the Chinese learned for the first time of other civilized states comparable to China.

In 114 B.C.E. Emperor Wu sent an army into Ferghana and gained recognition of Chinese overlordship in the area, thus obtaining control over the trade routes across Central Asia commonly called the **Silk Road** (see Map 7.1). The city-states along this route did not resist the Chinese presence. They could carry out the trade on which they depended more conveniently with Chinese garrisons to protect them than with rival tribes raiding them.

Silk Road The trade routes across Central Asia through which Chinese silk and other items were traded.

At the same time, Emperor Wu sent troops into northern Korea to establish military districts that would flank the Xiongnu on their eastern border. By 111 B.C.E. the Han government also had extended its rule south into Nam Viet, which extended from south China into what is now northern Vietnam. Thus during Emperor Wu's reign, the territorial reach of the Han state was vastly extended.

During the Han Dynasty China developed a **tributary system** to regulate contact with foreign powers. States and tribes beyond its borders sent envoys bearing gifts, often silk, and received gifts in return. Over the course of the dynasty the Han government's outlay on these gifts was huge, perhaps as much as 10 percent of state revenue. Although the tributary system was a financial burden to the Chinese, it reduced the cost of defense and offered China confirmation that it was the center of the civilized world.

tributary system A system first established during the Han Dynasty to regulate contact with foreign powers. States and tribes beyond its borders sent envoys bearing gifts and received gifts in return.

The silk given to the Xiongnu and other northern tributaries often entered the trading networks of Sogdian, Parthian, and Indian merchants, who carried it by caravans across Asia. Caravans returning to China carried gold, horses, and occasionally West Asian handicrafts. Through the trade along the Silk Road, the Chinese learned of new foodstuffs, including walnuts, pomegranates, sesame, and coriander, all of which came to be grown in China. (See "Global Trade: Silk," page 164.)

Maintaining a military presence so far from the center of China was expensive. To cut costs, the government set up self-supporting military colonies, recruited Xiongnu tribes to serve as auxiliary forces, and established vast government horse farms. Still, military

Ceramic Model of a Pigsty Chinese farmers regularly raised pigs, keeping them in walled-off pens and feeding them scraps. This Han Dynasty model of such a pigsty was placed in a tomb to represent the material goods one hoped the deceased would enjoy in the afterlife. (The Minneapolis Institute of Arts, Gift of Alan and Dena Naylor in memory of Thomas E. Leary)

expenses threatened to bankrupt the Han government.

Life in Han China

How were ordinary people's lives affected by the creation of a huge Han bureaucratic empire? The lucky ones who lived in Chang'an or Luoyang, the great cities of the empire, got to enjoy the material benefits of increased long-distance trade and a boom in the production of luxury goods.

The government did not promote trade per se. The Confucian elite, like ancient Hebrew wise men, considered trade necessary but lowly. Agriculture and crafts were more honorable because they produced something, but merchants merely took advantage of others' shortages to make profits as middlemen. This attitude justified the government's takeover of the grain, iron, and salt businesses. Still, the government indirectly promoted commerce by building cities and roads.

Markets were the liveliest places in the cities. Besides stalls selling goods of all kinds, markets offered fortune-tellers and entertainers. The markets also were used for the execution of criminals, to serve as a warning to onlookers.

Government patronage helped maintain the quality of craftsmanship in the cities. By the beginning of the first century C.E. China also had about fifty state-run ironworking factories. Chinese metalworking was the most advanced in the world at the time. In contrast to Roman blacksmiths, who hammered heated iron to make wrought iron tools, the Chinese knew how to liquefy iron and pour it into molds, producing tools with a higher carbon content that were harder and more durable.

Iron was replacing bronze in tools, but bronzeworkers still turned out a host of goods. Bronze was prized for jewelry, mirrors, and dishes. Bronze was also used for minting coins and for precision tools such as carpenters' rules and adjustable wrenches. Han metalsmiths were mass-producing superb crossbows long before the crossbow was dreamed of in Europe.

The bulk of the population in Han times and even into the twentieth century consisted of peasants living in villages of a few hundred households. Because the Han empire, much like the contemporaneous Roman Empire, drew its strength from a large population of free peasants who contributed both taxes and labor services to the state, the government had to try to keep peasants independent and productive.

Economic insecurity was a constant feature of Chinese peasant life. To fight peasant poverty, the government kept land taxes low, provided relief in time of famine, and promoted up-to-date agricultural methods. Still, many hard-pressed peasants were left to choose between migration to areas where new lands could be opened and quasi-servile status as the dependents of a magnate. Throughout the Han period Chinese farmers in search of land to till pushed into frontier areas, expanding Chinese domination at the expense of other ethnic groups, especially in central and south China.

GLOBAL TRADE

Silk

Silk was one of the earliest commodities to stimulate international trade. By 2500 B.C.E. Chinese farmers had domesticated *Bombyx mori*, the Chinese silkworm, and by 1000 B.C.E. they were making fine fabrics with complex designs. Sericulture (silkmaking) is labor-intensive. In order for silkworms to spin their cocoons, they have to be fed chopped leaves from mulberry trees every few hours, day and night, during the month between hatching and spinning. The cocoons consist of a single filament several thousand feet long but a minuscule 0.025 millimeter thick. More than two thousand cocoons are needed to make a pound of silk. After the cocoons are boiled to loosen the natural gum that binds the filament, several strands of filament are twisted together to make yarns.

What made silk the most valued of all textiles was its beauty and versatility. It could be made into sheer gauzes, shiny satins, multicolored brocades, and plush velvets. Korea and Japan not only imported Chinese silk but also began silk production themselves, and silk came to be used in both places in much the way it was used in China—for the clothes of the elite, for temple banners, and as a surface for writing and painting. Central Asia, Persia, India, and Southeast Asia also became producers of silk in distinctive local styles. Lacking suitable climates to produce silk, Mongolia and Tibet remained major importers of Chinese silks into modern times.

What makes the silk trade famous, however, is the trade across Asia to Europe. In Roman times silk carried by caravans across Asia or by ships across the Indian Ocean became a high-status luxury item, said to cost its weight in gold. To satisfy Roman taste, imported silk fabrics were unraveled and rewoven in Syrian workshops. Although the techniques of sericulture gradually spread through Asia, they remained a mystery in the West until the Byzantine emperor Justinian in the sixth century had two monks bring back silkworms from China along with knowledge of how to care for them and process their cocoons.

In medieval times most of the silk imported into Europe came from Persia, the Byzantine Empire, or the Arab world. Venetian merchants handled much of the trade. Some of this fabric still survives in ancient churches, where it was used for vestments and altar clothes and to wrap relics. In the eleventh century Roger I, king of Sicily, captured groups of silk-workers from Athens and Corinth and moved them to Sicily, initiating the production of silk in western Europe. Over the next couple of centuries, Italy became a major silk producer, joined by France in the fifteenth century.

With the development of the sea route between western Europe and China from the sixteenth century on, Europe began importing large quantities of Chinese silk, much of it as silk floss—raw silk—to supply Italian, French, and English silk weavers. In 1750 almost 77.2 tons of raw silk and nearly 20,000 bolts of silk cloth were carried from China to Europe. By this period the aristocracy of Europe regularly wore silk clothes, including silk stockings.

Mechanization of silkmaking began in Europe in the seventeenth century. The Italians developed machines to "throw" the silk—doubling and twisting raw silk into threads suitable for weaving. In the early nineteenth century the introduction of Jacquard looms using punched cards made complex patterns easier to weave.

In the 1920s the silk industry was hit hard by the introduction of synthetic fibers, especially rayon and nylon. In the 1940s women in the United States and Europe switched from silk stockings to the much less expensive nylon stockings.

The Chinese family in Han times was much like the Roman (see page 136) and the Indian (see page 61) families. In all three societies senior males had great authority, marriages were arranged by parents, and brides normally joined their husbands' families. Other practices were more distinctive to China, such as the universality of patrilineal family names, the practice of dividing land equally among the sons in a family, and the great emphasis placed on the virtue of filial piety. The brief *Classic of Filial Piety*, which claimed that filial piety was the root of all virtue, gained wide circulation in Han times, and one of the most commonly used texts for the education of women is Ban Zhao's *Admonitions for Women*, in which she extols the feminine virtues, such as humility. (See "Individuals in Society: The Ban Family," page 166.)

China and Rome

The empires of China and Rome (discussed in Chapter 6) were large, complex states governed by monarchs, bureaucracies, and standing armies. Both reached directly to the people

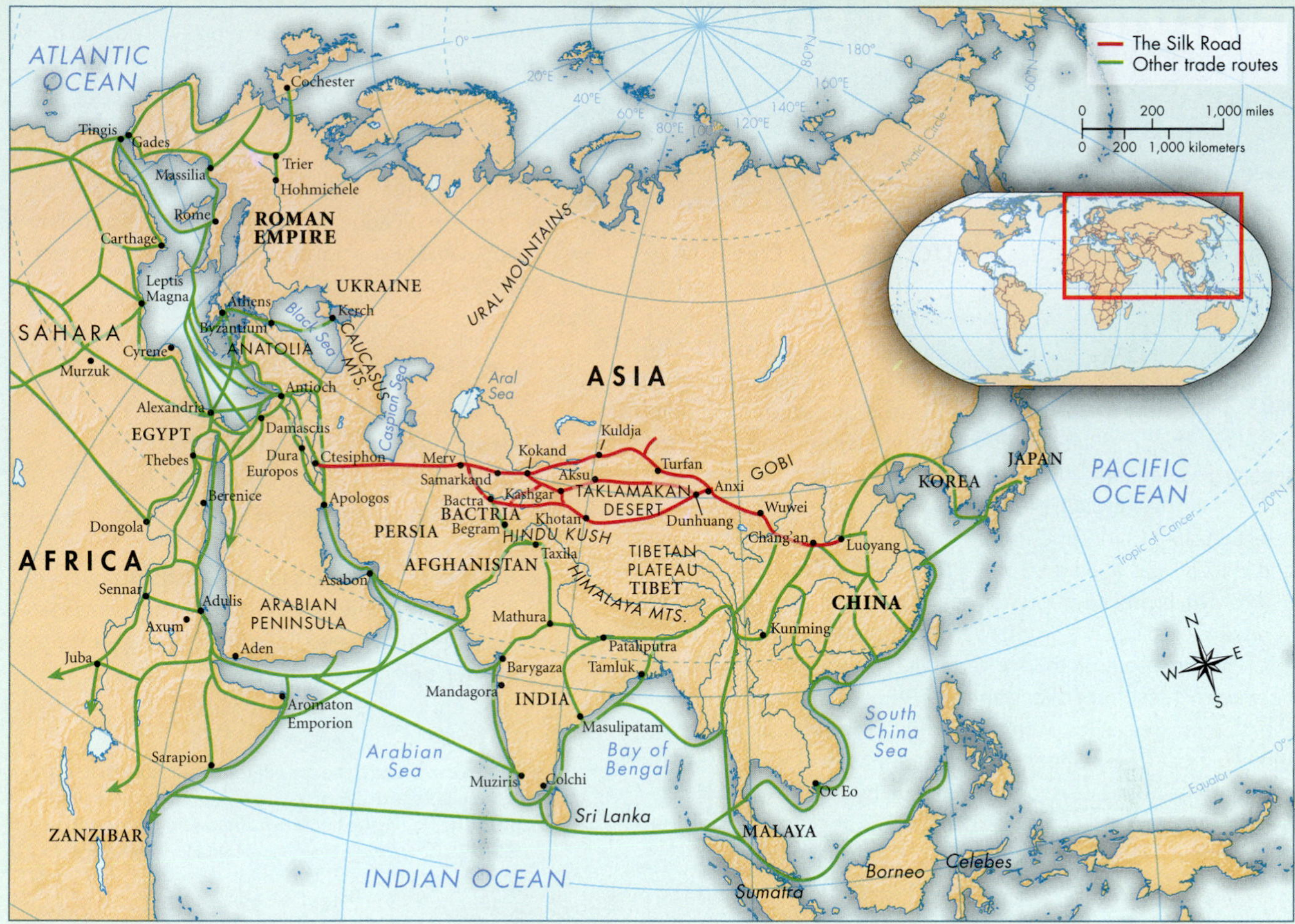

Map 7.2 The Silk Trade in the Seventh Century C.E.

European production of silk almost entirely collapsed. After China re-entered world trade in the early 1980s China rapidly expanded its silk production for export. By 2003 there were more than two thousand silk enterprises in China, employing a million workers and supplying 80 percent of the total world trade in silk.

through taxation and conscription policies, and both invested in infrastructure such as roads and waterworks. The empires faced the similar challenge of having to work hard to keep land from becoming too concentrated in the hands of hard-to-tax wealthy magnates. In both empires people in neighboring areas that came under political domination were attracted to the conquerors' material goods, productive techniques, and other cultural products, resulting in gradual cultural assimilation. China and Rome also had similar frontier problems and tried similar solutions, such as recruiting "barbarian" soldiers and settling soldier-colonists.

Nevertheless, the differences between Rome and Han China are worth as much notice as the similarities. The Roman Empire was linguistically and culturally more diverse than China. In China there was only one written language; people in the Roman Empire still wrote in Greek and several other languages, and people in the eastern Mediterranean could claim more ancient civilizations. China did not have comparable cultural rivals. Politically the dynastic principle was stronger in China than in Rome. Han emperors were never chosen by the army or by any institution comparable to the Roman senate, nor were there republican ideals in China. In contrast to the graduated forms of citizenship in Rome, Han

INDIVIDUALS IN SOCIETY

The Ban Family

BAN BIAO (3–54 C.E.), A SUCCESSFUL OFFICIAL from a family with an envied library, had three highly accomplished children: his twin sons, the general Ban Chao (32–102) and the historian Ban Gu (32–92), and his daughter, Ban Zhao (ca. 45–120). After distinguishing himself as a junior officer in campaigns against the Xiongnu, Ban Chao was sent in 73 C.E. to the Western Regions to see about the possibility of restoring Chinese overlordship there, lost several decades earlier. Ban Chao spent most of the next three decades in Central Asia. Through patient diplomacy and a show of force, he re-established Chinese control over the oasis cities of Central Asia, and in 92 he was appointed protector general of the area.

His twin brother Ban Gu was one of the most accomplished writers of his age, excelling in a distinctive literary form known as the rhapsody (*fu*). His "Rhapsody on the Two Capitals" is in the form of a dialogue between a guest from Chang'an and his host in Luoyang. It describes the palaces, spectacles, scenic spots, local products, and customs of the two great cities. Emperor Zhang (r. 76–88) was fond of literature and often had Ban Gu accompany him on hunts or travels. He also had him edit a record of the court debates he held on issues concerning the Confucian classics.

Ban Biao was working on the *History of the Western Former Han Dynasty*, when he died in 54. Ban Gu took over this project, modeling it on Sima Qian's *Records of the Grand Historian*. He added treatises on law, geography, and bibliography, the last a classified list of books in the imperial library.

Because of his connection to a general out of favor, Ban Gu was sent to prison in 92, where he soon died. At that time the *History of the Former Han Dynasty* was still incomplete. The emperor called on Ban Gu's widowed sister, Ban Zhao, to finish it. She came to the palace, where she not only worked on the history but also became a teacher of the women of the palace. According to the *History of the Later Han*, she taught them the classics, history, astronomy, and mathematics. In 106 an infant succeeded to the throne, and the widow of an earlier emperor became regent. This empress frequently turned to Ban Zhao for advice on government policies.

Ban Zhao credited her own education to her learned father and cultured mother and became an advocate of the education of girls. In her *Admonitions for Women* Ban Zhao objected that many families taught their sons to read but not their daughters. She did not claim girls should have the same education as boys; after all, "just as yin and yang differ, men and women have different characteristics." Women, she wrote, will do well if they cultivate the womanly virtues such as humility. "Humility means yielding and acting respectful, putting others first and oneself last, never mentioning one's own good deeds or denying one's own faults, enduring insults and bearing with mistreatment, all with due trepidation."* In subsequent centuries Ban Zhao's *Admonitions* became one of the most commonly used texts for the education of Chinese girls.

*Patricia Buckley Ebrey, ed., *Chinese Civilization: A Sourcebook*, rev. ed. (New York: Free Press, 1993), p. 75.

QUESTIONS FOR ANALYSIS

1. What inferences can you draw from the fact that a leading general had a brother who was a literary man?
2. What does Ban Zhao's life tell us about women in her society? How do you reconcile her personal accomplishments with the advice she gave for women's education?

Ban Zhao continued to be considered the ideal woman teacher into the eighteenth century, when this imaginary portrait depicted her taking up her brush among women and children. (National Palace Museum, Taipei, Taiwan © Cultural Relics Press)

China drew no distinctions between original and added territories. The social and economic structures also differed in the two empires. Slavery was much more important in Rome than in China, and merchants were more favored. Over time these differences put Chinese and Roman social and political development on different trajectories.

The Fall of the Han and the Age of Division

In the second century C.E. the Han government suffered a series of blows. A succession of child emperors required regents to rule in their place until they reached maturity, allowing the families of empresses to dominate the court. Emperors, once grown, turned to **eunuchs** (castrated palace servants) for help in ousting the empresses' families, only to find that the eunuchs were just as difficult to control. Then in 184 a millenarian religious sect rose in massive revolt. The armies raised to suppress the rebels soon took to fighting among themselves. After years of fighting, a stalemate was reached, with three warlords each controlling distinct territories in the north, the southeast, and the southwest. In 220 one of them forced the last of the Han emperors to abdicate, formally ending the Han Dynasty.

eunuchs Castrated males who played an important role as palace servants.

The period after the fall of the Han Dynasty is often referred to as the **Age of Division** (220–589). A brief reunification from 280 to 316 came to an end when non-Chinese who had been settling in north China since Han times seized the opportunity afforded by the political turmoil to take power. For the next two and a half centuries north China was ruled by one or more non-Chinese dynasties (the Northern Dynasties), and the south was ruled by a sequence of four short-lived Chinese dynasties (the Southern Dynasties) centered in the area of the present-day city of Nanjing.

Age of Division The period after the fall of the Han Dynasty, when China was politically divided.

In the south a hereditary aristocracy entrenched itself in the higher reaches of officialdom. These families intermarried only with families of equivalent pedigree and compiled lists and genealogies of the most eminent families. In this aristocratic culture, the arts of poetry and calligraphy flourished.

Establishing the capital at Nanjing, south of the Yangzi River, had a beneficial effect on the economic development of the south. To pay for an army and to support the imperial court and aristocracy, the government had to expand the area of taxable agricultural land, whether by settling migrants or converting the local inhabitants into taxpayers. The south, with its temperate climate and ample supply of water, offered nearly unlimited possibilities for such development.

The Northern Dynasties are interesting as the first case of alien rule in China. Ethnic tensions flared from time to time. In the late fifth century the Northern Wei (way) Dynasty (386–534) moved the capital from near the Great Wall to the ancient city of Luoyang, adopted Chinese-style clothing, and made Chinese the official language. But the armies remained in the hands of the Xianbei tribesmen. Soldiers who saw themselves as marginalized by the pro-Chinese reforms rebelled in 524. For the next fifty years north China was torn apart by struggles for power.

Quick Review
What challenges did the Qin and Han governments face?

How and why did Buddhism spread throughout East Asia?

In much the same period that Christianity was spreading out of its original home in ancient Israel, Buddhism was spreading beyond India. Buddhism came to Central, East, and Southeast Asia with merchants and missionaries along the overland Silk Road, by sea from India and Sri Lanka, and also through Tibet. Like Christianity, Buddhism was shaped by its contact with cultures in the different areas into which it spread, leading to several distinct forms.

Buddhism's Path Through Central Asia

Central Asia is a loose term used to refer to the vast area between the ancient civilizations of Persia, India, and China. Through most of recorded history, the region was ethnically and culturally diverse; it was home to urban centers, especially at the oases along the Silk Road, and to animal herders in the mountains and grasslands.

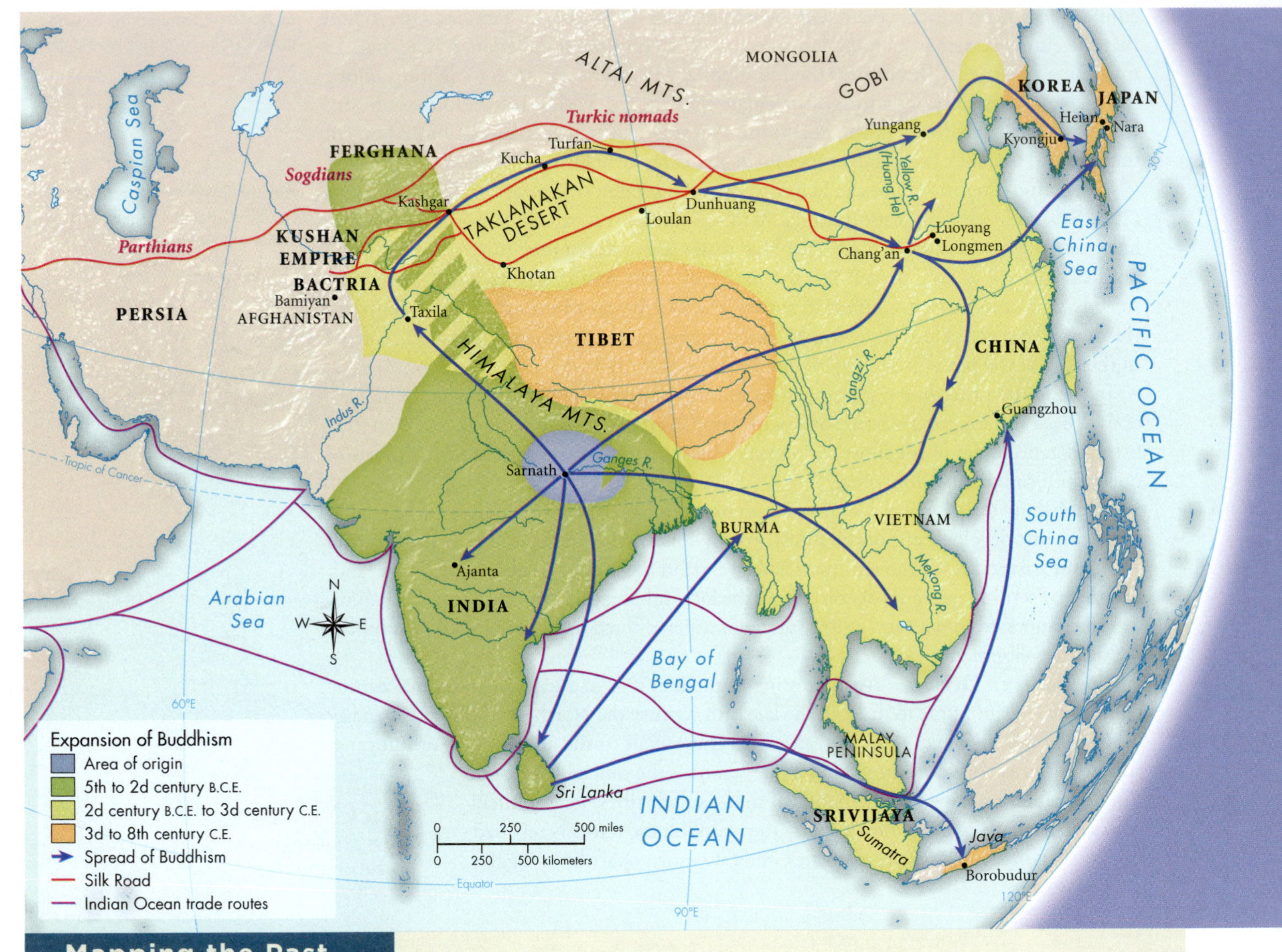

Mapping the Past

Map 7.3 The Spread of Buddhism, ca. 500 B.C.E.–800 C.E.

Buddhism spread throughout India in Ashoka's time and beyond India in later centuries. The different forms of Buddhism found in Asia today reflect this history. The Mahayana Buddhism of Japan came via Central Asia, China, and Korea, with a secondary later route through Tibet. The Theravada Buddhism of Southeast Asia came directly from India and indirectly through Sri Lanka.

ANALYZING THE MAP Trace the routes of the spread of Buddhism by time period. How fast did Buddhism spread?

CONNECTIONS Why do you think Buddhism spread more to the east of India than to the west?

Under Ashoka in India (see pages 72–73) Buddhism began to spread to Central Asia. This continued under the Kushan empire (ca. 50–250 C.E.), especially under the greatest Kushan king Kanishka I (ca. 100 C.E). In this region, where the influence of Greek art was strong, artists began to depict the Buddha in human form. Over the next several centuries most of the city-states of Central Asia became centers of Buddhism (Map 7.3).

The form of Buddhism that spread from Central Asia to China, Japan, and Korea was called Mahayana, which means "Great Vehicle" (see page 69), reflecting the claims of its adherents to a more inclusive form of the religion. Influenced by the Iranian religions then prevalent in Central Asia, Buddhism became more devotional. The Buddha came to be treated as a god, the head of an expanding pantheon of other Buddhas and bodhisattvas (Buddhas-to-be). With the growth of this pantheon, Buddhism became as much a religion for laypeople as for monks and nuns.

The Appeal and Impact of Buddhism in China

Why did Buddhism find so many adherents in China during the three centuries after the fall of the Han Dynasty in 220? In the unstable political environment, many people were open to new ideas. To Chinese scholars the Buddhist concepts of the reincarnation of souls, karma, and nirvana posed a stimulating intellectual challenge. To rulers the Buddhist religion offered a source of magical power and a political tool to unite Chinese and non-Chinese. In a rough and tumultuous age Buddhism's emphasis on kindness, charity, and eternal bliss was deeply comforting. As in India, Buddhism posed no threat to the social order, and the elite who were drawn to Buddhism encouraged its spread to people of all classes.

The monastic establishment grew rapidly in China. Like their Christian counterparts in medieval Europe, Buddhist monasteries played an active role in social, economic, and political life. Given the importance of family lines in China, becoming a monk was a major decision, since a man had to give up his surname and take a vow of celibacy, thus cutting himself off from the ancestral cult. Those not ready to become monks or nuns could pursue Buddhist goals as pious laypeople by performing devotional acts and making contributions to monasteries. Among the most generous patrons were rulers in both the north and south.

In China women turned to Buddhism as readily as men. Although birth as a female was considered lower than birth as a male, it was also viewed as temporary, and women were encouraged to pursue salvation on

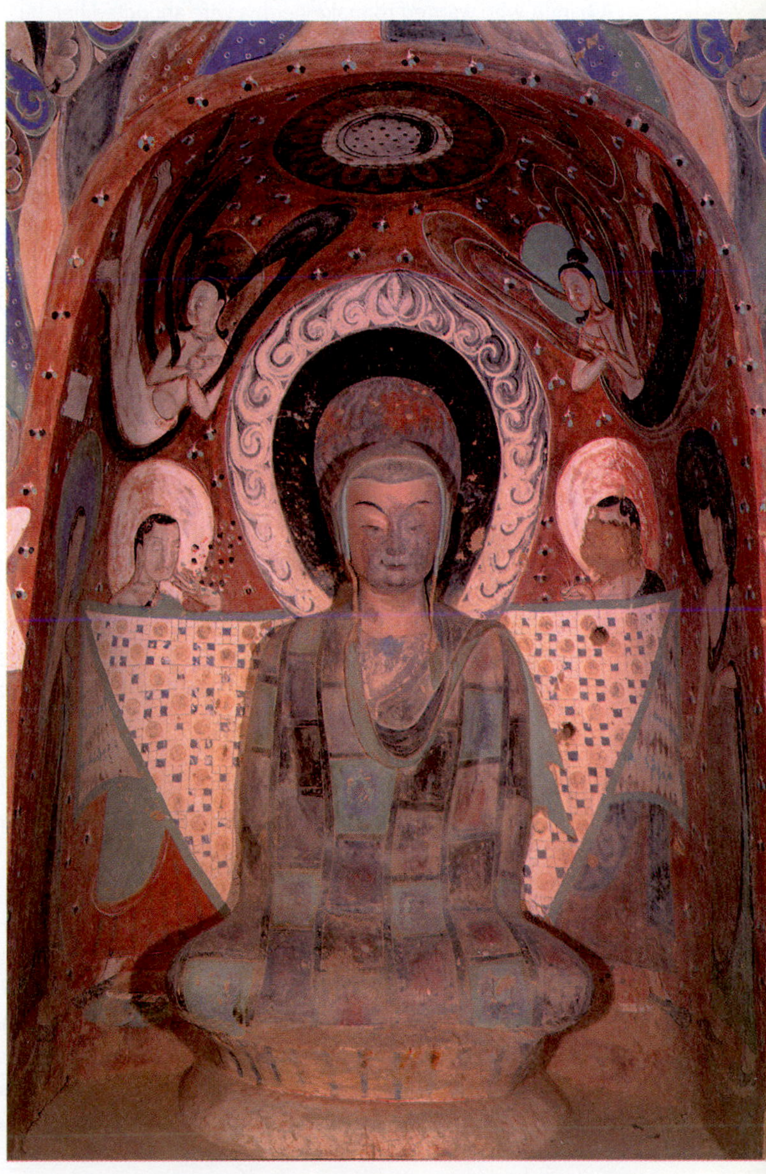

Meditating Monk This monk, wearing the traditional patchwork robe, sits in the crossed-legged meditation position. His small niche is to the left of the main image of the Buddha in cave 285 at Dunhuang, a cave completed in 539 under the patronage of a prince of the Northern Wei imperial house who was then the local governor. (Dunhuang Academy © Cultural Relics Press)

LISTENING TO THE PAST

Sixth-Century Biographies of Buddhist Nuns

Women drawn to Buddhism could leave secular life to become nuns. Most nuns lived with other nuns in convents, but they could also work to spread Buddhist teachings outside the cloister. The first collection of biographies of eminent nuns in China was written in 516. Among the sixty-five nuns whose lives it recounted are these three.

Kang Minggan

" Minggan's secular surname was Zhu, and her family was from Kaoping. For generations the family had venerated the [Buddhist] teachings known as the Great Vehicle.

A bandit who wanted to make her his wife abducted her, but, even though she suffered increasing torment, she vowed not to give in to him. She was forced to serve as a shepherdess far from her native home. Ten years went by and her longing for her home and family grew more and more intense, but there seemed to be no way back. During all this she kept her mind fixed on the Three Treasures, and she herself wished to become a nun.

One day she happened to meet a Buddhist monk, and she asked him to bestow on her the five fundamental precepts [of a Buddhist householder]. He granted her request and also presented her with a copy of the Bodhisattva Guanshiyin Scripture, which she then practiced chanting day and night without pause.

Deciding to return home to build a five-story pagoda, she fled to the east in great anxiety and distress. At first she did not know the road but kept traveling both day and night. When crossing over a mountain she saw a tiger lying only a few steps away from her. After momentary terror she composed her mind, and her hopes were more than met, for the tiger led the way for her, and, after the days had grown into weeks, she finally arrived in her home territory of Qing Province. As she was about to enter the village, the tiger disappeared, but at that moment, having arrived in the province, Minggan was again abducted, this time by Ming Bolian. When word reached her family, her husband and son ransomed her, but the family did not let her carry out her wishes [to enter the life of a Buddhist nun]. Only after three years of cultivating stringent religious practices was she able to follow her intention. As a nun, she especially concentrated on the cultivation of meditation, and she kept all the regulations of a monastic life without any transgressions. If she happened to commit a minor fault, she would confess it several mornings in a row, ceasing only after she received a sign or a good omen. Sometimes as a good omen she saw flowers rain down from the sky or she heard a voice in the sky or she saw a Buddha image or she had auspicious dreams.

As Minggan approached old age, her moral cultivation was even more strict and lofty. All the men and women north of the Yangtze River honored her as their spiritual teacher in whom they could take refuge.

In the spring of 348 of the Jin dynasty, she, together with Huichan and others — ten in all — traveled south, crossed the Yangtze River, and went to see the minister of public works, He Chong, in the capital of the Eastern Jin dynasty. As soon as he met them, he showed them great respect. Because at that time there were no convents in the capital region He Chong converted one of his private residences into a convent for them.

He asked Minggan, "What should the convent be named?"

She replied, "In the great realm of the Jin dynasty all the four Buddhist assemblies of monks, nuns, and male and female householders are now established for the first time. Furthermore, that which you as donor have established will bestow blessings and merit. Therefore, let us call the convent 'Establishing Blessings Convent.'" He Chong agreed to her suggestion. Not long afterward Minggan took sick and died. "

Daoqiong

" Daoqiong's secular surname was Jiang. Her family was from Danyang. When she was a little more than ten years old, she was already well educated in the classics and history, and after her full admission to the monastic assembly she became learned in the Buddhist writings as well and also diligently cultivated a life of asceticism. In the Taiyuan reign period [376–396] of the Eastern Jin dynasty, the empress admired her exalted conduct, and, whenever she wished to gain merit by giving gifts or by listening to religious exhortations, she most often depended on the convent where Daoqiong lived for such opportunities. Ladies of noble family vied with one another to associate with Daoqiong.

terms nearly equal to men. Joining a nunnery became an alternative for a woman who did not want to marry or did not want to stay with her husband's family in widowhood. (See "Listening to the Past: Sixth-Century Biographies of Buddhist Nuns," above.) Later, the only woman ruler of China, Empress Wu, invoked Buddhist principles to justify her role (see page 173), which reveals how significant a break with Confucianism Buddhism was for women.

In 431 she had many Buddhist images made and placed them everywhere: in Pengcheng Monastery, two gold Buddha images with a curtained dais and all accessories; in Pottery Office Monastery, a processional image of Maitreya, the future Buddha, with a jeweled umbrella and pendants; in Southern Establishing Joy Monastery, two gold images with various articles, banners, and canopies. In Establishing Blessings Convent, she had an image of the reclining Buddha made, as well as a hall to house it. She also had a processional image of the bodhisattva, Puxian [or Samantabhadra], made. Of all these items, there was none that was not extremely beautiful. Again, in 438, Daoqiong commissioned a gold Amitayus [or Infinite Life] Buddha, and in the fourth month and tenth day of that same year a golden light shone forth from the mark between the eyebrows of the image and filled the entire convent. The news of this event spread among religious and worldly alike, and all came to pay honor, and, gazing at the unearthly brilliance, there was none who was not filled with great happiness. Further, using the materials bequeathed to her by the Yuan empress consort, she extended the convent to the south to build another meditation hall. ”

In 910 a Buddhist nun of the Universal Light convent named Yanhui commissioned a painting of Guanyin and had her own portrait painted in the corner to show her devotion to the bodhisattva. Like other nuns, she had had her head shaved. (Courtesy of the Trustees of the British Museum)

Daozong

“ Daozong, whose family origins are unknown, lived in Three-Story Convent in Jiangling. As a child she had no intention of setting herself apart; as an adult she did not consider associating with others a defilement. She merely followed a course along the boundary between the wise and the foolish, and, although outwardly she seemed muddled, yet within she traversed hidden profundities.

On the full-moon night of the fifteenth day of the third month, in 463 . . . , Daozong, as an offering to the Buddha, purified herself in a fire fed by oil. Even though she was engulfed by flames up to her forehead, and her eyes and ears were nearly consumed, her chanting of the scriptures did not falter. Monastics and householders sighed in wonder; the demonic and upright were alike startled. When the country heard this news, everyone aspired to attain enlightenment. The appointed court scholar . . . , Liu Qiu, especially revered her and composed a Buddhist-style poetic verse to praise her. ”

Source: Kathryn Ann Tsai, trans., *Lives of the Nuns: Biographies of Chinese Buddhist Nuns from the Fourth to Sixth Centuries.*

QUESTIONS FOR ANALYSIS

1. Why were the lives of these three particular nuns considered worth recording? What was admirable or inspiring about their examples?
2. What do the nuns' spiritual journeys reveal about the virtues associated with Buddhist monastic life?
3. Do you see a gender element in these accounts? Were the traits that made a nun admirable also appropriate for monks?

Buddhism had an enormous impact on the visual arts in China, especially sculpture and painting. Before Buddhism, the Chinese had not set up statues of gods in temples, but now they decorated temples with a profusion of images. Inspired by the cave-temples of India and Central Asia, in China, too, caves were carved into rock faces to make temples.

Not everyone was won over by Buddhist teachings. Critics of Buddhism labeled it immoral, unsuited to China, and a threat to the state since monastery land was not taxed and

Quick Review
What explains the appeal of Buddhism to East Asians across the social and economic spectrum?

monks did not perform labor service. Twice in the north orders were issued to close monasteries and force monks and nuns to return to lay life, but these suppressions did not last long. No attempt was made to suppress belief in Buddhism, and the religion continued to thrive in the subsequent Sui and Tang periods.

What were the lasting accomplishments of the Sui and Tang Dynasties?

Political division was finally overcome when the Sui Dynasty conquered its rivals to reunify China in 581. Although the dynasty lasted only thirty-seven years, it left a lasting legacy in the form of political reform, the construction of roads and canals, and the institution of merit-based exams for the appointment of officials. The Tang Dynasty that followed would last for centuries and would build upon the Sui's accomplishments to create an era of impressive cultural creativity and political power.

The Sui Dynasty, 581–618

In the 570s and 580s, the long period of division in China was brought to an end under the leadership of the Sui (sway) Dynasty. Yang Jian, who both founded the Sui Dynasty and oversaw the reunification of China, was from a Chinese family that had intermarried with the non-Chinese elite of the north. In addition to conquering the south, the Sui reasserted Chinese control over northern Vietnam and campaigned into Korea and against the new force on the steppe, the Turks. The Sui strengthened central control of the government by curtailing the power of local officials to appoint their own subordinates and by instituting in 605 C.E. competitive written examinations for the selection of officials, a practice that would come to dominate the lives of educated men in later centuries.

Grand Canal A canal, built during the Sui Dynasty, that connected the Yellow and Yangzi Rivers, notable for strengthening China's internal cohesion and economic development.

The crowning achievement of the Sui Dynasty was the construction of the **Grand Canal**, which connected the Yellow and Yangzi River regions. The canal facilitated the shipping of tax grain from the prosperous Yangzi Valley to the centers of political and military power in north China. Henceforth the rice-growing Yangzi Valley and south China played an ever more influential role in the country's economic and political life, strengthening China's internal cohesion and facilitating maritime trade with Southeast Asia, India, and areas farther west.

Tang China, ca. 750 C.E.

Despite these accomplishments, the Sui Dynasty lasted for only two reigns. The ambitious projects of the two Sui emperors led to exhaustion and unrest, and in the ensuing warfare Li Yuan, a Chinese from the same northwest aristocratic circles as the founder of the Sui, seized the throne.

The Tang Dynasty, 618–907

The dynasty founded by Li Yuan, the Tang, was one of the high points of traditional Chinese civilization. Especially during this dynasty's first century, its capital, Chang'an, was the cultural center of East Asia. This position of strength gave the Chinese the confidence to be open to learning from the outside world, leading to a more cosmopolitan culture than in any other period before the twentieth century.

The first two Tang rulers, Gaozu (r. 618–626) and Taizong (r. 626–649), were able monarchs. Adding auxiliary troops composed of Turks, Tanguts, Khitans, and other non-Chinese led by their own chieftains to their armies, they campaigned into Korea, Vietnam, and Central Asia. In 630 the Chinese turned against their former allies, the Turks, gaining territory from them and winning for Taizong the title of Great Khan, so that for a short period he was simultaneously head of both the Chinese and the Turkish empires.

In the civil sphere Tang accomplishments far outstripped anything known in Europe until the growth of national states in the seventeenth century. Tang emperors subdivided the administration of the empire into departments. They built on the Sui precedent of using written examinations to select officials. Candidates had to master the Confucian classics and the rules of poetry, and they had to be able to analyze practical administrative and political matters. Government schools were founded to prepare the sons of officials and other young men for service as officials.

The mid-Tang Dynasty saw two women—Empress Wu and Consort Yang Guifei—rise to positions of great political power. Empress Wu was the consort of the weak and sickly Emperor Gaozong. After Gaozong suffered a stroke in 660, she took full charge. She continued to rule after Gaozong's death, summarily deposing her own two sons and dealing harshly with all opponents. In 690 she proclaimed herself emperor, the only woman who took that title in Chinese history. Although despised by later Chinese historians as an evil usurper, Empress Wu was an effective leader. It was not until she was over eighty that members of the court were able to force her out in favor of her son.

Her grandson, the emperor Xuanzong (r. 713–756), presided over a brilliant court and patronized leading poets, painters, and calligraphers in his early years. In his later years, however, after he became enamored of his consort Yang Guifei, he did not want to be bothered by the details of government. The emperor allowed Yang to place friends and relatives in important positions in the government. One of her favorites was the general An Lushan, who, after getting into a quarrel with Yang's brother over control of the government, rebelled in 755. Xuanzong had to flee the capital, and the troops that accompanied him forced him to have Yang Guifei executed.

The rebellion of An Lushan was devastating to the Tang Dynasty. Peace was restored only by calling on the Uighurs (WEE-grz), a Turkish people allied with the Tang, who looted the capital after taking it from the rebels. After the rebellion was finally suppressed in 763, the central government had to keep meeting the extortionate demands of the Uighurs. Many military governors came to treat their provinces as hereditary kingdoms and withheld tax returns from the central government. In addition,

Figurine of a Woman Notions of what makes women attractive have changed over the course of Chinese history. Figurines found in Tang tombs like this one show that full-figured women with plump faces were admired in the mid- and late Tang. Emperor Xuanzong's favorite, Yang Guifei, was said to be a plump woman, and the fashion is thought to have spread from the court. (Werner Forman/Art Resource, NY)

eunuchs gained increasing power at court and were able to prevent both the emperors and the Confucian officials from doing much about them.

Tang Culture

The reunification of north and south led to cultural flowering. The Tang capital cities of Chang'an and Luoyang became great metropolises; Chang'an and its suburbs grew to more than 2 million inhabitants (probably making it the largest city in the world at the time). The cities were laid out in rectangular grids and contained a hundred-odd walled "blocks" inside their walls. Like the gates of the city, the gates of each block were locked at night.

In these cosmopolitan cities, knowledge of the outside world was stimulated by the presence of envoys, merchants, and pilgrims from neighboring states. Because of the presence of foreign merchants, many religions were practiced, including Nestorian Christianity, Manichaeism, Zoroastrianism, Judaism, and Islam, although none of them spread into the Chinese population the way Buddhism had a few centuries earlier. Foreign fashions in hair and clothing were often copied, and foreign amusements such as the Persian game of polo found followings among the well-to-do. The introduction of new musical instruments and tunes from India, Iran, and Central Asia brought about a major transformation in Chinese music.

The Tang Dynasty was the great age of Chinese poetry. Skill in composing poetry was tested in the civil service examinations, and educated men had to be able to compose poems at social gatherings. The pain of parting, the joys of nature, and the pleasures of wine and friendship were all common poetic topics.

In Tang times Buddhism fully penetrated Chinese daily life. Stories of Buddhist origin became widely known, and Buddhist festivals became among the most popular holidays. Buddhist monasteries became an important part of everyday life. They ran schools for children. In remote areas they provided lodging for travelers. Merchants entrusted their money and wares to monasteries for safekeeping, in effect transforming the monasteries into banks and warehouses. The wealthy often donated money or land to support temples and monasteries, making monasteries among the largest landlords.

At the intellectual and religious level, Buddhism was developing in distinctly Chinese directions. Two schools that thrived were Pure Land and Chan. **Pure Land** appealed to laypeople because its simple act of calling on the Buddha Amitabha and his chief helper, the compassionate bodhisattva Guanyin, could lead to rebirth in Amitabha's paradise, the Pure Land. Among the educated elite the **Chan** school (known in Japan as Zen) also gained popularity. Chan teachings rejected the authority of the scriptures and claimed the superiority of mind-to-mind transmission of Buddhist truths. The "northern" Chan tradition emphasized meditation and monastic discipline. The "southern" tradition was even more iconoclastic, holding that enlightenment could be achieved suddenly through insight into one's own true nature, even without prolonged meditation.

Pure Land A school of Buddhism that taught that by calling on the Buddha Amitabha and his chief helper, one could achieve rebirth in Amitabha's Pure Land paradise.

Chan A school of Buddhism (known in Japan as Zen) that rejected the authority of the sutras and claimed the superiority of mind-to-mind transmission of Buddhist truths.

Opposition to Buddhism re-emerged in the late Tang period. In addition to concerns about the fiscal impact of removing so much land from the tax rolls and so many men from the labor service force, there were concerns about Buddhism's foreign origins. As China's international position weakened, xenophobia surfaced. During the persecution of 845, more than 4,600 monasteries and 40,000 temples and shrines were destroyed, and more than 260,000 Buddhist monks and nuns were forced to return to secular life. Although this ban was lifted after a few years, the monastic establishment never fully recovered. Buddhism retained a strong hold among laypeople, and basic Buddhist ideas like karma and reincarnation had become fully incorporated into everyday Chinese thinking. But Buddhism was never again as central to Chinese life.

Quick Review
How did the Sui and Tang build on the accomplishments of the Qin and Han?

How were elements of Chinese culture adapted throughout East Asia?

During the millennium from 200 B.C.E. to 800 C.E. China exerted a powerful influence on its immediate neighbors, who began forming states of their own. By Tang times China was surrounded by independent states in Korea, Manchuria, Tibet, the area that is now Yunnan province, Vietnam, and Japan. All of these states were much smaller than China in area and population, making China by far the dominant force politically and culturally until the nineteenth century. Nevertheless, each of these separate states developed a strong sense of uniqueness and independent identity.

The earliest information about each of these countries is found in Chinese sources. Han armies brought Chinese culture to Korea and Vietnam, but even in those cases much cultural borrowing was entirely voluntary as the elite, merchants, and craftsmen adopted the techniques, ideas, and practices they found appealing. In Japan much of the process of absorbing elements of Chinese culture was mediated via Korea. In Korea, Japan, and Vietnam the fine arts—painting, architecture, and ceramics in particular—were all strongly influenced by Chinese models. Tibet was as much in the Indian sphere of influence as in the Chinese and thus followed a somewhat different trajectory. Most significantly, it never adopted Chinese characters as its written language, nor was it as influenced by Chinese artistic styles as other areas. Moreover the form of Buddhism that became dominant in Tibet came directly from India, not through Central Asia and China.

In each area, Chinese-style culture was at first adopted by elites, but in time many Chinese products and ideas became incorporated into everyday life. By the eighth century the written Chinese language was used by educated people throughout East Asia. Educated Vietnamese, Koreans, and Japanese could communicate in writing when they could not understand each other's spoken languages. The books that educated people read included the Chinese classics, histories, and poetry, as well as Buddhist sutras translated into Chinese. The great appeal of Buddhism known primarily through Chinese translation was a powerful force promoting cultural borrowing.

Vietnam

Vietnam is today classed with the countries to its west as part of Southeast Asia, but its ties are at least as strong to China, and its climate is much like that of southernmost China—subtropical, with abundant rain and rivers. The Vietnamese first appear in Chinese sources as a people of south China called the Yue, who gradually migrated farther south as the Chinese state expanded. The people of the Red River Valley in northern Vietnam had achieved a relatively advanced level of Bronze Age civilization by the first century B.C.E. Power was held by hereditary tribal chiefs who served as civil, religious, and military leaders, with the king as the most powerful chief.

The collapse of the Qin Dynasty in 206 B.C.E. had an impact on this area because a former Qin general, Zhao Tuo (Trieu Da in Vietnamese), finding himself in the far south, set up his own kingdom of Nam Viet (Nan Yue in Chinese). This kingdom covered much of south China and was ruled by Trieu Da from his capital near the present site of Guangzhou. Its population consisted chiefly of the Viet people. After killing all officials loyal to the Chinese emperor, Trieu Da adopted the customs of the Viet and made himself the ruler of a vast state that extended as far south as modern-day Da Nang.

After almost a hundred years of diplomatic and military duels between the Han Dynasty and Trieu Da and his successors, Nam Viet was conquered in 111 B.C.E. by Chinese armies. Chinese administrators were assigned to replace the local nobility. Chinese political

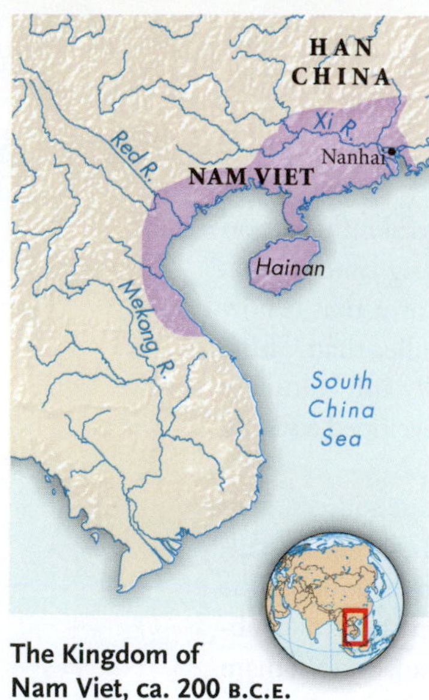

The Kingdom of Nam Viet, ca. 200 B.C.E.

institutions were imposed, and Confucianism was treated as the official ideology. The Chinese language was introduced as the medium of official and literary expression, and Chinese characters were adopted as the written form for the Vietnamese spoken language. The Chinese built roads, waterways, and harbors to facilitate communication within the region and to ensure that they maintained administrative and military control over it. Chinese art, architecture, and music had a powerful impact on their Vietnamese counterparts.

Chinese innovations that were beneficial to the Vietnamese were readily integrated into the indigenous culture, but the local elite were not reconciled to Chinese political domination. The most famous early revolt took place in 39 C.E., when two widows of local aristocrats, the Trung sisters, led an uprising against foreign rule. After overwhelming Chinese strongholds, they declared themselves queens of an independent Vietnamese kingdom. Three years later a powerful army sent by the Han emperor re-established Chinese rule.

China retained at least nominal control over northern Vietnam through the Tang Dynasty, and there were no real borders between China proper and Vietnam during this time. The local elite became culturally dual, serving as brokers between the Chinese governors and the native people.

Korea

Korea is a mountainous peninsula some 600 miles long extending south from Manchuria and Siberia. At its tip it is about 120 miles from Japan (Map 7.4). Archaeological, linguistic, and anthropological evidence indicates that the Korean people share a common ethnic origin with other peoples of North Asia, including those of Manchuria, Siberia, and Japan.

Korea began adopting elements of technology from China in the first millennium B.C.E., including bronze and iron technology. Chinese-Korean contact expanded during the Warring States Period when the state of Yan extended into part of Korea. In about 194 B.C.E. Wiman, an unsuccessful rebel against the Han Dynasty, fled to Korea and set up a state called Choson in what is now northwest Korea and southern Manchuria. In 108 B.C.E. this state was overthrown by the armies of the Han emperor Wu. Four prefectures were established there, and Chinese officials were dispatched to govern them.

The impact of the Chinese prefectures in Korea was similar to that of the contemporaneous Roman colonies in Britain in encouraging the spread of culture and political forms. The prefectures survived not only through the Han Dynasty, but also for nearly a century after the fall of the dynasty, to 313 C.E. The Chinese never controlled the entire Korean peninsula, however. The Han commanderies coexisted with the native Korean kingdom of Koguryŏ, founded in the first century B.C.E. After the Chinese colonies were finally overthrown, the kingdoms of Paekche and Silla emerged farther south on the peninsula in the third and fourth centuries C.E., leading to what is called the Three Kingdoms Period (313–668 C.E.). In all three Korean kingdoms Chinese was used as the language of government and learning. Each of the three kingdoms had hereditary kings, but their power was curbed by the existence of very strong hereditary elites.

Buddhism was officially introduced in Koguryŏ from China in 372 and in the other states not long after. Buddhism connected Korea to societies across Asia. Buddhist monks went back and forth between China and Korea. One even made the journey to India and back, and others traveled on to Japan to aid in the spread of Buddhism there.

When the Sui Dynasty finally reunified China in 589, it tried to establish control of at least a part of Korea, but the Korean kingdoms repeatedly repulsed Chinese attacks. The Tang government then tried allying itself with one state, Silla, to fight the others. Silla and

Tang jointly destroyed Paekche in 660 and Koguryŏ in 668. With its new resources Silla was able to repel Tang efforts to make Korea a colony but agreed to vassal status. The unification under Silla marked the first political unification of Korea.

For the next century Silla embarked on a policy of wholesale borrowing of Chinese culture and institutions. Annual embassies were sent to Chang'an, and large numbers of students studied in China. The Silla government was modeled on the Tang, although modifications were made to accommodate Korea's more aristocratic social structure.

Japan

The heart of Japan is four mountainous islands off the coast of Korea (see Map 7.4). Since the land is rugged and lacking in navigable waterways, the Inland Sea, like the Aegean in Greece, was the easiest avenue of communication in early times. Hence the land bordering the Inland Sea—Kyushu, Shikoku, and Honshu—developed as the political and cultural center of early Japan. Geography also blessed Japan with a moat—the Korea Strait and the Sea of Japan. Consequently, the Japanese for long periods were free to develop their way of life without external interference.

Japan's early development was closely tied to that of the mainland, especially to Korea. Physical anthropologists have discerned several major waves of immigrants into Japan. People of the Jōmon culture, established by about 10,000 B.C.E. after an influx of people from Southeast Asia, practiced hunting and fishing and fashioned clay pots. New arrivals from northeast Asia brought agriculture and a distinct culture called Yayoi (ca. 300 B.C.E.–300 C.E.). During the Han Dynasty objects of Chinese and Korean manufacture found their way into Japan, an indication that people were traveling back and forth as well. In the third century C.E. Chinese histories begin to report on the land called Wa made up of mountainous islands. It had numerous communities, markets, granaries, tax collection, and class distinctions.

Shinto The Way of the Gods; it was the native religion espoused by the Yamato rulers in Japan.

During the fourth through sixth centuries, new waves of migrants from Korea brought the language that evolved into Japanese. They also brought sericulture (silkmaking), bronze swords, crossbows, iron plows, and the Chinese written language. In this period a social order similar to Korea's emerged, dominated by a warrior aristocracy organized into clans. Each clan had its own chieftain, who marshaled clansmen for battle and served as chief priest. Over time the clans fought with each other, and their numbers were gradually reduced through conquest and alliance. By the fifth century the chief of the clan that claimed descent from the sun-goddess, located in the Yamato plain around modern Osaka, had come to occupy the position of Great King—or Queen, as female rulers were not uncommon in this period.

The Yamato rulers used their religion to subordinate the gods of their rivals, much as Hammurabi had used Marduk in Babylonia (see page 37). They established the chief shrine of the sun-goddess near the seacoast, where she could catch the first rays of the rising sun. Cults to other gods also were supported as long as they were viewed as subordinate to the sun-goddess. This native religion was later termed **Shinto**, the Way of the Gods. Buddhism was formally introduced in 538 C.E. and coexisted with the Shinto reverence for the spirits of ancestors and all living things.

Map 7.4 Korea and Japan, ca. 600 Korea and Japan are of similar latitude, but Korea's climate is more continental, with harsher winters. Of Japan's four islands, Kyushu is closest to Korea and mainland Asia.

Picturing the Past

Hōryūji Temple

Japanese Buddhist temples, like those in China and Korea, consisted of several buildings within a walled compound. The buildings of the Hōryūji Temple (built between 670 and 711, after Prince Shōtoku's original temple burned down) include the oldest wooden structures in the world and house some of the best early Buddhist sculpture in Japan. The three main buildings depicted here are the pagoda, housing relics; the main hall, with the temple's principal images; and the lecture hall, for sermons. The five-story pagoda could be seen from far away, much like the steeples of cathedrals in medieval Europe. (Michael Hitoshi/The Image Bank/Getty Images)

ANALYZING THE IMAGE How are the buildings arranged? How large is the compound? Do you see anything interesting about the roofs?

CONNECTIONS Do you think this temple was laid out primarily for the convenience of monks who resided there or more for lay believers coming to worship? How would their needs differ?

In the sixth century Prince Shōtoku (574–622) undertook a sweeping reform of the state designed to strengthen Yamato rule by adopting Chinese-style bureaucratic practices. His "Seventeen Principles" of 604 drew from both Confucian and Buddhist teachings. In it he likened the ruler to Heaven and instructed officials to put their duty to the ruler above the interest of their families. He instituted a ladder of official ranks similar to China's, admonished the nobility to avoid strife and opposition, and urged adherence to Buddhist precepts. Near his seat of government, Prince Shōtoku built the magnificent Hōryūji Temple and staffed it with monks from Korea. He also opened direct relations with China, sending four missions during the brief Sui Dynasty.

Nara Japan's capital and first true city; it was established in 710 and modeled on the Tang capital of Chang'an.

State-building efforts continued through the seventh century and culminated in the establishment in 710 of Japan's first long-term true city, the capital at **Nara**, north of modern Osaka. Nara, which was modeled on the Tang capital of Chang'an, gave its name to an era that lasted until 794 and that was characterized by the avid importation of Chinese ideas and methods. As Buddhism developed a stronghold in Japan, it inspired many trips to China to acquire sources and study at Chinese monasteries. Chinese and Korean craftsmen were often brought back to Japan, especially to help with the decoration of the many Buddhist temples then under construction. Musical instruments and tunes were imported as well, many originally from Central Asia. Chinese practices were instituted, such as the compilation of histories and law codes, the creation of provinces, and the appointment of governors to collect taxes from them. By 750 some seven thousand men staffed the central government.

Increased contact with the mainland had unwanted effects as well. In contrast to China and Korea, both part of the Eurasian landmass, Japan had been relatively isolated from many deadly diseases, so when diseases arrived with travelers, people did not have immunity. The great smallpox epidemic of 735–737 is thought to have reduced the population of about 5 million by 30 percent.

The Buddhist monasteries that ringed Nara were both religious centers and wealthy landlords, and the monks were active in the political life of the capital. Copying the policy of the Tang Dynasty in China, the government ordered every province to establish a Buddhist temple with twenty monks and ten nuns to chant sutras and perform other ceremonies on behalf of the emperor and the state. When an emperor abdicated in 749 in favor of his daughter, he became a Buddhist priest-monk, a practice many of his successors would later follow.

Quick Review
Which elements of Chinese culture were most appealing to its neighbors and why?

Connections

EAST ASIA was transformed in the years between the Qin unification in 221 B.C.E. and the end of the eighth century. The Han Dynasty and four centuries later the Tang Dynasty had proved that a centralized, bureaucratic monarchy could bring peace and prosperity to populations of 50 million or more spread across China proper. By 800 C.E. neighboring societies along China's borders, from Korea and Japan on the east to the Uighurs and Tibetans to the west, had followed China's lead, forming states and building cities. Buddhism had transformed the lives of all of these societies, bringing new ways of thinking about life and death and new ways of pursuing spiritual goals.

In the same centuries that Buddhism was adapting to and simultaneously transforming the culture of much of eastern Eurasia, comparable processes were at work in western Eurasia, where Christianity continued to spread, and in India where Brahmanism evolved into Hinduism. The spread of these religions was aided by increased contact between different cultures, facilitated in Eurasia by the merchants traveling the Silk Road or sailing the Indian Ocean. Where contact between cultures wasn't as extensive, as in Africa (discussed in Chapter 10), religious beliefs were more localized. The collapse of the Roman Empire in the west during this period was not unlike the collapse of the Han Dynasty, but in Europe the empire was never put back together at the level that it was in China, where the Tang Dynasty by many measures was more splendid than the Han. The story of these centuries in western Eurasia are taken up in the next two chapters, which trace the rise of Christianity and Islam and the movement of peoples throughout Europe and Asia. Before returning to the story of East Asia after 800 in Chapter 13, we will also examine the empires in Africa (Chapter 10) and the Americas (Chapter 11).

- **For a list of suggested readings for this chapter, visit** *bedfordstmartins.com/mckayworldunderstanding*.
- **For primary sources from this period, see** *Sources of World Societies*, Second Edition.
- **For Web sites, images, and documents related to topics in this chapter, see Make History at** *bedfordstmartins.com/mckayworldunderstanding*.

Chapter 7 **Study Guide**

To do these exercises online, go to bedfordstmartins.com/mckayworldunderstanding.

Step 1 GETTING STARTED

Below are basic terms about this period in global history. Can you identify each term below and explain why it matters?

TERMS	WHO (OR WHAT) AND WHEN	WHY IT MATTERS
Great Wall, p. 158		
Confucian classics, p. 161		
Records of the Grand Historian, p. 161		
Silk Road, p. 162		
tributary system, p. 162		
eunuchs, p. 167		
Age of Division, p. 167		
Grand Canal, p. 172		
Pure Land, p. 174		
Chan, p. 174		
Shinto, p. 177		
Nara, p. 178		

Step 2 MOVING BEYOND THE BASICS

The exercise below requires a more advanced understanding of the chapter material. Compare and contrast the Han and Roman Empires by filling in the chart below with descriptions of the society, economy, and government of the Han and Roman Empires (you may want to review Chapter 6 for this exercise). When you are finished, consider the following questions: What are the most important similarities and differences between the two empires? Based on your comparison of these two empires, what generalizations might you make about the emergence, expansion, and decline of empires?

	SOCIETY	ECONOMY	GOVERNMENT
Han Empire			
Roman Empire			

Step 3

PUTTING IT ALL TOGETHER

Now that you've reviewed key elements of the chapter, take a step back and try to see the big picture. Remember to use specific examples from the chapter in your answers.

IMPERIAL CHINA

- What role did political philosophy play in Chinese imperial government? How did Legalism shape Qin government? How did Confucianism shape Han government?
- What common aspirations and challenges linked the Qin, Han, Sui, and Tang Dynasties?

THE SPREAD OF BUDDHISM

- How did Buddhism change as it spread throughout East Asia? How did the malleability of Buddhism aid its spread?
- What role did monasticism play in the promotion and spread of Buddhism?

CHINA AND ITS NEIGHBORS

- Compare and contrast the adoption of Chinese culture in Korea, Vietnam, and Japan. How would you explain the similarities and differences you note?
- What role did Chinese military expansion play in the spread of Chinese culture? What role did commerce and trade play?

LOOKING BACK, LOOKING AHEAD

- Compare and contrast China under the Han and Tang with China under the Shang and Zhou. How did unification during the later period differ from unification during the earlier period?
- What role did Buddhism play in facilitating the emergence of shared culture in East Asia? In your opinion, does Christianity continue to play a similar role in contemporary Western societies? Why or why not?

In Yo ... nagine that you must explain Chapter 7 to someone who hasn't read it. What ... t points to include and why?

8

Continuity and Change in Europe and Western Asia

200–850

From the third century onward the Western Roman Empire slowly disintegrated. The last Roman emperor in the West, Romulus Augustus, was deposed by the Ostrogothic chieftain Odoacer (OH-duh-way-suhr) in 476, but much of the empire had already come under barbarian rule well before this. Scholars have long seen this era as one of the great turning points in Western history, but during the last several decades focus has shifted to continuities as well as changes. What is now usually termed "late antiquity" has been recognized as a period of creativity and adaptation in Europe and western Asia, not simply of decline and fall.

The two main agents of continuity were the Eastern Roman (or Byzantine) Empire and the Christian Church. The Byzantine Empire lasted until 1453, a thousand years longer than the Western Roman Empire. It preserved and transmitted much of Greco-Roman law, philosophy, and institutions. Missionaries and church officials spread Christianity within and far beyond the borders of what had been the Roman Empire, transforming a small sect into the most important and wealthiest institution in Europe. The main agent of change in late antiquity was the migration of barbarian groups throughout much of Europe and western Asia. They brought different social, political, and economic structures with them, but as they encountered Roman and Byzantine culture and became Christian, their own ways of doing things were also transformed.

French Reliquary of Sainte Foy Preachers who spread Christianity often told stories of heroic saints and martyrs, and placed their remains in reliquaries for people to venerate. This ninth-century reliquary contains the bones of Sainte Foy, a woman thought to have been martyred centuries earlier. (Erich Lessing/Art Resource, NY)

Chapter Preview

- How did the Byzantine Empire preserve the Greco-Roman legacy?
- How and why did Christian institutions change in late antiquity?
- How did Christianity spread and develop in late antiquity?
- How did the barbarians affect change in Europe and western Asia?

How did the Byzantine Empire preserve the Greco-Roman legacy?

The emperor Constantine (see page 151) had tried to maintain the unity of the Roman Empire, but during the fifth and sixth centuries the western and eastern halves drifted apart. Justinian (r. 527–565) temporarily regained Italy and North Africa from the Ostrogoths, but the costs were high. Justinian's wars exhausted the resources of the state, destroyed Italy's economy, and killed a large part of Italy's population. By the late sixth century, after Justinian's death, a weakened Italy had fallen to another Germanic tribe, the Lombards.

However, the Roman Empire continued in the East. The Eastern Roman or Byzantine Empire (Map 8.1) preserved the institutions and traditions of the old Roman Empire. Byzantium passed the intellectual heritage of Greco-Roman civilization on to later cultures and also developed its own distinctive characteristics.

Sources of Byzantine Strength

Byzantine emperors traced their lines back to Augustus (see page 137). While evolving into a Christian and Greek-speaking state with a multiethnic population centered in the eastern Mediterranean and the Balkans, the Byzantines retained the legal and administrative system of the empire centered at Rome. Thus, the senate that sat in Constantinople carried on the traditions of the old Roman senate. The army that defended the empire was the direct descendant of the old Roman legions.

Map 8.1 **The Byzantine and Sassanid Empires, ca. 600** Both the Byzantine and Sassanid Empires included territory that had earlier been part of the Roman Empire. The Sassanid Persians fought Roman armies before the founding of the Byzantine Empire. Later Byzantium and the Sassanids engaged in a series of wars that weakened both and brought neither lasting territorial acquisitions.

That army was kept very busy, for the Byzantine Empire survived waves of attacks by nomadic groups and rival empires. Why didn't one or a combination of these enemies capture Constantinople, as the Germanic tribes had taken Rome? Strong military leadership was one reason. Another was the city's location and excellent fortifications. Constantinople had the most powerful defenses in the ancient world. One defense was natural: the sea that surrounded Constantinople on three sides. The other defense was the walls that surrounded the city. Within the walls huge cisterns provided water, and vast gardens and grazing areas supplied vegetables and meat. Such strong fortifications and provisions meant that Constantinople's defenders could hold out far longer than a besieging army. In essence, the site chosen for the imperial capital in the fourth century enabled Constantinople to survive longer than it might have otherwise. Because the city survived, the empire, though reduced in territory, endured.

Chapter Chronology

226–651	Sassanid dynasty
325	Nicene Creed produced
340–419	Life of Saint Jerome
354–430	Life of Saint Augustine
380	Theodosius makes Christianity official religion of Roman Empire
ca. 385–461	Life of Saint Patrick
ca. 481–511	Reign of Clovis
527–565	Reign of Justinian
529	Writing of *The Rule of Saint Benedict*
541–543	"Justinian plague"
730–843	Iconoclastic controversy
768–814	Reign of Charlemagne
843	Treaty of Verdun ratified

The Sassanid Empire and Conflicts with Byzantium

For several centuries the Sassanid empire of Persia was Byzantium's most regular foe. In 226 Ardashir I (r. 226–243) founded the Sassanid dynasty, which lasted until 651, when it was overthrown by the Muslims. Ardashir expanded his territory and absorbed the Roman province of Mesopotamia.

Centered in the fertile Tigris-Euphrates Valley, the Sassanid empire depended on agriculture for its economic prosperity; its location also proved well suited for commerce (see Map 8.1). A lucrative caravan trade linked the Sassanid empire to the Silk Road and China (see page 164). Persian metalwork, textiles, and glass were exchanged for Chinese silks, and this trade brought about considerable cultural contact between the Sassanids and the Chinese.

The Sassanid Persians made Zoroastrianism the official state religion, and adherents to religions other than Zoroastrianism, such as Jews and Christians, faced discrimination. Religion and the state were inextricably tied together. The king's power rested on the support of nobles and Zoroastrian priests, who monopolized positions in the court and in the imperial bureaucracy. A highly elaborate court ceremonial and ritual exalted the status of the king and emphasized his semidivine pre-eminence over his subjects. (The Byzantine monarchy, the Roman papacy, and the Muslim caliphate subsequently copied aspects of this Persian ceremonial.)

An expansionist foreign policy brought Persia into frequent conflict with Byzantium, and neither side was able to achieve a clear-cut victory. The long wars financed by higher taxation, on top of the arrival of the plague (see page 187), compounded discontent in both Byzantine and Persian societies. Moreover, internal political instability weakened the Sassanid dynasty, and in the seventh century Persian territories were absorbed into the Islamic caliphate (see pages 213–214).

The Law Code of Justinian

Byzantine emperors organized and preserved Roman law, making a lasting contribution to the medieval and modern worlds. Roman law had developed from many sources—decisions by judges, edicts of emperors, legislation passed by the senate, and opinions of

INDIVIDUALS IN SOCIETY

Theodora of Constantinople

THE MOST POWERFUL WOMAN IN BYZANTINE history was the daughter of a bear trainer for the circus. Theodora (ca. 497–548) grew up in what her contemporaries regarded as an undignified and morally suspect atmosphere, and she worked as a dancer and actress, both dishonorable occupations in the Roman world. Despite her background, she caught the eye of Justinian, who was then a military leader and whose uncle (and adoptive father) Justin had himself risen from obscurity to become the ruler of the Byzantine Empire. Under Justinian's influence, Justin changed the law to allow an actress who had left her disreputable life to marry whom she liked, and Justinian and Theodora married in 525. When Justinian was proclaimed co-emperor with his uncle Justin on April 1, 527, Theodora received the rare title of *augusta*, empress. Thereafter her name was linked with Justinian's in the exercise of imperial power.

Most of our knowledge of Theodora's early life comes from the *Secret History*, a tell-all description of the vices of Justinian and his court written by Procopius around 550. Procopius was the official court historian and thus spent his days praising those same people. In the *Secret History*, however, he portrays Theodora and Justinian as demonic, greedy, and vicious, killing courtiers to steal their property. In scene after detailed scene, Procopius portrays Theodora as particularly evil, sexually insatiable, and cruel, a temptress who used sorcery to attract men, including the hapless Justinian.

In one of his official histories, *The History of the Wars of Justinian*, Procopius presents a very different Theodora. Riots between the supporters of two teams in chariot races had turned deadly, and Justinian wavered in his handling of the perpetrators. Both sides turned against the emperor, besieging the palace while Justinian was inside it. Shouting "*Nika!*" (Victory), the rioters swept through the city, burning and looting. Justinian's counselors urged flight, but, according to Procopius, Theodora rose and declared:

> *For one who has reigned, it is intolerable to be an exile. . . . If you wish, O Emperor, to save yourself, there is no difficulty: we have ample funds and there are the ships. Yet reflect whether, when you have once escaped to a place of security, you will not prefer death to safety. I agree with an old saying that the purple [that is, the color worn only by emperors] is a fair winding sheet [to be buried in].*

Justinian rallied, ordered more than thirty thousand men and women executed, and crushed the revolt.

Other sources describe or suggest Theodora's influence on imperial policy. Justinian passed a number of laws that improved the legal status of women, such as allowing women to own property and to be guardians over their own children. He forbade the exposure of unwanted infants, which happened more often to girls than to boys, since boys were valued more highly. Theodora presided at imperial receptions for Arab sheiks, Persian ambassadors, Germanic princesses from the West, and barbarian chieftains from southern Russia. When Justinian fell ill from the bubonic plague in 542, Theodora took over his duties. Justinian is reputed to have consulted her every day about all aspects of state policy, including religious policy regarding the doctrinal disputes that continued throughout his reign.

Theodora's influence over her husband and her power in the Byzantine state continued until she died, perhaps of cancer, twenty years before Justinian. Her influence may have even continued after death, for Justinian continued to pass reforms favoring women and, at the end of his life, accepted an interpretation of Christian doctrine she had favored. Institutions that she established, including hospitals and churches, continued to be reminders of her charity and piety.

Theodora has been viewed as a symbol of the use of beauty and cleverness to attain position and power, and also as a strong and capable co-ruler who held the empire together during riots, revolts, and deadly epidemics. Just as she fascinated Procopius, she continues to intrigue writers today, who make her a character not only in historical works, but also in science fiction and fantasy.

QUESTIONS FOR ANALYSIS

1. How would you assess the complex legacy of Theodora?
2. Since Procopius's public and private views of the empress are so different, should he be trusted at all as a historical source? Why?

A sixth-century mosaic of the empress Theodora, made of thousands of tiny cubes of glass, shows her with a halo — a symbol of power — and surrounded by officials, priests, and court ladies. (Scala/Art Resource, NY)

Sassanid Cameo In this cameo—a type of jewelry made by carving into a multicolored piece of rock—the Sassanid king Shapur and the Byzantine emperor Valerian fight on horseback, each identifiable by his distinctive clothing and headgear. This does not record an actual hand-to-hand battle, but uses the well-muscled rulers as symbols of their empires. (Erich Lessing/Art Resource, NY)

jurists expert in the theory and practice of law. By the fourth century Roman law had become a huge, bewildering mass. Its sheer bulk made it almost unusable.

To address this problem, the emperor Justinian appointed a committee to sort through and organize the laws, to harmonize the often differing opinions of Roman jurists, and to compile a handbook of civil law. The result was three works, the *Code*, the *Digest*, and the *Institutes*. Together, they are the backbone of the **corpus juris civilis**, the "body of civil law," which is the foundation of law for nearly every modern European nation.

corpus juris civilis The "body of civil law," it is composed of the *Code*, the *Digest*, and the *Institutes*.

Byzantine Intellectual Life

Just as they valued the law, the Byzantines prized education, and because of them many masterpieces of ancient Greek literature survived. Among members of the large reading public, history was a favorite subject.

The most remarkable Byzantine historian was Procopius (ca. 500–ca. 562). Procopius's *Secret History* is a vicious and uproarious attack on Justinian and his wife, the empress Theodora, which continued the wit and venom of earlier Greek and Roman writers. (See "Individuals in Society: Theodora of Constantinople," page 186.)

In mathematics and science the Byzantines discovered little that was new, though they passed Greco-Roman learning on to the Arabs. The best-known Byzantine scientific discovery was an explosive compound known as "Greek fire" made of crude oil mixed with resin and sulfur, which were heated and propelled by a pump through a bronze tube. As the liquid jet left the tube, it was ignited, somewhat like a modern flamethrower.

The Byzantines devoted a great deal of attention to medicine, and their general level of medical competence was far higher than that of western Europeans, for they could read about and use Hellenistic methods. Yet Byzantine physicians could not cope with the terrible disease, often called "the Justinian plague," that swept through the Byzantine Empire and parts of western Europe between 541 and 543. Probably originating in northwestern India and carried to the Mediterranean region by ships, the disease was similar to the bubonic plague. The epidemic had profound political as well as social consequences. It weakened Justinian's military resources, thus hampering his efforts to restore unity to the Mediterranean world. Losses from the plague also further weakened Byzantine and Persian forces that had long been fighting each other, contributing to their inability to offer more than token opposition to Muslim armies (see pages 213–214).

Life in Constantinople

By the tenth century Constantinople was the greatest city in the Christian world: the seat of the imperial court and administration, a large population center, and the pivot of a large volume of international trade. Given that the city was a natural geographical connecting point between East and West, its markets offered goods from many parts of the world. At the end of the eleventh century Constantinople may have been the world's third largest city, with only Córdoba in Spain and Kaifeng in China larger.

In Constantinople, the landed aristocracy always held the dominant social position. By contrast, merchants and craftsmen, even when they acquired considerable wealth, never won social prominence. Social rigidity did not, however, produce political stability. Between the accession of Emperor Heraclius in 610 and the fall of the city to western Crusaders in 1204 (see page 360), four separate dynasties ruled at Constantinople. Imperial government involved such intricate court intrigue, assassination plots, and military revolts that the word *byzantine* is sometimes used in English to mean extremely entangled and complicated politics.

What do we know about private life in Constantinople? The typical household in the city included family members and servants, some of whom were slaves. Artisans lived and worked in their shops, while clerks, civil servants, minor officials, and business people commonly dwelled in multistory buildings perhaps comparable to apartment complexes. Wealthy aristocrats resided in luxurious freestanding mansions.

In the homes of the upper classes, the segregation of women seems to have been the first principle of interior design. As in ancient Athens, private houses contained a *gynaeceum* (jihn-uh-SEE-um), or women's apartment, where women were kept strictly separated from the outside world. The fundamental reason for this segregation was the family's honor. As one Byzantine writer put it: "An unchaste daughter is guilty of harming not only herself but also her parents and relatives. That is why you should keep your daughters under lock and key. . . ."[1]

Marriage was part of a family's strategy for social advancement. Both the immediate family and the larger kinship group participated in the selection of a bride or a groom, choosing a spouse who might enhance the family's wealth or prestige.

Quick Review
What were the Byzantine Empire's most enduring accomplishments?

How and why did Christian institutions change in late antiquity?

As the Western Roman Empire disintegrated, the Christian Church survived and grew, becoming the most important institution in Europe. The church gained strength by taking more authority over religious issues away from the state. Also, the church's western realm, increasingly left to its own devices after the imperial capital moved from Rome to Constantinople, gained more power. Even so, the state continued to intervene in theological disputes. Meanwhile, new Christian orders emphasizing asceticism arose and made important contributions to religious and secular society.

The Evolution of Church Leadership and Orthodoxy

Believers in early Christian communities elected their leaders, but as the centuries passed appointment by existing church leaders or secular rulers became the common practice. During the reign of Diocletian (r. 284–305), the Roman Empire had been divided for administrative purposes into geographical units called **dioceses**, and Christianity adopted this pattern. Each diocese was headed by a bishop.

dioceses Geographic administrative districts of the church, each under the authority of a bishop and centered around a cathedral.

Some bishops brought significant administrative skills to the early Christian Church. Bishop Ambrose of Milan (339–397), for example, had a solid education, was a trained lawyer, and had once been the governor of a province. He was typical of the Roman aristocrats who held high public office, were converted to Christianity, and subsequently became bishops.

Because of his strong influence Ambrose came to be regarded as one of the fathers of the church, and his authority was regarded as second only to the Bible's in later centuries. Ambrose was a strong proponent of the position that the church was supreme in spiritual matters and the state in secular issues, an opinion shared by the church leadership as a whole. Although conflicts between religious and secular leaders were frequent, the church also received support from the emperors. In return the emperors expected the Christian Church's support in maintaining order and unity.

In the fourth century, disputes also arose within the Christian community over theological issues. Some disagreements had to do with the nature of Christ. For example, **Arianism**, which originated with Arius (ca. 250–336), a priest of Alexandria, held that Jesus was created by the will of God the Father and thus was not co-eternal with him or equal to him in power. Arian Christianity attracted many followers, including Greeks, Romans, and especially barbarian migrants to Europe who were converted by Arian Christian missionaries.

Arianism A theological belief, originating with Arius, a priest of Alexandria, that denied that Christ was co-eternal with God the Father.

Emperor Constantine, who legalized Christianity in 312, rejected the Arian interpretation and decided that religious disagreement meant civil disorder. In 325 he summoned a council of church leaders to Nicaea in Asia Minor and presided over it personally. The council produced the Nicene Creed, which defined the orthodox position that Christ is "eternally begotten of the Father" and of the same substance as the Father, an interpretation that is accepted today by the Roman Catholic Church, the Eastern Orthodox churches, and most Protestants. Arius and those who refused to accept the creed were banished, the first case of civil punishment for heresy. This participation of the emperor in a theological dispute within the church paved the way for later emperors to claim that they could do the same. Although Arian Christianity slowly died out among Greeks and Romans, it remained the most common form of Christianity among barbarian groups for centuries.

In 380 Theodosius went even further than Constantine and made Christianity the official religion of the empire. He stripped Roman pagan temples of statues, made the practice of the old Roman state religion a treasonable offense, and persecuted Christians who dissented from orthodox doctrine. Most significantly, he allowed the church to establish its own courts and develop its own body of law,

Sarcophagus of Helena This marble sarcophagus was made for Helena, the mother of Emperor Constantine, at her death. Its detailed carvings show victorious Roman horsemen and barbarian prisoners. Like her son, Helena became a Christian, and she was sent by Constantine on a journey to bring sacred relics from Jerusalem to Constantinople as part of his efforts to promote Christianity in the empire. (Vanni/Art Resource, NY)

called canon law. These courts, not the Roman government, had jurisdiction over the clergy and ecclesiastical disputes. The foundation for later growth in church power had thus been laid.

The Western Church and the Eastern Church

The leader of the church in the West, the bishop of Rome, became more powerful than his counterpart in the Byzantine East for a variety of reasons. The change began in the fourth century with the move of the imperial capital and the emperor from Rome to Constantinople. Because the bishop of Rome no longer had any real competition for leadership in the West, he began to exercise more influence there.

The power of successive bishops of Rome increased as they repeatedly called on the emperors at Constantinople for military support against barbarian invaders. Because the emperors had no troops to spare, they rarely could send such support. The Western Church thus became less dependent on the emperors' power and gradually took over political authority in central Italy, charging taxes, sending troops, and enforcing laws.

The bishops of Rome also stressed their special role within the church. They pointed to words spoken by Jesus to one of his disciples, Peter, and the fact that, according to tradition, Peter had lived in Rome and been its first bishop, to assert a privileged position in the church hierarchy, an idea called the Petrine Doctrine. As successors of Peter, they stated, the bishops of Rome—known as **popes**—should be supreme over other Christian communities. They urged other churches to appeal to Rome for the resolution of disputed issues.

popes Heads of the Roman Catholic Church, who became political as well as religious authorities. The period of a pope's term in office is called a "pontificate."

By contrast, in the East the emperor's jurisdiction over the church was fully acknowledged. As in Rome, there was a head of the church in Constantinople, called the patriarch, but he did not develop the same powers that the pope did in the West because there was never a similar power vacuum into which he needed to step. He and other high church officials were appointed by the emperor. The Eastern emperors looked on religion as a branch of the state. Following the pattern set by Constantine, the emperors summoned councils of bishops and theologians to settle doctrinal disputes. They and the Eastern bishops did not accept Rome's claim to primacy, and gradually the Eastern Christian Church, generally called the **Orthodox Church**, and the Roman Church began to diverge.

Orthodox Church Another name for the Eastern Christian Church, over which emperors continued to have power.

The Iconoclastic Controversy

In the centuries after Constantine the most serious dispute within the Orthodox Church concerned icons—images or representations of God the Father, Jesus, and the saints. Christian teaching held that icons fostered reverence and that Jesus and the saints could most effectively plead a cause to God the Father. (For more about the role of saints, see page 196.) Iconoclasts, those who favored the destruction of icons, argued that people were worshipping the image itself rather than what it signified. This, they claimed, constituted idolatry, a violation of one of the Ten Commandments, a religious and moral code sacred to Christians.

The result of this dispute was a terrible theological conflict, the **iconoclastic controversy**, that split the Byzantine world for a century. In 730 the emperor Leo III (r. 717–741) ordered the destruction of icons. The removal of these images from Byzantine churches provoked a violent reaction: entire provinces revolted, and the empire and Roman papacy severed relations. Since Eastern monasteries were the fiercest defenders of icons, Leo's son Constantine V (r. 741–775) seized their property, executed some of the monks, and forced other monks into the army. Theological disputes and civil disorder over the icons continued intermittently until 843, when the icons were restored.

iconoclastic controversy The conflict over the veneration of religious images in the Byzantine Empire.

The implications of the iconoclastic controversy extended far beyond strictly theological issues. Iconoclasm raised the question of the right of the emperor to intervene in religious disputes—a central problem in the relations between church and state. Iconoclasm antagonized the pope and served to encourage him in his quest for an alliance with the Frankish monarchy (see pages 201–202). This further divided the two parts of Christendom, and in 1054 a theological disagreement led the pope in Rome and the patriarch of Constantinople to excommunicate each other. The outcome was a continuing schism, or split, between the Roman Catholic and the Orthodox Churches.

Christian Monasticism

Like the great East Asian religions of Jainism and Buddhism (see pages 65–69), Christianity began and spread as a city religion. With time, however, some Christians started to feel that a life of asceticism (extreme material sacrifice, including fasting and the renunciation of sex) was a better way to show their devotion to Christ's teachings. Asceticism was—and is—a common part of many religious traditions, either as a temporary practice during especially holy times or as a permanent way of life.

Seeking to separate themselves from their families and normal social life, Christian ascetics withdrew from cities and moved to the Egyptian desert, where they sought God through prayer in caves and shelters in the desert or mountains. These individuals were called "hermits," from the Greek word *eremos*, meaning "desert," or "monks," from the Greek word *monos*, meaning "alone." Gradually, large groups of monks emerged in the deserts of Upper Egypt, creating a style of life known as "monasticism." Many devout women also were attracted to this eremitical type of monasticism, becoming nuns. Although monks and nuns led isolated lives, ordinary people soon recognized them as holy people and sought them as spiritual guides.

Church leaders did not really approve of eremitical life. Hermits sometimes claimed to have mystical experiences—direct communications with God. If hermits could communicate directly with the Lord, what need had they for priests, bishops, and the institutional church? The church hierarchy instead encouraged those who wanted to live ascetic lives of devotion to do so in communities. Consequently, in the fourth, fifth, and sixth centuries many different kinds of communal monasticism developed in Gaul, Italy, Spain, Anglo-Saxon England, and Ireland.

In 529 Benedict of Nursia (ca. 480–547) wrote a brief set of regulations for the monks who had gathered around him at Monte Cassino, between Rome and Naples. Benedict's guide for monastic life, known as *The Rule of Saint Benedict*, slowly replaced all others, and it has influenced all forms of organized religious life in the Roman Church. The guide outlined a monastic life of regularity, discipline, and moderation, with the day spent in prayer, study, and manual labor.

Saint Benedict Holding his *Rule* in his left hand, the seated and hooded patriarch of Western monasticism blesses a monk with his right hand. His monastery, Monte Cassino, is in the background. (Biblioteca Apostolica Vaticana, VAT.LAT.1202)

Why did the Benedictine form of monasticism eventually replace other forms of western monasticism? The monastic life as conceived by Saint Benedict struck a balance between asceticism and activity. It thus provided opportunities for men of entirely different abilities and talents — from mechanics and gardeners to literary scholars. The Benedictine form of religious life also proved congenial to women. Five miles from Monte Cassino at Plombariola, Benedict's twin sister Scholastica (ca. 480–543) adapted *The Rule of Saint Benedict* for her community of nuns.

Another reason for the dominance of Benedictine monasticism was its material success. In the seventh and eighth centuries Benedictine monasteries pushed back forests and wastelands, drained swamps, and experimented with crop rotation, making a significant contribution to the agricultural development of Europe. In the process they earned immense wealth. Monasteries also conducted schools for local young people. Local and royal governments drew on the services of the literate men and able administrators the monasteries produced.

Monasticism in the Greek Orthodox world differed in fundamental ways from the monasticism that evolved in western Europe. First, while *The Rule of Saint Benedict* gradually became the universal guide for all western European monasteries, each monastic house in the Byzantine world developed its own set of rules for organization and behavior. Second, education never became a central feature of the Greek houses. Since bishops and patriarchs of the Greek Church were recruited only from the monasteries, Greek houses did, however, exercise a cultural influence.

Quick Review
How did church-state relations shape the growth and development of both Roman and Orthodox Christianity?

How did Christianity spread and develop in late antiquity?

The growth of Christianity was tied not just to institutions such as the papacy and monasteries, but also to ideas. Initially, Christians rejected Greco-Roman culture. Gradually, however, Christian leaders and thinkers developed ideas that drew on classical influences. At the same time missionaries sponsored by bishops and monasteries spread Christian ideas and institutions far beyond the borders of the Roman and Byzantine Empires.

Christian Beliefs and the Greco-Roman Tradition

By the second century, church leaders began to incorporate elements of Greek and Roman philosophy and learning into Christian teachings (see pages 150–151). They found support for this incorporation in the written texts that circulated among Christians. In the third and fourth centuries these texts were brought together as the New Testament of the Bible, with general agreement about most of what should be included but sharp disputes about some books. Although some of Jesus's sermons as recorded in the Gospels (see page 148) urged followers to avoid worldly attachments, other parts of the Bible advocated acceptance of existing social, economic, and political structures. Christian thinkers built on these, adapting Christian teachings to fit with Roman realities and Roman ideas to fit with Christian aims.

Saint Jerome (340–419) translated the Bible's Old Testament and New Testament from Hebrew and Greek, respectively, into vernacular Latin (a form of Latin common among Christians of the time). Called the "Vulgate," his edition of the Bible served as the official translation until the sixteenth century, and scholars rely on it even today. Saint Jerome

Procession to a New Church In this sixth-century ivory carving, two men in a wagon, accompanied by a procession of people holding candles, carry relics of a saint to a Christian church under construction. New churches often received holy items when they were dedicated, and processions were common ways in which people expressed community devotion. (Cathedral Treasury, Trier. Photo: Ann Muenchow)

believed that Christians should study the best of ancient thought because it would direct their minds to God. He maintained that the best ancient literature should be interpreted in light of the Christian faith.

Christian attitudes toward gender and sexuality provide a good example of the ways early Christians challenged and then adopted the views of their contemporary world, modifying these as they did. In his plan of salvation Jesus considered women the equal of men. He attributed no disreputable qualities to women and did not refer to them as inferior creatures. On the contrary, women were among his earliest and most faithful converts.

Accordingly, women took an active role in the spread of Christianity, preaching, acting as missionaries, being martyred alongside men, and perhaps even baptizing believers. Because early Christians believed that the second coming of Christ was imminent, they devoted their energies to their new spiritual family of co-believers. Also, they often met in people's homes and called one another brother and sister, a metaphorical use of family terms that was new to the Roman Empire. Some women embraced the ideal of virginity and either singly or in monastic communities declared themselves "virgins in the service of Christ." All this made Christianity seem dangerous to many Romans, especially when becoming Christian led some young people to avoid marriage, which was viewed by Romans as the foundation of society and a necessity for maintaining the power of the paterfamilias (see page 136).

Not all Christian teachings represented a radical break from Roman tradition, however. In the first century male church leaders began to place restrictions on female believers. Paul (see page 150) and later writers forbade women to preach, and women were gradually excluded from holding official positions in Christianity other than in women's monasteries. In so limiting the activities of female believers Christianity was following well-established social patterns, just as it modeled its official hierarchy after that of the Roman Empire.

Christian teachings about sexuality also built on and challenged classical models. The church's unfavorable view of sexual activity involved an affirmation of the importance of a spiritual life, but it also incorporated hostility toward the body found in some Hellenistic philosophies. Just as spirit was superior to matter, the thinking went, the mind was superior to the body. Most Christian thinkers also taught that celibacy was the better life and that anything that distracted one's attention from the spiritual world performed an evil function. Most church fathers saw women as just such a distraction and temptation, and in some of their writings women are portrayed as evil. Same-sex relations—which were generally acceptable in the Greco-Roman world, especially if they were between socially unequal individuals—were also evil in the eyes of church fathers.

Saint Augustine

One thinker had an especially strong role in shaping Christian views about sexual activity and many other issues: Saint Augustine of Hippo (354–430), the most influential church father in the West. Augustine was born into an urban family in what is now Algeria in North Africa. His father was a pagan; his mother, Monica, a devout Christian. It was not until adulthood that he converted to his mother's religion, eventually becoming bishop of the city of Hippo Regius. Augustine gained renown as a preacher, a vigorous defender of orthodox Christianity, and the author of more than ninety-three books and treatises.

Augustine's autobiography, *The Confessions*, one of the most influential books in history, challenges Greco-Roman views of human behavior and morality. *The Confessions* describes Augustine's moral struggle, the conflict between his spiritual aspirations and his sensual self. Many Greek and Roman philosophers had taught that knowledge and virtue are the same: a person who knows what is right will do what is right. Augustine rejected this idea, arguing that people do not always act on the basis of rational knowledge. Instead, the basic or dynamic force in any individual is the will. When Adam ate the fruit forbidden by God in the Garden of Eden (Genesis 3:6), he committed the "original sin" and corrupted the will, wrote Augustine. Adam's sin was not simply his own but was passed on to all later humans through sexual intercourse. Augustine viewed sexual desire as the result of the disobedience of Adam and Eve, linking sexuality even more clearly with sin than had earlier church fathers. According to Augustine, because Adam disobeyed God, all human beings have an innate tendency to sin: their will is weak. But Augustine held that God restores the strength of the will through grace, which is transmitted in certain rituals that the church defined as **sacraments**. Augustine's ideas on sin, grace, and redemption became the foundation of all subsequent Western Christian theology, Protestant as well as Catholic.

sacraments Certain rituals of the church believed to act as a conduit of God's grace, such as the Eucharist and baptism.

Missionary Activity

Christ had said that his teaching was for all peoples, and Christians sought to make their faith catholic—that is, worldwide or believed everywhere. The Mediterranean served as the highway over which Christianity spread to the cities of the Byzantine Empire (Map 8.2). From there missionaries took Christian teachings to the countryside, and then to areas beyond the borders of the empire.

Because the religion of a region's chieftain or king determined the religion of the people, missionaries concentrated their initial efforts on these leaders and members of their families. Queens and other female members of the royal family were often the first converts in an area, and they influenced their husbands and brothers.

Tradition identifies the conversion of Ireland with Saint Patrick (ca. 385–461). After a vision urged him to Christianize Ireland, Patrick studied in Gaul and in 432 was consecrated a bishop. He then returned to Ireland, where he converted the Irish tribe by tribe, first baptizing the king.

The Christianization of the English really began in 597, when Pope Gregory I (pontificate 590–604) sent a delegation of monks to England. The conversion of the English had far-reaching consequences because Britain later served as a base for the Christianization

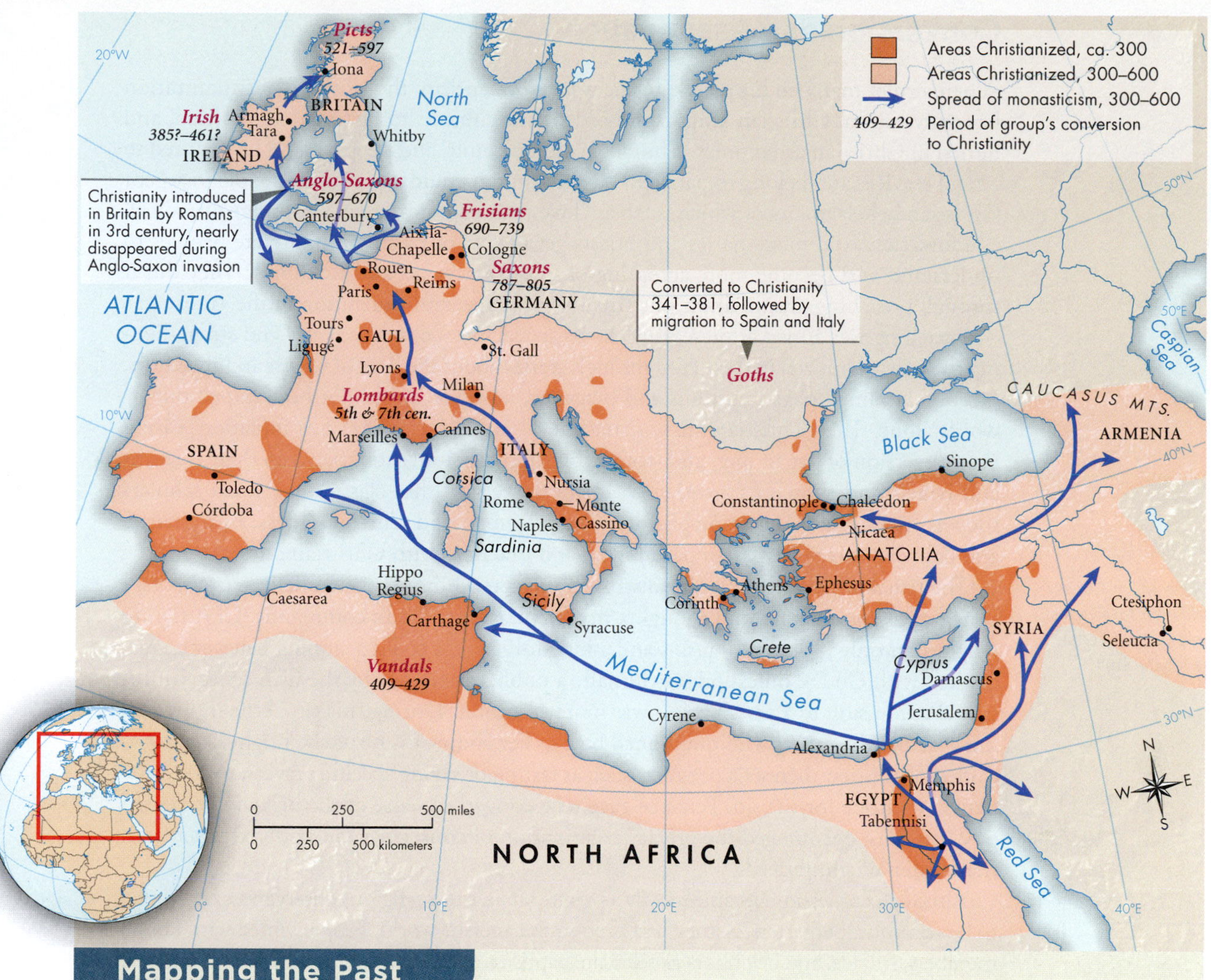

Mapping the Past

Map 8.2 The Spread of Christianity, ca. 300–800

Originating in the area near Jerusalem, Christianity spread throughout the Roman world.

ANALYZING THE MAP Based on the map, how did the roads and sea-lanes of the Roman Empire influence the spread of Christianity?

CONNECTIONS How does the map support the conclusion that Christianity began as an urban religion and then spread into more rural areas?

of Germany and other parts of northern Europe (see Map 8.2). By the tenth century the majority of people living on the European continent and the nearby islands were officially Christian, that is, they had received baptism.

In eastern Europe missionaries traveled far beyond the boundaries of the Byzantine Empire. In 863 the emperor Michael III (r. 842–867) sent the brothers Cyril (826–869) and Methodius (815–885) to preach Christianity in Moravia (an eastern region of the modern Czech Republic). Other missionaries succeeded in converting the Russians in the tenth century. Another Byzantine influence on Russia was the Slavic alphabet invented by Cyril (called the "Cyrillic alphabet"). This made possible the birth of Russian literature, and it is still in use today. Similarly, Byzantine art and architecture became the basis of and inspiration for Russian forms, particularly in the creation of religious icons.

Conversion and Assimilation

When a ruler marched his people to the waters of baptism, the work of Christianization had only begun. Christian kings could order their subjects to be baptized, married, and buried in Christian ceremonies. Churches could be built, and people could be required to attend services and belong to parishes, but the church could not compel people to accept Christian beliefs, many of which, such as "love your enemies," seemed strange or radical.

How, then, did missionaries and priests get masses of pagan and illiterate peoples to understand and become more accepting of Christian ideals and teachings? They did it through preaching, assimilation, the ritual of penance, and veneration of the saints.

Preaching was aimed at presenting the basic teachings of Christianity and strengthening the newly baptized in their faith through stories about the lives of Christ and the saints. Deeply ingrained pagan customs and practices, however, could not be stamped out by words alone. Thus Christian missionaries often pursued a policy of assimilation, easing the conversion of pagan men and women by stressing similarities between their customs and beliefs and those of Christianity. In the same way that classically trained scholars such as Jerome and Augustine blended Greco-Roman and Christian ideas, missionaries and converts mixed barbarian pagan ideas and practices with Christian ones.

penance Ritual in which Christians asked a priest for forgiveness for sins, and the priest set certain actions to atone for the sins.

The ritual of **penance** was also instrumental in teaching Christian beliefs, in this case concerning sins, actions and thoughts that went against God's commands. Christianity taught that only by confessing sins and asking forgiveness could a sinning believer be reconciled with God. Confession was initially a public ritual, but by the fifth century individual confession to a parish priest was more common. During this ritual the individual knelt before the priest, who questioned him or her about sins he or she might have committed. The priest then set a penance, such as fasting or saying specific prayers, to allow the person to atone for the sin. Penance gave new converts a sense of the behavior expected of Christians, encouraged the private examination of conscience, and offered relief from the burden of sinful deeds.

Although confession became mostly a private affair, most religious observances continued to be community matters, as they had been in the ancient world. People joined with family members, friends, and neighbors to celebrate baptisms and funerals, presided over by a priest.

saints People who were venerated for having lived or died in a way that was spiritually heroic or noteworthy.

Veneration of **saints** was another way that Christians formed stronger connections with their religion. Saints were understood to provide protection and assistance to worshippers, and parish churches often housed saints' relics, that is, bones, articles of clothing, or other objects associated with them. The relics served as links between the material world and the spiritual, and miracle stories about saints and their relics were an important part of Christian preaching and writing.

Although the decision to adopt Christianity was often made first by an emperor or king, actual conversion was a local matter, as people came to feel that the parish priest and the saints provided them with benefits in this world and the world to come. Christianity became an important means through which barbarian groups migrating into Europe gained access to at least some of Greco-Roman culture.

Quick Review
How did the expansion of Christianity contribute to changes in Christian beliefs and practices?

How did the barbarians affect change in Europe and western Asia?

The migration of peoples from one area to another has been a continuing feature of world history. One of the most enduring patterns of migration was the movement of peoples west and south from Central Asia and northern Europe beginning in the second century

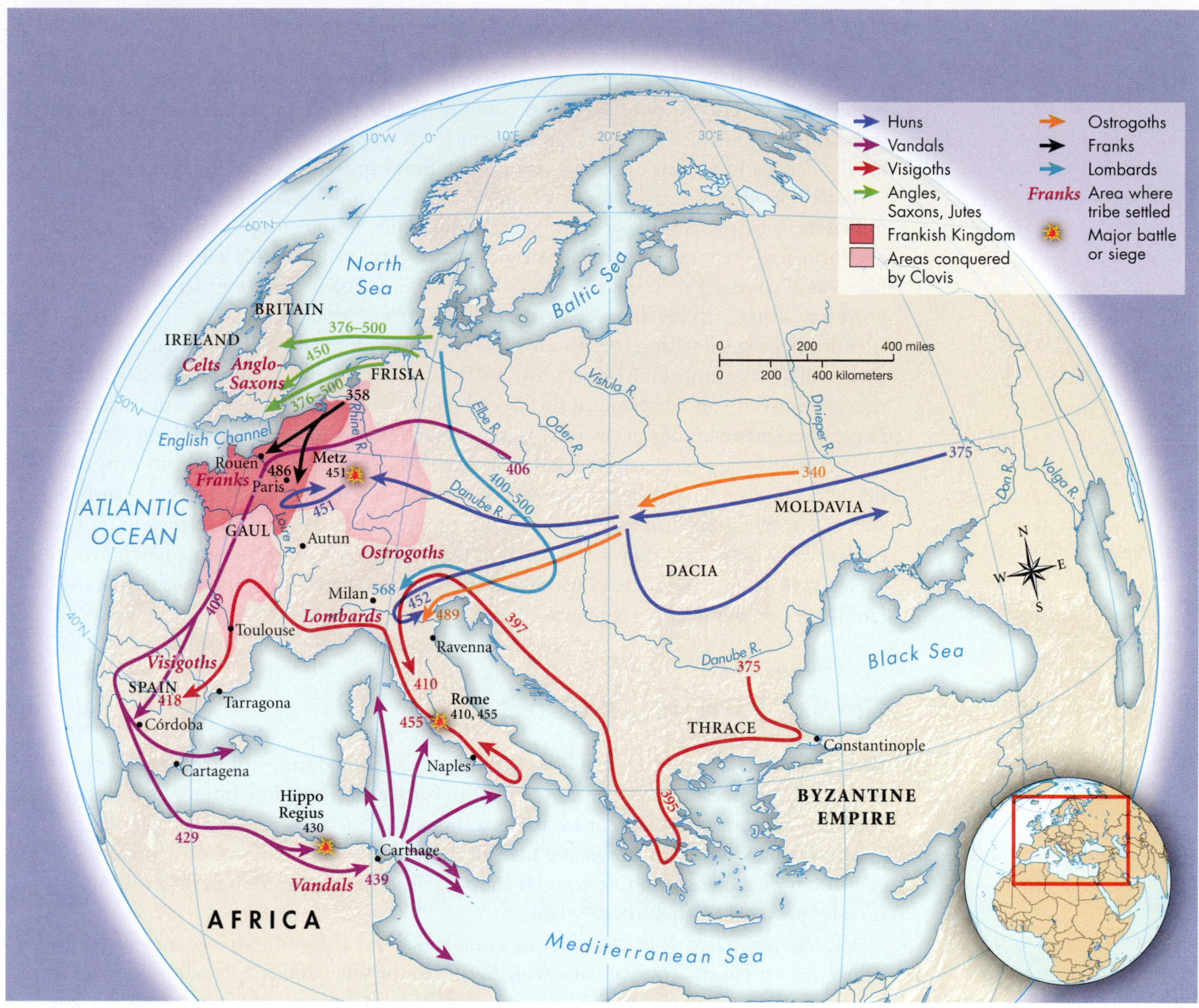

Map 8.3 The Barbarian Migrations, ca. 340–500 Various barbarian groups migrated throughout Europe and western Asia in late antiquity, pushed and pulled by a number of factors. Many of them formed loosely structured states, of which the Frankish kingdom would become the most significant.

C.E. (Map 8.3). The Greeks who encountered these peoples called them *barbaros* because they seemed to the Greeks to be speaking nonsense syllables—bar, bar, bar. ("Bar-bar" is the Greek equivalent of "blah-blah.") Although *barbaros* originally meant someone who did not speak Greek, gradually people labeled as such were also seen as unruly, savage, and primitive. The word brought this broader meaning with it when it came into Latin and other European languages.

Barbarians included many different ethnic groups with social and political structures, languages, laws, and beliefs developed in central and northern Europe and western Asia over many centuries. Among the largest barbarian groups were the Celts (whom the Romans called Gauls) and Germans. Celts, Germans, and other barbarians brought their traditions with them when they moved south and west, and these gradually combined with classical and Christian customs and beliefs to form a new type of society. From this cultural mix the Franks emerged as an especially influential force, and they built a lasting empire (see page 201).

Social and Economic Structures

For most barbarians, the basic social unit was the tribe, made up of kin groups, and tribe members believed that they were all descended from a common ancestor. Blood united them; kinship protected them. Kin groups were made up of families, which were responsible for the debts and actions of their members and for keeping the peace in general.

Barbarian groups usually resided in small villages, and climate and geography determined the basic patterns of agricultural and pastoral life. Many groups settled on the edges of clearings where they raised crops. Men and women tilled their fields with simple scratch plows and harvested their grain with small iron sickles. The kernels of grain were eaten as porridge, ground up for flour, or fermented into strong, thick beer.

Within the small villages, there were great differences in wealth and status. Free men and their families constituted the largest class, and the number of cattle these men possessed indicated their wealth and determined their social status. Free men also took part in tribal warfare. Slaves (prisoners of war) worked as farm laborers, herdsmen, and household servants.

Barbarian society was patriarchal: within each household the father had authority over his wife, children, and slaves. A woman was considered to be under the legal guardianship of a man, and she had fewer rights to own property than did Roman women in the late empire. However, once they were widowed (and there must have been many widows in such a violent, warring society), women sometimes assumed their husbands' rights over family property and took guardianship of their children.

Chiefs, Warriors, and Laws

Barbarian tribes were led by chieftains. Each chief was elected from among the male members of the strongest family. He led the tribe in war, settled disputes among its members, conducted negotiations with outside powers, and offered sacrifices to the gods. As barbarian groups migrated into and conquered parts of the Western Roman Empire, their chiefs became even more powerful. Often chiefs adopted the title of king, though this title implies broader power than they actually had.

Closely associated with the chief in some tribes was the comitatus (kuhm-ee-TAH-tuhs), or "war band." The warriors swore loyalty to the chief and fought alongside him in battle. Warriors may originally have been relatively equal to one another, but during the migrations and warfare of the second through the fourth centuries, the war band was transformed into a system of stratified ranks. When tribes settled down, warriors also began to acquire land. Social inequalities emerged and gradually grew stronger. These inequalities help explain the origins of the European noble class.

Early barbarian tribes had no written laws. Instead, law was based on custom and oral tradition. Beginning in the late sixth century, however, some tribal chieftains began to collect, write, and publish lists of their customs at the urging of Christian missionaries. The churchmen wanted to understand barbarian ways in order to assimilate the tribes to Christianity. Moreover, by the sixth century many barbarian chieftains needed regulations for the Romans under their jurisdiction as well as for their own people.

wergeld Compensatory payment for death or injury set in many barbarian law codes.

Barbarian law codes often included clauses designed to reduce interpersonal violence. Any crime that involved a personal injury was given a particular monetary value, called the **wergeld** (WUHR-gehld) (literally "man-money" or "money to buy off the spear"), that was to be paid by a person accused of a crime to the victim or the victim's family. If the accused agreed to pay the wergeld and if the victim or his or her family accepted the payment, there was peace. If the accused refused to pay the wergeld or if the victim or family refused to accept it, a blood feud ensued.

Like Greeks, Romans, and Hindus, barbarians worshipped hundreds of gods and goddesses with specialized functions. They regarded certain mountains, lakes, rivers, or

Anglo-Saxon Helmet This ceremonial bronze helmet from seventh-century England was found inside a ship buried at Sutton Hoo. The nearly 100-foot-long ship was dragged overland before being buried completely. It held one body and many grave goods, including swords, gold buckles, and silver bowls made in Byzantium. The unidentified person who was buried here was clearly wealthy and powerful, and so was very likely a chief. (Courtesy of the Trustees of the British Museum)

groves of trees as sacred because these were linked to deities. Rituals to honor the gods were held outdoors rather than in temples or churches, often at certain points in the yearly agricultural cycle. Among the Celts, religious leaders called druids had legal and educational as well as religious functions. Bards singing poems and ballads also passed down myths and stories of heroes and gods, which were written down much later.

Migrations and Political Change

Why did the barbarians migrate? In part, they were searching for more regular supplies of food, better farmland, and a warmer climate. Conflicts within and among barbarian groups also led to war and disruption, which motivated groups to move. Franks fought Alemanni (another Germanic tribe) in Gaul, while Visigoths fought Vandals in the Iberian peninsula and across North Africa. Roman expansion led to further movement of barbarian groups but also to the blending of cultures.

The spread of the Celts presents a good example of both conflict and assimilation. Celtic-speaking peoples had lived in central Europe since at least the fifth century B.C.E. and had spread out from there to the Iberian peninsula in the west, Hungary in the east, and the British Isles in the north. Celtic peoples conquered by the Romans often assimilated to Roman ways, adopting the Latin language and many aspects of Roman culture. Also, Celts and Romans intermarried, and many Celtic men became Roman citizens and joined the Roman army. By the fourth century C.E., however, Gaul and Britain were under pressure from Germanic groups moving westward. Roman troops withdrew from Britain, and Celtic-speaking peoples clashed with Germanic-speaking invaders, of whom the largest tribes were the Angles and the Saxons. Some Celtic-speakers moved farther west, to Brittany (modern northwestern France), Wales, Scotland, and Ireland. Others remained and intermarried with Germanic peoples, their descendants forming a number of small Anglo-Saxon kingdoms.

In eastern Europe, a significant factor in barbarian migration and the merging of various Germanic groups was pressure from nomadic steppe peoples from Central Asia, most prominently the Huns, who attacked the Black Sea area and the Eastern Roman Empire beginning in the fourth century. Under the leadership of their warrior-king Attila, the Huns swept into central Europe in 451, attacking Roman settlements in the Balkans and Germanic settlements along the Danube and Rhine Rivers. After Attila turned his army southward and crossed the Alps into Italy, a papal delegation, including Pope Leo I himself, asked him not to attack Rome. Though papal diplomacy was later credited with stopping

LISTENING TO THE PAST

Gregory of Tours, The Conversion of Clovis

Modern Christian doctrine holds that conversion is a process, the gradual turning toward Jesus and the teachings of the Christian Gospels. But in the early medieval world, conversion was perceived more as a one-time event determined by the tribal chieftain. If he accepted baptism, the mass conversion of his people followed. The selection here about the Frankish king Clovis is from The History of the Franks *by Gregory, bishop of Tours (ca. 504–594), written about a century after the events it describes.*

"The first child which Clotild bore for Clovis was a son. She wanted to have her baby baptized, and she kept urging her husband to agree to this. "The gods whom you worship are no good," she would say.

"They haven't even been able to help themselves, let alone others. . . . Take your Saturn, for example, who ran away from his own son to avoid being exiled from his kingdom, or so they say; and Jupiter, that obscene perpetrator of all sorts of mucky deeds, who couldn't keep his hands off other men, who had his fun with all his female relatives and couldn't even refrain from intercourse with his own sister. . . .

"You ought instead to worship Him who created at a word and out of nothing heaven, and earth, the sea and all that therein is, who made the sun to shine, who lit the sky with stars, who peopled the water with fish, the earth with beasts, the sky with flying creatures, by whose hand the race of man was made, by whose gift all creation is constrained to serve in deference and devotion the man He made." However often the Queen said this, the King came no nearer to belief. . . .

The Queen, who was true to her faith, brought her son to be baptized. . . . The child was baptized; he was given the name Ingomer; but no sooner had he received baptism than he died in his white robes. Clovis was extremely angry. He began immediately to reproach his Queen. "If he had been dedicated in the name of my gods," he said, "he would have lived without question; but now that he has been baptized in the name of your God he has not been able to live a single day!"

"I give thanks to Almighty God," replied Clotild, "the Creator of all things who has not found me completely unworthy, for He has deigned to welcome into his Kingdom a child conceived in my womb. . . ."

Some time later Clotild bore a second son. He was baptized Chlodomer. He began to ail and Clovis said, "What else do you expect? It will happen to him as it happened to his brother: no sooner is he baptized in the name of your Christ than he will die!" Clotild prayed to the Lord and at His commands the baby recovered.

Queen Clotild continued to pray that her husband might recognize the true God and give up his idol-worship. Nothing could persuade him to accept Christianity. Finally war broke out against the Alemanni and in this conflict he was forced by necessity to accept what he had refused of his own free will. It so turned out that when the two armies met on the battlefield there was a great slaughter and the troops of Clovis were rapidly being annihilated. He raised his eyes to heaven when he saw this, felt compunction in his heart and was moved to tears. "Jesus Christ," he said, "you who Clotild maintains to be the Son of the living God, you who deign to give help to those in travail and victory to those who trust in you, in faith I beg the glory of your help. If you will give me victory over my enemies, and if I may have evidence to that miraculous power which the people dedicated to your name say that they have experienced, then I will believe in you and I will be baptized in your name. I have called upon my own gods, but, as I see only too clearly, they have no intention of helping me. I therefore cannot believe that they possess any power for they do not come to the assistance of those who trust them. I now call upon you. I want to believe in you, but I must first be saved from my enemies." Even as he said this the Alemanni turned their backs and began to run away. As soon as they saw that their King was killed, they submitted to Clovis. "We beg you," they said, "to put an end to this slaughter. We are prepared

the advance of the Huns, dwindling food supplies for Hunnic troops, as well as a plague that had spread among them, were probably much more important factors. The Huns retreated from Italy, and within a year Attila was dead. Later leaders were not as effective, and the Huns never again played a significant role in European history. Their conquests had pushed many Germanic groups together, however, which transformed smaller bands of people into larger, more unified groups that could more easily pick the Western Roman Empire apart.

After they conquered an area, barbarians generally established rulership under kings (chieftains). The kingdoms did not have definite geographical borders, and their locations shifted as tribes moved. Eventually, barbarian kingdoms came to include Italy itself. The

Ninth-century ivory carving showing Clovis being baptized by Saint Remi (or Remigius). (Laurie Platt Winfrey/The Granger Collection, New York)

to obey you." Clovis stopped the war. He made a speech in which he called for peace. Then he went home. He told the Queen how he had won a victory by calling on the name of Christ. This happened in the fifteenth year of his reign (496).

The Queen then ordered Saint Remigius, Bishop of the town of Rheims, to be summoned in secret. She begged him to impart the word of salvation to the King. The Bishop asked Clovis to meet him in private and began to urge him to believe in the true God, Maker of heaven and earth, and to forsake his idols, which were powerless to help him or anyone else. The King replied: "I have listened to you willingly, holy father. There remains one obstacle. The people under my command will not agree to forsake their gods. I will go and put to them what you have just said to me." He arranged a meeting with his people, but God in his power had preceded him, and before he could say a word all those present shouted in unison: "We will give up worshipping our mortal gods, pious King, and we are prepared to follow the immortal God about whom Remigius preaches." This news was reported to the Bishop. He was greatly pleased and he ordered the baptismal pool to be made ready. . . . The baptistry was prepared, sticks of incense gave off clouds of perfume, sweet-smelling candles gleamed bright and the holy place of baptism was filled with divine fragrance. God filled the hearts of all present with such grace that they imagined themselves to have been transported to some perfumed paradise. King Clovis asked that he might be baptized first by the Bishop.

Like some new Constantine he stepped forward to the baptismal pool, ready to wash away the sores of his old leprosy and to be cleansed in flowing water from the sordid stains which he had borne so long.

King Clovis confessed his belief in God Almighty, three in one. He was baptized in the name of the Father, the Son, and the Holy Ghost, and marked in holy chrism [an anointing oil] with the sign of the Cross of Christ. More than three thousand of his army were baptized at the same time. ”

QUESTIONS FOR ANALYSIS

1. Who took the initiative in urging Clovis's conversion? What can we deduce from that?
2. According to this account, why did Clovis ultimately accept Christianity?
3. How does Gregory of Tours portray the workings of divine power in Clovis's conversion?
4. On the basis of this selection, do you consider *The History of the Franks* reliable? Why?

Western Roman emperors increasingly relied on barbarian commanders and their troops to maintain order. In 476 the barbarian chieftain Odoacer deposed Romulus Augustus, marking the official end of the Roman Empire in the West.

The Frankish Kingdom

Most barbarian kingdoms did not last very long, but one that did, and that came to have a decisive role in history, was that of the Franks. The Franks were a confederation of Germanic peoples who came from the northernmost part of the Roman Empire. In the fourth and fifth centuries they settled within the empire and allied with the Romans, some attaining high military and civil positions. The Franks believed that Merovech, a semi-legendary figure, founded their ruling dynasty, which was thus called **Merovingian** (mehr-uh-VIHN-jee-uhn).

Merovingian A dynasty founded in 481 by the Frankish chieftain Clovis in what is now France. *Merovingian* derives from *Merovech*, the name of the semi-legendary leader from whom Clovis claimed descent.

The reign of Clovis (ca. 481–511) was decisive in the development of the Franks as a unified people. Through military campaigns, Clovis acquired the central provinces of Roman Gaul and began to conquer southern Gaul from other Germanic tribes. His wife Clotild, a Roman Christian, converted her husband and supported the founding of churches and monasteries. Her actions typify the role women played in the Christianization of barbarian kingdoms. (See "Listening to the Past: Gregory of Tours, The Conversion of Clovis," page 200.)

Clovis's conversion to Roman Christianity brought him the crucial support of the bishops of Gaul in his campaigns against tribes that were still pagan or had accepted the Arian version of Christianity. As the defender of Roman Christianity against heretical tribes, Clovis went on to conquer the Visigoths, extending his domain to include much of what is now France and southwestern Germany.

When Clovis died, his kingdom was divided among his four sons, following Frankish custom. For the next two centuries rulers of the various kingdoms fought one another in civil wars, and other military leaders challenged their authority. So brutal were these wars that historians used to use the term *Dark Ages* to apply to the entire Merovingian period, although more recently they have noted that the Merovingians also developed new political institutions, so the era was not uniformly bleak.

Merovingian kings based some aspects of their government on Roman principles. For example, they adopted the Roman concept of the *civitas*—Latin for a city and its surrounding territory. A count presided over the civitas, raising troops, collecting royal revenues, and providing justice on the basis of local, not royal, law. At the king's court, an official called the mayor of the palace supervised legal, financial, and household officials; the mayor of the palace also governed in the king's absence. In the seventh century that position was held by members of an increasingly powerful family, the **Carolingians** (ka-ruh-LIHN-jee-uhns), who advanced themselves through advantageous marriages, a well-earned reputation for military strength, and the help of the church. Eventually the Carolingians replaced the Merovingians as rulers of the Frankish kingdom, cementing their authority when the Carolingian Charles Martel defeated Muslim invaders in 732 at the Battle of Poitiers (pwah-ty-AY) in central France.

Carolingians A dynasty of rulers that took over the Frankish kingdom from the Merovingians in the seventh century; *Carolingians* derives from the Latin word for "Charles," the name of several members of this dynasty.

Charlemagne's Conquests, ca. 768–814

The Battle of Poitiers helped the Carolingians acquire more support from the church, perhaps their most important asset. They further strengthened their ties to the church by supporting the work of missionaries and by allying themselves with the papacy against other Germanic tribes.

Charlemagne

The most powerful of the Carolingians was Charles the Great (r. 768–814), generally known as Charlemagne (SHAHR-luh-mayn). In the autumn of the year 800, Charlemagne visited Rome, where on Christmas Day Pope Leo III crowned him emperor. The event had momentous consequences. In taking as his motto *Renovatio romani imperi* (Revival of the Roman Empire), Charlemagne was

Picturing the Past

Charlemagne and His Wife

This illumination from a ninth-century manuscript portrays Charlemagne with one of his wives. Marriage was an important tool of diplomacy for Charlemagne, and he had a number of wives and concubines. (Erich Lessing/Art Resource, NY)

ANALYZING THE IMAGE What does Charlemagne appear to be doing? How would you characterize his wife's reaction?

CONNECTIONS Does this depiction of a Frankish queen match what you've read about female rulers in this era, such as Theodora and Clotild?

deliberately perpetuating old Roman imperial ideas while identifying with the new Rome of the Christian Church. The Byzantines regarded his papal coronation as rebellious and Charlemagne as a usurper. His crowning as emperor thus marks a decisive break between Rome and Constantinople.

Charlemagne's most striking characteristic was his phenomenal energy, which helps explain his great military achievements. Continuing the expansionist policies of his ancestors, he fought more than fifty campaigns, and by around 805 the Frankish kingdom included all of continental Europe except Spain, Scandinavia, southern Italy, and the Slavic fringes of the East.

The Treaty of Verdun, 483

For administrative purposes, Charlemagne divided his entire kingdom into counties. Each of the approximately six hundred counties was governed by a count, who had full military and judicial power and held his office for life but could be removed by the emperor for misconduct. As a link between local authorities and the central government, Charlemagne appointed officials called *missi dominici*, "agents of the lord king." Each year beginning in 802 two missi, usually a count and a bishop or abbot, visited assigned districts. They checked up on the counts and their districts' judicial, financial, and clerical activities.

Charlemagne's most enduring legacy was the cultural revival he set in motion, a revival that later historians called the "Carolingian Renaissance." The Carolingian Renaissance was a rebirth of interest in, study of, and preservation of the language, ideas, and achievements of classical Greece and Rome. Scholars at Charlemagne's capital of Aachen copied Greco-Roman and Christian books and manuscripts and built up libraries. Furthermore, Charlemagne urged monasteries to promote Christian learning, and both men's and women's houses produced beautiful illustrated texts, preserving Christian and classical works for subsequent generations.

Charlemagne left his vast empire to his sole surviving son, Louis the Pious (r. 814–840), who attempted to keep the empire intact. This proved to be impossible. Members of the nobility engaged in plots and open warfare against the emperor, often allying themselves with one of Louis's three sons. In 843, shortly after Louis's death, those sons agreed to the **Treaty of Verdun**, which divided the empire into three parts: Charles the Bald received the western part, Lothair the middle and the title of emperor, and Louis the eastern part, from which he acquired the title "the German." Though of course no one knew it at the time, this treaty set the pattern for political boundaries in Europe that has been maintained to today.

Treaty of Verdun A treaty ratified in 843 that divided Charlemagne's territories among his three surviving grandsons; their kingdoms set the pattern for the modern states of France, Italy, and Germany.

The weakening of central power was hastened by invasions and migrations from the north, south, and east. Thus Charlemagne's empire ended in much the same way that the Roman Empire had earlier, from a combination of internal weakness and external pressure.

Quick Review
How did the arrival of migrating peoples alter the social and political landscape of Europe and western Asia?

Connections

FOR CENTURIES THE END of the Roman Empire in the West was seen as a major turning point in history, the fall of the sophisticated and educated classical world to uncouth and illiterate tribes. Over the last several decades, however, many historians have put a greater emphasis on continuities. Barbarian kings relied on officials trained in Roman law, and Latin remained the language of scholarly communication and the Christian Church. Greco-Roman art and architecture still adorned the land, and people continued to use Roman roads, aqueducts, and buildings. In eastern Europe and western Asia, the Byzantine Empire preserved the traditions of the Roman Empire and protected the intellectual heritage of Greco-Roman culture for another millennium.

Very recently, however, some historians and archaeologists have returned to an emphasis on change. They note that people may have traveled on Roman roads after the end of the Roman Empire, but the roads were rarely maintained, and travel itself was much less secure than during the empire. Merchants no longer traded over long distances, so people's access to goods produced outside their local area plummeted. Knowledge about technological processes such as the making of glass and roof tiles declined or disappeared. Although there was intermarriage and cultural assimilation among Romans and barbarians, there was also violence and great physical destruction, even in Byzantium.

In the middle of the era covered in this chapter, a new force emerged that had a dramatic impact on much of Europe and western Asia — Islam. In the seventh and eighth centuries Sassanid Persia, much of the Byzantine Empire, and the barbarian kingdoms in the Iberian peninsula fell to Arab forces carrying this new religion. As we have seen in this chapter, a reputation as victors over Islam helped the Franks establish the most powerful state in Europe. As we will see in Chapter 14, Islam continued to shape European culture and politics in subsequent centuries. In terms of world history, the expansion of Islam may have been an even more dramatic turning point than the fall of the Roman Empire. Here, too, however, there were continuities, as the Muslims adopted and adapted Greek, Byzantine, and Persian political and cultural institutions.

- **For a list of suggested readings for this chapter, visit** *bedfordstmartins.com/mckayworldunderstanding*.
- **For primary sources from this period, see** *Sources of World Societies*, Second Edition.
- **For Web sites, images, and documents related to topics in this chapter, see Make History at** *bedfordstmartins.com/mckayworldunderstanding*.

Chapter 8 Study Guide

To do these exercises online, go to bedfordstmartins.com/mckayworldunderstanding.

Step 1

GETTING STARTED

Below are basic terms about this period in global history. Can you identify each term below and explain why it matters?

TERMS	WHO (OR WHAT) AND WHEN	WHY IT MATTERS
corpus juris civilis, p. 187		
dioceses, p. 189		
Arianism, p. 189		
popes, p. 190		
Orthodox Church, p. 190		
iconoclastic controversy, p. 190		
sacraments, p. 194		
penance, p. 196		
saints, p. 196		
wergeld, p. 198		
Merovingian, p. 202		
Carolingians, p. 202		
Treaty of Verdun, p. 204		

Step 2

MOVING BEYOND THE BASICS

The exercise below requires a more advanced understanding of the chapter material. Examine the role of the Byzantine Empire and the Christian Church in preserving the legacy of Greco-Roman civilization by filling in the chart below with descriptions of the contributions of the Byzantine Empire and the Christian Church in this context in two key areas: politics and government, and culture and ideas. When you are finished, consider the following questions: What aspects of Roman government were preserved by the Byzantine Empire? Why was the church so important to the preservation of the Greco-Roman legacy in the West? How did church and state work together to preserve the Greco-Roman legacy in the East?

	POLITICS AND GOVERNMENT	CULTURE AND IDEAS
Byzantine Empire		
Christian Church		

Step 3

PUTTING IT ALL TOGETHER

Now that you've reviewed key elements of the chapter, take a step back and try to see the big picture. Remember to use specific examples from the chapter in your answers.

THE BYZANTINE EMPIRE

- Compare and contrast the Western Roman Empire and the Eastern Roman Empire in the period just prior to the fall of the Western Roman Empire. Why was the Eastern Roman Empire able to withstand the pressure of barbarian migrations, while the Western Roman Empire was not?

- How did conflicts and connections with neighboring peoples shape the development of the Byzantine Empire?

THE SPREAD AND DEVELOPMENT OF CHRISTIANITY

- Is it more accurate to say that Rome was Christianized or that the Christian Church was Romanized? What evidence can you present to support your position?
- Why did so many barbarian elites aid in the spread of Christianity in Europe? What does the receptivity of such elites to Christianity tell us about barbarian society and culture?

MIGRATING PEOPLES

- How did barbarian society and culture compare to Roman society and culture? Were there any areas of similarity?
- How were Germanic and Roman influences combined in the structure and institutions of the Frankish kingdom?

LOOKING BACK, LOOKING AHEAD

- Compare and contrast Europe and western Asia before and after the fall of the Roman Empire in the West. What were the most important areas of continuity?
- How did the Byzantine Empire and the Christian Church lay the foundation in late antiquity for the subsequent medieval European civilization? What contributions did barbarian peoples make in this context?

In Your Own Words Imagine that you must explain Chapter 8 to someone who hasn't read it. What would be the most important points to include and why?

9

The Islamic World

600–1400

Around 610 in the city of Mecca in what is now Saudi Arabia, a merchant called Muhammad had a religious vision that inspired him to preach to the people of Mecca. By the time he died in 632, he had many followers in Arabia, and a century later his followers controlled what is now Syria, Palestine, Egypt, Iraq, Iran, northern India, North Africa, Spain, and southern France. Within another century Muhammad's beliefs had been carried across Central Asia to the borders of China and India. The speed with which Islam spread is one of the most amazing stories in world history, and scholars have pointed to many factors that must have contributed to its success. Military victories were rooted in strong military organization and the practice of establishing garrison cities in newly conquered territories. The religious zeal of new converts certainly played an important role. So too did the political weakness of many of the governments then holding power in the lands where Islam extended, such as the Byzantine government centered in Constantinople. Commerce and trade also spread the faith of Muhammad.

Egyptian Man Life remained gracious in the great cities of North Africa and the Middle East even as Islam brought new traditions. This image of a man wearing a turban is from an Egyptian wall painting dating to the eleventh century, during the Fatimid caliphate. (The Art Archive at Art Resource, NY)

Although its first adherents were nomads, Islam developed and flourished in a mercantile milieu. By land and sea, Muslim merchants transported a rich variety of goods across Eurasia. On the basis of the wealth that trade generated, a gracious, sophisticated, and cosmopolitan culture developed with centers at Baghdad and Córdoba. During the ninth, tenth, and eleventh centuries, the Islamic world witnessed enormous intellectual vitality and creativity, profoundly influencing the development of both Eastern and Western civilizations.

Chapter Preview

- Who was Muhammad and what did he teach?
- What explains the speed and scope of Islamic expansion?
- How and why did Islamic states change between 900 and 1400?
- What social distinctions were important in Muslim society?
- Why did trade thrive in Muslim lands?
- What new cultural developments emerged in this period?
- What characterized Muslim-Christian interactions?

Who was Muhammad and what did he teach?

Much of the Arabian peninsula, but not all, is desert. By the seventh century C.E. farming prevailed in the southwestern mountain valleys. In other scattered areas, oasis towns sustained sizable populations. Outside the towns were Bedouin (BEH-duh-uhn) nomadic tribes who moved from place to place, grazing their flocks. Though always small in number, Bedouins were the most important political and military force in the region, controlling trade and lines of communication. Mecca became the economic and cultural center of western Arabia, in part because pilgrims came to visit the Ka'ba, a temple containing a black stone thought to be a god's dwelling place as well as other holy objects connected to other gods. Muhammad's roots were in this region.

Arabian Social and Economic Structure

The basic social unit of the Bedouins and other Arabs was the tribe. Consisting of people connected through kinship, tribes provided protection and support in exchange for members' total loyalty. Like the Germanic peoples in the age of their migrations (see pages 196–204), Arab tribes were not static entities but rather continually evolving groups. A particular tribe might include both nomadic and sedentary members.

Dome of the Rock, Jerusalem Completed in 691 and revered by Muslims as the site where Muhammad ascended to Heaven, the Dome of the Rock is the oldest surviving Islamic sanctuary and, after Mecca and Medina, the holiest place in Islam. Although influenced by Byzantine and Persian architecture, it also has distinctly Arabic features, such as the 700 feet of carefully selected Qur'anic inscriptions and vegetal motifs that grace the top of the outer walls. (imagebroker.net/SuperStock)

As in other nomadic societies, nomads in Arabia depended on agriculturally productive communities for food and other supplies. Nomads paid for these goods with the products of their herds. Nomads acquired additional income by serving as desert guides and as guards for caravans, or by plundering caravans and extorting protection money.

In northern and central Arabia in the early seventh century, tribal confederations with their warrior elite were dominant. In the southern parts of the peninsula, however, religious aristocracies tended to hold political power. Many oasis or market towns contained members of one holy family who served the deity of the town and acted as guardians of the deity's shrine. Located in agricultural areas that were also commercial centers, the religious aristocracy had a stronger economic base than did the warrior-aristocrats. The political genius of Muhammad was to bind together these different tribal groups into a strong, unified state.

Chapter Chronology

622	Muhammad and his followers emigrate from Mecca to Medina
632	Muhammad dies; Abu Bakr becomes the first caliph
642	Muslim defeat of the Persians marks end of the Sassanid empire
651	Publication of the Qur'an
661	Ali assassinated; split between Shi'a and Sunnis
711	Muslims defeat Visigothic kingdom in Spain
722–1492	Progressive loss of most of Spain to the Christian reconquest (*reconquista*)
750–1258	Abbasid caliphate
762	Baghdad founded by Abbasids
800–1300	Height of Muslim learning and creativity
950–1100	Entry on a large scale of Turks into the Middle East
1055	Baghdad falls to Seljuk Turks
1099–1187	Christian Crusaders hold Jerusalem
1258	Mongols capture Baghdad and kill the last Abbasid caliph

Muhammad's Rise as a Religious Leader

Much like the earliest sources for Jesus, the earliest account of the life of Muhammad (ca. 570–632) comes from oral traditions passed down among followers and not written down for several decades or generations. According to these traditions, Muhammad was orphaned at the age of six. As a young man, he became a merchant in the caravan trade. Later he entered the service of a wealthy widow, Khadija, and their subsequent marriage brought him financial security. Muhammad was extremely pious and devoted to contemplation. At about age forty, Muhammad had a vision of an angelic being who commanded him to preach the revelations that God would be sending him. Muhammad began to preach to the people of Mecca, urging them to give up their idols and to submit to the one indivisible God. During his lifetime, Muhammad's followers wrote down his revelations and committed them to memory. In 651 they published the version of them that Muslims consider authoritative, the **Qur'an** (kuh-RAHN). Muslims revere the Qur'an for its sacred message and for the beauty of its Arabic language.

Qur'an The sacred book of Islam.

For the first two or three centuries after the death of Muhammad, there was considerable debate abut theological issues, such as the oneness of God, the role of the Scriptures, and Judgment Day, as well as about political issues, such as the authority of Muhammad and that of the caliph (KAY-lif; political ruler, successor to Muhammad). Likewise, religious scholars had to sort out and assess the **hadith** (huh-DEETH), collections of the sayings of or anecdotes about Muhammad. Muhammad's example as revealed in the hadith became the legal basis for the conduct of every Muslim. The life of Muhammad, who is also known as the Prophet, provides the "normative example," or **Sunna**, for the Muslim believer, the model of human behavior that became central to the Muslim way of life.

hadith Collections of the sayings of and anecdotes about Muhammad.

Sunna An Arabic term meaning "trodden path." The term refers to the deeds and sayings of Muhammad, which constitute the obligatory example for Muslim life.

The Tenets of Islam

Islam, the strict monotheistic faith that is based on the teachings of Muhammad, rests on the principle of the oneness and omnipotence of God (Allah). The word *Islam* means "surrender to God," and *Muslim* means "a person who submits." Muslims believe that

Muhammad was the last of the prophets, completing the work begun by Abraham, Moses, and Jesus.

Muslims believe that they worship the same God as Jews and Christians. Monotheism had flourished in Middle Eastern Semitic and Persian cultures for centuries before Muhammad. Islam appropriates much of the Old and New Testaments of the Bible but often retells the narratives with significant shifts in meaning. Muhammad insisted that he was not preaching a new message; rather, he was calling people back to the one true God, urging his contemporaries to reform their lives, to return to the faith of Abraham, the first monotheist.

Unlike the Old Testament, much of which is a historical narrative, or the New Testament, which is a collection of essays on the example and teachings of Jesus, the Qur'an is a collection of directives issued in God's name. Its organization is not strictly topical or chronological. To deal with seeming contradictions, later commentators explained the historical circumstances behind each revelation.

Five Pillars of Islam The basic tenets of the Islamic faith; they include reciting a profession of faith in God and in Muhammad as God's prophet, praying five times daily, fasting and praying during the month of Ramadan, making a pilgrimage to Mecca once in one's lifetime, and contributing alms to the poor.

The Qur'an prescribes a strict code of moral behavior. A Muslim must recite the profession of faith in God and in Muhammad as his prophet. A believer must also pray five times a day, fast and pray during the sacred month of Ramadan, make a pilgrimage (hajj) to the holy city of Mecca once during his or her lifetime, and give alms to the Muslim poor. These fundamental obligations are known as the **Five Pillars of Islam**.

Islam forbids alcoholic beverages and gambling. It condemns usury in business — that is, lending money and charging the borrower interest — and taking advantage of market demand for products by charging high prices. Muslim jurisprudence condemned licentious behavior by both men and women and specified the same punishments for both. (By contrast, contemporary Frankish law punished prostitutes, but not their clients.) Islam warns about Judgment Day and the importance of the life to come. Like the Christian Judgment Day, on that day God will separate the saved and the damned.

Quick Review
How did the beliefs at the heart of Muhammad's message challenge prevailing social and cultural norms?

What explains the speed and scope of Islamic expansion?

According to Muslim tradition, Muhammad's preaching at first did not appeal to many people. In preaching a transformation of the social order and calling for the destruction of the idols in the Ka'ba, Muhammad challenged the power of the local elite and the pilgrimage-based local economy. As a result, the townspeople of Mecca turned against him, and in 622 he and his followers were forced to flee to Medina, an event known as the *hijra* (hih-JIGH-ruh), or emigration.

At Medina, Muhammad attracted increasing numbers of believers, and his teachings began to have an impact. His followers supported themselves by raiding caravans en route to Mecca, setting off a violent conflict between Mecca and Medina. After eight years of strife, Mecca capitulated. Thus, by the time he died in 632, Muhammad had welded together all the Bedouin tribes.

umma A community of people who share a religious faith and commitment rather than a tribal tie.

Muhammad displayed genius as both a political strategist and a religious teacher. He gave Arabs the idea of a unique and unified **umma** (UH-muh), or community. The umma was to be a religious and political community led by Muhammad for the achievement of God's will on earth. In the early seventh century the southern Arab tribal confederations lacked cohesiveness and were constantly warring. The Islamic notion of an absolute higher authority transcended the boundaries of individual tribal units and fostered the political consolidation of the tribal confederations.

Islam's Spread Beyond Arabia

After the Prophet's death, Islam spread far beyond Arabia (Map 9.1). In the sixth century two powerful empires divided the Middle East: the Christian Greek-Byzantine Empire centered at Constantinople and the Zoroastrian Persian-Sassanid (suh-SAHN-uhd) Empire concentrated at Ctesiphon (near Baghdad in present-day Iraq). Although each empire maintained an official state religion, neither possessed religious unity. Both had sizable Jewish populations, and within Byzantium sects that Orthodox Greeks considered heretical were politically divisive forces. During the fourth through sixth centuries these two empires fought each other fiercely, each trying to expand its territories at the expense of the other. They also sought to control and tax the rich trade coming from Arabia and the Indian Ocean region. Many peripheral societies were drawn into the conflict. The resulting disorder facilitated the growth of Muslim states.

The second and third successors of Muhammad, Umar (r. 634–644) and Uthman (r. 644–656), launched a two-pronged attack against the Byzantine and Sassanid Empires. One force moved north against the Byzantine provinces of Syria and

Mapping the Past

Map 9.1 The Expansion of Islam, 622–900

The rapid expansion of Islam in a relatively short span of time testifies to the Arabs' superior fighting skills, religious zeal, and economic ambition as well as to their enemies' weakness. Plague, famine, and political troubles in Sassanid Persia contributed to Muslim victory there.

ANALYZING THE MAP Trace the routes of the spread of Islam by time period. How fast did it spread? How similar were the climates of the regions that became Muslim?

CONNECTIONS Which were the most powerful and populous of the societies that were absorbed into the Muslim world? What regions or societies were more resistant?

Palestine. From Syria, the Muslims conquered Egypt, taking the commercial and intellectual hub of Alexandria in 642. Simultaneously, Arab armies swept into the Sassanid Empire. The Muslim defeat of the Persians at Nihawand in 642 signaled the collapse of this empire (see Map 9.1).

The Muslims continued their drive eastward into Central Asia. The clash of Muslim horsemen with a Chinese army at the Talas River in 751 marked the farthest Islamic penetration into Central Asia (see Map 9.1). From southern Persia, a Muslim force marched into the Indus Valley in northern India and in 713 founded an Islamic community there. Beginning in the eleventh century Muslim dynasties from Ghazni in Afghanistan carried Islam deeper into the Indian subcontinent (see pages 306–307).

Likewise, to the west Arab forces moved across North Africa and crossed the Strait of Gibraltar. In 711 at the Guadalete River they easily defeated the Visigothic kingdom of Spain, and Muslims controlled most of Spain until the thirteenth century. Advances into France were stopped in 732 when the Franks defeated Arab armies in a battle near the city of Tours, and Muslim occupation of parts of southern France did not last long.

Reasons for the Spread of Islam

How can this rapid and remarkable expansion be explained? The internal view of Muslim historians was that God supported the Islamic faith and aided its spread. The external, especially European, view used to be that religious fervor was the main driving force. Today, few historians emphasize religious zeal alone but rather point to a combination of Arab military advantages and the political weaknesses of their opponents. The Byzantine and Sassanid Empires had just fought a grueling century-long war and had also been weakened by the plague. Equally important are the military strength and tactics of the Arabs. For example, rather than scattering as landlords of peasant farmers over conquered lands, Arab soldiers remained together in garrison cities, where their Arab ethnicity, tribal organization, religion, and military success set them apart. All soldiers were registered in the **diwān** (dih-WAHN), an administrative organ adopted from the Persians or Byzantines. Soldiers received a monthly ration of food for themselves and their families and an annual cash stipend. In return, they had to be available for military service. Except for the Berbers of North Africa, whom the Arabs could not pacify, Muslim armies initially did not seek to convert or recruit warriors from conquered peoples. In later campaigns to the east, many recruits were recent converts to Islam from Christian, Persian, and Berber backgrounds.

diwān A unit of government.

How did the conquered peoples make sense of their new subordinate situations? Jews and Christians tried to minimize the damage done to their former status and played down the gains of their new masters. Whereas Christians regarded the conquering Arabs as God's punishment for their sins, Jews saw the Arabs as instruments for their deliverance from Greek and Sassanid persecution.

While the conquered peoples figured out their situations as subordinates, Muslims had to figure out how to rule their new territories after Muhammad's death. The government they established is called the caliphate.

The Caliphate and the Split Between Shi'a and Sunni Alliances

When Muhammad died in 632, he left a large Muslim umma, but this community stood in danger of disintegrating into separate tribal groups. How was the vast empire that came into existence within one hundred years of his death to be governed? Neither the Qur'an nor the Sunna offered guidance for the succession.

In this crisis, according to tradition, a group of Muhammad's ablest followers elected Abu Bakr (573–634), a close supporter of the Prophet and his father-in-law, and hailed him as caliph, a term combining the ideas of leader, successor, and deputy (of the Prophet). This election marked the victory of the concept of a universal community of Muslim believers.

In the two years of his rule (632–634), Abu Bakr governed on the basis of his personal prestige within the Muslim umma. He sent out military expeditions, collected taxes, dealt with tribes on behalf of the entire community, and led the community in prayer. Gradually, under Abu Bakr's first three successors, Umar, Uthman, and Ali (r. 656–661), the caliphate emerged as an institution. Umar succeeded in exerting his authority over the Bedouin tribes involved in ongoing conquests. Uthman asserted the right of the caliph to protect the economic interests of the entire umma. Also, Uthman's publication of the definitive text of the Qur'an showed his concern for the unity of the umma. However, Uthman was from a Mecca family that had resisted the Prophet until the capitulation of Mecca in 630, and he aroused resentment when he gave favors to members of his family. Opposition to Uthman coalesced around Ali, and when Uthman was assassinated in 656, Ali was chosen to succeed him.

The issue of responsibility for Uthman's murder raised the question of whether Ali's accession was legitimate. Uthman's cousin Mu'awiya refused to recognize Ali as caliph. In the ensuing civil war, Ali was assassinated, and Mu'awiya (r. 661–680) assumed the caliphate. Mu'awiya founded the Umayyad Dynasty and shifted the capital of the Islamic state from Medina in Arabia to Damascus in Syria. Although electing caliphs remained the Islamic ideal, beginning with Mu'awiya, the office of caliph increasingly became hereditary. Two successive dynasties, the Umayyad (661–750) and the Abbasid (750–1258), held the caliphate.

From its inception the caliphate rested on the theoretical principle that Muslim political and religious unity transcended tribalism. Mu'awiya sought to enhance the power of the caliphate by making tribal leaders dependent on him for concessions and special benefits. At the same time, his control of a loyal and well-disciplined army enabled him to take the caliphate in an authoritarian direction. Through intimidation he forced the tribal leaders to accept his son Yazid as his heir, thereby establishing the dynastic principle of succession. By distancing himself from a simple life within the umma and withdrawing into the palace that he built at Damascus, and by surrounding himself with symbols and ceremony, Mu'awiya laid the foundations for an elaborate caliphal court.

The assassination of Ali and the assumption of the caliphate by Mu'awiya had another profound consequence. It gave rise to a fundamental division in the umma and in Muslim theology. Ali had claimed the caliphate on the basis of family ties — he was Muhammad's cousin and son-in-law. When Ali was murdered, his followers argued — partly because of

Ivory Chest of Pamplona, Spain The court of the Spanish Umayyads prized small, intricately carved ivory chests, often made in a royal workshop and used to store precious perfumes. This exquisite side panel depicts an eleventh-century caliph flanked by two attendants. An inscription on the front translates as "In the Name of God. Blessings from God, goodwill, and happiness." (Museo Navarra, Pamplona/Institut Amatller d'Art Hispanic)

imam The leader in community prayer.

Shi'a Arabic term meaning "supporters of Ali"; they make up one of the two main divisions of Islam.

Sunnis Members of the larger of the two main divisions of Islam; the division between Sunnis and Shi'a began in a dispute about succession to Muhammad, but over time many differences in theology developed.

ulama A group of religious scholars whom Sunnis trust to interpret the Qur'an and the Sunna.

the blood tie, partly because Muhammad had designated Ali **imam** (ih-MAHM), or leader in community prayer—that Ali had been the Prophet's designated successor. These supporters of Ali were called **Shi'a** (SHEE-uh), meaning "supporters" or "partisans" of Ali (Shi'a are also known as Shi'ites).

Those who accepted Mu'awiya as caliph insisted that the central issue was adhering to the practices and beliefs of the umma based on the precedents of the Prophet. They came to be called **Sunnis** (SOO-neez), which derived from *Sunna* (examples from Muhammad's life). When a situation arose for which the Qur'an offered no solution, Sunni scholars searched for a precedent in the Sunna, which gained an authority comparable to the Qur'an itself.

Both Sunnis and Shi'a maintain that authority within Islam lies first in the Qur'an and then in the Sunna. Who interprets these sources? Shi'a claim that the imam does, for he is invested with divine grace and insight. Sunnis insist that interpretation comes from the consensus of the **ulama**, the group of religious scholars.

Throughout the Umayyad period the Shi'a constituted a major source of discontent. They condemned the Umayyads as worldly and sensual rulers. The Abbasid (uh-BA-suhd) clan, which based its claim to the caliphate on the descent of Abbas, Muhammad's uncle, exploited the situation. The Abbasids agitated the Shi'a, encouraged dissension among tribal factions, and contrasted Abbasid piety with the pleasure-loving style of the Umayyads.

The Abbasid Caliphate

In 747 Abu' al-Abbas led a rebellion against the Umayyads, and in 750 he won general recognition as caliph. Damascus had served as the headquarters of Umayyad rule. Abu' al-Abbas's successor, al-Mansur (r. 754–775), founded the city of Baghdad in 762 and made it his capital. Thus the geographical center of the caliphate shifted eastward to former Sassanid territories. The first three Abbasid caliphs crushed their opponents, turned against many of their supporters, and created a new ruling elite drawn from newly converted Persian families that had traditionally served the ruler. The Abbasid revolution established a basis for rule and citizenship more cosmopolitan and Islamic than the narrow, elitist, and Arab basis that had characterized Umayyad government.

The Abbasids worked to identify their rule with Islam. They patronized the ulama, built mosques, and supported the development of Islamic scholarship. Although at first Muslims represented only a small minority of the conquered peoples, Abbasid rule provided the religious-political milieu in which Islam gained, over time, the allegiance of the vast majority of the populations from Spain to Afghanistan.

The Abbasids also borrowed heavily from Persian culture. Following Persian tradition, the Abbasid caliphs claimed to rule by divine right. A majestic palace with hundreds of attendants and elaborate court ceremonies deliberately isolated the caliph from the people he ruled. Subjects had to bow before the caliph, kissing the ground, a symbol of his absolute power.

Under the third caliph, Harun al-Rashid (r. 786–809), Baghdad emerged as a flourishing commercial, artistic, and scientific center. Its population of about a million people created a huge demand for goods and services, and Baghdad became an entrepôt (trading center) for textiles, slaves, and foodstuffs coming from Oman, East Africa, and India. The city also became intellectually influential. Harun al-Rashid organized the translation of Greek medical and philosophical texts. As part of this effort the Christian scholar Hunayn ibn Ishaq (808–873) translated Galen's medical works into Arabic and made Baghdad a center for the study and practice of medicine. Likewise, impetus was given to the study of astronomy. Above all, studies in Qur'anic textual analysis, history, poetry, law, and philosophy—all in Arabic—reflected the development of a distinctly Islamic literary and scientific culture.

An important innovation of the Abbasids was the use of slaves as soldiers. The caliph al-Mu'taşim (r. 833–842) acquired several thousand Turkish slaves who were converted to Islam and employed in military service. Slave soldiers—later including Slavs, Indians, and sub-Saharan blacks—became a standard feature of Muslim armies in the Middle East down to the twentieth century.

Administration of the Islamic Territories

The Islamic conquests brought into being a new imperial system. The Muslims adopted the patterns of administration used by the Byzantines in Egypt and Syria and by the Sassanids in Persia. Specifically, Arab **emirs**, or governors, were appointed and given overall responsibility for public order, maintenance of the armed forces, and tax collection. Below them, experienced native officials remained in office. Thus there was continuity with previous administrations.

emirs Arab governors who were given overall responsibility for public order, maintenance of the armed forces, and tax collection.

The Umayyad caliphate witnessed the further development of the imperial administration. At the head stood the caliph, who led military campaigns against unbelievers. Theoretically, he had the ultimate responsibility for the interpretation of the sacred law. In practice, however, the ulama interpreted the law as revealed in the Qur'an and the Sunna. In the course of time, the ulama's interpretations constituted a rich body of law, the **shari'a** (shuh-REE-uh), which covered social, criminal, political, commercial, and religious matters. The *qadis* (KAH-dees), or judges, who were well versed in the sacred law, carried out the judicial functions of the state. Nevertheless, Muslim law prescribed that all people have access to the caliph, and he set aside special times for hearing petitions and for directly redressing grievances.

shari'a Muslim law, which covers social, criminal, political, commercial, and religious matters.

The central administrative organ was the diwān, which collected the taxes that paid soldiers' salaries (see page 214) and financed charitable and public works, such as aid to the poor and the construction of mosques, irrigation works, and public baths. Another important undertaking was a relay network established to convey letters and intelligence reports rapidly between the capital and distant outposts.

The early Abbasid period witnessed considerable economic expansion and population growth, complicating the work of government. New and specialized departments emerged, each with a hierarchy of officials. The most important new official was the **vizier** (vuh-ZEER), a position that the Abbasids adopted from the Persians. The vizier was the caliph's chief assistant, advising the caliph on matters of general policy, supervising the bureaucratic administration, and, under the caliph, overseeing the army, the provincial governors, and relations with foreign governments.

vizier The caliph's chief assistant.

Quick Review
What characterized the states that emerged in the aftermath of the Islamic conquests?

How and why did Islamic states change between 900 and 1400?

In theory, the caliph and his central administration governed the whole empire, but in practice, the many parts of the empire enjoyed considerable local independence. As long as public order was maintained and taxes were forwarded, the central government rarely interfered. At the same time, the enormous distance between many provinces and the imperial capital made it difficult for the caliph to prevent provinces from breaking away. In time, regional dynasties emerged in much of the Islamic world, including Spain, Persia, Central Asia, northern India, and Egypt. None of these states repudiated Islam, but they did stop sending tax revenues to Baghdad. Moreover, most states became involved with costly wars against their neighbors in their attempts to expand. Sometimes these conflicts were worsened by Sunni-Shi'a antagonisms. All these developments, as well as invasions by Turks and Mongols, posed challenges to central Muslim authority.

Breakaway Territories and Shi'a Gains

One of the first territories to break away from the Baghdad-centered caliphate was Spain. In 755 an Umayyad prince set up an independent regime at Córdoba (see Map 9.1). Other territories soon followed. In 800 the emir in Tunisia in North Africa set himself up as an independent ruler and refused to place the caliph's name on the local coinage. And in 820 Tahir, the son of a slave, was rewarded with the governorship of Khurasan because he had supported the caliphate. Once he took office, Tahir ruled independently of Baghdad.

In 946 a Shi'a Iranian clan overran Iraq and occupied Baghdad. The caliph was forced to recognize the clan's leader as commander-in-chief and to allow the celebration of Shi'a festivals. A year later the caliph was accused of plotting against his new masters, snatched from his throne, dragged through the streets, and blinded. This incident marks the practical collapse of the Abbasid caliphate. Abbasid caliphs, however, remained as puppets of a series of military commanders and symbols of Muslim unity until the Mongols killed the last Abbasid caliph in 1258 (see page 219).

In another Shi'a advance, the Fatimids, a Shi'a dynasty that claimed descent from Muhammad's daughter Fatima, conquered North Africa then expanded into the Abbasid province of Egypt, founding the city of Cairo as their capital in 969. For the next century or so, Shi'a were in ascendancy in much of the western Islamic world.

The Fatamid Caliphate, 909–1171

The Ascendancy of the Turks

In the mid-tenth century the Turks began to enter the Islamic world in large numbers. First appearing in Mongolia in the sixth century, groups of Turks gradually appeared across the grasslands of Eurasia. Skilled horsemen, they became prime targets for Muslim slave raids, as they made good slave soldiers. Once they understood that Muslims could not be captured for slaves, more and more of them converted to Islam. The first to convert accepted Sunni Islam near Bukhara, then a great Persian commercial and intellectual center.

In the 1020s and 1030s Seljuk Turks overran Persia then pushed into Iraq and Syria. Baghdad fell to them on December 18, 1055, and the caliph became a puppet of the Turkish sultan. The Turkic elite rapidly gave up pastoralism and took up the sedentary lifestyle of the people they governed.

The Turks brought badly needed military strength to the Islamic world. They played a major part in recovering Jerusalem after it was held for nearly a century, from 1099 to 1187, by the European Crusaders (who had fought to take Christian holy lands back from the Muslims; see pages 357–360). They also were important in preventing the later Crusades from accomplishing much. Moreover, the Turks became staunch Sunnis and led a campaign against Shi'a.

The influx of Turks from 950 to 1100 also helped provide a new expansive dynamic. At the battle of Manzikert in 1071, Seljuk Turks broke through Byzantine border defenses, opening Anatolia to Turkish migration. Over the next couple of centuries, perhaps a million Turks entered the area. Seljuk Turks set up the Sultanate of Rum in Anatolia, which lasted until the Mongols invaded in 1243. Over time, many of the Christians in Anatolia converted to Islam and became fluent in Turkish.

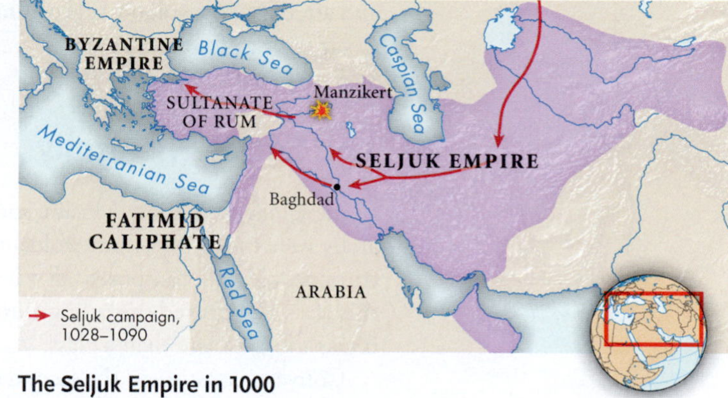

The Seljuk Empire in 1000

The Mongol Invasions

In the early thirteenth century the Mongols arrived in the Middle East. Originally from the grasslands of Mongolia, in 1206 they proclaimed Chinggis Khan (1162–1227) as their leader, and he welded Mongol, Tartar, and Turkish tribes into a strong confederation that rapidly subdued neighboring settled societies (see pages 298–302). After conquering much of north China, the Mongols swept westward, leaving a trail of blood and destruction.

In 1219–1221, when the Mongols first reached the Islamic lands, the areas from Persia through the Central Asian cities of Herat and Samarkand were part of the kingdom of Khwarizm. The ruler was a conqueror himself, having conquered much of Persia. He had the audacity to execute Chinggis's envoy, and Chinggis retaliated with a force of a hundred thousand soldiers that sacked city after city. Millions are said to have died.

Not many Mongol forces were left in Persia after the campaign of 1219–1221, and another army, sent in 1237, captured the Persian city of Isfahan. In 1251 the decision was taken to push farther west. Chinggis Khan's grandson, Hülegü (1217–1265) led an attack on the Abbasids in Baghdad, sacking and burning the city and killing the last Abbasid caliph in 1258. The fall of Damascus followed in 1260. Mamluk soldiers from Egypt, however, were able to withstand the Mongols and win a major victory at Ayn Jalut in Syria, which has been credited with saving Egypt and the Muslim lands in North Africa and perhaps Spain. At any rate, the desert ecology of the region did not provide suitable support for the Mongol armies, which required five horses for each soldier. Moreover, in 1260 the Great Khan (ruler of Mongolia and China) died, and the top Mongol generals withdrew to Mongolia for the selection of the next Great Khan.

Hülegü and his descendants ruled the central Muslim lands (referred to as the Il-Khanate) for eighty years. In 1295 his descendant Ghazan embraced Islam and worked for the revival of Muslim culture. As the Turks had done earlier, the Mongols, once converted, injected new vigor into the faith and spirit of Islam.

Quick Review
How and why did divisions emerge within the Islamic world after 900?

What social distinctions were important in Muslim society?

When the Prophet appeared, Arab society consisted of independent Bedouin tribal groups. Heads of families elected the *sheik*, or tribal chief. He was usually chosen from among elite warrior families who believed their bloodlines made them superior. According to the Qur'an, however, birth counted for nothing; piety was the only criterion for honor. The idea of social equality was a basic Muslim doctrine.

When Muhammad defined social equality, he was thinking about equality among Muslims alone. But even among Muslims, a sense of pride in ancestry could not be destroyed by a stroke of the pen. Claims based on birth remained strong among the first Muslims, and after Islam spread outside of Arabia, full-blooded Arab tribesmen regarded themselves as superior to foreign converts.

The Social Hierarchy

In the Umayyad period, Muslim society was distinctly hierarchical. At the top of the hierarchy were the caliph's household and the ruling Arab Muslims. Descended from Bedouin tribespeople and composed of warriors, veterans, governing officials, and town settlers, this class constituted the ruling elite. Because birth continued to determine membership, it was more a caste than a class.

Converts constituted the second class in Islamic society, one that grew slowly over time. Converts to Islam had to attach themselves to one of the Arab tribes in a subordinate capacity. From the Muslim converts eventually came the members of the commercial and learned professions—merchants, traders, teachers, doctors, artists, and interpreters of the shari'a. Second-class citizenship led some Muslim converts to adopt Shi'ism (see page 216). Even so, over the centuries, converts to Islam intermarried with their Muslim conquerors. Gradually, assimilation united peoples of various ethnic backgrounds.

dhimmis A term meaning "protected peoples"; they included Jews, Christians, and Zoroastrians.

Dhimmis (zih-MEEZ)—including Jews, Christians, and Zoroastrians—formed the third stratum. Considered "protected peoples" because they worshipped only one God, they were allowed to practice their religions, maintain their houses of worship, and conduct their business affairs as long as they gave unequivocal recognition to Muslim political supremacy and paid a small tax. Because many Jews and Christians were well educated, they were often appointed to high positions in government. Restrictions placed on Christians and Jews were not severe, and outbursts of violence against them were rare. However, their social position deteriorated during the Crusades and the Mongol invasions, when there was a general rise of religious loyalties. At those times, Muslims suspected the dhimmis, often rightly, of collaborating with the enemies of Islam.

How did the experience of Jews under Islam compare with that of Jews living in Christian Europe? Recent scholarship shows that in Europe Jews were first marginalized in the Christian social order then completely expelled from it. In Islam Jews, though marginalized, participated fully in commercial and professional activities, some attaining economic equality with their Muslim counterparts. The seventeenth Sura (chapter) of the Qur'an, titled Bani Isra'il, "The Children of Israel," accords to the Jews a special respect because they were "the people of the Book." Also, Islamic culture was urban and commercial and gave the merchant considerable respect; medieval Christian culture was basically rural and agricultural, and it did not revere the businessperson.

Slavery

Slavery had long existed in the ancient Middle East, and the Qur'an accepted slavery much the way the Old and New Testaments did. But the Qur'an also prescribes just and humane treatment of slaves, explicitly encouraging the freeing of slaves and the offering of opportunities for slaves to buy their own freedom. In fact, the freeing of slaves was thought to pave the way to paradise.

Muslim expansion ensured a steady flow of slaves captured in war. Women slaves worked as cooks, cleaners, laundresses, and nursemaids. A few performed as singers, musicians, and dancers. Many female slaves also served as concubines. Not only rulers but also high officials and rich merchants owned many concubines. Down the economic ladder, artisans and tradesmen often had a few concubines who assumed domestic as well as sexual duties.

According to tradition, the seclusion of women in a harem protected their virtue (see page 225), and when men had the means, the harem was secured by eunuch (castrated) guards. The use of eunuch guards seems to have been a practice Muslims adopted from the Byzantines and Persians. Early Muslim law forbade castration, so in the early Islamic period Muslims secured eunuchs from European, African, and Central Asian slave markets. In contrast to China, where only the emperor could have eunuch servants, the well-to-do in the Muslim world could purchase them to guard their harems.

Muslims also employed eunuchs as secretaries, tutors, and commercial agents, possibly because eunuchs were said to be more manageable and dependable than men with ordinary desires. Male slaves, eunuchs or not, were also set to work as longshoremen on the docks, as oarsmen on ships, in construction crews, in workshops, and in mines.

As already noted, male slaves also fought as soldiers. In the ninth century the rulers of Tunisia formed a special corps of black military slaves, and at the end of that century the Tulunid rulers of Egypt built an army of black slaves. The Fatimid rulers of Egypt (969–1171) raised large black battalions, and a Persian visitor to Cairo between 1046 and 1049 estimated an army of 100,000 slaves, of whom 30,000 were black soldiers.

Separating Men and Women in a Mosque In this mid-sixteenth-century illustration of the interior of a mosque, a screen separates the women, who are wearing veils and tending children, from the men. The women can hear what is being said, but the men cannot see them. (Bodleian Library, University of Oxford, Ms. Ouseley Add 24, fol. 55v)

Slavery in the Islamic world differed in a number of fundamental ways from the slavery later practiced in the Americas. First, race had no particular connection to slavery among Muslims. Second, slavery in the Islamic world was not the basis for plantation agriculture, as it was in the southern United States, the Caribbean, and Brazil in the eighteenth and nineteenth centuries. Finally, slavery was rarely hereditary in the Muslim world. Most slaves who were taken from non-Muslim peoples later converted, which often led to emancipation. The children of female slaves by Muslim masters were by definition Muslim and thus free. To give Muslim slavery the most positive possible interpretation, one could say that it provided a means to fill certain socioeconomic and military needs and that it assimilated rather than segregated outsiders.

Women in Classical Islamic Society

Before Islam, Arab tribal law gave women virtually no legal status. Girls were sold into marriage by their guardians, and their husbands could terminate the union at will. Also, women had virtually no property or succession rights. Seen from this perspective, the Qur'an sought to improve the social position of women.

The hadith—records of what Muhammad said and did, and what believers in the first two centuries after his death believed he said and did (see page 211)—usually depict women in terms of moral virtue, domesticity, and saintly ideals; they also show some prominent women in political roles. For example, Aisha, daughter of the first caliph and probably

LISTENING TO THE PAST

Abu Hamid Al-Ghazali, The Etiquette of Marriage

Abu Hamid Al-Ghazali (1058–1111) was a Persian philosopher, theologian, jurist, and Sufi, and a prolific author of more than seventy books. His magnum opus, the Revival of the Religious Sciences, *is divided into four parts:* Acts of Worship, Norms of Daily Life, The Ways to Perdition, *and* The Ways of Salvation. *The passages on marriage presented here are only a small part of* Norms of Daily Life, *a lengthy treatise full of quotations from the Qur'an and traditions about the words and actions of Muhammad. His writings reflect the trend toward more patriarchal readings of Muslim teachings.*

" There are five advantages to marriage: procreation, satisfying sexual desire, ordering the household, providing companionship, and disciplining the self in striving to sustain them. The first advantage — that is, procreation — is the prime cause, and on its account marriage was instituted. The aim is to sustain lineage so that the world would not want for humankind. . . .

It was for the purpose of freeing the heart that marriage with the bondmaid was permitted when there was fear of hardship, even though it results in enslaving the son, which is a kind of attrition; such marriage is forbidden to anyone who can obtain a free woman. However, the enslaving of a son is preferable to destroying the faith, for enslavement affects temporarily the life of the child, while committing an abomination results in losing the hereafter; in comparison to one of its days the longest life is insignificant. . . .

It is preferable for a person with a temperament so overcome by desire that one woman cannot curb it to have more than one woman, up to four. For God will grant him love and mercy, and will appease his heart by them; if not, replacing them is recommended. Seven nights after the death of Fatimah, Ali got married. It is said that al-Hasan, the son of Ali, was a great lover having married more than two hundred women. Perhaps he would marry four at a time, and perhaps he would divorce four at a time replacing them with others. . . .

The fourth advantage [of marriage]: being free from the concerns of household duties, as well as of preoccupation with cooking, sweeping, making beds, cleaning utensils, and means for obtaining support. . . .

Ali used to say, "The worst characteristics of men constitute the best characteristics of women; namely, stinginess, pride, and cowardice. For if the woman is stingy, she will preserve her own and her husband's possessions; if she is proud, she will refrain from addressing loose and improper words to everyone; and if she is cowardly, she will dread everything and will therefore not go out of her house and will avoid compromising situations for fear of her husband. . . ."

Some God-fearing men as a precaution against delusion would not marry off their daughters until they are seen. Al-Amash said, "Every marriage occurring without looking ends in worry and sadness." It is obvious that looking does not reveal character, religion, or wealth; rather, it distinguishes beauty from ugliness. . . .

The Messenger of God declared that "The best women are those whose faces are the most beautiful and whose dowries are the smallest." He enjoined against excessiveness in dowries. The Messenger of God married one of his wives for a dowry of ten dirhams and household furnishings that consisted of a hand mill, a jug, a pillow made of skin stuffed with palm fibers, and a stone; in the case of another, he feasted with two measures of barley; and for another, with two measures of dates and two of mush. . . .

It is incumbent upon the guardian also to examine the qualities of the husband and to look after his daughter so as not to give her in marriage to one who is ugly, ill-mannered, weak in faith, negligent in upholding her rights, or unequal to her in descent. The Prophet has said, "Marriage is enslavement; let one, therefore, be careful in whose hands he places his daughter." . . .

Muhammad's favorite wife, played a leading role in rallying support for the movement opposing Ali, who succeeded Uthman in 656 (see page 215). Likewise, Umm Salama, a member of a wealthy and prominent clan in Mecca, first supported Ali, then switched sides and supported the Umayyads.[1] (See "Listening to the Past: Abu Hamid Al-Ghazali, The Etiquette of Marriage," above.)

The Qur'an, like the religious writings of other traditions, represents moral precept rather than social practice, and the texts are open to different interpretations. Modern scholars tend to agree that the Islamic sacred book intended women to be the spiritual and sexual equals of men and gave them considerable economic rights. In the early Umayyad period, moreover, women played active roles in the religious, economic, and political life of the community. They owned property. They had freedom of movement and traveled widely.

1308 Persian edition of the *Alchemy of Happiness*, titled in the original Arabic version the *Revival of Religious Sciences*. (Bibliothèque nationale de France)

The Prophet asked his daughter Fatimah, "What is best for a woman?" She replied, "That she should see no man, and that no man should see her." So he hugged her and said they were "descendants one of another" [Qur'an 3:33]. Thus he was pleased with her answer. . . .

The Prophet permitted women to go to the mosques; the appropriate thing now, however, is to prevent them [from doing so], except for the old [ones]. Indeed such [prevention] was deemed proper during the days of the companions; A'ishah declared, "If the Prophet only knew of the misdeeds that women would bring about after his time, he would have prevented them from going out." . . .

If [a man] has several wives, then he should deal equitably with them and not favor one over the other; should he go on a journey and desire to have one [of his wives] accompany him, he should cast lots among them, for such was the practice of the Messenger. If he cheats a woman of her night, he should make up for it, for making up for it is a duty upon him. . . .

Let [a man] proceed with gentle words and kisses. The Prophet said, "Let none of you come upon his wife like an animal, and let there be an emissary between them." He was asked, "What is this emissary, O Messenger of God?" He said, "The kiss and [sweet] words."

One should not be overjoyed with the birth of a male child, nor should he be excessively dejected over the birth of a female child, for he does not know in which of the two his blessings lie. Many a man who has a son wishes he did not have him, or wishes that he were a girl. The girls give more tranquility and [divine] remuneration, which are greater.

Concerning divorce, let it be known that it is permissible; but of all permissible things, it is the most detestable to Almighty God. ”

Source: Madelain Farah, *Marriage and Sexuality in Islam: A Translation of Al-Ghazālī's Book on the Etiquette of Marriage from the Ihyā'* (Salt Lake City: University of Utah Press, 1984), pp. 53, 63, 64, 66, 85–86, 88–89, 91, 95–96, 100, 103, 106, 113, 116, slightly modified.

QUESTIONS FOR ANALYSIS

1. In what ways are the views toward marriage and gender expressed by Al-Ghazali similar to those seen in other traditions?
2. Were there situations in which the author did not think it was appropriate to do what Muhammad and his early followers did? What was his reasoning?

They participated with men in public religious rituals and observances. But this Islamic ideal of women and men having equal value to the community did not last, and, as Islamic society changed, the precepts of the Qur'an were interpreted in more patriarchal ways.

By the Abbasid period, the status of women had declined. The practices of the Byzantine and Persian lands that had been conquered, including seclusion of women, were absorbed. The supply of slave women increased substantially. Some scholars speculate that as wealth replaced ancestry as the criterion of social status, men more and more viewed women as possessions, as a form of wealth.

Men were also seen as dominant in their marriages. The Qur'an states that "men are in charge of women because Allah hath made the one to excel the other, and because they (men) spend of their property (for the support of women). So good women are obedient, guarding in secret that which Allah hath guarded."[2] A tenth-century interpreter, Abu Ja'far Muhammad ibn-Jarir al-Tabari, commented on that passage this way:

> *Men are in charge of their women with respect to disciplining (or chastising) them, and to providing them with restrictive guidance concerning their duties toward God and themselves (i.e., the men), by virtue of that by which God has given excellence (or preference) to the men over their wives: i.e., the payment of their dowers to them, spending of their wealth on them, and providing for them in full.*[3]

A thirteenth-century commentator on the same Qur'anic passage goes into more detail and argues that women are incapable of and unfit for any public duties, such as participating in religious rites, giving evidence in the law courts, or being involved in any public political decisions. This view came to be accepted, and later interpreters further categorized the ways in which men were superior to women.

The Sunni aphorism "There shall be no monkery in Islam" captures the importance of marriage in Muslim culture and the Muslim belief that a sexually frustrated person is dangerous to the community. Islam had no roles for the celibate. In the Muslim world, as in China, every man and woman is expected to marry unless physically incapable or financially unable. Marriage is seen as a safeguard of virtue, essential to the stability both of the family and of society.

As in medieval Europe and traditional India and China, in Muslim society families or guardians, not the prospective bride and groom, identified suitable marriage partners and finalized the contract. Because it was absolutely essential that the bride be a virgin, marriages were arranged shortly after the onset of the girl's menstrual period at age twelve or thirteen. Husbands were perhaps ten to fifteen years older. Youthful marriages ensured a long period of fertility.

A wife's responsibilities depended on the wealth and occupation of her husband. A farmer's wife helped in the fields, ground the corn, carried water, prepared food, and did the myriad of tasks necessary in rural life. Shopkeepers' wives in the cities sometimes helped in business. In an upper-class household, the lady supervised servants, looked after all domestic arrangements, and did whatever was needed for her husband's comfort.

In every case, children were the wife's special domain. A mother exercised authority over her children and enjoyed their respect. As in Chinese culture, the prestige of the young wife depended on the production of children—especially sons—as rapidly as possible. A wife's failure to have children was one of the main reasons for a man to take a second wife or to divorce his wife entirely.

Like the Jewish tradition, Muslim law permits divorce. Although divorce is allowed, it is not encouraged. One commentator cited the Prophet as saying, "The lawful thing which God hates most is divorce."[4]

In contrast to the traditional Christian view of sexual activity as something inherently shameful, Islam maintains a healthy acceptance of sexual pleasure for both males and females. The Qur'an permits a man to have four wives, provided that all are treated justly. As in other societies that allowed men to take several wives, only wealthy men could afford to do so. The vast majority of Muslim males were monogamous because they had difficulty enough supporting one wife.

In many present-day Muslim cultures, few issues are more sensitive than the veiling and seclusion of women. These practices have their roots in pre-Islamic times, and they took firm hold in classical Islamic society. As Arab conquerors subjugated various peoples, they adopted some of the vanquished peoples' customs. Veiling was probably of Byzantine or Persian origin. The head veil seems to have been the mark of freeborn urban women; wearing it distinguished them from slave women. Country and desert women did not wear veils because they interfered with work. The veil also indicated respectability and modesty.

Gradually, the custom of covering women extended beyond the veil. Eventually, all parts of a woman's body were considered best covered in public.

An even greater restriction on women than veiling was the practice of purdah, literally, seclusion behind a screen or curtain—the harem system. The practice of secluding women in a harem also derives from Arabic contacts with Persia and other Eastern cultures. Scholars do not know precisely when the harem system began, but by 800 women in more prosperous households stayed out of sight. The harem became another symbol of male prestige and prosperity, as well as a way to distinguish upper-class women from peasants.

Quick Review
How did social, religious, and gender hierarchies shape Islamic life?

Why did trade thrive in Muslim lands?

Islam looked favorably on profit-making enterprises. From 1000 to 1500 there was less ideological resistance to striving for profit in trade and commerce in the Muslim world than in the Christian West or the Confucian East. Also in contrast to the social values of the medieval West and the Confucian East, Muslims tended to look with disdain on agricultural labor. Muhammad had earned his living in business as a representative of the city of Mecca, which carried on a brisk trade from southern Palestine to southwestern Arabia.

The Qur'an, moreover, has no prohibition against trade with Christians or other unbelievers. In fact, non-Muslims, including the Jews of Cairo and the Armenians in the central Islamic lands, were prominent in mercantile networks.

Waterways served as the main commercial routes of the Islamic world (Map 9.2). They included the Mediterranean and Black Seas; the Caspian Sea and the Volga River, which gave access deep into Russia; the Aral Sea, from which caravans departed for China; the Gulf of Aden; and the Arabian Sea and the Indian Ocean, which linked the Persian Gulf region with eastern Africa, the Indian subcontinent, and eventually Indonesia and the Philippines.

Cairo was a major Mediterranean entrepôt for intercontinental trade. Foreign merchants from Central Asia, Persia, Iraq, northern Europe (especially Venice), the Byzantine Empire, and Spain sailed up the Nile to the Aswan region, traveled east from Aswan by caravan to the Red Sea, and then sailed down the Red Sea to Aden, where they entered the Indian Ocean on their way to India. They exchanged textiles, glass, gold, silver, and copper for Asian spices, dyes, and drugs and for Chinese silks and porcelains. Muslim and Jewish merchants dominated the trade with India, and all spoke and wrote Arabic. Their commercial practices included the *sakk*, an Arabic word that is the root of the English *check*, an order to a banker to pay money held on account to a third party; the practice can be traced to Roman Palestine. Muslims also developed other business innovations, such as the bill of exchange, a written order from one person to another to pay a specified sum of money to a designated person or party, and the idea of the joint stock company, an arrangement that lets a group of people invest in a venture and share its profits (and losses) in proportion to the amount each has invested.

Trade also benefited from improvements in technology. The adoption from the Chinese of the magnetic compass greatly helped navigation of the Arabian Sea and the Indian Ocean. The construction of larger ships led to a shift in long-distance cargoes from luxury goods such as pepper, spices, and drugs to bulk goods such as sugar, rice, and timber.

In this period Egypt became the center of Muslim trade, benefiting from the decline of Iraq caused by the Mongol capture of Baghdad and the fall of the Abbasid caliphate (see page 219). Beginning in the late twelfth century Persian and Arab seamen sailed down

Map 9.2 The Expansion of Islam and Its Trading Networks in the Thirteenth and Fourteenth Centuries By 1500 Islam had spread extensively in North and East Africa, and into the Balkans, the Caucasus, Central Asia, India, and island Southeast Asia. Muslim merchants played a major role in bringing their religion as they extended their trade networks. They were active in the Indian Ocean long before the arrival of Europeans.

the east coast of Africa and established trading towns between Somalia and Sofala (see pages 254–258). These thirty to fifty urban centers—each merchant-controlled, fortified, and independent—linked Zimbabwe in southern Africa with the Indian Ocean trade and the Middle Eastern trade.

Quick Review
How did Islamic attitudes toward merchants and commerce shape the economy of the Islamic world?

Until the sixteenth century much more world trade went through Muslim than European hands. One byproduct of the extensive trade through Muslim lands was the spread of useful plants. Cotton, sugar cane, and rice spread from India to other places with suitable climates. Citrus fruits made their way to Muslim Spain from Southeast Asia and India. The value of this trade contributed to the prosperity of the Abbasid era.

What new cultural developments emerged in this period?

Long-distance trade provided the wealth that made possible a sophisticated culture in the cities of the Muslim world. (See "Individuals in Society: Ibn Battuta," page 228.) Education helped foster achievements in the arts and sciences, Sufism brought a new spiritual and intellectual tradition.

The Cultural Centers of Baghdad and Córdoba

The cities of Baghdad and Córdoba, at their peak in the tenth century, stand out as the finest examples of cosmopolitan Muslim civilization. On Baghdad's streets thronged a kaleidoscope of races, creeds, costumes, and cultures, an almost infinite variety of peoples from Asia, Africa, and Europe. Shops and marketplaces offered a dazzling and exotic array of goods from all over the world. This brilliant era provided the background for the tales that appear in *The Thousand and One Nights*. Though filled with folklore, including the tales of Aladdin and Sinbad, the *Arabian Nights* (as it is also called) has provided many of the images through which Europeans have understood the Islamic world.

Córdoba in southern Spain competed with Baghdad for the cultural leadership of the Islamic world. In the tenth century no city in Asia or Europe could equal dazzling Córdoba. Its streets were well paved and lighted, and the city had an abundant supply of freshwater. With a population of about 1 million, Córdoba contained 1,600 mosques, 900 public baths, 213,177 houses for ordinary people, and 60,000 mansions for the elite. In its 80,455 shops, 13,000 weavers produced textiles that were internationally famous. Córdoba was also a great educational center with twenty-seven free schools and a library containing 400,000 volumes. (By contrast, the great Benedictine abbey of Saint-Gall in Switzerland had about 600 books.) Moreover, Córdoba's scholars made contributions in chemistry, medicine and surgery, music, philosophy, and mathematics.

Education and Intellectual Life

Muslim culture valued learning, especially religious learning, because knowledge provided the guidelines by which men and women should live. Parents, thus, established elementary schools for the training of their children. After the caliph Uthman (see page 215) ordered the preparation of an approved text of the Qur'an and had copies of it made, the Qur'an became the basic text. From the eighth century onward formal education for young men involved reading, writing, and the study of the Qur'an, believed essential for its religious message and for its training in proper grammar and syntax.

Islam is a religion of the law, and the institution for instruction in Muslim jurisprudence was the **madrasa** (muh-DRA-suh), the school for the study of Muslim law and religion. Many madrasas were founded throughout the Muslim world between 1000 and 1350.

madrasa A school for the study of Muslim law and religious science.

Schools were urban phenomena. Wealthy merchants endowed them, providing salaries for teachers, stipends for students, and living accommodations for both. The teacher served as a guide to the correct path of living. All Islamic higher education rested on a close relationship between teacher and students, so in selecting a teacher, the student (or his father) considered the character and intellectual reputation of the teacher, not that of the institution. Students built their subsequent careers on the reputation of their teachers.

Learning depended heavily on memorization and recitation of Islamic texts, the most important being the Qur'an. Students, of course, learned to write, for they had to record

INDIVIDUALS IN SOCIETY

Ibn Battuta

IN 1354 THE SULTAN OF MOROCCO APPOINTED A scribe to write an account of the travels of Abu' Abdallah Ibn Battuta (1304–1368), who between 1325 and 1354 had traveled through most of the Islamic world. The two men collaborated. The result was a travel book written in Arabic and later hailed as the richest eyewitness account of fourteenth-century Islamic culture. It has often been compared to the slightly earlier *Travels* of the Venetian Marco Polo (see page 303).

Ibn Battuta was born in Tangier to a family of legal scholars. As a youth, he studied Muslim law, gained fluency in Arabic, and acquired the qualities considered essential for a civilized Muslim gentleman: courtesy, manners, and the social polish that eases relations among people.

At age twenty-one he left Tangier to make the *hajj* (pilgrimage) to Mecca. He crossed North Africa and visited Alexandria, Cairo, Damascus, and Medina. Reaching Mecca in October 1326, he immediately praised God for his safe journey, kissed the Holy Stone at the Ka'ba, and recited the ritual prayers. There he decided to see more of the world.

In the next four years Ibn Battuta traveled to Iraq and to Basra and Baghdad in Persia, then returned to Mecca before sailing down the coast of Africa as far as modern Tanzania. On the return voyage he visited Oman and the Persian Gulf region, then traveled by land across central Arabia to Mecca. Strengthened by his stay in the holy city, he decided to go to India by way of Egypt, Syria, and Anatolia; across the Black Sea to the plains of western Central Asia, detouring to see Constantinople; back to the Asian steppe; east to Khurasan and Afghanistan; and down to Delhi in northern India.

For eight years Ibn Battuta served as a judge in the service of the sultan of Delhi. In 1341 the sultan chose him to lead a diplomatic mission to China. After the expedition was shipwrecked off the southeastern coast of India, Ibn Battuta traveled through southern India, Sri Lanka, and the Maldive Islands. Then he went to China, stopping in Bengal and Sumatra before reaching the southern coast of China, then under Mongol rule. Returning to Mecca in 1346, he set off for home, getting to Morocco in 1349. After a brief trip across the Strait of Gibraltar to Granada, he undertook his last journey, by camel caravan across the Sahara to Mali in the west African Sudan (see page 249), returning home in 1354. Scholars estimate that he had traveled about seventy-five thousand miles.

Ibn Battuta had a driving intellectual curiosity to see and understand the world. At every stop, he sought the learned jurists and pious men at the mosques and madrasas. He marveled at the Lighthouse of Alexandria, then in ruins; at the vast harbor at Kaffa (in southern Ukraine on the Black Sea), whose two hundred Genoese ships were loaded with silks and slaves for the markets at Venice, Cairo, and Damascus; and at the elephants in the sultan's procession in Delhi, which carried machines that tossed gold and silver coins to the crowds.

Ibn Battuta must have had an iron constitution. Besides walking long distances on his land trips, he endured fevers, dysentery, malaria, the scorching heat of the Sahara, and the freezing cold of the steppe. His thirst for adventure was stronger than his fear of nomadic warriors and bandits on land and the dangers of storms and pirates at sea.

A traveler, perhaps Ibn Battuta, as depicted on a 1375 European map. (The Granger Collection, New York)

Source: R. E. Dunn, *The Adventures of Ibn Battuta: A Muslim Traveler of the Fourteenth Century* (Berkeley: University of California Press, 1986).

QUESTIONS FOR ANALYSIS

1. Trace the routes of Ibn Battuta's travels on Map 9.2 (page 226).
2. How did a common Muslim culture facilitate Ibn Battuta's travels?

the teacher's commentary on a particular work. But the overwhelming emphasis was on the oral transmission of knowledge.

Because Islamic education focused on particular books, when the student had mastered a text to his teacher's satisfaction, the teacher issued the student a certificate stating that he had studied the book or collection of traditions with his teacher. The certificate allowed the student to transmit a text to the next generation on the authority of his teacher.

As the importance of books suggests, the Muslim transmission and improvement of papermaking techniques had special significance to education. For centuries the Chinese had been making paper from rags and from the fibers of hemp, jute, bamboo, and other plants. After these techniques spread westward, Muslim papermakers improved on them by adding starch to fill the pores in the surfaces of the sheets. Even before the invention of printing, papermaking had a revolutionary impact on the collection and diffusion of knowledge and thus on the transformation of society.

Muslim higher education, apart from its fundamental goal of preparing men to live wisely and in accordance with God's law, aimed at preparing them to perform religious and legal functions as Qur'an—or hadith—readers; as preachers in the mosques; as professors, educators, or copyists; and especially as judges. Judges issued fatwas, or legal opinions, in the public courts; their training was in the Qur'an, hadith, or some text forming part of the shari'a.

Islamic culture was ambivalent on the issue of female education. Women were excluded from participating in the legal, religious, or civic occupations for which the madrasa prepared young men. Moreover, educational theorists insisted that men should study in a sexually isolated environment because feminine allure would distract them. Nevertheless, many young women received substantial educations from their parents or family members; the initiative invariably rested with their fathers or older brothers. According to one biographical dictionary covering the lives of 1,075 women, 411 of them had memorized the Qur'an, studied with a particular teacher, and received a certificate. After marriage, responsibility for a woman's education belonged to her husband.

How does Islamic higher education during the twelfth through fourteenth centuries compare with that available in Europe or China at the same time (see pages 365–366, 327–332)? There are some striking similarities and some major differences. In both Europe and the Islamic countries, religious authorities ran most schools, while in China the government, local villages, and lineages ran schools, and private tutoring was very common. In the Islamic world, as in China, the personal relationship of teacher and student was seen as key to education. In Europe the reward for satisfactorily completing a course of study was a degree granted by the university. In China, at the very highest levels, the state ran a civil service examination system that rewarded achievement with appointments in the state bureaucracy. In Muslim culture, by contrast, it was not the school or the state but the individual teacher whose evaluation mattered and who granted certificates.

Still, there were also some striking similarities in the practice of education. Students in all three cultures had to master a sacred language (Latin, Arabic, or classical Chinese). In all three cultures education rested heavily on the study of basic religious, legal, or philosophical texts. Also in all three cultures memorization played a large role in the acquisition and transmission of learning. Furthermore, teachers in all three societies lectured on particular passages, and leading teachers might disagree fiercely about the correct interpretations of a particular text, forcing students to question, to think critically, and to choose among divergent opinions. All these similarities in educational practice contributed to cultural cohesion and ties among the educated living in scattered localities.

In the Muslim world the spread of the Arabic language, not only among the educated classes but also among all the people, was the decisive element in the creation of a common culture. Recent scholarship demonstrates that after the establishment of the Islamic empire, the major influence in the cultural transformation of the Byzantine–Sassanid–North African and the Central Asian worlds was language. The Arabic language proved more important than religion in this regard. Whereas conversion to Islam was gradual, linguistic conversion went much faster. Islamic rulers required tribute from monotheistic peoples—the Persians and Greeks—but they did not force them to change their religions. Conquered peoples were, however, compelled to submit to a linguistic conversion—to adopt the Arabic language. In time Arabic produced a cohesive and "international" culture over a large part of the Eurasian world.

As a result of Muslim creativity and vitality, modern scholars consider the years from 800 to 1300 to be one of the most brilliant periods in the world's history. Near the beginning of this period the Persian scholar al-Khwarizmi (d. ca. 850) harmonized Greek and Indian findings to produce astronomical tables that formed the basis for later Eastern and Western research. Al-Khwarizmi also studied mathematics, and his textbook on algebra (from the Arabic *al-Jabr*) was the first work in which the word *algebra* is used to mean the "transposing of negative terms in an equation to the opposite side."

Muslim medical knowledge far surpassed that of the West. Muslim medical science reached its peak in the work of Ibn Sina of Bukhara (980–1037), known in the West as Avicenna. His *al-Qanun* codified all Greco-Arabic medical thought, described the contagious nature of tuberculosis and the spreading of diseases, and listed 760 drugs.

Muslim scholars also wrote works on geography, jurisprudence, and philosophy. Al-Kindi (d. ca. 870) was the first Muslim thinker to try to harmonize Greek philosophy and the religious precepts of the Qur'an. He sought to integrate Islamic concepts of human beings and their relations to God and the universe with the principles of ethical and social conduct discussed by Plato and Aristotle. Ibn Rushid, or Averroës (1126–1198), of Córdoba, a judge in Seville and later the royal court physician, paraphrased and commented on the works of Aristotle. He insisted on the right to subject all knowledge, except the dogmas of faith, to the test of reason and on the essential harmony of religion and philosophy.

The Mystical Tradition of Sufism

Like the world's other major religions—Buddhism, Hinduism, Judaism, and Christianity—Islam also developed a mystical tradition: Sufism (SOO-fizm). It arose in the ninth and tenth centuries as a popular reaction to the materialism and worldliness of the later Umayyad regime. Sufis sought a personal union with God—divine love and knowledge through intuition rather than through rational deduction and study of the shari'a.

Between the tenth and the thirteenth centuries groups of Sufis gathered around prominent leaders called *shaykhs*; members of these groups were called *dervishes*. Dervishes entered hypnotic or ecstatic trances, either through the constant repetition of certain prayers or through physical exertions such as whirling or dancing.

Some Sufis acquired reputations as charismatic holy men to whom ordinary Muslims came seeking spiritual consolation, healing, charity, or political mediation between tribal and factional rivals. Other Sufis became known for their writings. Probably the most famous medieval Sufi was the Spanish mystic-philosopher Ibn al'Arabi (1165–1240). He traveled widely in Spain, North Africa, and Arabia seeking masters of Sufism. In Mecca he received a "divine commandment" to begin his major work, *The Meccan Revelation*, which evolved into a personal encyclopedia of 560 chapters. In 1223, after visits to Egypt, Anatolia, Baghdad, and Aleppo, Ibn al'Arabi concluded his pilgrimage through the Islamic world at Damascus, where he produced *The Bezels [Edges] of Wisdom*, considered one of the greatest works of Sufism.

Quick Review
How did Islamic ideas about education shape Islamic intellectual life?

Picturing the Past

Sufi Collective Ritual

Collective or group rituals, in which Sufis tried through ecstatic experiences to come closer to God, have always fascinated outsiders, including non-Sufi Muslims. Here the sixteenth-century Persian painter Sultan Muhammad illustrates the writing of the fourteenth-century lyric poet Hafiz. Notice the various musical instruments and the delicate floral patterns so characteristic of Persian art. (Edinburgh University Library, Scotland/With kind permission of the University of Edinburgh/The Bridgeman Art Library)

ANALYZING THE IMAGE What sort of architectural space is depicted here? What distinctions do you see among the people in terms of how they dress and what they are doing?

CONNECTIONS How common are music and dance in religion? What do they provide?

What characterized Muslim-Christian interactions?

During the early centuries of its development, Islam came into contact with the other major religions of Eurasia — Hinduism in India, Buddhism in Central Asia, Zoroastrianism in Persia, and Judaism and Christianity in western Asia and Europe. However, the relationship that did the most to define Muslim identity was the one with Christianity. The close physical proximity and the long history of military encounters undoubtedly contributed to making the Christian-Muslim encounter so important to both sides.

European Christians and Middle Eastern Muslims shared a common cultural heritage from the Judeo-Christian past. In the classical period of Islam, Muslims learned about Christianity from the Christians they met in conquered territories; from the Old and New Testaments; from Jews; and from Jews and Christians who converted to Islam. Before 1400 a wide spectrum of Muslim opinion about Jesus and Christians existed. At the time of the Crusades and of the Christian reconquest of Muslim Spain (the *reconquista*, 722–1492), polemical anti-Christian writings appeared. In other periods, Muslim views were more positive.

In the medieval period Christians and Muslims met frequently in business and trade. Commercial contacts gave Europeans, notably the Venetians, familiarity with Muslim art and architecture. Likewise, when in the fifteenth century Muslim artists in the Ottoman Empire and in Persia became acquainted with Western artists, they admired and imitated them. Also, Christians very likely borrowed aspects of their higher education practices from Islam.

In the Christian West, Islam had the greatest cultural impact in Andalusia in southern Spain. Between roughly the eighth and twelfth centuries, Muslims, Christians, and Jews lived in close proximity in Andalusia, and some scholars believe the period represents a remarkable era of interfaith harmony. Many Christians adopted Arabic patterns of speech and dress, gave up the practice of eating pork, and developed a special appreciation for

Mozarabs Christians who adopted some Arabic customs but did not convert.

Arabic music and poetry. These assimilated Christians, called **Mozarabs** (moh-ZAR-uhbz), did not attach much importance to the doctrinal differences between the two religions.

However, Mozarabs soon faced the strong criticism of both Muslim scholars and Christian clerics. Muslim teachers feared that close contact between people of the two religions would lead to Muslim contamination and become a threat to the Islamic faith. Christian bishops worried that a knowledge of Islam would lead to confusion about essential Christian doctrines. Both Muslim scholars and Christian theologians argued that assimilation led to moral decline.

Thus, beginning in the late tenth century, Muslim regulations closely defined what Christians and Muslims could do. Because of their status as unbelievers, Mozarabs had to live in special sections of cities; could not learn the Qur'an, employ Muslim workers or servants, or build new churches; and had to be buried in their own cemeteries. A Muslim who converted to Christianity immediately incurred a sentence of death. By about 1250 the Christian reconquest of Muslim Spain had brought most of the Iberian Peninsula under Christian control. With their new authority Christian kings set up schools that taught both Arabic and Latin to train missionaries.

Beyond Andalusian Spain, mutual animosity limited contact between people of the two religions. The Muslim assault on Christian Europe in the eighth and ninth centuries left a legacy of bitter hostility. Europeans' perception of Islam as a menace helped inspire the Crusades of the eleventh through thirteenth centuries (see pages 357–361).

Despite the conflicts between the two religions, Muslim scholars often wrote sympathetically about Jesus. For example, the great historian al Tabari (d. 923), relying on Arabic sources, wrote positively of Jesus's life, focusing on his birth and crucifixion. Also, Ikhwan al-Safa, an eleventh-century Islamic brotherhood, held that in his preaching Jesus deliberately rejected the harsh punishments reflected in the Jewish Torah and tried to be the healing physician teaching by parables and trying to touch people's hearts by peace and love. In terms of more critical views of Christianity, al Tabari used Old Testament books to prove Muhammad's prophethood. The prominent theologian and qadi (judge) of Teheran, Abd al-Jabbar (d. 1024), though not critical of Jesus, argued that Christians failed to observe the laws of Moses and Jesus, and thus, distorted Jesus's message.

Mozarabic Bible
In this page from a tenth-century Mozarabic Bible, Moses is depicted closing the passage through the Red Sea, thus drowning the Egyptians. (The Art Archive at Art Resource, NY)

In the Christian West, both positive and negative views of Islam appeared in literature. The Bavarian knight Wolfram von Eschenbach's *Parzival* and the Englishman William Langland's *Piers the Plowman* reveal broad-mindedness and tolerance toward Muslims. Some travelers in the Middle East were impressed by the kindness and generosity of Muslims and with the strictness and devotion with which Muslims observed their faith. Frequently, however, Christian literature portrayed Muslims as the most dreadful of Europe's enemies, guilty of every kind of crime. In his *Inferno*, for example, the great Florentine poet Dante (1265–1321) placed Muhammad in the ninth circle of Hell, near Satan himself, where he was condemned as a spreader of discord and scandal and suffered perpetual torture.

Even when they rejected each other most forcefully, the Christian and Muslim worlds had a significant impact on each other. Art styles, technology, and even institutional practices spread in both directions. During the Crusades Muslims adopted Frankish weapons and methods of fortification. Christians in contact with Muslim scholars recovered ancient Greek philosophical texts that survived only in Arabic translation.

Quick Review
How did Muslims and Christians come into contact with each other, and how did they view each other?

Connections

DURING THE FIVE CENTURIES that followed Muhammad's death, his teachings came to be revered in large parts of the world from Spain to Afghanistan. Although in some ways similar to the earlier spread of Buddhism out of India and Christianity out of Palestine, in the case of Islam, military conquests played a large part in the extension of Muslim lands. Still, conversion was never complete; both Christians and Jews maintained substantial communities within Muslim lands. Moreover, cultural contact among Christians, Jews, and Muslims was an important element in the development of each culture.

Muslim civilization in these centuries drew from many sources, including Persia and Byzantium, and in turn had broad impact beyond its borders. Muslim scholars preserved much of early Greek philosophy and science through translation into Arabic. Trade connected the Muslim lands both to Europe and to India and China.

During the first and second centuries after Muhammad, Islam spread along the Mediterranean coast of North Africa, which had been part of the Roman world. The next chapter explores other developments in the enormous and diverse continent of Africa during this time. Many of the written sources that tell us about the African societies of these centuries were written in Arabic by visitors from elsewhere in the Muslim world. Muslim traders traveled through many of the societies in Africa north of the Congo, aiding the spread of Islam to the elites of many of these societies. Ethiopia was an exception, as Christianity spread there from Egypt before the time of Muhammad and retained its hold in subsequent centuries. Africa's history is introduced in the next chapter.

- **For a list of suggested readings for this chapter, visit** *bedfordstmartins.com/mckayworldunderstanding*.
- **For primary sources from this period, see** *Sources of World Societies*, Second Edition.
- **For Web sites, images, and documents related to topics in this chapter, see Make History at** *bedfordstmartins.com/mckayworldunderstanding*.

Chapter 9 Study Guide

To do these exercises online, go to bedfordstmartins.com/mckayworldunderstanding.

Step 1 GETTING STARTED

Below are basic terms about this period in global history. Can you identify each term below and explain why it matters?

TERMS	WHO (OR WHAT) AND WHEN	WHY IT MATTERS
Qur'an, p. 211		
hadith, p. 211		
Sunna, p. 211		
Five Pillars of Islam, p. 212		
umma, p. 212		
diwān, p. 214		
imam, p. 216		
Shi'a, p. 216		
Sunnis, p. 216		
ulama, p. 216		
emirs, p. 217		
shari'a, p. 217		
vizier, p. 217		
dhimmis, p. 220		
madrasa, p. 227		
Mozarabs, p. 232		

Step 2 MOVING BEYOND THE BASICS

The exercise below requires a more advanced understanding of the chapter material. Examine the relationship between Islamic beliefs and social, economic, and cultural developments in the Islamic world by filling in the first column of the chart below with a description of the core Islamic beliefs. Then fill in the remaining three columns with descriptions of the impact of those beliefs on social, economic, and cultural developments. When you are finished, consider the following questions: How did the advent of Islam impact the status of women in Islamic lands? How did Islamic attitudes toward trade shape the economy of Islamic lands? How did Islamic beliefs influence education and scholarship in the Islamic world?

CORE ISLAMIC BELIEFS	IMPACT ON SOCIAL DEVELOPMENTS	IMPACT ON ECONOMIC DEVELOPMENTS	IMPACT ON CULTURAL DEVELOPMENTS

Step 3

PUTTING IT ALL TOGETHER

Now that you've reviewed key elements of the chapter, take a step back and try to see the big picture. Remember to use specific examples from the chapter in your answers.

THE ORIGINS OF ISLAM

- What characterized the social and economic environment in which Muhammad lived and preached?
- What are the core teachings of Islam? How do they compare to the core teachings of Christianity and Judaism?

ISLAMIC EXPANSION

- Argue for or against the following proposition: "The single most important factor explaining the rapid expansion of Islamic territories was the religious fervor of Muslim leaders and their armies." What evidence can you present to support your position?
- What explains the fragmentation of the Islamic world after 900? How did internal factors contribute to this trend? What about external threats?

ISLAMIC SOCIETY, COMMERCE, AND CULTURE

- Compare and contrast Roman (Chapter 6) and Islamic slavery. What role did slaves play in each society? How would you explain the similarities and differences you note?
- Compare and contrast Islamic and Confucian ideas (Chapter 7) about merchants and trade. How did such attitudes shape the social and economic trajectories of the Islamic and Chinese civilizations?

LOOKING BACK, LOOKING AHEAD

- What older Persian and Byzantine institutions and ideas did Islamic states incorporate into their own governments? How were those ideas and institutions modified by Islamic beliefs and practices?
- What connections can you make between the history of Muslim-Christian interactions and the contemporary relationship between Western and Islamic societies? How do long-held beliefs shape each society's view of the other?

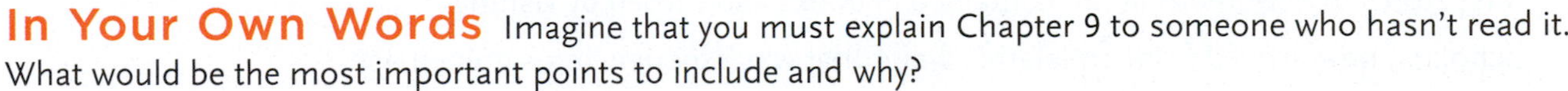

In Your Own Words Imagine that you must explain Chapter 9 to someone who hasn't read it. What would be the most important points to include and why?

10

African Societies and Kingdoms

1000 B.C.E.–1500 C.E.

Until fairly recently, most of the outside world knew little about the African continent, its history, or its people. The sheer size of the continent, along with tropical diseases and the difficulty of navigating Africa's rivers inland, limited travel there to a few intrepid Muslim adventurers such as Ibn Battuta. Ethnocentrism and racism led many in the West to fill in this gap in knowledge with the assumption that early Africa was home to "primitive," inferior societies. But recent scholarship has allowed us to learn more about early African civilizations, and we are able to appreciate the richness, diversity, and dynamism of those cultures. We know now that between about 400 and 1500 some highly centralized, bureaucratized, and socially stratified civilizations developed in Africa alongside communities with a looser form of social organization that were often held together simply through common bonds of kinship.

In West Africa there arose during this period several large empires that were closely linked to the trans-Saharan trade in salt, gold, cloth, ironware, ivory, and other goods. After 700 this trade connected West Africa with the Muslim societies of North Africa and the Middle East. Vast stores of new information, contained in books and carried by visiting scholars, now arrived from an Islamic world that was experiencing a golden age.

Meanwhile, Bantu-speaking peoples carried ironworking and the domestication of crops and animals from modern Cameroon to Africa's southern tip. They established kingdoms, such as Great Zimbabwe, in the interior, while one group, the Swahili, established large and prosperous city-states along the Indian Ocean coast.

Ife Ruler West African kings, such as the one shown in this bronze torso of a Yoruban king, or *Oni*, from the thirteenth or fourteenth century, were usually male. (© Jerry Thompson)

Chapter Preview

- How did geography shape the history of Africa's diverse peoples?
- How did the advent of settled agriculture affect early societies?
- What role did the trans-Saharan trade play in West African history?
- What kingdoms and empires emerged in Africa between 800 and 1500?

How did geography shape the history of Africa's diverse peoples?

The world's second largest continent (after Asia), Africa covers 20 percent of the earth's land surface. The student beginning the study of African history should bear in mind the enormous diversity of African peoples and cultures both within and across regions. African peoples are not now and never have been homogeneous. This rich diversity helps explain why the study of African history is so exciting and challenging.

Africa's Geographical and Human Diversity

Five main climatic zones roughly divide the continent (Map 10.1). Fertile land with unpredictable rainfall borders parts of the Mediterranean coast in the north and the southwestern coast of the Cape of Good Hope in the south. Inland from these areas lies dry steppe country with little plant life. The steppe gradually gives way to Africa's great deserts: the Sahara in the north and the Namib (NAH-mihb) and Kalahari in the south. The savanna—flat grassland—extends in a swath across the widest part of the continent, across parts

Map 10.1 The Geography of Africa Africa's climate zones have always played a critical role in the history of the continent and its peoples. These zones mirror each other north and south of the equator: tropical forest, savanna, subdesert, desert, and Mediterranean climate.

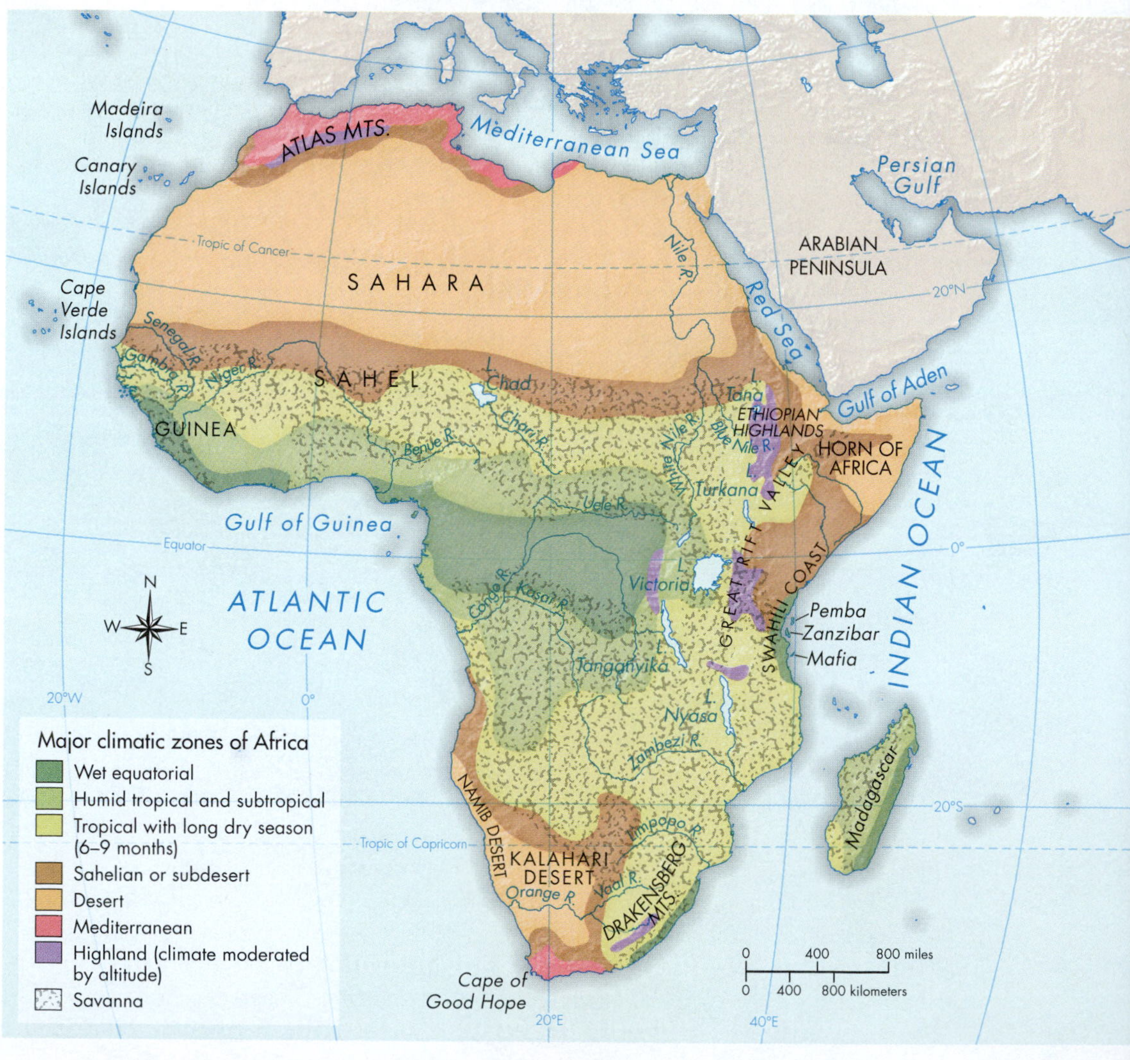

of south-central Africa, and along the eastern coast. It accounts for perhaps 55 percent of the African continent. Tropical rain forests stretch along coastal West Africa and on both sides of the equator in central Africa. Africa's climate is mostly tropical, with subtropical climates limited to the northern and southern coasts and to regions of high elevation. Rainfall is seasonal on most of the continent and is very sparse in desert and semidesert areas.

Geography and climate have significantly shaped African economic development. In the eastern African plains the earliest humans hunted wild animals. The drier steppe regions favored herding. Wetter savanna regions, like the Nile Valley, encouraged grain-based agriculture. Tropical forests favored hunting and gathering and, later, root-based agriculture. Rivers and lakes supported economies based on fishing.

Africa's peoples are as diverse as the continent's topography. In North Africa contacts with Asian and European civilizations date back to the ancient Phoenicians, Greeks, and Romans (see Chapters 5 and 6). Groups living on the coast or along trade routes had the greatest degree of contact with outside groups. The native Berbers of North Africa, living along the Mediterranean, intermingled with many different peoples—with Muslim Arabs, who first conquered North Africa in the seventh and eighth centuries C.E. (see page 213); with Spanish Muslims and Jews, many of whom settled in North Africa after their expulsion from Spain in 1492 (see page 387); and with sub-Saharan blacks with whom they traded across the Sahara Desert. The peoples living along the Swahili coast in East Africa developed a maritime civilization and had rich commercial contacts with southern Arabia, the Persian Gulf, India, China, and the Malay Archipelago.

Black Africans inhabited the region south of the Sahara, an area of savanna and rain forest. Short-statured peoples, sometimes inaccurately referred to as Pygmies, inhabited the equatorial rain forests. South of those forests, in the continent's southern third, lived the Khoisan (KOY-sahn), a small people with yellow-brown skin color who primarily were hunters but also had domesticated livestock.

Chapter Chronology

ca. 1000 B.C.E.–1500 C.E.	Bantu-speakers expand across central and southern Africa
ca. 600 C.E.	Christian missionaries convert Nubian rulers
642 C.E.	Muslim conquest of Egypt; Islam introduced to Africa
650–1500 C.E.	Slave trade from sub-Saharan Africa to the Mediterranean
700–900 C.E.	Berbers develop caravan routes
ca. 900–1100 C.E.	Kingdom of Ghana; bananas and plantains arrive in Africa from Asia
ca. 1100–1400 C.E.	Great Zimbabwe built, flourishes
ca. 1200–1450 C.E.	Kingdom of Mali
ca. 1312–1337 C.E.	Reign of Mansa Musa in Mali
1314–1344 C.E.	Reign of Amda Siyon in Ethiopia
1324–1325 C.E.	Mansa Musa's pilgrimage to Mecca

Egypt, Race, and Being African

When Europeans first started exploring sub-Saharan Africa's interior in the nineteenth century, they were amazed at the quality of the art and architecture they came across. In response they developed the Hamitic thesis, which argued that Africans were not capable of such work, so a "Hamitic race" related to the Caucasian race must have settled in Africa in the distant past, bringing superior technology and knowledge, and then blended into nearby African populations or departed. Although completely discredited today, the Hamitic thesis survived throughout much of the twentieth century.

As is evident from the nineteenth century's artificial construction of a Hamitic race, popular usage of the term *race* has often been imprecise and inaccurate. The application of general characteristics and patterns of behavior to peoples based on perceptions of physical differences is one of the legacies of imperialism and colonialism. Anthropologists have long insisted that when applied to geographical, national, religious, linguistic, or cultural groups, the concept of race is inappropriate and has been refuted by the scientific data. But issues of race continue to engender fierce debate. Nowhere in African studies has this debate been more strident than over questions relating to Egyptian identity and civilization, and Africa's contribution to European civilization.

Geographically, Egypt, located in North Africa, is part of the African continent. But from ancient times down to the present, scholars have debated whether racially and culturally Egypt is part of the Mediterranean world or part of the African world. More recently, the debate has also included the question of whether Egyptians of the first century B.C.E. made contributions to the Western world in architecture, mathematics, philosophy, science, and religion, and, if so, whether they were black people.

Some African and African American scholars have argued that much Western historical writing since the eighteenth century has been a "European racist plot" to destroy evidence that would recognize African accomplishments. They have amassed architectural and linguistic evidence, as well as a small mountain of quotations from Greek and Roman writers and from the Bible, to insist that the ancient Egyptians belonged to the black race. Against this view, another group of scholars holds that the ancient Egyptians were Caucasians. They believe that Phoenician, Berber, Libyan, Hebrew, and Greek peoples populated Egypt and created its civilization.

Quick Review
How did Africa's geographical diversity contribute to the diversity of its human populations?

A third proposition, perhaps the most plausible, holds that ancient Egypt, at the crossroads of three continents, was a melting pot of different cultures and peoples. Many diverse peoples contributed to the great achievements of Egyptian culture. Moderate scholars believe that black Africans resided in ancient Egypt, primarily in Upper Egypt (south of what is now Cairo), but that other racial groups constituted the majority of the population.

How did the advent of settled agriculture affect early societies?

The introduction of new crops from Asia and methods of settled agriculture profoundly changed many African societies, although the range of possibilities was greatly dependent on local variations in climate and geography. Bantu-speakers took the knowledge of domesticated livestock and agriculture as well as the ironworking skills that developed in northern and western Africa and spread them south across central and southern Africa. The most prominent feature of early West African society was a strong sense of community based on blood relationships and on religion. Extended families made up the villages that collectively formed small kingdoms.

Settled Agriculture and Its Impact

Agriculture began very early in Africa. Knowledge of plant cultivation moved west from ancient Judaea (southern Palestine), arriving in the Nile Delta in Egypt about the fifth millennium B.C.E. Settled agriculture then traveled down the Nile Valley and moved west across the Sahel to the central and western Sudan. By the first century B.C.E. settled agriculture existed in West Africa. From there it spread to the equatorial forests. Gradually most Africans evolved a sedentary way of life. Hunting-and-gathering societies survived only in scattered parts of Africa, particularly in the central rain forest region and in southern Africa.[1]

The evolution from a hunter-gatherer life to a settled life had profound effects. In contrast to nomadic conditions, settled societies made shared or common needs more apparent, and those needs strengthened ties among extended families. Agricultural and pastoral populations also increased, though scholars speculate that this increase was not steady, but rather fluctuated over time. Nor is it clear that the growth in numbers of people was accompanied by a commensurate increase in agricultural output.

Early African societies were similarly influenced by the spread of ironworking, though scholars dispute the route by which this technology spread to sub-Saharan Africa. Whatever the route, ancient iron tools found at the village of Nok on the Jos Plateau in present-day Nigeria seem to prove a knowledge of ironworking in West Africa by at least 700 B.C.E. The Nok culture, which enjoys enduring fame for its fine terra-cotta (baked clay) sculptures, flourished from about 800 B.C.E. to 200 C.E.

Nok Woman Hundreds of terra-cotta sculptures such as the head of this woman survive from the Nok culture, which originated in the central plateau of northern Nigeria in the first millennium B.C.E. (Werner Forman/Art Resource, NY)

Bantu Migrations

The spread of ironworking is linked to the migrations of Bantu-speaking peoples. Today the overwhelming majority of people living south of the Congo River speak a **Bantu** language. Because very few Muslims or Europeans penetrated into the interior, and few Bantu-speakers wrote down their languages, very few written sources for the early history of central and southern Africa survive. Lacking written sources, modern scholars have tried to reconstruct the history of the Bantu-speakers on the basis of linguistics, oral traditions, archaeology, and anthropology. Botanists and zoologists have played particularly critical roles in providing information about early diets and environments.

Bantu Speakers of a Bantu language living south and east of the Congo River.

Bantu-speaking peoples originated in the Benue region, the borderlands of modern Cameroon and Nigeria. In the second millennium B.C.E. they began to spread south and east into the forest zone of equatorial Africa. Why they began this movement is still a matter of dispute among historians. Some hold that rapid population growth sent people in search of land. Others believe that the evolution of centralized kingdoms allowed rulers to expand their authority, while causing newly subjugated peoples to flee in the hope of regaining their independence.

Bantu Migrations, ca. 1000 B.C.E.–1500 C.E.

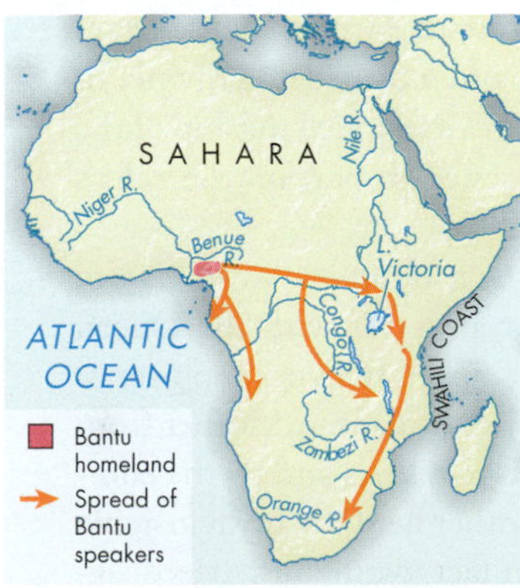

During the next fifteen hundred years, Bantu-speakers migrated throughout the savanna, adopted mixed agriculture, and learned ironworking. Mixed agriculture (cultivating cereals and raising livestock) and ironworking were practiced in western East Africa (the region of modern Burundi) in the first century B.C.E. In the first millennium C.E. Bantu-speakers migrated into eastern and southern Africa. Here the Bantu-speakers, with their iron weapons, either killed, drove off, or assimilated the hunting-gathering peoples they met. Some of the earlier assimilated inhabitants gradually adopted a Bantu language, contributing to the spread of Bantu culture.

The settled cultivation of cereals, the keeping of livestock, and the introduction of new crops — together with

Bantu-speakers' intermarriage with indigenous peoples—led over a long time to considerable population increases and the need to migrate farther. The so-called Bantu migrations should not be seen as a single movement sweeping across Africa from west to east to south and displacing all peoples in their path. Rather, those migrations were a series of group interactions between Bantu-speakers and pre-existing peoples in which bits of culture, languages, economies, and technologies were shared and exchanged to produce a wide range of cultural variation across central and southern Africa.[2]

The Bantu-speakers' expansion and subsequent land settlement that dominated eastern and southern African history in the first fifteen hundred years of the Common Era wasn't uniform. Enormous differences in the quality of the environment resulted in very uneven population distribution. The largest concentration of people seems to have been in the region bounded on the west by the Congo River and on the north, south, and east by Lake Edward, Lake Victoria, and Mount Kilimanjaro, comprising parts of modern Uganda, Rwanda, and Tanzania. There the agricultural system rested on sorghum and yam cultivation. Between 900 and 1100 bananas and plantains (a starchy form of the banana) arrived from Asia. Because little effort was needed for their cultivation and the yield was much higher than for yams, bananas soon became the Bantu people's staple crop. The rapid growth of the Bantu-speaking population led to further migration southward and eastward. By the eighth century Bantu-speaking people had crossed the Zambezi River and had begun settling in the region of present-day Zimbabwe. By the fifteenth century they had reached Africa's southeastern coast.

Life in the Kingdoms of the Western Sudan, ca. 1000 B.C.E.–800 C.E.

Sudan The African region surrounded by the Sahara, the Gulf of Guinea, the Atlantic Ocean, and the mountains of Ethiopia.

The **Sudan** is the region bounded by the Sahara to the north, the Gulf of Guinea to the south, the Atlantic Ocean to the west, and the highlands of Ethiopia to the east (see Map 10.1). In the savanna of the western Sudan—where the Bantu migrations originated—a series of dynamic kingdoms emerged in the millennium before European intrusion began in the 1400s and 1500s.

Between 1000 B.C.E. and 200 C.E. the peoples of the western Sudan made the momentous shift from nomadic hunting to settled agriculture. Food supply affects population, and the peoples of the region increased dramatically in number. By 400 C.E. the entire savanna (see Map 10.1), particularly the areas around Lake Chad, the Niger River bend, and present-day central Nigeria, had a large population.

Families and clans affiliated by blood kinship lived together in villages or small city-states. The basic social unit was the extended family. A chief, in consultation with a council of elders, governed a village. Some villages seem to have formed kingdoms. Village chiefs were responsible to regional heads, who answered to provincial governors, who in turn were responsible to a king. The chiefs and their families formed an aristocracy.

Kingship in the Sudan may have emerged from the priesthood. African kings always had religious sanction or support for their authority and were often considered divine. In this respect, early African kingship bears a strong resemblance to Germanic kingship of the same period (discussed in Chapter 14): the king's authority rested in part on the ruler's ability to negotiate with outside powers, such as the gods.

Among the Asante in modern-day Ghana, one of the most prominent West African peoples, the king was considered divine but shared some royal power with the Queen Mother. She was a full member of the governing council and enjoyed full voting power in various matters of state. The future king was initially chosen by the Queen Mother from eligible royal candidates, and then had to be approved by both his elders and by the commoners. Among the Yoruba in modern Nigeria the Queen Mother held the royal insignia and could withhold it if the future king did not please her. In fact, women exercised significant power and autonomy in many African societies. The institutions of female chiefs, known as *iyalode* among the Yoruba and *omu* among the Igbo in modern Nigeria, were established to represent women in the political process.

Religious practices in the western Sudan, like African religions elsewhere, were animistic and polytheistic. Most people believed that a supreme being had created the universe and was the source of all life. Most African religions also recognized ancestral spirits, which people believed might seek God's blessings for the prosperity and security of their families and communities as long as these groups behaved appropriately. Some African religions believed as well that nature spirits lived in such things as the sky, forests, rocks, and rivers. These spirits controlled the forces of nature and had to be appeased. Because special ceremonies were necessary to satisfy the spirits, special priests with the knowledge and power to communicate with them through sacred rituals were needed. The heads of families and villages were often priests. Each family head was responsible for ceremonies honoring the dead and living members of the family.[2]

Kinship patterns and shared religious practices helped to bind together the early African kingdoms of the western Sudan. The spread of Islam across the Sahara by at least the ninth century C.E., however, created a north-south religious and cultural divide in the western Sudan. Islam advanced across the Sahel into modern Mauritania, Mali, Burkina Faso, Niger, northern Nigeria, and Chad, but halted when it reached the savanna and forest zones of West Africa. The societies in the south maintained their traditional animistic religious practices. Muslim empires lying along the great northern bend of the Niger River evolved into formidable powers ruling over sizable territory as they seized control of the southern termini of the trans-Saharan trade. What made this long-distance trade possible was the "ship of the desert," the camel.

Quick Review
What kinds of states and societies emerged in Africa after the introduction of settled agriculture?

What role did the trans-Saharan trade play in West African history?

The expression "trans-Saharan trade" refers to the north-south trade across the Sahara (see Map 10.2). The camel had an impact on this trade comparable to the very important impact of horses and oxen on European agriculture. Camels are well suited for desert transportation. They can carry about five hundred pounds as far as twenty-five miles a day, and they can go for days without drinking, living on the water stored in their stomachs. The trans-Saharan trade brought lasting economic and social change to Africa, facilitating the spread of Islam via Muslim Arab traders, and affected the development of world commerce.

The Berbers of North Africa

Sometime in the fifth century C.E. the North African **Berbers** fashioned a saddle for use on the camel. The saddle gave the Berbers and later the region's Arabian inhabitants maneuverability on the animal and thus a powerful political and military advantage: they came to dominate the desert and to create lucrative routes across it.

Berbers North African peoples who controlled the caravan trade between the Mediterranean and the Sudan.

Between 700 and 900 C.E. the Berbers developed a network of caravan routes between the Mediterranean coast and the Sudan (see Map 10.2). The Arab Berber merchants from North Africa who controlled the caravan trade carried dates, salt from the Saharan salt mines, and some manufactured goods—silk and cotton cloth, beads, mirrors—to the

Trans-Saharan Trade A Berber caravan driver adjusts the salt block on his camel in a timeless ritual of the trans-Saharan trade. (© James Michael Dorsey)

Sudan. These products were exchanged for the much-coveted commodities of the West African savanna—gold, ivory, gum, kola nuts, and enslaved West African men and women who were sold to Muslim slave markets in Morocco, Algiers, Tripoli, and Cairo.

Effects of Trade on West African Society

The steady growth of trans-Saharan trade had three important effects on West African society. First, trade stimulated gold mining. Parts of modern-day Senegal, Nigeria, and Ghana contained rich veins of gold, and by the eleventh century nine tons of gold were exported to the Mediterranean coast and Europe annually. Most of this metal went to Egypt. From there it was transported down the Red Sea and eventually to India (see Map 9.2 on page 226) to pay for the spices and silks demanded by Mediterranean commerce. In this way, African gold linked the entire world, exclusive of the Western Hemisphere.

Second, trade in gold and other goods created a desire for slaves. Slaves were West Africa's second most valuable export (after gold). Slaves worked the gold and salt mines, and in Muslim North Africa, southern Europe, and southwestern Asia there was a high demand for household slaves among the elite. African slaves, like their early European and Asian counterparts, seem to have been peoples captured in war. Recent research suggests, moreover, that large numbers of black slaves were also recruited for Muslim military service through the trans-Saharan trade. High death rates from disease, manumission, and the assimilation of some blacks into Muslim society meant that the demand for slaves remained high for centuries. Table 10.1 shows the scope of the trans-Saharan slave trade. The total number of blacks enslaved over an 850-year period may be tentatively estimated at more than 4 million.[3]

Slavery in Muslim societies, as in European and Asian countries before the fifteenth century, was not based on skin color. Muslims also enslaved Caucasians who had been purchased, seized in war, or kidnapped from Europe. Wealthy Muslim households in Córdoba, Alexandria, and Tunis often included slaves of a number of races, all of whom had been completely cut off from their cultural roots. Likewise, West African kings who sold blacks to northern traders also bought a few white slaves—Slavic, British, and Turkish—for their own domestic needs. Race had little to do with the practice of slavery at this time.

TABLE 10.1 Estimated Magnitude of Trans-Saharan Slave Trade, 650–1500

Years	Annual Average of Slaves Traded	Total
650–800	1,000	150,000
800–900	3,000	300,000
900–1100	8,700	1,740,000
1100–1400	5,500	1,650,000
1400–1500	4,300	430,000

Source: R. A. Austen, "The Trans-Saharan Slave Trade: A Tentative Census," in *The Uncommon Market: Essays in the Economic History of the Atlantic Slave Trade*, ed. H. A. Gemery and J. S. Hogendorn (New York: Academic Press, 1979). Used with permission.

The third important effect on West African society was the role of trans-Saharan trade in stimulating the development of urban centers. Scholars date the growth of African cities from around the early ninth century. Families that had profited from trade tended to congregate in the border zones between the savanna and the Sahara. They acted as middlemen between the miners to the south and Muslim merchants from the north. By the early thirteenth century these families had become powerful black merchant dynasties. Muslim traders from the Mediterranean settled permanently in the trading depots, from which they organized the trans-Saharan caravans. The concentration of people stimulated agriculture and the craft industries. Gradually cities of sizable population emerged. Jenne, Gao, and Timbuktu, which enjoyed commanding positions on the Niger River bend, became centers of the export-import trade. Sijilmasa grew into a thriving market center. Koumbi Saleh, with between fifteen thousand and twenty thousand inhabitants, was probably the largest city in the western Sudan in the twelfth century. Between 1100 and 1400 these cities played a dynamic role in the commercial life of West Africa and Europe and became centers of intellectual creativity.

The Spread of Islam in Africa

Perhaps the most significant consequence of the trans-Saharan trade was the introduction of Islam to West African society. In the eighth century Arab invaders overran all of coastal North Africa. They introduced the Berbers living there to the religion of Islam (see page 213), and gradually the Berbers became Muslims. As traders, these Berbers carried Islam to sub-Saharan West Africa. From the eleventh century onward militant Almoravids, a coalition of fundamentalist western Saharan Berbers, preached Islam to the rulers of Ghana, Mali, Songhai, and Kanem-Bornu, who, admiring Muslim administrative techniques and wanting to protect their kingdoms from Muslim Berber attacks, accepted Islamic conversion. Some merchants also sought to preserve their elite mercantile status with the Berbers by adopting Islam. By the tenth century Muslim Berbers controlled the north-south trade routes to the savanna. By the eleventh century African rulers of Gao and Timbuktu had accepted Islam. The king of Ghana was also influenced by Islam. Muslims quickly became integral to West African government and society. Hence in the period from roughly 1000 to 1400, Islam in West Africa was a class-based religion with conversion inspired by political or economic motives.

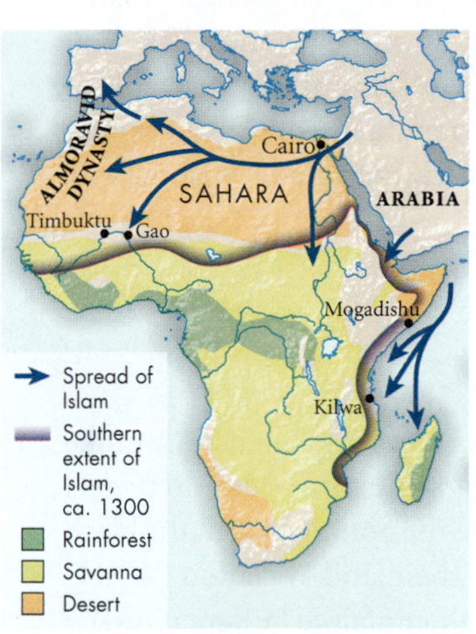

The Spread of Islam in Africa

Conversion to Islam introduced West Africans to a rich and sophisticated culture. By the late eleventh century Muslims were guiding the ruler of Ghana in the operation of his administrative machinery. Because efficient government depends on the preservation of records, the arrival of Islam in West Africa marked the advent of written documents there. African rulers corresponded with Arab and North African Muslim architects, theologians, and other intellectuals, who advised them on statecraft and religion. Islam accelerated the development of the West African empires of the ninth through fifteenth centuries.

After the Muslim conquest of Egypt in 642 (see page 214), Islam spread southward from Egypt up the Nile Valley and west to Darfur and Wadai. This Muslim penetration came not by military force but, as in the trans-Saharan trade routes in West Africa, by gradual commercial passage.

Muslim expansion from the Arabian peninsula across the Red Sea to the Horn of Africa, then southward along the coast of East Africa, represents a third direction of Islam's growth in Africa. From ports on the Red Sea and the Gulf of Aden, maritime trade carried Islam to East Africa and the Indian Ocean. Muslims founded the port city of **Mogadishu**, today Somalia's capital. In the twelfth century Mogadishu developed into a Muslim sultanate (a country ruled by a sultan). Archaeological evidence, confirmed by Arabic sources, reveals a rapid Islamic expansion along Africa's east coast in the thirteenth century as far south as Kilwa.

Mogadishu A Muslim port city in East Africa founded between the eighth and tenth centuries; today it is the capital of Somalia.

Quick Review
How did the trans-Saharan trade connect Africa to the larger world and what were the consequences of those connections?

What kingdoms and empires emerged in Africa between 800 and 1500?

stateless societies African societies bound together by ethnic or blood ties rather than being political states.

All African societies shared one basic feature: a close relationship between political and social organization. Ethnic or blood ties bound clan members together. What scholars call **stateless societies** were culturally homogeneous ethnic societies, generally organized around kinship groups. The smallest ones numbered fewer than a hundred people and were nomadic hunting groups. Larger stateless societies of perhaps several thousand people, such as the Tiv in modern central Nigeria, lived a settled and often agricultural or herding life. These societies lacked a central authority figure, such as a king, a capital city, or a military. A village or group of villages might recognize a chief who held very limited powers and whose position was not hereditary, but more commonly they were governed by local councils, whose members were either elders or persons of merit. Although stateless societies functioned successfully, their weakness lay in their inability to organize and defend themselves against attack by the powerful armies of neighboring kingdoms or by the European powers of the colonial era.

While stateless societies were relatively common in Africa, the period from about 800 to 1500 is best known as the age of Africa's great empires (Map 10.2). It witnessed the flowering of several powerful African states. In the western Sudan the large empires of Ghana, Mali, and Songhai developed. On the east coast emerged powerful city-states based on commerce and, like Sudan, very much influenced by Islam. In Ethiopia, in central East Africa, kings relied on the Christian faith of their people to strengthen political authority. In southern Africa the empire of Great Zimbabwe, built on the gold trade with the east coast, flourished.

The Kingdom of Ghana, ca. 900–1100

Ghana From the word for ruler, the name of a large and influential African kingdom inhabited by the Soninke people.

The nucleus of the territory that became the kingdom of **Ghana** was inhabited by Soninke people who called their ruler *ghana*, or war chief. By the late eighth century Muslim traders and other foreigners applied the king's title to the region where the Soninke lived, the black kingdom south of the Sahara. The Soninke themselves called their land Wagadou (WAH-guh-doo). Only the southern part of Wagadou received enough rainfall to be agriculturally productive, and it was in this area that the civilization of Ghana developed (see Map 10.2). Skillful farming and an efficient system of irrigation led to the production of abundant crops, which eventually supported a population of as many as two hundred thousand.

In 992 Ghana captured the Berber town of Awdaghost, strategically situated on the trans-Saharan trade route. Thereafter Ghana controlled the southern portion of a major caravan route. Before the year 1000, the rulers of Ghana had extended their influence almost to the Atlantic coast and had captured a number of small kingdoms in the south and east. By the early eleventh century the Ghanaian king exercised sway over a territory approximately the size of Texas. No other power in the West African region could successfully challenge him.

Throughout this vast West African area, all authority sprang from the king. Religious ceremonies and court rituals emphasized the king's sacredness and were intended to strengthen his authority. The king's position was hereditary in the matrilineal line — that is, the ruling king's heir was one of the king's sister's sons.

A council of ministers assisted the king in the work of government, and from the ninth century on most of these ministers were Muslims. Detailed evidence about the early Ghanaian bureaucracy has not survived, but scholars suspect that separate agencies were responsible for taxation, royal property, foreigners, forests, and the army. The royal

Mapping the Past

Map 10.2 African Kingdoms and Trade, ca. 800–1500

Throughout world history powerful kingdoms have generally been closely connected to far-flung trade networks.

ANALYZING THE MAP Which kingdoms, empires, and city-states were linked to the trans-Saharan trade network? Which were connected to the Indian Ocean trade network? To the Portuguese route?

CONNECTIONS How were the kingdoms, empires, and city-states shown on this map shaped by their proximity to trade routes?

administration was well served by ideas, skills, and especially literacy brought from the North African and Arab Muslim worlds. The king and his people, however, clung to their ancestral religion and basic cultural institutions.

Koumbi Saleh The city in which the king of Ghana held his court.

The king of Ghana held his court in the large and vibrant city of **Koumbi Saleh**, which the eleventh-century Spanish Muslim geographer al-Bakri (1040?–1094) actually describes as two towns—one in which the king and the royal court lived, and the other Muslim. Al-Bakri provides a valuable picture of the Muslim part of the town in the eleventh century:

> *The city of Ghana consists of two towns lying on a plain, one of which is inhabited by Muslims and is large, possessing twelve mosques—one of which is a congregational mosque for Friday prayer; each has its imam, its muezzin and paid reciters of the Quran. The town possesses a large number of jurisconsults and learned men.*[4]

Either for their own protection or to preserve their special identity, the Muslims of Koumbi Saleh lived separately from the African artisans and tradespeople. The Muslim community in Ghana must have been large and prosperous to have supported twelve mosques. Muslim religious leaders exercised civil authority over their fellow Muslims. The imam was the religious leader who conducted the ritual worship, especially the main prayer service on Fridays (see page 216). The muezzin led the prayer responses after the imam (see page 224). The presence of the religious leaders and of other learned Muslims suggests that Koumbi Saleh was a city of vigorous intellectual activity.

The administration and defense of Ghana's vast territories was expensive. To support the kingdom, the royal estates—some hereditary, others conquered in war—produced annual revenue, mostly in the form of foodstuffs for the royal household. The king also received tribute annually from subordinate chieftains. Customs duties on goods entering and leaving the country generated revenues. Salt was the largest import. Berber merchants paid a tax to the king on the cloth, metalwork, weapons, and other goods that they brought into the country from North Africa; in return these traders received royal protection from bandits. African traders bringing gold into Ghana from the south also paid the customs duty.

Finally, the royal treasury held a monopoly on the export of gold. The gold industry was undoubtedly the king's largest source of income. It was on gold that the fame of medieval Ghana rested. The ninth-century Persian geographer al-Ya-qubi wrote, "Its king is mighty, and in his lands are gold mines. Under his authority are various other kingdoms—and in all this region there is gold."[5]

The governing aristocracy—the king, his court, and Muslim administrators—occupied the highest rung on the Ghanaian social ladder. On the next rung stood the merchant class. Considerably below the merchants stood the farmers, cattle breeders, gold mine supervisors, and skilled craftsmen and weavers—what today might be called the middle class. Some merchants and miners must have enjoyed great wealth, but, as in all aristocratic societies, money alone did not suffice. High status was based on blood and royal service. On the social ladder's lowest rung were slaves, who worked in households, on farms, and in the mines. As in Asian and European societies of the time, slaves accounted for only a small percentage of the population.

Apart from these social classes stood the army. According to al-Bakri, "the king of Ghana can put 200,000 warriors in the field, more than 40,000 being armed with bow and arrow." Like most medieval estimates, this is probably a gross exaggeration. The king of Ghana, however, did maintain at his palace a standing force of a thousand men, comparable to the bodyguards of the emperors of the Roman Republic. In wartime this regular army was augmented by levies of soldiers from conquered peoples and by the use of slaves and free reserves. The force that the king could field was sizable, if not as huge as al-Bakri estimated.

The reasons for ancient Ghana's decline are still a matter of much debate. By al-Bakri's time there were other increasingly powerful neighbors, such as the Mandinka to challenge Ghana's influence in the region. The most commonly accepted theory for Ghana's rapid decline held, however, that the Berber Almoravid dynasty of North Africa invaded and conquered Ghana around 1100 and forced its rulers and people to convert to Islam. A close study of this question has recently concluded that while Almoravid and Islamic pressures certainly disrupted the empire, weakening it enough for its incorporation into the rising Mali empire, there was no Almoravid military invasion and subsequent forced conversion to Islam.[6]

The Kingdom of Mali, ca. 1200–1450

There can be no doubt that Ghana and its capital of Koumbi Saleh were in decline between 1100 and 1200. The kingdom of Ghana split into several small kingdoms that feuded among themselves. One people, the Mandinka from the kingdom of Kangaba on the upper Niger River, gradually asserted their dominance over these kingdoms. The Mandinka had long been part of the Ghanaian empire, and the Mandinka and Soninke belonged to the same language group. Kangaba formed the core of the new empire of Mali. Building on Ghanaian foundations, Mali developed into a better-organized and more powerful state than Ghana.

The kingdom of Mali owed its greatness to two fundamental assets. First, its strong agricultural and commercial base provided for a large population and enormous wealth. Second, Mali had two rulers, Sundiata (soon-JAH-tuh) and Mansa Musa, who combined military success with exceptionally creative personalities.

The earliest surviving evidence about the Mandinka, dating from the early eleventh century, indicates that they were extremely successful at agriculture. Consistently large harvests throughout the twelfth and thirteenth centuries meant a plentiful supply of food, which encouraged steady population growth. The geographical location of the Mandinka on the upper Niger River (see Map 10.2) also placed them in an ideal position in West African trade. Earlier, during the period of Ghanaian hegemony, the Mandinka had acted as middlemen in the gold and salt traffic flowing north and south. In the thirteenth century Mandinka traders formed companies, traveled widely, and gradually became a major force in the entire West African trade.

The founder of Mali, Sundiata (r. ca. 1230–1255) set up his capital at Niani, transforming the city into an important financial and trading center. He then embarked on a policy of imperial expansion. Through a series of military victories, Sundiata and his successors absorbed into Mali other territories of the former kingdom of Ghana and established hegemony over the trading cities of Gao, Jenne, and Walata.

These expansionist policies were continued in the fourteenth century by Sundiata's descendant Mansa Musa (r. ca. 1312–1337), early Africa's most famous ruler. Mansa Musa fought many campaigns and checked every attempt at rebellion. Ultimately his influence extended northward to several Berber cities in the Sahara, eastward to the trading cities of Timbuktu and Gao, and westward as far as the Atlantic Ocean. Throughout his territories, he maintained strict royal control over the rich trans-Saharan trade. Thus this empire, roughly twice the size of the Ghanaian kingdom and containing perhaps 8 million people, brought Mansa Musa fabulous wealth.

The Expansion of Mali, ca. 1200–1450

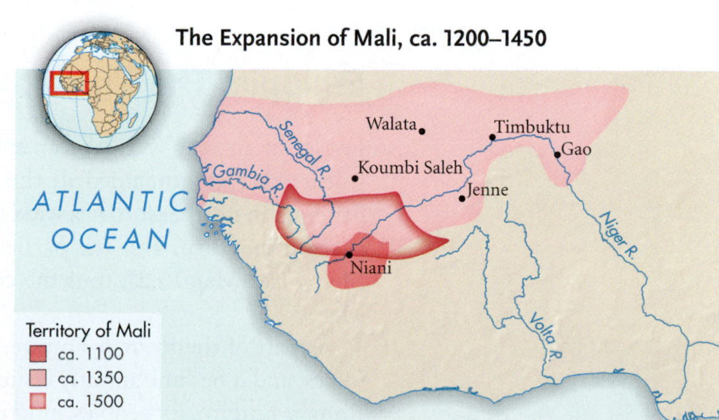

Mansa Musa built on the foundations of his predecessors. The stratified aristocratic structure of Malian society perpetuated the pattern set in Ghana, as did the system of provincial administration and annual tribute. The emperor took responsibility for the territories that formed the heart of the empire and appointed governors to rule the outlying provinces or dependent kingdoms. But Mansa Musa made a significant innovation: in a practice strikingly similar to a system used in both China and France at the time, he appointed members of the royal family as provincial governors. He could count on their loyalty, and they received valuable experience in the work of government.

In another aspect of administration, Mansa Musa also differed from his predecessors. He became a devout Muslim. Although most of the Mandinka clung to their ancestral animism, Islamic practices and influences in Mali multiplied.

The most celebrated event of Mansa Musa's reign was his pilgrimage to Mecca in 1324–1325, during which he paid a state visit to the sultan of Egypt. Mansa Musa's entrance into Cairo was magnificent. Preceded by five hundred slaves, each carrying a six-pound staff of gold, he followed with a huge host of retainers, including one hundred elephants each bearing one hundred pounds of gold. The emperor lavished his wealth on the citizens of the Egyptian capital.

For the first time, the Mediterranean world gained concrete knowledge of Mali's wealth and power, and the black kingdom began to be known as one of the world's great empires. Mali retained this international reputation into the fifteenth century. Musa's pilgrimage also had significant consequences within Mali. He gained some understanding of the Mediterranean countries and opened diplomatic relations with the Muslim rulers of Morocco and Egypt. His zeal for the Muslim faith and Islamic culture increased. Musa brought back from Arabia the distinguished architect al-Saheli, whom he commissioned to build new mosques at Timbuktu and other cities. These mosques served as centers for the conversion of Africans to Islam.

Timbuktu Originally a campsite for desert nomads, it grew into a thriving city under Mansa Musa, king of Mali and Africa's most famous ruler.

Timbuktu began as a campsite for desert nomads, but under Mansa Musa, it grew into a thriving trading post, or entrepôt (AHN-truh-poh), attracting merchants and traders from North Africa and all parts of the Mediterranean world. They brought with them cosmopolitan attitudes and ideas. In the fifteenth century Timbuktu developed into a great center for scholarship and learning. Architects, astronomers, poets, lawyers, mathematicians, and theologians flocked there. One hundred fifty schools, for men only, were devoted to Qur'anic studies. The school of Islamic law enjoyed a distinction in Africa comparable to the prestige of the school at Cairo. The vigorous traffic in books that flourished in Timbuktu made them the most common items of trade. Timbuktu's tradition and reputation for African scholarship lasted until the eighteenth century.

Moreover, in the fourteenth and fifteenth centuries many Arab and North African Muslim intellectuals and traders married native African women. These unions brought into being a group of racially mixed people. The necessity of living together harmoniously, the traditional awareness of diverse cultures, and the cosmopolitan atmosphere of Timbuktu all contributed to a rare degree of racial toleration and understanding.

The third great West African empire, Songhai, succeeded Mali in the fourteenth century. It encompassed the old empires of Ghana and Mali and extended its territory farther north and east to become one of the largest African empires in history (see Map 10.2).

Ethiopia: The Christian Kingdom of Aksum

Just as the ancient West African empires were significantly affected by Islam and the Arab culture that accompanied it, the African kingdoms that arose in modern Sudan and Ethiopia in northeast Africa were heavily influenced by Egyptian culture, and they influenced it in return. This was particularly the case in ancient Nubia. Nubia's capital was at Meroë (see Map 10.2); thus the country is often referred to as the Nubian kingdom of Meroë.

As part of the Roman Empire, Egypt was subject to Hellenistic and Roman cultural forces, and it became an early center of Christianity. Nubia, however, was never part of the Roman Empire; its people clung to ancient Egyptian religious ideas. Christian mission-

Christianity and Islam in Ethiopia The prolonged contest between the two religions in Ethiopia was periodically taken to the battlefield. This drawing from the eighteenth century by an Ethiopian artist shows his countrymen (left) advancing victoriously and celebrates national military success. (© British Library Board. OR 533 f50v)

aries went to the Upper Nile region and succeeded in converting the Nubian rulers around 600 C.E. By that time, there were three separate Nubian states, of which the kingdom of Nobatia, centered at Dongola, was the strongest. The Christian rulers of Nobatia had close ties with the kingdom of **Aksum** in Ethiopia, and through this relationship Egyptian culture spread to Ethiopia.

Aksum A kingdom in northwestern Ethiopia that was a sizable trading state and the center of Christian culture.

The Kingdom of Aksum, ca. 600

Two-thirds of the country consists of the Ethiopian highlands, the rugged plateau region of East Africa. The Great Rift Valley divides this territory into two massifs (mountain masses), of which the Ethiopian Plateau is the larger. Sloping away from each side of the Great Rift Valley are a series of mountains and valleys. Together with this mountainous environment, the three Middle Eastern religions—Judaism, Christianity, and Islam—have influenced Ethiopian society, each bringing symbols of its cultural identity via trade and contact with its neighbors in the Upper Nile, including Nobatia, and via its proximity to the Middle East.

By the first century C.E. the kingdom of Aksum in northwestern Ethiopia was a sizable trading state. Merchants at Adulis, its main port on the Red Sea, sold ivory, gold, emeralds, rhinoceros horns, shells, and slaves to the Sudan, Arabia, Yemen, and various cities across the Indian Ocean in exchange for glass, ceramics, fabrics, sugar, oil, spices, and precious gems. Adulis contained temples, stone-built houses, and irrigated agriculture. Between the first and eighth centuries Aksum served as the capital of

INDIVIDUALS IN SOCIETY

Amda Siyon

SCHOLARS CONSIDER AMDA SIYON (R. 1314–1344) the greatest ruler of Ethiopia's Solomonic dynasty. Yet we have no image or representation of him. We know nothing of his personal life, though if he followed the practice of most Ethiopian kings, he had many wives and children. Nor do we know anything about his youth and education. The evidence of what he did, however, suggests a tough military man who personified the heroic endurance and physical pain expected of warriors. According to a chronicle of Siyon's campaign against the Muslim leader of Ifat, he

> *clove the ranks of the rebels and struck so hard that he transfixed two men as one with the blow of his spear, through the strength of God. Thereupon the rebels scattered and took to flight, being unable to hold their ground in his presence.*

Amda Siyon reinforced control over his kingdom's Christian areas. He then expanded into neighboring regions of Shewa, Gojam, and Damot. Victorious there, he gradually absorbed the Muslim states of Ifat and Hedya to the east and southeast. These successes gave him effective control of the central highlands and also the Indian Ocean trade routes to the Red Sea (see Map 10.2). He governed in a quasi-feudal fashion. Theoretically the owner of all land, he assigned *gults*, or fiefs, to his ablest warriors. In return for nearly complete authority in their regions, these warrior-nobles conscripted soldiers for the king's army, required agricultural services from the farmers working on their land, and collected taxes in kind.

Ethiopian rulers received imperial coronation at Aksum, but their kingdom had no permanent capital. Rather, the ruler and court were peripatetic. They constantly traveled around the country to check the warrior-nobles' management of the gults, to crush revolts, and to impress ordinary people with royal dignity.

Territorial expansion had important economic and religious consequences. Amda Siyon concluded trade agreements with Muslims by which they were allowed to trade with his country in return for Muslim recognition of his authority, and their promise to accept his administration and pay taxes. Economic growth followed. As a result of these agreements, the flow of Ethiopian gold, ivory, and slaves to Red Sea ports for export to the Islamic heartlands and to South Asia accelerated. Profits from commercial exchange improved people's lives, or at least the lives of the upper classes.

Monk-missionaries from traditional Christian areas flooded newly conquered regions, stressing that Ethiopia was a new Zion, or second Israel; a Judeo-Christian nation defined by religion. Ethiopian Christianity focused on the divinity of the Old Testament Jehovah, rather than on the humanity of the New Testament Jesus. Jewish dietary restrictions, such as the avoidance of pork and shellfish, shaped behavior, and the holy Ark of the Covenant had a prominent place in the liturgy.

Colorful biblical scenes adorn the interior of the Urai Kidane Miharet Church, one of the many monasteries established by Amda Siyon. (Ariadne Van Zandberger/The Africa Image Library, photographersdirect.com)

But the monks also taught New Testament values, especially the importance of charity and spiritual reform. Following the Byzantine pattern, the Ethiopian priest-king claimed the right to summon church councils and to issue doctrinal degrees. Christianity's stress on monogamous marriage, however, proved hard to enforce. As in other parts of Africa (and in Islamic lands, China, and South Asia), polygyny remained common, at least among the upper classes.

Sources: G. W. B. Huntingford, ed., *The Glorious Victories of Amda Seyon* (Oxford: Oxford University Press, 1965), pp. 89–90; H. G. Marcus, *A History of Ethiopia*, updated ed. (Berkeley: University of California Press, 2002); J. Iliffe, *Africans: The History of a Continent*, 2d ed. (New York: Cambridge University Press, 2007).

QUESTIONS FOR ANALYSIS

1. What features mark Ethiopian culture as unique and distinctive among early African societies?
2. Referring to Solomonic Ethiopia, assess the role of legend in history.

an empire extending over much of what is now northern Ethiopia. The empire's prosperity rested on trade.

The expansion of Islam into northern Ethiopia in the eighth century (see page 245) weakened Aksum's commercial prosperity. The Arabs first ousted the Greek Byzantine merchants who traded on the Dahlak Archipelago (in the southern Red Sea), and converted the islands' inhabitants. Then, Muslims attacked and destroyed Adulis. Some Aksumites converted to Islam; many others found refuge in the rugged mountains north of the kingdom, where they were isolated from outside contacts. Thus began the insularity that characterized later Ethiopian society.

Tradition ascribes to Frumentius (ca. 300–380 C.E.), a Syrian Christian trader, the introduction of Coptic Christianity, an Orthodox form of Christianity that originated in Egypt, into Ethiopia. Kidnapped as a young boy en route from India to Tyre (in southern Lebanon), Frumentius was taken to Aksum, given his freedom, and appointed tutor to the future king, Ezana. Upon Ezana's accession to the throne, Frumentius went to Alexandria, Egypt, where he was consecrated the first bishop of Aksum around 340 C.E. He then returned to Ethiopia with some priests to spread Christianity. Shortly after members of the royal court accepted Christianity, it became the Ethiopian state religion. Ethiopia's future was to be inextricably tied up with Christianity, a unique situation in black Africa.

Ethiopia's acceptance of Christianity led to the production of ecclesiastical documents and royal chronicles, making Ethiopia the first black African society that can be studied from written records. The Scriptures were translated into Ge'ez (gee-EHZ), an ancient language and script used in Ethiopia and Aksum. Pagan temples were dedicated to Christian saints; and, as in early medieval Ireland and in the Orthodox Church of the Byzantine world, the monasteries were the main cultural institutions of the Christian faith in Ethiopia. As the Ethiopian state expanded, vibrant monasteries provided inspiration for the establishment of convents for nuns, as in medieval Europe (see page 353).

Monastic records provide fascinating information about early Ethiopian society. Settlements were made on the warm and moist plateau lands, not in the arid lowlands or the river valleys. Farmers used a scratch plow (unique in sub-Saharan Africa) to cultivate wheat and barley, and they regularly rotated those cereals. Plentiful rainfall seems to have helped produce abundant crops, which in turn led to population growth. In contrast to people in most of sub-Saharan Africa, both sexes probably married young. Because of ecclesiastical opposition to polygyny, monogamy was the norm, other than for kings and the very rich. The abundance of land meant that young couples could establish independent households. Widely scattered farms, with the parish church as the central social unit, seem to have been the usual pattern of existence.

Above the broad class of peasant farmers stood warrior-nobles. Their wealth and status derived from their fighting skills, which kings rewarded with grants of estates and with the right to collect tribute from the peasants. To acquire lands and to hold warriors' loyalty, Ethiopian kings had to pursue a policy of constant territorial expansion. (See "Individuals in Society: Amda Siyon" on page 252.) Nobles maintained order in their regions, supplied kings with fighting men, and displayed their superior status by the size of their households and their generosity to the poor.

Sometime in the fourteenth century six scribes in the Tigrayan highlands of Ethiopia combined oral tradition, Jewish and Islamic commentaries, apocryphal (noncanonical) Christian texts, and the writings of the early Christian Church fathers to produce the *Kebra Negast* (The Glory of Kings). This history served the authors' goals: it became an Ethiopian national epic, glorifying a line of rulers descended from the Hebrew king Solomon (see page 48), arousing patriotic feelings, and linking Ethiopia's identity to the Judeo-Christian tradition. From the tenth to the sixteenth centuries, and even in the Ethiopian constitution of 1955, rulers of Ethiopia claimed that they belonged to the Solomonic line of succession. Thus the church and state in Ethiopia were inextricably linked.

Picturing the Past

The Queen of Sheba and King Solomon

Sheba, Queen Makeda, figured prominently in European as well as Ethiopian art. Created in about 1180 by a French artist as part of a series of biblical scenes for an abbey in Austria, this image shows Solomon receiving gifts from Sheba's servants. The inscription surrounding the scene reads "Solomon joins himself to the Queen of Sheba and introduces her to his faith." (Erich Lessing/Art Resource, NY)

ANALYZING THE IMAGE What are King Solomon and Queen Sheba wearing and holding? How are the other figures depicted, and what are they doing?

CONNECTIONS What does the style of this image suggest about the background of the artist, and about the audience for whom the image was intended?

Ethiopia's high mountains isolated the kingdom and hindered access from the outside, but through trade, word gradually spread about the Christian devotion of this African kingdom. Twelfth-century Crusaders returning from the Middle East told of a powerful Christian ruler, Prester John, whose lands lay behind Muslim lines and who was eager to help restore the Holy Land to Christian control. The story of Prester John sparked European imagination and led to exploration aimed at finding his legendary kingdom, which was eventually identified with Ethiopia. In the later thirteenth century the dynasty of the Solomonic kings witnessed a literary and artistic renaissance particularly notable for works of hagiography (biographies of saints), biblical exegesis (critical explanation or interpretation of the Bible), and manuscript illumination. The most striking feature of Ethiopian society in the period from 500 to 1500 was the close relationship between the church and the state. Christianity inspired fierce devotion and tended to equate doctrinal heresy with political rebellion, thus reinforcing central monarchical power.

The East African City-States

Like Ethiopia, the city-states of East Africa were shaped by their proximity to the trade routes of the Red Sea and Indian Ocean. Greco-Roman ships traveled from Adulis on the Red Sea around the tip of the Gulf of Aden and down the portion of the East African coast that the Greeks called Azania in modern-day Kenya and Tanzania (see Map 10.2). These ships carried manufactured goods—cotton cloth, copper and brass, iron tools, and gold and silver plate. At the African coastal emporiums, Mediterranean merchants exchanged these goods for cinnamon, myrrh and frankincense, captive slaves, and animal byproducts such as ivory, rhinoceros horns, and tortoise shells. The ships then headed back north and, somewhere around Cape Guardafui on the Horn of Africa, caught the monsoon winds eastward to India, where ivory was in great demand.

In the early centuries of the Common Era many merchants and seamen from the Mediterranean settled in East African coastal towns. Succeeding centuries saw the arrival of more traders. The great emigration from Arabia after the death of Muhammad accelerated Muslim penetration of the area, which the Arabs called the Zanj, "land of the blacks," a land inhabited by a Bantu-speaking peoples also called the Zanj. Along the coast, Arabic Muslims established small trading colonies whose local peoples were ruled by kings and practiced various animistic religions. Eventually—whether through Muslim political hegemony or gradual assimilation—the coastal peoples slowly converted to Islam. Indigenous African religions, however, remained strong in the continent's interior. (See "Listening to the Past: A Tenth-Century Muslim Traveler Describes Parts of the East African Coast," page 256.)

Migrants from the Arabian peninsula and the Malay Archipelago had a profound influence on the lives of the coastal people of East Africa. Beginning in the late twelfth century fresh waves of Arabs and of Persians from Shiraz poured down the coast, first settling at Mogadishu, then pressing southward to Kilwa. Everywhere they landed, they introduced Islamic culture to the indigenous population. Similarly, from the first to the fifteenth centuries Indonesians crossed the Indian Ocean and settled on the African coast and on the large island of Madagascar, or Malagasy, an Indonesian name. All these immigrants intermarried with Africans, and the resulting society combined Asian, African, and especially Islamic traits. The East African coastal culture was called **Swahili**, after a Bantu language whose vocabulary and poetic forms exhibit a strong Arabic influence. The thirteenth-century Muslim mosque at Mogadishu and the fiercely Muslim populations of Mombasa and Kilwa in the fourteenth century attest to strong Muslim influence.

Swahili The East African coastal culture, named after a Bantu language whose vocabulary and poetic forms exhibit strong Arabic influences.

By the late thirteenth century **Kilwa** had become the most powerful city on the coast, exercising political hegemony as far north as Pemba and as far south as Sofala (see Map 10.2). In the fourteenth and fifteenth centuries the coastal cities were great commercial empires comparable to the Italian city-state of Venice (discussed in Chapter 14). Like Venice, Swahili cities such as Kilwa, Mombasa, and Pemba were situated on islands just offshore. The tidal currents that isolated them from the mainland also protected them from landside attack.

Kilwa The most powerful city on the east coast of Africa by the late thirteenth century.

From among the rich mercantile families that controlled the coastal cities arose a ruler who by the fourteenth century had taken the Arabic title *sheik*. The sheik governed both the island city of Kilwa and the nearby mainland. Farther inland, tribal chiefs ruled with the advice of councils of elders.

Approaching the East African coastal cities in the late fifteenth century, Portuguese traders were astounded at their enormous wealth and prosperity. This wealth rested on the

Copper Coin from Mogadishu, Twelfth Century Islamic proscriptions against representation of the human form prevented the use of rulers' portraits on coinage, unlike the practice of the Romans, Byzantines, and Sassanids. Instead, Islamic coins since the Umayyad period were decorated exclusively with writing. Sultan Haran ibn Sulayman of Kilwa on the East African coast minted this coin, a symbol of the region's Muslim culture and of its rich maritime trade. (Courtesy of the Trustees of the British Museum)

LISTENING TO THE PAST

A Tenth-Century Muslim Traveler Describes Parts of the East African Coast

Other than Ethiopia, early African societies left no written accounts of their institutions and cultures, so modern scholars rely for information on the chronicles of travelers and merchants. Outsiders, however, come with their own preconceptions, attitudes, and biases. They tend to measure what they visit and see by the conditions and experiences with which they are familiar.

Sometime in the early tenth century the Muslim merchant-traveler Al Mas'udi (d. 945 C.E.), in search of African ivory, visited Oman, the southeast coast of Africa, and Zanzibar. He referred to all the peoples he encountered as Zanj, a term that was also applied to the maritime Swahili culture of the area's towns. Al Mas'udi's report, excerpted here, offers historians a wealth of information about these peoples.

"Omani seamen cross the strait [of Berbera, off northern Somalia] to reach Kanbalu island [perhaps modern Pemba], located in the sea of Zanj. The island's inhabitants are a mixed population of Muslims and idolatrous Zanj. . . . I have sailed many seas, the Chinese sea, the Rum sea [Mediterranean], the Khazar [Caspian Sea], the Kolzom [Red Sea], and the sea of Yemen. I have encountered dangers without number, but I know no sea more perilous than the sea of Zanj. Here one encounters a fish called el-Owal (whale). . . . The sailors fear its approach, and both day and night they strike pieces of wood together or beat drums to drive it away. . . . The Zanj sea also contains many other fish species possessing the most varied shapes and forms. . . . Ambergris* is found in great quantities along the Zanj coast and also along the coastline of Shihr in Arabia. . . . The best ambergris is found in the islands and on the shores of the Zanj sea: it is round, of a pale blue tint, sometimes the size of an ostrich egg, sometimes a little less. Lumps of it are swallowed by the whale, . . . When the sea becomes very rough the whale vomits up large rock size balls of ambergris. When it tries to gulp them down again it chokes to death and its body floats to the surface. Quickly the men of Zanj, or from other lands, who have been waiting for a favorable moment, draw the fish near with harpoons and tackle, cut open its stomach, and extract the ambergris. The pieces found in its intestines emit a nauseating odor, and Iraqi and Persian chemists call these *nedd*: but the fragments found near the back are much purer as these have been longer inside the body. . . .

The lands of the Zanj provide the people with wild leopard skins that they wear and that they export to Muslim countries. These are the largest leopard skins and make the most beautiful saddles. The Zanj also export tortoise-shell for making combs, and ivory is likewise employed for this purpose. The giraffe is the most common animal found in these lands. . . . They [the Zanj] settled in this country, and spread south to Sofala, which marks the most distant frontier of this land and the terminus of the ship voyages made from Oman and Siraf on the Zanj sea. Just as the China sea ends with the land of Japan, the limits of the sea of Zanj are the lands of Sofala and the Waqwaq, a region with a warm climate and fertile soil that produces gold in abundance and many other marvelous things. This is where the Zanj built their capital and chose their king, who they call *Mfalme*, the traditional title for their sovereigns. The *Mfalme* rules over all other Zanj kings, and commands 300,000 cavalrymen. The Zanj employ the ox as a beast of burden, for their country contains no horses, mules or camels, and they do not even know of these animals. Nor do they know of snow or hail. . . . The territory of the Zanj commences where a branch diverts from the upper Nile and continues to the land of Sofala and the Waqwaq. Their villages extend for about 700 parasangs in length and breadth along the coast. The country is divided into valleys, mountains and sandy deserts. It abounds in wild elephants but you will not see a single tame one. The Zanj employ them neither for war nor for anything else. . . . When they want to catch them, they throw in the water the leaves, bark and branches of a particular tree that grows in their country: then they hide in ambush until the elephants come to drink. The tainted water burns them and makes them drunk, causing them to fall down and be unable to get up. The Zanj then rush upon them, armed with very long spears, and kill them for their tusks. Indeed, the lands of the Zanj produce tusks each weighing fifty pounds and more. They generally go to Oman, and are then sent on to China and India. These are the two primary destinations, and if they were not, ivory would be abundant in Muslim lands.

In China the kings and military and civil officers ride in ivory palanquins:† no official or dignitary would dare to enter the royal presence in an iron palanquin. Only ivory can serve on this occasion. Thus they prefer straight tusks to curved . . . They also burn ivory before their idols and incense their altars with its perfume, just as Christians use the Mary incense and other scents in their churches. The Chinese derive no other benefit from the elephant, and believe it brings bad fortune when used for domestic purposes or war. In India ivory is much in demand. There dagger handles, as well as curved sword-scabbards, are fashioned from ivory. But ivory is chiefly used in the manufacture of chessmen and backgammon pieces. . . .

The merchant trade along the East African coast still relies on dhows, whose design has remained virtually unchanged since Al Mas'udi's time. (Ken Welsh/age footstock/Robert Harding World Imagery)

Although the Zanj are always hunting the elephant and collecting its ivory, they still make no use of ivory for their own domestic needs. For their finery they use iron rather than gold and silver, and oxen, as we mentioned above, as beasts of burden or for war, as we use camels or horses. The oxen are harnessed like horses and run at the same speed.

To return to the Zanj and their kings, these are known as *Wfalme*, meaning son of the Great Lord. They refer thus to their king because he has been selected to govern them fairly. As soon as he exerts tyrannical power or strays from the rule of law they put him to death and exclude his descendants from accession to the throne. They claim that through his wrongful actions he ceases to be the son of the Master, that is, the King of Heaven and Earth. They give God the name *Maliknajlu*, meaning the Sovereign Master.

The Zanj express themselves eloquently, and have preachers in their own language. Often a devout man will stand in the center of a large crowd and exhort his listeners to render themselves agreeable to God and to submit to his commands. He depicts for them the punishments their disobedience exposes them to, and recalls the example of their ancestors and former kings. These people possess no religious code: their kings follow custom and govern according to traditional political practices.

The Zanj eat bananas, which are as abundant as they are in India; but the staples in their diets are millet and a plant called *kalari* that is pulled from the earth like truffles. It is similar to the cucumber of Egypt and Syria. They also eat honey and meat. Every man worships what he pleases, be it a plant, an animal or a mineral.‡ The coconut grows on many of the islands: its fruit is eaten by all the Zanj peoples. One of these islands, situated one or two days' sail off the coast, contains a Muslim population and an hereditary royal family. This is the island of Kanbalu, which we have already mentioned. ”

Source: Al Mas'udi, *Les Prairies d'Or*, C. Barbier de Meynard and Pavet de Courteille, trans. Arab to French (Paris: the Imperial Printers, 1861, 1864), vol I: 231, 234, 333-335; vol. III: 2, 3, 5-9, 26-27, 29, 30-31. Roger B. Beck, trans. French to English.

*A solid, waxy, flammable substance, produced in the digestive system of sperm whales, not initially swallowed as Al Mas'udi purports. Principally used in perfumery, and not to be confused with amber, the fossil resin used in the manufacture of ornamental objects such as beads and women's combs.

†An enclosed litter attached to poles that servants supported on their shoulders.

‡These are forms of animism.

QUESTIONS FOR ANALYSIS

1. What does Al Mas'udi's report tell us about the Zanj peoples and their customs? How would you describe his attitude toward them?
2. What commodities were most sought after by Muslim traders? Why? Where were they sold?

sheik's monopolistic control of all trade in the area. Some coastal cities manufactured goods for export: Mogadishu produced cloth for the Egyptian market; Mombasa and Malindi processed iron tools; and Sofala made cottons for the interior trade. The bulk of the cities' exports, however, consisted of animal products—leopard skins, tortoise shell, ambergris, ivory—and gold. The gold originated in the Mutapa region south of the Zambezi River, where the Bantu mined it. As in tenth-century Ghana, gold was a royal monopoly in the fourteenth-century coastal city-states. The Mutapa kings received it as annual tribute, prohibited outsiders from entering the mines or participating in the trade, and controlled shipments down the Zambezi to the coastal markets. Kilwa's prosperity rested on its traffic in gold.

African goods satisfied the global aristocratic demand for luxury goods. In Arabia leopard skins were made into saddles, shells were made into combs, and ambergris was used in the manufacture of perfumes. Because African elephants' tusks were larger and more durable than the tusks of Indian elephants, African ivory was in great demand in India for sword and dagger handles, carved decorative objects, and the ceremonial bangles used in Hindu marriage rituals. Wealthy Chinese valued African ivory for use in the construction of sedan chairs. In exchange for these natural products, the Swahili cities bought in, among many other items: incense, glassware, glass beads, and carpets from Arabia; textiles, spices, rice, and cotton from India; and grains, fine porcelain, silk, and jade from China.

Slaves were another export from the East African coast. The trade accelerated with the establishment of Muslim settlements in the eighth century and continued down to the arrival of the Portuguese in the late fifteenth century, who provided a market for African slaves in the New World (discussed in Chapter 15). In fact, the global market for slaves would fuel the East African coastal slave trade until at least the beginning of the twentieth century. As in West Africa, traders obtained slaves primarily through raids and kidnapping.

The Arabs called the northern Somalia coast *Ras Assir* (Cape of Slaves). From there, Arab traders transported slaves northward up the Red Sea to the markets of Arabia and Persia. Muslim dealers also shipped blacks from the region of Zanzibar across the Indian Ocean to markets in India. Rulers of the Deccan Plateau in central India used large numbers of black slave soldiers in their military campaigns. Slaves also worked on the docks and dhows (typical Arab lateen-rigged ships) in the Muslim-controlled Indian Ocean. They also served as domestic servants and concubines throughout South and East Asia.

As early as the tenth century sources mention persons with "lacquer-black bodies" in the possession of wealthy families in Song China.[7] In 1178 a Chinese official noted in a memorial to the emperor that Arab traders were shipping thousands of blacks from East Africa to the Chinese port of Guangzhou (Canton) by way of the Malay Archipelago. The Chinese employed these slaves as household servants, as musicians, and, because East Africans were often expert swimmers, as divers to caulk the leaky seams of ships below the water line.

By the thirteenth century Africans living in many parts of South and East Asia had made significant economic and cultural contributions to their societies. It appears, however, that in Indian, Chinese, and East African markets, slaves were never as valuable a commodity as ivory. Thus the volume of the Eastern slave trade did not approach that of the trans-Saharan slave trade.[8]

Southern Africa and Great Zimbabwe

Southern Africa, bordered on the northwest by the Kalahari Desert and on the northeast by the Zambezi River (see Map 10.2), enjoys a mild and temperate climate. Desert conditions prevail along the Atlantic coast, which gets less than five inches of annual rainfall.

Ruins of Great Zimbabwe Considered the most impressive monument in the African interior south of the Ethiopian highlands, these ruins of Great Zimbabwe consist of two complexes of dry-stone buildings, some surrounded by a massive serpentine wall 32 feet high and 17 feet thick at its maximum. Among the archaeological finds are monoliths crowned by soapstone birds (left). This 14½-inch-high monolith also appears to have an alligator-like creature on its side. Scholars debate the significance of these birds: Were they symbols of royal power? Messengers from the spiritual world to the terrestrial? What does the alligator mean? (photo: Robert Harding World Imagery/SuperStock; bird: Courtesy of the National Archives of Zimbabwe)

Eastward toward the Indian Ocean, rainfall increases, amounting to between fifty to ninety inches a year in some places. Temperate grasslands characterize the highlands in the interior. Considerable variations in climate occur throughout much of southern Africa from year to year.

Southern Africa has enormous mineral resources: gold, copper, diamonds, platinum, and uranium. Preindustrial peoples mined some of these deposits in open excavations down several feet, but fuller exploitation required modern technology.

Located at the southern extremity of the Afroeurasian landmass, southern Africa has a history that is very different from the histories of West Africa, the Nile Valley, and the East African coast. Unlike the rest of coastal Africa, southern Africa remained far removed from the outside world until the Portuguese arrived in the late fifteenth century—with one important exception. Bantu-speaking people reached southern Africa in the eighth century. They brought skills in ironworking and mixed farming (settled crop production plus cattle and sheep raising) and immunity to the kinds of diseases that later decimated the Amerindians of South America (discussed in Chapter 16).

The earliest residents of southern Africa were hunters and gatherers. In the first millennium C.E. new farming techniques from the north arrived. Lack of water and timber (both needed to produce the charcoal used in iron smelting) slowed the spread of iron technology and tools and thus of crop production in southwestern Africa. These advances reached the western coastal region by 1500. By that date, Khoisan-speakers were farming in the arid western regions. The area teemed with wild game. To the east, descendants of Bantu-speaking immigrants grew sorghum, raised cattle and sheep, and fought with iron-headed spears. However, disease-bearing insects such as the tsetse (SET-see) fly, which causes sleeping sickness, attacked the cattle and sheep and retarded their domestication.

The nuclear family was the basic social unit among early southern African peoples, who practiced polygyny and traced descent in the male line. Several families formed bands numbering between twenty and eighty people. Such bands were not closed entities; people in neighboring territories identified with bands speaking the same language. As in most preindustrial societies, a division of labor existed whereby men hunted and women cared for children and raised edible plants. People lived in caves or in camps made of portable material, and they moved from one watering or hunting region to another as seasonal or environmental needs required.

Great Zimbabwe A ruined South African city discovered by a German explorer in 1871; it is considered the most powerful monument south of the Nile Valley and Ethiopian highlands.

In 1871 a German explorer came upon the ruined city of **Great Zimbabwe** southeast of what is now Masvingo in Zimbabwe. Archaeologists consider Great Zimbabwe the most impressive monument in Africa south of the Nile Valley and the Ethiopian highlands. The ruins consist of two vast complexes of dry-stone buildings, a fortress, and an elliptically shaped enclosure commonly called the Temple. Stone carvings, gold and copper ornaments, and Asian ceramics once decorated the buildings. The ruins extend over sixty acres and are encircled by a massive wall. The entire city was built from local granite between the eleventh and fifteenth centuries without any outside influence.

Great Zimbabwe was the political and religious capital of a vast empire. During the first millennium C.E. settled crop cultivation, cattle raising, and work in metal led to a steady buildup in population in the Zambezi-Limpopo region. The area also contained a rich gold-bearing belt. Gold ore lay near the surface; alluvial gold lay in the Zambezi River tributaries. In the tenth century the inhabitants collected the alluvial gold by panning and washing; after the year 1000, the gold was worked in open mines with iron picks. Traders shipped the gold eastward to Sofala (see Map 10.2). Great Zimbabwe's wealth and power rested on this gold trade.

Great Zimbabwe declined in the fifteenth century, perhaps because the area had become agriculturally exhausted and could no longer support the large population. Some people migrated northward and settled in the Mazoe River Valley, a tributary of the Zambezi. This region also contained gold, and the settlers built a new empire in the tradition of Great Zimbabwe. This empire's rulers were called "Mwene Mutapa," and their power was also based on the gold trade down the Zambezi River to Indian Ocean ports. It was this gold that the Portuguese sought when they arrived on the East African coast in the late fifteenth century.

Quick Review
What role did international trade play in the development of Africa's kingdoms and empires?

Connections

BECAUSE OUR ANCESTORS first evolved in Africa, Africa's archaeological record is rich with material artifacts, such as weapons, tools, ornaments, and eating utensils. But its written record is much less complete, and thus the nonmaterial dimensions of human society — human interaction in all its facets — is much more difficult to reconstruct. The only exception is in Egypt, where hieroglyphic writings give us a more complete picture of Egyptian society than of nearly any other ancient culture.

Not until the Phoenicians, Greeks, and Romans were there written accounts of the peoples of North and East Africa. These accounts document Africa's early connections and contributions to the vast trans-Saharan and Indian Ocean trading networks that stretched from Europe to China. This trade brought wealth to the kingdoms, empires, and city-states that developed alongside the routes. But the trade in ideas most profoundly connected the growing African states to the wider world, most notably through Islam, which arrived by the eighth century, and Christianity, which developed a foothold in Ethiopia.

Prior to the late fifteenth century Europeans had little knowledge about African societies. All this would change during the European Age of Discovery. Chapter 16 traces the expansion of Portugal from a small and poor European nation to an overseas empire, as it established trading posts and gained control of the African gold trade. Portuguese expansion led to competition, spurring Spain and then England to strike out for gold of their own in the New World. The acceleration of this conquest would forever shape the history of Africa and the Americas (discussed in Chapters 11 and 16) and intertwine them via the African slave trade that fueled the labor needs of the colonies in the New World.

- **For a list of suggested readings for this chapter, visit** *bedfordstmartins.com/mckayworldunderstanding*.
- **For primary sources from this period, see** *Sources of World Societies*, Second Edition.
- **For Web sites, images, and documents related to topics in this chapter, see Make History at** *bedfordstmartins.com/mckayworldunderstanding*.

Chapter 10 Study Guide

To do these exercises online, go to bedfordstmartins.com/mckayworldunderstanding.

Step 1

GETTING STARTED

Below are basic terms about this period in global history. Can you identify each term below and explain why it matters?

TERMS	WHO (OR WHAT) AND WHEN	WHY IT MATTERS
Bantu, p. 241		
Sudan, p. 242		
Berbers, p. 243		
Mogadishu, p. 245		
stateless societies, p. 246		
Ghana, p. 246		
Koumbi Saleh, p. 248		
Timbuktu, p. 250		
Aksum, p. 251		
Swahili, p. 255		
Kilwa, p. 255		
Great Zimbabwe, p. 260		

Step 2

MOVING BEYOND THE BASICS

The exercise below requires a more advanced understanding of the chapter material. Examine the role of geographic and climatic diversity in African history by filling in the chart below with descriptions of the society, government, and economy of each of Africa's five main climatic zones. When you are finished consider the following questions: In which regions did settled agriculture lead to population growth and urbanization? Which regions had the strongest economic and cultural connections to societies outside of Africa? Which regions were most isolated from the outside world? How did geography and climate shape the patterns you have noted?

	SOCIETY	GOVERNMENT	ECONOMY
Fertile northern and southern coastal regions			
Steppe lands			
Deserts			
Savanna			
Tropical rain forests			

Step 3

PUTTING IT ALL TOGETHER

Now that you've reviewed key elements of the chapter, take a step back and try to see the big picture. Remember to use specific examples from the chapter in your answers.

GEOGRAPHY AND AGRICULTURE

- How did geography and climate shape the spread of agriculture in Africa?
- What common characteristics were shared by settled agricultural societies across Africa? What role did Bantu-speaking peoples play in linking diverse African societies?

THE TRANS-SAHARAN TRADE

- What role did West Africa play in international commerce between 800 and 1500 C.E.?
- How did the growth of the trans-Saharan trade stimulate political and religious change in West Africa?

KINGDOMS AND EMPIRES

- How did Islam shape the political development of West Africa?
- Compare and contrast Ethiopia and the East African city-states. How would you explain the differences you note?

LOOKING BACK, LOOKING AHEAD

- How has the paucity of indigenous written records shaped our understanding of early African history?
- How might the advent of the Atlantic slave trade in the sixteenth century and European imperialism in Africa in the nineteenth century have affected Western assumptions about conditions in Africa prior to 1500?

In Your Own Words Imagine that you must explain Chapter 10 to someone who hasn't read it. What would be the most important points to include and why?

11

The Americas

2500 B.C.E.–1500 C.E.

The first humans settled in the Americas between 40,000 and 15,000 B.C.E. after emigrating from Asia. The melting of glaciers 13,000 to 11,000 years ago separated the Americas and Afroeurasia, and the Eastern and Western Hemispheres developed in isolation from one another. There were many parallels, however. In both areas people initially gathered and hunted their food, and then some groups began to plant crops, adapting plants that were native to the areas they settled. Techniques of plant domestication spread, allowing for population growth because harvested crops provided a more regular food supply than did gathered food. In certain parts of both hemispheres, efficient production and transportation of food supplies led to the growth of cities, with monumental buildings honoring divine and human power, specialized production of a wide array of products, and marketplaces where those products were exchanged. New products included improved military equipment, which leaders used to enhance their authority and build up the large political entities we call kingdoms and empires. The power of those leaders also often rested on religious ideas, so that providing service to a king or obeying the laws he set forth was viewed as a way to honor the gods. In the Western Hemisphere strong and prosperous empires developed first in Mesoamerica—consisting of present-day Mexico and Central America—and then in the Andes.

Moche Portrait Vessel
A Moche artist captured the commanding expression of a ruler in this ceramic vessel. The Moche were one of many cultures in Peru that developed technologies that were simultaneously useful and beautiful, including brightly colored cloth and intricately fit stone walls. (Private Collection/Photo © Boltin Picture Library/The Bridgeman Art Library)

Chapter Preview

- How did early peoples of the Americas adapt to its diverse environments?
- What characterized early societies in the Americas?
- What kinds of societies emerged in the Americas in the classical era?
- Who were the Aztecs and how did they build an empire?
- What were the strengths and weaknesses of the Inca Empire?

How did early peoples of the Americas adapt to its diverse environments?

Mesoamerica The term used by scholars to designate the area of present-day Mexico and Central America.

As in the development of early human cultures worldwide, the environment shaped the formation of settlements in the Americas. North America includes arctic tundra, dry plains, coastal wetlands, woodlands, deserts, and temperate rain forests. **Mesoamerica** is dominated by high plateaus with a temperate climate and good agricultural land bounded by coastal plains. The Caribbean coast of Central America is characterized by thick jungle lowlands, heavy rainfall, and torrid heat. South America has extremely varied terrain. The entire western coast is edged by the Andes, while three-fourths of the continent is lowland plains. South America's Amazon River is bordered by tropical lowland rain forests. Not surprisingly, the varied environments of the Americas contributed to the great diversity of peoples, cultures, and linguistic groups.

Settling the Americas

The traditions of many American Indian peoples teach that their group originated independently, often through the actions of a divine figure. Many creation accounts, including that of the book of Genesis in the Bible, begin with people who are created out of earth and receive assistance from supernatural beings who set out certain ways the people are supposed to behave. Both Native American and biblical creation accounts continue to have deep spiritual importance for many people.

Map 11.1 The Settling of the Americas Before 10,000 B.C.E. Genetic evidence is currently providing new information about the ways that people migrated across the Bering Strait through the region known as Beringia. It suggests that this occurred in waves, and that people settled in Beringia for a while before going on, and also migrated back to Asia.

Archaeological and DNA evidence indicates that the earliest humans came to the Americas from Siberia and East Asia, but exactly when and how this happened is hotly debated. The traditional account is that people crossed the Bering Strait from what is now Russian Siberia to what is now Alaska sometime between 15,000 and 13,000 B.C.E. (Map 11.1). This was the end of the last Ice Age, so more of the world's water was frozen and ocean levels were much lower than they are today. The migrants traveled southward through North America between two large ice sheets that were slowly melting and retreating. They lived by gathering and hunting, using spears with distinctive fluted stone tips that archaeologists term "Clovis points" after the town in New Mexico where they were first discovered.

There is some difference of opinion about exactly when the Clovis culture flourished, with some scholars accepting 11,000 B.C.E. as the height of Clovis technology and others 9000 B.C.E. Disagreements regarding the age of the Clovis culture are significant because they are part of a much broader debate about the traditional account of migration to the Americas. Archaeologists working at Monte Verde along the coast of Chile have excavated a site that they date to about 12,000 B.C.E., and perhaps much earlier. This site is ten thousand miles from the Bering Land bridge, which would have meant a very fast walk. Monte Verde and a few other sites are leading increasing numbers of archaeologists to conclude that migrants over the land bridge were preceded by people coming originally from Asia who traveled along the coast in skin boats, perhaps as early as 40,000 B.C.E. The coasts that they traveled along are far under water today, so archaeological evidence is difficult to obtain, but DNA and other genetic evidence has lent support to the theory of coastal migration. However and whenever people got to the Western Hemisphere, they lived by gathering, fishing, and hunting, as did everyone throughout the world at that point.

Chapter Chronology

ca. 40,000–13,000 B.C.E.	Initial human migration to the Americas (date disputed)
ca. 8000 B.C.E.	Beginnings of agriculture
ca. 2500 B.C.E.	First cities in Norte Chico region of Peru
ca. 2000 B.C.E	Earliest mound building in North America
ca. 1500–300 B.C.E.	Olmec culture
ca. 1200 B.C.E.	Emergence of Chavin culture
ca. 200 B.C.E.–600 C.E.	Hopewell culture
ca. 100–800 C.E.	Moche culture
ca. 450 C.E.	Peak of Teotihuacán's influence
ca. 600–900 C.E.	Peak of Maya culture
ca. 1050–1250 C.E.	Construction of mounds at Cahokia
1325 C.E.	Construction of Aztec city of Tenochtitlán begins
ca. 1450 C.E.	Height of Aztec culture
ca. 1500 C.E.	Inca Empire reaches its largest extent

The Development of Agriculture

About 8000 B.C.E. people in some parts of the Americas began raising crops as well as gathering wild produce. As in the development of agriculture in Afroeurasia, people initially planted the seeds of native plants. At some point people living in what is now southern Mexico began raising what would become the most important crop in the Americas — maize, which we generally call corn.

People bred various types of maize for different purposes and for different climates, making it the staple food throughout the highlands of Mesoamerica. They often planted maize along with squash, beans, and other crops in a field called a milpa (MIHL-puh); the beans use the maize stalks for support as they grow and also fix nitrogen in the soil, acting as a natural fertilizer. Crops can be grown in milpas year after year, in contrast to single-crop planting in which rotation is needed so as not to exhaust the soil.

Maize was viewed as the source of human life and therefore came to have a symbolic and religious meaning. It featured prominently in sculptures of gods and kings, and it was often associated with a specific deity, the corn god. Ceremonies honoring this god were held regularly.

In central Mexico, along with milpas, people also built *chinampas* (chee-NAHM-pahs), floating gardens. They dredged soil from the bottom of a lake or pond, placed the soil on mats of woven twigs, and then planted maize and other crops in the soil. Chinampas were enormously productive, yielding up to three harvests a year.

Knowledge of maize cultivation and maize seeds themselves spread from Mesoamerica into both North and South America. By 3000 B.C.E. farmers in what is now Peru and Uruguay were planting maize, and by 2000 B.C.E. farmers in southwest North America were as well. The crop then spread into the Mississippi Valley and to northeastern North America, where farmers bred slightly different variants for the different growing conditions. After 1500 C.E. maize cultivation spread to Europe, Africa, and Asia as well, becoming an essential food crop there.

The expansion of maize was the result of contacts between different groups that can be traced through trade goods as well. Copper from the Great Lakes, used for jewelry and ornaments, was a particularly valuable item and was traded throughout North America, reaching Mexico by 3000 B.C.E. Obsidian from the Rocky Mountains, used for blades, was traded widely, as were shells and later pottery.

Lime Container from the Andes This 9-inch gold bottle for holding lime, made between 500 C.E. and 1000 C.E., shows a seated female figure with rings in her ears and beads across her forehead and at her neck, wrists, knees, and ankles. Lime helped release the active ingredients in coca, which was used by many peoples of South America in rituals and to withstand bodily discomfort. Pieces of coca leaves were placed in the mouth with small amounts of powdered lime made from seashells, and then chewed. (Image © The Metropolitan Museum of Art/Art Resource, NY)

Various cultivars of maize were developed for many different climates, but maize was difficult to grow in high altitudes. Thus in the high Andes, people relied on potatoes, with the earliest evidence of people eating potatoes dating from about 11,000 B.C.E. Potatoes first grew wild and then were cultivated, and selective breeding produced many different varieties. The slopes on which potatoes were grown were terraced with stone retaining walls, keeping the hillsides from sliding. High-altitude valleys were connected to mountain life and vegetation to form a single interdependent agricultural system, called "vertical archipelagos," capable of supporting large communities. Such vertical archipelagos often extended more than thirty-seven miles from top to bottom. Potatoes ordinarily cannot be stored for long periods, but Andean peoples developed a product called *chuñu*, freeze-dried potatoes made by subjecting potatoes alternately to nightly frosts and daily sun. Chuñu will keep unspoiled for several years. Coca (the dried leaves of a plant native to the Andes from which cocaine is derived), chewed in moderation as a dietary supplement, enhanced people's stamina and their ability to withstand the cold that was part of living at high altitudes.

Maize will also not grow well in hot, wet climates. In the Amazon rain forest manioc, a tuber that can be cooked in many ways, became the staple food instead. It was planted along with other crops, including fruits, nuts, and various types of palm trees. Just how many people Amazonian agriculture supported before the introduction of European diseases (see "Connections" on page 287) is hotly debated by anthropologists, but increasing numbers see the original tropical rain forest not as a pristine wilderness, but as an ecosystem managed effectively by humans for thousands of years.

Farming in the Americas was not limited to foodstuffs. Beginning about 2500 B.C.E. people living along the coast of Peru used irrigation to raise cotton, and textiles became an important part of Peruvian culture. Agriculture in the Americas was extensive, though it was limited by the lack of an animal that could be harnessed to pull a plow. People throughout the Americas domesticated dogs for hunting, and in the Andes they domesticated llamas and alpacas to carry loads through the mountains. But no native species allowed itself to be harnessed as horses, oxen, and water buffalo did in Asia and Europe, which meant that all agricultural labor was human-powered.

Quick Review
How did settled agriculture spread in the Americas and what kinds of agriculture were developed in the Americas' diverse environments?

What characterized early societies in the Americas?

Agricultural advancement had definitive social and political consequences. Careful cultivation of the land brought a reliable and steady food supply, which contributed to a relatively high fertility rate. As a result, population in the Americas grew steadily and may have reached about 15 million by the first century B.C.E. This growth in population allowed for the creation of the first urban societies.

Inca Khipu, ca. 1400 C.E. This khipu, a collection of colored, knotted strings, recorded numeric information and allowed Inca administrators to keep track of the flow of money, goods, and people in their large empire. Every aspect of the khipu—the form and position of the knots, the colors and spin of the string—may have provided information. Administrators read them visually and by running their hands through them, as Braille text is read today. (Museo Arqueologico Rafael Larco Herrera, Lima, Peru)

Mounds, Towns, and Trade in North and South America

By 2500 B.C.E. some groups in North America began to build massive earthworks, mounds of earth and stone serving a variety of purposes (see page 275). The Ohio and Mississippi River Valleys contain the richest concentration of mounds, but these earthworks have been found from the Great Lakes down to the Gulf of Mexico (see Map 11.1). One early large mound at Poverty Point, Louisiana, on the banks of the Mississippi dates from about 1300 B.C.E. The area was home to perhaps five thousand people and was inhabited for hundreds of years, with trade goods brought in by canoe and carved stone beads exported.

Large structures for political and religious purposes began to be built earlier in South America than in North America. By about 2500 B.C.E. cities grew along river valleys on the coast of Peru in the region called Norte Chico (NAWR-tay CHEE-koh). Stepped pyramids, some more than ten stories high, dominated these settlements, and they were built at about the same time as the pyramids in Egypt. Cities in Norte Chico often used irrigation to water crops. People who lived along the coast relied extensively on fish and shellfish, which they traded with residents of inland cities for the cotton needed to make nets. The largest city, Caral, had many stone plazas, houses, and temples. Cotton was used in Norte Chico for many other things, including the earliest example yet discovered of a **khipu** (also spelled *quipu*), a collection of knotted strings that was used to record information. Later Peruvian cultures, including the Incas, developed ever more complex khipu, using them to represent tax obligations, census records, and other numeric data.

khipu An intricate system of knotted and colored strings used by early Peruvian cultures to store information such as census and tax records.

Along with khipu, Norte Chico culture also developed religious ideas and representations of deities that influenced many Andean cultures. Religious ceremonies, as well as other festivities, in Norte Chico likely involved music, as a large number of bone flutes have been discovered.

The earliest cities in the Andes were built by the Chavin people beginning about 1200 B.C.E. These people built stone pyramids and other types of monumental architecture. They worked gold and silver into human and animal figurines, trading these and other goods to coastal peoples.

Olmec Contributions to Mesoamerican Culture	
Ritual ball games	Sacrifice at sacred ceremonial sites
Large pyramid-shaped buildings	Calendar that traced celestial phenomena
Huge stone heads of rulers or gods	Symbolic writing system

Olmec Agriculture, Technology, and Religion

Olmecs The oldest of the early advanced Mesoamerican civilizations.

The **Olmecs** created the first society with cities in Mesoamerica. The word *Olmec* comes from an Aztec term for the peoples living in southern Veracruz and western Tabasco, Mexico, between about 1500 and 300 B.C.E.

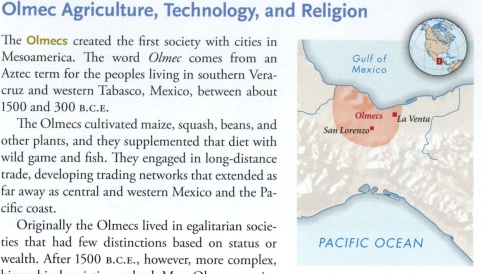

The Olmecs, ca. 1500–300 B.C.E.

The Olmecs cultivated maize, squash, beans, and other plants, and they supplemented that diet with wild game and fish. They engaged in long-distance trade, developing trading networks that extended as far away as central and western Mexico and the Pacific coast.

Originally the Olmecs lived in egalitarian societies that had few distinctions based on status or wealth. After 1500 B.C.E., however, more complex, hierarchical societies evolved. Most Olmecs continued to live in small villages along the rivers of the region, while their leaders resided in large cities, including those today known as San Lorenzo and La Venta. These cities contained palaces for the elite, large plazas, temples, water reservoirs, and carved stone drains for the disposal of wastes. They also contained special courts on which men played a game with a hard rubber ball that was both religious ritual and sport.

Around 900 B.C.E. San Lorenzo, the center of early Olmec culture, was destroyed, probably by migrating peoples from the north, and power passed to La Venta in Tabasco. Archaeological excavation at La Venta has uncovered a huge volcano-shaped pyramid. The upward thrust of this monument, like ziggurats in Mesopotamia or cathedrals in medieval Europe, may have represented the human effort to get closer to the gods. Built of huge stone slabs, the Great Pyramid required, scholars estimate, some eight hundred thousand hours of human labor. It testifies to the region's good harvests, which were able to support a labor force large enough to build such a monument.

Quick Review
What role did large settlements featuring monumental structures play in early American societies?

What kinds of societies emerged in the Americas in the classical era?

Maya A highly developed Mesoamerican culture centered in the Yucatán peninsula of Mexico. The Maya created the most intricate writing system in the Western Hemisphere.

The urban culture of the Olmecs and other Mesoamerican peoples influenced subsequent Mesoamerican societies. Especially in what became known as the classical era (300–900 C.E.), various groups developed large states centered on cities, with high levels of technological and intellectual achievement. The city-states established by the **Maya** were the longest lasting, but others were significant as well. Peoples living in North America built communities that, although smaller than those in Mesoamerica, featured significant achievements, such as the use of irrigation to enhance agricultural production.

Palace Doorway Lintel at Yaxchilan, Mexico Lady Xoc, principal wife of King Shield-Jaguar, who holds a torch over her, pulls a thorn-lined rope through her tongue to sanctify with her blood the birth of a younger wife's child—reflecting the importance of blood sacrifice in Maya culture. The elaborate headdresses and clothes of the couple show their royal status. (Photograph K2887 © Justin Kerr)

Maya Agriculture and Trade

Linguistic evidence suggests that the first Maya were a small North American Indian group that emigrated from the area that is now southern Oregon and northern California to the western highlands of Guatemala. Between the third and second millennia B.C.E. various groups, including the Cholans and Tzeltalans, broke away from the parent group and moved north and east into the Yucatán peninsula. The Cholan-speaking Maya, who occupied the area during the time of great cultural achievement, apparently created the culture.

Maya communities relied on agriculture. The staple crop in Mesoamerica was maize, often raised in multiple-crop milpas with other foodstuffs. The Maya also practiced intensive agriculture in raised, narrow, rectangular plots that they built above the low-lying, seasonally flooded land bordering rivers.

The raised-field and milpa systems yielded food sufficient to support large population centers. The entire Maya region could have had as many as 14 million inhabitants. In various Maya settlements (Map 11.2), archaeologists have uncovered the palaces of nobles, elaborate pyramids where nobles were buried, engraved pillars, masonry temples, altars, sophisticated polychrome pottery, and courts for games played with a rubber ball. The largest site, Tikal, may have had forty thousand people and served as a religious and ceremonial center.

At these population centers, public fairs for trading merchandise accompanied important religious festivals. The extensive trade among Maya communities, plus a common language, promoted unity among the peoples of the region and gave them a common sense of identity. Merchants trading beyond Maya regions, such as with the Zapotecs of the Valley of Oaxaca and with the Teotihuacános of the central valley of Mexico, were considered state ambassadors bearing "gifts" to royal neighbors, who reciprocated with their own "gifts." Since this long-distance trade played an important part in international relations, the merchants conducting it were high nobles or even members of the royal family.

The extensive networks of rivers and swamps in the area ruled by the Maya were the main arteries of transportation. Wide roads also linked Maya centers. Trade produced considerable wealth that seems to have been concentrated in a noble class, for the Maya had no distinctly mercantile class. They did have a sharply defined hierarchical society. A hereditary elite owned private land, defended society, carried on commercial activities, exercised political power, and directed religious rituals. Artisans and scribes made up the next social level. The rest of the people were farmers, unskilled laborers, and slaves, the latter including prisoners of war.

Wars were fought in Maya society for a variety of reasons. Long periods without rain caused crop failure, which led to famine and then war with other centers for food. Certain

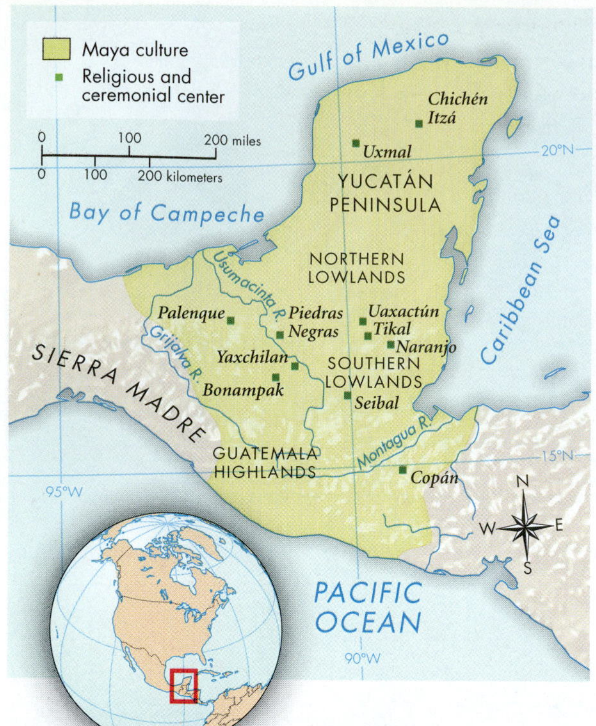

Map 11.2 The Maya World, 300–900 C.E. The Maya built dozens of cities linked together in trading networks of roads and rivers. Only the largest of them are shown here.

cities, such as Tikal, extended their authority over larger areas through warfare with neighboring cities. Within the same communities, domestic strife between factions over the succession to the kingship or property led to violence.

Maya Science and Religion

The Maya developed the most complex writing system in the Americas, a script with nearly a thousand characters that represent concepts and sounds. With this script important events and observations were recorded in books made of bark paper and deerskin, on stone pillars archaeologists term "steles," on pottery, and on the walls of temples and other buildings. The deciphering of this writing over the last fifty years has demonstrated that the inscriptions are historical documents recording the births, accessions, marriages, wars, and deaths of Maya kings and nobles, in contrast to the earliest writings from Mesopotamia, which are tax records for payments to the temple (see page 30). The writing and pictorial imagery often represent the same events, allowing for a fuller understanding of Maya dynastic history.

Learning about Maya religion through written records is more difficult. In the sixteenth century Spanish religious authorities ordered all books of Maya writing to be destroyed, viewing them as demonic. Only three (and part of a fourth) survived, because they were already in Europe. These texts provide information about religious rituals and practices, as well as astronomical calculations. Further information comes from the ***Popul Vuh*** (poh-POHL VOO), or *Book of Council*, a book of mythological narratives and dynastic history written in the middle of the sixteenth century in the Maya language but in European script, which Spanish friars had taught to Maya students. Like the Bible in Judeo-Christian tradition, the *Popul Vuh* gives the Maya view of the creation of the world, concepts of good and evil, and the entire nature and purpose of the living experience.

Popul Vuh The *Book of Council*, a collection of mythological narratives and dynastic histories that constitutes the primary record of the Maya civilization.

Maya religious practice emphasized performing rituals at specific times, which served as an impetus for further refinements of the calendar. From careful observation of the earth's movements around the sun, the Maya devised a calendar of eighteen 20-day months and one 5-day month, for a total of 365 days. They also used a second calendar with a cycle of 260 days, perhaps inherited from the Olmecs. When these two cyclical calendars coincided, which happened once every fifty-two years, the Maya celebrated with a period of feasting, ball-game competitions, and religious observance. These observances—and those at other times as well—included human sacrifice to honor the gods and demonstrate the power of earthly kings. The actions of those kings were recorded using yet a third calendar, which counted in a linear fashion forward from a specific date.

The Maya devised a form of mathematics based on the vigesimal (20) rather than the decimal (10) system. More unusual was their use of the number zero, which allows for more complex calculations than are possible in number systems without it. The zero may have actually been discovered by the Olmecs, who used it in figuring their calendar, but the Maya used it mathematically as well. The Maya's proficiency with numbers made them masters of abstract knowledge—notably in astronomy, mathematics, calendric development, and the recording of history.

Maya civilization lasted about a thousand years, reaching its peak between approximately 600 and 900 C.E., the period when the Tang Dynasty was flourishing in China, Islam was spreading in the Middle East, and Carolingian rulers were extending their sway in Europe. Between the eighth and tenth centuries the Maya abandoned their cultural and ceremonial centers, and Maya civilization collapsed. Archaeologists and historians attribute the decline to a combination of agricultural failures due to land exhaustion and drought; overpopulation; disease; and constant wars fought to achieve economic and political goals. These wars brought widespread destruction, which aggravated agrarian problems. Royalty also suffered from the decline in Maya civilization: just as in good times kings attributed moral authority and prosperity to themselves, so in bad times, when military, economic, and social conditions deteriorated, they were blamed.

Growth and Assimilation of the Teotihuacán and Toltec Cultures

The Maya were not alone in creating a complex culture in Mesoamerica during the classic period. In modern-day Monte Albán in southern Mexico, Zapotecan-speaking peoples established a great religious center whose temples and elaborately decorated tombs testify to the wealth of the nobility. To the north of Monte Albán, Teotihuacán (tay-oh-tee-wah-KAHN) in central Mexico witnessed the flowering of a remarkable civilization built by a new people from regions east and south of the Valley of Mexico. In about 450 C.E. the city of Teotihuacán had a population of over two hundred thousand—more than any European city at the time. The inhabitants were stratified into distinct social classes. The rich and powerful resided in houses of palatial splendor in a special precinct. Ordinary working people, tradespeople, artisans, and obsidian craftsmen lived in apartment compounds, or barrios, on the edge of the city. Agricultural laborers lived outside the city. Teotihuacán became the center of trade and culture for all of Mesoamerica.

In the center of the city stood several great pyramids, which the Aztecs later referred to as the Pyramids of the Sun and the Moon. The Pyramid of the Sun is the world's third-largest pyramid, only a bit smaller than the largest ancient Egyptian pyramid. Exactly what deities were worshipped there is unknown, although they appear to have included the feathered serpent god worshipped by many Mesoamerican peoples, called Quetzalcoatl (kwet-suhl-kuh-WAH-tuhl) or "quetzal serpent" by the Aztecs.

Around 750 C.E. less-developed peoples from the southwest burned Teotihuacán, and the city-state fell apart. This collapse, plus that of the Maya in about 900 B.C.E., marks the end of the classical period in Mesoamerica for most scholars, just as the end of the Roman Empire in the West marks the end of the classical era in Europe (see Chapter 6). As in Europe, a period of disorder, militarism, and domination by smaller states followed.

The Toltecs, ca. 900–1200 C.E.

Whereas nature gods and their priests seem to have governed the great cities of the earlier period, militant gods and warriors dominated the petty states that now arose. Among these states, the most powerful heir to Teotihuacán was the Toltec confederation, a weak union of strong states. The Toltecs admired the culture of their predecessors and sought to absorb and preserve it. Through intermarriage, they assimilated with the Teotihuacán people. In fact, every new Mesoamerican confederation became the cultural successor of earlier confederations.

Under Topiltzin (r. ca. 980–1000), the Toltecs extended their hegemony over most of central Mexico. After the reign of Topiltzin, however, troubles beset the Toltec state. Drought led to crop failure. Northern peoples, the Chichimecas, attacked the borders in waves. Weak, incompetent rulers could not quell domestic uprisings. When the last Toltec king committed suicide in 1174, the Toltec state collapsed.

Hohokam, Hopewell, and Mississippian Societies

Mesoamerican trading networks extended into southwestern North America, where by 300 B.C.E. the Hohokam people and other groups were using irrigation canals, dams, and terraces to enhance their farming of the arid land (Map 11.3). The Hohokam built plat-

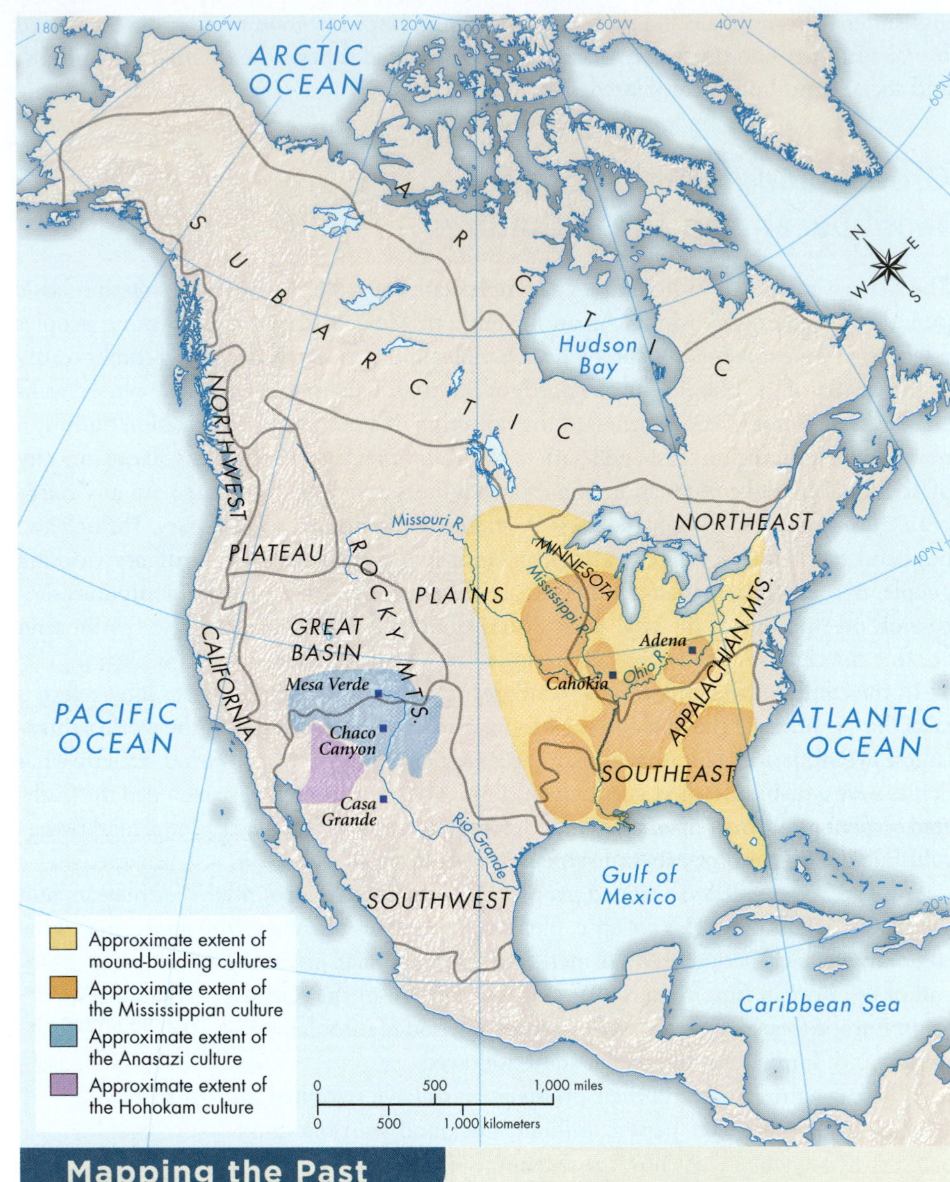

Mapping the Past

Map 11.3 Major North American Agricultural Societies, ca. 600–1500 C.E.

Many North American groups used agriculture to increase the available food supply and allow greater population density and the development of urban centers. Shown here are three of these cultures: the Mississippian, Anasazi, and Hohokam.

ANALYZING THE MAP How did the location of the Mississippian and other mound-building cultures facilitate trade?

CONNECTIONS The climate and natural vegetation of North America in this period did not differ significantly from those of today. What different types of challenges might these have posed for crop-raising in the three societies shown here?

forms for ceremonial purposes and, like the Olmecs and other Mesoamerican peoples, played games with rubber balls. The balls themselves were imported, and turquoise and other precious stones were exported in return. Religious ideas came along with trade goods. Along with local divinities, the feathered serpent god became important to desert peoples. Other groups, including the Anasazi (ah-nuh-SAH-zee), the Yuma, and later the Pueblo and Hopi also built settlements in this area. Mesa Verde, the largest Anasazi town, had a population of about twenty-five hundred living in houses built into and on cliff walls. Roads connected Mesa Verde to other Anasazi towns. Drought, deforestation, and soil erosion led to decline in both the Hohokam and Anasazi cultures, increasing warfare between towns.

To the east, the mound building introduced at settlements along the Mississippi River around 2000 B.C.E. spread more widely in the valleys of other rivers. One of the most important mound-building cultures was that of the Hopewell (200 B.C.E.–600 C.E.), named for a town in Ohio near where the most extensive mounds were built. Some mounds were burial chambers for priests, leaders, and other high-status individuals, or for thousands of more average people. Others were platforms for the larger houses of important people. Still others were simply huge mounds of earth shaped like animals or geometric figures, which may have served some sort of ceremonial purpose. Mound building thus had many purposes: to honor the gods, to remember the dead, and to make distinctions between leaders and common folk.

Hopewell earthworks also included canals that enabled trading networks to expand, bringing products from the Caribbean far into the interior. Those trading networks also carried maize, allowing more intensive agriculture to spread throughout the eastern woodlands of North America.

At Cahokia (kuh-HOE-kee-uh), near the confluence of the Mississippi and Missouri Rivers in Illinois, archaeologists have uncovered the largest mound of all, part of a ceremonial center and city that housed perhaps thirty-eight thousand people. Work on this complex of mounds, plazas, and houses—which covered five and a half square miles—began about 1050 C.E. and was completed about 1250 C.E.

The mounds at Cahokia are the most impressive physical achievement of the **Mississippian** mound builders, who built cities and mounds throughout much of the eastern United States. What do the mounds tell us about Mississippian societies? The largest mounds served as burial chambers for leaders and, in many cases, for the leaders' male and female servants, who were sacrificed in order to assist the leader in the afterlife. Mounds also

Mississippian An important mound-building culture that thrived between 800 and 1500 C.E. in a territory that extended from the Mississippi River to the Appalachian Mountains. The largest mound produced by this culture is found at Cahokia, Illinois.

Great Serpent Mound, Adams County, Ohio Made by people in the Hopewell culture, this 1,254-foot-long mound in the form of a writhing snake has its "head" at the highest point, suggesting an open mouth ready to swallow a huge egg formed by a heap of stones. (Georg Gerster/Photo Researchers, Inc.)

contain valuable artifacts, such as jewelry made from copper from Michigan, mica (a mineral used in building) from the Appalachians, obsidian from the Rocky Mountains, conch shells from the Caribbean, and pipestone from Minnesota.

From these burial items, archaeologists have deduced that mound culture was hierarchical and that power was increasingly centralized. The leader had religious responsibilities and also managed long-distance trade and gift-giving. The exchange of goods was not perceived as a form of commerce but as a means of showing respect and of establishing bonds among diverse groups. Large towns housed several thousand inhabitants and served as political and ceremonial centers. They controlled surrounding villages of a few hundred people but did not grow into large, politically unified city-states the way Tikal and Teotihuacán did.

Mississippian mound builders relied on agriculture to support their complex cultures, and by the time Cahokia was built, maize agriculture had spread to the Atlantic coast. Particularly along riverbanks and the coastline, fields of maize, beans, and squash surrounded large, permanent villages containing many houses, all surrounded by walls made of earth and timber. Hunting and fishing provided animal protein, but the bulk of people's food came from farming. For recreation, people played various ball games and chunkey, a game in which spears were thrown at a disk rolled across the ground. As in Mesoamerica, these games were sometimes played in large arenas with many spectators, who frequently gambled on the outcome.

Mississippian people's artifacts reveal their religious ideas. Along with the visible world, the Mississippian cosmos included an Overworld and an Underworld filled with supernatural beings; the three worlds were linked together by an axis usually portrayed as a tree or a striped pole. The forces and beings of both spiritual worlds, which often took the form of falcons, serpents, panthers, or creatures that combined parts from various animals, were honored through ceremonies and rituals, and they offered supernatural power to humans who performed these rites correctly.

At its peak in about 1150 Cahokia was the largest city north of Mesoamerica. However, construction of an interior wooden fence around the city denuded much of the surrounding countryside of trees, which made spring floods worse and eventually destroyed much of the city. An earthquake at the beginning of the thirteenth century furthered the destruction, and the city never recovered. The worsening climate of the fourteenth century that brought famine to Europe probably also contributed to Cahokia's decline, and the site's population dispersed. Throughout Mississippian areas the fifteenth century brought increased warfare, as evidenced by the building of walls and defensive works around towns, and more migration. Iroquois-speaking peoples in particular migrated south from what is now New York into the valleys of the Ohio River and its tributaries, sometimes displacing groups that had been living in these areas through warfare. In the fifteenth or early sixteenth century a group of Iroquois nations formed an association known as the Iroquois League to lessen intergroup violence. This league was a powerful force when European colonists first entered these areas.

Quick Review
What common characteristics linked the major societies of Mesoamerica and North America in the classical era?

Who were the Aztecs and how did they build an empire?

Nahuatl The language of both the Toltecs and the Aztecs.

The Aztecs provide a spectacular example of a culture that adopted many things from earlier peoples and also adapted them to create an even more powerful state. Around 1300 a group of **Nahuatl**-speaking (NAH-watt) people are believed to have migrated southward from what is now northern Mexico, settling on the shores and islands of Lake Texcoco in the central valley of Mexico (Map 11.4). Here they built the twin cities of Tenochtitlán (tay-nawch-teet-LAHN) and Tlatelolco, which by 1500 were probably larger than any city in Europe except Istanbul. As they migrated, these people, who were later called the Aztecs, conquered many neighboring city-states and established an empire later termed the Aztec Empire. The word *Aztec* was not used at the time, however, and most scholars now prefer the term **Mexica** to refer to the empire and its people; we use both terms here.

Mexica The dominant ethnic group of what is now Mexico, who created an empire based on war and religion that reached its height in the mid-1400s; in the nineteenth century the people became known as Aztecs.

Religion and War in Aztec Society

In Mexica society, religion was the dynamic factor that transformed other aspects of the culture: economic security, social mobility, education, and especially war. The state religion of the Aztecs initially gave them powerful advantages over other groups in central Mexico; it inspired them to conquer vast territories in a remarkably short time. War came to be seen as a religious duty; through it nobles, and occasionally commoners, honored the gods, gained prestige, and often acquired wealth.

The Mexicas worshipped a number of gods and goddesses as well as some deities that had dual natures as both male and female. Like many polytheists, Mexicas took the deities of people they encountered into their own pantheon or mixed their attributes with those of existing gods. Quetzalcoatl, for example, the feathered serpent god found among

Map 11.4 The Aztec (Mexica) Empire in 1519 The Mexica migrated into the central valley of what is now Mexico from the north, conquering other groups and establishing an empire, later called the Aztec Empire. The capital of the Aztec Empire was Tenochtitlán, built on islands in Lake Texcoco.

INDIVIDUALS IN SOCIETY

Tlacaélel

THE HUMMINGBIRD GOD HUITZILOPOCHTLI WAS originally a somewhat ordinary god of war and of young men, but in the fifteenth century he was elevated in status among the Mexica. He became increasingly associated with the sun and gradually became the Mexicas' most important deity. This change appears to have been primarily the work of Tlacaélel, the very long-lived chief adviser to the emperors Itzcóatl (r. 1427–1440), Montezuma I (r. 1440–1469), and Axayacatl (r. 1469–1481). Tlacaélel first gained influence during wars in the 1420s in which the Mexicas defeated the rival Tepanecs, after which he established new systems of dividing military spoils and enemy lands. At the same time, he advised the emperor that new histories were needed in which the destiny of the Mexica people was made clearer. Tlacaélel ordered the destruction of older historical texts, and under his direction the new chronicles connected Mexicas' fate directly to Huitzilopochtli. Mexica writing was primarily pictographic, drawn and then read by specially trained scribes who used written records as an aid to oral presentation, especially for legal issues, historical chronicles, religious and devotional poetry, and astronomical calculations.

According to these new texts, the Mexicas had been guided to Lake Texcoco by Huitzilopochtli; there they saw an eagle perched on a cactus, which a prophecy foretold would mark the site of their new city. Huitzilopochtli kept the world alive by bringing the sun's warmth, but to do this he required the Mexicas, who increasingly saw themselves as the "people of the sun," to provide a steady offering of human blood.

The worship of Huitzilopochtli became linked to cosmic forces as well as daily survival. In Nahua tradition, the universe was understood to exist in a series of five suns, or five cosmic ages. Four ages had already passed, and their suns had been destroyed; the fifth sun, the age in which the Mexicas were now living, would also be destroyed unless the Mexicas fortified the sun with the energy found in blood. Warfare thus not only brought new territory under Mexica control but also provided sacrificial victims to nourish the sun god. With these ideas, Tlacaélel created what Miguel León-Portilla, a leading contemporary scholar of Nahuatl religion and philosophy, has termed a "mystico-militaristic" conception of Aztec destiny.

Human sacrifice was practiced in many cultures of Mesoamerica, including the Olmec and the Maya as well as the Mexica, before the changes introduced by Tlacaélel, but the number of victims is believed to have increased dramatically during the last period of Mexica rule. A huge pyramid-shaped temple in the center of Tenochtitlán, dedicated to Huitzilopochtli and the water god Tlaloc, was renovated and expanded many times, the last in 1487. Each expansion was dedicated by priests sacrificing war captives. Similar ceremonies were held regularly throughout the year on days dedicated to Huitzilopochtli and were attended by many observers, including representatives from neighboring states as well as masses of Mexicas. According to many accounts, victims were placed on a stone slab, and their hearts were cut out with an obsidian knife; the officiating priest then held the heart up as an offering to the sun. Sacrifices were also made to other gods at temples elsewhere in Tenochtitlán, and perhaps in other cities controlled by the Mexicas.

Estimates of the number of people sacrificed to Huitzilopochtli and other Mexica gods vary enormously and are impossible to verify. Both Mexica and later Spanish accounts clearly exaggerated the numbers, but most historians today assume that between several hundred and several thousand people were killed each year.

Sources: Miguel León-Portilla, *Pre-Columbian Literatures of Mexico* (Norman: University of Oklahoma Press, 1969); Inga Clendinnen, *Mexicas: An Interpretation* (Cambridge: Cambridge University Press, 1991).

QUESTIONS FOR ANALYSIS

1. How did the worship of Huitzilopochtli contribute to Aztec expansion? To hostility toward the Aztecs?
2. Why might Tlacaélel have seen it as important to destroy older texts as he created this new Aztec mythology?

Tlacaélel emphasized human sacrifice as one of the Aztecs' religious duties. (Scala/Art Resource, NY)

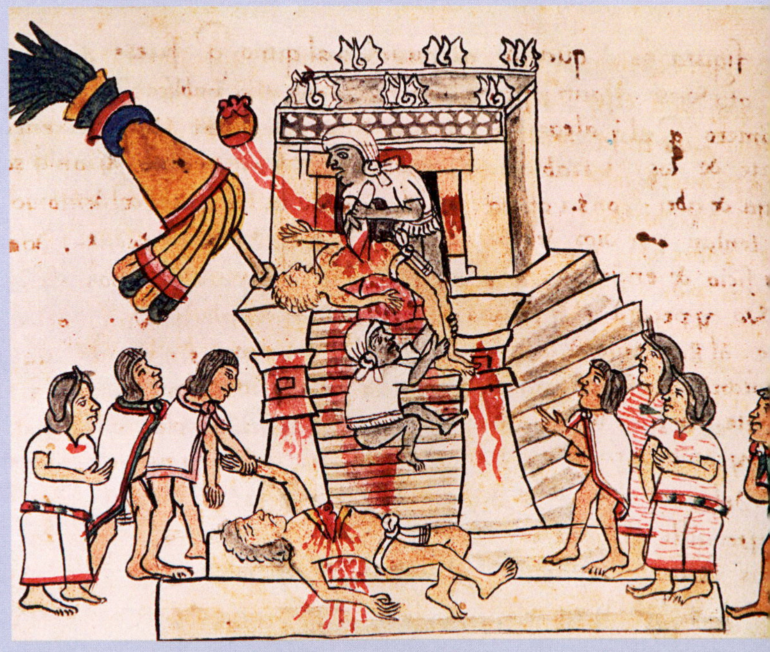

many Mesoamerican groups, was generally revered by the Mexicas as a creator deity and a source of knowledge.

Among the deities venerated by Mexica and other Mesoamerican groups was Huitzilopochtli (weet-zeel-oh-POHCH-tlee), a young warrior-god whose name translates fully as "Blue Hummingbird of the South" (or "Blue Hummingbird on the Left") and who symbolized the sun blazing at high noon. The sun, the source of all life, had to be kept moving in its orbit if darkness was not to overtake the world. To keep it moving, Aztecs believed, the sun had to be frequently fed precious fluids—that is, human blood. Therefore, human sacrifice was seen as a sacred duty, essential for the preservation and prosperity of humankind. (See "Individuals in Society: Tlacaélel," page 278.)

Most victims were war captives, for the Aztecs controlled their growing empire by sacrificing prisoners seized in battle, by taking hostages from among defeated peoples as ransom against future revolt, and by demanding that subject states provide an annual tribute of people to be sacrificed to Huitzilopochtli. In some years it was difficult to provide enough war captives, so other types of people, including criminals and slaves, were sacrificed as well. Additionally, unsuccessful generals, corrupt judges, and careless public officials were routinely sacrificed.

The Mexica state religion required constant warfare for two basic reasons. One was to meet the gods' needs for human sacrifice; the other was to acquire warriors for the next phase of imperial expansion. Moreover, defeated peoples had to pay tribute in foodstuffs to support rulers, nobles, warriors, and the imperial bureaucracy. The vanquished supplied laborers for agriculture, the economic basis of Mexica society. Likewise, conquered peoples had to produce workers for the construction and maintenance of the entire Aztec infrastructure—roads, dike systems, aqueducts, causeways, and royal palaces. Finally, merchants also benefited from warfare, for it opened new markets for traders' goods in subject territories.

Social Distinctions Among Aztecs

Few sharp social distinctions existed among the Aztecs during their early migrations, but by the early sixteenth century Aztec society had changed. A stratified social structure had come into being, and the warrior aristocracy exercised great authority. Generals, judges, and governors of provinces were appointed by the emperor from among his servants who had earned reputations as war heroes. These great lords, or tecuhtli (teh-COOT-lee), dressed luxuriously and lived in palaces. Acting as provincial governors, they exercised full political, judicial, and military authority on the emperor's behalf. In their territories they maintained order, settled disputes, and judged legal cases; oversaw the cultivation of land; and made sure that tribute—in food or gold—was paid. The governors also led troops in wartime. These functions resembled those of feudal lords in western Europe during the Middle Ages. Just as only nobles in France and England could wear fur and carry swords, just as gold jewelry and elaborate hairstyles for women distinguished royal and noble classes in African kingdoms, so in Mexica societies only the tecuhtli could wear jewelry and embroidered cloaks. As the empire expanded, the growth of a strong mercantile class led to an influx of tropical wares and luxury goods. These goods contributed to the elegant and extravagant lifestyle that the upper classes enjoyed.

Beneath the great nobility of military leaders and imperial officials was the class of warriors. Theoretically, every free man could be a warrior, but in practice the sons of nobles were more likely to become warriors because of their fathers' positions and influence in the state. At the age of six, boys entered a school that trained them for war. They were taught to fight, learned to live on little food and sleep, and to accept pain without complaint. At about age eighteen, a warrior fought his first campaign. If he captured a prisoner for ritual sacrifice, he acquired the title *iyac*, or warrior. If in later campaigns he succeeded in

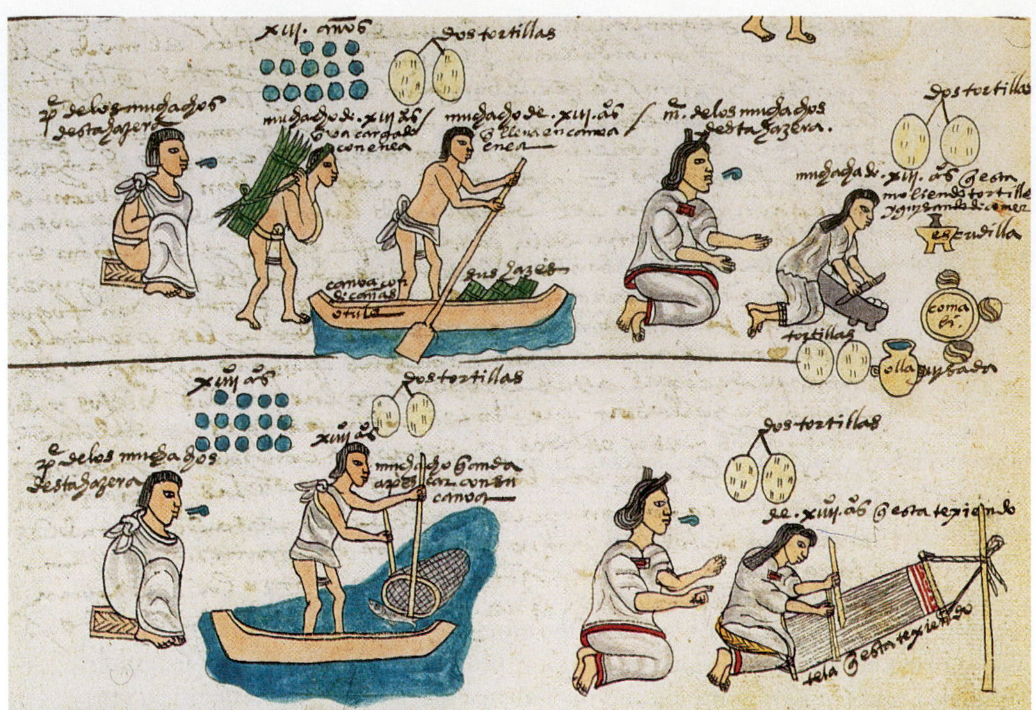

Picturing the Past

Aztec Adolescents

This scene of adults supervising the tasks that young people at each age (indicated by dots) were expected to learn appeared in a painted book made by Mexica artists in the middle of the sixteenth century. It includes Nahuatl and Spanish words, including "dos [two] tortillas," the basic amount of food the artists thought was appropriate for these adolescents. (The Bodleian Library, University of Oxford, MS Arch. Selden. A.1, fol. 60r)

ANALYZING THE IMAGE What tasks are boys expected to learn? What tasks are girls expected to learn? What do these differences suggest about Aztec society?

CONNECTIONS This painting was made about a generation after the Spanish conquest, so that in some ways it represents an idealized past rather the current reality. How might this have shaped the artists' views of adolescence?

killing or capturing four of the enemy, he became a *tequiua*—one who shared in the booty and thus was a member of the nobility. If a young man failed in several campaigns to capture the required four prisoners, he became a *macehualli* (plural *macehualtin*), a commoner.

The macehualtin made up the vast majority of the population. Members of this class performed all sorts of agricultural, military, and domestic services, and they carried heavy public burdens not required of noble warriors. Unlike nobles, priests, orphans, and slaves, macehualtin paid taxes. Macehualtin in the capital, however, possessed certain rights: they held their plots of land for life, and they received a small share of the tribute paid by the provinces to the emperor.

Beneath the macehualtin were the *tlalmaitl*, the landless workers or serfs. Some social historians speculate that this class originated during the period of migrations and upheavals following the end of the classical period (see page 273), when weak and defenseless people placed themselves under the protection of strong warriors, just as European peasants had become serfs after the end of the Roman Empire (see Chapter 6). The tlalmaitl provided agricultural labor, paid rents in kind, and were bound to the soil—they could not move off the land. In many ways the tlalmaitl resembled the serfs of western Europe, but unlike serfs they performed military service when called on to do so. They enjoyed some rights as citizens and generally were accorded more respect than slaves.

Slaves were the lowest social class. Like Asian, European, and African slaves, most were prisoners captured in war or kidnapped from enemy tribes. But Aztecs who stole from a temple or private house or plotted against the emperor could also be enslaved, and people in serious debt sometimes voluntarily sold themselves into slavery. Female slaves often became their masters' concubines. Mexica slaves differed fundamentally from European ones, for they could possess goods; save money; buy land, houses, and even slaves for their own service; and purchase their freedom. If a male slave married a free woman, their offspring were free, and most slaves eventually gained their freedom. Mexica slavery, therefore, had some humane qualities and resembled slavery in Islamic societies (see Chapter 9).

Women of all social classes played important roles in Mexica society, but those roles were restricted largely to the domestic sphere. Almost all Mexica people married, men at about twenty and women several years earlier. As in premodern Asian and European societies, parents selected their children's spouses, using neighborhood women as go-betweens. Save for the few women vowed to the service of the temple, marriage and the household were a woman's fate, and marriage represented social maturity for both sexes. Pregnancy became the occasion for family and neighborhood feasts, and a successful birth launched celebrations lasting from ten to twenty days.

Alongside the secular social classes stood the temple priests. Huitzilopochtli and each of the numerous lesser gods were attended to by many priests who oversaw the upkeep of the temple, assisted at religious ceremonies, and performed ritual sacrifices. Priests were also believed to be capable of foretelling the future from signs and omens. Temples possessed enormous wealth in gold and silver ceremonial vessels, statues, buildings, and land. From the temple revenues and resources, the priests supported schools, aided the poor, and maintained hospitals. The chief priests had the ear of the emperor and often exercised great power and influence.

The emperor stood at the peak of the social pyramid. A small oligarchy of the chief priests, warriors, and state officials made the selection from among the previous emperor's sons. If none of the sons proved satisfactory, a brother or nephew of the emperor was chosen, but election was always restricted to the royal family.

The Aztec emperor was expected to be a great warrior who had led Mexica and allied armies into battle. All his other duties pertained to the welfare of his people. It was up to the emperor to see that justice was done; he was the final court of appeal. He also held ultimate responsibility for ensuring an adequate food supply.

The City of Tenochtitlán

Tenochtitlán A large and prosperous Aztec city that was built starting in 1325.

As of 1500 **Tenochtitlán** had about 60,000 households and a total population of around 250,000, making it one of the largest cities in the world. At the time, no European city and few Asian cities could boast a population even half that size. The total Aztec Empire has been estimated at around 5 million inhabitants, with the total population of Mesoamerica at between 20 and 30 million.

Originally built on salt marshes, Tenochtitlán was approached by four great causeways that connected it with the mainland. Openings in the causeways, covered by bridges, provided places for boats to pass through. Stone and adobe walls surrounded the city itself, making it somewhat like medieval Constantinople, highly defensible and capable of resisting a prolonged siege (see Chapter 8). Wide, straight streets as well as canals plied by boats and canoes crisscrossed the city. Lining the roads and canals stood thousands of rectangular one-story houses. Although space was limited, many small gardens and parks dotted the city. A large aqueduct carried pure water from distant springs and supplied fountains in the parks. Streets and canals opened onto public squares and marketplaces. At one side of the central square of Tenochtitlán stood the great temple of Huitzilopochtli. Built as a pyramid and approached by three flights of 120 steps each, the temple was about one hundred feet high and dominated the city's skyline.

Quick Review
What role did warfare play in Aztec society and culture?

What were the strengths and weaknesses of the Inca Empire?

The Inca civilization developed and flourished in the Andean valleys of highland Peru. Like the Aztecs, the Incas started as a small militaristic group. But they grew in numbers and power as they conquered surrounding groups, eventually establishing one of the most extraordinary empires in the world. Gradually, Inca culture spread throughout Peru.

Earlier Peruvian Cultures

Moche A Native American culture that thrived along Peru's northern coast between 100 and 800 C.E. The culture existed as a series of city-states.

Inca achievements built on those of cultures that preceded them in the Andes and on the Peruvian coast. These included the Chavin civilization (see page 269) and the **Moche** (MO-cheh) civilization, which flourished along a 250-mile stretch of Peru's northern coast between 100 and 800 C.E. Rivers that flowed out of the Andes into the valleys allowed the Moche people to develop complex irrigation systems, with which they raised food crops and cotton. Each Moche valley contained a large ceremonial center with palaces and pyramids surrounded by settlements of up to ten thousand people.

Politically, Moche civilization was made up of a series of small city-states rather than one unified state, and warfare was common among them. As in Aztec culture, war provided victims for human sacrifice. Beginning about 500, the Moche suffered several severe El Niños, the changes in ocean current patterns in the Pacific that bring both searing drought and flooding. Their leaders were not able to respond effectively to the devastation, and the cities lost population.

The Moche civilization was one of several that were able to carve out slightly larger empires than their predecessors, the Chavin. These newer civilizations built cities around large public plazas, with temples, palaces, and elaborate stonework. Using terraces and other means to increase the amount of arable soil, they grew potatoes and other crops, even at very high altitudes. Enough food was harvested to feed not only the farmers themselves but also massive armies, administrative bureaucracies, and thousands of industrial workers.

Inca Imperialism and Its Religious Basis

Incas The Andean people who created a large empire that was at its peak around 1500 and was held together by an extensive system of roads.

Who were the **Incas**? *Inca* was originally the name of the governing family of a group that settled in the basin of Cuzco. From that family, the name was gradually extended to all peoples living in the Andes valleys. The Incas themselves used the word to identify their ruler or emperor. Here the term is used for both the ruler and the people. As with the Aztecs, so with the Incas: religious ideology was the force that transformed the culture, and it also created pressure for imperialist expansion.

The Inca Empire, 1532

The Incas believed their ruler descended from the sun-god and that the health and prosperity of the state depended on him. Dead rulers were thought to link the people to the sun-god. When the ruler died, his corpse was preserved as a mummy in elaborate clothing and housed in a sacred and magnificent chamber.

As a group, the descendants of a dead ruler managed his lands and sources of income and used the revenues to care for his mummy, maintain his cult, and support themselves. The costs of maintaining the cult were high; therefore, the next ruler had to find new sources of income through higher taxes or imperial expansion.

Around 1000 C.E. the Incas were one of many small groups fighting among themselves for land and water. The cult of royal mummies provided the impetus for expanding Inca power. The desire for conquest provided incentives for courageous (or ambitious) nobles: those who were victorious in battle and gained new territories for the state could expect lands, additional wives, servants, herds of llamas, gold, silver, fine clothes, and other symbols of high status. Even common soldiers who distinguished themselves in battle could be rewarded with booty and raised to noble status. The imperial interests of the emperor paralleled those of other social groups. Under Pachacuti Inca and his successors, Inca domination was gradually extended by warfare to the frontier of present-day Ecuador and Colombia in the north and to the Maule River in present-day Chile in the south, an area of about 350,000 square miles. Eighty provinces, scores of ethnic groups, and 16 million people came under Inca control. A remarkable system of roads held the empire together.

Conquered peoples were forced to adopt the Inca language, which the Spanish called **Quechua** (KEH-chuh-wuh), and this was another way in which the Inca way of life was spread throughout the Andes. Though not written until the Spanish in Peru adopted it as a second official language, Quechua had replaced local languages by the seventeenth and eighteenth centuries and is still spoken by most Peruvians today.

Quechua The official language of the Incas, it is still spoken by most Peruvians today.

Both the Aztecs and the Incas ruled very ethnically diverse peoples. Whereas the Aztecs tended to control their subject peoples through terror, the Incas governed by means of imperial unification. They imposed not only their language but also their entire panoply of gods. Magnificent temples scattered throughout the expanding empire housed images of these gods. Priests led prayers and elaborate rituals, and on such occasions as a terrible natural disaster or a great military victory, they sacrificed human beings to the gods.

Imperial unification was also achieved through the forced participation of local chieftains in the central bureaucracy and through a policy of colonization. To prevent rebellion in newly conquered territories, Inca rulers transferred all the inhabitants of these territories to other parts of the empire, replacing them with workers who had lived longer under Inca rule. The rulers also drafted men from conquered territories for distant wars, breaking up kin groups that had existed in Andean society for centuries.

An excellent system of roads facilitated the transportation of armies and the rapid communication of royal orders by runners. The roads followed straight lines wherever possible but also crossed pontoon bridges and tunneled through hills. Like Persian and Roman roads, these great feats of Inca engineering linked an empire. On these roads, Inca officials, tax collectors, and accountants traveled throughout the empire, using increasingly elaborate

LISTENING TO THE PAST

Felipe Guaman Poma de Ayala, *The First New Chronicle and Good Government*

According to his own self-description, Felipe Guaman Poma de Ayala (1550?–1620?) was a member of an indigenous noble family in Peru. His native language was Quechua, but he was baptized as a Christian, learned to read and write Spanish, and served as an assistant to a Spanish friar and a Spanish judge. He saw and experienced firsthand the abuses of the Spanish authorities in what had been the Inca Empire. In the early seventeenth century he began writing and illustrating what became his masterpiece, a handwritten book of almost eight hundred pages of text and nearly four hundred line drawings addressed to the king of Spain that related the history of the Inca Empire and the realities of Spanish rule. Finishing in about 1615, he hoped to send the book to Spain, where it would convince the king to make reforms that would bring about the "good government" of the book's title. (The book apparently never reached the king, though it did make it to Europe. It was discovered in the Danish Royal Library in Copenhagen in 1908; how it got there is unknown.) Guaman Poma's descriptions of Inca life before the conquest are shaped by his purpose, but they also portray some important aspects of Andean culture that appear from other sources to have been quite accurate. In the following section, Guaman Poma sets out certain traditional age-group categories of Inca society, which he terms "paths," ten for men and ten for women. Through these, he gives us a glimpse of Inca values and everyday activities, and suggests that this orderly structure underlay Inca power.

" The first path was that of the brave men, the soldiers of war. They were thirty-three years of age (they entered this path as young as twenty-five, and left it at fifty). These brave men were held very much apart and distinguished in every manner possible. The Inca [the Inca ruler] selected some of these Indians to serve in his battles and wars. He selected some from among these brave Indians to settle as *mitmacs* (foreigners) in other provinces, giving them more than enough land, both pasture and cropland, to multiply, and giving each of them a woman from the same land. He did this to keep his kingdom secure; they served as overseers. He selected some of these brave Indians to serve as plowmen and as skilled workers in every task that was necessary for the Inca and the other lords, princes, noblemen, and ladies of this kingdom; those selected in this way were called *mitmac* (foreigners). Others of these brave men were selected to work in the mines and for other labor, toil, and obligations. . . .

The Fifth Path was that of the *sayapayac* [those who stand upright]. These were the Indians of the watch, aged from eighteen to twenty years. They served as messenger boys between one pueblo and another, and to other nearby places in the valley. They also herded flocks, and accompanied the Indians of war and the great lords and captains. They also carried food. . . .

The Eighth Path was that of boys aged from five to nine years. These were the "boys who play" (*puellacoc wamracuna*). They served their mothers and fathers in whatever ways they could, and bore many whippings and thumpings; they also served by playing with the toddlers and by rocking and watching over the babies in cradles. . . .

The Tenth Path was that of those called *wawa quirawpi cac* (newborn babies at the breast, in cradles), from the age of one month. It is right for others to serve them; their mothers must necessarily serve them for no other person can give milk to these children. . . .

The First Path was that of the married women and widows called *auca camayocpa warmin* [the warriors' women], whose occupation is weaving fine cloth for the Inca, the other lords, the captains, and the soldiers. They were thirty-three years of age when they married; up until then, they remained virgins and maidens. . . . These wives of brave men were not free [from tribute obligations]. These women had the occupation of weaving fine *awasca* cloth and spinning yarn; they assisted the commons in their pueblos and provinces, and they assisted with everything their titled noble lords decreed. . . .

The Sixth Path was that of those called *coro tasquicunas, rotusca tasqui*, which means "young girls

khipus (see page 269) to record financial and labor obligations, the output of fields, population levels, land transfers, and other numerical records.

Although the pressure for growth of the Inca Empire continued unabated, it produced stresses. For example, open lands began to be scarce, so the Incas attempted to penetrate the tropical Amazon forest east of the Andes, an effort that led to repeated military disasters. Traditionally, the Incas waged wars with highly trained armies drawn up in massed formation and fought pitched battles on level ground, often engaging in hand-to-hand combat. But in dense jungles the troops could not maneuver or maintain order against enemies us-

Guaman Poma's line drawing shows a woman on the "first path," weaving fine cloth on a back-strap loom. (Nick Saunders/Barbara Heller Photo Library, London/Art Resource, NY)

with short-cropped hair." They were from twelve to eighteen years of age and served their fathers, mothers, and grandmothers. They also began to serve the great ladies so that they could learn to spin yarn and weave delicate materials. They served as animal herders and workers in the fields, and in making *chica* [corn beer] for their fathers and mothers, and they assisted in other occupations insofar as they could, helping out. . . . they were filled with obedience and respect, and were taught to cook, spin, and weave. Their hair was kept cropped until they reached the age of thirty, when they were married and given the dowry of their destitution and poverty.

The Seventh Path was that of the girls called flower pickers. . . . They picked flowers to dye wool for *cumpis*, cloth, and other things, and they picked the edible herbs mentioned above, which they dried out and stored in the warehouse to be eaten the following year. These girls were from nine to twelve years of age. . . .

The Ninth Path was that of the girls aged one and two, who were called *llucac warmi wawa* ("young girls who crawl."). They do nothing; instead, others serve them. Better said, they ought to be served by their mothers, who should be exempt [from tribute] because of the work of raising their children. Their mothers have to walk around carrying them, and never let go of their hands. "

Source: Felipe Guaman Poma de Ayala, *The First New Chronicle and Good Government*, selected, translated, and annotated by David Frye, pp. 70, 72, 74, 75, 77, 80, 81, 82.

QUESTIONS FOR ANALYSIS

1. The "First Path" among both men and women is the one with the highest status. Judging by the way Guaman Poma describes these, what do the Incas especially value? How do his descriptions of other paths support your conclusions about this?
2. In what ways are the paths set out for boys and men different from those for girls and women? In what ways are they similar? What does this suggest about Inca society?
3. Guaman Poma wrote this about eighty years after the Spanish conquest of Peru. How does the date and the colonial setting affect our evaluation of this work as a source?

ing guerrilla tactics and sniping at them with deadly blowguns. Another source of stress was revolts among subject peoples in conquered territories. Even the system of roads and message-carrying runners couldn't keep up with the administrative needs of the empire. The average runner could cover about 50 leagues, or 175 miles, per day—a remarkable feat of physical endurance, especially at a high altitude—but the larger the empire became, the greater the distances to be covered. The round-trip from the capital at Cuzco to Quito in Ecuador, for example, took from ten to twelve days, so that an emperor might have to base urgent decisions on incomplete or out-of-date information. The empire was overextended.

When the Inca Huayna Capac died in 1525, his throne was bitterly contested by two of his sons, Huascar and Atahualpa. Huascar's threat to do away with the cult of royal mummies led the nobles—who often benefited from managing land and wealth for a deceased ruler—to throw their support behind Atahualpa. In the civil war that began in 1532, Atahualpa easily prevailed, but the conflict weakened the Incas. On his way to his coronation at Cuzco, Atahualpa encountered Francisco Pizarro and 168 Spaniards who had recently entered the kingdom. The Spaniards quickly became the real victors in the Inca kingdom (see page 422).

The Clan-Based Structure of Inca Society

The *ayllu* (EYE-yoo), or clan, served as the fundamental social unit of Inca society. All members of the ayllu owed allegiance to the *curacas*, or clan leaders, who conducted relations with outsiders. The ayllu held specific lands granted by village or provincial authorities on a long-term basis, and individual families tended to work the same plots for generations. Cooperation in the cultivation of the land and intermarriage among members of the ayllu wove people into a tight web of connections. (See "Listening to the Past: Felipe Guaman Poma de Ayala, *The First New Chronicle and Good Government*," page 284.)

In return for the land, every family had to provide crops for the Inca nobles, bureaucracy, and religious personnel, and also send a person to provide a certain number of days per year of labor. This labor tax, called the *mit'a* (MEE-tuh), was rotated among households in an ayllu throughout the year, and it was similar to the labor obligations required of peasant families in Europe. The government also made an ayllu responsible for maintaining state-owned granaries, which distributed grain in times of shortage and famine, and supplied assistance in natural disasters.

As the Inca Empire expanded, it imposed this pattern of social and labor organization on newly conquered indigenous peoples. After the conquest, the Spaniards adopted the Incas' ways of organizing their economy and administration, just as the Incas (and, in Mesoamerica, the Aztecs) had built on earlier cultures.

The state required everyone to marry and even decided when and sometimes whom a person should marry. Women married in their late teens, men when they were a little older. The marriage ceremony was followed by a large wedding feast at which the state presented the bride and groom with two sets of clothing, one for everyday wear and the other for festive occasions. Sometimes, marriage was used as a symbol of conquest; Inca rulers and nobles married the daughters of elite families among the peoples they conquered. Very high-ranking Inca men sometimes had many wives, but marriage among common people was generally monogamous.

The backbreaking labor of ordinary people in the fields and mines made possible the luxurious lifestyle of the great Inca nobility. The nobles—called *orejones*, or "big ears," by the Spanish because they pierced their ears and distended the lobes with heavy jewelry—were the ruling Inca's kinsmen. Lesser nobles included the curacas, royal household servants, public officials, and religious leaders.

In the fifteenth century Inca rulers ordered that allegiance be paid to the ruler at Cuzco rather than to the curacas, and they relocated the entire populations of certain regions and disrupted clan groups, which led to resentment. As the empire expanded, there arose a noble class of warriors, governors, and local officials whose support the ruling Inca secured with gifts of land, precious metals, and llamas and alpacas. The nobility was exempt from agricultural work and from other kinds of public service.

Quick Review
How did the Inca maintain control of their vast empire, and why did that control begin to break down?

Connections

RESEARCH ON ALL the cultures discussed in this chapter is providing new information every year, provoking vigorous debates among scholars. Archaeologists are discovering new objects and reinterpreting the sites where they were found, historians are learning to better read indigenous writing systems, biologists are using more complex procedures to study genetic linkages, anthropologists are integrating information from oral histories and preserved traditions, and scholars in other disciplines are using both traditional and new methods to expand their understanding. In no other chapter of this book are the basic outlines of what most people agree happened changing as fast as they are for the Americas. Together the various fields of study have produced a history of the Western Hemisphere in the centuries before 1500 that looks more like the history of the Eastern Hemisphere than it did twenty years ago. We now know that there were large, settled agricultural communities in many parts of North and South America that traded ideas and goods with one another, and that the empires of Mesoamerica and the Andes were as rich and powerful as any in Asia, Africa, or Europe.

The parallel paths of the two hemispheres were radically changed by Columbus's arrival and the events that followed, however. The greater availability of metals, especially iron, in the Eastern Hemisphere meant that the military technology of the Europeans who came to the Western Hemisphere was more deadly than anything indigenous peoples had developed. Even more deadly, however, were the germs Europeans brought with them, from which the people of the Western Hemisphere died in astounding numbers. In some cases one or two indigenous people who had made contact with Europeans would spread disease throughout the native population. As a result, when Europeans arrived in the home areas of these people they would find deserted villages with only a few residents. Often, they could not imagine how so few people could have built huge earth mounds or massive stone works. Therefore, they speculated that these structures must have been built by wandering Egyptians or Israelites, a tribe of giants, or (in the early twentieth century) space aliens, giving rise to myths that have been slow to die.

- **For a list of suggested readings for this chapter, visit** *bedfordstmartins.com/mckayworldunderstanding*.
- **For primary sources from this period, see** *Sources of World Societies*, Second Edition.
- **For Web sites, images, and documents related to topics in this chapter, see Make History at** *bedfordstmartins.com/mckayworldunderstanding*.

Chapter 11 **Study Guide**

To do these exercises online, go to bedfordstmartins.com/mckayworldunderstanding.

Step 1

GETTING STARTED

Below are basic terms about this period in global history. Can you identify each term below and explain why it matters?

TERMS	WHO (OR WHAT) AND WHEN	WHY IT MATTERS
Mesoamerica, p. 266		
khipu, p. 269		
Olmecs, p. 270		
Maya, p. 270		
Popul Vuh, p. 272		
Mississippian, p. 275		
Nahuatl, p. 276		
Mexica, p. 277		
Tenochtitlán, p. 281		
Moche, p. 282		
Incas, p. 282		
Quechua, p. 283		

Step 2

MOVING BEYOND THE BASICS

The exercise below requires a more advanced understanding of the chapter material. Compare and contrast the three major civilizations of the Americas by filling in the chart below with descriptions of the role trade, warfare, and religion played in the society and culture of each civilization. When you are finished consider the following questions: What common characteristics did these civilizations share? What political purposes were served by trade and religion in each civilization? Why was warfare endemic in all three civilizations?

	TRADE	WARFARE	RELIGION
Maya			
Aztec			
Inca			

Step 3 PUTTING IT ALL TOGETHER

Now that you've reviewed key elements of the chapter, take a step back and try to see the big picture. Remember to use specific examples from the chapter in your answers.

EARLY DEVELOPMENT OF AMERICAN SOCIETIES

- How did geography and climate shape migration and settlement patterns in the Americas?
- How did the Olmec help lay the foundation for later Mesoamerican societies?

THE CLASSICAL ERA

- How did trade link the societies of the Americas during the classical era?
- Compare and contrast the classical societies of Mesoamerica and North America. How would you explain the similarities and differences you note?

AZTEC AND INCA EMPIRES

- Compare and contrast the imperial expansion of the Aztecs and the Incas. What factors created pressure for continued expansion in each empire?

- Compare and contrast imperial government in the Aztec and Inca Empires. How did each empire control subject peoples and exploit their labor and resources?

LOOKING BACK, LOOKING AHEAD

- What important similarities are there between the histories of the Western and Eastern Hemispheres prior to 1500? How would you account for these similarities?
- How might European conquest and colonization of the Americas after 1500 have shaped our view of the civilizations of the Americas as they existed *prior* to 1500?

In Your Own Words Imagine that you must explain Chapter 11 to someone who hasn't read it. What would be the most important points to include and why?

12

Cultural Exchange in Central and Southern Asia

to 1400

The large expanse of Asia treated in this chapter underwent profound changes during the centuries examined here. The Central Asian grasslands gave birth to nomadic confederations capable of dominating major states—first the Turks, then later, even more spectacularly, the Mongols. The nomads' mastery of the horse and mounted warfare gave them a military advantage that agricultural societies could rarely match. From the fifth century on, groups of Turks appeared along the fringes of the settled societies of Eurasia, from China and Korea to India and Persia. Often Turks were recruited as auxiliary soldiers; sometimes they gained the upper hand. By the tenth century many were converting to Islam.

Mongol Woman Women played influential roles among the Mongols. The Mongol woman portrayed in this painting is Chabi, wife of Khubilai Khan. Like other Mongols, she maintained Mongol dress even though she spent much of her time in China. (National Palace Museum, Taipei, Taiwan © Cultural Relics Press)

Much more dramatic was the rise of the Mongols under the charismatic leadership of Chinggis Khan in the late twelfth and early thirteenth centuries. A military genius, with a relatively small army, Chinggis subdued one society after another from Byzantium to the Pacific. For a century Mongol hegemony fostered unprecedented East-West trade and contact.

Arab and Turkish armies brought Islam to India, but the Mongols never gained power there. In the Indian subcontinent, regional cultures flourished. Although Buddhism declined around 1100–1200, Hinduism continued to flourish. India continued to be the center of a very active seaborne trade, and this trade helped carry Indian ideas and practices to Southeast Asia. Buddhism was adopted in much of Southeast Asia, along with other ideas and techniques from India. The maritime trade in spices and other goods brought increased contact with the outside world to all but the most isolated of islands in the Pacific.

Chapter Preview

- How did Central Asian nomads conquer nearby settled civilizations?
- How did the Mongols build and govern a Eurasian empire?
- How did the Mongol conquests facilitate cultural exchange?
- What was the result of India's encounters with Turks and Mongols?
- How did states develop along the trade routes of Southeast Asia and beyond?

How did Central Asian nomads conquer nearby settled civilizations?

One experience Rome, Persia, India, and China all shared was conflict with Central Asian **nomads**. Central Asia was dominated by the **steppe**, arid grasslands that stretched from modern Hungary, through southern Russia and across Central Asia and adjacent parts of China, to Mongolia and parts of today's northeast China. Initially small in number, the nomadic peoples of this region would use their military superiority to conquer first other nomads, then the settled societies they encountered. In the process, they created settled empires of their own that drew on the cultures they absorbed.

nomads Groups of people who move from place to place in search of food, water, and pasture for their animals, usually following the seasons.

steppe Grasslands that are too dry for crops but support pasturing animals; they are common across much of the center of Eurasia.

Nomadic Society

Too dry for crop agriculture, the grasslands could support only a thin population of nomadic herders who lived off their flocks of sheep, goats, camels, horses, or other animals. In their search for water and good pastures, nomadic groups often came into violent conflict with other nomadic groups pursuing the same resources. Groups on the losing end, especially if they were small, faced the threat of extermination or slavery, which prompted them to make alliances with other groups or move far away. Groups on the winning end of intertribal conflicts could exact tribute from those they defeated, sometimes so much that they could devote themselves entirely to war, leaving the work of tending herds to their slaves and vassals.

To get the products of nearby agricultural societies, especially grain, woven textiles, iron, tea, and wood, nomadic herders would trade their own products, such as horses and furs. When trade was difficult, they would turn to raiding to seize what they needed. Much of the time nomadic herders raided other nomads, but nearby agricultural settlements were common targets as well. The nomads' skill as horsemen and archers made it difficult for farmers and townsmen to defend against them.

Political organization among nomadic herders was generally very simple. Clans—members of an extended family—had chiefs, as did tribes (coalitions of clans). Leadership within a group was based on military prowess and was often settled by fighting. Occasionally a charismatic leader would emerge who was able to extend alliances to form confederations of tribes. Large confederations rarely lasted more than

Manichean Priests Many religions spread through Central Asia before it became predominantly Muslim after 1300. This fragment of a tenth- to twelfth-century illustrated document, found at the Silk Road city of Turfan, is written in the Uighur language and depicts Manichean priests. (Archives Charmet/The Bridgeman Art Library)

a century or so, however, and when they broke up, tribes again spent much of their time fighting with each other.

The Turks

In 552 a group called Turks who specialized in metalworking rebelled against their overlords, the Rouruan, whose empire dominated the region from the eastern Silk Road cities of Central Asia through Mongolia. The Turks quickly supplanted the Rouruan as overlords of the Silk Road in the east. When the first Turkish khagan (ruler) died a few years later, the Turkish empire was divided between his younger brother, who took the western part (modern Central Asia), and his son, who took the eastern part (modern Mongolia).

The Eastern Turks frequently raided China and just as often fought among themselves. The Chinese history of the Sui Dynasty records that "The Turks prefer to destroy each other rather than to live side-by-side. They have a thousand, nay ten thousand clans who are hostile to and kill one another. They mourn their dead with much grief and swear vengeance."[1] In the early seventh century the empire of the Eastern Turks ran up against the growing military might of the Tang Dynasty in China and soon broke apart.

In the eighth century a Turkic people called the Uighurs formed a new empire based in Mongolia that survived about a century. It had close ties to Tang China, providing military aid but also extracting large payments in silk. During this period many Uighurs adopted religions then current along the Silk Road, notably Buddhism, Nestorian Christianity, and Manichaeism. In the ninth century this Uighur empire was destroyed by another Turkic people from north of Mongolia called the Kyrghiz (KIHR-guhz). Some fled to what is now western China. Setting up their capital city in Kucha, these Uighurs created a remarkably stable and prosperous kingdom that lasted four centuries (ca. 850–1250). Documentary and archaeological evidence reveals a complex urban civilization in which Buddhism, Manichaeism, and Christianity existed side by side, practiced by Turks as well as by Tokharians, Sogdians, and other Iranian peoples.

Farther west in Central Asia other groups of Turks, such as the Karakhanids, Ghaznavids, and Seljuks, rose to prominence. Often local Muslim forces would try to capture them, employ them as slave soldiers, and convert them. By the mid- to late tenth century many were serving in the Islamic Abbasid armies. Also in the tenth century Central Asian Turks began converting to Islam (which protected them from being abducted as slaves). Then they took to raiding unconverted Turks.

In the mid-eleventh century the Turks had gained the upper hand in the caliphate, and the caliphs became little more than figureheads. From there Turkish power was extended into Syria, Palestine, and Asia Minor. In 1071 Seljuk Turks inflicted a devastating defeat on the Byzantine army in eastern Anatolia (see page 218). Other Turkish confederations established themselves in Afghanistan and extended their control into north India (see page 307).

In India, Persia, and Anatolia, the formidable military skills of nomadic Turkish warriors made it possible for them to become overlords of settled societies. By the end of the thirteenth century

Chapter Chronology

ca. 320–480	Gupta Empire in India
ca. 380–450	Life of India's greatest poet, Kalidasa
ca. 450	White Huns invade northern India
ca. 500–1400	India's medieval age; caste system reaches its mature form
552	Turks rebel against Rouruan and rise to power in Central Asia
ca. 780	Borobudur temple complex begun in Srivijaya
802–1432	Khmer Empire of Cambodia
ca. 850–1250	Kingdom of the Uighurs
1030	Turks control north India
ca. 1100–1200	Buddhism declines in India
ca. 1200–1300	Easter Island society's most prosperous period
1206	Temujin proclaimed Chinggis Khan; Mongol language recorded; Delhi sultanate established
ca. 1240	*The Secret History of the Mongols*
1276	Mongol conquest of Song China
ca. 1300	Plague spreads throughout Mongol Empire
1398	Timur takes control of the Delhi sultanate

Major Central Asian Nomadic Confederations
Third century B.C.E.: Xiongnu (or Huns)
Fourth and fifth centuries C.E.: Turks
Twelfth century C.E.: Mongols

nomad power prevailed through much of Eurasia. Just as the Uighurs developed a hybrid urban culture along the eastern end of the Silk Road, the Turks of Central and West Asia created an Islamic culture that drew from both Turkish and Iranian sources. Nevertheless, despite the presence of Turkish overlords all along the southern fringe of the steppe, no one group of Turks was able to unite them all into a single political unit. That feat had to wait for the next major power on the steppe, the Mongols.

The Mongols

In the twelfth century ambitious Mongols did not aspire to match the Turks or other groups that had migrated west, but rather wanted to be successors to the Khitans and Jurchens, nomadic groups that had stayed in the east and mastered ways to extract resources from China. In the tenth and eleventh centuries the Khitans had accomplished this; in the twelfth century the Jurchens had overthrown the Khitans and extended their reach even deeper into China. The Khitans and Jurchens formed hybrid nomadic-urban states, with northern sections where tribesmen continued to live in the traditional way and southern sections politically controlled by the non-Chinese rulers but settled largely by taxpaying Chinese. Both Khitan and Jurchen elites became culturally dual, adept in Chinese ways as well as in their own traditions.

The Mongols lived north of these hybrid nomadic-settled societies and maintained their traditional ways. Chinese, Persian, and European observers have all left descriptions of the daily life of the Mongols, which they found strikingly different from their own. The daily life of the peasants of China, India, Vietnam, and Japan, all tied to the soil, had much more in common with each other than with the Mongol pastoralists. Before considering the military conquests of the Mongols, it is useful to look more closely at their way of life.

Mongol Daily Life

yurts Tents in which the pastoral nomads lived; they could be quickly dismantled and loaded onto animals or carts.

Before their great conquests the Mongols, like other steppe nomads, did not have cities, towns, or villages. Rather, they moved with their animals between winter and summer pastures. To make their settlements portable, the Mongols lived in round tents called **yurts** rather than in houses. The yurts, about twelve to fifteen feet in diameter, were constructed of light wooden frames covered by layers of wool felt, greased to make them waterproof. A group of families traveling together would set up their yurts in a circle open to the south and draw up their wagons in a circle around the yurts for protection.

Because the steppe was too cold and dry for agriculture, the Mongol diet consisted mostly of animal products, including meat, cheese, and fermented alcoholic drinks made from milk. Without granaries to store food, the Mongols' survival was endangered when weather or diseases of their animals threatened their food supply. When grain or vegetables could be obtained through trade, they were added to the diet. Wood was scarce, so dried animal dung or grasses fueled the cook fires.

Mongol women had to work very hard and had to be able to care for the animals when the men were away hunting or fighting. They normally drove the carts and set up and dismantled the yurts. They also milked the sheep, goats, and cows and made the butter and cheese. In addition, they made and repaired clothes. Women, like men, had to be expert riders, and many also learned to shoot. They participated actively in family decisions, especially as wives and mothers. In *The Secret History of the Mongols*, a work written in Mongolian in about 1240, the mother and wife of the Mongol leader Chinggis Khan frequently make impassioned speeches on the importance of family loyalty. (See "Listening to the Past: The Abduction of Women in *The Secret History of the Mongols*," page 296.)

Mongol Yurt A Chinese artist in the thirteenth or fourteenth century captured the essential features of a Mongol yurt to illustrate the story of a Chinese woman who married a nomad. (Image © The Metropolitan Museum of Art/Art Resource, NY)

Mongol men kept as busy as the women. They made carts and wagons and the frames for the yurts. They also made harnesses for the horses and oxen, leather saddles, and the equipment needed for hunting and war, such as bows and arrows. Men also had charge of the horses, and they milked the mares. One specialist among the nomads was the blacksmith, who made stirrups, knives, and other metal tools.

Kinship underlay most social relationships among the Mongols. Normally each family occupied a yurt, and groups of families camping together were usually related along the male line (brothers, uncles, nephews, and so on). More distant patrilineal relatives were recognized as members of the same clan and could call on each other for aid. People from the same clan could not marry each other, so men had to get wives from other clans. When a woman's husband died, she would be inherited by another male in the family, such as her husband's brother or his son by another woman. Tribes were groups of clans, often distantly related. Both clans and tribes had chiefs who would make decisions on where to graze and when to retaliate against another tribe that had stolen animals or people. Women were sometimes abducted for brides. When tribes stole men from each other, they normally made them into slaves, and slaves were forced to do much of the heavy work. They would not necessarily remain slaves their entire lives, however, as their original tribes might be able to recapture them or make exchanges for them, or their masters might free them.

Even though population was sparse in the regions where the Mongols lived, conflict over resources was endemic. Defending against attacks and retaliating against raids was as much a part of the Mongols' daily life as caring for their herds and trading with nearby settlements.

As with the Turks and other steppe nomads, religious practices centered around the shaman, a religious expert believed to be able to communicate with the gods. The high god of the Mongols was Heaven/Sky, but they recognized many other gods as well. Some groups of Mongols, especially those closer to settled communities, converted to Buddhism, Nestorian Christianity, or Manichaeism.

Quick Review
How did the society, values, and lifestyle of Central Asian nomads differ from their settled counterparts in Eurasia?

LISTENING TO THE PAST

The Abduction of Women in *The Secret History of the Mongols*

Within a few decades of Chinggis Khan's death, oral traditions concerning his rise were written down in the Mongolian language. They begin with the cycles of revenge among the tribes in Mongolia, many of which began when women were abducted for wives. These passages relate how Temujin's (Chinggis Khan's) father Yesugei seized Hogelun, Temujin's future mother, from a passing Merkid tribesman; how twenty years later three Merkids in return seized women from Temujin; and Temujin's revenge.

That year Yesugei the Brave was out hunting with his falcon on the Onan. Yeke Chiledu, a nobleman of the Merkid tribe, had gone to the Olkhunugud people to find himself a wife, and he was returning to the Merkid with the girl he'd found when he passed Yesugei hunting by the river. When he saw them riding along Yesugei leaned forward on his horse. He saw it was a beautiful girl. Quickly he rode back to his tent and just as quick returned with his two brothers, Nekun Taisi and Daritai Odchigin. When Chiledu saw the three Mongols coming he whipped his dun-colored horse and rode off around a nearby hill with the three men behind him. He cut back around the far side of the hill and rode to Lady Hogelun, the girl he'd just married, who stood waiting for him at the front of their cart. "Did you see the look on the faces of those three men?" she asked him. "From their faces it looks like they mean to kill you. As long as you've got your life there'll always be girls for you to choose from. There'll always be women to ride in your cart. As long as you've got your life you'll be able to find some girl to marry. When you find her, just name her Hogelun for me, but go now and save your own life!" Then she pulled off her shirt and held it out to him, saying: "And take this to remember me, to remember my scent." Chiledu reached out from his saddle and took the shirt in his hands. With the three Mongols close behind him he struck his dun-colored horse with his whip and took off down the Onan River at full speed.

The three Mongols chased him across seven hills before turning around and returning to Hogelun's cart. Then Yesugei the Brave grasped the reins of the cart, his elder brother Nekun Taisi rode in front to guide them, and the younger brother Daritai Odchigin rode along by the wheels. As they rode her back toward their camp, Hogelun began to cry, . . . and she cried till she stirred up the waters of the Onan River, till she shook the trees in the forest and the grass in the valleys. But as the party approached their camp Daritai, riding beside her, warned her to stop: "This fellow who held you in his arms, he's already ridden over the mountains. This man who's lost you, he's crossed many rivers by now. You can call out his name, but he can't see you now even if he looks back. If you tried to find him now you won't even find his tracks. So be still now," he told her. Then Yesugei took Lady Hogelun to his tent as his wife. . . .

[Some twenty years later] one morning just before dawn Old Woman Khogaghchin, Mother Hogelun's servant, woke with a start, crying: "Mother! Mother! Get up! The ground is shaking, I hear it rumble. The Tayichigud must be riding back to attack us. Get up!"

Mother Hogelun jumped from her bed, saying: "Quick, wake my sons!" They woke Temujin and the others and all ran for the horses. Temujin, Mother Hogelun, and Khasar each took a horse. Khachigun, Temuge Odchigin, and Belgutei each took a horse. Bogorchu took one horse and Jelme another. Mother Hogelun lifted the baby Temulun onto her saddle. They saddled the last horse as a lead and there was no horse left for [Temujin's wife] Lady Borte. . . .

Old Woman Khogaghchin, who'd been left in the camp, said: "I'll hide Lady Borte." She made her get into a black covered cart. Then she harnessed the cart to a speckled ox. Whipping the ox, she drove the cart away from the camp down the Tungelig. As the first light of day hit them, soldiers rode up and told them to stop. "Who are you?" they asked her, and Old Woman Khogaghchin answered: "I'm a servant of Temujin's. I've just come from shearing his sheep. I'm on my way back to my own tent to make felt from the wool." Then they asked her: "Is Temujin at his tent? How far is it from here?" Old Woman Khogaghchin said: "As for the tent, it's not far. As for Temujin, I couldn't see whether he was there or not. I was just shearing his sheep out back." The soldiers rode off toward the camp, and Old Woman Khogaghchin whipped the ox. But as the cart moved faster its axletree snapped. "Now we'll have to run for the woods on foot," she thought, but before she could start the soldiers returned. They'd made [Temujin's half brother] Belgutei's mother their captive, and had her slung over one of their horses with her feet swinging down. They rode up to the old woman shouting: "What have you got in that cart!" "I'm just carrying wool," Khogaghchin replied, but an old soldier turned to the younger ones and said, "Get off your horses and see what's in there." When they opened the door of the cart they found Borte inside. Pulling her out, they forced Borte and Khogaghchin to ride on their horses, then they all set out after Temujin. . . .

The men who pursued Temujin were the chiefs of the three Merkid clans, Toghtoga, Dayin Usun, and Khagatai Darmala. These three had come to get their revenge, saying: "Long ago Mother Hogelun was stolen from our brother, Chiledu." When they couldn't catch Temujin they said to each other: "We've got our revenge. We've taken their wives from them," and they rode down from Mount Burkhan Khaldun back to their homes. . . .

Chinggis and his wife Borte are seated together at a feast in this fourteenth-century Persian illustration. (Bibliothèque nationale de France/The Bridgeman Art Library)

Having finished his prayer Temujin rose and rode off with Khasar and Belgutei. They rode to [his father's sworn brother] Toghoril Ong Khan of the Kereyid camped in the Black Forest on the Tula River. Temujin spoke to Ong Khan, saying: "I was attacked by surprise by the three Merkid chiefs. They've stolen my wife from me. We've come to you now to say, 'Let my father the Khan save my wife and return her.'" . . .

[Temujin and his allies] moved their forces from Botoghan Bogorjin to the Kilgho River where they built rafts to cross over to the Bugura Steppe, into [the Merkid] Chief Toghtoga's land. They came down on him as if through the smoke-hole of his tent, beating down the frame of his tent and leaving it flat, capturing and killing his wives and his sons. They struck at his door-frame where his guardian spirit lived and broke it to pieces. They completely destroyed all his people until in their place there was nothing but emptiness. . . .

As the Merkid people tried to flee from our army running down the Selenge with what they could gather in the darkness, as our soldiers rode out of the night capturing and killing the Merkid, Temujin rode through the retreating camp shouting out: "Borte! Borte!"

Lady Borte was among the Merkid who ran in the darkness and when she heard his voice, when she recognized Temujin's voice, Borte leaped from her cart. Lady Borte and Old Woman Khogaghchin saw Temujin charge through the crowd and they ran to him, finally seizing the reins of his horse. All about them was moonlight. As Temujin looked down to see who had stopped him he recognized Lady Borte. In a moment he was down from his horse and they were in each other's arms, embracing. ”

Source: Paul Kahn, trans., *The Secret History of the Mongols: The Origin of Chingis Khan*. Copyright © 1984. Reprinted with permission of Paul Kahn.

QUESTIONS FOR ANALYSIS

1. What do you learn from these stories about the Mongol way of life?
2. "Marriage by capture" has been practiced in many parts of the world. Can you infer from these stories why such a system would persist? What was the impact of such practices on kinship relations?
3. Can you recognize traces of the oral origins of these stories?

How did the Mongols build and govern a Eurasian empire?

In the mid-twelfth century the Mongols were just one of many peoples in the eastern grasslands, neither particularly numerous nor especially advanced. Why then did the Mongols suddenly emerge as an overpowering force on the historical stage? One explanation is ecological. A drop in the mean annual temperature created a subsistence crisis. As pastures shrank, the Mongols and other nomads had to look beyond the steppe to get more of their food from the agricultural world. A second reason for their sudden rise was the appearance of a single individual, the brilliant but utterly ruthless Temujin (ca. 1162–1227), later and more commonly called Chinggis Khan (sometimes spelled Genghis or Ghengis).

Chinggis Khan

In Temujin's youth his father had built a modest tribal following. When Temujin's father was poisoned by a rival, his followers, not ready to follow a boy of twelve, drifted away, leaving Temujin and his mother and brothers in a vulnerable position. Temujin slowly collected followers. In 1182 Temujin was captured and carried in a cage to a rival's camp. After a daring midnight escape, he led his followers to join a stronger chieftain whom his father had once aided. With the chieftain's help, Temujin began avenging the insults he had received.

Temujin proved to be a natural leader, and as he subdued the Tartars, Kereyids, Naimans, Merkids, and other Mongol and Turkish tribes, he built up an army of loyal followers. In 1206, at a great gathering of tribal leaders, Temujin was proclaimed **Chinggis Khan**, or Great Ruler. Chinggis decreed that Mongol, until then an unwritten language, be written down in the script used by the Uighur Turks. With this script a record was made of the Mongol laws and customs. Another measure adopted at this assembly was a postal relay system to send messages rapidly by mounted courier, suggesting that Chinggis already had ambitions to rule a vast empire.

Chinggis Khan The title given to the Mongol ruler Temujin in 1206 and later to his successors; it means Great Ruler.

With the tribes of Mongolia united, the energies previously devoted to infighting and vendettas were redirected to exacting tribute from the settled populations nearby, starting with the Jurchen (Jin) state that extended into north China (see Map 13.2, page 327). Because of his early experiences with intertribal feuding, Chinggis mistrusted traditional tribal loyalties, and as he fashioned a new army, he gave it a new, non-tribal structure. He conscripted soldiers from all the tribes and assigned them to units that were composed of members from different tribes. He selected commanders for each unit whom he could remove at will, although he allowed commanders to pass their posts to their sons.

After Chinggis subjugated a city, he would send envoys to cities farther out to demand submission and threaten destruction. Those who opened their city gates and submitted without fighting could become allies and retain local power, but those who resisted faced the prospect of mass slaughter. He despised city dwellers and would sometimes use them as living shields in the next battle. After the Mongol armies swept across north China in 1212–1213, ninety-odd cities lay in rubble. Beijing, captured in 1215, burned for more than a month. Not surprisingly many governors of cities and rulers of small states hastened to offer submission.

Chinggis preferred conquest to administration and did not stay in north China to set up an administrative structure. He left that to subordinates and turned his attention westward, to Central Asia and Persia, then dominated by different groups of Turks. In 1218 Chinggis proposed to the Khwarizm shah of Persia that he accept Mongol overlordship and establish trade relations. The shah, to show his determination to resist, ordered the envoy and the merchants who had accompanied him killed. The next year Chinggis led an army of one hundred thousand soldiers west to retaliate. Mongol forces destroyed the shah's army and sacked one Persian city after another, demolishing buildings and massacring hundreds of thousands of people.

After returning from Central Asia, Chinggis died in 1227 during the siege of a city in northwest China. Before he died, he instructed his sons not to fall out among themselves but instead to divide the spoils.

Chinggis's Successors

Although Mongol leaders traditionally had had to win their positions, after Chinggis died the empire was divided into four states called **khanates**, with one of the lines of his descendants taking charge of each one (Map 12.1). Chinggis's third son, Ögödei, assumed the title of khan, and he directed the next round of invasions.

khanates The states ruled by a khan; the four units into which Chinggis divided the Mongol Empire.

In 1237 representatives of all four lines led 150,000 Mongol, Turkish, and Persian troops into Europe. During the next five years they gained control of Moscow and Kievan Russia and looted cities in Poland and Hungary. They were poised to attack deeper into Europe when they learned of the death of Ögödei in 1241. To participate in the election of a new khan, the army returned to the Mongols' new capital city, Karakorum.

Once Ögödei's son was certified as his successor, the Mongols turned their attention to Persia and the Middle East. In 1256 a Mongol army took northwest Iran, then pushed on to the Abbasid capital of Baghdad. When it fell in 1258, the last Abbasid caliph was murdered, and the population was put to the sword. The Mongol onslaught was successfully resisted, however, by both the Delhi sultanate (see page 307) and the Mamluk rulers in Egypt (see page 219).

Under Chinggis's grandson Khubilai Khan (r. 1260–1294) the Mongols completed their conquest of China. First they surrounded the Song Empire in central and south China (discussed in Chapter 13) by taking its westernmost province in 1252, as well as Korea to its east in 1258, destroying the Nanzhao kingdom in modern Yunnan in 1254, and then continuing south and taking Annam (northern Vietnam) in 1257. During their advance toward the Chinese capital of Hangzhou, the Mongols ordered the total slaughter of the people of the major city of Changzhou, and in 1276 the Chinese empress dowager surrendered in hopes of sparing the people of the capital a similar fate.

Mongol Conquests

1206	Temujin made Chinggis Khan
1215	Fall of Beijing (Jurchens)
1219–1220	Fall of Bukhara and Samarkand in Central Asia
1227	Death of Chinggis
1237–1241	Raids into eastern Europe
1257	Conquest of Annam (northern Vietnam)
1258	Conquest of Abbasid capital of Baghdad; conquest of Korea
1260	Khubilai succeeds to khanship
1274	First attempt at invading Japan
1276	Surrender of Song Dynasty (China)
1281	Second attempt at invading Japan
1293	Mongol fleet unsuccessful in invasion of Java
mid-14th century	Decline of Mongol power

Mapping the Past

Map 12.1 The Mongol Empire

The creation of the vast Mongol Empire facilitated communication across Eurasia and led to both the spread of deadly plagues and the transfer of technical and scientific knowledge. After the death of Chinggis Khan in 1227, the empire was divided into four khanates ruled by different lines of his successors. In the 1270s the Mongols conquered southern China, but most of their subsequent campaigns did not lead to further territorial gains.

ANALYZING THE MAP Trace the campaigns of the Mongols. Which ones led to acquisition of territory, and which ones did not?

CONNECTIONS Would the division of the Mongol Empire into separate khanates have made these areas easier for the Mongols to rule? What drawbacks might it have had from the Mongols' point of view?

Having overrun China and Korea, Khubilai turned his eyes toward Japan. In 1274 a force of 30,000 soldiers and support personnel sailed from Korea to Japan. In 1281 a combined Mongol and Chinese fleet of about 150,000 made a second attempt to conquer Japan. On both occasions the Mongols managed to land but were beaten back by Japanese samurai armies. Each time fierce storms destroyed the Mongol fleets. A decade later, in 1293, Khubilai tried sending a fleet to the islands of Southeast Asia, including Java, but it met with no more success than the fleets sent to Japan.

Why were the Mongols so successful against so many different types of enemies? Even though their population was tiny compared to the populations of the large agricultural societies they conquered, their tactics, their weapons, and their organization all gave them advantages. Like other nomads before them, they were superb horsemen and excellent archers. Their horses were extremely nimble, able to change direction quickly, thus allowing the Mongols to maneuver easily and ride through infantry forces armed with swords, lances, and javelins. Usually only other nomadic armies, like the Turks, could stand up well against the Mongols.

The Mongols were also open to trying new military technologies. To attack walled cities, they learned how to use catapults and other engines of war. At first they employed Chinese catapults, but when they learned that those used by the Turks in Afghanistan were more powerful, they adopted the better model. The Mongols also used exploding arrows and gunpowder projectiles developed by the Chinese.

The Mongols made good use of intelligence and tried to exploit internal divisions in the countries they attacked. Thus, in north China they appealed to the Khitans, who had been defeated by the Jurchens a century earlier, to join them in attacking the Jurchens. In Syria they exploited the resentment of Christians against their Muslim rulers.

The 1258 Fall of Baghdad This illustration from a fourteenth-century Persian manuscript shows the Mongol army attacking the walled city of Baghdad. Note the use of catapults on both sides. (Bildarchiv Preussischer Kulturbesitz/Art Resource, NY)

The Mongols as Rulers

The success of the Mongols in ruling vast territories was due in large part to their willingness to incorporate other ethnic groups into their armies and governments. Whatever their original country or religion, those who served the Mongols loyally were rewarded. Uighurs, Tibetans, Persians, Chinese, and Russians came to hold powerful positions in the Mongol government. Chinese helped breach the walls of Baghdad in the 1250s, and Muslims operated the catapults that helped reduce Chinese cities in the 1270s.

Since, in Mongol eyes, the purpose of fighting was to gain riches, they regularly would loot the settlements they conquered, taking whatever they wanted, including the residents. Land would be granted to military commanders, nobles, and army units to be governed and exploited as the recipients wished. Those working the land would be given to them as serfs. The Mongols built a capital city called Karakorum in modern Mongolia, and to bring it up to the level of the cities they conquered, they transported skilled workers from those cities. For instance, after Bukhara and Samarkand were captured in 1219–1220, some thirty thousand artisans were seized and transported to Mongolia.

In time, however, the Mongols came to realize that simply appropriating the wealth and human resources of the settled lands was not as good as extracting regular revenue from them. A Chinese-educated Khitan who had been working for the Jurchens in China explained to the Mongols that collecting taxes from farmers would be highly profitable. The Mongols gave this a try, but soon political rivals convinced the khan that he would gain even more by letting Central Asian Muslim merchants bid against each other for licenses to collect taxes any way they could, a system called **tax-farming**. Ordinary Chinese found this method of tax collecting much more oppressive than traditional Chinese methods, since there was little to keep the tax collectors from seizing everything they could.

tax-farming Assigning the collection of taxes to whoever bids the most for the privilege.

By the second half of the thirteenth century there was no longer a genuine pan-Asian Mongol Empire. Much of Asia was in the hands of Mongol successor states, but these were generally hostile to each other. Khubilai was often at war with the khanate of Central Asia, then held by his cousin Khaidu, and he had little contact with the khanate of the Golden Horde in south Russia. The Mongols adapted their methods of government to the existing traditions of each place they ruled, and the regions now went their separate ways.

In China the Mongols resisted assimilation and purposely avoided many Chinese practices. The rulers conducted their business in the Mongol language and spent their summers in Mongolia. Khubilai discouraged Mongols from marrying Chinese and took only Mongol women into the palace. Some Mongol princes preferred to live in yurts erected on the palace grounds rather than in the grand palaces constructed at Beijing. Chinese were treated as legally inferior not only to the Mongols but also to all other non-Chinese.

In Central Asia, Persia, and Russia the Mongols tended to merge with the Turkish groups already there and, like them, converted to Islam. Russia in the thirteenth century was not a strongly centralized state, and the Mongols allowed Russian princes and lords to continue to rule their territories as long as they turned over adequate tribute. In the Middle East the Mongol Il-khans (as they were known in Persia) were more active as rulers, again continuing the traditions of the caliphate. In Mongolia itself, however, Mongol traditions were maintained.

Mongol control in each of the khanates lasted about a century. In the mid-fourteenth century the Mongol dynasty in China deteriorated into civil war, and in the 1360s the Mongols withdrew back to Mongolia. There was a similar loss of Mongol power in Persia and Central Asia. Only on the south Russian steppe was the Golden Horde able to maintain its hold for another century.

As Mongol rule in Central Asia declined, a new conqueror emerged, Timur, also known as Tamerlane (Timur the Lame). Not a nomad but a highly civilized Turkish noble, Timur in the 1360s struck out from his base in Samarkand into Persia, north India (see page 309), southern Russia, and beyond. His armies used the terror tactics that the Mongols had perfected, massacring the citizens of cities that resisted. In the decades after his death in 1405, however, Timur's empire went into decline.

Quick Review
What purposes did Mongol conquest serve, and how did their style of government reflect these goals?

How did the Mongol conquests facilitate cultural exchange?

The Mongol governments did more than any earlier political entities to encourage the movement of people and goods across Eurasia. With these vast movements came cultural accommodation as the Mongols, their conquered subjects, and their trading partners learned from one another. This cultural exchange included both physical goods and the sharing of ideas. It also facilitated the spread of the plague and the unwilling movement of enslaved captives.

The Movement of Peoples

The Mongols had never looked down on merchants the way the elites of many traditional states did, and they welcomed the arrival of merchants from distant lands. Even when different groups of Mongols were fighting among themselves, they usually allowed caravans to pass without harassing them.

The Mongol practice of transporting skilled people from the lands they conquered also brought people into contact with each other in new ways. Besides those forced to move, the Mongols recruited administrators from China, Persia, and the Middle East. Especially prominent were the Uighur Turks of Chinese Central Asia, whose familiarity with Chinese civilization and fluency in Turkish were extremely valuable in facilitating communication.

The Mongols were remarkably open to religious experts from all the lands they encountered. More Europeans made their way as far as Mongolia and China in the Mongol period than ever before. Popes and kings sent envoys to the Mongol court in the hope of enlisting the Mongols on their side in their long-standing conflict with Muslim forces over the Holy Land. European visitors were also interested in finding Christians who had been cut off from the West by the spread of Islam, and in fact there were considerable numbers of Nestorian Christians in Central Asia.

Depictions of Europeans The Mongol Empire, by facilitating travel across Asia, increased knowledge of faraway lands. Rashid al-Din's *History of the World* included a history of the Franks, illustrated here with images of Western popes (left) conferring with Byzantine emperors (right). (Topkapi Saray Museum, Ms. H.1654, fol. 303a)

The most famous European visitor to the Mongol lands was the Venetian Marco Polo (ca. 1254–1324). In his famous *Travels*, Marco Polo described all the places he visited or learned about during his seventeen years away from home. He reported being warmly received by Khubilai, who impressed him enormously. He was also awed by the wealth and splendor of Chinese cities and spread the notion of Asia as a land of riches. In Marco Polo's lifetime, some skeptics did not believe his tale, and even today some scholars speculate that he may have learned about China from Persian merchants he met in the Middle East without actually going to China. Regardless of the final verdict on Marco Polo's veracity, there is no doubt that the great popularity of his book contributed to European interest in finding new routes to Asia.

The Spread of Disease, Goods, and Ideas

The rapid transfer of people and goods across Central Asia spread more than ideas and inventions. It also spread diseases, the most deadly of which was the plague known in Europe as the Black Death, which most scholars identify today as the bubonic plague. In the early fourteenth century, transmitted by rats and fleas, the plague began to spread from

Central Asia into West Asia, the Mediterranean, and western Europe. When the Mongols were assaulting the city of Kaffa in the Crimea in 1346, they were infected by the plague and had to withdraw. In retaliation, they purposely spread the disease to their enemy by catapulting the bodies of victims into the city of Kaffa. Soon the disease was carried from port to port throughout the Mediterranean by ship. The confusion of the mid-fourteenth century that led to the loss of Mongol power in China, Iran, and Central Asia undoubtedly owes something to the effect of the spread of the plague and other diseases. (For more on the Black Death, see Chapter 14.)

Traditionally, the historians of each of the countries conquered by the Mongols portrayed them as a scourge. Russian historians, for instance, saw this as a period of bondage that set Russia back and cut it off from western Europe. Among contemporary Western historians, it is now more common to celebrate the genius of the Mongol military machine and treat the spread of ideas and inventions as an obvious good, probably because we see global communication as a good in our own world. There is no reason to assume, however, that people benefited equally from the improved communications and the new political institutions of the Mongol era. Merchants involved in long-distance trade prospered, but those enslaved and transported hundreds or thousands of miles from home would have seen themselves as the most pitiable of victims.

The places that were ruled by Mongol governments for a century or more—China, Central Asia, Persia, and Russia—do not seem to have advanced at a more rapid rate during that century than they did in earlier centuries, either economically or culturally. By Chinese standards Mongol imposition of hereditary status distinctions was a step backward from a much more mobile and open society, and placing Persians, Arabs, or Tibetans over Chinese did not arouse interest in foreign cultures. Much more foreign music and foreign styles in clothing, art, and furnishings were integrated into Chinese civilization in Tang times than in Mongol times.

In terms of the spread of technological and scientific ideas, Europe seems to have been by far the main beneficiary of increased communication, largely because in 1200 it lagged farther behind than the other areas. Chinese inventions such as printing, gunpowder, and the compass spread westward. Persian and Indian expertise in astronomy and mathematics also spread. In terms of the spread of religions, Islam probably gained the most. It came to dominate in Chinese Central Asia, which had previously been Buddhist.

Another element promoting Eurasian connection was maritime trade, which linked all the societies of the Indian Ocean and East Asia. The products of China and other areas of the East introduced to Europe by merchants like Marco Polo whetted the appetites of Europeans for goods from the East, and the demand for Asian goods eventually culminated in the great age of European exploration and expansion (discussed in Chapter 16). By comparison, in areas the Mongols had directly attacked, protecting their own civilization became a higher priority than drawing from the outside to enrich or enlarge it.

Quick Review
What were the most important consequences of the regional exchange promoted and facilitated by the Mongols?

Stop here

What was the result of India's encounters with Turks and Mongols?

South Asia, although far from the heartland of the steppe, still felt the impact of the arrival of the Turks in Central Asia. Over the course of many centuries, horsemen from both the east and the west (Scythians, Huns, Turks, and Mongols) all sent armies south to raid or invade north India. After the Mauryan Empire broke apart in 185 B.C.E. (see page 73), India was politically divided into small kingdoms for several centuries. Only the Guptas in the fourth century would emerge to unite much of north India, though their rule was cut short by the invasion of the Huns in about 450. In the centuries that followed, India witnessed the development of regional cultures and was profoundly shaped by Turkish nomads from Central Asia who brought their culture and, most importantly, Islam to India. Despite these events, the lives of most Indians remained unchanged, with the majority of the people living in villages in a society defined by caste.

The Gupta Empire, ca. 320–480

In the early fourth century a state emerged in the Ganges plain that was able to bring large parts of north India under its control. The rulers of this Indian empire, the Guptas, consciously modeled their rule after that of the Mauryan Empire, and the founder took the name of the founder of that dynasty, Chandragupta. Although the Guptas never controlled as much territory as the Mauryans had, they united north India and received tribute from states in Nepal and the Indus Valley, thus giving large parts of India a period of peace and political unity.

The Guptas' administrative system was not as centralized as that of the Mauryans. In the central regions they drew their revenue from a tax on agriculture and maintained monopolies on key products such as metals and salt (reminiscent of Chinese practice). They also exacted labor service for the construction and upkeep of roads, wells, and irrigation systems. More distant areas were assigned to governors who were allowed considerable leeway, and governorships often became hereditary. Areas still farther away were encouraged to become vassal states, able to participate in the splendor of the capital and royal court in subordinate roles and to engage in profitable trade, but not required to turn over much in the way of revenue.

The Gupta kings were patrons of the arts. Poets composed epics for the courts of the Gupta kings, and other writers experimented with prose romances and popular tales. India's greatest poet, Kalidasa (ca. 380–450), like Shakespeare, wrote poems as well as plays in verse. His most highly esteemed play, *Shakuntala*, concerns a daughter of a hermit who enthralls a king who is out hunting. The king sets up house with her, then returns to his court and, owing to a curse, forgets her. Only much later does he acknowledge their child as his true heir. Equally loved is Kalidasa's one-hundred-verse poem "The Cloud Messenger" about a demigod who asks a passing cloud to carry a message to his wife, from whom he has long been separated.

The Gupta Empire, ca. 320–480

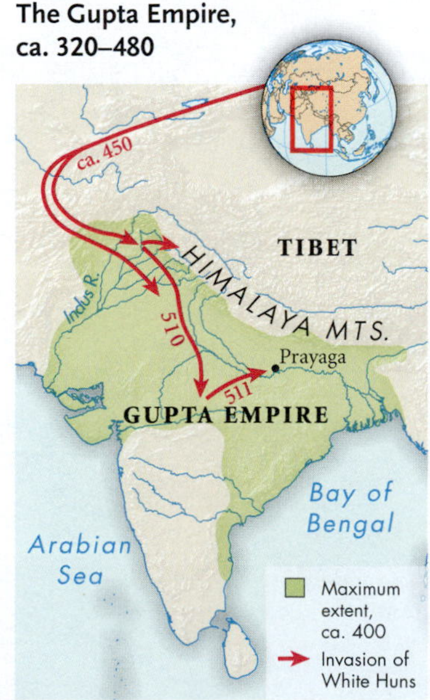

In mathematics, too, the Gupta period could boast of impressive intellectual achievements. The so-called Arabic numerals are actually of Indian origin. Indian mathematicians developed the place-value notation system, with separate columns for ones, tens, and hundreds, as well as a zero sign to indicate the absence of units in a given column. This system greatly facilitated calculation and spread as far as Europe by the seventh century.

The Gupta rulers were Hindus, but they tolerated all faiths. Buddhist pilgrims from other areas of Asia reported that Buddhist monasteries with hundreds or even thousands of monks and nuns flourished in the cities. The success of Buddhism did not hinder Hinduism with its many gods, which remained popular among ordinary people.

The great crisis of the Gupta Empire was the invasion of the Huns (Xiongnu). The migration of these nomads from Central Asia shook much of Eurasia. Around 450 a group of them known as the White Huns thundered into India. Although the Huns failed to uproot the Gupta Empire, they dealt the dynasty a fatal blow.

India's Medieval Age and the First Encounter with Islam

After the decline of the Gupta Empire, India once again broke into separate kingdoms that were frequently at war with each other. Most of the dynasties of India's medieval age (ca. 500–1400) were short-lived, but a balance of power was maintained between the major regions of India, with none gaining enough of an advantage to conquer the others (Map 12.2).

Political division fostered the development of regional cultures. Literature came to be written in India's regional languages, among them Marathi, Bengali, and Assamese. Commerce continued as before, and the coasts of India remained important in the sea trade of the Indian Ocean.

The first encounters with Islam occurred in this period. In 711 the Umayyad governor of Iraq sent a force with six thousand horses and six thousand camels to seize the Sind area in western India (modern day Pakistan). The western part of India remained part of the caliphate for centuries, but Islam did not spread much beyond this foothold. During the

Map 12.2 South and Southeast Asia in the Thirteenth Century The extensive coastlines of South and Southeast Asia and the predictable monsoon winds aided seafaring in this region. Note the Strait of Malacca, through which most east-west sea trade passed.

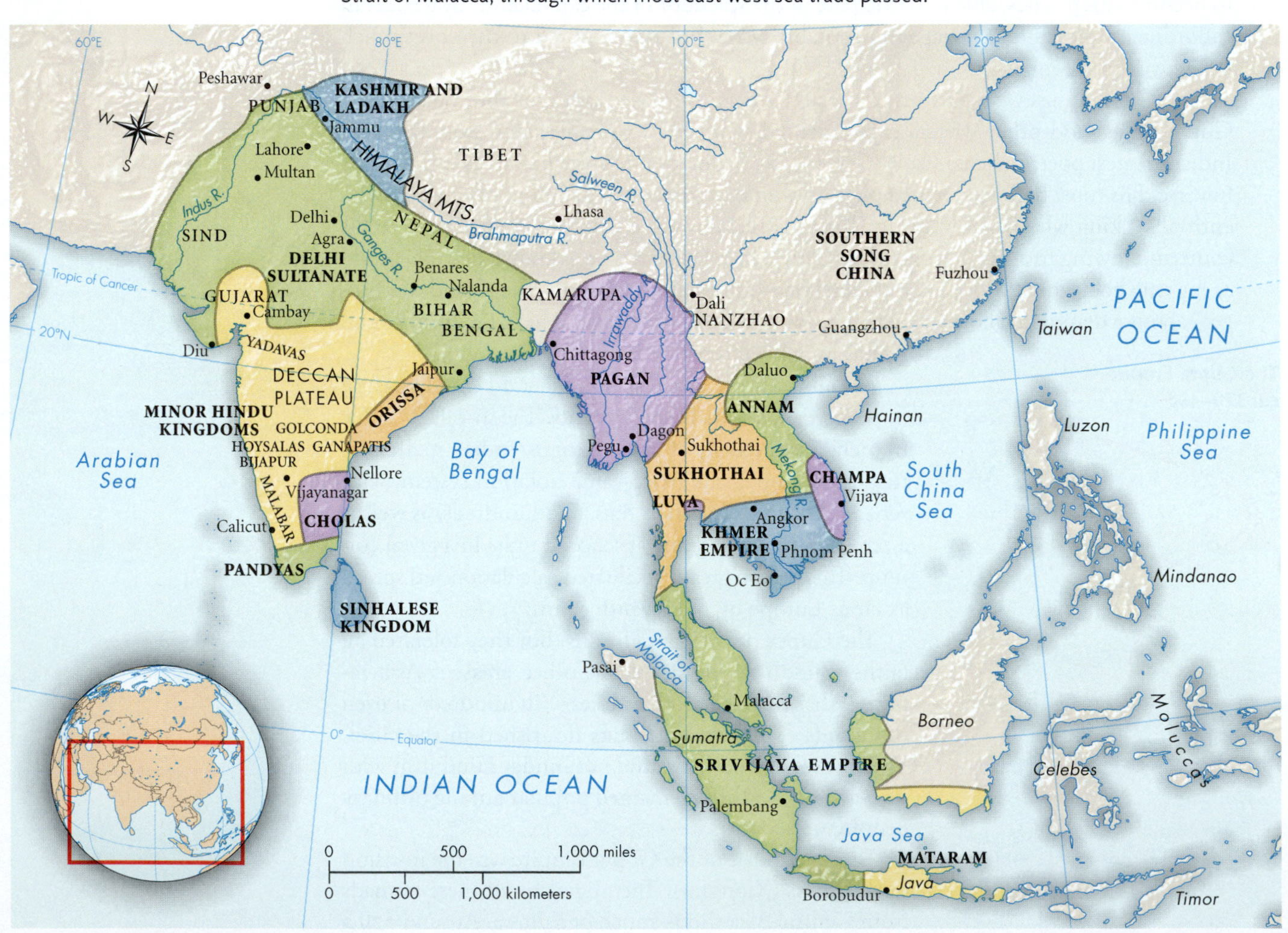

ninth and tenth centuries Turks from Central Asia moved into the region of today's northeastern Iran and western Afghanistan, then known as Khurasan. Converts to Islam, they first served as military forces for the caliphate in Baghdad, but as its authority weakened (see page 293), they made themselves rulers of an effectively independent Khurasan and frequently sent raiding parties into north India. Beginning in 997, Mahmud of Ghazni (r. 997–1030) led seventeen annual forays into India from his base in modern Afghanistan. His goal was plunder to finance his wars against other Turkish rulers in Central Asia. Eventually even the Arab conquerors of the Sind fell to the Turks. By 1030 the Indus Valley, the Punjab, and the rest of northwest India were in the grip of the Turks.

After an initial period of raids and destruction of temples, the Muslim Turks came to an accommodation with the Hindus, who were classed as a **protected people**, like the Christians and Jews, and allowed to follow their religion. They had to pay a special tax but did not have to perform military service. Local chiefs and rajas were often allowed to remain in control of their domains as long as they paid tribute. Most Indians looked on the Muslim conquerors as a new ruling caste, capable of governing and taxing them but otherwise peripheral to their lives. The myriad castes largely governed themselves, isolating the newcomers.

protected people The Muslim classification used for Hindus, Christians, and Jews; they were allowed to follow their religions but had to pay a special tax.

Nevertheless, over the course of several centuries Islam gained a strong hold on north India, especially in the Indus Valley (modern Pakistan) and in Bengal at the mouth of the Ganges River (modern Bangladesh). Moreover, the sultanate seems to have had a positive effect on the economy. Much of the wealth confiscated from temples was put to more productive use, and India's first truly large cities emerged. The Turks also were eager to employ skilled workers, giving new opportunities to low-caste manual and artisan labor.

The Muslim rulers were much more hostile to Buddhism than to Hinduism, seeing Buddhism as a competitive proselytizing religion. In 1193 a Turkish raiding party destroyed the great Buddhist university at Nalanda in Bihar. Buddhist monks were killed or forced to flee to Buddhist centers in Southeast Asia, Nepal, and Tibet. Buddhism, which had thrived for so long in peaceful and friendly competition with Hinduism, went into decline in its native land.

Hinduism, however, remained as strong as ever. South India was largely unaffected by these invasions, and traditional Hindu culture flourished there under native kings ruling small kingdoms. (See "Individuals in Society: Bhaskara the Teacher," page 308.) Temple-centered Hinduism flourished, as did devotional cults and mystical movements. This was a great age of religious art and architecture in India. Extraordinary temples covered with elaborate bas-relief were built in many areas.

The Delhi Sultanate

In the twelfth century a new line of Turkish rulers arose in Afghanistan, led by Muhammad of Ghur (d. 1206). Muhammad captured Delhi and extended his control nearly throughout north India. When he fell to an assassin in 1206, one of his generals, the former slave Qutb-ud-din, took over and established a government at Delhi, separate from the government in Afghanistan. This sultanate of Delhi lasted for three centuries, even though dynasties changed several times.

A major accomplishment of the Delhi sultanate was holding off the Mongols. Although the Turks by this time were highly cosmopolitan and no longer nomadic, they had retained their martial skills and understanding of steppe warfare. Chinggis Khan and his troops entered the Indus Valley in 1221 in pursuit of the shah of Khurasan. The sultan wisely kept out of the way, and when Chinggis Khan left some troops in the area, the sultan made no attempt to challenge them. Two generations later, in 1299, a Mongol khan launched a campaign into India with two hundred thousand men, but the sultan of the time was able to defeat them. Two years later the Mongols returned and camped at Delhi for two

INDIVIDUALS IN SOCIETY

Bhaskara the Teacher

IN INDIA, AS IN MANY OTHER SOCIETIES, astronomy and mathematics were closely linked, and many of the most important mathematicians served their rulers as astronomers. Bhaskara (1114–ca. 1185) was such an astronomer-mathematician. For generations his Brahmin family had been astronomers at the Ujjain astronomical observatory in north-central India, and his father had written a popular book on astrology.

Bhaskara was a highly erudite man. A disciple wrote that he had thoroughly mastered eight books on grammar, six on medicine, six on philosophy, five on mathematics, and the four Vedas. Bhaskara eventually wrote six books on mathematics and mathematical astronomy. They deal with solutions to simple and quadratic equations and show his knowledge of trigonometry, including the sine table and relationships between different trigonometric functions, and even some of the basic elements of calculus. Earlier Indian mathematicians had explored the use of zero and negative numbers. Bhaskara developed these ideas further, in particular improving on the understanding of division by zero.

A court poet who centuries later translated Bhaskara's book titled *The Beautiful* explained its title by saying Bhaskara wrote it for his daughter named Beautiful (Lilavati) as consolation when his divination of the best time for her to marry went awry. Whether Bhaskara did or did not write this book for his daughter, many of the problems he provides in it have a certain charm:

> *On an expedition to seize his enemy's elephants, a king marched two yojanas the first day. Say, intelligent calculator, with what increasing rate of daily march did he proceed, since he reached his foe's city, a distance of eighty yojanas, in a week?**
>
> *Out of a heap of pure lotus flower, a third part, a fifth, and a sixth were offered respectively to the gods Siva, Vishnu, and the Sun; and a quarter was presented to Bhavani. The remaining six lotuses were given to the venerable preceptor. Tell quickly the whole number of lotus.*†
>
> *If eight best variegated silk scarfs, measuring three cubits in breadth and eight in length, cost a hundred nishkas, say quickly, merchant, if thou understand trade, what a like scarf, three and a half cubits long and half a cubit wide will cost.*‡

In the conclusion to *The Beautiful*, Bhaskara wrote:

> *Joy and happiness is indeed ever increasing in this world for those who have* The Beautiful *clasped to their throats, decorated as the members are with neat reduction of fractions, multiplication, and involution, pure and perfect as are the solutions, and tasteful as is the speech which is exemplified.*

Bhaskara had a long career. His first book on mathematical astronomy, written in 1150 when he was thirty-six, used mathematics to calculate solar and lunar eclipses or planetary conjunctions. Thirty-three years later he was still writing on the subject, this time providing simpler ways to solve problems encountered before. Bhaskara wrote his books in Sanskrit, already a literary language rather than a vernacular language, but even in his own day some of them were translated into other Indian languages.

Within a couple of decades of his death, a local ruler endowed an educational institution to study Bhaskara's works, beginning with his work on mathematical astronomy. In the text he had inscribed at the site, the ruler gave the names of Bhaskara's ancestors for six generations, as well as of his son and grandson, who had continued in his profession.

*Quotations from Haran Chandra Banerji, *Colebrooke's Translation of the Lilanvanti*, 2d ed. (Calcutta: The Book Co., 1927), pp. 80–81, 30, 51, 200. The answer is that each day he must travel 22/7 yojanas farther than the day before.

†The answer is 120.

‡The answer, from the formula $x = (1 \times 7 \times 1 \times 100) / (8 \times 3 \times 8 \times 2 \times 2)$, is given in currencies smaller than the nishka: 14 drammas, 9 panas, 1 kakini, and 6⅔ cowry shells. (20 cowry shells = 1 kakini, 4 kakini = 1 pana, 16 panas = 1 dramma, and 16 drammas = 1 nishka.)

QUESTIONS FOR ANALYSIS

1. What might have been the advantages of making occupations like astronomer hereditary in India?
2. How does Bhaskara link joy and happiness to mathematical concepts?

The observatory where Bhaskara worked in Ujjain today stands in ruins. (Dinodia Photo Library)

months, but they eventually left without taking the sultan's fort. Another Mongol raid in 1306–1307 also was successfully repulsed.

During the fourteenth century, however, the Delhi sultanate was in decline and proved unable to ward off the armies of Timur (see page 302), who took Delhi in 1398. Timur's chronicler reported that when the troops drew up for battle outside Delhi, the sultanate had 10,000 horsemen, 20,000 foot soldiers, and 120 war elephants. Though alarmed at the sight of the elephants, Timur's men dug trenches to trap them and shot at their drivers. The sultan fled, leaving the city to surrender. Timur took as booty all the elephants, loading them with treasures seized from the city.

Timur's invasion left a weakened sultanate. The Delhi sultanate endured under different rulers until 1526, when it was conquered by the Mughals, a Muslim dynasty that would rule over most of northern India from the sixteenth into the nineteenth century.

Life in Medieval India

Local institutions played a much larger role in the lives of the overwhelming majority of people in medieval India than did the state. Craft guilds oversaw conditions of work and trade; local councils handled law and order at the town or village level; and local castes gave members a sense of belonging and identity.

Like peasant societies elsewhere, including in China, Japan, and Southeast Asia, agricultural life in India ordinarily meant village life. The average farmer worked a small plot of land outside the village. All the family members pooled their resources under the direction of the head of the family. These joint efforts strengthened family solidarity.

The agricultural year began with spring plowing. The traditional plow, drawn by two oxen wearing yokes and collars, had an iron-tipped share and a handle with which the farmer guided it. Rice, the most important and popular grain, was sown at the beginning of the long rainy season. Beans, lentils, and peas grew during the cold season and were harvested in the spring, when fresh food was scarce. Cereal crops such as wheat, barley, and millet provided carbohydrates and other nutrients. Sugarcane was another important crop. Some families cultivated vegetables, spices, fruit trees, and flowers in their gardens.

Farmers also raised livestock. Most highly valued were cattle, which were raised for plowing and milk, hides, and horns, but Hindus did not slaughter them for meat. Like the Islamic and Jewish prohibition on the consumption of pork, the eating of beef was forbidden among Hindus.

Local craftsmen and tradesmen lived and worked in specific parts of a town or village. They were frequently organized into guilds, with guild heads and guild rules. The textile industries were particularly well developed. Silk (which had entered India from China), linen, wool, and cotton fabrics were produced in large quantities and traded throughout India and beyond. The cutting and polishing of precious stones was another industry associated closely with foreign trade.

In the cities shops were open to the street; families lived on the floors above. The busiest tradesmen dealt in milk and cheese, oil, spices, and perfumes. Equally prominent but disreputable were tavern keepers. In addition to these tradesmen and merchants, a host of peddlers shuffled through towns and villages selling everything from needles to freshly cut flowers.

In this period the caste system reached its mature form. Within the broad division into the four *varna* (strata) of Brahmin, Kshatriya, Vaishya, and Shudra (see page 61), the population was subdivided into numerous castes, or **jati**. Each caste had a proper occupation. In addition, its members married only within the caste and ate only with other members. Members of high-status castes feared pollution from contact with lower-caste individuals and had to undertake rituals of purification to remove the taint.

jati The thousands of Indian castes.

Men at Work This stone frieze from the Buddhist stupa in Sanchi depicts Indian men doing a variety of everyday jobs. Although the stone was carved to convey religious ideas, we can use it as a source for such details of daily life as the sort of clothing men wore while working and how they carried loads. (Dinodia Photo Library)

Eventually Indian society comprised perhaps as many as three thousand castes. Each caste had its own governing body, which enforced the rules of the caste. Those incapable of living up to the rules were expelled, becoming outcastes. These unfortunates lived hard lives, performing tasks that others considered unclean or lowly.

Villages were often walled, as in north China and the Middle East. The streets were unpaved, and cattle and sheep roamed as freely as people. The pond outside the village was its main source of water and also a spawning ground for fish, birds, and mosquitoes. After the farmers returned from the fields in the evening, the village gates were closed until morning.

The life of the well-to-do is described in the *Kamasutra* (Book on the Art of Love). Comfortable surroundings provided a place for wealthy men to enjoy poetry, painting, and music in the company of like-minded friends. Courtesans well-trained in entertaining men added to their pleasures. A man who had more than one wife was advised not to let one wife speak ill of the other and to try to keep each of them happy by taking them to gardens, giving them presents, telling them secrets, and loving them well.

For all members of Indian society regardless of caste, marriage and family were the focus of life. As in China, the family was under the authority of the eldest male, who might take several wives, and ideally sons stayed home with their parents after they married. The family affirmed its solidarity by the religious ritual of honoring its dead ancestors—a ritual that linked the living and the dead, much like ancestor worship in China (see page 82). People commonly lived in extended families: grandparents, uncles and aunts, cousins, and nieces and nephews all lived together in the same house or compound.

Children in poor households worked as soon as they were able. Children in wealthier households faced the age-old irritations of learning reading, writing, and arithmetic. Less attention was paid to daughters than to sons, though in more prosperous families they were often literate. Because girls who had lost their virginity could seldom hope to find good husbands and thus would become financial burdens and social disgraces to their families, daughters were customarily married as children, with consummation delayed until they reached puberty.

A wife was expected to have no life apart from her husband. A widow was expected to lead the hard life of the ascetic, sleeping on the ground; eating only one simple meal a day, without meat, wine, salt, or honey; wearing plain undyed clothes without jewelry; and shaving her head. She was viewed as inauspicious to everyone but her children, and she did not attend family festivals. Among high-caste Hindus, a widow would be praised for throwing herself on her husband's funeral pyre. Buddhist sects objected to this practice, called **sati**, but some Hindu religious authorities declared that by self-immolation a widow could expunge both her own and her husband's sins, so that both would enjoy eternal bliss in Heaven.

sati A practice whereby a high-caste Hindu woman would throw herself on her husband's funeral pyre.

Within the home the position of a wife often depended on her own intelligence and strength of character. Wives were supposed to be humble, cheerful, and diligent even toward worthless husbands. As in other patriarchal societies, however, occasionally a woman ruled the household. For women who did not want to accept the strictures of married life, the main way out was to join a Buddhist or Jain religious community (see pages 169–170).

Quick Review
How did the arrival of Islamic conquerors change Indian life? What aspects of Indian life endured?

How did states develop along the trade routes of Southeast Asia and beyond?

Much as Roman culture spread to northern Europe and Chinese culture spread to Korea, Japan, and Vietnam, in the first millennium C.E. Indian learning, technology, and material culture spread to Southeast Asia, both mainland and insular. The spread of Indian culture was facilitated by the growth of maritime trade, but this interchange did not occur uniformly, and by 1400 there were still isolated societies in this region, most notably in the Pacific islands east of Indonesia.

Southeast Asia is a tropical region that is more like India than China, with temperatures hovering around 80°F and rain falling dependably throughout the year. The topography of mainland Southeast Asia is marked by north-south mountain ranges separated by river valleys. It was easy for people to migrate south along these rivers but harder for them to cross the heavily forested mountains that divided the region into areas that had limited contact with each other. The indigenous population was originally mostly Malay, but migrations over the centuries brought many other peoples, including speakers of Austro-Asiatic, Austronesian, and Sino-Tibetan-Burmese languages, some of whom moved to the islands offshore and farther into the Pacific Ocean.

State Formation and Indian Influences

Southeast Asia was long a crossroads. Traders from China, India, Africa, and Europe either passed through the region when traveling from the Indian to the Pacific Ocean, or came for its resources, notably spices. (See "Global Trade: Spices," page 312.)

The northern part of modern Vietnam was under Chinese political control off and on from the second century B.C.E. to the tenth century C.E. (see page 175), but Indian influence was of much greater significance for the rest of Southeast Asia. The first state to appear in historical records, called Funan by Chinese visitors, had its capital in southern Vietnam.

GLOBAL TRADE

Spices

Spices, from ancient times on, were a major reason for both Europeans and Chinese to trade with South and Southeast Asia. Pepper, nutmeg, cloves, cinnamon, and other spices were in high demand not only because they could be used to flavor food but also because they were thought to have positive pharmacological properties. Unlike other highly desired products of India and farther east — such as sugar, cotton, rice, and silk — no way was found to produce the spices close to where they were in demand. Because of the location where these spices were produced, this trade was from earliest times largely a maritime trade conducted through a series of middlemen.

Two types of pepper grew in India and Southeast Asia. Black pepper is identical to our familiar peppercorns. "Long pepper," from a related plant, was hotter. The Mediterranean world imported its pepper from India; China imported it from Southeast Asia. After the discovery of the New World, the importation of long pepper declined, as the chili pepper found in Mexico was at least as spicy and grew well in Europe and China.

Cloves and nutmeg entered the repertoire of spices somewhat later than pepper. They are interesting because they could be grown in only a handful of small islands in the eastern part of the Indonesian archipelago. Merchants in China, India, Arab lands, and Europe got them through intermediaries and did not know where they were grown. An Arab source from about 1000 C.E. reported that cloves came from an island near India that had a Valley of Cloves, and that they were acquired by a silent barter. The sailors would lay the items they were willing to trade out on the beach, and the next morning they would find cloves in their place.

The demand for these spices in time encouraged Chinese, Indian, and Arab seamen to make the trip to the Strait of Malacca or east Java. Malay seamen in small craft such as outrigger canoes would bring the spices the thousand or more miles to the major ports where foreign merchants would purchase them. This trade was important to the prosperity of the Srivijaya kingdom.

In the Mongol era, travelers like Marco Polo, Ibn Battuta, and Odoric of Pordenone (in modern Italy) reported on the cultivation and marketing of spices in the various places they visited. Ibn Battuta reported seeing the trunks of cinnamon trees floated down rivers in India. Odoric reported that pepper was picked like grapes from groves so huge it would take eighteen days to walk around them. Marco Polo referred to the 7,459 islands in the China Sea that local mariners could navigate and that produced a great variety of spices as well as aromatic wood. He also reported that spices, including pepper, nutmeg, and cloves, could be acquired at the great island of Java, perhaps not understanding that they had often been shipped from the innumerable small islands to Java.

Gaining direct access to the spices of the East was one of the motivations behind Christopher Columbus's voyages. Not long after, Portuguese sailors did reach India by sailing around Africa, and soon the Dutch were competing with them for control of the spice trade and setting up rival trading posts. Pepper was soon successfully planted in other tropical places, including Brazil. India, however, has remained the largest exporter of spices to this day.

In the first to sixth centuries C.E. Funan extended its control over much of Indochina and the Malay Peninsula. Merchants from northwest India would offload their goods and carry them across the narrowest part of the Malay Peninsula. The ports of Funan offered food and lodging to the merchants as they waited for the winds to shift to continue their voyages. Brahmin priests and Buddhist monks from India settled along with the traders, serving the Indian population and attracting local converts. Rulers often invited Indian priests and monks to serve under them, using them as foreign experts knowledgeable about law, government, architecture, and other fields.

After the decline of Funan, maritime trade continued to grow, and petty kingdoms appeared in many places. Indian traders frequently established small settlements, generally located on the coast. Contact with the local populations led to intermarriage and the creation of hybrid cultures. Local rulers often adopted Indian customs and values, embraced Hinduism and Buddhism, and learned **Sanskrit**, India's classical literary language. Sanskrit gave different peoples a common mode of written expression, much as Chinese did in East Asia and Latin did in Europe.

Sanskrit India's classical literary language.

When Indian traders, migrants, and adventurers entered mainland Southeast Asia, they encountered both long-settled peoples and migrants moving southward from the frontiers of China. As in other such extensive migrations, the newcomers fought one another as often

Map 12.3 The Spice Trade, ca. 100 B.C.E.–1500 C.E.

as they fought the native populations. In 939 the north Vietnamese became independent of China and extended their power southward along the coast of present-day Vietnam. The Thais had long lived in what is today southwest China and north Burma. In the eighth century the Thai tribes united in a confederacy and expanded northward against Tang China. Like China, however, the Thai confederacy fell to the Mongols in 1253. Still farther west another tribal people, the Burmese, migrated to the area of modern Burma in the eighth century. They also established a state, which they ruled from their capital, Pagan, and came into contact with India and Sri Lanka.

The most important mainland state was the Khmer (kuh-MAIR) Empire of Cambodia (802–1432), which controlled the heart of the region. The Khmers were indigenous to the area. Their empire eventually extended south to the sea and the northeast Malay Peninsula. Indian influence was pervasive; the impressive temple complex at Angkor Wat built in the early twelfth century was dedicated to the Hindu god Vishnu. Social organization, however, was modeled not on the Indian caste system but on indigenous traditions of social hierarchy. A large part of the population was of slave status, many descended from non-Khmer mountain tribes defeated by the Khmers. Generally successful in a long series of wars with the Vietnamese, the Khmers reached the peak of their power in 1219 and then gradually declined.

Picturing the Past

Bayan Relief, Angkor

Among the many relief sculptures at the temples of Angkor are depictions of royal processions, armies at war, trade, cooking, cockfighting, and other scenes of everyday life. In the relief shown here, the boats and fish convey something of the significance of the sea to life in Southeast Asia. (Robert Wilson, photographer)

READING THE IMAGE Find the boat. What do the people on it seem to be doing? What fish and animals do you see in the picture? Can you find the alligator eating a fish?

CONNECTIONS Why would a ruler devote so many resources to decorating the walls of a temple? Why include scenes like this one?

The Srivijaya Maritime Trade Empire

Srivijaya A maritime empire that held the Strait of Malacca and the waters around Sumatra, Borneo, and Java.

Far different from these land-based states was the maritime empire of **Srivijaya** (sree-vih-JUH-yuh), based on the island of Sumatra in modern Indonesia. From the sixth century on, it held the important Strait of Malacca, through which most of the sea traffic between China and India passed. This state, held together as much by alliances as by direct rule, was in many ways like the Gupta state of the same period in India, securing its prominence and binding its vassals and allies through its splendor and the promise of riches through trade.

Much as the Korean and Japanese rulers adapted Chinese models (see pages 177–178), the Srivijayan rulers drew on Indian traditions to justify their rule and organize their state. The Sanskrit writing system was used for government documents, and Indians were often employed as priests, scribes, and administrators. Using Sanskrit overcame the barriers raised by the many different native languages of the region. Indian mythology took hold, as did Indian architecture and sculpture. Kings and their courts, the first to embrace Indian culture, consciously spread it to their subjects.

After several centuries of prosperity, Srivijaya suffered a stunning blow in 1025. The Chola state in south India launched a large naval raid and captured the Srivijayan king and capital. Unable to hold their gains, the Indians retreated, but the Srivijaya Empire never regained its vigor.

During the era of the Srivijayan kingdom, other kingdoms flourished as well in island Southeast Asia. Borobudur, the magnificent Buddhist temple complex, was begun under patronage of Javan rulers in around 780. This stone monument depicts the ten tiers of Buddhist cosmology. When pilgrims made the three-mile-long winding ascent, they passed numerous sculpted reliefs depicting the journey from ignorance to enlightenment.

Buddhism became progressively more dominant in Southeast Asia after 800. Mahayana Buddhism became important in Srivijaya and Vietnam, but Theravada Buddhism, closer to the original Buddhism of early India, became the dominant form in the rest of mainland Southeast Asia. Buddhist missionaries from India and Sri Lanka played a prominent role in these developments. Local converts continued the process by making pilgrimages to India and Sri Lanka to worship and to observe Indian life for themselves.

The Spread of Indian Culture in Comparative Perspective

The social, cultural, and political systems developed in India, China, and Rome all had enormous impact on neighboring peoples whose cultures were originally not as technologically advanced. Some of the mechanisms for cultural spread were similar in all three cases, but differences were important as well.

In the case of Rome and both Han and Tang China, strong states directly ruled outlying regions, bringing their civilizations with them. India's states, even its largest empires, such as the Mauryan and Gupta, did not have comparable bureaucratic reach. Outlying areas tended to be in the hands of local lords who had consented to recognize the overlordship of the stronger state. Moreover, most of the time India was politically divided.

The expansion of Indian culture into Southeast Asia thus came not from conquest and extending direct political control, but from the extension of trading networks, with missionaries following along. This made it closer to the way Japan adopted features of Chinese culture, often through the intermediary of Korea. In both cases, the cultural exchange was largely voluntary, as the Japanese or Southeast Asians sought to adopt more up-to-date technologies (such as writing) or were persuaded of the truth of religious ideas they learned from foreigners.

The Settlement of the Pacific Islands

Through most of Eurasia, societies became progressively less isolated over time. But in 1400 there still remained many isolated societies, especially in the islands east of modern Indonesia. As discussed in Chapter 1, *Homo sapiens* began settling the western Pacific islands very early, reaching Australia by 50,000 years ago and New Guinea by 35,000 years ago. The process did not stop there, however. The ancient Austronesians (speakers of Austronesian languages) were skilled mariners who used double-canoes and brought pottery, the root vegetable taro, pigs, and chickens to numerous islands of the Pacific in subsequent centuries, generally following the coasts. Their descendants, the Polynesians, learned how to sail into the open ocean. They reached Tahiti and the Marquesas Islands in the central Pacific by about 200 C.E. Undoubtedly, seafarers were sometimes blown off their intended course, but communities would not have developed unless the original groups had included women as well as men, so probably in many cases they were looking for new places to live.

Settlement of the Pacific Islands

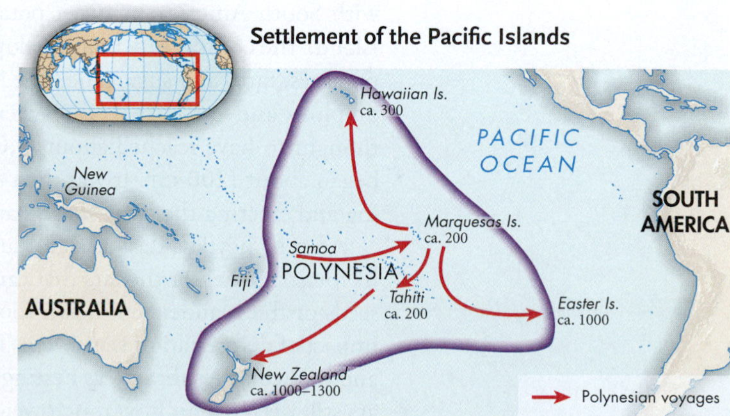

Easter Island Statues Archaeologists have excavated and restored many of Easter Island's huge statues, which display remarkable stylistic consistency, with the head disproportionately large and the legs not visible. (JP De Mann/Robert Harding World Imagery)

After reaching the central Pacific, Polynesians continued to fan out, in some cases traveling a thousand or more miles away. They reached the Hawaiian Islands in about 300 C.E., Easter Island in perhaps 1000, and New Zealand not until about 1000–1300. There even were groups who sailed west, eventually settling in Madagascar between 200 and 500.

In the more remote islands, such as Hawai'i, Easter Island, and New Zealand, the societies that developed were limited by the small range of domesticated plants and animals that the settlers brought with them and those that were indigenous to the place. Easter Island is perhaps the most extreme case. Only 15 miles wide at its widest point (only 63 square miles in total area), it is 1,300 miles from the nearest inhabited island (Pitcairn) and 2,240 miles from the coast of South America. At some point there was communication with South America, as sweet potatoes originally from there made their way to Easter Island. The community that developed on the island raised chickens and cultivated sweet potatoes, taro, and sugarcane. The inhabitants also engaged in deep-sea fishing, catching dolphins and tuna. Their tools were made of stone, wood, or bone. The population is thought to have reached about 15,000 at Easter Island's most prosperous period, which began about 1200 C.E. It was then that its people devoted remarkable efforts to fashioning and erecting the large stone statues that still dot the island.

After its heyday, Easter Island suffered severe environmental stress with the decline of its forests. Whether the rats that came with the original settlers ate too many of the trees' seeds or the islanders cut down too many of the trees to transport the stone statues, the impact of deforestation was severe. The islanders could not make boats to fish in the ocean, and bird colonies shrank, as nesting areas decreased, also reducing the food supply. Scholars still disagree on how much weight to give the many different elements that contributed to a decline in the prosperity of Easter Island from the age when the statues were erected.

Certainly, early settlers of an island could have drastic impact on its ecology. When Polynesians first reached New Zealand, they found large birds up to ten feet tall. They hunted them so eagerly that within a century the birds had all but disappeared. Hunting seals and sea lions also led to their rapid depletion. But the islands of New Zealand were much larger than Easter Island, and in time the Maori (the indigenous people of New Zealand) found more sustainable ways to feed themselves, depending more and more on agriculture.

Quick Review
What kinds of states formed in Southeast Asia, and what role did trade have in state formation in the region?

Connections

THE SOCIETIES OF EURASIA became progressively more connected to each other during the centuries discussed in this chapter. One element promoting connection was the military superiority of the nomadic warriors of the steppe, first the Turks, then the Mongols, who conquered many of the settled civilizations near them. Through conquest they introduced their culture and, in the case of the Turks, the religion of Islam to India.

Another element was maritime trade, which connected all the societies of the Indian Ocean and East Asia. As the Mongol Empire declined, maritime trading routes became an even more important part of the African, European, and Asian economic integration, with long-lasting consequences for the Afroeurasian trading world (see Chapter 16). Maritime trade was also one of the key elements in the spread of Indian culture to both mainland and insular Southeast Asia. Other elements connecting these societies included Sanskrit as a language of administration and missionaries who brought both Hinduism and Buddhism far beyond their homelands. Some societies did remain isolated, probably none more than the remote islands of the Pacific, such as Hawai'i, Easter Island, and New Zealand.

East Asia was a key element in both the empires created by nomadic horsemen and the South Asian maritime trading networks. As discussed in Chapter 13, before East Asia had to cope with the rise of the Mongols, it experienced one of its most prosperous periods, during which China, Korea, and Japan became more distinct culturally. China's economy boomed during the Song Dynasty, and the scholar-official class, defined through the civil service examination, came more and more to dominate culture. In Korea and Japan, by contrast, aristocrats and military men gained ascendancy. Although China, Korea, and Japan all drew on both Confucian and Buddhist teachings, they ended up with elites as distinct as the Chinese scholar-official, the Korean aristocrat, and the Japanese samurai.

- **For a list of suggested readings for this chapter, visit** *bedfordstmartins.com/mckayworldunderstanding*.
- **For primary sources from this period, see** *Sources of World Societies*, Second Edition.
- **For Web sites, images, and documents related to topics in this chapter, see Make History at** *bedfordstmartins.com/mckayworldunderstanding*.

Chapter 12 **Study Guide**

To do these exercises online, go to bedfordstmartins.com/mckayworldunderstanding.

Step 1

GETTING STARTED

Below are basic terms about this period in global history. Can you identify each term below and explain why it matters?

TERMS	WHO (OR WHAT) AND WHEN	WHY IT MATTERS
nomads, p. 292		
steppe, p. 292		
yurts, p. 294		
Chinggis Khan, p. 298		
khanates, p. 299		
tax-farming, p. 302		
protected people, p. 307		
jati, p. 309		
sati, p. 311		
Sanskrit, p. 312		
Srivijaya, p. 314		

Step 2

MOVING BEYOND THE BASICS

The exercise below requires a more advanced understanding of the chapter material. Examine the connections Central Asian nomads helped forge among the civilizations of Eurasia by filling in the chart below with descriptions of the impact of nomadic invaders on religion, government, and commerce in China and India. When you are finished, consider the following questions: What role did nomadic peoples play in stimulating cultural and commercial exchange in China and India? How did nomadic peoples use local governmental structures and political elites to facilitate their rule of conquered territories? How were nomadic peoples themselves changed by their contact with the settled peoples?

	RELIGION	GOVERNMENT	COMMERCE
Nomadic influences in China			
Nomadic influences in India			

Step 3 PUTTING IT ALL TOGETHER

Now that you've reviewed key elements of the chapter, take a step back and try to see the big picture. Remember to use specific examples from the chapter in your answers.

CENTRAL ASIAN NOMADS

- What military advantages explain the ability of Central Asian nomads to defeat the large armies of settled peoples?
- In what ways did nomadic and settled peoples cooperate in Eurasia? Under what circumstances did cooperation turn into conflict?

THE MONGOLS

- What light does the rise of Chinggis Khan to power shed on the nature of Mongol politics and society?
- How did Mongol military and political activities accelerate regional exchange? Who gained and who lost as a result of Mongol activities?

INDIA AND SOUTHEAST ASIA

- How did the arrival of Islamic conquerors alter the Indian religious landscape?

- How and why did Indian culture spread in Southeast Asia? How did the relationship between India and Southeast Asia differ from the relationship between China and its neighbors?

LOOKING BACK, LOOKING AHEAD

- How had the settled states of Eurasia responded to the threat posed by nomadic peoples prior to the rise of the Turks and the Mongols? Why did the Turks and the Mongols prove more dangerous than other nomadic confederations?
- How did the Mongols contribute to the process of global integration, a process that accelerated in the centuries after their decline?

In Your Own Words Imagine that you must explain Chapter 12 to someone who hasn't read it. What would be the most important points to include and why?

13

States and Cultures in East Asia

800–1400

During the six centuries between 800 and 1400, East Asia was the most advanced region of the world. For several centuries the Chinese economy had grown spectacularly, and China's methods of production were highly advanced in fields as diverse as rice cultivation, the production of iron and steel, and the printing of books. China's system of government was also advanced for its time. In the Song period the principle that the government should be in the hands of educated scholar-officials, selected through competitive written civil service examinations, became well established. Song China's great wealth and sophisticated government did not give it a military advantage, however, and in this period China had to pay tribute to militarily more powerful northern neighbors, the Khitans, the Jurchens, and finally the Mongols, who conquered all of China in 1279.

First Song Emperor China enjoyed a period of great cultural and economic development under the Song Dynasty, whose founder, Taizu, is depicted in this painting. (The Granger Collection, New York)

During the previous millennium basic elements of Chinese culture had spread beyond China's borders, creating a large cultural sphere centered on the use of Chinese as the language of civilization. Beginning around 800, however, the pendulum shifted toward cultural differentiation in East Asia as Japan, Korea, and China developed in distinctive ways. In both Korea and Japan, court aristocrats were dominant both politically and culturally, and then aristocrats lost out to generals with power in the countryside. By 1200 Japan was dominated by warriors—known as samurai. In both Korea and Japan, Buddhism retained a very strong hold, one of the ties that continued to link the countries of East Asia.

Chapter Preview

- What led to a Chinese economic revolution and what was its impact?
- How did government and society change in the Song and Yuan Dynasties?
- How did Korean society and culture develop under the Koryŏ Dynasty?
- What characterized Japan's Heian Period?
- What were the causes and consequences of military rule in Japan?

What led to a Chinese economic revolution and what was its impact?

Chinese historians traditionally viewed dynasties as following a standard cyclical pattern. Founders were vigorous men able to recruit capable followers to serve as officials and generals. Externally they would extend China's borders; internally they would bring peace. Their taxes would be fair. Over time, however, emperors born in the palace would get used to luxury and lack the founders' strength and wisdom. Families with wealth or political power would find ways to avoid taxes, forcing the government to impose heavier taxes on the poor. As a result, impoverished peasants would flee; the morale of those in the government and armies would decline; and the dynasty would find itself able neither to maintain internal peace nor to defend its borders.

dynastic cycle The theory that Chinese dynasties go through a predictable cycle from early vigor and growth to subsequent decline as administrators become lax and the well-off find ways to avoid paying taxes, cutting state revenues.

Viewed in terms of this theory of the **dynastic cycle**, by 800 the Tang Dynasty (see pages 172–174) was in decline. It had ruled China for nearly two centuries, and its high point was in the past. A massive rebellion had wracked it in the mid-eighth century, and the Uighur Turks and Tibetans were menacing its borders. Many of the centralizing features of the government had been abandoned, with power falling more and more to regional military governors.

Historically, Chinese political theorists always assumed that a strong, centralized government was better than a weak one or than political division, but if anything the Tang toward the end of its dynastic cycle seems to have been both intellectually and economically more

City Life A well-developed system of river and canal transport kept the Song capital well supplied with goods from across China, as shown in this detail from a 17-foot-long hand scroll painted in the twelfth century. (Palace Museum, Beijing)

vibrant than the early Tang had been. Less control from the central government seems to have stimulated trade and economic growth. Between 742 and 1100, China's population doubled, reaching 100 million and making China the largest country in the world at the time.

Chapter Chronology

794–1185	Heian period in Japan
804	Two Japanese Buddhist monks, Saichō and Kūkai, travel to China
935–1392	Koryŏ Dynasty in Korea
960–1279	Song Dynasty in China; emergence of scholar-official class; invention of movable type
995–1027	Fujiwara Michinaga dominant at Heian court
ca. 1000–1010	*The Tale of Genji*
1069	Wang Anshi introduces sweeping political and economic reforms
1119	First reported use of compass
1120s	First government-issued paper money introduced by Song
1126	Song loss of north China to the Jurchens; Song capital relocated to Hangzhou
1130–1200	Zhu Xi, Neo-Confucian philosopher
1185–1333	Kamakura Shogunate in Japan; Zen Buddhism flourishes
1234–1368	Mongols' Yuan Dynasty in China
ca. 1275–1292	Marco Polo travels in China

Agricultural prosperity and denser settlement patterns aided commercialization of the economy. Peasants in Song China no longer merely aimed at self-sufficiency. They had found that producing for the market made possible a better life. Peasants sold their surpluses and used their profits to buy charcoal, tea, oil, and wine. In many places farmers specialized in commercial crops, such as sugar, oranges, cotton, silk, and tea. (See "Global Trade: Tea," page 324.) The need to transport the products of interregional trade stimulated the inland and coastal shipping industries, providing employment for shipbuilders and sailors as well as business opportunities for enterprising families with enough capital to purchase a boat.

As marketing increased, demand for money grew enormously, leading eventually to the creation of the world's first paper money. To avoid the weight and bulk of coins for large transactions, local merchants in late Tang times started trading receipts from deposit shops where they had left money or goods. The early Song authorities awarded a small set of these shops a monopoly on the issuing of these certificates of deposit, and in the 1120s the government took over the system, producing the world's first government-issued paper money.

With the intensification of trade, merchants became progressively more specialized and organized. They set up partnerships and joint stock companies, with a separation of owners (shareholders) and managers. In the large cities merchants were organized into guilds according to the type of product sold, and they arranged sales from wholesalers to shop owners and periodically set prices. When government officials wanted to requisition supplies or assess taxes, they dealt with the guild heads.

Foreign trade also flourished in the Song period. In 1225 the superintendent of customs at the coastal city of Quanzhou wrote an account of the foreign places Chinese merchants visited. It includes sketches of major trading cities from Srivijaya and Malabar in Southeast Asia to Cairo and Baghdad in the Middle East. In this period Chinese ships began to displace Indian and Arab merchants in the South Seas. Ship design was improved in several ways. Watertight bulkheads improved buoyancy and protected cargo. Stern-mounted rudders improved steering. Some of the ships were powered by both oars and sails and were large enough to hold several hundred men.

Also important to oceangoing travel was the perfection of the **compass**. The way a magnetic needle would point north had been known for some time, but in Song times the needle was reduced in size and attached to a fixed stem (rather than floated in water). In some cases it was put in a small protective case with a glass top, making it suitable for sea travel. The first reports of a compass used in this way date to 1119.

compass A tool developed in Song times to aid in navigation at sea; it consisted of a magnetic needle that would point north that was placed in a small protective case.

The Song also witnessed many advances in industrial techniques. Heavy industry, especially iron, grew astoundingly. With advances in metallurgy, iron production reached around 125,000 tons per year in 1078, a sixfold increase over the output in 800. Much of the iron was put to military purposes. Mass-production methods were used to make iron armor in small, medium, and large sizes. High-quality steel for swords was made through high-temperature metallurgy. The needs of the army also brought Chinese

GLOBAL TRADE

Tea

Tea is made from the young leaves and leaf buds of *Camellia sinensis*, a plant native to the hills of southwest China. As an item of trade, tea has a very long history. Already by Han times (206 B.C.E.–220 C.E.) tea was being grown and drunk in southwest China, and for several centuries thereafter it was looked on as a local product of the region with useful pharmacologic properties, such as countering the effects of wine. By Tang times (608–907) it was being widely cultivated in the Yangzi River Valley and was a major item of interregional trade.

The most intensive time for tea production was the harvest season, since young leaves were of much more value than mature ones. Mobilized for about a month each year, women would come out to help pick the tea. Not only were Chinese tea merchants among the wealthiest merchants, but from the late eighth century on, taxes on tea became a major source of government revenue.

Tea circulated in several forms, loose and compressed (brick), powder and leaf. The cost of tea varied both by form and by region of origin. In Song times (960–1279), the cheapest tea could cost as little as 18 cash per catty, the most expensive 275. In Kaifeng in the 1070s the most popular type was loose tea powdered at water mills. The tea exported from Sichuan to Tibet, however, was formed into solid bricks for ease of transport.

The Song Dynasty established a government monopoly on tea. Only those who purchased government licenses could legally trade in tea. The dynasty also used its control of tea to ensure a supply of horses, needed for military purposes. The government could do this because the countries on its borders that produced the best horses — Tibet, Central Asia, Mongolia, and so on — were not suitable for growing tea. Thus the Song government insisted on horses for tea.

Tea reached Korea and Japan as a part of Buddhist culture. Buddhist monks drank it to help them stay awake during long hours of recitation or meditation. Tea was first introduced to Japan by a Buddhist priest around 804, but tea consumption did not become widespread until the twelfth century, when Zen monasteries popularized its use. By the fourteenth century tea imported from China was still prized, but the Japanese had begun to appreciate the distinctive flavors of teas from different regions of Japan. With the development of the tea ceremony, tea drinking became an art in Japan, with much attention to the selection and handling of tea utensils. In both Japan and Korea, offerings of tea became a regular part of offerings to ancestors, as they were in China.

Tea did not become important in Europe until the seventeenth century. Tea first reached Russia in 1618, when a Chinese embassy presented some to the tsar. Under agreements between the Chinese and Russian governments, camel trains would arrive in China laden with furs and would return carrying tea, taking about a year for the round trip. By 1700 Russia was receiving more than 600 camel loads of tea annually. By 1800 it was receiving more than 6,000 loads, amounting to more than 3.5 million pounds. Tea reached western Europe in the sixteenth century, both via Arabs and via Jesuit priests traveling on Portuguese ships.

In Britain, where tea drinking would become a national institution, tea was first drunk in coffeehouses. By the end of the seventeenth century tea made up more than 90 percent of China's exports to England. In the eighteenth century tea drinking spread to homes and tea gardens. Queen Anne (r. 1702–1714) was credited with starting the custom of drinking tea instead of ale for breakfast. Afternoon tea became a central feature of British social life in the nineteenth century.

Already by the end of the eighteenth century Britain imported so much tea from China that it worried about the

engineers to experiment with the use of gunpowder. In the twelfth-century wars against the Jurchens, those defending a besieged city used gunpowder to propel projectiles at the enemy.

The quickening of the economy fueled the growth of cities. Dozens of cities had fifty thousand or more residents, and quite a few had more than a hundred thousand — very large populations compared to other places in the world at the time. Both the capitals, Kaifeng (kigh-fuhng) and Hangzhou (hahng-joh), are estimated to have had in the vicinity of a million residents.

The medieval economic revolution shifted the economic center of China south to the Yangzi River drainage area. This area had many advantages over the north China plain. Rice, which grew in the south, provides more calories per unit of land and therefore allows denser settlement. The milder temperatures often allowed two crops to be grown on

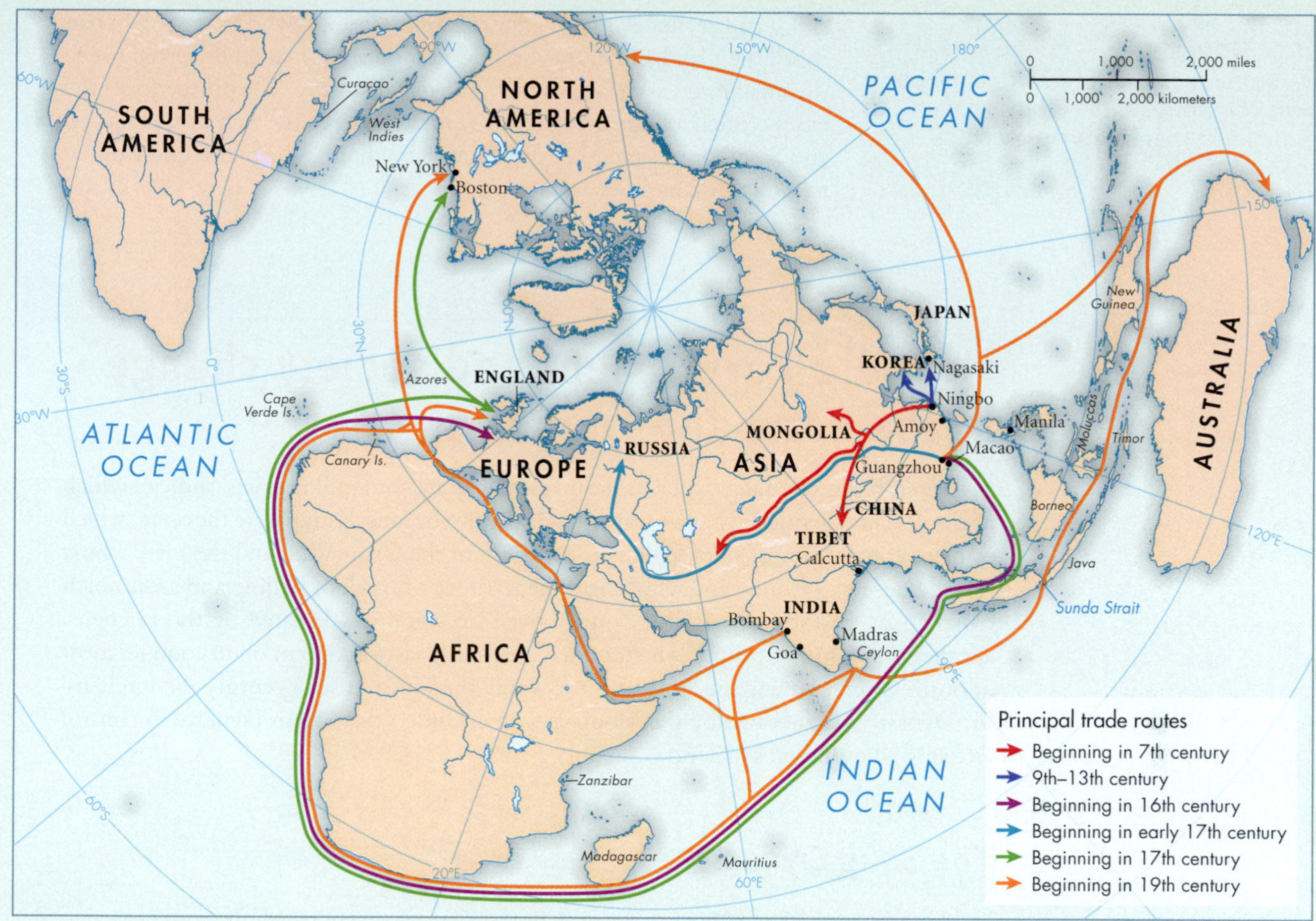

Map 13.1 The Tea Trade

outflow of silver to pay for it. Efforts to balance trade with China involved promoting the sale of Indian opium to China and efforts to grow tea in British colonies. Using tea seeds collected in China and a tea plant indigenous to India's Assam province, both India and Sri Lanka eventually grew tea successfully. By the end of the nineteenth century huge tea plantations had been established in India, and India surpassed China as an exporter of tea.

The spread of the popularity of drinking tea also stimulated the desire for fine cups to drink it from. Importation of Chinese ceramics, therefore, often accompanied adoption of China's tea customs.

the same plot of land, first a summer and then a winter crop. The abundance of rivers and streams facilitated shipping, which reduced the cost of transportation and thus made regional specialization economically more feasible. In the first half of the Song Dynasty, the capital was still at Kaifeng in the north, close to the Grand Canal (see page 172), which linked the capital to the rich south.

Ordinary people benefited from the Song economic revolution in many ways. There were more opportunities for the sons of farmers to leave agriculture and find work in cities. Those who stayed in agriculture had a better chance to improve their situations by taking up sideline production of wine, charcoal, paper, or textiles. Energetic farmers who grew cash crops such as sugar, tea, mulberry leaves (for silk), and cotton (recently introduced from India) could grow rich. Greater interregional trade led to the availability of more goods at the rural markets held every five or ten days.

Quick Review
How did rural prosperity and population growth contribute to the intensification of trade and urbanization in medieval China?

Of course, not everyone grew rich. Poor farmers who fell into debt had to sell their land, and if they still owed money they could be forced to sell their daughters as maids, concubines, or prostitutes. The prosperity of the cities created a huge demand for women to serve the rich in these ways, and Song sources mention that criminals would kidnap girls and women to sell in distant cities at huge profits.

How did government and society change in the Song and Yuan Dynasties?

In the tenth century Tang China broke up into separate contending states, some of which had non-Chinese rulers. The two states that proved to be long-lasting were the Song, which came to control almost all of China proper south of the Great Wall, and the Liao, whose ruling house was Khitan and which held the territory of modern Beijing and areas north (Map 13.2). In the early twelfth century the Liao state was defeated by the Jurchens, another non-Chinese people, who founded the Jin Dynasty and went on to conquer most of north China, leaving the Song to control only the south. After a century the Jurchens' Jin Dynasty was defeated by the Mongols who extended their Yuan Dynasty to control virtually all of China by 1276.

The Song Dynasty

The founder of the Song Dynasty, Taizu (r. 960–976), was a general whose troops elevated him to emperor (somewhat reminiscent of Roman practice). Taizu worked to make sure that such an act could not happen in the future by placing the armies under central government control. To curb the power of his generals, he retired or rotated them and assigned civil officials to supervise them. In time these civil bureaucrats came to dominate every aspect of Song government and society. The civil service examination system established during the Sui Dynasty (see page 172) was greatly expanded to provide the dynasty with a constant flow of men trained in the Confucian classics.

Curbing the generals' power ended warlordism but did not solve the military problem of defending against the nomadic Khitans's Liao Dynasty to the north. After several attempts to push the Liao back beyond the Great Wall, the Song agreed to make huge annual payments of gold and silk to the Khitans, in a sense paying them not to invade. Even so, the Song rulers had to maintain a standing army of more than a million men. By the middle of the eleventh century military expenses consumed half the government's revenues. Song had the industrial base to produce swords, armor, and arrowheads in huge quantities, but they had difficulty maintaining enough horses and well-trained horsemen.

In the early twelfth century the military situation rapidly worsened when the Khitan state was destroyed by another tribal confederation led by the Jurchens. Although the Song allied with the Jurchens, the Jurchens quickly realized how easy it would be to defeat the Song. When they marched into the Song capital in 1126, they captured the emperor, and he died eight years later in captivity. Song forces rallied around one of his sons who escaped capture, and this prince reestablished a Song court in the south at Hangzhou (see Map 13.2). This Southern Song Dynasty controlled only about two-thirds of the former Song territories, but the social, cultural, and intellectual life there remained vibrant until the Song fell to the Mongols in 1279.

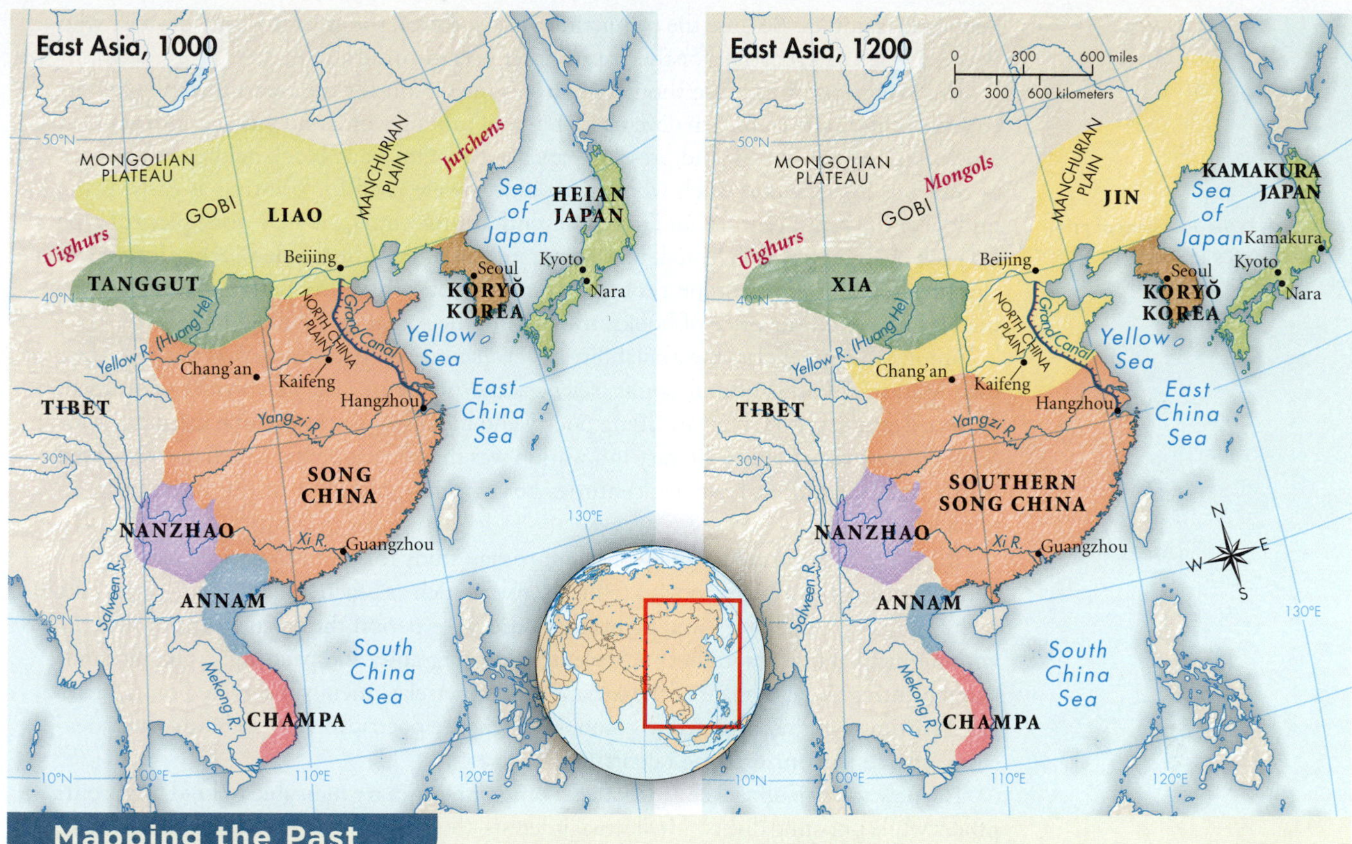

Mapping the Past

Map 13.2 East Asia in 1000 and 1200

The Song Empire did not extend as far as its predecessor, the Tang, and faced powerful rivals to the north — the Liao Dynasty of the Khitans and the Xia Dynasty of the Tanguts. Koryŏ Korea maintained regular contact with Song China, but Japan, by the late Heian period, was no longer deeply involved with the mainland. By 1200 military families dominated both Korea and Japan, but the borders were little changed. On the mainland, the Liao Dynasty had been overthrown by the Jurchens' Jin Dynasty, which also seized the northern third of the Song Empire. Because the Song relocated its capital to Hangzhou in the south, this period is called the Southern Song period.

ANALYZING THE MAP What are the countries of East Asia in 1000? What are the major differences in 1200?

CONNECTIONS What connections do you see between the length of their northern borders and the histories of China, Korea, and Japan?

The Scholar-Officials and Neo-Confucianism

The Song period saw the full flowering of one of the most distinctive features of Chinese civilization, the **scholar-official class** certified through highly competitive civil service examinations. This elite was both broader and better educated than the elites of earlier periods in Chinese history. Once the **examination system** was fully developed, aristocratic habits and prejudices largely disappeared. Ancestry did not matter as much when office depended more on study habits than on connections.

The examination system came to carry such prestige that the number of scholars entering each competition escalated rapidly, from fewer than 30,000 early in the eleventh century, to nearly 80,000 by the end of that century, to about 400,000 by the dynasty's end. To prepare for the examinations, men had to memorize the classics, master specific forms of composition, including poetry, and be ready to discuss policy issues, citing appropriate

scholar-official class Chinese educated elite that included both scholars and officials. The officials had usually gained office by passing the highly competitive civil service examination. Scholars without office had often studied for the examinations but failed repeatedly.

examination system A system of selecting officials based on competitive written examinations.

historical examples. Because the competition was so fierce, the great majority of those who devoted years to preparing for the exams never became officials.

The invention of printing should be given some credit for the trend toward a better-educated elite. Tang craftsmen developed the art of carving words and pictures into wooden blocks, inking the blocks, and pressing paper onto them. Each block held an entire page of text and illustrations. Such whole-page blocks were used for printing as early as the middle of the ninth century, and in the eleventh century **movable type** (one piece of type for each character) was invented, but it was rarely used because whole-block printing was cheaper. In China as in Europe a couple of centuries later, the introduction of printing dramatically lowered the price of books, thus aiding the spread of literacy.

movable type A system of printing in which one piece of type is used for each unique character.

Among the upper class the availability of cheaper books enabled scholars to amass their own libraries. Works on philosophy, science, and medicine also were avidly consumed, as were Buddhist texts. Han and Tang poetry and historical works became the models for Song writers. One popular literary innovation was the encyclopedia, which first appeared in the Song period, at least five centuries before the publication of the first European encyclopedia.

The life of the educated man involved more than study for the civil service examinations and service in office. Many took to refined pursuits such as practicing the arts—especially poetry writing, calligraphy, and painting. In the Song period the engagement of the elite with the arts led to extraordinary achievement in calligraphy and painting, especially landscape painting. A large share of the social life of upper-class men was centered on these refined pastimes, as they gathered to compose or criticize poetry, to view each other's art treasures, and to patronize young talents.

The new scholar-official elite produced some extraordinary men able to hold high court offices while pursuing diverse intellectual interests. (See "Individuals in Society: Shen Gua," page 330.) Ouyang Xiu spared time in his busy official career to write love songs and histories. Sima Guang, besides serving as prime minister, wrote a narrative history of China from the Warring States Period (403–221 B.C.E.) to the founding of the Song Dynasty. Su Shi wrote more than twenty-seven hundred poems and eight hundred letters while active in opposition politics. He was also an esteemed painter, calligrapher, and theorist of the arts. Su Song, another high official, constructed an eighty-foot-tall mechanical clock. As in Renaissance Europe a couple of centuries later (discussed in Chapter 15), gifted men made advances in a wide range of fields.

These highly educated men accepted the Confucian responsibility to aid the ruler in the governing of the country. In this period, however, this commitment tended to embroil them in unpleasant factional politics. In 1069 the chancellor Wang Anshi proposed a series of sweeping reforms designed to raise revenues and help small farmers. Many well-respected scholars and officials thought that Wang's policies would do more harm than good and resisted enforcing them. Animosities grew as critics were assigned offices far from the capital. Later, when they returned to power, they retaliated against those who had pushed them out, escalating the conflict.

Besides politics, scholars also debated issues in ethics and metaphysics. For several centuries Buddhism had been more vital than Confucianism. Beginning in the late Tang period Confucian teachers began claiming that the teachings of the Confucian sages contained all the wisdom one needed and that a true Confucian would reject Buddhist teachings. During the eleventh century many Confucian teachers urged students to set their sights not on exam success but on the higher goals of attaining the wisdom of the sages.

Neo-Confucianism, as this movement is generally termed, was more fully developed in the twelfth century by the immensely learned Zhu Xi (joo shee) (1130–1200). Besides serving in office, he wrote, compiled, or edited almost a hundred books; corresponded with dozens of other scholars; and still regularly taught groups of disciples, many of whom stayed with him for years at a time. Although he was treated as a political threat during his lifetime, within decades of his death his writings came to be considered orthodox, and

Neo-Confucianism The revival of Confucian thinking that began in the eleventh century, characterized by the goal of attaining the wisdom of the sages, not exam success.

Picturing the Past

On a Mountain Path in Spring

With spare, sketchy strokes, the court painter Ma Yuan (ca. 1190–1225) depicts a scholar on an outing accompanied by his boy servant carrying a lute. The scholar gazes into the mist, his eyes attracted by a bird in flight. The poetic couplet was inscribed by Emperor Ningzong (r. 1194–1124), at whose court Ma Yuan served. It reads: "Brushed by his sleeves, wild flowers dance in the wind. / Fleeing from him, hidden birds cut short their songs." (National Palace Museum, Taipei, Taiwan © Cultural Relics Press)

ANALYZING THE IMAGE Find the key elements in this picture: the scholar, the servant boy, the bird, the willow tree. Are these elements skillfully conveyed? Are there other elements in the painting that you find hard to read?

CONNECTIONS What do you think is the reason for writing a poetic couplet on this painting? Does it enhance the experience of viewing the painting or detract from it?

in subsequent centuries candidates for the examinations had to be familiar with his commentaries on the classics.

Women's Lives in Song Times

Families who could afford it usually tried to keep their wives and daughters within the walls of the house, rather than let them work in the fields or in shops or inns. At home there was plenty for them to do. Not only was there the work of tending children and preparing meals, but spinning, weaving, and sewing were considered women's work and took a great deal of time. Families that raised silkworms also needed women to do much of the work of coddling the worms and getting them to spin their cocoons. Within the home women generally had considerable say and took active interest in issues such as the selection of marriage partners for their children.

INDIVIDUALS IN SOCIETY

Shen Gua

IN THE ELEVENTH CENTURY IT WAS NOT RARE for Chinese men of letters to have broad interests, but few could compare to Shen Gua (1031–1095), a man who tried his hand at everything from mathematics, geography, economics, engineering, medicine, divination, and archaeology to military strategy and diplomacy.

In his youth Shen Gua traveled widely with his father, who served as a provincial official, which added to his knowledge of geography. In 1063 he passed the civil service examinations, and in 1066 he received a post in the capital, just before Wang Anshi's rise to power. He generally sided with Wang in the political disputes of the day. He eventually held high astronomical, ritual, and financial posts and became involved in waterworks and the construction of defense walls. He was sent as an envoy to the Khitans in 1075 to try to settle a boundary dispute. When a military campaign that he advised failed in 1082, he was demoted and later retired to write.

It is from his book of notes that we know the breadth of his interests. In one note Shen describes how, on assignment to inspect the frontier, he made a relief map of wood and glue-soaked sawdust to show the mountains, roads, rivers, and passes. The emperor was so impressed when he saw it that he ordered all the border prefectures to make relief maps. Elsewhere Shen describes the use of petroleum and explains how to make movable type from clay. Shen Gua often applied a mathematical approach to issues that his contemporaries did not think of in those terms. He once computed the total number of possible situations on a Go board, and another time he calculated the longest possible military campaign given the limits of human carriers, who had to carry their own food as well as food for the soldiers.

Shen Gua is especially known for his scientific explanations. He explained the deflection of the compass from due south. He identified petrified bamboo and from its existence argued that the region where it was found must have been much warmer and more humid in ancient times. He argued against the theory that tides are caused by the rising and setting of the sun, demonstrating that they correlate with the cycles of the moon. He proposed switching from a lunar calendar to a solar one of 365 days, saying that even though his contemporaries would reject his idea, "surely in the future some will adopt my idea." To convince his readers that the sun and the moon were spherical, not flat, he suggested that they cover a ball with fine powder on one side and then look at it obliquely. The powder was the part of the moon illuminated by the sun, and as the viewer looked at it obliquely, the white part would be crescent shaped, like a waxing moon. Shen Gua, however, did not realize that the sun and moon had entirely different orbits, and he explained why they did not collide by positing that both were composed of *qi* (vital energy) and had form but not substance.

Shen Gua also wrote on medicine and criticized his contemporaries for paying more attention to old treatises than to clinical experience. Yet he, too, was sometimes stronger on theory than on observation. In one note he argued that longevity pills could be made from cinnabar. He reasoned that if cinnabar could be transformed in one direction, it ought to be susceptible to transformation in the opposite direction as well. Therefore, since melted cinnabar causes death, solid cinnabar should prevent death.

QUESTIONS FOR ANALYSIS

1. How did Shen Gua's travels add to his curiosity about the material world?
2. In what ways could Shen Gua have used his scientific interests in his work as a government official?
3. How does Shen Gua's understanding of the natural world compare to that of the early Greeks? (See Chapter 5, pages 114–117.)

Shen Gua played Go with white and black markers on a grid-like board like this one. (Library of Congress, LC-USZC4-8471/8472)

Woman Attendant The Song emperors were patrons of a still-extant temple in northern China that enshrined a statue of the "holy mother," the mother of the founder of the ancient Zhou Dynasty. The forty-two maids who attend her, one of whom is shown here, seem to have been modeled on the palace ladies who attended Song emperors. (© Cultural Relics Press)

Women tended to marry between the ages of sixteen and twenty. Their husbands were, on average, a couple of years older than they were. Marriages were arranged by their parents. Before a wedding took place, written agreements were exchanged, listing the prospective bride's and groom's birth dates, parents, and grandparents; the gifts that would be exchanged; and the dowry the bride would bring. The goal was to match families of approximately equal status, but a young man who had just passed the civil service exams would be considered a good prospect even if his family had little wealth.

A few days before the wedding the bride's family sent her dowry to the groom's family. On the day of the wedding, the groom and some of his friends and relatives went to the bride's home to get her. She would be elaborately dressed and would tearfully bid farewell to everyone in her family. She was carried to her new home in a fancy sedan chair to the sound of music. Meanwhile the groom's family's friends and relatives had gathered at his home, ready to greet the bridal party. The bride would kneel and bow to her new parents-in-law and later also to the tablets representing her husband's ancestors. Later they were shown to their new bedroom, where the bride's dowry had already been placed, and people tossed beans or rice on the bed, symbolizing the desired fertility. After teasing them, the guests left them alone and went out to the courtyard for a wedding feast.

The young bride's first priority was to try to win over her mother-in-law, since everyone knew that mothers-in-law were hard to please. One way to do this was to quickly bear a son for the family. Within the patrilineal system, a woman fully secured her position in the family by becoming the mother of one of the men. Every community had older women skilled in midwifery who were called to help when a woman went into labor. If the family was well-to-do, arrangements might be made for a wet nurse to help her take care of the newborn.

Women frequently had four, five, or six children, but likely one or more would die in infancy. If a son reached adulthood and married before the woman herself was widowed, she would be considered fortunate, for she would have always had an adult man who could take care of business for her—first her husband, then her grown son. But in the days when infectious diseases took many people in their twenties and thirties, it was not uncommon for a woman to be widowed while in her twenties, when her children were still very young.

A woman with a healthy and prosperous husband faced another challenge in middle age: her husband could bring home one or more **concubines**. Wives outranked concubines and could give them orders in the house, but a concubine had her own ways of getting back through her hold on the husband. The children born to a concubine were considered just as much children of the family as the wife's children, and if the wife had had only daughters and the concubine had a son, the wife would find herself dependent on the concubine's son in her old age.

concubine A woman contracted to a man as a secondary spouse; although subordinate to the wife, her sons were considered legitimate heirs.

As a woman's children grew up, she would start thinking of suitable marriage partners. A woman's life became easier once she had a daughter-in-law to do the cooking and cleaning. Many found more time for religious devotions at this stage of their lives. Their sons, still living with them, could be expected to look after them and do their best to make their late years comfortable.

Neo-Confucianism is sometimes blamed for a decline in the status of women in Song times, largely because one of the best known of the Neo-Confucian teachers, Cheng Yi, once told a follower that it would be better for a widow to die of starvation than to lose her virtue by remarrying. In later centuries this saying was often quoted to justify pressuring widows, even very young ones, to stay with their husbands' families and not remarry. In Song times, however, widows frequently remarried.

foot binding The practice of binding the feet of girls with long strips of cloth to keep them from growing large.

It is true that **foot binding** began during the Song Dynasty, but it was not recommended by Neo-Confucian teachers; rather it was associated with the pleasure quarters and with women's efforts to beautify themselves. Foot binding spread gradually during Song times but was probably still largely an elite practice. In later centuries it became extremely common in north and central China, eventually spreading to all classes. Women with bound feet were less mobile than women with natural feet, but only those who could afford servants bound their feet so tightly that walking was difficult.

China Under Mongol Rule

As discussed in Chapter 12, the Mongols conquered China in stages, gaining much of north China by 1215 and all of it by 1234, but not taking the south till the 1270s. The north suffered the most devastation. The non-Chinese rulers in the north, the Jin Dynasty of the Jurchen thought they had the strongest army known to history, and they certainly had one of the largest. Yet Mongol tactics frustrated them. The Mongols would take a city, plunder it, and then withdraw, letting the Jin take it back and deal with the resulting food shortages and destruction. Under these circumstances, Jurchen power rapidly collapsed.

Not until Khubilai was Great Khan was the Song Dynasty defeated and south China brought under the control of the Mongol's Yuan Dynasty. Non-Chinese rulers had gained control of north China several times in Chinese history, but none of them had been able to secure control of the region south of the Yangzi River, which required a navy. By the 1260s Khubilai had put Chinese shipbuilders to work building a fleet, crucial to his victory over the Song (see page 301).

Blue-and-White Jars of the Yuan Period Chinese ceramics had long been in demand outside of China, and an innovation of the Mongol period—decorating white porcelain with underglaze designs in blue—proved especially popular. Persia imported large quantities of Chinese blue-and-white ceramics, and Korean, Japanese, and Vietnamese potters took up versions of the style themselves. (© The Trustees of the British Museum/Art Resource NY)

Life in China under the Mongols was much like life in China under earlier alien rulers. Some were deprived of their land, business, or freedom and suffered real hardship. Yet people still spoke Chinese, followed Chinese customs in financial dealings, participated in traditional religious practices, and turned to local landowners when in need. Teachers still taught students the classics, scholars continued to write books, and books continued to be printed.

The Mongols, like other foreign rulers before them, did not see anything particularly desirable in the social mobility of Chinese society. Preferring stability, they assigned people hereditary occupations, occupations that came with obligations to the state. Besides these occupational categories, the Mongols classified the population into four grades, with the Mongols occupying the top grade. Next came various non-Chinese, such as the Uighurs and Persians. Below them were Chinese former subjects of the Jurchen, called the Han. At the bottom were the former subjects of the Song, called southerners.

The reason for codifying ethnic differences this way was to preserve the Mongols' privileges as conquerors. Chinese were not allowed to take Mongol names, and great efforts were made to keep them from passing as Mongols or marrying Mongols. To keep Chinese from rebelling, they were forbidden to own weapons or congregate in public.

As the Mongols captured Chinese territory, they recruited Chinese into their armies and government. Although some refused to serve the Mongols, others argued that the Chinese would fare better if Chinese were the administrators and could shield Chinese society from the most brutal effects of Mongol rule. A few Confucian scholars devoted themselves to the task of patiently teaching Mongol rulers the principles of Confucian government.

Nevertheless, government service, which had long been central to the identity and income of the educated elite in China, was not as widely available under the Mongols. The Mongols reinstituted the civil service examinations in 1315, but filled only about 2 percent of the positions in the bureaucracy through it and reserved half of those places for Mongols.

The scholar-official elite without government employment turned to alternative ways to support themselves. Those who did not have land to live off of found work as physicians, teachers, priests, or writers. Many took leadership roles at the local level, such as founding academies for Confucian learning or promoting local charitable ventures. Through such activities, scholars out of office could assert the importance of civil over military values and see themselves as trustees of the Confucian tradition.

Since the Mongols wanted to extract wealth from China, they had every incentive to develop the economy. They encouraged trade both within China and beyond its borders and tried to keep paper money in circulation. They repaired the Grand Canal, which had been ruined during their initial conquest of north China. Chinese industries with strong foreign markets, such as porcelain, thrived. Nevertheless, the economic expansion of late Tang and Song times did not continue under the alien rule of the Jurchen and Mongols. The combination of war, disease, and a shrinking economy led to a population decline, probably of tens of millions.

The Mongols' Yuan Dynasty began a rapid decline in the 1330s as disease, rebellions, and poor leadership led to disorder throughout the country. When a Chinese strongman succeeded in consolidating the south, the Mongol rulers retreated to Mongolia before he could take Beijing. By 1368 the Yuan Dynasty had given way to a new Chinese-led dynasty: the Ming.

Quick Review
How did Chinese life under the Mongols differ from Chinese life under the Song?

How did Korean society and culture develop under the Koryŏ Dynasty?

During the Silla period Korea was strongly tied to Tang China and avidly copied China's model (see pages 176–177). This changed along with much else in North Asia between 800 and 1400. In this period Korea lived more in the shadows of the powerful nomad states of the Khitans, Jurchens, and Mongols than of the Chinese.

The Silla Dynasty began to decline after the king was killed in a revolt in 780. For the next 155 years, rebellions and coups d'état followed one after the other, as different groups of nobles placed their candidates on the throne and killed as many of their opponents as they could. As conditions deteriorated, serfs absconded in large numbers, and independent merchants and seamen of humble origins came to dominate the three-way trade between China, Korea, and Japan.

The dynasty that emerged from this confusion was called Koryŏ (KAW-ree-oh) (935–1392). During this time Korea developed more independently of the Chinese model than it had in Silla times, just as contemporary Japan was doing (see the next section). This was not because the Chinese model was rejected; the Koryŏ capital was laid out on the Chinese model, and the government was closely patterned on the Tang system. But despite Chinese influence, Korean society remained deeply aristocratic.

The Koryŏ Dynasty, 935–1392

The founder of the dynasty, Wang Kon (877–943), was a man of relatively obscure maritime background, and he needed the support of the old aristocracy to maintain control. His successors introduced civil service examinations on the Chinese model, as well as examinations for Buddhist clergy, but because the aristocrats were the best educated and the government schools admitted only the sons of aristocrats, this system served primarily to solidify their control. Like the Heian aristocrats in Japan (see pages 336–338), the Koryŏ aristocrats wanted to stay in the capital and only reluctantly accepted posts in the provinces.

At the other end of the social scale, the number of people in the serf-slave stratum seems to have increased. This lowborn stratum included not only privately held slaves but also large numbers of government slaves as well as government workers in mines, porcelain factories, and other government industries. Sometimes entire villages or groups of villages were considered lowborn. There were occasional slave revolts, and some manumitted (freed) slaves did rise in status, but prejudice against anyone with slave ancestors was strong. In China and Japan, by contrast, slavery was a much more minor element in the social landscape.

The commercial economy declined in Korea during this period, showing that it was not closely linked to China's then booming economy. Except for the capital, there were no cities of commercial importance, and in the countryside the use of money declined. One industry that did flourish was ceramics. Connoisseurs have long appreciated the elegance of the pale green Koryŏ celadon pottery, decorated with designs executed in inlaid white or gray clay.

Buddhism remained strong throughout Korea, and monasteries became major centers of art and learning. As in Song China and Kamakura Japan, Chan (Zen) and Tiantai (Tendai) were the leading Buddhist teachings (see pages 174, 338). The founder of the Koryŏ Dynasty attributed the dynasty's success to the Buddha's protection, and he and his successors were ardent patrons of the church. As in medieval Europe, aristocrats who entered the church occupied the major abbacies. Monasteries played the same roles as they did in China and Japan, such as engaging in money lending and charitable works. As in Japan (but not China), some monasteries accumulated military power.

The Koryŏ Dynasty was preserved in name long after the ruling family had lost most of its power. In 1170 the palace guards massacred the civil officials at court and placed a new king on the throne. The coup leaders scrapped the privileges that had kept the aristocrats in power and appointed themselves to the top posts. After incessant infighting among the

Wooden Blocks for Printing The Heainsa Buddhist Temple in Korea has preserved the 80,000 woodblocks used to print the huge Buddhist canon in the thirteenth century. The monk shown here is replacing a block. All the blocks are carved on both sides and stabilized by wooden frames that have kept them from warping. (© OUR PLACE THE WORLD HERITAGE COLLECTION, www.ourplaceworldheritage.com)

generals and a series of coups, in 1196 the general Ch'oe Ch'ung-hon took control. The domination of Korea by the Ch'oe family was much like the contemporaneous situation in Japan, where warrior bands were seizing power. Moreover, because the Ch'oe were content to dominate the government while leaving the Koryŏ king on the throne, they had much in common with the Japanese shoguns, who followed a similar strategy.

Although Korea adopted many ideas from China, it could not so easily adopt the Chinese assumption that it was the largest, most powerful, and most advanced society in the world. Korea, from early times, recognized China as being in many ways senior to it, but when strong non-Chinese states emerged to its north in Manchuria, Korea was ready to accommodate them as well. Koryŏ's first neighbor to the north was the Khitan state of Liao, which in 1010 invaded and sacked the capital. To avoid destruction, Koryŏ acceded to vassal status, but Liao invaded again in 1018. This time Koryŏ was able to repel the nomadic Khitans. Afterward a defensive wall was built across the Korean peninsula south of the Yalu River. When the Jurchens and their Jin Dynasty supplanted the Khitans's Liao Dynasty, Koryŏ agreed to send them tribute as well.

As mentioned in Chapter 12, Korea was conquered by the Mongols, and the figurehead Koryŏ kings were moved to Beijing. This was a time of hardship for the Korean people. In the year 1254 alone, the Mongols enslaved two hundred thousand Koreans and took them away. Ordinary people in Korea suffered grievously when their land was used as a launching pad for the huge Mongol invasions of Japan. In this period Korea also suffered from frequent attacks by Japanese pirates, somewhat like the depredations of the Vikings, in Europe a little earlier (see page 348). The Mongol overlords did little to provide protection, and the harried coastal people had little choice but to retreat inland.

When Mongol rule in China fell apart in the mid-fourteenth century, it declined in Korea as well. Chinese rebels opposing the Mongols entered Korea and even briefly captured the capital in 1361. When the Ming Dynasty was established in China in 1368, the

LISTENING TO THE PAST

The Pillow Book of Sei Shonagon

Beginning in the late tenth century Japan produced a series of great women writers. At the time women were much freer than men to write in vernacular Japanese, giving them a large advantage. Lady Murasaki, author of the novel The Tale of Genji, *is the most famous of the women writers of the period, but her contemporary Sei Shonagon is equally noteworthy. Sei Shonagon served as a lady in waiting to Empress Sadako during the last decade of the tenth century (990–1000). Her only known work is* The Pillow Book, *a collection of notes, character sketches, anecdotes, descriptions of nature, and eccentric lists such as boring things, awkward things, hateful things, and things that have lost their power.*

The Pillow Book *portrays the lovemaking/marriage system among the aristocracy more or less as it is depicted in* The Tale of Genji. *Marriages were arranged for family interests, and a man could have more than one wife. Wives and their children commonly stayed in their own homes, where their husbands and fathers would visit them. But once a man had an heir by his wife, there was nothing to prevent him from establishing relations with other women. Some relationships were long-term, but many were brief, and men often had several lovers at the same time. Some women became known for their amorous conquests, others as abandoned women whose husbands ignored them. The following passage from* The Pillow Book *looks on this lovemaking system with amused detachment.*

“It is so stiflingly hot in the Seventh Month that even at night one keeps all the doors and lattices open. At such times it is delightful to wake up when the moon is shining and to look outside. I enjoy it even when there is no moon. But to wake up at dawn and see a pale sliver of a moon in the sky — well, I need hardly say how perfect that is.

I like to see a bright new straw mat that has just been spread out on a well-polished floor. The best place for one's three-foot curtain of state is in the front of the room near the veranda. It is pointless to put it in the rear of the room, as it is most unlikely that anyone will peer in from that direction.

It is dawn and a woman is lying in bed after her lover has taken his leave. She is covered up to her head with a light mauve robe that has a lining of dark violet; the colour of both the outside and the lining is fresh and glossy. The woman, who appears to be asleep, wears an unlined orange robe and a dark crimson skirt of stiff silk whose cords hang loosely by her side, as if they have been left untied. Her thick tresses tumble over each other in cascades, and one can imagine how long her hair must be when it falls freely down her back.

Nearby another woman's lover is making his way home in the misty dawn. He is wearing loose violet trousers, an orange hunting costume, so lightly coloured that one can hardly tell whether it has been dyed or not, a white robe of still silk, and a scarlet robe of glossy, beaten silk. His clothes, which are damp from the mist, hang loosely about him. From the dishevelment of his side locks one can tell how negligently he must have tucked his hair into the black lacquered headdress when he got up. He wants to return and write his next-morning letter before the dew on the morning glories has had time to vanish; but the path seems endless, and to divert himself he hums "the sprouts in the flax fields."

As he walks along, he passes a house with an open lattice. He is on his way to report for official duty, but cannot help stopping to lift up the blind and peep into the room. It amuses him to think that a man has probably been spending the night here and has only recently got up to leave, just as happened to himself. Perhaps that man too had felt the charm of the dew.

Looking around the room, he notices near the woman's pillow an open fan with a magnolia frame and purple paper; and at the foot of her curtain of state he sees some narrow strips of Michinoku paper and

Quick Review
What impact did the Jurchens, Khitans, and Mongols have on Korean society and government?

Koryŏ court was unsure how to respond. In 1388 a general, Yi Song-gye, was sent to oppose a Ming army at the northwest frontier. When he saw the strength of the Ming, he concluded that making an alliance was more sensible than fighting, and he led his troops back to the capital, where in 1392 he usurped the throne, founding the Choson Dynasty.

What characterized Japan's Heian period?

As described in Chapter 7, during the seventh and eighth centuries the Japanese ruling house pursued a vigorous policy of adopting useful ideas, techniques, and policies from the more advanced civilization of China. The rulers built a splendid capital along Chinese lines in Nara and fostered the growth of Buddhism. Monasteries grew so powerful in Nara,

also some other paper of a faded colour, either orange-red or maple.

The woman senses that someone is watching her and, looking up from under her bedclothes, sees a gentleman leaning against the wall by the threshold, a smile on his face. She can tell at once that he is the sort of man with whom she need feel no reserve. All the same, she does not want to enter into any familiar relations with him, and she is annoyed that he should have seen her asleep.

"Well, well, Madam," says the man, leaning forward so that the upper part of his body comes behind her curtains, "what a long nap you're having after your morning adieu! You really are a lie-abed!"

"You call me that, Sir," she replied, "only because you're annoyed at having had to get up before the dew had time to settle."

Their conversation may be commonplace, yet I find there is something delightful about the scene.

Now the gentleman leans further forward and, using his own fan, tries to get hold of the fan by the woman's pillow. Fearing his closeness, she moves further back into her curtain enclosure, her heart pounding. The gentleman picks up the magnolia fan and, while examining it, says in a slightly bitter tone, "How standoffish you are!"

But now it is growing light; there is a sound of people's voices, and it looks as if the sun will soon be up. Only a short while ago this same man was hurrying home to write his next-morning letter before the mists had time to clear. Alas, how easily his intentions have been forgotten!

While all this is afoot, the woman's original lover has been busy with his own next-morning letter, and now, quite unexpectedly, the messenger arrives at her house. The letter is attached to a spray of bush-clover, still damp with dew, and the paper gives off a delicious aroma of incense. Because of the new visitor, however, the woman's servants cannot deliver it to her.

Finally it becomes unseemly for the gentleman to stay any longer. As he goes, he is amused to think that a similar scene may be taking place in the house he left earlier that morning. ”

During the Heian period, noblewomen were fashion-conscious. Wearing numerous layers of clothing gave women the opportunity to choose different designs and colors for their robes. The layers also kept them warm in drafty homes. (The Museum Yamato Bunkakan)

Source: Ivan Morris, trans., *The Pillow Book of Sei Shonagon* (New York: Penguin Books, 1970), pp. 60–62.

QUESTIONS FOR ANALYSIS

1. What sorts of images does Sei Shonagon evoke to convey an impression of a scene?
2. What can you learn from this passage about the material culture of Japan in this period?
3. Why do you think Sei Shonagon was highly esteemed as a writer?

however, that in less than a century the court decided to move away from them and encourage other sects of Buddhism.

The new capital was built about twenty-five miles away at Heian (HAY-ahn; modern Kyoto). Like Nara, Heian was modeled on the Tang capital of Chang'an. For the first century at Heian the government continued to follow Chinese models, but it turned away from them with the decline of the Tang Dynasty in the late ninth century. The last official embassy to China made the trip in 894. During the Heian period (794–1185) Japan witnessed a literary and cultural flowering under the rule of the Fujiwara family.

Fujiwara Rule

Only the first two Heian emperors were much involved in governing. By 860 political management was taken over by a series of regents from the Fujiwara family, who supplied most of the empresses in this period. Fujiwara dominance represented the privatization of political power and a return to clan politics. Political history thus took a very different course in Japan than in China, where, when a dynasty weakened, military strongmen would compete to depose the emperor and found their own dynasties. In Japan for the next thousand years, political contenders sought to manipulate the emperors rather than supplant them.

The Fujiwaras reached the apogee of their glory under Fujiwara Michinaga (r. 995–1027). He dominated the court for more than thirty years as the father of four empresses, the uncle of two emperors, and the grandfather of three emperors. He acquired great landholdings and built fine palaces for himself and his family. After ensuring that his sons could continue to rule, he retired to a Buddhist monastery, all the while continuing to maintain control.

By the end of the eleventh century several emperors who did not have Fujiwara mothers found a device to counter Fujiwara control: they abdicated but continued to exercise power by controlling their young sons on the throne. This system of rule has been called **cloistered government** because the retired emperors took Buddhist orders, while maintaining control of the government from behind the scenes. Thus for a time the imperial house was a contender for political power along with other aristocratic groups.

cloistered government A system in which an emperor retired to a Buddhist monastery but continued to exercise power by controlling his young son on the throne.

Aristocratic Culture

A brilliant aristocratic culture developed in the Heian period. It was strongly focused on the capital at Heian, where nobles, palace ladies, and imperial family members lived a highly refined and leisured life. In their society niceties of birth, rank, and breeding counted for everything. From their diaries we know of the pains aristocratic women took in their dress. Even among men, presentation and knowing how to dress tastefully was more important than skill with a horse or sword. The elegance of one's calligraphy and the allusions in one's poems were matters of intense concern to both men and women at court. Courtiers did not like to leave the capital, and some like the court lady Sei Shonagon shuddered at the sight of ordinary working people. (See "Listening to the Past: *The Pillow Book* of Sei Shonagon," page 336.)

In this period a new script was developed for writing Japanese phonetically. Each symbol was based on a simplified Chinese character and represented one of the syllables used in Japanese. Although "serious" essays, histories, and government documents continued to be written in Chinese, less formal works such as poetry and memoirs were written in Japanese. Mastering the new writing system took much less time than mastering writing in Chinese and aided the spread of literacy, especially among women in court society. In fact, the literary masterpiece of this period is ***The Tale of Genji***, written in Japanese by Lady Murasaki over several years (ca. 1000–1010). This long narrative depicts a cast of characters enmeshed in court life, with close attention to dialogue and personality.

The Tale of Genji A Japanese literary masterpiece about court life written by Lady Murasaki.

In the Heian period women played important roles at all levels of society. Women educated in the arts and letters could advance at court as attendants to the ruler's empress and other consorts. Women could inherit property from their parents, and they would compete with their brothers for shares of the family property. In political life, marrying a daughter to an emperor or shogun (see page 339) was one of the best ways to gain power, and women often became major players in power struggles.

Buddhism remained very strong throughout the Heian period. A mission sent to China in 804 included two monks in search of new texts. One of the monks, Saichō, spent time at the monasteries on Mount Tiantai and brought back the Buddhist teachings associated with that mountain (called Tendai in Japanese). Tendai's basic message is that all living beings share the Buddha nature and can be brought to salvation. Tendai practices include strict monastic discipline, prayer, textual study, and meditation. Once back in Japan, Saichō established a monastery on Mount Hiei outside Kyoto, which grew to be one of the most important monasteries in Japan. By the twelfth century this monastery and its many branch temples had vast lands and a powerful army of monk-soldiers to protect its interests. Whenever the monastery felt that its interests were at risk, it sent the monk-soldiers into the capital to parade its sacred symbols in an attempt to intimidate the civil authorities.

Kūkai, the other monk on the 804 mission to China, came back with texts from another school of Buddhism—Shingon, "True Word," a form of **Esoteric Buddhism**. Esoteric Buddhism is based on the idea that teachings containing the secrets of enlightenment had been secretly transmitted from the Buddha. An adept (expert) can gain access to these mysteries through initiation into the mandalas (cosmic diagrams), mudras (gestures), and mantras (verbal formulas). On his return to Japan, Kūkai attracted many followers and was allowed to establish a monastery at Mount Kōya, south of Osaka. The popularity of Esoteric Buddhism was a great stimulus to Buddhist art.

Esoteric Buddhism A sect of Buddhism that maintains that the secrets of enlightenment have been secretly transmitted from the Buddha and can be accessed through initiation into the mandalas, mudras, and mantras.

Quick Review
What values and beliefs were reflected in Japanese culture during the Heian period?

What were the causes and consequences of military rule in Japan?

The gradual rise of a warrior elite over the course of the Heian period finally brought an end to the domination of the Fujiwaras and other Heian aristocratic families. In 1156 civil war broke out between the Taira and Minamoto warrior clans based in western and eastern Japan, respectively. Both clans relied on skilled warriors, later called samurai, who were rapidly becoming a new social class. A samurai and his lord had a double bond: in return for the samurai's loyalty and service, the lord granted him land or income. From 1159 to 1181 a Taira named Kiyomori dominated the court. His relatives became governors of more than thirty provinces, managed some five hundred tax-exempt estates, and amassed a fortune in the trade with Song China and Koryŏ Korea. Still, the Minamoto clan managed to defeat the Taira, and the Minamoto leader, Yoritomo, became **shogun**, or general-in-chief. With him began the Kamakura Shogunate (1185–1333). This period is often referred to as Japan's feudal period because it was dominated by a military class whose members were tied to their superiors by bonds of loyalty and supported by landed estates rather than salaries.

The Shogun Minamoto Yoritomo in Court Dress This wooden sculpture, 27.8 inches tall (70.6 cm), was made about a half century after Yoritomo's death for use in a shrine dedicated to his memory. The bold shapes convey Yoritomo's dignity and power. (Tokyo National Museum/image: TNM Image Archives)

shogun The Japanese general-in-chief, whose headquarters was the shogunate.

Military Rule

The similarities between military rule in Japan and feudalism in medieval Europe during roughly the same period have fascinated scholars, as have the very significant differences. In Europe feudalism emerged out of the fusion of Germanic and Roman social institutions and flowered under the impact of Muslim and Viking invasions. In Japan military rule evolved from a combination of the native warrior tradition and Confucian ethical principles of duty to superiors.

The emergence of the samurai was made possible by the development of private landholding. The government land allotment system, copied from Tang China, began breaking down in the eighth century (much as it did in China). By the ninth century local lords began escaping imperial taxes and control by commending (formally giving) their land to tax-exempt entities such as monasteries, the imperial family, and certain high-ranking officials. The local lord then received his land back as a tenant and paid his protector a small rent. The monastery or privileged individual received a steady income from the land, and the local lord escaped imperial taxes and control. By the end of the thirteenth century most land seems to have been taken off the tax rolls this way. Each plot of land could thus have several people with rights to shares of its produce, ranging from the cultivator, to a local lord, to an estate manager working for him, to a regional strongman, to a noble or temple in the capital. Unlike peasants in medieval Europe, where similar practices of commendation occurred, those working the land in Japan never became serfs. Moreover, Japanese lords rarely lived on the lands they had rights in, unlike English or French lords who lived on their manors.

Bushido Literally, the "way of the warrior"; the code of conduct by which samurai were expected to live.

Samurai resembled European knights in several ways. Both were armed with expensive weapons, and both fought on horseback. Just as the knight was supposed to live according to the chivalric code, so Japanese samurai were expected to live according to **Bushido** (or "way of the warrior"), a code that stressed military honor, courage, stoic acceptance of hardship, and, above all, loyalty. Disloyalty brought social disgrace, which the samurai could avoid only through *seppuku*, ritual suicide by slashing his belly.

The Kamakura Shogunate derives its name from Kamakura, a city near modern Tokyo that was the seat of the Minamoto clan. The founder, Yoritomo, ruled the country much the way he ran his own estates, appointing his retainers to newly created offices. To cope with the emergence of hard-to-tax estates, he put military land stewards in charge of seeing to the estates' proper operation. To bring order to the lawless countryside, he appointed military governors to oversee the military and enforce the law in the provinces.

Yoritomo's wife Masako protected the interests of her own family, the Hōjōs, especially after Yoritomo died. She went so far as to force her first son to abdicate when he showed signs of preferring the family of his wife to the family of his mother. She later helped her brother take power away from her father. Thus the process of reducing power holders to figureheads went one step further in 1219 when the Hōjō family reduced the shogun to a figurehead. The Hōjō family held the reins of power until 1333.

Kamakura Shogunate, 1185–1333

The Mongols' two massive seaborne invasions in 1274 and 1281 (see page 301) were a huge shock to the shogunate. The Kamakura government was hard-pressed to gather adequate resources for its defense. Temples were squeezed, farmers were taken away from their fields to build walls, and warriors were promised generous rewards in return for their service. Although the Hōjō regents, with the help of a "divine wind" (*kamikaze*), repelled the Mongols, they were unable to reward their vassals in the traditional way because little booty was found among the wreckage of the Mongol fleets. Discontent grew among the samurai, and by the fourteenth century the entire political system was breaking down, with both the imperial and the shogunate families fighting among themselves.

The factional disputes among Japan's leading families remained explosive until 1331, when the emperor Go-Daigo tried to recapture real power. His attempt sparked an uprising by the great families, local lords, samurai, and even Buddhist monasteries, which had thousands of samurai retainers. Go-Daigo destroyed the Kamakura Shogunate in 1333 but soon lost the loyalty of his followers. By 1338 one of his most important military supporters, Ashikaga Takauji, had turned on him and established the Ashikaga Shogunate, which lasted until 1573. Takauji's victory was also a victory for the samurai, who took over civil authority throughout Japan.

Cultural Trends

The cultural distance between the elites and the commoners narrowed a little during the Kamakura period. Buddhism was vigorously spread to ordinary Japanese by energetic preachers. Honen (1133–1212) propagated the Pure Land teaching, preaching that paradise could be reached through simple faith in the Buddha and repeating the name of the Buddha Amitabha. His follower Shinran (1173–1263) taught that monks should not shut themselves off in monasteries but should marry and have children. A different path was promoted by Nichiren (1222–1282), who proclaimed that to be saved people had only to invoke sincerely the Lotus Sutra, one of the most important of the Buddhist sutras. These lay versions of Buddhism found a receptive audience among ordinary people in the countryside.

It was also during the Kamakura period that **Zen** came to flourish in Japan. Zen teachings originated in Tang China, where they were known as Chan (see page 174). Rejecting the authority of the sutras, Zen teachers claimed the superiority of mind-to-mind transmission of Buddhist truth. One school of Zen held that enlightenment could be achieved suddenly through insight into one's own true nature. This school taught rigorous meditation and the use of kōan riddles to unseat logic and free the mind for enlightenment. This teaching found eager patrons among the samurai, who were attracted to its discipline and strong master-disciple bonds.

Zen A school of Buddhism that emphasized meditation and truths that could not be conveyed in words.

Buddhism remained central to the visual arts. Many temples in Japan still house fine sculptures done in this period. In painting, narrative hand scrolls brought to life the miracles that faith could bring and the torments of Hell awaiting unbelievers. All forms of literature were depicted in these scrolls, including *The Tale of Genji*, war stories, and humorous anecdotes.

During the Kamakura period war tales continued the tradition of long narrative prose works. *The Tale of the Heike* tells the story of the fall of the Taira family and the rise of the Minamoto clan. The tale reached a large and mostly illiterate audience because blind minstrels would chant sections to the accompaniment of a lute. The story is suffused with the Buddhist idea of the transience of life and the illusory nature of glory. Yet it also celebrates strength, courage, loyalty, and pride.

After stagnating in the Heian period, agricultural productivity began to improve in the Kamakura period, and the population grew, reaching perhaps 8.2 million by 1333. Much like farmers in contemporary Song China, Japanese farmers in this period adopted new strains of rice, often double-cropped in warmer regions, made increased use of fertilizers, and improved irrigation for paddy rice. Besides farming, ordinary people made their livings as artisans, traders, fishermen, and entertainers. Although trade in human beings was banned, those who fell into debt might sell themselves or their children, and professional

The Itinerant Preacher Ippen The monk Ippen spread Pure Land teaching as he traveled through Japan urging people to call on the Amitabha Buddha through song and dance. This detail from a set of twelve paintings done in 1299, a decade after his death, shows him with his belongings on his back as he approaches a village. (Tokyo National Museum/image: TNM Image Archives)

Quick Review
What were the most important political, social, and cultural consequences of the emergence of the samurai as a dominant force in Japanese life?

slave traders kidnapped women and children. A vague category of outcastes occupied the fringes of society, in a manner reminiscent of India. Buddhist strictures against killing and Shinto ideas of pollution probably account for the exclusion of butchers, leatherworkers, morticians, and lepers, but other groups, such as bamboo whisk makers, were also traditionally excluded for no obvious reason.

Connections

EAST ASIA FACED many internal and external challenges between 800 and 1400, and the ways the societies responded to them shaped their subsequent histories. In China the first four centuries of this period were a time of economic growth, urbanization, the spread of printing, and the expansion of the educated class. In Korea and Japan aristocracy and military rule were more typical of the era. All three areas, but especially China and Korea, faced an unprecedented challenge from the Mongols, with Japan less vulnerable because it did not share a land border. The challenges of the period did not hinder creativity in the literary and visual arts; among the greatest achievements of this era are the women's writings of Heian Japan, such as *The Tale of Genji*, and landscape painting of both Song and Yuan China.

Europe during these six centuries, the subject of the next chapter, also faced invasions from outside. Europe had a social structure more like that of Korea and Japan than of China, with less centralization and a more dominant place in society for military men. The centralized church in Europe, however, was unlike anything known in East Asian history. These centuries in Europe saw a major expansion of Christendom, especially to Scandinavia and eastern Europe, both through conversion and migration. Although there were scares that the Mongols would penetrate deeper into Europe, the greatest challenge in Europe was the Black Death and the huge loss of life that it caused.

- **For a list of suggested readings for this chapter, visit** *bedfordstmartins.com/mckayworldunderstanding*.
- **For primary sources from this period, see** *Sources of World Societies*, Second Edition.
- **For Web sites, images, and documents related to topics in this chapter, see Make History at** *bedfordstmartins.com/mckayworldunderstanding*.

Chapter 13 Study Guide

To do these exercises online, go to bedfordstmartins.com/mckayworldunderstanding.

Step 1 GETTING STARTED

Below are basic terms about this period in global history. Can you identify each term below and explain why it matters?

TERMS	WHO (OR WHAT) AND WHEN	WHY IT MATTERS
dynastic cycle, p. 322		
compass, p. 323		
scholar-official class, p. 327		
examination system, p. 327		
movable type, p. 328		
Neo-Confucianism, p. 328		
concubine, p. 331		
foot binding, p. 332		
cloistered government, p. 338		
The Tale of Genji, p. 338		
Esoteric Buddhism, p. 339		
shogun, p. 339		
Bushido, p. 340		
Zen, p. 341		

Step 2 MOVING BEYOND THE BASICS

The exercise below requires a more advanced understanding of the chapter material. Examine the divergence of China, Korea, and Japan in the medieval period by filling in the chart below with descriptions of the major social, political, and cultural developments in the three states during the period covered in this chapter. When you are finished, consider the following questions: What role did nomadic peoples play in shaping Chinese, Korean, and Japanese history during this period? How would you characterize the political elites of each of these states? What connections remained between these three states, despite their divergence?

	SOCIETY	POLITICS	CULTURE
China			
Korea			
Japan			

Step 3

PUTTING IT ALL TOGETHER

Now that you've reviewed key elements of the chapter, take a step back and try to see the big picture. Remember to use specific examples from the chapter in your answers.

CHINA

- In what ways did late Tang and Song China defy the expectations of traditional Chinese historians?
- Why, despite its growth and prosperity, did China become increasingly vulnerable to nomadic confederations under the Song?

KOREA

- In what ways was Korean society different from Chinese and Japanese society?
- How did Korea's leaders react to the presence of powerful nomadic confederations on their borders?

JAPAN

- Compare and contrast Japanese elite culture during the Heian period with Chinese elite culture under the Song. How would you explain the differences you note?
- How and why did the power of Japanese samurai increase during the medieval period?

LOOKING BACK, LOOKING AHEAD

- Compare and contrast the place of China in the East Asian world before and after the period covered in this chapter. How would you explain the differences you note?
- From 1500 on, East Asia would face an unprecedented maritime challenge from European states. How might developments in the period covered in this chapter have affected the ability of East Asian states to meet this challenge?

In Your Own Words Imagine that you must explain Chapter 13 to someone who hasn't read it. What would be the most important points to include and why?

14

Europe in the Middle Ages

800–1450

By the fifteenth century scholars in northern Italy began to think that they were living in a new era, one in which the glories of ancient Greece and Rome were being reborn. What separated their time from classical antiquity, in their opinion, was a long period of darkness and barbarism, to which a seventeenth-century professor gave the name "Middle Ages." In this conceptualization, the history of Europe was divided into three periods—ancient, medieval, and modern—an organization that is still in use today. Later, the history of other parts of the world was sometimes fit into this three-period schema as well, with discussions of the "classical" period in Maya history, of "medieval" India and China, and of "modern" everywhere.

Today historians often question whether labels of past time periods for one culture work on a global scale, and some scholars are uncertain about whether "Middle Ages" is a just term even for European history. They assert that the Middle Ages was not simply a period of stagnation between two high points but rather a time of enormous intellectual energy and creative vitality. While agrarian life continued to dominate Europe, political structures that would influence later European history began to form, and Christianity continued to spread. People at the time did not know that they were living in an era that would later be labeled "middle" or sometimes even "dark," and we can wonder whether they would have shared this negative view of their own times.

Hedwig of Bavaria Like other noble women in medieval Europe, Hedwig played a wide variety of roles. She ruled when her husband was away and founded monasteries to facilitate the spread of Christianity. (The John Paul Getty Museum, Los Angeles, Ms Ludwig XI, fol.12v [detail], Court Atelier of Duke Ludwig I of Liegnitz and Brieg [illuminator], *Vita beatae Hedwigis*, 1353. Tempera colors, colored washes and ink bound between wood boards covered with red-stained pigskin, 34.1 x 24.8 cm)

Chapter Preview

- How did medieval rulers try to create larger and more stable territories?
- How did the Christian Church enhance its power and create new practices?
- What were the motives, course, and consequences of the Crusades?
- What characterized European society in the Middle Ages?
- What were the key educational and cultural developments?
- Why have the later Middle Ages been seen as a time of calamity and crisis?

How did medieval rulers try to create larger and more stable territories?

The growth of Germanic kingdoms such as those of the Merovingians and the Carolingians (see Chapter 8) is generally viewed as the beginning of "medieval" politics in Europe, and that is why we begin this chapter with the ninth century. In 800 Charlemagne, the most powerful of the Carolingians, was crowned the Holy Roman emperor. After his death his empire was divided among his grandsons, and their kingdoms were weakened by nobles vying for power. In addition, beginning around 800 western Europe was invaded by several different groups. Local nobles were the strongest power, and common people turned to them for protection. By the eleventh century, however, rulers in some parts of Europe reasserted authority and slowly built centralized states.

Invasions and Migrations

From the moors of Scotland to the mountains of Sicily, there arose in the ninth century the prayer, "Save us, O God, from the violence of the Northmen." The Northmen were pagan Germanic peoples from Norway, Sweden, and Denmark who came to be known as Vikings.

Viking assaults began around 800, and by the mid-tenth century the Vikings had brought large sections of continental Europe and Britain under their sway. In the east they sailed the rivers of Russia as far as the Black Sea. In the west they established permanent settlements in Iceland and short-lived ones in Greenland and Newfoundland in Canada (Map 14.1).

The Vikings were superb seamen with advanced methods of boatbuilding. Propelled either by oars or by sails, Viking ships could carry between forty and sixty men — enough to harass an isolated monastery or village. Against these ships, the Carolingian Empire, with no navy, was helpless. At first the Vikings attacked and sailed off laden with booty. Later, on returning, they settled down and colonized the areas they had conquered, often marrying local women and adopting the languages and some of the customs of their new homes.

Along with the Vikings, groups of central European steppe peoples known as Magyars (MAG-yahrz) also raided villages in the late ninth century, taking plunder and captives and forcing leaders to pay tribute. Moving westward, small bands of Magyars on horseback reached far into Europe. They subdued northern Italy, compelled Bavaria and Saxony to pay tribute, and penetrated into the Rhineland and Burgundy. They settled in the area that is now

Animal Headpost from a Viking Ship Skilled woodcarvers produced ornamental headposts for ships, sledges, wagons, and bedsteads. The fearsome quality of many carvings suggests that they were intended to ward off evil spirits and to terrify. (© University Museum of Cultural Heritage, Oslo. Photographer: Eirik Irgens Johnsen)

Hungary, became Christian, and in the eleventh century allied with the papacy.

From North Africa, the Muslims also began new encroachments in the ninth century. They already ruled most of Spain and now conquered Sicily, driving northward into central Italy and the south coast of France.

What was the impact of these invasions? From the perspective of those living in what had been Charlemagne's empire, these attacks contributed to increasing disorder and violence. Italian, French, and English sources often describe this period as one of terror and chaos. People in other parts of Europe might have had a different opinion. In Muslim Spain and Sicily scholars worked in thriving cities, and new crops such as cotton and sugar enhanced ordinary people's lives. In eastern Europe states such as Moravia and Hungary became strong kingdoms. A Viking point of view might be the most positive, for by 1100 descendants of the Vikings not only ruled their homelands in Norway, Sweden, and Denmark but also ruled northern France, England, Sicily, Iceland, and Russia, with an outpost in Greenland and occasional voyages to North America.

Chapter Chronology

722–1492	Reconquista, the Christian reconquest of Spain from Muslims
ca. 800–950	Viking, Magyar, and Muslim attacks on Europe
1066–1087	Reign of William the Conqueror
1086	*Domesday Book*
1095–1270	Crusades
1180–1270	Height of construction of cathedrals in France
1215	Magna Carta
1225–1274	Life of Saint Thomas Aquinas, author of *Summa Theologica*
1309–1376	Papacy in Avignon
1315–1322	Famine in northern Europe
ca. 1337–1453	Hundred Years' War
1347	Black Death arrives in Europe
1358	Jacquerie peasant uprising in France
1378–1417	Great Schism
1381	English Peasants' Revolt
1429	Joan of Arc leads French troops to victory at Orléans

Feudalism and Manorialism

The large-scale division of Charlemagne's empire led to a decentralization of power at the local level. Civil wars weakened the power and prestige of kings, who could do little about regional violence. Likewise, the invasions of the ninth century, especially those of the Vikings, weakened royal authority. The Frankish kings were unable to halt the invaders, and the local aristocracy had to assume responsibility for defense. Thus, in the ninth and tenth centuries great aristocratic families increased their authority in their local territories, and distant and weak kings could not interfere. Common people turned for protection to the strongest power, the local nobles.

The most powerful nobles were those who gained warriors' allegiance, often symbolized in a ceremony in which a warrior (knight) swore his loyalty as a **vassal**—from a Celtic term meaning "servant"—to the more powerful individual, who became his lord. In return for the vassal's loyalty, aid, and military assistance, the lord promised him protection and material support. This support most often came in the form of land, called a **fief** (*feudum* in Latin). The fief, which might contain forests, churches, and towns, technically still belonged to the lord, and the vassal had only the use of it. Peasants living on a fief produced the food and other goods necessary to maintain the knight.

vassal A knight who has sworn loyalty to a particular lord.

fief A portion of land, the use of which was given by a lord to a vassal in exchange for the latter's oath of loyalty.

Though historians debate this, fiefs appear to have been granted extensively first by Charles Martel (688–741) and then by his successors, including Charlemagne and his grandsons. These fiefs went to the most powerful nobles, who often took the title of count. As the Carolingians' control of their territories weakened, the practice of granting fiefs moved to the local level, with lay lords, bishops, and abbots as well as kings granting fiefs. This system, later named **feudalism**, was based on personal ties of loyalty cemented by grants of land rather than on allegiance to an abstract state or governmental system.

The economic power of the warrior class rested on landed estates, which were worked by peasants under a system of **manorialism**. Free farmers surrendered themselves and their land to the lord's jurisdiction in exchange for protection. The land was given back to them to farm, but they were tied to the land by various payments and services. Most significantly,

feudalism A medieval European political system that defines the military obligations and relations between a lord and his vassals and involves the granting of fiefs.

manorialism The economic system that governed rural life in medieval Europe, in which the landed estates of a lord were worked by the peasants under the lord's jurisdiction in exchange for his protection.

Mapping the Past

Map 14.1 Invasions and Migrations of the Ninth Century

This map shows the Viking, Magyar, and Arab invasions and migrations in the ninth century. Compare it with Map 8.3 (page 197) on the barbarian migrations of late antiquity to answer the following questions.

ANALYZING THE MAP What similarities do you see in the patterns of migration in these two periods? What significant differences?

CONNECTIONS How did Viking expertise in shipbuilding and sailing make their migrations different from those of earlier Germanic tribes? How did this set them apart from the Magyar and Muslim invaders of the ninth century?

serf A peasant who lost his or her freedom and became permanently bound to the landed estate of a lord.

a peasant lost his or her freedom and became a **serf**, part of the lord's permanent labor force. Unlike slaves, serfs were personally free, but they were bound to the land and unable to leave it without the lord's permission.

The transition from freedom to serfdom was slow, but by around 1000 the majority of western Europeans were serfs. While serfs ranged from the highly prosperous to the desperately poor, all had lost their freedom. In eastern Europe the transition was slower but longer lasting. Western European peasants began to escape from serfdom in the later Middle Ages, at the very point that serfs were more firmly tied to the land in eastern Europe, especially in eastern Germany, Poland, and Russia.

The Restoration of Order

The eleventh century witnessed the beginnings of political stability in western Europe. Foreign invasions gradually declined, and in some parts of Europe lords in control of large territories built up their power even further, becoming kings over growing and slowly centralizing states. As rulers expanded their territories and extended their authority, they developed larger governmental institutions and armies to maintain control, as well as taxation systems to pay for them. These new institutions and practices laid the foundations for modern national states. Political developments in England, France, and Germany provide good examples of the beginnings of the national state in the central Middle Ages.

Under the pressure of Viking invasions in the ninth and tenth centuries, the seven kingdoms of Anglo-Saxon England united under one king. At the same time, England was divided into local shires, or counties, each under the jurisdiction of a sheriff appointed by the king. When Edward the Confessor (r. 1042–1066) died, his cousin, Duke William of Normandy, a French-speaking descendant of the Vikings, crossed the channel and won the English throne by defeating his Anglo-Saxon rival Harold Godwinson at the Battle of Hastings. Later dubbed "the Conqueror," William (r. 1066–1087) subdued the rest of the country and distributed land to his Norman followers. He retained the Anglo-Saxon institution of sheriff.

In 1085 William decided to conduct a systematic survey of the entire country to determine how much wealth there was and who had it. The resulting record, called the *Domesday Book* (DOOMZ-day), provided William and his descendants with vital information for governing the country. Completed in 1086, the book is an invaluable source of social and economic information about medieval Europe.

In 1128 William's granddaughter Matilda married a powerful French noble, Geoffrey of Anjou. Their son, who became Henry II of England, inherited provinces in northwestern France from his father. When Henry married the great heiress Eleanor of Aquitaine in 1152, he claimed lordship over Aquitaine and other provinces in southwestern France as well. The histories of England and France were thus closely intertwined in the Middle Ages.

In the early twelfth century France consisted of a number of nearly independent provinces, each governed by its local ruler. The work of unifying France began under Philip II (r. 1180–1223), known as Philip Augustus. By the end of his reign Philip was effectively master of northern France, and by 1300 most of the provinces of modern France had been added to the royal domain through diplomacy, marriage, war, and inheritance.

In central Europe the German king Otto I (r. 936–973) defeated many other lords to build up his power, based on an alliance with and control of the church. Otto asserted the right to control church appointments, and bishops and abbots had to perform feudal homage for the lands that accompanied their positions. German rulers were not able to build up centralized power, however. Under Otto I and his successors, a loose confederation stretching from the North Sea to the Mediterranean developed. In this confederation, later called the Holy Roman Empire, the emperor shared power with princes, dukes, counts, city officials, archbishops, and bishops.

Frederick Barbarossa (r. 1152–1190) of the house of Hohenstaufen tried valiantly to make the Holy Roman Empire a united state. He made alliances with the high nobles and even compelled the great churchmen to become his vassals. When he tried to enforce his authority over the cities of northern Italy, however, they formed a league against him in alliance with the pope and defeated him. Frederick's absence from the German part of his empire allowed the princes and other rulers of independent provinces to consolidate their power there as well.

The Norman Conquest, 1066

Law and Justice

Throughout Europe in the twelfth and thirteenth centuries, the law was a hodgepodge of customs, feudal rights, and provincial practices. Rulers wanted to blend these elements into a uniform system of rules acceptable and applicable to all their peoples, though their success in doing so varied.

The French king Louis IX (r. 1226–1270) was famous in his time for his concern for justice. Each French province, even after being made part of the kingdom of France, retained its unique laws and procedures. But Louis IX created a royal judicial system, establishing the Parlement of Paris, a kind of supreme court that heard appeals from lower courts.

Under Henry II (r. 1154–1189), England developed and extended a common law—a law common to and accepted by the entire country. No other country in medieval Europe did so. Each year Henry sent out circuit judges (royal officials who traveled in a given circuit or district) to hear civil and criminal cases. Wherever the king's judges sat, there sat the king's court. Slowly, the king's court gained jurisdiction over all property disputes and criminal actions.

Henry's son John (r. 1199–1216) met with serious disappointment after taking the throne. He lost the French province of Normandy to Philip Augustus in 1204 and spent the rest of his reign trying to win it back. Saddled with heavy debt from his father and brother Richard (r. 1189–1199), John's efforts to raise more revenue created an atmosphere of resentment. When John's military campaign failed in 1214, it was clear that the French lands that had once belonged to the English king were lost for good. The barons revolted and in 1215 forced him to attach his seal to the Magna Carta—the "Great Charter," which became the cornerstone of English justice and law.

To contemporaries the Magna Carta was intended to redress the grievances that particular groups had against King John. It came to have much broader significance, however, and every English king in the Middle Ages reissued the Magna Carta. It came to signify the principle that everyone, including the king and the government, must obey the law.

Quick Review
What were the consequences of the ninth and tenth century invasions, and how did medieval rulers reassert their authority in the eleventh and twelfth centuries?

How did the Christian Church enhance its power and create new practices?

Like kings and emperors, eleventh and twelfth century popes sought to consolidate their power, although such efforts were sometimes challenged by secular rulers. Despite such challenges, monasteries continued to be important places for learning and devotion, and new religious orders were founded. Also, Christianity expanded into Europe's northern and eastern regions, and Christian rulers expanded their holdings in Muslim Spain.

Papal Reforms

During the ninth and tenth centuries the church came under the control of kings and feudal lords, who chose church officials in their territories, granting them fiefs that provided an income and expecting loyalty and service in return. Church offices were sometimes sold outright—a practice called *simony*. Although the Roman Church encouraged clerical celibacy, many priests were married or living with women. Not surprisingly, clergy who had bought their positions or had been granted them for political reasons provided little spiritual guidance, and their personal lives were rarely models of high moral standards. The popes themselves often paid more attention to their families' political fortunes or their own pleasures than to the institutional or spiritual health of the church.

Serious efforts to change all this began in the eleventh century. A series of popes believed that secular or lay control over the church was largely responsible for the lack of moral leadership, so they proclaimed the church independent from secular rulers. The Lateran Council of 1059 decreed that the authority and power to elect the pope rested solely in the college of cardinals, a special group of priests from the major churches in and around Rome. The college retains that power today.

Pope Gregory VII (pontificate 1073–1085) vigorously championed reform and the expansion of papal power. He ordered all priests to give up their wives and children or face dismissal, invalidated the ordination of church officials who had purchased their offices, and placed nuns under firmer control of male authorities. He was the first pope to emphasize the political authority of the papacy, ordering that any church official selected or appointed by a layperson should be deposed, and any layperson, including rulers, who appointed a church official should be excommunicated—cut off from the sacraments and the Christian community.

European rulers immediately protested this restriction of their power, and the strongest reaction came from Henry IV, the ruler of Germany. Henry continued to appoint officials, and Gregory responded by excommunicating bishops who supported Henry and threatening to depose him. In January 1077 Henry arrived at the pope's residence in Canossa in northern Italy and, according to legend, stood outside in the snow for three days seeking forgiveness. As a priest, Gregory was obliged to readmit the emperor into the Christian community. Although Henry bowed before the pope, he actually won a victory, maintaining authority over his subjects and in 1084 being crowned the Holy Roman emperor.

Monastic Life

By the eighth century monasteries and convents dotted the European landscape, and during the ninth and tenth centuries they were often the target of Viking attacks or raids by local looters seeking valuable objects. Some religious communities fled and dispersed, while others fell under the control and domination of local feudal lords. Powerful laymen appointed themselves or their relatives as abbots, took the lands and goods of monasteries, and spent monastic revenues.

Medieval monasteries fulfilled the needs of the feudal system in other ways as well. They provided noble boys with education and opportunities for ecclesiastical careers. Although a few men who rose in the ranks of church officials were of humble origins, most were from high-status families. Social class also defined the kinds of religious life open to women. Kings and nobles usually established convents for their female relatives and other elite women, and the position of abbess, or head of a convent, became the most powerful position a woman could hold in medieval society. (See "Individuals in Society: Hildegard of Bingen," page 354.) People of lower social standing did live and work in monasteries, but as lay brothers and sisters who performed manual labor, not religious duties.

Routines within individual monasteries varied widely. In every monastery, however, daily life centered on the liturgy or Divine Office, psalms, and other prayers. Praying was looked on as a vital service, as crucial as the labor of peasants and the military might of nobles. Prayers were said for peace, rain, good harvests, the civil authorities, the monks' and nuns' families, and their benefactors. Monastic patrons in turn lavished gifts on the monasteries, which often became very wealthy, controlling large tracts of land and the peasants who farmed them.

The combination of lay control and wealth created problems for monasteries as monks and nuns concentrated on worldly issues and levels of spiritual observance and intellectual

INDIVIDUALS IN SOCIETY

Hildegard of Bingen

THE TENTH CHILD OF A LESSER NOBLE FAMILY, Hildegard (1098–1179) was turned over to the care of an abbey in the Rhineland when she was eight years old. There she learned Latin and received a good education. She spent most of her life in various women's religious communities, two of which she founded herself. When she was a child, she began having mystical visions, often of light in the sky, but told few people about them. In middle age, however, her visions became more dramatic: "And it came to pass . . . when I was 42 years and 7 months old, that the heavens were opened and a blinding light of exceptional brilliance flowed through my entire brain. And so it kindled my whole heart and breast like a flame, not burning but warming . . . and suddenly I understood of the meaning of expositions of the books."* She wanted the church to approve of her visions and wrote first to St. Bernard of Clairvaux, who answered her briefly and dismissively, and then to Pope Eugenius, who encouraged her to write them down. Her first work was *Scivias* (Know the Ways of the Lord), a record of her mystical visions that incorporates extensive theological learning (see the illustration).

Obviously possessed of leadership and administrative talents, Hildegard left her abbey in 1147 to found the convent of Rupertsberg near Bingen. There she produced *Physica* (On the Physical Elements) and *Causa et Curae* (Causes and Cures), scientific works on the curative properties of natural elements; poems; a mystery play; and several more works of mysticism. She carried on a huge correspondence with scholars, prelates, and ordinary people. When she was over fifty, she left her community to preach to audiences of clergy and laity, and she was the only woman of her time whose opinions on religious matters were considered authoritative by the church.

Hildegard's visions have been explored by theologians and also by neurologists, who judge that they may have originated in migraine headaches, as she reports many of the same phenomena that migraine sufferers do: auras of light around objects, areas of blindness, feelings of intense doubt and intense euphoria. The interpretations that she develops come from her theological insight and learning, however, not from her illness. That same insight also emerges in her music, which is what she is best known for today. Eighty of her compositions survive — a huge number for a medieval composer — most of them written to be sung by the nuns in her convent, so they have strong lines for female voices. Many of her songs and chants have been recorded recently by various artists and are available on compact disk, as downloads, and on several Web sites.

*From *Scivias*, trans. Mother Columba Hart and Jane Bishop, *The Classics of Western Spirituality* (New York/Mahwah: Paulist Press, 1990).

QUESTIONS FOR ANALYSIS

1. Why do you think Hildegard might have kept her visions secret at first? Why do you think she eventually sought church approval for them?
2. In what ways were Hildegard's accomplishments extraordinary given women's general status in the Middle Ages?

Inspired by heavenly fire, Hildegard begins to dictate her visions to her scribe. The original of this elaborately illustrated copy of *Scivias* disappeared from Hildegard's convent during World War II, but fortunately a facsimile had already been made. (Private Collection/The Bridgeman Art Library)

activity declined. Several waves of reform improved the situation in some monasteries, but when deeply impressed laypeople showered gifts on monasteries with good reputations, monastic observance and spiritual fervor again declined.

In the thirteenth century the growth of cities provided a new challenge for the church. Many urban people thought that the church did not meet their spiritual needs. They turned instead to heresies — that is, to versions of Christianity outside of those approved by the papacy. Ironically, many of these belief systems denied the value of material wealth. Combating **heresy** became a principal task of new religious orders, most prominently the Dominicans and Franciscans, who preached and ministered to city dwellers; the Dominicans also staffed the papal Inquisition, a special court designed to root out heresy.

heresy An opinion, belief, or action counter to doctrines that church leaders defined as correct; heretics could be punished by the church.

Popular Religion

Religion had an extraordinary impact on the daily lives of ordinary people in medieval Europe. Religious practices varied widely from country to country and even from province to province. But nowhere was religion a one-hour-a-week affair.

For Christians, the village church was the center of community life, with the parish priest in charge of a host of activities. Every Sunday and on holy days the villagers attended Mass, breaking the painful routine of work. The feasts that accompanied baptisms, weddings, funerals, and other celebrations were commonly held in the churchyard. Popular religion consisted largely of rituals heavy with symbolism. For example, before slicing a loaf of bread, the pious woman tapped the sign of the cross on it with her knife. Before planting began on local lands, the village priest customarily went out and sprinkled the fields with water, symbolizing refreshment and life. The entire calendar was designed with reference to Christmas, Easter, and Pentecost.

The Christian calendar was also filled with saints' days. Saints were individuals who had lived particularly holy lives and were honored locally or more widely for their connection with the divine. The cult of the saints, which developed in a rural and uneducated environment, represents a central feature of popular culture in the Middle Ages. People believed that the saints possessed supernatural powers that enabled them to perform miracles, and each saint became the special property of the locality in which his or her relics — remains or possessions — rested. In return for the saint's healing powers and support, peasants would offer prayers, loyalty, and gifts.

Most people in medieval Europe were Christian, but there were small Jewish communities scattered through many parts of Europe, as well as Muslims in the Iberian Peninsula, Sicily, other Mediterranean islands, and southeastern Europe. Increasing suspicion and hostility marked relations among believers in different religions throughout the Middle Ages, but there were also important similarities in the ways that European Christians, Jews, and Muslims understood and experienced their faiths. In all three traditions, every major life transition, such as marriage or the birth of a child, was marked by a ceremony that involved religious officials or spiritual elements. In all three faiths, death was marked by religious rituals, and the living had obligations to the dead, including prayers and special mourning periods.

The Expansion of Christianity

The eleventh and twelfth centuries saw not only reforms in monasticism and the papacy but also an expansion of Christianity into Scandinavia, the Baltic lands, eastern Europe, and Spain that had profound cultural consequences. As it occurred, more and more Europeans began to think of themselves as belonging to a realm of Christianity that was political as well as religious, a realm they called Christendom.

Córdoba Mosque and Cathedral The huge arches of the Great Mosque at Córdoba dwarf the cathedral built in its center after the city was conquered by Christian armies in 1236. During the reconquista, Christian kings often transformed mosques into churches, often by simply adding Christian elements such as crosses and altars to existing structures. (dbimages/Alamy)

Christian influences entered Scandinavia and the Baltic lands primarily through the creation of dioceses (church districts headed by bishops). This took place in Denmark in the tenth and eleventh centuries, and the institutional church spread rather quickly due to the support offered by the strong throne. Dioceses were established in Norway and Sweden in the eleventh century, and in 1164 Uppsala, Sweden, long the center of the pagan cults of Odin and Thor, became a Catholic archdiocese.

Otto I (see page 351) planted a string of dioceses along his northern and eastern frontiers, hoping to pacify the newly conquered Slavs in eastern Europe. However, frequent Slavic revolts illustrate the people's resentment of German lords and clerics and indicate that the church did not easily penetrate the region.

The church also moved into central Europe, first into Bohemia in the tenth century and from there into Poland and Hungary in the eleventh century. In the twelfth and thirteenth centuries thousands of Germanic settlers poured into eastern Europe from the west.

The Reconquista, 722–1492

The Iberian Peninsula was another area of Christian expansion. About 950 Caliph Abd al-Rahman III (912–961) ruled most of the peninsula. Christian Spain consisted of a number of small kingdoms. When civil wars erupted among Rahman's descendants, Muslim lands were split among several small kingdoms, making it easier for Christians to take over these lands. By 1248 Christians held all of the peninsula save for the small state of Granada in the south. As the Christians advanced, they changed the face of Spanish cities, transforming mosques into cathedrals.

Fourteenth-century clerical propagandists would call the movement to expel the Muslims the **reconquista**

reconquista A fourteenth-century term used to describe the Christian crusade to wrest Spain back from the Muslims from 722 to 1492; clerics believed it was a sacred and patriotic mission.

(reconquest)—a sacred and patriotic crusade to wrest the country from "alien" Muslim hands. This religious idea became part of Spanish political culture and of the national psychology. Rulers of the Christian kingdoms of Spain increasingly passed legislation discriminating against Muslims and Jews as well as against those whose ancestors were Muslim or Jewish. As a consequence of the reconquista (ray-kon-KEES-tah), the Spanish and Portuguese also learned how to administer vast tracts of newly acquired territory. In the sixteenth century they used their claims about the rightful dominance of Christianity to justify their colonization of new territories overseas, and relied on their experiences at home to provide models of how to govern.

Quick Review
How did the growth and prosperity of the Catholic Church complicate and, in some cases, undermine its religious and spiritual mission?

What were the motives, course, and consequences of the Crusades?

The expansion of Christianity in the Middle Ages was not limited to Europe but extended to the eastern Mediterranean in what were later termed the **Crusades**. Occurring in the late eleventh and early twelfth centuries, the Crusades were wars sponsored by the papacy to recover the holy city of Jerusalem from the Muslims. Although people of all ages and classes participated in the Crusades, so many knights joined in that crusading became a distinctive feature of the upper-class lifestyle.

Crusades Holy wars sponsored by the papacy for the recovery of the Holy Land from the Muslims.

Background and Motives

In the eleventh century the papacy had strong reasons for wanting to launch an expedition against Muslims in the East. If the pope could muster a large army against the enemies of Christianity, his claim to be the leader of Christian society in the West would be strengthened. Moreover, in 1054 a serious theological disagreement had split the Greek Church of Byzantium and the Roman Church of the West. The pope believed that a crusade would lead to strong Roman influence in Greek territories and eventually the reunion of the two churches.

Popes and other church officials gained support for war in defense of Christianity by promising spiritual benefits to those who joined a campaign or died fighting. Church leaders said that these people would be forgiven for their sins without having to do penance. Preachers communicated these ideas widely and told stories about warrior-saints who slew hundreds of enemies.

In the late eleventh century the Seljuk Turks took over Palestine, defeating both Arabic and Byzantine armies. The Byzantine emperor at Constantinople appealed to western European Christians for support. The emperor's appeal fit well with papal aims, and in 1095 Pope Urban II called for a great Christian holy war against the infidels. He urged Christian knights who had been fighting one another to direct their energies against those he claimed were the true enemies of God, the Muslims.

The Course of the Crusades

Thousands of people of all classes responded to Urban's call. The First Crusade was successful, mostly because of the dynamic enthusiasm of the participants, who had little more than religious zeal. They knew little of the geography or climate of the Middle East, and the

LISTENING TO THE PAST

An Arab View of the Crusades

The Crusades helped shape the understanding that Arabs and Europeans had of each other and all subsequent relations between the Christian West and the Arab world. To medieval Christians, the Crusades were papally approved military expeditions to recover holy places in Palestine; to the Arabs, these campaigns were "Frankish wars" or "Frankish invasions" for the acquisition of territory.

Early in the thirteenth century, Ibn Al-Athir (1160–1223), a native of Mosul, an important economic and cultural center in northern Mesopotamia (modern Iraq), wrote a history of the First Crusade. He relied on Arab sources for the events he described. Here is his account of the Crusaders' capture of Antioch.

"The power of the Franks first became apparent when in the year 478/1085–86* they invaded the territories of Islam and took Toledo and other parts of Andalusia [in Spain]. Then in 484/1091 they attacked and conquered the island of Sicily and turned their attention to the African coast. Certain of their conquests there were won back again, but they had other successes, as you will see.

In 490/1097 the Franks attacked Syria. This is how it all began: Baldwin, their King, a kinsman of Roger the Frank who had conquered Sicily, assembled a great army and sent word to Roger saying: "I have assembled a great army and now I am on my way to you, to use your bases for my conquest of the African coast. Thus you and I shall become neighbors."

Roger called together his companions and consulted them about these proposals. "This will be a fine thing for them and for us!" they declared, "for by this means these lands will be converted to the Faith!" At this Roger raised one leg and farted loudly, and swore that it was of more use than their advice. "Why?" "Because if this army comes here it will need quantities of provisions and fleets of ships to transport it to Africa, as well as reinforcements from my own troops. Then, if the Franks succeed in conquering this territory they will take it over and will need provisioning from Sicily. This will cost me my annual profit from the harvest. If they fail they will return here and be an embarrassment to me here in my own domain." . . .

He summoned Baldwin's messenger and said to him: "If you have decided to make war on the Muslims your best course will be to free Jerusalem from their rule and thereby win great honor. I am bound by certain promises and treaties of allegiance with the ruler of Africa." So the Franks made ready to set out to attack Syria.

Another story is that the Fatimids of Egypt were afraid when they saw the Seljuqids extending their empire through Syria as far as Gaza, until they reached the Egyptian border and Atsiz invaded Egypt itself. They therefore sent to invite the Franks to invade Syria and so protect Egypt from the Muslims.† But God knows best.

When the Franks decided to attack Syria they marched east to Constantinople, so that they could cross the straits and advance into Muslim territory by the easier, land route. When they reached Constantinople, the Emperor of the East refused them permission to pass through his domains. He said: "Unless you first promise me Antioch, I shall not allow you to cross into the Muslim empire." His real intention was to incite them to attack the Muslims, for he was convinced that the Turks, whose invincible control over Asia Minor he had observed, would exterminate every one of them. They accepted his conditions and in 490/1097 they crossed the Bosphorus at Constantinople. . . . They . . . reached Antioch, which they besieged.

When Yaghi Siyan, the ruler of Antioch, heard of their approach, he was not sure how the Christian people of the city would react, so he made the Muslims go outside the city on their own to dig trenches, and the next day sent the Christians out alone to continue the task. When they were ready to return home at the end of the day he refused to allow them. "Antioch is yours," he said, "but you will have to leave it to me until I see what happens between us and the Franks." "Who will protect our children and our wives?" they said. "I shall look after them for you." So they resigned themselves to their fate, and lived in the Frankish camp for nine months, while the city was under siege.

Yaghi Siyan showed unparalleled courage and wisdom, strength and judgment. If all the Franks who died had survived they would have overrun all the lands of Islam. He protected the families of the Christians in Antioch and would not allow a hair of their heads to be touched.

Crusaders could never agree on a leader. Adding to these disadvantages, supply lines were never set up, starvation and disease wracked the army, and the Turks slaughtered hundreds of noncombatants. Nevertheless, the army pressed on, defeating the Turks in several battles, and after a monthlong siege it took Jerusalem in July 1099 (Map 14.2). Fulcher of Chartres, a chaplain on the First Crusade, described the scene: "If you had been there your feet would have been stained to the ankles in the blood of the slain. What shall I say? None of them were left alive. Neither women nor children were spared."[1]

In this vivid battle scene from a chronicle written in 1218 by an English monk, Christians and Muslims, both wearing chain mail, fight at close quarters. Slain warriors and a dead horse, common sights on the battlefield, lie underneath them. (© Corpus Christi College, Oxford, U.K./The Bridgeman Art Library)

After the siege had been going on for a long time the Franks made a deal with . . . a cuirass [breastplate]-maker called Ruzbih whom they bribed with a fortune in money and lands. He worked in the tower that stood over the riverbed, where the river flowed out of the city into the valley. The Franks sealed their pact with the cuirass-maker, God damn him! and made their way to the water-gate. They opened it and entered the city. Another gang of them climbed the tower with their ropes. At dawn, when more than 500 of them were in the city and the defenders were worn out after the night watch, they sounded their trumpets. . . . Panic seized Yaghi Siyan and he opened the city gates and fled in terror, with an escort of thirty pages. His army commander arrived, but when he discovered on enquiry that Yaghi Siyan had fled, he made his escape by another gate. This was of great help to the Franks, for if he had stood firm for an hour, they would have been wiped out. They entered the city by the gates and sacked it, slaughtering all the Muslims they found there. This happened in jumada I (491/April/May 1098). . . .

It was the discord between the Muslim princes . . . that enabled the Franks to overrun the country. ”

Source: *Arab Historians of the Crusades*, selected and translated from the Arabic sources by Francesco Gabrieli. Translated from the Italian by E. J. Costello. © 1969 by Routledge & Kegan Paul Ltd. Reproduced by permission of Taylor & Francis Books UK and The University of California Press.

*Muslims traditionally date events from Muhammad's hegira, or emigration, to Medina, which occurred in 622 according to the Christian calendar.

†Although Muslims, Fatimids were related doctrinally to the Shi'ites, but the dominant Sunni Muslims considered the Fatimids heretics.

QUESTIONS FOR ANALYSIS

1. Most Christian histories of the Crusades begin with Pope Urban II's call in 1095. What does Ibn Al-Athir see as the beginning? How would this make his view of the Crusades different from that of Christian chroniclers?
2. How does Ibn Al-Athir characterize the Christian leaders Roger and Baldwin? How does this compare with his characterization of Yaghi Siyan, the Muslim ruler of Antioch?
3. To what does Ibn Al-Athir attribute the fall of Antioch? What does this suggest about his view of Christian military capabilities?

With Jerusalem taken, four small "Crusader states"—Jerusalem, Edessa, Tripoli, and Antioch—were established, and castles and fortified towns were built in these states to defend against Muslim reconquest. Reinforcements arrived in the form of pilgrims and fighters from Europe, so that there was constant coming and going by land and more often by sea after the Crusaders conquered port cities.

Between 1096 and 1270 the crusading ideal was expressed in eight papally approved expeditions, though none after the First Crusade accomplished very much. The Muslim states

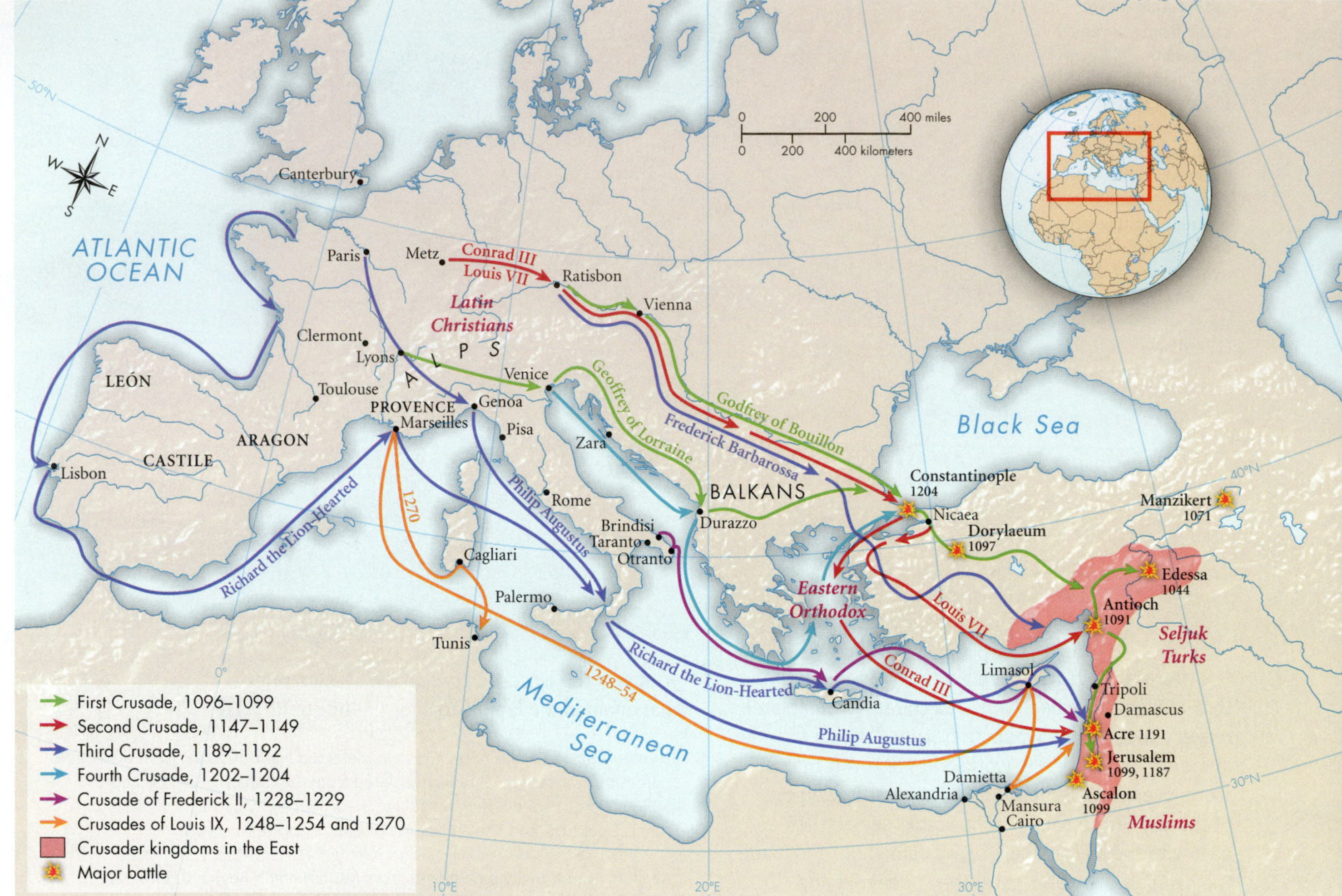

Map 14.2 The Crusades, 1096–1270 The Crusaders took many different sea and land routes on their way to Jerusalem, often crossing the lands of the Byzantine Empire, which led to conflict with Eastern Christians. The Crusader kingdoms in the East lasted only briefly.

in the Middle East were politically fragmented when the Crusaders first came, and it took them about a century to reorganize. They did so dramatically under Saladin (Salah al-Din). In 1187 the Muslims retook Jerusalem, but the Christians kept their hold on port towns, and Saladin allowed pilgrims safe passage to Jerusalem. From that point on, the Crusader states were more important economically than politically or religiously, giving Italian and French merchants direct access to Eastern products.

After the Muslims retook Jerusalem the crusading movement faced other setbacks. During the Fourth Crusade (1202–1204), Crusaders stopped in Constantinople, and when they were not welcomed, they sacked the city. The Byzantine Empire splintered into three parts and soon consisted of little more than the city of Constantinople. Moreover, the assault of one Christian people on another made the split between the Greek and Latin Churches permanent and discredited the entire crusading movement in the eyes of many Christians.

In the late thirteenth century Turkish armies, after gradually conquering all other Muslim rulers, turned against the Crusader states. In 1291 the Christians' last stronghold, the port of Acre, fell. Knights then needed a new battlefield for military actions, which some found in Spain, where the rulers of Aragon and Castile continued fighting Muslims until 1492.

Consequences of the Crusades

The Crusades testified to the religious enthusiasm of the High Middle Ages and the influence of the papacy, gave kings and the pope opportunities to expand their bureaucracies, and provided an outlet for nobles' dreams of glory. The Crusades also introduced some Europeans to Eastern luxury goods and proved a boon to Italian merchants.

Despite these advantages, the Crusades had some seriously negative sociopolitical consequences. For one thing, they proved to be a disaster for Jewish-Christian relations. Inspired by the ideology of holy war, Christian armies on their way to Jerusalem on the First Crusade joined with local mobs to attack Jewish families and communities. Later Crusades brought similar violence, enhanced by accusations that Jews engaged in the ritual murder of Christians to use their blood in religious rites.

Legal restrictions on Jews gradually increased throughout Europe. Jews were forbidden to have Christian servants or employees, to hold public office, to appear in public on Christian holy days, or to enter Christian parts of town without a badge marking them as Jews. They were prohibited from engaging in any trade with Christians except money-lending—which only fueled popular resentment—and were banished from England and France.

The Crusades also left an inheritance of deep bitterness in Christian-Muslim relations. Each side dehumanized the other. (See "Listening to the Past: An Arab View of the Crusades," page 358.) Whereas Europeans perceived the Crusades as sacred religious movements, Muslims saw them as expansionist and imperialistic. The ideal of a sacred mission to conquer or convert Muslim peoples entered Europeans' consciousness and became a continuing goal. When in 1492 Christopher Columbus sailed west, he used the language of the Crusades in his diaries, and he hoped to establish a Christian base in India from which a new crusade against Islam could be launched (see Chapter 16).

Quick Review
What role did religious fervor play in the Crusades? What about political and economic considerations?

What characterized European society in the Middle Ages?

In the late ninth century medieval intellectuals described Christian society as composed of those who pray (the monks), those who fight (the nobles), and those who work (the peasants). They asserted that the three categories of citizens had been established by God and that every person had been assigned a fixed place in the social order.

This three-category model does not fully describe medieval society; there were degrees of wealth and status within each group. Also, the model does not take townspeople and the emerging commercial classes into consideration, and it completely excludes those who were not Christian. Furthermore, those who used the model, generally bishops and other church officials, ignored the fact that each of these groups was made up of both women and men. Despite—or perhaps because of—these limitations, the model of the three categories was a powerful mental construct. Therefore, we can use it to organize our investigation of life in the Middle Ages, broadening it to include groups and issues that medieval authors did not. (See page 353 for a discussion of the life of monks and nuns—"those who pray.")

The Life and Work of Peasants

The men and women who worked the land in the Middle Ages made up probably more than 90 percent of the population. Medieval theologians lumped everyone who worked the land into the category of "those who work," but in fact there were many levels of peasants,

Agricultural Work In this scene from a German manuscript written about 1190, men and women of different ages are sowing seeds and harvesting grain. All residents of a village, including children, engaged in agricultural tasks. (Rheinisches Landesmuseum, Bonn/The Bridgeman Art Library)

ranging from outright slaves to free and very rich farmers. Most peasants were serfs, required to stay in the village and perform a certain amount of labor each week on the lord's land. Serfs frequently had to pay arbitrary levies, as for marriage or inheritance of property. A free person had to do none of these things. For his or her landholding, rent had to be paid to the lord, but a free person could move and live as he or she wished.

Serfdom was a hereditary condition, though many serfs did secure their freedom, and the economic revival that began in the eleventh century (see pages 364–365) allowed many to buy their freedom. Further opportunities for increased personal freedom came when lords organized groups of villagers to migrate to sparsely settled frontier areas or to cut down forests or fill in swamps so that there was more land available for farming. Those who participated often gained a reduction in traditional manorial obligations and an improvement of their social and legal conditions.

In the Middle Ages most European peasants, free and unfree, lived in family groups in small villages that were part of a manor, the estate of a lord (see page 349). The manor was the basic unit of medieval rural organization and the center of rural life. In western and central Europe, peasant households consisted of one married couple, their children (including stepchildren), and perhaps one or two other relatives, such as a grandparent or unmarried aunt. In southern and eastern Europe, extended families were more likely to live in the same household or very near one another. Between one-third and one-half of children died before age five, though many people lived into their sixties.

The arable land of the manor was divided between the lord and the peasantry, with the lord's portion known as the demesne (dih-MAYN) or home farm. A peasant family's land was not usually one particular field but a scattering of strips across many fields, some of which would be planted in grain, some in other crops, and some left unworked to allow the soil to rejuvenate. That way if one field yielded little, strips in a different field might be more bountiful.

The peasants' work was typically divided according to gender. Men and boys were responsible for clearing new land, plowing, and caring for large animals; women and girls

Saint Maurice Some of the individuals who were held up to young men as models of ideal chivalry were probably real, but their lives were embellished with many stories. One such individual was Saint Maurice (d. 287), a soldier apparently executed by the Romans for refusing to renounce his Christian faith. He first emerges in the Carolingian period, and later he was held up as a model knight and declared a patron of the Holy Roman Empire and protector of the imperial army in wars against the pagan Slavs. His image was used on coins, and his cult was promoted by the archbishops of Magdeburg, who moved his relics to their cathedral. Until 1240 he was portrayed as a white man, but after that he was usually represented as a black man, as in this sandstone statue from Magdeburg Cathedral (ca. 1250). We have no idea why this change happened. (The Menil Collection)

were responsible for the care of small animals, spinning, and food preparation. Both sexes harvested and planted, though often there were gender-specific tasks within each of these major undertakings. Women and men worked in the vineyards and in the harvest and preparation of crops needed by the textile industry. Beginning in the eleventh century water mills and windmills aided in some tasks, especially grinding grain, and an increasing use of horses rather than oxen speeded up plowing.

The mainstay of the diet for peasants everywhere—and for all other classes—was bread. Peasants also ate vegetables, but animals were too valuable to be used for food on a regular basis. Ale was the universal drink of common people, and it provided needed calories and some relief from the difficult and monotonous labor that filled people's lives. In many places, severe laws forbidding hunting and trapping in the forests restricted deer and other game to the king and nobility.

The Life and Work of Nobles

The nobility, though a small fraction of the total population, strongly influenced all aspects of medieval culture. In the early Middle Ages noble status was limited to a very few families, but in the eleventh century knights in service to kings began to claim such status because it gave them special legal privileges. Nobles generally paid few taxes, and they had power over the people living on their lands. They maintained order, resolved disputes, and protected their dependents from attacks. They appointed officials who oversaw agricultural production. The liberty and privileges of the noble were inheritable.

Originally, most knights focused solely on military skills, but gradually a different ideal of knighthood emerged, usually termed **chivalry**. Chivalry was a code of conduct originally devised by the clergy to transform the typically crude and brutal behavior of the knightly class. Qualities associated with chivalry included loyalty, bravery, generosity, honor, graciousness, mercy, and eventually gallantry toward women. The chivalric ideal—and it was an ideal, not a standard pattern of behavior—created a new standard of masculinity for nobles, in which loyalty and honor remained the most important qualities, but graceful dancing and intelligent conversation were not considered unmanly.

chivalry A code of conduct that was supposed to govern the behavior of a knight.

Noblewomen played a large and important role in the functioning of the estate. They were responsible for managing the household's "inner economy"—cooking, brewing, spinning, weaving, and caring for yard animals. When the lord was away for long periods, his wife became the sole manager of the family properties. Often the responsibilities of the estate fell permanently to her if she became a widow.

Towns, Cities, and the Growth of Commercial Interests

The rise of towns and the growth of a new business and commercial class were a central part of Europe's recovery after the disorders of the tenth century. The development of towns was to lay the foundations for Europe's transformation, centuries later, from a rural agricultural society into an urban industrial society—a change with global implications.

Medieval towns had a few characteristics in common, one being that walls enclosed them. Most towns were first established as trading centers, with a marketplace in the middle, and they were likely to have a mint for coining money and a court for settling disputes. In each town, many people inhabited a small, cramped area. As population increased, towns rebuilt their walls, expanding the living space to accommodate growing numbers. Residents bargained with lords to make the town politically independent, which gave them the right to hold legal courts, select leaders, and set taxes.

Townspeople also tried to acquire liberties, above all personal freedom, for themselves. It gradually developed that serfs who fled their manors for towns and were able to find work and avoid recapture became free of personal labor obligations. In this way the growth of towns contributed to a slow decline of serfdom in western Europe, although the complete elimination of serfdom would take centuries.

Merchants constituted the most powerful group in most towns, and they were often organized into merchant guilds, which prohibited nonmembers from trading, pooled members' risks, monopolized city offices, and controlled the economy of the town. Towns became centers of production as well, and artisans in particular trades formed their own **craft guilds**. Members of the craft guilds determined the quality, quantity, and price of the goods produced and the number of apprentices and journeymen affiliated with the guild. Formal membership in guilds was generally limited to men, but women often worked in guild shops without official membership.

craft guilds Associations of artisans organized to regulate the quality, quantity, and price of the goods produced as well as the number of affiliated apprentices and journeymen.

Artisans generally made and sold products in their own homes, with production taking place on the ground floor. The family lived above the business on the second or third floor. As the business and the family expanded, additional stories were added.

Most medieval towns and cities developed with little planning or attention to sanitation. Horses and oxen dropped tons of dung on the streets every year. It was universal practice in the early towns to dump household waste, both animal and human, into the road in front of one's house. Despite such unpleasant aspects of urban life, people wanted to get into medieval towns because they represented opportunities for economic advancement, social mobility, and improvement in legal status.

The Expansion of Trade and the Commercial Revolution

The growth of towns went hand in hand with a remarkable expansion of trade as artisans and craftsmen manufactured goods for local and foreign consumption. Most trade centered in towns and was controlled by merchants. They began to pool their money to finance trading expeditions, sharing the profits and also sharing the risks. If disaster struck, an investor's loss was limited to the amount of that individual's investment, a legal concept termed "limited liability" that is essential to the modern capitalist economy.

Italian cities, especially Venice, led the West in trade in general and dominated trade with Asia and North Africa. Venetian ships carried salt from the Venetian lagoon; pepper and other spices from North Africa; and slaves, silk, and purple textiles from the East to northern and western Europe. Merchants from other cities in northern Italy such as Florence and Milan were also important traders, and they developed new methods of accounting and record keeping that facilitated the movement of goods and money. The commercial towns of Flanders were

Factors Contributing to the Growth of Towns
A rise in population
Increased agricultural output
Relative peace and political stability
The expansion of trade and commerce

The Hanseatic League, ca. 1300–1400

also leaders in long-distance trade and built up a vast industry in the manufacture of cloth, aided by ready access to wool from England, which was just across the channel. The availability of raw wool also encouraged the development of cloth manufacture within England itself, and commercial families in manufacturing towns grew fabulously rich.

In much of northern Europe, the Hanseatic League, a mercantile association of towns formed to achieve mutual security and exclusive trading rights, controlled trade. During the thirteenth century perhaps two hundred cities from Holland to Poland joined the league, but Lübeck always remained the dominant member. League ships carried furs, wax, copper, fish, grain, timber, and wine. These goods were exchanged for other products, mainly cloth and salt, from western cities. At cities such as Bruges and London, Hanseatic merchants secured special concessions exempting them from all tolls and allowing them to trade at local fairs. Hanseatic merchants also established foreign trading centers.

These developments added up to what is often called the **commercial revolution**. In giving the transformation this name, historians point not only to an increase in the sheer volume of trade and in the complexity and sophistication of business procedures but also to the new attitude toward business and making money. Some even detect a "capitalist spirit" in which making a profit was regarded as a good thing in itself, regardless of the uses to which that profit was put.

commercial revolution The transformation of the economic structure of Europe, beginning in the eleventh century, from a rural, manorial society to a more complex mercantile society.

The commercial revolution created a great deal of new wealth, which did not escape the attention of kings and other rulers. Wealth could be taxed, and through taxation kings could create strong and centralized states. The commercial revolution also provided the opportunity for thousands of serfs in western Europe to improve their social position; however, many people continued to live hand to mouth on low wages. Also, it is important to remember that most towns remained small throughout the Middle Ages. Feudal nobility and churchmen continued to determine the preponderant social attitudes, values, and patterns of thought and behavior.

Quick Review
How did the growth of towns and commerce challenge the existing medieval social model?

What were the key educational and cultural developments?

The towns that became centers of trade and production in the High Middle Ages also developed into cultural and intellectual centers. Trade brought in new ideas as well as merchandise, and in many cities a new type of educational institution—the university—emerged, meeting the needs of the new bureaucratic states and the church for educated administrators. As universities emerged, so did other cultural advancements, such as new forms of architecture and literature.

Universities and Scholasticism

Since the time of the Carolingian Empire, monasteries and cathedral schools had offered the only formal instruction available. Monasteries, geared to religious concerns, were located in rural environments. In contrast, schools attached to cathedrals were frequently situated in cities, where people of many backgrounds stimulated the growth and exchange of ideas. In the eleventh century in Bologna and other Italian cities wealthy businessmen established municipal schools, and in the twelfth century municipal schools in Italy and cathedral schools in France developed into much larger universities, a transformation parallel to the opening of madrasas in Muslim cities (see page 227).

The growth of the University of Bologna coincided with a revival of interest in Roman law. The study of Roman law as embodied in Justinian's *Code* (see page 185) had never completely died out in the West, but this sudden burst of interest seems to have been inspired by Irnerius (ca. 1055–ca. 1130), a great teacher at Bologna.

At the Italian city of Salerno, interest in medicine had persisted for centuries. Greek and Muslim physicians there had studied the use of herbs as cures and had experimented with surgery. The twelfth century ushered in a new interest in Greek medical texts and in the work of Arab and Greek doctors. Ideas from this medical literature spread throughout Europe from Salerno and became the basis of training for physicians at other medieval universities.

Although medicine and law were important academic disciplines in the Middle Ages, theology was "the queen of sciences," so termed because it involved the study of God, who was said to make all knowledge possible. Paris became the place to study theology, and in the first decades of the twelfth century students from all over Europe crowded into the cathedral school of Notre Dame in that city.

Scholastics Medieval professors who developed a method of thinking, reasoning, and writing in which questions were raised and authorities cited on both sides of a question.

University professors were known as "schoolmen" or **Scholastics**. They developed a method of thinking, reasoning, and writing in which questions were raised and authorities cited on both sides of a question. The goal of the Scholastic method was to arrive at definitive answers and to provide a rational explanation for what was believed on faith.

One of the most famous Scholastics was Peter Abélard (1079–1142). Fascinated by logic, which he believed could be used to solve most problems, Abélard used a method of systematic doubting in his writing and teaching. As he put it, "By doubting we come to questioning, and by questioning we perceive the truth." Other scholars merely asserted theological principles; Abélard discussed and analyzed them.

Thirteenth-century Scholastics devoted an enormous amount of time to collecting and organizing knowledge on all topics. These collections were published as summa (SOO-muh), or reference books. Thomas Aquinas (1225–1274), a professor at the University of Paris, produced the most famous collection, the *Summa Theologica*, which deals with a vast number of theological questions.

In northern Europe—at Paris and later at Oxford and Cambridge in England—university faculties grouped themselves according to academic disciplines, or schools: law, medicine, arts, and theology. Students lived in privately endowed residential colleges and were considered to be lower-level members of the clergy. This clerical status, along with widely held ideas about women's lesser intellectual capabilities, meant that university education was restricted to men.

At all universities, the standard method of teaching was the lecture. With this method the professor read an authoritative text. He then explained and interpreted the passage. Examinations were given after three, four, or five years of study, when the student applied for a degree. Examinations were oral and very difficult. If the candidate passed, he was awarded the first, or bachelor's, degree. Further study enabled the graduate to try for the master's and doctor's degrees. Degrees were technically licenses to teach. Most students, however, did not become teachers. They staffed the expanding royal and papal administrations.

Cathedrals and a New Architectural Style

As we have seen, religious devotion was expressed through daily rituals, holiday ceremonies, and the creation of new institutions such as universities and religious orders. People also wanted permanent visible representations of their piety, and both church and city leaders

Notre Dame Cathedral, Paris, begun 1163 This view offers a fine example of the twin towers (left), the spire, the great rose window over the south portal (center), and the flying buttresses that support the walls and the vaults. Like hundreds of other churches in medieval Europe, it was dedicated to the Virgin Mary. With a spire rising more than 300 feet, Notre Dame was the tallest building in Europe at the time of its construction. (David R. Frazier/Photo Researchers, Inc.)

wanted physical symbols of their wealth and power. These aims found their most spectacular outlet in the building of cathedrals.

In the tenth and eleventh centuries cathedrals were built in a style that resembled ancient Roman architecture, with massive walls, rounded stone arches, and small windows—features later labeled Romanesque. In the twelfth century a new style spread out from central France. It was dubbed **Gothic** by later Renaissance architects who thought that only the uncouth Goths could have invented such a disunified style. The basic features of Gothic architecture—pointed arches, high ceilings, and exterior supports called flying buttresses that carried much of the weight of the roof—allowed unprecedented interior lightness. Stained-glass windows were cut into the stone, so that the interior, one French abbot exclaimed, "would shine with the wonderful and uninterrupted light of most sacred windows, pervading the interior beauty."[2] Between 1180 and 1270 in France alone, eighty cathedrals, about five hundred abbey churches, and tens of thousands of parish churches were constructed in this new style. They are testimony to the faith and piety of medieval people and also to the civic pride of urban residents, for towns competed with one another to build the largest and most splendid cathedral.

Gothic The term for the architectural and artistic style that prevailed in Europe from the mid-twelfth to the sixteenth century.

Cathedrals served secular as well as religious purposes. Local guilds met in the cathedrals to arrange business deals, and municipal officials held political meetings there. Pilgrims slept there, lovers courted there, and traveling actors staged plays there. First and foremost, however, the cathedral was intended to teach the people the doctrines of Christian faith through visual images such as those found in stained-glass windows and religious statuary. In this way architecture became the servant of theology.

Troubadour Poetry

troubadours Medieval poets in southern Europe who wrote and sang lyrical verses. The word *troubadour* comes from the Provençal word *trobar*, which in turn derives from the Arabic *taraba*, meaning "to sing" or "to sing poetry."

Educational and religious texts were typically written in Latin, but poems, songs, and stories were written down in local dialects and celebrated things of concern to ordinary people. In southern Europe, especially in the area of southern France known as Provence, poets who called themselves **troubadours** wrote lyric verses celebrating love, desire, beauty, and gallantry. They sang them at the courts of nobles and rulers.

Troubadour poets celebrated "courtly love," the pure or perfect love a knight was supposed to feel for his lady. In courtly love poetry, the writer praises his or her love object, idealizing the beloved and promising loyalty and great deeds. Poetry in praise of love originated in the Muslim culture of the Iberian Peninsula, where heterosexual romantic love had long been the subject of poems and songs. Southern France was a border area where Christian and Muslim cultures mixed; Spanish Muslim poets sang at the courts of Christian nobles, and Provençal poets picked up their romantic themes.

Quick Review
What values, beliefs, and priorities were reflected in medieval scholarship, architecture, and literature?

Why have the later Middle Ages been seen as a time of calamity and crisis?

Between 1300 and 1450 Europeans experienced a frightful series of shocks: climate change, economic decline, plague, war, social upheaval, and increased crime and violence. Death and preoccupation with death made the fourteenth century one of the most wrenching periods of history in Europe.

The Great Famine and the Black Death

In the first half of the fourteenth century Europe experienced a series of climate changes, especially the beginning of a period of colder and wetter weather that historical geographers label the "little ice age." Its effects were dramatic and disastrous. Population had steadily increased in the twelfth and thirteenth centuries, but with colder weather, poor harvests led to scarcity and starvation. The costs of grain, livestock, and dairy products rose sharply. Almost all of northern Europe suffered a terrible famine between 1315 and 1322. Thus, when a virulent new disease, later called the **Black Death** (Map 14.3), struck Europe in 1347, malnutrition made its population especially vulnerable to its predations.

Black Death The plague that first struck Europe in 1347, killing perhaps one-third of the population.

Most historians and almost all microbiologists identify the disease that spread in the fourteenth century as the bubonic plague, although some think it might have been a different dreadful disease. Plague normally afflicts rats. Fleas living on the infected rats pass the bacteria that cause the plague on to the next rat they bite. Usually the disease is limited to rodents, but at certain points in history the fleas have jumped from their rodent hosts to humans and other animals.

The disease had dreadful effects on the body. The classic symptom was a painful bubo, or growth the size of a nut or an apple in the armpit, in the groin, or on the neck. If the

The Spread of the Black Death to Europe
1331: Plague first described in southwestern China
1340s: Plague reaches Black Sea ports, spread by Mongol armies and merchants
October 1347: Genoese ships bring the plague from the Crimea to the Sicilian port of Messina

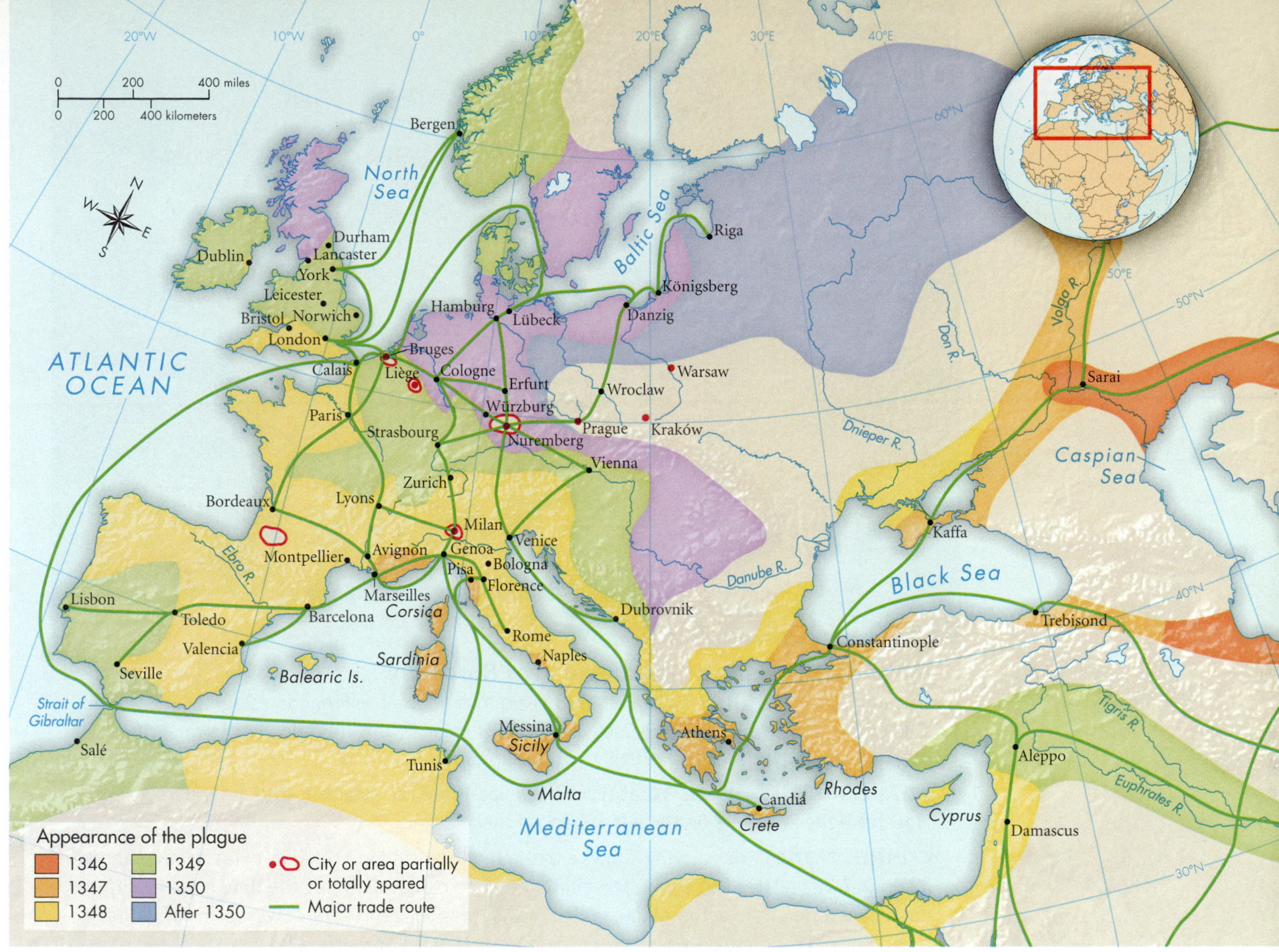

Map 14.3 The Course of the Black Death in Fourteenth-Century Europe The plague followed trade routes as it spread into and across Europe. A few cities that took strict quarantine measures were spared.

bubo was drained, the victim had a chance of recovery. The secondary stage was the appearance of black blotches caused by bleeding under the skin. Finally, the victim began to cough violently and spit blood, and death followed in two or three days. Physicians could sometimes ease the pain but had no cure.

Most people — lay, scholarly, and medical — believed that the Black Death was caused by poisons or by "corrupted air" that carried the disease from place to place. They sought to keep poisons from entering the body by smelling or ingesting strong-smelling herbs, and they tried to remove the poisons through bloodletting. They also prayed and did penance. Anxiety and fears about the plague caused people to look for scapegoats, and they found them in the Jews, who they believed had poisoned the wells of Christian communities and thereby infected the drinking water. This charge led to the murder of thousands of Jews across Europe.

Because population figures for the period before the arrival of the plague do not exist for most countries and cities, only educated guesses can be made about mortality rates. Of a total English population of perhaps 4.2 million, probably 1.4 million died of the Black Death in its several visits. In Italy densely populated cities endured incredible losses. Florence lost between one-half and two-thirds of its population when the plague visited in 1348. The disease recurred intermittently in the 1360s and 1370s, and it reappeared many times, as late as the early 1700s in Europe.

Picturing the Past

Siege of the Castle of Mortagne near Bordeaux

This miniature of a battle in the Hundred Years' War shows the French besieging an English-held castle. Medieval warfare usually consisted of small skirmishes and attacks on castles. (© British Library Board, MS Royal 14 e. IV f. 23)

ANALYZING THE IMAGE What types of weapons are the attackers and defenders using? How have the attackers on the left enhanced their position?

CONNECTIONS This painting shows a battle that occurred in 1377, but it was painted about a hundred years later and shows the military technology available at the time it was painted, not at the time of the actual siege. Which of the weapons represent newer forms of military technology? What impact would you expect them to have on warfare?

In the short term the economic effects of the plague were severe because the death of many peasants disrupted food production. But in the long term the dramatic decline in population eased pressure on the land, and wages and per capita wealth rose for those who survived. The psychological consequences of the plague were profound. Some people sought release in wild living, while others turned to the severest forms of asceticism and frenzied religious fervor.

The Hundred Years' War

While the plague ravaged populations in Asia, North Africa, and Europe, a long international war in western Europe added further death and destruction. England and France had engaged in sporadic military hostilities from the time of the Norman Conquest in 1066 (see page 351), and in the middle of the fourteenth century these became more intense. From 1337 to 1453 the two countries intermittently fought one another in what was the longest war in European history, ultimately dubbed the Hundred Years' War.

The Hundred Years' War had a number of causes. Both England and France claimed the duchy of Aquitaine in southwestern France, and the English king Edward III argued that, as the grandson of an earlier French king, he should have rightfully inherited the French throne. Nobles in provinces on the borders of France who were worried about the growing power of the French king supported Edward, as did wool merchants and cloth makers in Flanders who depended on English wool. The governments of both England and France manipulated public opinion to support their side in the war, with each country portraying the other as evil.

The war, fought almost entirely in France, consisted mainly of a series of random sieges and raids. During the war's early stages, England was highly successful, primarily through the use of longbows fired by well-trained foot soldiers against mounted knights and, after 1375, by early cannons. By 1419 the English had advanced to the walls of Paris. Nonetheless, while England scored the initial victories, France won the war.

The ultimate French success rests heavily on the actions of a French peasant girl, Joan of Arc, whose vision and military leadership revived French fortunes and led to victory. Born in 1412, Joan grew up in a pious household. During adolescence she began to hear voices, which she later said belonged to Saint Michael, Saint Catherine, and Saint Margaret. In 1428 these voices told her that the dauphin of France—Charles VII, who was uncrowned as king because of the English occupation—had to be crowned and the English expelled from France. Joan went to the French court and secured the support of the dauphin to travel, dressed as a knight, with the French army to the besieged city of Orléans.

At Orléans, Joan inspired and led French attacks, and the English retreated. As a result of her successes, Charles made Joan co-commander of the entire army, and she led it to a string of military victories in the summer of 1429; many cities surrendered without a fight. Two months after the victory at Orléans, Charles VII was crowned king at Reims.

Joan and the French army continued their fight against the English. In 1430 England's allies, the Burgundians, captured Joan and sold her to the English, and the French did not intervene. The English wanted Joan eliminated for obvious political reasons, but the primary charge against her was heresy, and the trial was conducted by church authorities. In 1431 the court condemned her as a heretic, and she was burned at the stake in the marketplace at Rouen. The French army continued its victories without her, and demands for an end to the war increased among the English, who were growing tired of the mounting loss of life and the flow of money into a seemingly bottomless pit. Slowly the French reconquered Normandy and finally ejected the English from Aquitaine. At the war's end in 1453, only the town of Calais remained in English hands.

The long war had a profound impact on the two countries. In England and France the war promoted nationalism—the feeling of unity and identity that binds together a people. It led to technological experimentation, especially with gunpowder weaponry, whose firepower made the protective walls of stone castles obsolete. However, such weaponry also made warfare increasingly expensive. The war also stimulated the development of the English Parliament. Between 1250 and 1450 representative assemblies from several classes of society flourished in many European countries, but only the English Parliament became a powerful national body. Edward III's constant need for money to pay for the war compelled him to summon it many times, and its representatives slowly built up their powers.

Challenges to the Church

In times of crisis or disaster people of all faiths have sought the consolation of religion, but in the fourteenth century the official Christian Church offered little solace. While local clergy eased the suffering of many, a dispute over who was the legitimate pope weakened the church as an institution. In 1309 pressure by the French monarchy led the pope to move his permanent residence to Avignon in southern France. This marked the start of seven successive papacies in Avignon. These popes, all of whom were French, concentrated on bureaucratic and financial matters to the exclusion of spiritual objectives.

In 1376 one of the French popes returned to Rome, and when he died there several years later Roman citizens demanded an Italian pope who would remain in Rome. The

The Great Schism, 1378–1417

cardinals elected Urban VI, but his tactless and arrogant manner caused them to regret their decision. The cardinals slipped away from Rome and declared Urban's election invalid because it had come about under threats from the Roman mob. They elected a French cardinal who took the name Clement VII (pontificate 1378–1394) and set himself up at Avignon in opposition to Urban. There were thus two popes, a situation that was later termed the Great Schism.

The powers of Europe aligned themselves with Urban or Clement along strictly political lines. France recognized the Frenchman, Clement; England, France's historic enemy, recognized Urban. The rest of Europe lined up behind one or the other. In the end the schism weakened the religious faith of many Christians and brought church leadership into serious disrepute.

A first attempt to heal the schism led to the installation of a third pope and a threefold split, but finally a church council meeting at Constance (1414–1418) successfully deposed the three schismatic popes and elected a new leader, who took the name Martin V (pontificate 1417–1431). The schism was over, but those who had hoped that the council would also reform problems in the church were disappointed. In the later fifteenth century the papacy concentrated on building up its wealth and political power in Italy rather than on the concerns of the whole church. As a result, many people decided that they would need to rely on their own prayers and pious actions rather than on the institutional church for their salvation.

Peasant and Urban Revolts

The difficult conditions of the fourteenth and fifteenth centuries spurred a wave of peasant and urban revolts across Europe. In 1358, when French taxation for the Hundred Years' War fell heavily on the poor, the frustrations of the French peasantry exploded in a massive uprising called the Jacquerie (zhah-kuh-REE). Adding to the anger over taxes was the toll taken by the plague and by the famine that had struck some areas. Crowds swept through the countryside, slashing the throats of nobles, burning their castles, raping their wives and daughters, and killing or maiming their livestock. Artisans, small merchants, and parish priests joined the peasants, and residents of both urban and rural areas committed terrible destruction. For several weeks the nobles were on the defensive, until the upper class united to repress the revolt with merciless ferocity. Thousands of the "Jacques," innocent as well as guilty, were cut down.

Taxes and other grievances also led to the 1381 English Peasants' Revolt, involving tens of thousands of people. The Black Death had dramatically reduced the supply of labor, and peasants had demanded higher wages and fewer manorial obligations. Parliament countered with a law freezing wages and binding workers to their manors. Although the law was difficult to enforce, it contributed to an atmosphere of discontent, which was further enhanced by popular preachers who proclaimed that great disparities between rich and poor went against Christ's teachings. Moreover, decades of aristocratic violence, much of it perpetrated against the weak peasantry, had bred hostility and bitterness.

In 1380 Parliament imposed a poll tax on all citizens to fund the Hundred Years' War, sparking a revolt. Beginning with assaults on the tax collectors, the uprising in England followed much the same course as had the Jacquerie in France. Castles and manors were sacked; manorial records were destroyed; nobles were murdered. Urban discontent merged with rural violence. Apprentices and journeymen, frustrated because the highest positions in the guilds were closed to them, rioted.

The boy-king Richard II (r. 1377–1399) met the leaders of the revolt, agreed to charters ensuring the peasants' freedom from manorial obligations, tricked them with false promises, and then proceeded to crush the uprising with terrible ferocity. The nobility tried to use this defeat to restore the ancient obligations of serfdom, but the increasingly commercialized economy made that difficult, and serfdom slowly disappeared in England, though peasants remained poor.

Conditions in England and France were not unique. In Florence in 1378 the *ciompi*, or poor propertyless workers, revolted, and serious social unrest occurred in Lübeck, Brunswick, and other German cities. In Spain in 1391 massive uprisings in Seville and Barcelona took the form of vicious attacks on Jewish communities. Rebellions and uprisings everywhere revealed deep peasant and worker frustration with the socioeconomic conditions of the time.

Quick Review
How did natural and manmade disasters combine to make the fourteenth century a time of social and economic upheaval?

Connections

MEDIEVAL EUROPE continues to fascinate us today. We go to medieval banquets, fairs, and even weddings; visit castle-themed hotels and amusement parks; watch movies about knights and their conquests; play video games in which we become warriors, trolls, or sorcerers; and read stories with themes of great quests, some set in the Middle Ages and some set in places that just seem medieval. From all these amusements the Middle Ages emerges as a strange and wonderful time. Characters from other parts of the world often heighten the exoticism: a Muslim soldier joins the fight against a common enemy, a Persian princess rescues the hero and his sidekick, a Buddhist monk teaches martial arts techniques. These characters from outside Europe are fictional, but they also represent aspects of reality, because medieval Europe was not isolated, and political and social structures similar to those in Europe developed elsewhere.

In reality few of us would probably want to live in the real Middle Ages, when most people worked in the fields all day, a banquet meant a piece of tough old rooster instead of the usual meal of pea soup and black bread, and even wealthy lords lived in damp and drafty castles. We do not really want to return to a time when one-third to one-half of all children died before age five and alcohol was the only real pain reliever. But the contemporary appeal of the Middle Ages is an interesting phenomenon, particularly because it stands in such sharp contrast to the attitude of educated Europeans who lived in the centuries immediately afterward. They were the ones who dubbed the period "middle" and viewed the soaring cathedrals as dreadful "Gothic." They saw their own era as the one to be celebrated, and the Middle Ages as best forgotten.

- **For a list of suggested readings for this chapter, visit** *bedfordstmartins.com/mckayworldunderstanding*.
- **For primary sources from this period, see** *Sources of World Societies*, Second Edition.
- **For Web sites, images, and documents related to topics in this chapter, see Make History at** *bedfordstmartins.com/mckayworldunderstanding*.

Chapter 14 Study Guide

To do these exercises online, go to bedfordstmartins.com/mckayworldunderstanding.

Step 1

GETTING STARTED

Below are basic terms about this period in global history. Can you identify each term below and explain why it matters?

TERMS	WHO (OR WHAT) AND WHEN	WHY IT MATTERS
vassal, p. 349		
fief, p. 349		
feudalism, p. 349		
manorialism, p. 349		
serf, p. 350		
heresy, p. 355		
reconquista, p. 356		
Crusades, p. 357		
chivalry, p. 363		
craft guilds, p. 364		
commercial revolution, p. 365		
Scholastics, p. 366		
Gothic, p. 367		
troubadours, p. 368		
Black Death , p. 368		

Step 2

MOVING BEYOND THE BASICS

The exercise below requires a more advanced understanding of the chapter material. Examine the social structure of medieval Europe by filling in the chart below with descriptions of the characteristics and lifestyle of the medieval peasantry, nobility, and clergy, as well as important developments and trends affecting the group's composition and status. When you are finished, consider the following questions: How accurate was the medieval model that divided society into those who work, those who fight, and those who pray? How might you modify this model to create a better picture of the reality of medieval life?

	CHARACTERISTICS AND LIFESTYLE	DEVELOPMENTS AND TRENDS
Peasants		
Nobility		
Clergy		

Step 3

PUTTING IT ALL TOGETHER

Now that you've reviewed key elements of the chapter, take a step back and try to see the big picture. Remember to use specific examples from the chapter in your answers.

POLITICAL CONSOLIDATION AND RELIGIOUS REFORM

- What was the relationship between feudalism and manorialism? How did the two systems work together to shape the medieval social and political world?
- How and why did the agendas of secular rulers and the papacy clash in the Middle Ages?

SOCIETY, ECONOMY, AND CULTURE

- How did serfdom differ from slavery? How and why did western European peasants gain increased personal liberty over the course of the Middle Ages?
- What made the rise of universities possible? How might larger social and economic trends have contributed to their emergence?

THE LATER MIDDLE AGES

- What were the social, economic, and cultural consequences of the plague?

- What factors combined to undermine European's faith in religious and political authorities? How did peasant and urban revolts reflect this lack of confidence?

LOOKING BACK, LOOKING AHEAD

- Argue for or against the following statement. "The Middle Ages are best understood as a period of transition, a low point of decline and disorder between the twin peaks of Classical and Renaissance civilization." What evidence can you present in support of your argument?

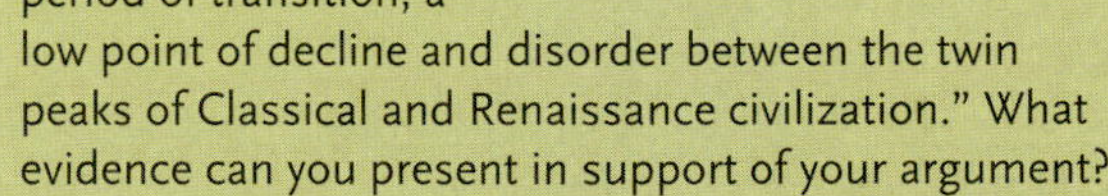

- What role might the Crusades play in contemporary Muslim-Christian relations? What connections might Muslims or Christians today make between the Crusades and the global policies of Western nations in the twenty and twenty-first centuries?

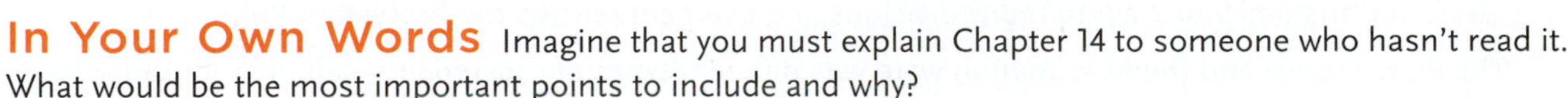

In Your Own Words Imagine that you must explain Chapter 14 to someone who hasn't read it. What would be the most important points to include and why?

15

Europe in the Renaissance and Reformation

1350–1600

While disease, famine, and war marked the fourteenth century in much of Europe, the era also witnessed the beginnings of remarkable changes in many aspects of intellectual and cultural life. First in Italy and then elsewhere, artists and writers thought that they were living in a new golden age, later termed the Renaissance, French for *rebirth*. The word *renaissance* was used initially to describe art that seemed to recapture, or perhaps even surpass, the classical past, and then came to be used for many aspects of life of the period. The new attitude diffused slowly out of Italy, with the result that the Renaissance "happened" at different times in different parts of Europe. It shaped the lives of Europe's educated elites, although families, kin networks, religious beliefs, and the rhythms of the agricultural year still remained important.

Portrait of Baldassare Castiglione Individual portraits like this one by the Italian artist Raphael expressed the ideals of the Renaissance: elegance, balance, proportion, and self-awareness. (© Samuel Courtauld Trust, The Courtauld Gallery, London/The Bridgeman Art Library)

Religious reformers carried out even more dramatic changes. Calls for reform of the Christian Church began very early in its history and continued throughout the Middle Ages. In the sixteenth century these calls gained wide acceptance, due not only to religious issues and problems within the church but also to political and social factors. Western Christianity broke into many divisions, a movement termed the Protestant Reformation. The Renaissance and the Reformation were very different types of movements, but both looked back to a time they regarded as purer and better than their own, and both offered opportunities for strong individuals to shape their world in unexpected ways. Both have also been seen as key elements in the creation of the "modern" world.

Chapter Preview

- What were the major cultural developments of the Renaissance?
- What were the key social hierarchies in Renaissance Europe?
- How did the nation-states of western Europe evolve in this period?
- What were the central beliefs of Protestant reformers?
- How did the Catholic Church respond to the advent of Protestantism?
- Why did religious violence escalate in this period?

What were the major cultural developments of the Renaissance?

Renaissance A French word meaning rebirth, used to describe a cultural movement that began in fourteenth-century Italy and looked back to the classical past.

The **Renaissance** was characterized by self-conscious awareness among fourteenth- and fifteenth-century Italians, particularly scholars and writers known as humanists, that they were living in a new era. Their ideas influenced education and were spread through the new technology of the printing press. Interest in the classical past and in the individual also shaped Renaissance art in terms of style and subject matter. Also important to Renaissance art were the wealthy patrons who helped fund it.

Wealth and Power in Renaissance Italy

patronage Financial support of writers and artists by cities, groups, and individuals, often to produce specific works or works in specific styles.

Economic growth laid the material basis for the Italian Renaissance and its cultural achievements. Ambitious merchants gained political power to match their economic power and then used their money and power to buy luxuries and hire talent in a **patronage** system. Through this system cities, groups, and individuals commissioned writers and artists to produce specific works. Thus, economics, politics, and culture were interconnected.

The Renaissance began in the northern Italian city of Florence, which possessed enormous wealth. From their position as tax collectors for the papacy, Florentine mercantile families began to dominate European banking, setting up offices in major European and North African cities. The resulting profits allowed banking families to control the city's politics and culture. Although Florence was officially a republic, starting in 1434 the great Medici (MEH-duh-chee) banking family held power almost continually for centuries. They supported an academy for scholars and a host of painters, sculptors, poets, and architects.

In other Italian cities as well, wealthy merchants and bankers built magnificent palaces and became patrons of the arts, hiring not only architects to design and build these palaces but also artists to fill them with paintings and sculptures, and musicians and composers to fill them with music. Attractions like these appealed to the rich, social-climbing residents of Venice, Florence, Genoa, and Rome, who came to see life more as an opportunity for enjoyment than as a painful pilgrimage to Heaven.

This cultural flowering took place amid political turmoil. In the fifteenth century five powers dominated the Italian peninsula: Venice, Milan, Florence, the Papal States, and the kingdom of Naples. These powers competed for territory and tried to extend their authority over smaller city-states. While the states of northern Europe were moving toward centralization and consolidation, Italian politics resembled a jungle where the powerful dominated the weak.

In one significant respect, however, the Italian city-states anticipated future relations among competing European states after 1500. Whenever one Italian state appeared to gain a predominant position within the peninsula, other states combined to establish a balance of power against the major threat. In the formation of these alliances, Renaissance Italians invented the machinery of modern diplomacy: permanent embassies with resident ambassadors in capitals where political relations and commercial ties needed continual monitoring.

Although the resident ambassador was one of the great political achievements of the Italian Renaissance, diplomacy did not prevent invasions of Italy. These began in

Italian States, 1494

1494 as Italy became the focus of international ambitions and the battleground of foreign armies, and Italian cities suffered severely from continual warfare for decades. Thus the failure of the city-states to form some type of federal system, to consolidate, or at least to establish a common foreign policy led to centuries of subjugation by outsiders.

Chapter Chronology

1434–1737	Medici family in power in Florence
1450s	Development of movable metal type in Germany
1469	Marriage of Isabella of Castile and Ferdinand of Aragon
1492	Spain conquers Granada; practicing Jews expelled from Spain
1508–1512	Michelangelo paints ceiling of the Sistine Chapel
1513	Niccolò Machiavelli writes *The Prince*
1521	Diet of Worms
1521–1555	Charles V's wars against Valois kings
1525	Peasant revolts in Germany
1527	Henry VIII of England asks Pope Clement VII to annul his marriage to Catherine of Aragon
1536	John Calvin publishes *The Institutes of the Christian Religion*
1540	Founding of the Society of Jesus (Jesuits)
1545–1563	Council of Trent
1555	Peace of Augsburg
1558–1603	Reign of Elizabeth I in England
1560–1660	Height of European witch-hunt
1568–1578	Civil war in the Netherlands
1572	Saint Bartholomew's Day massacre
1598	Edict of Nantes

The Rise of Humanism

The realization that something new and unique was happening first came to writers in the fourteenth century, especially to the Italian poet and humanist Francesco Petrarch (frahn-CHEH-skoh PEH-trahrk; 1304–1374). For Petrarch, the barbarian migrations (see pages 196–201) had caused a sharp cultural break with the glories of Rome and inaugurated what he called the "dark ages." Along with many of his contemporaries, Petrarch sought to reconnect with the classical past, and he believed that such efforts were bringing on a new golden age.

Petrarch and other poets, writers, and artists showed a deep interest both in the physical remains of the Roman Empire and in classical Latin texts. The study of Latin classics became known as the *studia humanitates*, usually translated as "liberal studies" or the "liberal arts." People who advocated it were known as *humanists*, and their program as **humanism**. Like all programs of study, humanism contained an implicit philosophy: that human nature and achievements were worthy of contemplation. Humanists did not reject religion, however. Instead they sought to synthesize Christian and classical teachings, pointing out the harmony between them.

humanism A program of study designed by Italians that emphasized the critical study of Latin and Greek literature with the goal of understanding human nature.

Humanists and other Renaissance thinkers were especially interested in individual achievement. They were particularly drawn to individuals who had risen above their background to become brilliant, powerful, or unique. (See "Individuals in Society: Leonardo da Vinci," page 383.) Such individuals had the admirable quality of *virtù* (ver-TOO), which is not virtue in the sense of moral goodness, but the ability to shape the world around them according to their will.

Humanists thought that their recommended course of study in the classics would provide essential skills for future diplomats, lawyers, military leaders, businessmen, and politicians, as well as for writers and artists. They also taught that taking an active role in the world should be the aim of all educated individuals and that education was not simply for private or religious purposes, but to benefit the public good.

Humanists put their educational ideas into practice. They opened schools and academies in Italian cities and courts in which pupils learned Latin and Greek and studied the classics. These classics, humanists taught, would provide models of how to write clearly, argue effectively, and speak persuasively. Gradually humanist education became the basis for intermediate and advanced education for well-to-do urban boys and men.

Humanists disagreed about education for women. Many saw the value of exposing women to classical models of moral behavior and reasoning, but they also wondered whether a program of study that emphasized eloquence and action was proper for women, whose sphere was generally understood to be private and domestic. Nonetheless, through tutors or programs of self-study a few women did become educated in the classics.

Procession of the Magi, 1461 This segment of a huge fresco by the Italian artist Bennozzo Gozzoli covering three walls of a chapel in the Medici palace in Florence shows members of the Medici family and other contemporary individuals in a procession accompanying the biblical three wise men (*magi* in Italian) as they brought gifts to the infant Jesus. Reflecting the self-confidence of his patrons, Gozzoli places several members of the Medici family at the head of the procession, accompanied by their grooms. (Erich Lessing/Art Resource, NY)

Humanists looked to the classical past for political as well as literary models. The best-known political theorist of this era was Niccolò Machiavelli (1469–1527), who worked as an official for the city of Florence until he was ousted in a power struggle. He spent the rest of his life writing, and his most famous work is the short political treatise *The Prince* (1513). Using the examples of classical and contemporary rulers, *The Prince* argues that the function of a ruler (or a government) is to preserve order and security. To preserve the state a ruler should use whatever means necessary—brutality, lying, manipulation—but he should not do anything that would make the populace turn against him, since that could destabilize the state. "It is much safer for the prince to be feared than loved," Machiavelli advised, "but he ought to avoid making himself hated."[1]

Christian Humanism

In the last quarter of the fifteenth century, students from northern Europe flocked to Italy, absorbed the "new learning" of humanism, and carried it back to their own countries. Northern humanists shared the Italians' ideas about the wisdom of ancient texts and felt even more strongly that the best elements of classical and Christian cultures should be combined. These **Christian humanists**, as they were later called, saw humanist learning as a way to bring about reform of the church and to deepen people's spiritual lives.

Christian humanists Humanists from northern Europe who thought that the best elements of classical and Christian cultures should be combined and saw humanist learning as a way to bring about reform of the church and deepen people's spiritual lives.

The Englishman Thomas More (1478–1535) began life as a lawyer, studied the classics, and entered government service. His most famous work, *Utopia* (1516), describes a community on an island somewhere beyond Europe where the problems that plagued More's fellow citizens, such as poverty, hunger, and religious intolerance do not exist. *Utopia* was widely read by learned Europeans in the Latin in which More wrote it, and later in vernacular translations, and its title quickly became the standard word for any idealized imaginary society.

Better known by contemporaries than Thomas More was the Dutch humanist Desiderius Erasmus (1466?–1536) of Rotterdam. His fame rested largely on his exceptional knowledge of Greek and the Bible. For Erasmus, education was the key to moral and intellectual improvement, and true Christianity was an inner attitude of the spirit, not a set of outward actions.

Printing and Its Social Impact

Although the fourteenth-century humanist Petrarch and the sixteenth-century humanist Erasmus had many similar ideas, the immediate impact of their ideas was very different because of one thing: the printing press with movable metal type. While Petrarch's works spread slowly from person to person by hand copying, Erasmus's works spread quickly through printing, in which hundreds or thousands of identical copies could be made in a short time.

Printing with movable type was invented in China (see page 328), and movable metal type was first developed in thirteenth-century Korea. Printing with movable metal type was independently developed in Germany in the middle of the fifteenth century as a combination of existing technologies. Several metal-smiths, most prominently Johann Gutenberg (ca. 1400–1468), transformed the metal stamps used to mark signs on jewelry into type that could be covered with ink and used to mark symbols onto a page. The printing revolution was also enabled by the ready availability of paper, which was made using techniques that had originated in China and spread from Muslim Spain to the rest of Europe.

The effects of the invention of movable-type printing were not felt overnight. Nevertheless, within a half century of the publication of Gutenberg's Bible of 1456, movable type had brought about radical changes. Historians estimate that somewhere between 8 million and 20 million books were printed in Europe between 1456 and 1500, many more than the total number of books that had been produced in the West during the many millennia between the invention of writing and 1456.

Printing transformed both the private and the public lives of Europeans. In the public realm, government and church leaders both used and worried about printing. They printed laws, declarations of war, battle accounts, and propaganda, but they also attempted to censor or ban books and authors whose ideas they thought were wrong. These efforts were rarely effective.

In the private realm, printing enabled people to read identical books so that they could more easily discuss the ideas that the books contained. Although most of the earliest books and pamphlets dealt with religious subjects, printers produced anything that would sell. Illustrations increased a book's sales, so they published both history and pornography full of woodcuts and engravings. Additionally, single-page broadsides and flysheets allowed public events and "wonders" such as comets and two-headed calves to be experienced vicariously by the stay-at-home. Since books and other printed materials were read aloud to illiterate listeners, print bridged the gap between the written and oral cultures.

Because many laypeople could not read Latin, printers put out works in Italian, French, Spanish, and English, fostering standardization in these languages. Works in these languages were also performed on stage, for plays of all types were popular everywhere. In London the works of William Shakespeare (1564–1616) were especially popular (see page 430).

Art and the Artist

No feature of the Renaissance evokes greater admiration than its artistic masterpieces. In Renaissance Italy wealthy merchants, bankers, popes, and princes commissioned art as a means of glorifying themselves and their families. As a result of patronage certain artists gained great fame, leading many historians to view the Renaissance as the beginning of the concept of the artist as genius. In the Middle Ages people believed that only God created, albeit through individuals, and artistic originality was not particularly valued. By contrast, Renaissance artists and humanists came to think that a work of art was the deliberate creation of a unique personality, of an individual who transcended traditions, rules, and theories.

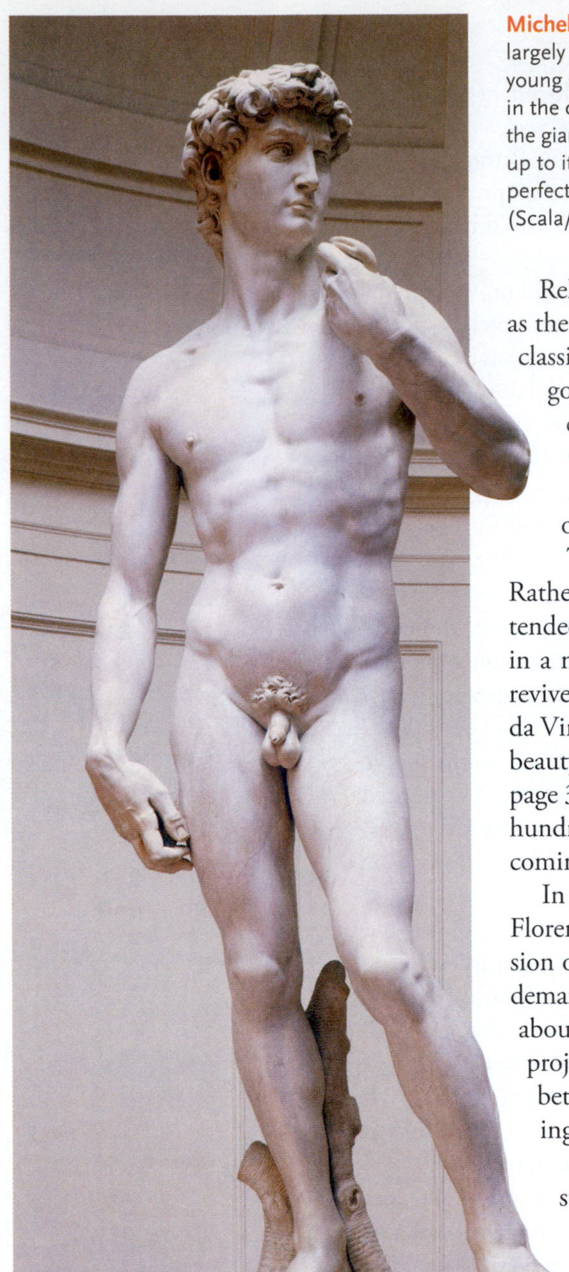

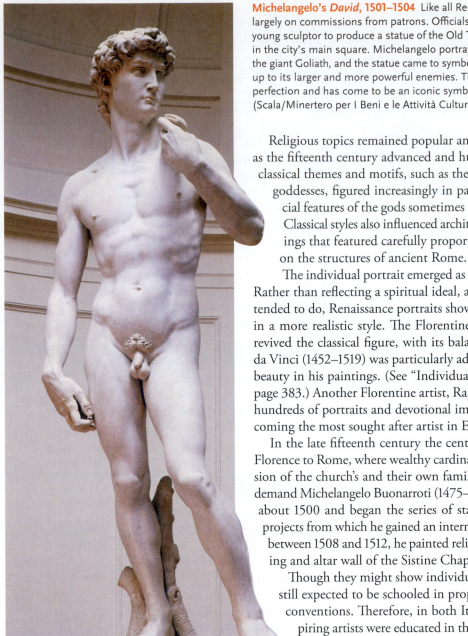

Michelangelo's *David*, 1501–1504 Like all Renaissance artists, Michelangelo worked largely on commissions from patrons. Officials of the city of Florence contracted the young sculptor to produce a statue of the Old Testament hero David to be displayed in the city's main square. Michelangelo portrayed David anticipating his fight against the giant Goliath, and the statue came to symbolize the republic of Florence standing up to its larger and more powerful enemies. The *David* captures ideals of human perfection and has come to be an iconic symbol of Renaissance artistic brilliance. (Scala/Minertero per I Beni e le Attività Culturali/Art Resource, NY)

Religious topics remained popular among both patrons and artists, but as the fifteenth century advanced and humanist ideas spread more widely, classical themes and motifs, such as the lives and loves of pagan gods and goddesses, figured increasingly in painting and sculpture, with the facial features of the gods sometimes modeled on those of living people. Classical styles also influenced architecture, as architects designed buildings that featured carefully proportioned arches and domes modeled on the structures of ancient Rome.

The individual portrait emerged as a distinct genre in Renaissance art. Rather than reflecting a spiritual ideal, as medieval painting and sculpture tended to do, Renaissance portraits showed human ideals, often portrayed in a more realistic style. The Florentine sculptor Donatello (1386–1466) revived the classical figure, with its balance and self-awareness. Leonardo da Vinci (1452–1519) was particularly adept at portraying female grace and beauty in his paintings. (See "Individuals in Society: Leonardo da Vinci," page 383.) Another Florentine artist, Raphael Sanzio (1483–1520), painted hundreds of portraits and devotional images in his relatively short life, becoming the most sought after artist in Europe.

In the late fifteenth century the center of Renaissance art shifted from Florence to Rome, where wealthy cardinals and popes wanted visual expression of the church's and their own families' power and piety. To meet this demand Michelangelo Buonarroti (1475–1564) went to Rome from Florence about 1500 and began the series of statues, paintings, and architectural projects from which he gained an international reputation. Most famously, between 1508 and 1512, he painted religiously themed frescoes on the ceiling and altar wall of the Sistine Chapel.

Though they might show individual genius, Renaissance artists were still expected to be schooled in proper artistic techniques and stylistic conventions. Therefore, in both Italy and northern Europe most aspiring artists were educated in the workshops of older artists. By the later sixteenth century formal academies were also established to train artists. Like universities, artistic workshops and academies were male-only settings. Several women did become well-known as painters during the Renaissance, but they were trained by their artist fathers and often quit painting when they married.

Women were not alone in being excluded from the institutions of Renaissance culture. Though a few talented artists such as Leonardo and Michelangelo emerged from artisanal backgrounds, most scholars and artists came from families with at least some money. The audience for artists' work was also exclusive, limited mostly to educated and prosperous citizens. In general a small, highly educated minority of literary humanists and artists created the culture of and for a social elite. In this way the Renaissance maintained, and even enhanced, a gulf between the learned minority and the uneducated multitude that has survived for many centuries.

Quick Review

How did humanism shape the art, literature, and scholarship of fifteenth- and sixteenth-century Europe?

INDIVIDUALS IN SOCIETY

Leonardo da Vinci

The enigmatic smile and smoky quality of Leonardo da Vinci's *Lady with an Ermine* can be found in many of Leonardo's works. (Czartoryski Museum, Krakow/ The Bridgeman Art Library)

WHAT MAKES A GENIUS? AN INFINITE CAPACITY for taking pains? A divine spark as manifested by talents that far exceed the norm? Or is it just "one percent inspiration and ninety-nine percent perspiration," as Thomas Edison said? To most observers, Leonardo da Vinci was one of the greatest geniuses in the history of the Western world. In fact, Leonardo was one of the individuals that the Renaissance label "genius" was designed to describe: a special kind of human being with exceptional creative powers.

Leonardo (who, despite the title of a recent bestseller, is always called by his first name) was born in Vinci, near Florence, the illegitimate son of Caterina, a local peasant girl, and Ser Piero da Vinci, a notary public. Leonardo was raised by his father; Ser Piero secured Leonardo's apprenticeship with the painter and sculptor Andrea del Verrocchio in Florence. In 1472, when Leonardo was just twenty years old, he was listed as a master in Florence's "Company of Artists."

Leonardo's most famous portrait, *Mona Lisa*, shows a woman with an enigmatic smile that the sixteenth-century artist and writer Giorgio Vasari described as "so pleasing that it seemed divine rather than human." The portrait, probably of the young wife of a rich Florentine merchant (her exact identity is hotly debated), may be the best-known painting in the history of art. Another work of Leonardo's, *The Last Supper*, has been called "the most revered painting in the world."

Leonardo's reputation as a genius does not rest simply on his paintings, however, which are few in number, but rather on the breadth of his abilities and interests. In these, he is often understood to be the first "Renaissance man," a phrase we still use for a multitalented individual. He wanted to reproduce what the eye can see, and he drew everything he saw around him. Trying to understand how the human body worked, Leonardo studied live and dead bodies, doing autopsies and dissections to investigate muscles and circulation. He carefully analyzed the effects of light and experimented with perspective, which gave his drawings and paintings a realistic, three-dimensional look.

Leonardo used his drawings as the basis for his paintings and also as a tool of scientific investigation. He drew plans for hundreds of inventions, many of which would become reality centuries later, such as the helicopter, tank, machine gun, and parachute. He was hired by one of the powerful new rulers in Italy, Duke Ludovico Sforza of Milan, to design practical things that the duke needed, including weapons, fortresses, and water systems, as well as to produce works of art. Leonardo left Milan when Sforza was overthrown in war and spent the last years of his life painting, drawing, and designing for the pope and the French king.

Leonardo experimented with new materials for painting and sculpture, some of which worked and some of which did not. The experimental method he used to paint *The Last Supper* caused the picture to deteriorate rapidly, and it began to flake off the wall as soon as it was finished. Leonardo regarded it as never quite completed, for he could not find a model for the face of Christ that would evoke the spiritual depth he felt it deserved. His gigantic equestrian statue in honor of Ludovico's father, Duke Francesco Sforza, was never made. He planned to write books on many subjects but never finished any of them, leaving only notebooks. Leonardo once said that "a painter is not admirable unless he is universal." The patrons who supported him — and he was supported very well — perhaps wished that his inspirations would have been a bit less universal in scope, or at least accompanied by more perspiration.

Sources: Giorgio Vasari, *Lives of the Artists*, vol. 1, trans. G. Bull (London: Penguin Books, 1965); S. B. Nuland, *Leonardo da Vinci* (New York: Lipper/Viking, 2000).

QUESTIONS FOR ANALYSIS

1. In what ways do the notion of a genius and the notion of a Renaissance man support one another? In what ways do they contradict one another? Which seems a better description of Leonardo?
2. Has the idea of artistic genius changed since the Renaissance? If so, how?

What were the key social hierarchies in Renaissance Europe?

The division between the educated and uneducated was one of many social hierarchies evident in the Renaissance. Other hierarchies built on those of the Middle Ages, but also developed new features that contributed to modern social hierarchies, such as those of race, class, and gender.

Race and Slavery

Renaissance people did not use the word *race* the way we do, but often used *race*, *people*, and *nation* interchangeably for ethnic, national, and religious groups. They did make distinctions based on skin color that were in keeping with later conceptualizations of race, but these distinctions were interwoven with other characteristics when people thought about human differences.

Ever since the time of the Roman Republic, a few black Africans had lived in western Europe. They had come, along with white slaves, as the spoils of war. After the collapse of the Roman Empire and throughout the Middle Ages, Muslim and Christian merchants continued to import black slaves. The black population was especially concentrated in the cities of the Iberian Peninsula, where African slaves sometimes gained their freedom.

Picturing the Past

***Laura de Dianti*, 1523**

The Venetian artist Titian shows a young Italian woman with a gorgeous blue dress and an elaborate pearl and feather headdress accompanied by a young black page with a gold earring. Slaves from Africa and the Ottoman Empire were common in wealthy Venetian households. (Courtesy, Friedrich Kisters, Heinz Kisters Collection)

ANALYZING THE IMAGE How does the artist convey the message that this woman comes from a wealthy family? How does he use the skin color of the slave to highlight the woman's fair skin, which was part of Renaissance ideals of female beauty?

CONNECTIONS Household slaves worked at various tasks, but they were also symbols of the exotic. What other elements does Titian include in the painting to represent foreign places and the wealth brought to Venice by overseas trade? What does this painting suggest about Venetian attitudes toward slaves, who were part of that trade?

By the mid-sixteenth century blacks, slave and free, constituted roughly 3 percent of the Portuguese population, and because of intermarriage cities such as Lisbon had significant numbers of people of mixed African and European descent.

In Renaissance Portugal, Spain, and Italy, African slaves supplemented the labor force in virtually all occupations. Slaves also formed the primary workforce on the sugar plantations set up by Europeans on the Atlantic islands in the late fifteenth century (see page 425). European aristocrats sometimes had themselves painted with their black servants to indicate their wealth or, in the case of noblewomen, to highlight their fair skin.

Until their voyages down the African coast in the late fifteenth century, Europeans had little concrete knowledge of Africans and their cultures. They perceived Africa as the home of people isolated by heresy and Islam from superior European civilization. Africans' contact, even as slaves, with Christian Europeans would improve the blacks, they believed. The expanding slave trade reinforced negative preconceptions about the inferiority of black Africans.

Wealth and the Nobility

The word *class* was not used in the Renaissance to describe social division, but by the thirteenth century, and even more so by the fifteenth, the idea of a changeable hierarchy based on wealth was emerging alongside the medieval concept of orders (see page 361). This was particularly true in towns where, with the rise of trade and commerce, townspeople could now gain status through wealth. Wealthy merchants oversaw vast trading empires, held positions of political power, and lived in splendor rivaling that enjoyed by the richest nobles. The development of a hierarchy of wealth did not mean an end to the hierarchy of orders, however, and even poorer nobles still had higher status than merchants.

Gender Roles

Toward the end of the fourteenth century learned men (and a few women) began what was termed the **debate about women** (*querelle des femmes*), an argument about women's character and nature that would last for centuries. Misogynist critiques of women denounced females as devious, domineering, and demanding. In response, several authors compiled long lists of famous and praiseworthy women. Some writers were interested not only in defending women but also in exploring the reasons behind women's secondary status.

debate about women A discussion, which began in the later years of the fourteenth century, that attempted to answer fundamental questions about gender and to define the role of women in society.

Beginning in the sixteenth century the debate about women also became one about female rulers, because in Spain, England, France, and Scotland women served as advisers to child kings or ruled in their own right. There were no successful rebellions against female rulers simply because they were women, but in part this was because female rulers, especially Queen Elizabeth I of England, emphasized qualities regarded as masculine—physical bravery, stamina, wisdom, duty—whenever they appeared in public.

The dominant notion of the "true" man was that of the married head of household, so men whose class and age would have normally conferred political power but who remained unmarried were sometimes excluded from ruling positions. Actual marriage patterns in Europe left many women unmarried until late in life, but this did not lead to greater equality. Women who worked for wages, as was typical, earned about half to two-thirds of what men did even for the same work. Of all the ways in which Renaissance society was hierarchically arranged—by class, age, level of education, rank, race, occupation—gender was regarded as the most "natural" distinction and therefore the most important one to defend.

Quick Review
What role did race, wealth, and gender play in determining status and opportunity in Renaissance Europe?

How did the nation-states of western Europe evolve in this period?

The High Middle Ages had witnessed the origins of many of the basic institutions of the modern state. Sheriffs, inquests, juries, circuit judges, professional bureaucracies, and representative assemblies all trace their origins to the twelfth and thirteenth centuries. The linchpin for the development of states, however, was strong monarchy. Beginning in the fifteenth century rulers used aggressive methods to build up their governments. They began the work of reducing violence, curbing unruly nobles, and establishing domestic order. Here, we examine how monarchies throughout western Europe built and maintained power.

France

The Hundred Years' War left France drastically depopulated, commercially ruined, and agriculturally weak (see page 372). Nonetheless, Charles VII (r. 1422–1461) revived the monarchy and France. He reorganized the royal council, giving increased influence to middle-class men, and strengthened royal finances through such taxes as the *gabelle* (on salt) and the *taille* (on land). By establishing regular companies of cavalry and archers—recruited, paid, and inspected by the state—Charles created the first permanent royal army.

Two further developments strengthened the French monarchy. The marriage of Louis XII (r. 1498–1515) and Anne of Brittany added the large western duchy of Brittany to the state. Louis XII's successor, Francis I (r. 1515–1547), and Pope Leo X reached a mutually satisfactory agreement about church and state powers in 1516 that gave French kings the power to control the appointment and thus the policies of church officials in the kingdom.

England

English society suffered severely in the fourteenth and fifteenth centuries. Population, decimated by the Black Death, continued to decline. Between 1455 and 1471 adherents of the ducal houses of York and Lancaster waged civil wars over control of the English throne. These conflicts were commonly called the Wars of the Roses. The chronic disorder hurt trade, agriculture, and domestic industry, and the authority of the monarchy sank lower than it had been in centuries.

The Yorkist Edward IV (r. 1461–1483) succeeded in defeating the Lancastrian forces and after 1471 began to reconstruct the monarchy and consolidate royal power. Henry VII (r. 1485–1509) of the Welsh house of Tudor worked to restore royal prestige, to crush the power of the nobility, and to establish order and law at the local level. Because the government halted the long period of anarchy, it won the key support of the merchant and agricultural upper middle class. Early in his reign Henry VII summoned several meetings of Parliament, primarily to confirm laws, but the center of royal authority was the royal council, which governed at the national level. There Henry VII revealed his distrust of the nobility: very few great lords were among the king's closest advisers, who instead were lesser landowners and lawyers.

Henry VII rebuilt the monarchy. He encouraged the cloth industry and built up the English merchant marine. He crushed an invasion from Ireland, secured peace with Scotland through the marriage of his daughter Margaret to the Scottish king, and enhanced English prestige through the marriage of his eldest son, Arthur, to Catherine of Aragon, the daughter of Ferdinand and Isabella of Spain. When Henry VII died in 1509, he left a country at peace, a substantially augmented treasury, and the position of the crown much enhanced.

Spain

While England and France laid the foundations of unified nation-states during the Renaissance, Spain remained a conglomerate of independent kingdoms. Even the wedding in 1469 of Isabella of Castile and Ferdinand of Aragon did not bring about administrative unity. Isabella and Ferdinand were, however, able to exert their authority in ways similar to the rulers of France and England. They curbed aristocratic power by excluding aristocrats and great territorial magnates from the royal council, and instead appointed only men of middle-class background. They also secured from the Spanish pope Alexander VI the right to appoint bishops in Spain and in the Hispanic territories in America, enabling them to establish the equivalent of a national church. In 1492 their armies conquered Granada, the last territory held by Arabs in southern Spain.

Ferdinand and Isabella's rule also marked the start of a dark chapter in Spanish history, greater persecution of the Jews. In the Middle Ages the kings of France and England had expelled the Jews from their kingdoms, and many had sought refuge in Spain. During the reconquista (see page 356), Christian kings in Spain had renewed Jewish rights and privileges; in fact, Jewish industry, intelligence, and money had supported royal power. Nonetheless, a strong undercurrent of resentment of Jewish influence and wealth festered.

In the fourteenth century anti-Semitism in Spain was aggravated by anti-Jewish preaching, by economic dislocation, and by the search for a scapegoat during the Black Death. Anti-Semitic pogroms swept Spain, and perhaps 40 percent of the Jewish population was killed or forced to convert. Those who converted were called *conversos* (kuhn-VEHR-sohz) or New Christians. Conversos were often well-educated and held prominent positions in government, the church, medicine, law, and business.

Such successes bred resentment. Aristocrats resented their financial dependence on conversos; the poor hated the converso tax collectors; and churchmen doubted the sincerity of their conversions. Queen Isabella shared these suspicions, and she and Ferdinand received permission from Pope Sixtus IV to establish a special Inquisition. Investigations and trials began immediately, with officials of the Inquisition looking for conversos who showed any sign of incomplete conversion, such as not eating pork.

Most conversos identified themselves as sincere Christians; many came from families that had received baptism generations before. In response, officials of the Inquisition developed a new type of anti-Semitism. A person's status as a Jew, they argued, could not be changed by religious conversion, but was in the person's blood and was heritable, so Jews could never be true Christians. Under what were known as "purity of blood" laws, having "pure Christian blood" became a requirement for noble status.

In 1492, shortly after the conquest of Granada, Isabella and Ferdinand issued an edict expelling all practicing Jews from Spain. Of the community of perhaps 200,000 Jews, 150,000 fled. Absolute religious orthodoxy and "purity of blood" served as the theoretical foundation of the Spanish national state.

The Habsburgs

War and diplomacy were important ways that states increased their power in sixteenth-century Europe, but so was marriage. Because almost all of Europe was ruled by hereditary dynasties, claiming and holding resources involved shrewd marital strategies.

The benefits of an advantageous marriage can be seen most dramatically with the Habsburgs. The Holy Roman emperor Frederick III, a Habsburg who was the ruler of most of Austria, arranged for his son Maximilian to marry Europe's most prominent heiress, Mary of Burgundy, in 1477; she inherited the Netherlands, Luxembourg, and the county of Burgundy in what is now eastern France. Through this union with the rich and powerful duchy of Burgundy, the Austrian house of Habsburg, already the strongest ruling family in the empire, became an international power.

Maximilian learned the lesson of marital politics well, marrying his son and daughter to the children of Ferdinand and Isabella, the rulers of Spain, much of southern Italy, and eventually the Spanish New World empire. His grandson Charles V (1500–1558) fell heir to a vast and incredibly diverse collection of states and peoples (Map 15.1). Charles was convinced that it was his duty to maintain the political and religious unity of Western Christendom. This conviction would be challenged far more than Charles ever anticipated.

Quick Review
How did monarchs in France, England, and Spain consolidate their authority in this period, and what goals and strategies did these monarchs have in common?

Map 15.1 The Global Empire of Charles V, ca. 1556 Charles V exercised theoretical jurisdiction over more European territory than anyone since Charlemagne. He also claimed authority over large parts of North and South America, although actual Spanish control was weak in much of this area.

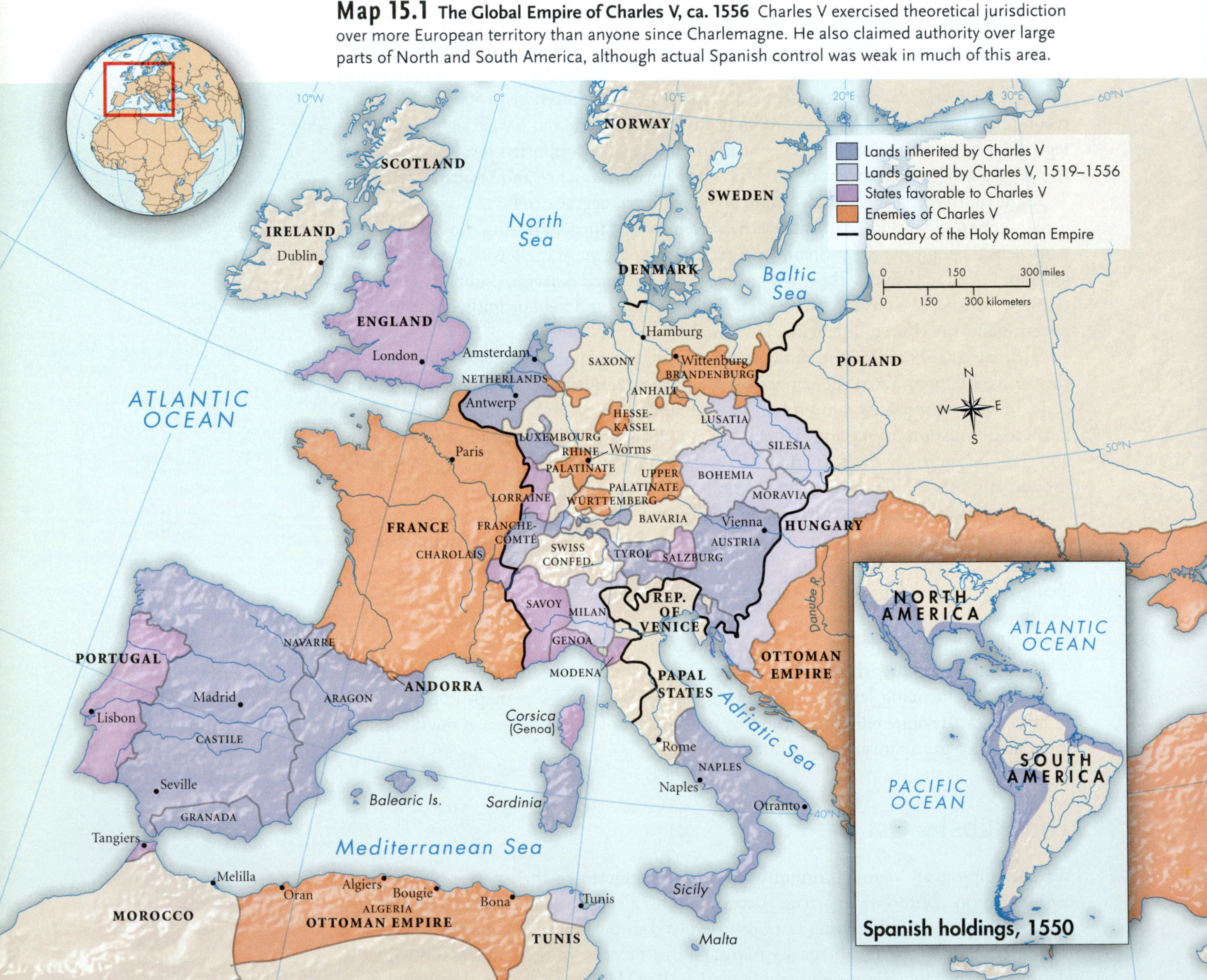

CHAPTER LOCATOR What were the major cultural developments of the Renaissance?

What were the central beliefs of Protestant reformers?

Calls for reform in the church came from many quarters in early-sixteenth-century Europe—from educated laypeople and urban residents, from villagers and artisans, and from church officials themselves. This dissatisfaction helps explain why the ideas of Martin Luther found a ready audience. Within a decade of his first publishing his ideas in Germany, much of central Europe and Scandinavia had broken with the Catholic Church in a movement that came to be known as the **Protestant Reformation**. In addition, even more radical concepts of the Christian message were being developed and linked to calls for social change.

Protestant Reformation A religious reform movement that began in the early sixteenth century that split the Western Christian Church.

Criticism of the Church

Sixteenth-century Europeans were deeply pious. Despite—or perhaps because of—the depth of their piety, many people were also highly critical of the Roman Catholic Church and its clergy. Papal conflicts with rulers and the Great Schism (see page 372) badly damaged the prestige of church leaders. Papal tax collection methods were also attacked, and some criticized the papacy itself as an institution. Anticlericalism, or opposition to the clergy, was widespread.

In the early sixteenth century critics of the church concentrated their attacks on clerical immorality, poorly trained or barely literate priests, and clerical absenteeism. In regard to absenteeism, many clerics, especially higher ecclesiastics, held several benefices (or offices) simultaneously—a practice termed pluralism. However, they seldom visited the communities served by the benefices, let alone performed the spiritual responsibilities those offices entailed.

There was also local resentment of clerical privileges and immunities. Priests, monks, and nuns were exempt from civic responsibilities, such as defending the city and paying taxes. Yet religious orders frequently held large amounts of urban property. City governments were increasingly determined to integrate the clergy into civic life. This brought city leaders into opposition with bishops and the papacy, which for centuries had stressed the independence of the church from lay control.

Martin Luther

By itself, widespread criticism of the church did not lead to the dramatic changes of the sixteenth century. Those resulted from the personal religious struggle of a University of Wittenberg professor and Augustinian friar, Martin Luther (1483–1546).

Martin Luther was a very conscientious friar, but he was plagued by anxieties about sin and his ability to meet God's demands. Through his study of Saint Paul's letters in the New Testament, he gradually arrived at a new understanding of Christian doctrine. His understanding is often summarized as "faith alone, grace alone, scripture alone." He believed that salvation and justification (righteousness in God's eyes) come through faith, and that faith is a free gift of God, not the result of human effort. God's word is revealed only in biblical scripture, not in the traditions of the church.

At the same time Luther was engaged in his spiritual struggle, Pope Leo X authorized a special Saint Peter's indulgence to finance his building plans in Rome. An **indulgence** was a document, signed by the pope or another church official, that substituted for penance. The archbishop who controlled the area in which Wittenberg was located, Albert of Mainz,

indulgence A papal statement granting remission of a priest-imposed penalty for sin. (No one knew what penalty God would impose after death.)

Selling Indulgences A German single-page pamphlet shows a monk offering an indulgence, with the official seals of the pope attached, as people run to put their money in the box in exchange for his promise of heavenly bliss, symbolized by the dove above his head. Indulgences were sold widely in Germany, and they were the first Catholic practice that Luther criticized openly. This pamphlet also attacks the sale of indulgences, calling it devilish and deceitful, a point of view expressed in the woodcut by the peddler's riding on a donkey, an animal that had long been used as a symbol of ignorance. Indulgences were often printed as fill-in-the-blank forms. This one, purchased in 1521, has space for the indulgence seller's name at the top, the buyer's name in the middle, and the date at the bottom. (woodcut: akg-images; indulgence: Visual Connection Archive)

also promoted the sale of indulgences, in his case to pay off a debt he had incurred to be named bishop of several additional territories.

Luther was severely troubled that many people believed that they had no further need for repentance once they had purchased indulgences. He wrote a letter to Archbishop Albert on the subject and enclosed in Latin "Ninety-five Theses on the Power of Indulgences." His argument was that indulgences undermined the seriousness of the sacrament of penance and competed with the preaching of the Gospel. Luther intended the theses for academic debate, but by December 1517 they had been translated from Latin into German and were read throughout the Holy Roman Empire.

Luther was ordered to go to Rome, but he was able to avoid this because the ruler of the territory in which he lived protected him. The pope nonetheless ordered him to recant many of his ideas, and Luther publicly burned the letter containing the papal order. In this highly charged atmosphere, emperor Charles V summoned Luther to appear before the **Diet of Worms**. When ordered to recant at this assembly, Luther flatly refused, citing the authority of Scripture and his own conscience.

Diet of Worms An assembly of the Estates of the Holy Roman Empire convened by Charles V in the German city of Worms. It was here, in 1521, that Martin Luther refused to recant his writings.

Protestant Originally meaning "a follower of Luther," this term came to be generally applied to all non-Catholic western European Christians.

Protestant Thought and Its Appeal

As he developed his ideas, Luther gathered followers, who came to be called Protestants. At first **Protestant** meant "a follower of Luther," but with the appearance of many protesting sects, it became a general term applied to all non-Catholic western European Christians.

Catholic teaching held that salvation is achieved by both faith and good works. Protestants held that salvation comes by faith alone, irrespective of good works or the sacraments. God, not people, initiates salvation. (See "Listening to the Past: Martin Luther, *On Christian Liberty*," page 392.) Second, Protestants believed that authority rests in the Bible alone, not in the Bible and traditional church teachings as Catholics maintained. Third, Protestants held that the church is a spiritual priesthood of all believers, an invisible fellowship not fixed in any place or person, which differed markedly from the Roman Catholic practice of looking to a clerical, hierarchical institution headed by the pope in Rome. Finally, the medieval church had stressed the superiority of the monastic and religious life over the secular. Luther disagreed and argued that every person should serve God in his or her individual calling.

Pulpits and printing presses spread Luther's message all over Germany, where it found a receptive audience in all social classes. Educated people and humanists were attracted by Luther's ideas. He advocated a simpler personal religion based on faith, a return to the spirit of the early church, the centrality of the Scriptures in the liturgy and in Christian life, and the abolition of elaborate ceremonies—precisely the reforms the Christian humanists had been calling for. His insistence that everyone should read and reflect on the Scriptures attracted the literate middle classes, including many priests and monks who became clergy in the new Protestant churches. Luther's ideas also appealed to townspeople who envied the church's wealth and resented paying for it. After cities became Protestant, the city council taxed the clergy and placed them under the jurisdiction of civil courts.

Scholars in many disciplines have attributed Luther's fame and success to the invention of the printing press, which rapidly reproduced and made known his ideas. Many printed works included woodcuts and other illustrations, so that even those who could not read could grasp the main ideas. Hymns were also important means of conveying central points of doctrine, as was Luther's translation of the New Testament into German in 1523.

The Radical Reformation and the German Peasants' War

In the sixteenth century the practice of religion remained a public matter. The ruler determined the official form of religious practice in his (or occasionally her) jurisdiction. Almost everyone believed that the presence of a faith different from that of the majority represented a political threat to the security of the state. Few believed in religious liberty; people with different ideas had to convert or leave.

Some individuals and groups rejected the idea that church and state needed to be united, however, and they sought to create a voluntary community of believers as they understood it to have existed in New Testament times. In terms of theology and spiritual practices, these individuals and groups varied widely, though they are generally termed "radicals" for their insistence on a more extensive break with prevailing ideas. Some adopted the custom of baptizing adult believers—for which they were given the title of "Anabaptists" or re-baptizers by their enemies—while others saw all outward sacraments or rituals as misguided. Some groups attempted communal ownership of property, living very simply and rejecting anything they thought unbiblical. Some reacted harshly to members who deviated from the group's accepted practices, but others argued for complete religious toleration and individualism.

Religious radicals were met with fanatical hatred and bitter persecution, including banishment and execution. Both Protestant and Catholic authorities felt threatened by the social, political, and economic implications of radicals' religious ideas and by their rejection of a state church, which the authorities saw as key to maintaining order.

Another group to challenge state authorities was the peasantry. In the early sixteenth century the economic condition of peasants varied from place to place but was generally worse than it had been in the fifteenth century and was deteriorating. Peasants demanded

LISTENING TO THE PAST

Martin Luther, *On Christian Liberty*

The idea of liberty or freedom has played a powerful role in the history of human society and culture, but the meaning and understanding of liberty have undergone continual change and interpretation. In the Roman world, where slavery was a basic institution, liberty meant the condition of being a free man, independent of obligations to a master. In the Middle Ages, possessing liberty meant having special privileges or rights that other persons or institutions did not have. A lord or a monastery, for example, might speak of his or its liberties, and citizens in London were said to possess the "freedom of the city," which allowed them to practice trades and own property without interference. Likewise, the first chapter of Magna Carta (1215), often called the "Charter of Liberties," states: "Holy Church shall be free and have its rights entire and its liberties *inviolate," meaning that the English Church was independent of the authority of the king.*

The idea of liberty also has a religious dimension, and the reformer Martin Luther formulated a classic interpretation of liberty in his treatise On Christian Liberty *(sometimes translated as* On the Freedom of a Christian*), arguably his finest piece. Written in Latin for the pope but translated immediately into German and published widely, it contains the main themes of Luther's theology: the importance of faith, the relationship of Christian faith and good works, the dual nature of human beings, and the fundamental importance of scripture. Luther writes that Christians were freed through Christ, not by their own actions, from sin and death.*

" Christian faith has appeared to many an easy thing; nay, not a few even reckon it among the social virtues, as it were; and this they do because they have not made proof of it experimentally, and have never tasted of what efficacy it is. For it is not possible for any man to write well about it, or to understand well what is rightly written, who has not at some time tasted of its spirit, under the pressure of tribulation; while he who has tasted of it, even to a very small extent, can never write, speak, think, or hear about it sufficiently. . . .

I hope that . . . I have attained some little drop of faith, and that I can speak of this matter, if not with more elegance, certainly with more solidity. . . .

A Christian man is the most free lord of all, and subject to none; a Christian man is the most dutiful servant of all, and subject to everyone.

Although these statements appear contradictory, yet, when they are found to agree together, they will do excellently for my purpose. They are both the statements of Paul himself, who says, "Though I be free from all men, yet have I made myself a servant unto all" (I Corinthians 9:19), and "Owe no man anything but to love one another" (Romans 13:8). Now love is by its own nature dutiful and obedient to the beloved object. Thus even Christ, though Lord of all things, was yet made of a woman; made under the law; at once free and a servant; at once in the form of God and in the form of a servant.

Let us examine the subject on a deeper and less simple principle. Man is composed of a twofold nature, a spiritual and a bodily. As regards the spiritual nature, which they name the soul, he is called the spiritual, inward, new man; as regards the bodily nature, which they name the flesh, he is called the fleshly, outward, old man. The Apostle speaks of this: "Though our outward man perish, yet the inward man is renewed day by day" (II Corinthians 4:16). The result of this diversity is that in the Scriptures opposing statements are made concerning the same man, the fact being that in the same man these two men are opposed to one another; the flesh lusting against the spirit, and the spirit against the flesh (Galatians 5:17).

We first approach the subject of the inward man, that we may see by what means a man becomes justified, free, and a true Christian; that is, a spiritual, new, and inward man. It is certain that absolutely none among outward things, under whatever name they may be reckoned, has any influence in producing Christian righteousness or liberty, nor, on the other hand, unrighteousness or slavery. This can be shown by an easy argument.

What can it profit to the soul that the body should be in good condition, free, and full of life, that it should eat, drink, and act according to its pleasure, when even the most impious slaves of every kind of vice are prosperous in these matters? Again, what harm can ill health, bondage, hunger, thirst, or any other outward evil, do to the soul, when even the most pious of men, and the freest in the purity of their conscience, are harassed by these things? Neither of these states of things has to do with the liberty or the slavery of the soul.

And so it will profit nothing that the body should be adorned with sacred vestment, or dwell in holy places, or be occupied in sacred offices, or pray, fast, and abstain from certain meats, or do whatever works can be done through the body and in the body. Something widely different will be necessary for the justification and liberty of the soul, since the things I have spoken of can be done by an impious person, and only hypocrites are produced by devotion to these things. On the other hand, it will not at all injure the soul that the body should be clothed in profane raiment, should dwell in profane places, should eat and drink in the ordinary fashion, should not pray

On effective preaching, especially to the uneducated, Luther urged the minister "to keep it simple for the simple." (Church of St. Marien, Wittenberg/The Bridgeman Art Library)

aloud, and should leave undone all the things above mentioned, which may be done by hypocrites.

. . . One thing, and one alone, is necessary for life, justification, and Christian liberty; and that is the most Holy Word of God, the Gospel of Christ, as He says, "I am the resurrection and the life; he that believeth in me shall not die eternally" (John 9:25), and also, "If the Son shall make you free, ye shall be free indeed" (John 8:36), and "Man shall not live by bread alone, but by every word that proceedeth out of the mouth of God" (Matthew 4:4).

Let us therefore hold it for certain and firmly established that the soul can do without everything except the Word of God, without which none at all of its wants is provided for. But, having the Word, it is rich and wants for nothing, since that is the Word of life, of truth, of light, of peace, of justification, of salvation, of joy, of liberty, of wisdom, of virtue, of grace, of glory, and of every good thing. . . .

But you will ask, "What is this Word, and by what means is it to be used, since there are so many words of God?" I answer, "The Apostle Paul (Romans 1) explains what it is, namely the Gospel of God, concerning His Son, incarnate, suffering, risen, and glorified through the Spirit, the Sanctifier." To preach Christ is to feed the soul, to justify it, to set it free, and to save it, if it believes the preaching. For faith alone, and the efficacious use of the Word of God, bring salvation. "If thou shalt confess with thy mouth the Lord Jesus, and shalt believe in thine heart that God hath raised Him from the dead, thou shalt be saved" (Romans 9:9); . . . and "The just shall live by faith" (Romans 1:17). . . .

But this faith cannot consist of all with works; that is, if you imagine that you can be justified by those works, whatever they are, along with it. . . . Therefore, when you begin to believe, you learn at the same time that all that is in you is utterly guilty, sinful, and damnable, according to that saying, "All have sinned, and come short of the glory of God" (Romans 3:23). . . . When you have learned this, you will know that Christ is necessary for you, since He has suffered and risen again for you, that, believing on Him, you might by this faith become another man, all your sins being remitted, and you being justified by the merits of another, namely Christ alone.

. . . [A]nd since it [faith] alone justifies, it is evident that by no outward work or labour can the inward man be at all justified, made free, and saved; and that no works whatever have any relation to him. . . . Therefore the first care of every Christian ought to be to lay aside all reliance on works, and strengthen his faith alone more and more, and by it grow in knowledge, not of works, but of Christ Jesus, who has suffered and risen again for him, as Peter teaches (I Peter 5). ”

Source: *Luther's Primary Works*, ed. H. Wace and C. A. Buchheim (London: Holder and Stoughton, 1896). Reprinted in *The Portable Renaissance Reader*, ed. James Bruce Ross and Mary Martin McLaughlin (New York: Penguin Books, 1981), pp. 721–726.

QUESTIONS FOR ANALYSIS

1. What did Luther mean by liberty?
2. Why, for Luther, was scripture basic to Christian life?

limitations on the new taxes and services their noble landlords were imposing. They believed that their demands conformed to the Scriptures and cited Luther as a theologian who could prove that they did.

Wanting to prevent rebellion, Luther initially sided with the peasants, blasting the lords for robbing their subjects. But when rebellion broke out, the peasants who expected Luther's support were soon disillusioned. Freedom for Luther meant independence from the authority of the Roman Church, not opposition to legally established secular powers. Convinced that rebellion would hasten the end of civilized society, he wrote the tract *Against the Murderous, Thieving Hordes of the Peasants*, which said, in part, "Let everyone who can smite, slay, and stab [the peasants], secretly and openly, remembering that nothing can be more poisonous, hurtful or devilish than a rebel."[2] The nobility crushed the revolt, which became known as the German Peasants' War of 1525. That year, historians estimate, more than seventy-five thousand peasants were killed.

The peasants' war greatly strengthened the authority of lay rulers. Because Luther turned against the peasants who revolted, the Reformation lost much of its popular appeal after 1525, though peasants and urban rebels sometimes found a place for their social and religious ideas in radical groups. Peasants' economic conditions did moderately improve, however. For example, in many parts of Germany, enclosed fields, meadows, and forests were returned to common use instead of being controlled by noble landlords.

Marriage and Women's Roles

Luther and other Protestants believed that a priest's or nun's vows of celibacy went against human nature and God's commandments. Luther married a former nun, Katharina von Bora (1499–1532), who quickly had several children. Most other Protestant reformers also married, and their wives had to create a new and respectable role for themselves — pastor's

Martin Luther and Katharina von Bora Lucas Cranach the Elder painted this double marriage portrait to celebrate Luther's wedding in 1525 to Katharina von Bora, a former nun. The artist was one of the witnesses at the wedding and, in fact, had presented Luther's marriage proposal to Katharina. The couple quickly became a model of the ideal marriage, and many churches wanted their portraits. More than sixty similar paintings, with slight variations, were produced by Cranach's workshop and hung in churches and wealthy homes. (Uffizi, Florence/Scala/Art Resource, NY)

wife—to overcome being viewed as simply a new type of priest's concubine. They were expected to be models of wifely obedience and Christian charity.

Catholics viewed marriage as a sacramental union that, if validly entered into, could not be dissolved. Protestants saw marriage as a contract in which each partner promised the other support, companionship, and the sharing of mutual goods. Most Protestants came to allow divorce. Divorce remained rare, however, because marriage was such an important social and economic institution.

Protestants did not break with medieval scholastic theologians in their view that, within marriage, women were to be subject to men. A few women took the Protestant idea about the priesthood of all believers to heart and wrote religious pamphlets and hymns, but no sixteenth-century Protestants officially allowed women to hold positions of religious authority. Monarchs such as Elizabeth I of England and female territorial rulers of the states of the Holy Roman Empire did determine religious policies, however.

Because the Reformation generally brought the closing of monasteries and convents, marriage became virtually the only occupation for upper-class Protestant women. Recognizing this, women in some convents fought the Reformation or argued that they could still be pious Protestants within convent walls. Most nuns left, however, and we do not know what happened to them. The Protestant emphasis on marriage made unmarried women (and men) suspect, for they did not belong to the type of household regarded as the cornerstone of a proper, godly society.

The Reformation and German Politics

Criticism of the church was widespread in Europe in the early sixteenth century, and calls for reform came from many areas. Yet such movements could be more easily squelched by the strong central governments of Spain, France, and England. The Holy Roman Empire, in contrast, included hundreds of largely independent states in which the emperor had far less authority than did the monarchs of western Europe. Thus local rulers in the empire continued to exercise great power.

Germany was one place where local leadership remained strong, and Luther's ideas appealed to its rulers for a variety of reasons. Though Germany was not a nation, people did have an understanding of being German because of their language and traditions. Luther frequently used the phrase "we Germans" in his attacks on the papacy, and his appeal to national feeling influenced many rulers. Also, while some German rulers were sincerely attracted to Lutheran ideas, material considerations swayed many others to embrace the new faith. The rejection of Roman Catholicism and the adoption of Protestantism would mean the legal confiscation of church lands and property. Thus many political authorities in the empire used the religious issue to extend their financial and political power and to enhance their independence from the emperor.

The Habsburg Charles V, elected as emperor in 1521, was a vigorous defender of Catholicism, so it is not surprising that the Reformation led to religious wars. Protestant territories in the empire formed military alliances, and the emperor could not oppose them effectively given other military engagements. In southeastern Europe Habsburg troops were already fighting the Ottoman Turks. Habsburg soldiers were also engaged in a series of wars with the Valois (VAL-wah) kings of France. The cornerstone of French foreign policy in the sixteenth and seventeenth centuries was the desire to keep the German states divided. Thus Europe witnessed the paradox of the Catholic king of France supporting Lutheran princes in their challenge to his fellow Catholic, Charles V. The Habsburg-Valois wars advanced the cause of Protestantism and promoted the political fragmentation of the German Empire.

Finally, in 1555, Charles agreed to the Peace of Augsburg, which officially recognized Lutheranism and ended religious war in Germany for many decades. Under this treaty,

Allegory of the Tudor Dynasty The unknown creator of this work intended to glorify the virtues of the Protestant succession; the painting has no historical reality. Henry VIII (seated) hands the sword of justice to his Protestant son Edward VI. At left the Catholic Queen Mary and her husband Philip of Spain are followed by Mars, god of war, signifying violence and civil disorder. At right the figures of Peace and Plenty accompany the Protestant Elizabeth I, symbolizing England's happy fate under her rule. (Yale Center for British Art, Paul Mellon Collection/The Bridgeman Art Library)

the political authority in each territory of the Holy Roman Empire was permitted to decide whether the territory would be Catholic or Lutheran. Most of northern and central Germany became Lutheran, while southern Germany was divided between Lutheran and Catholic. Charles V abdicated in 1556, transferring power over his Spanish and Netherlandish holdings to his son Philip II and his imperial power to his brother Ferdinand.

England's Shift Toward Protestantism

States within the Holy Roman Empire and the kingdom of Denmark-Norway were the earliest territories to accept the Protestant Reformation, but by the later 1520s religious change also came to England, France, and eastern Europe. In all these areas, a second generation of reformers, most prominently John Calvin (see page 397), built on earlier ideas to develop their own theology and plans for institutional change.

As on the continent, the Reformation in England had economic and political as well as religious causes. The impetus for England's break with Rome was the desire of King Henry VIII (r. 1509–1547) for a new wife. When the personal matter of his need to divorce his first wife became enmeshed with political issues, a complete break with Rome resulted.

In 1527, after eighteen years of marriage, Henry's wife Catherine of Aragon had failed to produce a male child, and Henry had also fallen in love with a court lady-in-waiting, Anne Boleyn. So Henry petitioned Pope Clement VII for an annulment of his marriage to Catherine. When the pope stalled, Henry decided to remove the English Church from papal authority. In this way, he was able to get the annulment and marry Anne.

Henry used Parliament to legalize the Reformation in England and to make himself the supreme head of the Church of England. Anne had a daughter, Elizabeth, but failed to produce a son, so Henry VIII charged her with adulterous incest and in 1536 had her beheaded. His third wife, Jane Seymour, gave Henry the desired son, Edward, but she died in childbirth. Henry went on to three more wives.

Between 1535 and 1539, influenced by his chief minister, Thomas Cromwell, Henry dissolved the English monasteries in order to gain their wealth. Hundreds of former church properties were sold to the middle and upper classes, strengthening the upper classes and tying them to the crown. Despite the speed of official change from Catholicism to Protestantism, people rarely "converted" overnight. Instead, they responded to the local consequences of the shift from Catholicism—for example, the closing of a monastery, the ending of masses for the dead—with a combination of resistance, acceptance, and collaboration.

In the short reign of Henry's sickly son Edward VI (r. 1547–1553), strongly Protestant ideas exerted a significant influence on the religious life of the country. The equally brief reign of Mary Tudor (r. 1553–1558), the devoutly Catholic daughter of Catherine of Aragon, witnessed a sharp move back to Catholicism, and many Protestants fled to the continent. Mary's death raised to the throne her half-sister Elizabeth (r. 1558–1603) and inaugurated the beginning of religious stability.

Elizabeth had been raised a Protestant, but at the start of her reign sharp differences existed in England. On the one hand, Catholics wanted a Roman Catholic ruler. On the other hand, a vocal number of returning exiles, known as "Puritans," wanted all Catholic elements in the Church of England eliminated. Elizabeth chose a middle course between Catholic and Puritan extremes, and the Anglican Church, as the Church of England was called, moved in a moderately Protestant direction.

Calvinism and Its Moral Standards

John Calvin (1509–1564) was born in Noyon in northwestern France. As a young man he studied law, but in 1533 he experienced a religious crisis, as a result of which he converted from Catholicism to Protestantism. Calvin believed that God had specifically selected him to reform the church. Accordingly, he accepted an invitation to assist in the reformation of the city of Geneva. There, beginning in 1541, Calvin worked to establish a Christian society ruled by God through civil magistrates and reformed ministers.

Calvin's ideas are embodied in *The Institutes of the Christian Religion*, first published in 1536 and modified several times afterward. The cornerstone of Calvin's theology was his belief in the absolute sovereignty and omnipotence of God and the total weakness of humanity. Calvin did not ascribe free will to human beings because that would detract from the sovereignty of God. According to his beliefs, men and women could not actively work to achieve salvation; rather, God decided at the beginning of time who would be saved and who damned. This viewpoint constitutes the theological principle called **predestination**.

predestination Calvin's teaching that, by God's decree, some persons are guided to salvation and others to damnation; that God has called us not according to our works but according to his purpose and grace.

Calvin aroused Genevans to a high standard of morality. In the reformation of the city, the Genevan Consistory, a group of laymen and pastors, was assembled "to keep watch over every man's life [and] to admonish amiably those whom they see leading a disorderly life."[3] Although all municipal governments in early modern Europe regulated citizens' conduct, none did so with the severity of Geneva's Consistory under Calvin's leadership. Absence from sermons, criticism of ministers, dancing, card playing, family quarrels, and heavy drinking were all investigated and punished by the Consistory.

Religious refugees from France, England, Spain, Scotland, and Italy visited Calvin's Geneva. Subsequently, the Reformed Church of Calvin served as the model for the Presbyterian Church in Scotland, the Huguenot (HYOO-guh-naht) Church in France, and the Puritan churches in England and New England.

For Calvinists, one's own actions could do nothing to change one's fate, but many people came to believe that hard work, thrift, and proper moral conduct could be signs that an individual was among the "elect" chosen for salvation. Any occupation or profession could be a God-given calling, and work should be done with diligence and dedication. These factors helped to make Calvinism the most dynamic force in sixteenth- and seventeenth-century Protestantism.

Quick Review
How did the religious landscape of Europe in 1555 differ from the religious landscape in 1517?

How did the Catholic Church respond to the advent of Protestantism?

Between 1517 and 1547 Protestantism made remarkable advances. Nevertheless, the Roman Catholic Church made a significant comeback. After about 1540 no new large areas of Europe, other than the Netherlands, accepted Protestant beliefs (Map 15.2). Many historians see the developments within the Catholic Church after the Protestant Reformation as two interrelated movements, one a drive for internal reform linked to earlier reform efforts, and the other a Counter-Reformation that opposed Protestantism. In both movements, papal reforms and new religious orders were important agents.

Papal Reforms and the Council of Trent

In 1542 Pope Paul III (pontificate 1534–1549) established the Supreme Sacred Congregation of the Roman and Universal Inquisition, often called the Holy Office, with jurisdiction over the Roman Inquisition, a powerful instrument of the Catholic Reformation. The Inquisition was a committee of six cardinals with judicial authority over all Catholics and the power to arrest, imprison, and execute. Within the Papal States, the Inquisition effectively destroyed heresy (and some heretics).

Pope Paul III also called a general council, which met intermittently from 1545 to 1563 at Trent, an imperial city close to Italy. It was called not only to reform the church but also to secure reconciliation with the Protestants. Lutherans and Calvinists were invited to participate, but their insistence that the Scriptures be the sole basis for discussion made reconciliation impossible.

Nonetheless, the decrees of the Council of Trent laid a solid basis for the spiritual renewal of the Catholic Church. It gave equal validity to the Scriptures and to tradition as sources of religious truth and authority. It reaffirmed the seven sacraments and the traditional Catholic teaching on transubstantiation (the transformation of bread and wine into the body and blood of Christ in the Eucharist). It tackled the disciplinary matters that had disillusioned the faithful, requiring bishops to reside in their own dioceses, suppressing pluralism and the selling of church offices, and forbidding the sale of indulgences. The council also required every diocese to establish a seminary for educating and training clergy. Finally, great emphasis was placed on preaching to and instructing the laity, especially the uneducated. For four centuries the doctrinal and disciplinary legislation of Trent served as the basis for Roman Catholic faith, organization, and practice.

New Religious Orders

Just as seminaries provided education, so did new religious orders, which aimed to raise the moral and intellectual level of the clergy and people. The Ursuline (UHR-suh-luhn) order

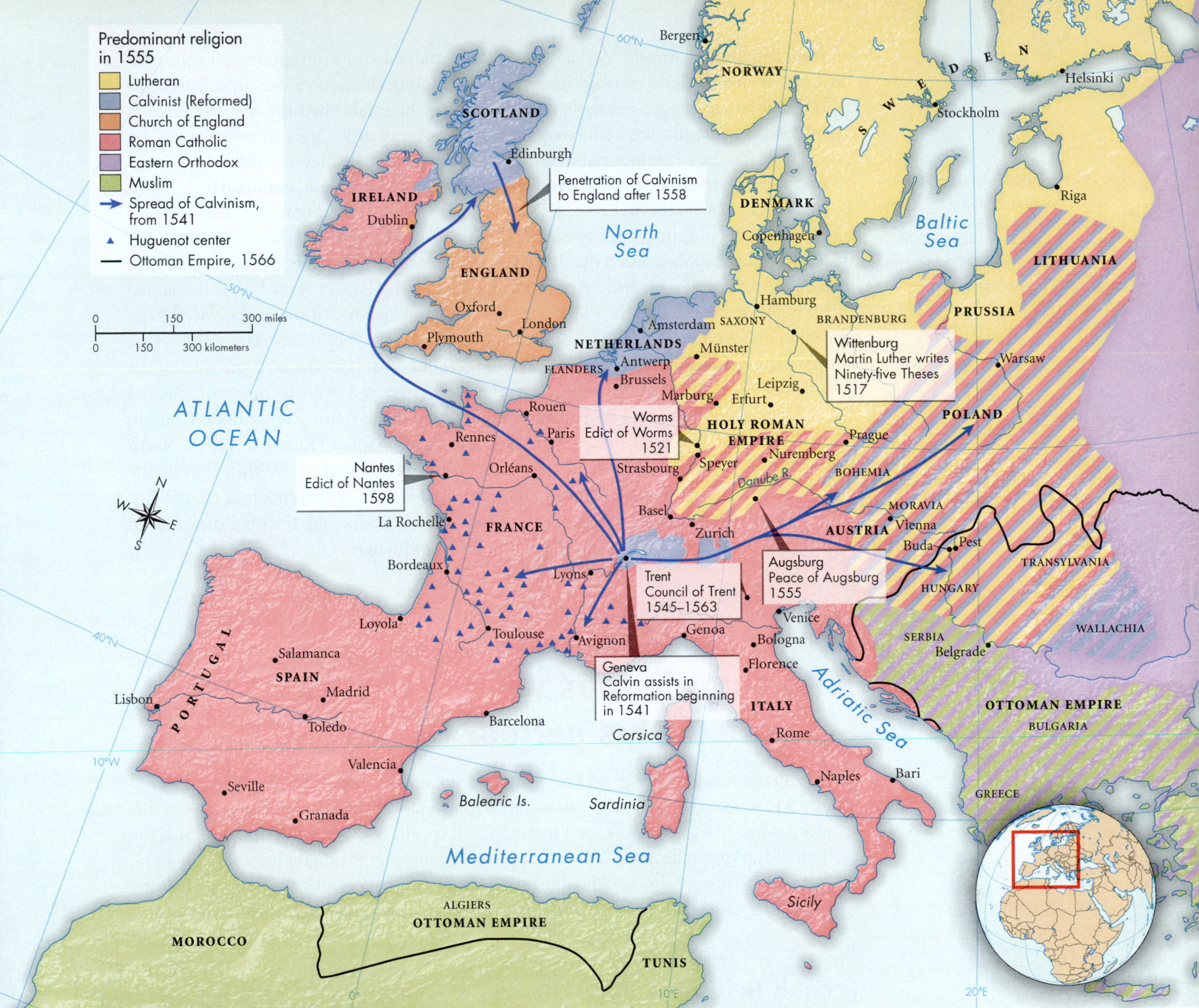

Mapping the Past

Map 15.2 Religious Divisions in Europe, ca. 1555

The Reformation shattered the religious unity of Western Christendom. The situation was even more complicated than a map of this scale can show. Many cities within the Holy Roman Empire, for example, accepted a different faith than did the surrounding countryside; Augsburg, Basel, and Strasbourg were all Protestant, though surrounded by territory ruled by Catholic nobles.

ANALYZING THE MAP Which countries were most religiously diverse in Europe? Which were least diverse?

CONNECTIONS Where was the first arena of religious conflict in Europe, and why did it develop there and not elsewhere? To what degree can nonreligious factors be used as an explanation of the religious divisions that developed in sixteenth-century Europe?

of nuns, founded by Angela Merici (1474–1540), attained enormous prestige for the education of women. Merici worked for many years among the poor, sick, and uneducated around her native Brescia in northern Italy. In 1535 she established the first women's religious order concentrating exclusively on teaching young girls. After receiving papal approval in 1565, the Ursulines rapidly spread to France and the New World.

Jesuits Members of the Society of Jesus, founded by Ignatius Loyola and approved by the papacy in 1540, whose goal was the spread of the Roman Catholic faith through humanistic schools and missionary activity.

Another important new order was the Society of Jesus, or **Jesuits**. Founded by Ignatius Loyola (1491–1556) in 1540, this order played a powerful international role in strengthening Catholicism in Europe and spreading the faith around the world. While recuperating from a wound, Loyola studied the life of Christ and other religious books and decided to give up his military career and become a soldier of Christ. The Society of Jesus developed into a highly centralized, tightly knit organization whose professed members vowed to go anywhere the pope said they were needed and "help souls." They established schools that adopted the modern humanist curricula and methods and that educated the sons of the nobility as well as the poor. The Jesuits attracted many recruits and achieved phenomenal success for the papacy and the reformed Catholic Church, carrying Christianity to India and Japan before 1550 and to Brazil, North America, and the Congo in the seventeenth century. Within Europe the Jesuits brought almost all of southern Germany and much of eastern Europe back to Catholicism. Also, as confessors and spiritual directors to kings, Jesuits exerted great political influence.

Quick Review
How did the Catholic Reformation alter the Catholic Church? What were the most important areas of change and continuity?

Why did religious violence escalate in this period?

In 1559 France and Spain signed the Treaty of Cateau-Cambrésis, which ended the long conflict known as the Habsburg-Valois wars. However, over the next century religious differences led to riots, civil wars, and international conflicts. Especially in France and the Netherlands, Protestants and Catholics opposed one another through preaching, teaching, and violence. This era also saw the most virulent witch persecutions in European history, as both Protestants and Catholics tried to make their cities and states more godly.

French Religious Wars

King Francis I's treaty with the pope (see page 386) gave the French crown a rich supplement of money and offices, and also a vested financial interest in Catholicism. Significant numbers of French people, however, were attracted to Calvinism. Calvinism drew converts from among reform-minded members of the Catholic clergy, the middle classes, and artisan groups. Additionally, some French nobles became Calvinist, either because of religious conviction or because this allowed them to oppose the monarchy. By the middle of the sixteenth century perhaps one-tenth of the French population had become **Huguenots**, the name given to French Calvinists.

Huguenots French Calvinists.

Both Calvinists and Catholics believed that the others' books, services, and ministers polluted the community. Preachers communicated these ideas in sermons, triggering violence at the baptisms, marriages, and funerals of the other faith. Armed clashes between Catholic royalist nobles and Calvinist antimonarchical nobles occurred in many parts of France.

Calvinist teachings called the power of sacred images into question, and mobs in many cities destroyed statues, stained-glass windows, and paintings. Catholic mobs responded

Massacre of the Huguenots, 1573 The Italian artist Giorgio Vasari depicts the Saint Bartholomew's Day massacre in Paris, one of many bloody events in the religious wars that accompanied the Reformation. Here Admiral Coligny, a leader of the French Protestants (called Huguenots) is hurled from a window while his followers are slaughtered. This fresco was commissioned by Pope Gregory XIII to decorate a hall in the Vatican Palace in Rome. Both sides used visual images to win followers and celebrate their victories. (Vatican Palace/Scala/Art Resource, NY)

by defending the sacred images, and crowds on both sides killed their opponents, often in gruesome ways.

A savage Catholic attack on Calvinists in Paris on August 24, 1572—Saint Bartholomew's Day—followed the usual pattern. The occasion was the marriage of the king's sister Margaret of Valois to the Protestant Henry of Navarre, which was intended to help reconcile Catholics and Huguenots. Instead, Huguenot wedding guests in Paris were massacred, and other Protestants were slaughtered by mobs. Religious violence spread to the provinces, where thousands were killed. The Saint Bartholomew's Day massacre led to a civil war that dragged on for fifteen years. As a result of the conflict, agriculture in many areas was destroyed, commercial life declined severely, and starvation and death haunted the land.

What ultimately saved France was a small group of moderates of both faiths called **politiques** (POH-lee-teeks) who believed that only the restoration of a strong monarchy could reverse the trend toward collapse. The politiques also favored officially recognizing the Huguenots. The death of the French queen Catherine de' Medici, followed by the assassination of her son King Henry III, paved the way for the accession of Henry of Navarre, a politique who became Henry IV (r. 1589–1610).

Henry's willingness to sacrifice religious principles to political necessity saved France. He converted to Catholicism but also, in 1598, issued the Edict of Nantes (nahnt), which granted liberty of conscience (freedom of thought) and liberty of public worship to Huguenots in 150 fortified towns. By helping restore internal peace in France, the reign of Henry IV and the Edict of Nantes paved the way for French kings to claim absolute power in the seventeenth century.

Civil Wars in the Netherlands

In the Netherlands a movement for church reform developed into a struggle for Dutch independence. The Catholic emperor Charles V had inherited the seventeen provinces that compose present-day Belgium and the Netherlands (see page 388). In the Netherlands, as elsewhere, corruption in the Roman Catholic Church and the critical spirit of the Renaissance provoked pressure for reform, and Lutheran ideas took root. Charles V had grown up in the Netherlands, however, and he was able to limit the impact of the new ideas. Charles V abdicated in 1556 and transferred power over the Netherlands to his son Philip II, who had grown up in Spain. Although Philip, like his father, opposed Protestantism, Protestant ideas, particularly those of Calvin, spread in the Netherlands.

politiques Catholic and Protestant moderates who sought to end the religious violence in France by restoring a strong monarchy and granting official recognition to the Huguenots.

In the 1560s Spanish authorities attempted to suppress Calvinist worship and raised taxes, which sparked riots and a wave of iconoclasm. In response, Philip II sent twenty thousand Spanish troops, and from 1568 to 1578 civil war raged in the Netherlands between Catholics and Protestants and between the seventeen provinces and Spain. Eventually the ten southern provinces came under the control of the Spanish Habsburg forces.

Union of Utrecht The alliance of seven northern provinces of the Netherlands, all of which were Protestant, that declared independence from Spain and formed the United Provinces of the Netherlands.

The seven northern provinces, led by Holland, formed the **Union of Utrecht** (the United Provinces), and in 1581 they declared their independence from Spain. The north was Protestant, and the south remained Catholic. Philip did not accept the independence of the north, and war continued. England was even drawn into the conflict, supplying money and troops to the United Provinces. Hostilities ended in 1609 when Spain agreed to a truce that recognized the independence of the United Provinces.

The Great European Witch-Hunt

Insecurity created by the religious wars contributed to persecution for witchcraft, which actually began before the Reformation in the 1480s but became especially common about 1560. Both Protestants and Catholics tried and executed those accused of being witches.

The heightened sense of God's power and divine wrath in the Reformation era was an important factor in the witch-hunts, but other factors were also significant. In the later Middle Ages, many educated Christians added a demonological component to existing ideas about witches. Witches were no longer simply people who used magical power to do harm and get what they wanted, but rather people used by the Devil to do what he wanted. Some demonological theorists also claimed that witches were organized in an international conspiracy to overthrow Christianity.

Trials involving this new notion of witchcraft as diabolical heresy began in Switzerland and southern Germany in the late fifteenth century; became less numerous in the early decades of the Reformation, when Protestants and Catholics were busy fighting each other; and then picked up again about 1560, spreading to much of western Europe and to European colonies in the Americas. Scholars estimate that during the sixteenth and seventeenth centuries somewhere between 40,000 and 60,000 people were executed for witchcraft.

Though the gender balance of the accused varied widely in different parts of Europe, between 75 and 85 percent of those tried and executed were women, whom some demonologists viewed as weaker and so more likely to give in to the Devil. Tensions within families, households, and neighborhoods also played a role in witchcraft accusations, as grievances and jealousies led to accusations. Suspects were questioned and tortured by legal authorities, and they often implicated others. The circle of the accused grew, sometimes into a much larger hunt that historians have called a "witch panic." Panics were most common in the part of Europe that saw the most witch accusations in general—the Holy Roman Empire, Switzerland, and parts of France.

Even in the sixteenth century a few individuals questioned whether witches could ever do harm, make a pact with the Devil, or engage in the wild activities attributed to them. Furthermore, doubts about whether secret denunciations were valid or torture would ever yield a truthful confession gradually spread among the same authorities who had so vigorously persecuted witches. By about 1660, prosecutions for witchcraft became less common. The last official execution for witchcraft in England was in 1682, though the last one in the Holy Roman Empire was not until 1775.

Quick Review
What role did local, national, and international politics play in the religious violence of the sixteenth and seventeenth centuries?

Connections

THE RENAISSANCE AND THE REFORMATION are often seen as key to the creation of the modern world. The radical changes of these times contained many elements of continuity, however. Artists, humanists, and religious reformers looked back to the classical era and early Christianity for inspiration, viewing those times as better and purer than their own. Political leaders played important roles in cultural and religious developments, just as they had for centuries in Europe and other parts of the world.

The events of the Renaissance and Reformation thus were linked with earlier developments, and they were also closely connected with another important element in the modern world: European exploration and colonization (discussed in Chapter 16). Renaissance monarchs paid for expeditions' ships, crews, and supplies, expecting a large share of any profits gained and increasingly viewing overseas territory as essential to a strong state. Only a week after Martin Luther stood in front of Charles V at the Diet of Worms declaring his independence in matters of religion, Ferdinand Magellan, a Portuguese sea captain using Spanish ships, was killed by indigenous people in a group of islands off the coast of southeast Asia. Charles V had provided the backing for Magellan's voyage, the first to circumnavigate the globe. Magellan viewed one of the purposes of his trip as the spread of Christianity, and later in the sixteenth century institutions created as part of the Catholic Reformation, including the Jesuit order and the Inquisition, would operate in European colonies overseas as well as in Europe itself. The desire for fame, wealth, and power that was central to the Renaissance, and the religious zeal central to the Reformation, were thus key to the European voyages and to colonial ventures as well.

- **For a list of suggested readings for this chapter, visit** *bedfordstmartins.com/mckayworldunderstanding*.
- **For primary sources from this period, see** *Sources of World Societies*, Second Edition.
- **For Web sites, images, and documents related to topics in this chapter, see Make History at** *bedfordstmartins.com/mckayworldunderstanding*.

Chapter 15 **Study Guide**

To do these exercises online, go to bedfordstmartins.com/mckayworldunderstanding.

Step 1

GETTING STARTED

Below are basic terms about this period in global history. Can you identify each term below and explain why it matters?

TERMS	WHO (OR WHAT) AND WHEN	WHY IT MATTERS
Renaissance, p. 378		
patronage, p. 378		
humanism, p. 379		
Christian humanists, p. 380		
debate about women, p. 385		
Protestant Reformation, p. 389		
indulgence, p. 389		
Diet of Worms, p. 390		
Protestant, p. 390		
predestination, p. 397		
Jesuits, p. 400		
Huguenots, p. 400		
politiques, p. 401		
Union of Utrecht, p. 402		

Step 2

MOVING BEYOND THE BASICS

The exercise below represents a more advanced understanding of the chapter material. Examine the key differences between Catholic and Protestant beliefs and practices by filling in the chart below with descriptions of Catholic and Protestant views of salvation, the nature and role of the clergy, and the nature and role of the church. When you are finished, consider the following questions: How did Protestantism build on humanism? How did Protestant beliefs challenge Catholic institutions? Why did European states inevitably become involved in the theological conflicts of the Reformation?

	VIEWS OF SALVATION	NATURE AND ROLE OF CLERGY	NATURE AND ROLE OF THE CHURCH
Protestantism			
Catholicism			

Step 3 PUTTING IT ALL TOGETHER

Now that you've reviewed key elements of the chapter, take a step back and try to see the big picture. Remember to use specific examples from the chapter in your answers.

THE RENAISSANCE

- How did Renaissance ideas about individuals and their potential differ from those that prevailed in the Middle Ages?
- How did political and economic considerations shape the emergence, development, and spread of the Renaissance?

THE PROTESTANT REFORMATION

- How did Protestantism differ from earlier calls for theological and institutional reform of the Catholic Church? What explains Protestantism's remarkable success?
- What groups found Protestantism most appealing? Why?

THE CATHOLIC REFORMATION AND RELIGIOUS VIOLENCE

- Should the Catholic Reformation be considered a success? Why or why not?
- What connections can you make between the various forms of religious violence (riots, wars, witchcraft trials) that plagued sixteenth and seventeenth-century Europe? What common factors and conditions contributed to each of these types of religious violence?

LOOKING BACK, LOOKING AHEAD

- How did medieval developments prepare the way for the Renaissance and the Reformation? What were the most important areas of continuity between medieval and early modern Europe?
- Many scholars and thinkers have seen the Renaissance and Reformation as marking the beginning of the "modern" Western world. Do you agree with this assessment? Why or why not?

In Your Own Words Imagine that you must explain Chapter 15 to someone who hasn't read it. What would be the most important points to include and why?

16

The Acceleration of Global Contact

1450–1600

Before 1500 Europeans were relatively marginal players in a centuries-old trading system that linked Africa, Asia, and Europe. Elite classes everywhere prized Chinese porcelains and silks, while wealthy Chinese wanted ivory and black slaves from East Africa and exotic goods and peacocks from India. African people wanted textiles from India and cowrie shells from the Maldives. Europeans craved spices and silks, but they had few desirable goods to offer their trading partners.

The Indian Ocean was the locus of these desires and commercial exchanges, which sparked competition among Arab, Persian, Turkish, Indian, African, Chinese, and European merchants and adventurers. They fought each other for the trade that brought great wealth. They also jostled with Muslim scholars, Buddhist teachers, and Christian missionaries, who competed for the religious adherence of the peoples of Sumatra, Java, Borneo, and the Philippine Islands.

Mexica Noble This image from the early-seventeenth-century indigenous *Codex Ixtlilxochitl* shows a Mexica noble holding flowers and a tube of tobacco in his right hand. His jewelry and decorated cape emphasize his wealth and social standing. (Codex Ixtlilxochitl, Facsimile edition by ADEVA, Graz, Austria)

The European search for better access to Asian trade goods led to a new overseas empire in the Indian Ocean and the accidental discovery of the Western Hemisphere. With this discovery South and North America soon joined an international network of trade centers and political empires, which Europeans came to dominate. The era of globalization had begun, creating new forms of cultural exchange, assimilation, conversion, and resistance. Europeans sought to impose their cultural values on the peoples they encountered while struggling to comprehend them and their societies. The Age of Discovery from 1450 to 1650, as the time of these encounters is known, laid the foundations for the modern world as we know it today.

Chapter Preview

- How did trade link the peoples of Africa, Asia, and Europe prior to 1492?
- How and why did Europeans undertake voyages of expansion?
- What was the impact of conquest?
- How did expansion shape values and beliefs in Europe and the Americas?

How did trade link the peoples of Africa, Asia, and Europe prior to 1492?

Historians now recognize that a type of world economy, known as the Afroeurasian trade world, linked the products and people of Europe, Asia, and Africa in the fifteenth century. Prior to 1492, the West was not the dominant player in world trade. Nevertheless, wealthy Europeans were eager consumers of luxury goods from the East, which they received through Venetian and Genoese middlemen.

The Trade World of the Indian Ocean

The Indian Ocean was the center of the Afroeurasian trade world, serving as a crossroads for commercial and cultural exchanges between China, India, the Middle East, Africa, and Europe (Map 16.1). From the seventh through the fourteenth centuries, the volume of this trade steadily increased, declining only during the years of the Black Death.

Merchants congregated in a series of multicultural, cosmopolitan port cities strung around the Indian Ocean. Most of these cities had some form of autonomous self-government, and mutual self-interest had largely limited violence and attempts to monopolize trade. The most developed area of this commercial web was made up of the ports surrounding the South China Sea. In the fifteenth century the port of Malacca became a great commercial entrepôt (AHN-truh-poh), a trading post to which goods were shipped for storage while awaiting redistribution to other places.

The Mongol emperors opened the doors of China to the West, encouraging Europeans to do business there. After the Mongols fell to the Ming Dynasty in 1368, China entered a period of agricultural and commercial expansion, population growth, and urbanization. Historians agree that China had the most advanced economy in the world until at least the start of the eighteenth century.

China also took the lead in exploration, sending Admiral Zheng He's fleet as far west as Egypt. (See "Individuals in Society: Zheng He," page 410.) From 1405 to 1433, each of his seven expeditions involved hundreds of ships and tens of thousands of men. The purpose of the voyages was primarily diplomatic, to enhance China's prestige and seek tribute-paying alliances. The voyages came to a sudden halt after the deaths of Zheng and the emperor who initiated his voyages, probably due to court opposition to their high cost and contact with foreign peoples.

By ending large-scale exploration on China's part, this decision marked a turning point in history. Nonetheless, Zheng He's voyages left a legacy of increased Chinese trading in the South China Sea and Indian Ocean. Following Zheng He's voyages, tens of thousands of Chinese emigrated to the Philippines, where they acquired commercial dominance of the island of Luzon by 1600.

Another center of Indian Ocean trade was India, the crucial link between the Persian Gulf and the Southeast Asian and East Asian trade networks. Trade among ports bordering the Indian Ocean was revived in the Middle Ages by Arab merchants who circumnavigated India on their way to trade in the South China Sea. The need for stopovers led to the establishment of trading posts at Gujarat and on the Malabar coast, where the cities of Calicut and Quilon became thriving commercial centers.

The inhabitants of India's Coromandel coast traditionally looked to Southeast Asia, where they had ancient trading and cultural ties. Hinduism and Buddhism arrived in Southeast Asia from India during the Middle Ages, and a brisk trade between Southeast Asian and Coromandel port cities persisted from that time until the arrival of the Portuguese in the sixteenth century. India itself was an important contributor of goods to the world trading system. Most of the world's pepper was grown in India, and Indian cotton and silk textiles were also highly prized.

Chapter Chronology

1450–1650	Age of Discovery
1492	Columbus lands on San Salvador
1494	Treaty of Tordesillas ratified
1518	Atlantic slave trade begins
1519–1521	Spanish conquest of Aztec capital of Tenochtitlán
1533	Pizarro conquers Inca Empire
1571	Spanish found port of Manila in the Philippines
1580	Michel de Montaigne's *Essays* published
1602	Dutch East India Company established

Peoples and Cultures of the Indian Ocean

Indian Ocean trade connected peoples from the Malay Peninsula (the southern extremity of the Asian continent), India, China, and East Africa, among whom there was an enormous variety of languages, cultures, and religions. In spite of this diversity, certain sociocultural similarities linked these peoples, especially in Southeast Asia.

For example, by the fifteenth century, inhabitants of what we call Indonesia, Malaysia, the Philippines, and the many islands in between all spoke languages of the Austronesian family, reflecting continuing interactions among them. A common environment led to a diet based on rice, fish, palms, and palm wine. In comparison to India, China, or even Europe after the Black Death, Southeast Asia was sparsely populated. People were concentrated in port cities and in areas of intense rice cultivation.

Another difference between Southeast Asia and India, China, and Europe was the higher status of women in the region. Women took the primary role in planting and harvesting rice, giving them authority and economic power. At marriage, which typically occurred around age twenty, the groom paid the bride (or sometimes her family) a sum of money called **bride wealth**, which remained under her control. This practice was in sharp contrast to the Chinese, Indian, and European dowry, which came under the husband's control. Property was administered jointly, in contrast to the Chinese principle and Indian practice that wives had no say in the disposal of family property. All children, regardless of gender, inherited equally.

bride wealth In early modern Southeast Asia, a sum of money the groom paid the bride or her family at the time of marriage, in contrast to the husband's control of dowry in China, India, and Europe.

Respect for women carried over to the commercial sphere. Women participated in business as partners and independent entrepreneurs, even undertaking long commercial sea voyages. When Portuguese and Dutch men settled in the region and married local women, their wives continued to play important roles in trade and commerce.

In contrast to most parts of the world other than Africa, Southeast Asian peoples had an accepting attitude toward premarital sexual activity, and no premium was placed on virginity at marriage. Divorce carried no social stigma, and it was easy if a pair proved incompatible. Either the woman or the man could initiate a divorce, and common property and children were divided.

Trade with Africa and the Middle East

On the east coast of Africa, Swahili-speaking city-states engaged in the Indian Ocean trade, exchanging ivory, rhinoceros horn, tortoise shells, copra (dried coconut), and slaves for textiles, spices, cowrie shells, porcelain, and other goods. Peopled by confident and urbane merchants, East African cities were known for their prosperity and culture.

Mansa Musa This detail from the Catalan Atlas of 1375 depicts a king of Mali, Mansa Musa, who was legendary for his wealth in gold. European desires for direct access to the trade in sub-Saharan gold helped inspire Portuguese exploration of the west coast of Africa in the fifteenth century. (Bridgeman-Giraudon/Art Resource, NY)

INDIVIDUALS IN SOCIETY

Zheng He

IN 1403 THE CHINESE EMPEROR YONGLE ordered his coastal provinces to build a vast fleet of ships, with construction centered at Longjiang near Nanjing. The inland provinces were to provide wood for the ships and float it down the Yangzi River. Thirty thousand shipwrights, carpenters, sailmakers, ropers, and caulkers worked in a frenzy. As work progressed, Yongle selected a commander for the fleet. The emperor chose Zheng He (1371–1433), despite fearing that the thirty-five-year-old was too old for so politically important an expedition. The decision rested on Zheng's unquestioned loyalty, strength of character, energy, ability, and eloquence. These qualities apparently were expected to compensate for Zheng's lack of seamanship.

The southwestern province of Yunnan, where Zheng was born, had a large Muslim population, and he was raised in that faith. When the then prince Zhi Di defeated the Mongols in Yunnan, Zheng's father was killed in the related disorder. The young boy was taken prisoner and, as was the custom, castrated. Raised in Zhi Di's household, he learned to read and write, studied Confucian writings, and accompanied the prince on all military expeditions. By age twenty Zheng was not the soft, effeminate stereotype of the eunuch; rather he was "seven feet tall and had a waist five feet in circumference. His cheeks and forehead were high . . . [and] he had glaring eyes . . . [and] a voice loud as a bell. . . . He was accustomed to battle." Zheng must have looked imposing. A devout Muslim, he persuaded the emperor to place mosques under imperial protection after a period of persecution. On his travels, he prayed at mosques at Malacca and Hormuz. Unable to sire sons, he adopted a nephew. When Zheng became a naval commander under Yongle, he was the first eunuch in Chinese history to hold such an important position.

The fleet for Zheng's first expedition was composed of 317 ships, including junks, supply ships, water tankers, warships, transports for horses, and patrol boats, and carried twenty-eight thousand sailors and soldiers; it was the largest naval force in world history before World War I. Because it bore tons of beautiful porcelains, elegant silks, lacquer ware, and exquisite artifacts to be exchanged for goods abroad, it was called the "treasure fleet."

Between 1405 and 1433, Zheng led seven voyages, which combined the emperor's diplomatic, political, geographical, and commercial goals (see Map 16.1). During the voyages he worked toward Yongle's goal of securing China's hegemony over tributary states and collecting pledges of loyalty from them. Zheng also sought information on winds, tides, distant lands, and rare plants and animals, and he sailed as far west as Egypt to gather it. Because smallpox epidemics had recently hit China, another purpose of his voyages was to gather pharmacological products. An Arab text on drugs and therapies was secured and translated into Chinese. He also brought back a giraffe and mahogany, a wood ideal for ships' rudders because of its hardness.

Just before his death, Zheng recorded his accomplishments on stone tablets. The expeditions had unified "seas and continents . . . the countries beyond the horizon from the ends of the earth have all become subjects . . . and the distances and routes between distant lands may be calculated," implying that China had accumulated considerable geographical information. From around the Indian Ocean, official tribute flowed to the Ming court as a result of Zheng's efforts. A vast immigration of Chinese people into Southeast Asia, sometimes called the Chinese diaspora, came into being after the expeditions. Immigrants carried with them Chinese culture, including social customs, diet, and practical objects of Chinese technology — calendars, books, scales for weights and measures, and musical instruments. With legends collected about him and monuments erected to him, Zheng became a great cult hero.

Source: Louise Levathes, *When China Ruled the Seas: The Treasure Fleet of the Dragon Throne, 1405–1433* (New York: Oxford University Press, 1996).

QUESTIONS FOR ANALYSIS

1. What do the voyages of the treasure fleet tell us about China in the fifteenth century?
2. What was Zheng He's legacy?

Zheng He (right), voyager to India, Persia, Arabia, and Africa. (From Lo Monteng, *The Western Sea Cruises of Eunuch San Pao*, 1597)

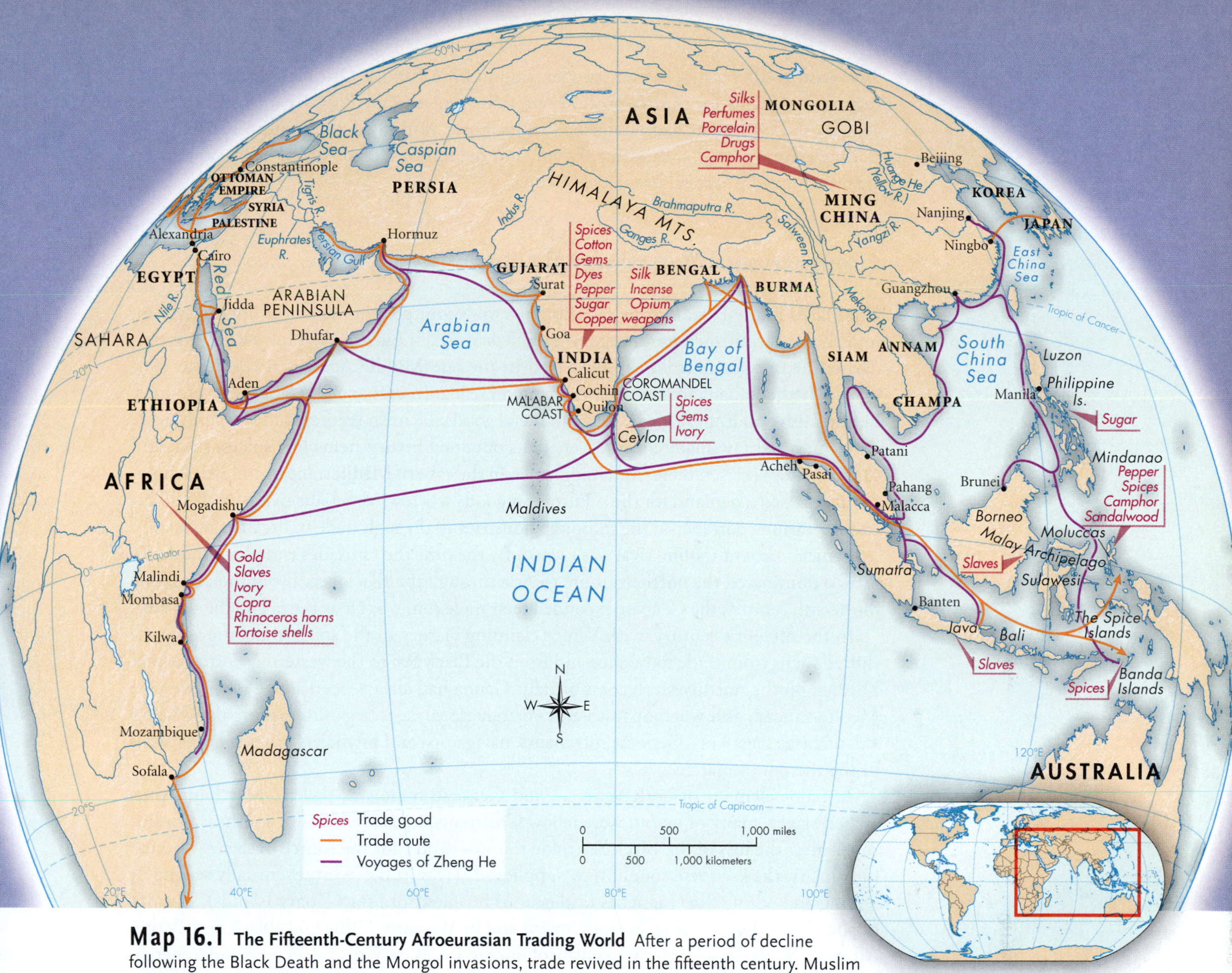

Map 16.1 The Fifteenth-Century Afroeurasian Trading World After a period of decline following the Black Death and the Mongol invasions, trade revived in the fifteenth century. Muslim merchants dominated trade, linking ports in East Africa and the Red Sea with those in India and the Malay Archipelago. The Chinese admiral Zheng He's voyages (1405–1433) followed the most important Indian Ocean trade routes, hoping to impose Ming dominance of trade and tribute.

West Africa also played an important role in world trade. In the fifteenth century most of the gold that reached Europe came from Sudan in West Africa and, in particular, from the kingdom of Mali near present-day Ghana. Transported across the Sahara by Arab and African traders, the gold was sold in the ports of North Africa. Other trading routes led to the Egyptian cities of Alexandria and Cairo, where the Venetians held commercial privileges.

Inland nations that sat astride the north-south caravan routes grew wealthy from this trade. In the mid-thirteenth century the kingdom of Mali emerged as an important player on the overland trade route. In later centuries, however, the diversion of gold away from the trans-Sahara routes would weaken the inland states of Africa politically and economically.

Gold was one important object of trade; slaves were another. Arabic and African merchants took West African slaves to the Mediterranean to be sold in European, Egyptian, and Middle Eastern markets and also brought eastern Europeans to West Africa as slaves. In addition, Indian and Arabic merchants traded slaves in the coastal regions of East Africa.

The Middle East served as an intermediary for trade between Europe, Africa, and Asia and was also an important supplier of goods for foreign exchange, especially silk and cotton.

Two great rival empires, the Persian Safavids and the Turkish Ottomans, dominated the region, competing for control over western trade routes to the East. By the mid-sixteenth century the Ottomans had established control over eastern Mediterranean sea routes to trading centers in Syria, Palestine, Egypt, and the rest of North Africa. Their power also extended into Europe as far west as Vienna.

Genoese and Venetian Middlemen

Compared to the East, Europe constituted a minor outpost in the world trading system, for European craftsmen produced few products to rival those of Asia. However, Europeans desired luxury goods from the East, and in the late Middle Ages such trade was controlled by the Italian city-states of Venice and Genoa. In exchange for European products like Spanish and English wool, German metal goods, Flemish textiles, and silk cloth made with imported raw materials, the Venetians obtained luxury items like spices, silks, and carpets. They accessed these from middlemen in the eastern Mediterranean and Asia Minor. Because Eastern demand for these European goods was low, Venetians made up the difference by earning currency in the shipping industry and through trade in firearms and slaves.

Venice's ancient trading rival was Genoa. By the time the Crusades ended around 1270, Genoa dominated the northern route to Asia through the Black Sea. From then until the fourteenth century, the Genoese expanded their trade routes as far as Persia and the Far East.

In the fifteenth century, with Venice claiming victory in the spice trade, the Genoese shifted focus from trade to finance and from the Black Sea to the western Mediterranean. Located on the northwestern coast of Italy, Genoa had always been active in the western Mediterranean, and when Spanish and Portuguese voyages began to explore the western Atlantic (see page 414), Genoese merchants, navigators, and financiers provided their skills to the Iberian monarchs.

A major element of both Venetian and Genoese trade was slavery. Merchants purchased slaves, many of whom were fellow Christians, in the Balkans of southeastern Europe. After the loss of the Black Sea trade routes—and thus the source of slaves—to the Ottomans, the Genoese sought new supplies of slaves in the West, eventually seizing or buying and selling the Guanches (indigenous peoples from the Canary Islands), Muslim prisoners and Jewish refugees from Spain, and by the early 1500s both black and Berber Africans. With the growth of Spanish colonies in the New World, Genoese and Venetian merchants became important players in the Atlantic slave trade.

Italian experience in colonial administration, the slave trade, and international trade and finance served as a model for the Iberian states as they pushed European expansion to new heights. Mariners, merchants, and financiers from Venice and Genoa—most notably Christopher Columbus—played crucial roles in bringing the fruits of this experience to the Iberian Peninsula and to the New World.

Quick Review
What goods did each of the major participants in the Afroeurasian trade system supply?

How and why did Europeans undertake voyages of expansion?

In the fifteenth and early sixteenth centuries, Europeans launched new voyages of exploration, commerce, and conquest out of a desire to spread Christianity, to undo Italian and Ottoman domination of trade with the East, and to tap entirely new sources of wealth. Ultimately, their efforts landed them in the New World.

Causes of European Expansion

Europeans sought to expand their international reach for many reasons. By the middle of the fifteenth century, Europe was experiencing a revival of population and economic activity after the lows of the Black Death. This revival created demands for luxury goods, especially spices, from the East. However, the conquest of Constantinople by the Ottomans gave the Muslim empire control of trade routes to the east and blocked the fulfillment of European demands. Europeans thus needed to find new sources of precious metal to trade with the Ottomans or to find trade routes that bypassed the Ottomans.

Religious fervor was another important catalyst for expansion. The passion and energy ignited by the Christian reconquista of the Iberian Peninsula encouraged the Portuguese and Spanish to continue the Christian crusade. In 1492 Spain conquered Granada, the last remaining Muslim state on the Iberian Peninsula. Just seven months later, Columbus departed across the Atlantic.

Combined with eagerness to gain wealth and to spread Christianity were the desire for glory and the urge to chart new waters. Scholars have frequently described the European discoveries as a manifestation of Renaissance curiosity about the physical universe. The journals kept by European voyagers attest to their motives and fascination with the new peoples and places they visited. When the Portuguese explorer Vasco da Gama reached the port of Calicut, India, in 1498 and a native asked what he wanted, he replied, "Christians and spices."[1]

Eagerness for exploration was heightened by a lack of opportunity at home. After the reconquista, young men of the Spanish upper classes found their economic and political opportunities greatly limited. The ambitious turned to the sea to seek their fortunes.

Whatever the reasons, the voyages were made possible by the growth of government power. The Spanish monarchy was stronger than before and in a position to support foreign ventures. In Portugal explorers also looked to the monarchy, to Prince Henry the Navigator in particular (page 414), for financial support and encouragement. Monarchs shared many of the motivations of explorers. In addition, competition among European monarchs was an important factor in encouraging the steady stream of expeditions that began in the late fifteenth century.

Ordinary men chose to join these voyages to escape poverty at home, to continue a family trade, or to find better lives as illegal immigrants in the colonies. However, common sailors were ill-paid, and life at sea meant danger, hunger, and overcrowding. For months at a time, 100 to 120 people lived and worked in a space of 1,600 to 2,000 square feet.

The people who stayed at home had a powerful impact on the process and a strong interest in it. Royal ministers and factions at court influenced monarchs to provide or deny support for exploration. The small number of people who could read served as an audience for tales of fantastic places and unknown peoples. One of the most popular books of the time was the fourteenth-century text *The Travels of Sir John Mandeville*, which purported to be a firsthand account of the author's travels

The Travels of Sir John Mandeville The author of this tale claimed to be an English knight who traveled extensively in the Middle East and Asia from the 1320s to the 1350s. Although historians now consider the work a skillful fiction, it had a great influence on how Europeans understood the world at the time. This illustration, from an edition published around 1410, depicts Mandeville approaching a walled city on the first stage of his voyage to Constantinople. (© British Library Board, Add 24289, f14v)

in the Middle East, India, and China. These fantastic tales of cannibals, one-eyed giants, men with the heads of dogs, and other marvels were believed for centuries. Columbus took a copy of Mandeville and the equally popular and more reliable *The Travels of Marco Polo* on his voyage in 1492.

Technology and the Rise of Exploration

caravel A small, maneuverable, three-mast sailing ship developed by the Portuguese in the fifteenth century that gave the Portuguese a distinct advantage in exploration and trade.

Ptolemy's *Geography* Second century C.E. work that synthesized the classical knowledge of geography and introduced the concepts of longitude and latitude. Reintroduced to Europeans in 1410 by Arab scholars, its ideas allowed cartographers to create more accurate maps.

Technological developments in shipbuilding, navigation, and weaponry provided another impetus for European expansion. In the course of the fifteenth century, the Portuguese developed the **caravel**, a small, light, three-mast sailing ship. The caravel was maneuverable, sturdy, and could be sailed with a small crew. When fitted with cannon, it could dominate larger vessels.

Great strides in cartography and navigational aids were also made during this period. Around 1410 Arab scholars reintroduced Europeans to **Ptolemy's *Geography***. Written in the second century, the work synthesized the geographical knowledge of the classical world. It represented a major improvement over medieval cartography, showing the world as round and introducing the idea of latitude and longitude to plot position accurately. It also contained significant errors. Unaware of the Americas, Ptolemy showed the world as much smaller than it is, so that Asia appeared not very distant from Europe.

The magnetic compass enabled sailors to determine their direction and position at sea. The astrolabe, an instrument invented by the ancient Greeks and perfected by Muslim navigators, was used to determine the altitude of the sun and other celestial bodies. It permitted mariners to plot their latitude, that is, their precise position north or south of the equator.

Like the astrolabe, Europeans borrowed much of the technology for their voyages from the East. Gunpowder, the compass, and the sternpost rudder were Chinese inventions. The lateen sail, which allowed European ships to tack against the wind, was a product of the Indian Ocean trade world. Advances in cartography also drew on the rich tradition of Judeo-Arabic mathematical and astronomical learning in Iberia. In exploring new territories, European sailors thus called on techniques and knowledge developed over centuries in China, the Muslim world, and trading centers along the Indian Ocean.

The Expanding Portuguese Empire

Portugal was a small and poor nation on the margins of European life. Yet Portugal had a long history of seafaring and navigation. Blocked from access to western Europe by Spain, the Portuguese turned to the Atlantic, whose waters they knew better than did other Europeans.

In the early phases of Portuguese exploration, Prince Henry (1394–1460), a younger son of the king, played a leading role. A nineteenth-century scholar dubbed Henry "the Navigator" because of his support for the study of geography and navigation and for the annual expeditions he sponsored down the western coast of Africa.

Portugal's conquest of Ceuta, an Arab city in northern Morocco, in 1415 marked the beginning of European overseas expansion. In the 1420s, under Henry's direction, the Portuguese began to settle the Atlantic islands of Madeira (ca. 1420) and the Azores (1427). In 1443 they founded their first African commercial settlement at

Portuguese Expansion into Africa

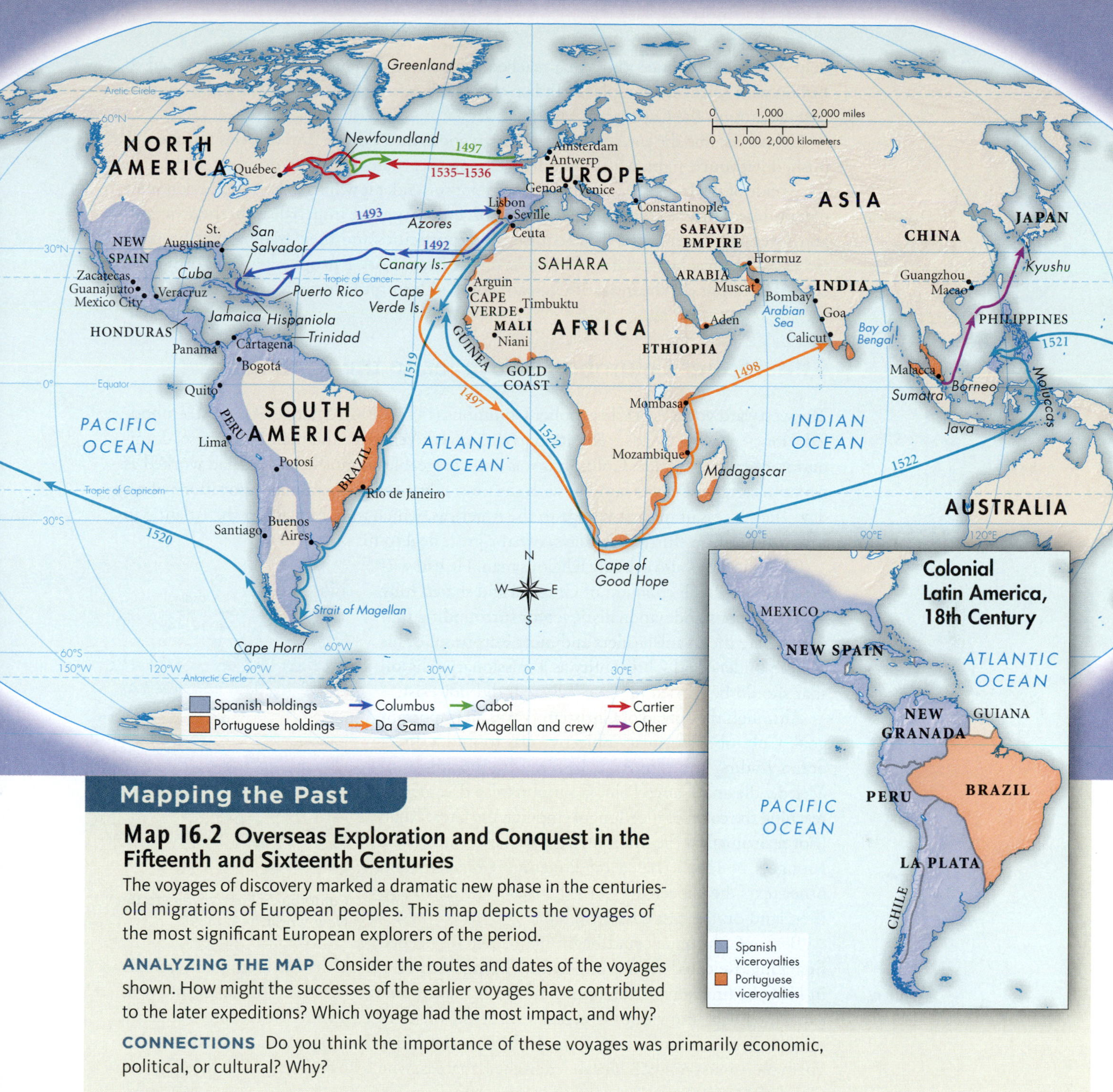

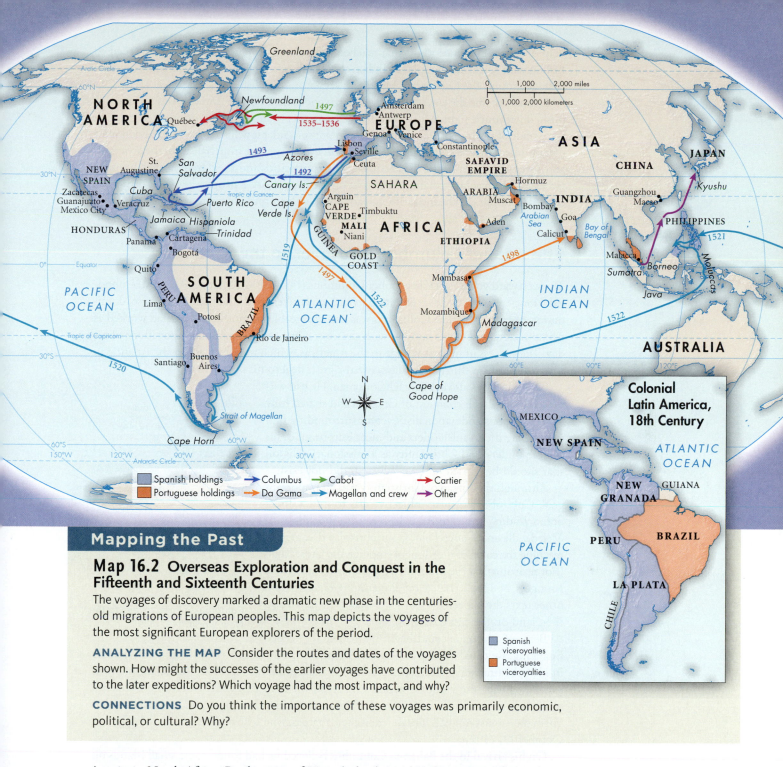

Mapping the Past

Map 16.2 Overseas Exploration and Conquest in the Fifteenth and Sixteenth Centuries

The voyages of discovery marked a dramatic new phase in the centuries-old migrations of European peoples. This map depicts the voyages of the most significant European explorers of the period.

ANALYZING THE MAP Consider the routes and dates of the voyages shown. How might the successes of the earlier voyages have contributed to the later expeditions? Which voyage had the most impact, and why?

CONNECTIONS Do you think the importance of these voyages was primarily economic, political, or cultural? Why?

Arguin in North Africa. By the time of Henry's death in 1460, his support for exploration was vindicated by thriving sugar plantations on the Atlantic islands, the first arrival of enslaved Africans in Portugal (see page 425), and new access to African gold.

The Portuguese next established trading posts and forts on the gold-rich Guinea coast and penetrated into the African continent all the way to Timbuktu (Map 16.2). By 1500 Portugal controlled the flow of African gold to Europe.

The Portuguese then pushed farther south down the west coast of Africa. In 1487 Bartholomew Diaz (ca. 1451–1500) rounded the Cape of Good Hope at the southern tip, but was forced to turn back. A decade later Vasco da Gama (ca. 1469–1524) succeeded in rounding the Cape while commanding a fleet in search of a sea route to India. With the help of an Indian guide, da Gama reached the port of Calicut in India. He returned to Lisbon with spices and samples of Indian cloth. Thereafter, a Portuguese convoy set out for passage around the Cape every March.

Lisbon became the entrance port for Asian goods into Europe, but this was not accomplished without a fight. Muslim-controlled port city-states had long dominated the rich spice trade of the Indian Ocean, and they did not surrender it willingly. Portuguese conquest of a number of these cities laid the foundation for Portuguese imperialism in the sixteenth and seventeenth centuries. The acquisition of port cities and their trade routes brought riches to Portugal but had limited impact on the lives of Asian peoples beyond Portuguese coastal holdings. In the meantime, Spain also had begun the quest for an empire.

Christopher Columbus's Voyages to the Americas

The westward voyages of Christopher Columbus (1451–1506), a native of Genoa, embodied a long-standing Genoese ambition to circumvent Venetian, and then Portuguese, domination of eastward trade. Columbus was knowledgeable about the sea. He had worked as a mapmaker, and he was familiar with the most advanced navigational innovations of his day. The success of his first voyage to the Americas, which took him across the Atlantic to the Caribbean in thirty-three days, owed a great deal to his seamanship.

Columbus was also a deeply religious man. He had witnessed the Spanish conquest of Granada and shared fully in the religious and nationalistic fervor surrounding that event. Like the Spanish rulers and most Europeans of his age, he understood Christianity as a missionary religion that should be carried to places where it did not exist.

Columbus's First Voyage to the New World, 1492–1493

Although the spread of Christianity was an important goal, Columbus's primary objective was to find a direct ocean trading route to Asia. Inspired by the stories of Mandeville and Marco Polo, Columbus also dreamed of reaching the court of the Mongol emperor, the Great Khan (not realizing that the Ming Dynasty had overthrown the Mongols in 1368). Based on Ptolemy's *Geography* and other texts, he expected to pass the islands of Japan and then land on the east coast of China.

Before Columbus could begin his voyage he needed financing. Rejected for funding by the Portuguese in 1483 and by Ferdinand and Isabella in 1486, he finally won the support of the Spanish monarchy in 1492. The Spanish crown agreed to make him viceroy over any territory he might discover and to give him one-tenth of the material rewards of the journey. With this backing, Columbus and his small fleet left Spain on August 3, 1492. He landed in the Bahamas, which he christened San Salvador, on October 12, 1492.

On his arrival in the Bahamas Columbus believed he had found some small islands off the east coast of Japan. In a letter he wrote to Ferdinand and Isabella on his return to Spain, Columbus described the natives as handsome, peaceful, and primitive. Believing he was in the Indies, he called them "Indians," a name that was later applied to all inhabitants of the Americas. Columbus concluded that they would make good slaves and could quickly be converted to Christianity. (See "Listening to the Past: Columbus Describes His First Voyage," page 418.)

Scholars have identified the inhabitants of the islands as the Taino (TIGH-noh) people, speakers of the Arawak language, who inhabited Hispaniola (modern-day Haiti and the Dominican Republic) and other islands in the Caribbean. Columbus received reassuring reports from Taino villagers of the presence of gold and of a great king in the vicinity.

From San Salvador, Columbus sailed southwest, believing that this course would take him to Japan or the coast of China. He landed instead on Cuba on October 28. Deciding that he must be on the mainland of China near the coastal city of Quinsay (now Hangzhou), he sent a small embassy inland with letters from Ferdinand and Isabella and instructions to locate the grand city.

The landing party found only small villages. Confronted with this disappointment, Columbus focused on trying to find gold or other valuables among the peoples he had discovered. The sight of Taino people wearing gold ornaments on Hispaniola seemed to prove that gold was available in the region. In January, confident that its source would soon be found, he headed back to Spain to report on his discovery.

Over the next decades, the Spanish would follow a policy of conquest and colonization in the New World (see pages 420–422). On his second voyage, Columbus forcibly subjugated the island of Hispaniola and enslaved its indigenous peoples. On this and subsequent voyages, he brought with him settlers for the new Spanish territories. Columbus himself, however, had little interest in or capacity for governing. Arriving in Hispaniola on this third voyage, he found revolt had broken out against his brother. A royal expedition sent to investigate returned the brothers to Spain in chains. Although Columbus was quickly cleared of wrongdoing, he did not recover his authority over the territories.

To the end of his life in 1506, Columbus believed that he had found small islands off the coast of Asia. He never realized that he had found a vast continent unknown to Europeans, except for a fleeting Viking presence centuries earlier. He could not know that the lands he discovered would become a crucial new arena for international trade and colonization, with grave consequences for native peoples.

Later Explorers

The Florentine navigator Amerigo Vespucci (veh-SPOO-chee; 1454–1512) realized what Columbus had not. Writing about his discoveries on the coast of modern-day Venezuela, Vespucci was the first to describe America as a continent separate from Asia. In recognition of Amerigo's bold claim, the continent was named for him.

World Map of Diogo Ribeiro, 1529 This map integrates the wealth of new information provided by European explorers in the decades after Columbus's 1492 voyage. Working on commission for the Spanish king Charles V, mapmaker Diogo Ribeiro incorporated new details on Africa, South America, India, the Malay Archipelago, and China. Note the inaccuracy in his placement of the Moluccas, or Spice Islands, which are much too far east. This "mistake" was intended to serve Spain's interests in trade negotiations with the Portuguese. (Biblioteca Apostolica Vaticana, BORG.III)

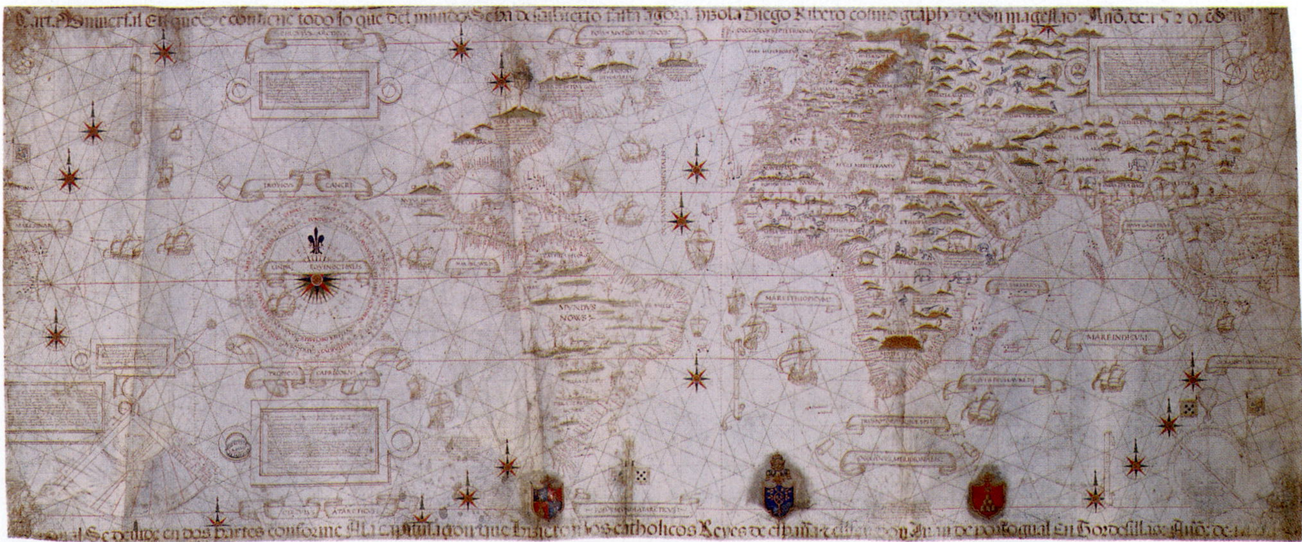

LISTENING TO THE PAST

Columbus Describes His First Voyage

On his return voyage to Spain in February 1493, Christopher Columbus composed a letter intended for wide circulation and had copies of it sent ahead to Isabella, Ferdinand, and others when the ship docked at Lisbon. Because the letter sums up Columbus's understanding of his achievements, it is considered the most important document of his first voyage.

" Since I know that you will be pleased at the great success with which the Lord has crowned my voyage, I write to inform you how in thirty-three days I crossed from the Canary Islands to the Indies, with the fleet which our most illustrious sovereigns gave me. I found very many islands with large populations and took possession of them all for their Highnesses; this I did by proclamation and unfurled the royal standard. No opposition was offered.

I named the first island that I found "San Salvador," in honour of our Lord and Saviour who has granted me this miracle. . . . When I reached Cuba, I followed its north coast westwards, and found it so extensive that I thought this must be the mainland, the province of Cathay.* . . . From there I saw another island eighteen leagues eastwards which I then named "Hispaniola."† . . .

Hispaniola is a wonder. The mountains and hills, the plains and meadow lands are both fertile and beautiful. They are most suitable for planting crops and for raising cattle of all kinds, and there are good sites for building towns and villages. The harbours are incredibly fine and there are many great rivers with broad channels and the majority contain gold.‡ The trees, fruits and plants are very different from those of Cuba. In Hispaniola there are many spices and large mines of gold and other metals.§ . . .

The inhabitants of this island, and all the rest that I discovered or heard of, go naked, as their mothers bore them, men and women alike. A few of the women, however, cover a single place with a leaf of a plant or piece of cotton which they weave for the purpose. They have no iron or steel or arms and are not capable of using them, not because they are not strong and well built but because they are amazingly timid. All the weapons they have are canes cut at seeding time, at the end of which they fix a sharpened stick, but they have not the courage to make use of these, for very often when I have sent two or three men to a village to have conversation with them a great number of them have come out. But as soon as they saw my men all fled immediately, a father not even waiting for his son. And this is not because we have harmed any of them; on the contrary, wherever I have gone and been able to have conversation with them, I have given them some of the various things I had, a cloth and other articles, and received nothing in exchange. But they have still remained incurably timid. True, when they have been reassured and lost their fear, they are so ingenuous and so liberal with all their possessions that no one who has not seen them would believe it. If one asks for anything they have they never say no. On the contrary, they offer a share to anyone with demonstrations of heartfelt affection, and they are immediately content with any small thing, valuable or valueless, that is given them. I forbade the men to give them bits of broken crockery, fragments of glass or tags of laces, though if they could get them they fancied them the finest jewels in the world.

I hoped to win them to the love and service of their Highnesses and of the whole Spanish nation and to persuade them to collect and give us of the things which they possessed in abundance and which we needed. They have no religion and are not idolaters; but all believe that power and goodness dwell in the sky and they are firmly convinced that I have come from the sky with these ships and people. In this belief they gave me a good reception everywhere, once they had overcome their fear; and this is not because they are stupid — far from it, they are men of great intelligence, for they navigate all those seas, and give a marvellously good account of everything — but because they have never before seen men clothed or ships like these. . . .

In all these islands the men are seemingly content with one woman, but their chief or king is allowed more than twenty. The women appear to work more than the men and I have not been able to find out if they have private property. As far as I could see whatever a man had was shared among all the rest and

Treaty of Tordesillas The 1494 agreement giving Spain everything west of an imaginary line drawn down the Atlantic and giving Portugal everything to the east.

To settle competing claims to the Atlantic discoveries, Spain and Portugal turned to Pope Alexander VI. The resulting **Treaty of Tordesillas** (tor-duh-SEE-yuhs) in 1494 gave Spain everything to the west of an imaginary line drawn down the Atlantic and Portugal everything to the east. This arbitrary division worked in Portugal's favor when in 1500 an expedition led by Pedro Alvares Cabral, en route to India, landed on the coast of Brazil, which Cabral claimed as Portuguese territory.

Spain had not given up the search for a western passage to Asia. In 1519 Charles V of Spain commissioned Ferdinand Magellan (1480–1521) to find a direct sea route to the spices of the Moluccas, islands off the southeast coast of Asia. Magellan sailed southwest across

this particularly applies to food. . . . In another island, which I am told is larger than Hispaniola, the people have no hair. Here there is a vast quantity of gold, and from here and the other islands I bring Indians as evidence.

In conclusion, to speak only of the results of this very hasty voyage, their Highnesses can see that I will give them as much gold as they require, if they will render me some very slight assistance; also I will give them all the spices and cotton they want. . . . I will also bring them as much aloes as they ask and as many slaves, who will be taken from the idolaters. I believe also that I have found rhubarb and cinnamon and there will be countless other things in addition. . . .

So all Christendom will be delighted that our Redeemer has given victory to our most illustrious King and Queen and their renowned kingdoms, in this great matter. They should hold great celebrations and render solemn thanks to the Holy Trinity with many solemn prayers, for the great triumph which they will have, by the conversion of so many peoples to our holy faith and for the temporal benefits which will follow, for not only Spain, but all Christendom will receive encouragement and profit.

This is a brief account of the facts.

Written in the caravel off the Canary Islands.**

15 February 1493

At your orders

THE ADMIRAL ”

Source: J. M. Cohen, ed. and trans., *The Four Voyages of Christopher Columbus* (Penguin Classics, 1958), pp. 115–123. Copyright © J. M. Cohen, 1969, London. Reproduced by permission of Penguin Books Ltd.

*Cathay is the old name for China. In the logbook and later in this letter Columbus accepts the native story that Cuba is an island that they can circumnavigate in something more than twenty-one days, yet he insists here and during the second voyage that it is in fact part of the Asiatic mainland.

†Hispaniola is the second largest island of the West Indies; Haiti occupies the western third of the island, the Dominican Republic the rest.

Christopher Columbus, by Ridolfo Ghirlandaio. Friend of Raphael and teacher of Michelangelo, Ghirlandaio (1483–1561) enjoyed distinction as a portrait painter, and so we can assume that this is a good likeness of the older Columbus. (Scala/Art Resource, NY)

‡This did not prove to be true.

§These statements are also inaccurate.

**Actually, Columbus was off Santa Maria in the Azores.

QUESTIONS FOR ANALYSIS

1. How did Columbus explain the success of his voyage?
2. What was Columbus's view of the Native Americans he met?
3. Evaluate his statements that the Caribbean islands possessed gold, cotton, and spices.
4. Why did Columbus cling to the idea that he had reached Asia?

the Atlantic to Brazil, and after a long search along the coast he located the treacherous strait off the southern tip of South America that now bears his name (see Map 16.2). After passing through the strait, his fleet sailed up the west coast of South America and then headed west into the Pacific toward the Malay Archipelago. Some of these islands were conquered in the 1560s and named the Philippines for Philip II of Spain.

Terrible storms, disease, starvation, and violence haunted the expedition, and only one of Magellan's five ships returned to Spain. Magellan himself was killed in a skirmish in the Philippines. In 1522 the sole remaining ship, with only eighteen men aboard, returned to Spain, having traveled from the east by way of the Indian Ocean, the Cape of Good

Hope, and the Atlantic. The voyage—the first to circumnavigate the globe—had taken close to three years.

Despite the losses, this voyage revolutionized Europeans' understanding of the world by demonstrating the vastness of the Pacific. Magellan's expedition also made Spain rethink its plans for overseas commerce and territorial expansion. Clearly, the westward passage to the Indies was too long and dangerous for commercial purposes. Thus Spain soon abandoned the attempt to oust Portugal from the Eastern spice trade and concentrated on exploiting its New World territories.

The English and French also set sail across the Atlantic during the early days of exploration, in their case to search for a northwest passage to the Indies. In 1497 John Cabot (ca. 1450–1499), a Genoese merchant living in London, discovered Newfoundland. The next year he returned and explored the New England coast. These forays proved futile, and at that time the English established no permanent colonies in the territories they explored. Early French exploration of the Atlantic was equally frustrating. Between 1534 and 1541 Frenchman Jacques Cartier (1491–1557) made several voyages and explored the St. Lawrence region of Canada, searching for a passage to the wealth of Asia. When this hope proved vain, the French turned to a new source of profit within Canada itself: trade in beavers and other furs. French fisherman also competed with the Spanish and English for the teeming schools of cod they found in the Atlantic waters around Newfoundland.

Spanish Conquest in the New World

conquistador Spanish for "conqueror"; Spanish soldier-explorer, such as Hernando Cortés and Francisco Pizarro, who sought to conquer the New World for the Spanish crown.

Mexica Empire Also known as the Aztec Empire, a large and complex Native American civilization in modern Mexico and Central America that possessed advanced mathematical, astronomical, and engineering technology.

After Columbus's voyages Spanish explorers penetrated farther into the New World. This territorial expansion began in 1519, when the Spanish governor in Cuba sent an expedition, under the command of the **conquistador** (kahn-KEES-tuh-dor) Hernando Cortés (1485–1547), to what is now Mexico. Accompanied by six hundred men, sixteen horses, and ten cannon, Cortés was to launch the conquest of the **Mexica Empire**. Its people were later called the Aztecs, but now most scholars prefer to use the term *Mexica* to refer to them and their empire.

The Mexica Empire was ruled by Montezuma II (r. 1502–1520) from his capital at Tenochtitlán (tay-nawch-teet-LAHN), now Mexico City. Larger than any European city of the time, it was the heart of a sophisticated, advanced civilization.

Soon after Cortés landed on the Mexican coast on April 21, 1519, his camp was visited by delegations of Mexica leaders bearing gifts and news of their great emperor. Impressed by the wealth of the local people, Cortés decided to defy his orders from the governor in Cuba, which restricted him to trading and exploration, and set up a settlement, Veracruz, under his own authority. He then burned his ships to prevent any disloyal or frightened followers from returning to Cuba.

The Mexica state religion necessitated constant warfare against neighboring peoples to secure captives for religious sacrifices and laborers for agricultural and building projects. Conquered peoples were required to pay tribute to the Mexica state through their local chiefs. Realizing that he could exploit dissension over this practice to his own advantage, Cortés forged an alliance with the Tlaxcala (tlah-SKAH-lah) and other subject kingdoms. In October a combined Spanish-Tlaxcalan force occupied the city of Cholula and massacred many thousand inhabitants. Strengthened by this display of power, Cortés made alliances with other native kingdoms. In November 1519, with a few hundred Spanish men and some six thousand indigenous warriors, he marched on Tenochtitlán.

Invasion of Tenochtitlán, 1519–1521

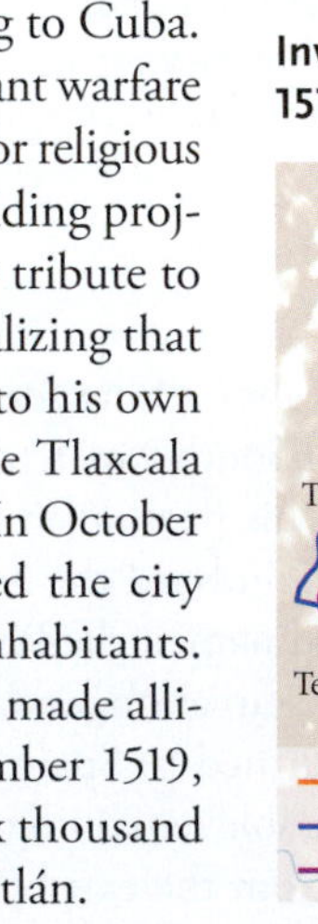

Picturing the Past

Doña Marina Translating for Hernando Cortés During His Meeting with Montezuma

In April 1519 Doña Marina (or La Malinche as she is known in Mexico) was among twenty women given to the Spanish as slaves. Fluent in Nahuatl (NAH-wha-tuhl) and Yucatec Mayan (spoken by a Spanish priest accompanying Cortés), she acted as an interpreter and diplomatic guide for the Spanish. She had a close relationship with Cortés and bore his son, Don Martín Cortés, in 1522. This image was created by Tlaxcalan artists shortly after the conquest of Mexico and represents one indigenous perspective on the events. (The Granger Collection, New York)

ANALYZING THE IMAGE What role does Doña Marina (far right) appear to be playing in this image? Does she appear to be subservient or equal to Cortés (right, seated)? How did the painter indicate her identity as non-Spanish?

CONNECTIONS How do you think the native rulers negotiating with Cortés might have viewed Doña Marina? What about a Spanish viewer of this image? What does the absence of other women suggest about the role of women in these societies?

Montezuma refrained from attacking the Spaniards as they advanced toward his capital and welcomed Cortés and his men into Tenochtitlán. Other native leaders attacked the Spanish, but Montezuma relied on the advice of his state council, itself divided, and on the dubious loyalty of tribute-paying communities subjugated by the Mexica. Montezuma's long hesitation proved disastrous. When Cortés took Montezuma hostage, the emperor's influence over his people crumbled.

During the ensuing attacks and counterattacks, Montezuma was killed. The Spaniards and their allies escaped from the city and began gathering forces and making new alliances against the Mexica. In May 1510 Cortés led a second, much larger assault on Tenochtitlán. The Spanish victory in late summer 1521 was hard-won and greatly aided by the effects of smallpox, which had weakened and reduced the Mexica population. After the defeat of Tenochtitlán, Cortés and other conquistadors began the systematic conquest of Mexico. Over time a series of indigenous kingdoms fell under Spanish domination, although not without decades of resistance.

Inca Empire The vast and sophisticated Peruvian empire centered at the capital city of Cuzco that was at its peak from 1438 until 1532.

More surprising than the defeat of the Mexicas was the fall of the remote **Inca Empire** in Peru. Like the Mexicas, they had created a vast empire that rivaled that of the Europeans in population and complexity. However, by the time of the Spanish invasion the Inca Empire had been weakened by a civil war over succession and an epidemic of disease, possibly smallpox.

The Spanish conquistador Francisco Pizarro (ca. 1475–1541) landed on the northern coast of Peru on May 13, 1532, the very day Atahualpa (ah-tuh-WAHL-puh) won control of the empire after five years of fighting his brother for the throne. As Pizarro advanced across the Andes toward Cuzco, the capital of the Inca Empire, Atahualpa was also heading there for his coronation.

Atahualpa sent envoys to greet the Spanish and invite them to meet him in the provincial town of Cajamarca. His plan was to lure the Spaniards into a trap, seize their horses and ablest men for his army, and execute the rest. Instead, the Spaniards ambushed and captured him, collected an enormous ransom in gold, and then executed him in 1533. The Spanish then marched on to Cuzco, profiting once again from internal conflicts to form alliances with local peoples. When Cuzco fell in 1533, the Spanish plundered immense riches in gold and silver.

As with the Mexica, decades of violence and resistance followed the defeat of the Incan capital. Nevertheless, the Spanish conquest opened a new chapter in European relations with the New World. It was not long before rival European nations attempted to forge their own overseas empires.

Quick Review
How did previous knowledge of and experience with the Afroeurasian trade system shape European expansion in the fifteenth and early sixteenth centuries?

What was the impact of conquest?

The growing European presence in the New World transformed its land and its peoples forever. Violence and disease wrought devastating losses, while surviving peoples encountered new political, social, and economic organizations imposed by Europeans. Although the exchange of goods and people between Europe and the New World brought diseases to the Americas, it also gave both the New and Old Worlds new crops that eventually altered consumption patterns across the globe.

As important, for the first time, a truly global economy emerged in the sixteenth and seventeenth centuries, and it forged new links among far-flung peoples, cultures, and societies. The ancient civilizations of Europe, Africa, the Americas, and Asia confronted each other in new and rapidly evolving ways. Those confrontations often led to conquest, forced migration, and brutal exploitation, but they also contributed to cultural exchange and renewal.

Colonial Administration

Columbus, Cortés, and Pizarro had claimed the lands they had discovered for the Spanish crown. How were these lands governed? Already in 1503, the Spanish had granted the port of Seville a monopoly over all traffic to the New World and established the House of Trade to oversee economic matters. In 1524 Spain added to this body the Royal and Supreme

Council of the Indies, with authority over all colonial affairs subject to approval by the king. Spanish territories themselves were divided into **viceroyalties** or administrative divisions (see Map 16.2).

Spanish Viceroyalties in the New World
New Spain: Created in 1525 with Mexico City as its capital
Peru: Created in 1542 with Lima as its capital
New Granada: Created in 1717 with Bogotá as its capital
La Plata: Created in 1776 with Buenos Aires as its capital

Within each territory, the viceroy, or imperial governor, exercised broad military and civil authority as the direct representative of Spain. The viceroy presided over the *audiencia* (ow-dee-EHN-see-ah), a board of judges that served as his advisory council and the highest judicial body. Later, King Charles III (r. 1759–1788) introduced the system of intendants to Spain's New World territories. These royal officials possessed broad military, administrative, and financial authority within their intendancies, smaller divisions within each viceroyalty, and were responsible not to the viceroy but to the monarchy in Madrid.

viceroyalties The name for the four administrative units of Spanish possessions in the Americas: New Spain, Peru, New Granada, and La Plata.

The Portuguese governed their colony of Brazil in a similar manner. After the union of the crowns of Portugal and Spain in 1580, Spanish administrative forms were introduced. Local officials called *corregidores* (kuh-REH-gih-dawr-eez) held judicial and military powers. Royal policies placed severe restrictions on Brazilian industries that might compete with those of Portugal and Spain.

The Impact of European Settlement on the Lives of Indigenous Peoples

Before Columbus's arrival, the Americas were inhabited by thousands of groups of indigenous peoples with different languages and cultures. These groups ranged from hunter-gatherer tribes organized into tribal confederations to large-scale agriculture-based empires connecting bustling cities and towns.

The lives of these indigenous peoples were radically transformed by the arrival of Europeans. In the sixteenth century perhaps two hundred thousand Spaniards immigrated to the New World. To work the cattle ranches, sugar plantations, and silver mines these settlers established, the conquistadors first turned to the indigenous peoples.

The Spanish quickly established the **encomienda system**, in which the Crown granted the conquerors the right to employ groups of Native Americans as laborers or to demand tribute from them in exchange for providing food and shelter. In practice, the encomiendas (ehn-koh-mee-EHN-duhz) were a legalized form of slavery.

encomienda system A system whereby the Spanish crown granted the conquerors the right to forcibly employ groups of Indians; it was a disguised form of slavery.

The new conditions and hardships imposed by conquest and colonization resulted in enormous native population losses. The major cause of death was disease. Having little or no resistance to diseases brought from the Old World, the inhabitants of the New World fell victim to smallpox, typhus, influenza, and other illnesses. Another factor behind the decline in population was overwork. Unaccustomed to forced labor, native workers died in staggering numbers. Moreover, forced labor diverted local people from tending to their own crops, leading to malnutrition, reduced fertility rates, and starvation. Malnutrition

Silver Mine at Potosí The incredibly rich silver mines at Potosí (in modern-day Bolivia) contributed to the intensification of the African slave trade. In New Spain millions of indigenous laborers suffered brutal conditions and death in the silver mines. (Courtesy of The Hispanic Society of America)

Mixed Races The unprecedented mixing of peoples in the Spanish New World colonies inspired great fascination. An elaborate terminology emerged to describe the many possible combinations of indigenous, African, and European blood, which were known collectively as *castas*. This painting belongs to a popular genre of the eighteenth century depicting couples composed of individuals of different ethnic origin and the children produced of their unions. (Schalkwijk/Art Resource, NY)

and hunger in turn lowered resistance to disease. Finally, many indigenous peoples also died through outright violence in warfare.[2]

The Franciscan Bartolomé de Las Casas (1474–1566) documented the brutal treatment of indigenous peoples at the hands of the Spanish, claiming that "of three millions of people which Hispaniola itself did contain, there are left remaining alive scarce three hundred persons."[3] Las Casas and other missionaries asserted that the Indians had human rights, and through their persistent pressure the Spanish emperor Charles V abolished the worst abuses of the encomienda system in 1531.

The pattern of devastating disease and population loss established in the Spanish colonies was repeated everywhere Europeans settled. The best estimate is that the native population declined from roughly 50 million in 1492 to around 9 million by 1700. It is important to note, however, that native populations and cultures did survive the conquest period, sometimes by blending with European incomers and sometimes by maintaining cultural autonomy.

For colonial administrators the main problem posed by the astronomically high death rate was the loss of a subjugated labor force to work the mines and sugar plantations. The search for fresh sources of labor gave birth to the new tragedy of the Atlantic slave trade (see page 425).

The Columbian Exchange

Columbian exchange The exchange of animals, plants, and diseases between the Old and the New Worlds.

The travel of people and goods between the Old and New Worlds led to an exchange of animals, plants, and diseases, a complex process known as the **Columbian exchange**. As we have seen, the introduction of new diseases to the Americas had devastating consequences. But other results of the exchange brought benefits not only to the Europeans but also to native peoples.

Everywhere they settled, the Spanish and Portuguese brought and raised wheat with labor provided by the encomienda system. Grapes and olives brought over from Spain did well in parts of Peru and Chile. Perhaps the most significant introduction to the diet of Native Americans came via the meat and milk of the livestock that the early conquistadors brought with them, including cattle, sheep, and goats. The horse enabled both the Spanish conquerors and native populations to travel faster and farther as well as to transport heavy loads.

In turn, Europeans returned home with many food crops that became central elements of their diet. Crops originating in the Americas included tomatoes as well as many varieties of beans, squash, pumpkins, and peppers. One of the most important of such crops was maize (corn). By the late seventeenth century maize had become a staple in Spain, Portugal, southern France, and Italy, and in the eighteenth century it became one of the chief foods of southeastern Europe. Even more valuable was the nutritious white potato, which slowly spread from west to east—to Ireland, England, and France in the seventeenth century, and to Germany, Poland, Hungary, and Russia in the eighteenth, contributing everywhere to a rise in population.

While the exchange of foods was a great benefit to both cultures, the introduction of European pathogens to the New World had a disastrous impact on the native population. The wave of catastrophic epidemic disease that swept the Western Hemisphere after 1492 can be seen as an extension of the swath of devastation wreaked by the Black Death in the 1300s, first on Asia and then on Europe. The world after Columbus was thus unified by disease as well as by trade and colonization.

Sugar and Early Transatlantic Slavery

As Portuguese explorers began their voyages along the western coast of Africa, one of the first commodities they sought was slaves. In 1444 the first ship returned to Lisbon with a cargo of enslaved Africans. While the first slaves were simply seized by small raiding parties, Portuguese merchants soon found that it was easier to trade with African leaders, who were accustomed to dealing in slaves captured through warfare with neighboring powers. From 1490 to 1530 Portuguese traders brought between three hundred and two thousand black slaves to Lisbon each year.

In this stage of European expansion, the history of slavery became intertwined with the history of sugar. Originally sugar was an expensive luxury that only the very affluent could afford, but population increases and greater prosperity in the fifteenth century led to increasing demand. The establishment of sugar plantations on the Canary and Madeira Islands in the fifteenth century testifies to this demand.

Sugar was a particularly difficult crop to produce for profit. Sugar cultivation was extremely labor intensive and, because sugarcane has a virtually constant growing season, there was no fallow period when workers could recuperate. The demands of sugar production were increased with the invention of roller mills to crush the cane more efficiently. Yields could be augmented, but only if a sufficient labor force was found to supply the mills. Europeans solved the labor problem by forcing first native islanders and then enslaved Africans to perform the backbreaking work.

The transatlantic slave trade began in 1518 when Spanish king Charles I authorized traders to bring African slaves to New World colonies. The Portuguese brought the first slaves to Brazil around 1550; by 1600 four thousand were being imported annually. After its founding in 1621, the Dutch West India Company transported thousands of Africans to Brazil and the Caribbean, mostly to work on sugar plantations. In the late seventeenth century, with the chartering of the Royal African Company, the English got involved in bringing slaves to Barbados and other English colonies in the Caribbean and mainland North America.

Before 1700, when slavers decided it was better business to improve conditions, some 20 percent of slaves died on the voyage from Africa to the Americas.[4] The most common cause of death was dysentery induced by poor-quality food and water, lack of sanitation, and intense crowding. On sugar plantations, death rates among slaves from illness and exhaustion were extremely high, leading to a constant stream of new shipments of slaves from Africa. Driven by rising demands for sugar, cotton, tobacco, and other plantation crops, the tragic transatlantic slave trade reached its height in the eighteenth century.

The Transatlantic Slave Trade

The Birth of the Global Economy

With Europeans' discovery of the Americas and their exploration of the Pacific, the entire world was linked for the first time in history by seaborne trade. The opening of that trade brought into being three successive commercial empires: the Portuguese, the Spanish, and the Dutch.

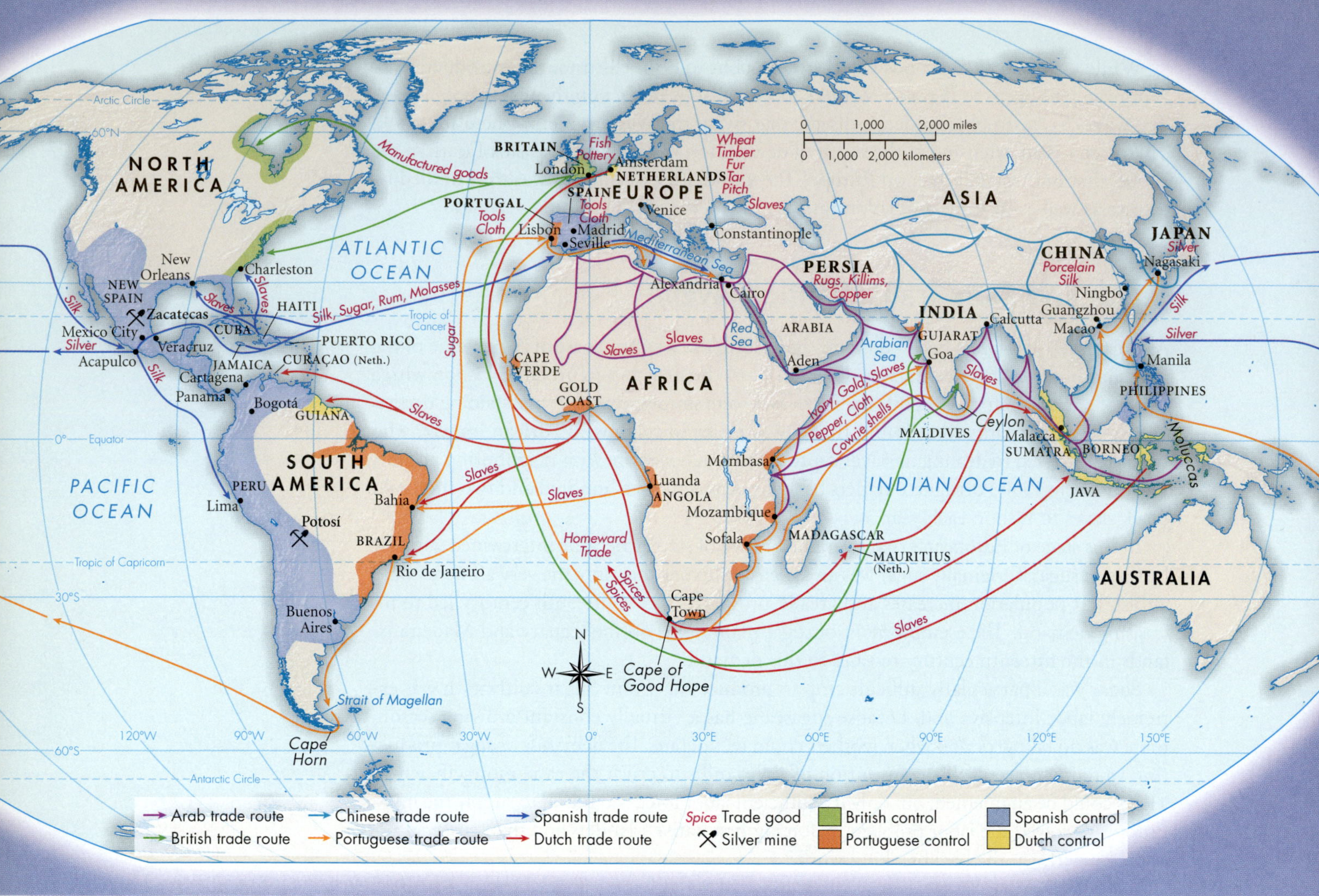

Map 16.3 Seaborne Trading Empires in the Sixteenth and Seventeenth Centuries By the mid-seventeenth century trade linked all parts of the world except for Australia. Notice that trade in slaves was not confined to the Atlantic but involved almost all parts of the world.

The Portuguese were the first worldwide traders. In the sixteenth century they controlled the sea route to India (Map 16.3). From their fortified bases at Goa on the Arabian Sea and at Malacca on the Malay Peninsula, ships carried goods to the Portuguese settlement at Macao in the South China Sea. From Macao Portuguese ships loaded with Chinese silks and porcelains sailed to the Japanese port of Nagasaki and to the Philippine port of Manila, where Chinese goods were exchanged for Spanish silver from New Spain. Throughout Asia the Portuguese traded in slaves. Back to Portugal they brought Asian spices that had been purchased with textiles produced in India and with gold and ivory from East Africa. They also shipped back sugar from their colony in Brazil, produced by African slaves whom they had transported across the Atlantic.

Becoming an imperial power a few decades later than the Portuguese, the Spanish were determined to claim their place in world trade. This was greatly facilitated by the discovery of silver, first at Potosí in modern-day Bolivia and later in Mexico. Silver poured into Europe through the Spanish port of Seville, contributing to steep inflation across Europe. Demand for silver also created a need for slaves to work in the mines. (See "Global Trade: Silver," page 428.)

The Spanish Empire in the New World was basically land-based, but across the Pacific the Spaniards built a seaborne empire centered at Manila in the Philippines. The city of Manila served as the transpacific bridge between Spanish America and China. In Manila, Spanish traders used silver from American mines to purchase Chinese silk for European markets.

In the seventeenth century the Dutch challenged the Spanish and Portuguese Empires, emerging by the end of the century as the most powerful worldwide seaborne trading power. The Dutch Empire was built on spices, and the Dutch East India Company was founded in 1602 with the stated intention of capturing the spice trade from the Portuguese.

The Dutch set their sights on gaining direct access to and control of the Indonesian sources of spices. In return for assisting Indonesian princes in local squabbles and disputes with the Portuguese, the Dutch won broad commercial concessions. Through agreements, seizures, and outright war, they gained control of the western access to the Indonesian archipelago in the first half of the seventeenth century. Gradually they achieved political domination over the archipelago itself. By the 1660s the Dutch had managed to expel the Portuguese from Ceylon and other East Indian islands, thereby establishing control of the lucrative spice trade.

Quick Review
What factors contributed to the precipitous drop in American indigenous populations following European conquest?

How did expansion shape values and beliefs in Europe and the Americas?

The age of overseas expansion heightened Europeans' contacts with the rest of the world. These contacts gave birth to new ideas about the inherent superiority or inferiority of different races, in part to justify European participation in the slave trade. Two great writers of the period both captured and challenged these views. The essays of Michel de Montaigne epitomized a new spirit of skepticism and cultural relativism, while the plays of William Shakespeare reflected his efforts to come to terms with the cultural complexities of his day. Religion became another means of cultural contact, as European missionaries aimed to spread Christianity in both the New World and East Asia, with mixed results.

New Ideas About Race

At the beginning of the transatlantic slave trade, most Europeans would have thought of Africans, if they thought of them at all, as savages and barbarians. They grouped Africans into the despised categories of pagan heathens or Muslim infidels. As Europeans turned to Africa for new sources of slaves, they drew on beliefs about Africans' primitiveness and barbarity to defend slavery and even argue that enslavement benefited Africans by bringing the light of Christianity to heathen peoples.

Over time the institution of slavery fostered a new level of racial inequality. Africans gradually became seen as utterly distinct from and wholly inferior to Europeans. In a transition from rather vague assumptions about African's non-Christian religious beliefs and general lack of civilization, Europeans developed increasingly rigid ideas of racial superiority and inferiority to safeguard the growing profits gained from plantation slavery. Black skin became equated with slavery itself as Europeans at home and in the colonies convinced themselves that blacks were destined by God to serve them as slaves in perpetuity.

After 1700 the emergence of new methods of observing and describing nature led to the use of science to define race. From referring to a nation or an ethnic group, henceforth "race" would be used to describe supposedly biologically distinct groups of people whose physical differences produced differences in culture, character, and intelligence, differences that justified the enslavement of "inferior" races.

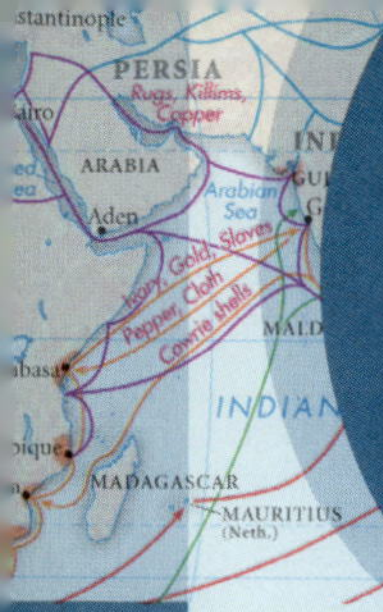

GLOBAL TRADE

Silver

Silver in vast quantities was discovered in 1545 by the Spanish, at an altitude of fifteen thousand feet, at Potosí in unsettled territory conquered from the Inca Empire. A half-century later, 160,000 people lived in Potosí, making it about the size of the city of London. In the second half of the sixteenth century the mine (in present-day Bolivia) yielded perhaps 60 percent of all the silver mined in the world. From Potosí and the mines at Zacatecas and Guanajuato in Mexico, huge quantities of precious metals poured forth.

Mining became the most important industry in the colonies. The Spanish crown claimed the quinto, one-fifth of all precious metals mined in South America, and gold and silver yielded the Spanish monarchy 25 percent of its total income. Seville was the official port of entry for all Spanish silver, although a lively smuggling trade existed.

The real mover of world trade was not Europe, however, but China, which in this period had a population approaching 100 million. By 1450 the collapse of its paper currency led the Ming government to shift to a silver-based currency. Instead of rice, the traditional form of payment, all Chinese now had to pay their taxes in silver. The result was an insatiable demand for the world's production of silver.

Japan was China's original source, and the Japanese continued to ship large quantities of silver ore until the depletion of its mines near the end of the seventeenth century. The discovery of silver in the New World provided a vast and welcome new supply for the Chinese market. In 1571 the Spanish founded a port city at Manila in the Philippines to serve as a bridge point for bringing silver to Asia. Throughout the seventeenth century Spanish galleons annually carried 2 million pesos (or more than fifty tons) of silver from Acapulco to Manila, where Chinese merchants carried it on to China. Even more silver reached China through exchange with European merchants who purchased Chinese goods using silver shipped across the Atlantic.

In exchange for silver, the Chinese traded high-quality finished goods much desired by elites across the world, including fine silks, porcelain, and spices. To ensure continued demand for their products, enterprising Chinese merchants adapted them to Western tastes.

Silver had a mixed impact on the regions involved. Spain's immense profits from silver paid for the tremendous expansion of its empire and for the large armies that defended it. However, the easy flow of money also dampened economic innovation. It exacerbated the rising inflation Spain was already experiencing in the mid-sixteenth century. When the profitability of the silver mines diminished in the 1640s, Spain's power was fundamentally undercut.

China experienced similarly mixed effects. On the one hand, the need for finished goods to trade for silver led to the rise of a merchant class and a new specialization of regional production. On the other hand, the inflation resulting from the influx of silver weakened the finances of the Ming Dynasty. As the purchasing power of silver declined in China, so did the value of silver taxes. The ensuing fiscal crisis helped bring down the Ming and led to the rise of the Qing in 1644. Ironically, the two states that benefited the most from silver also experienced political decline as a direct result of their reliance on it.

Silver ore mined at Potosí thus built the first global trade system in history. Previously, a long-standing Afroeurasian trading world had involved merchants and consumers from the three Old World continents. Once Spain opened a trade route across the Pacific through Manila, all continents except Australia and Antarctica were enduringly linked.

Michel de Montaigne and Cultural Curiosity

Racism was not the only possible reaction to the new worlds emerging in the sixteenth century. Decades of religious fanaticism, bringing civil anarchy and war, led both Catholics and Protestants to doubt that any one faith contained absolute truth. Added to these doubts was the discovery of peoples in the New World who had radically different ways of life. These shocks helped produce ideas of skepticism and cultural relativism in the sixteenth and seventeenth centuries. Skepticism is a school of thought founded on doubt that total certainty or definitive knowledge is ever attainable. Cultural relativism suggests that one culture is not necessarily superior to another, just different. Both notions found expression in the work of Frenchman Michel de Montaigne (MEE-shel duh mahn-TAYN; 1533–1592).

Montaigne developed a new literary genre, the essay—from the French *essayer*, meaning "to test or try"—to express his thoughts and ideas. Published in 1580, Montaigne's *Essays* consisted of short personal reflections. Intending to be accessible to ordinary people, Montaigne wrote in French rather than in Latin and used an engaging conversational style.

Map 16.4 The Global Silver Trade

Silver remained a crucial element in world trade through the nineteenth century. When Mexico won independence from Spain in 1821, it began to mint its own silver dollar, which became the most prized coin in trade in East Asia. By the beginning of the twentieth century, when the rest of the world had adopted gold as the standard of currency, only China and Mexico remained on the silver standard, testimony to the central role this metal had played in their histories.

Montaigne's essay "On Cannibals" reveals the impact of overseas discoveries on his consciousness. In contrast to the prevailing views of the time, he rejected the notion that one culture is superior to another. Speaking of native Brazilians, he wrote:

> *I find that there is nothing barbarous and savage in this nation [Brazil], . . . except, that everyone gives the title of barbarism to everything that is not according to his usage; as, indeed, we have no other criterion of truth and reason, than the example and pattern of the opinions and customs of the place wherein we live.*[5]

In his own time and throughout the seventeenth century, few would have agreed with Montaigne's challenging of European superiority. The publication of his ideas, however, contributed to a basic shift in attitudes. Montaigne inaugurated an era of doubt. "Wonder," he said, "is the foundation of all philosophy, research is the means of all learning, and ignorance is the end."[6]

William Shakespeare and His Influence

In addition to marking the introduction of the essay as a literary genre, the period fostered remarkable creativity in other branches of literature. England—especially in the late sixteenth and early seventeenth centuries—witnessed remarkable literary expression.

The undisputed master of the period was the dramatist William Shakespeare, whose genius lay in the originality of his characterizations, the diversity of his plots, his understanding of human psychology, and his unsurpassed gift for language. Born in 1564, Shakespeare was a Renaissance man with a deep appreciation of classical culture, individualism, and humanism.

Like Montaigne's, Shakespeare's work reveals the impact of new connections between Europeans and peoples of other cultures. The title character of *Othello* is described as a "Moor of Venice." In Shakespeare's day, the word *moor* referred to Muslims of Moroccan or North African origin, including those who had migrated to the Iberian Peninsula. It could also be applied, though, to natives of the Iberian Peninsula who converted to Islam or to non-Muslim Berbers in North Africa. To complicate things even more, references in the play to Othello as "black" in skin color have led many to believe that Shakespeare intended him to be a sub-Saharan African. This confusion in the play reflects the uncertainty in Shakespeare's own day about racial and religious classifications.

The character of Othello is both vilified in racist terms by his enemies and depicted as a brave warrior, a key member of the city's military leadership, and a man capable of winning the heart of an aristocratic white woman. Shakespeare's play thus demonstrates both the intolerance of contemporary society and the possibility for some individuals to look beyond racial stereotypes.

Shakespeare's last play, *The Tempest*, displays a similar interest in race and race relations. The plot involves the stranding on an island of sorcerer Prospero and his daughter, Miranda. There Prospero finds and raises Caliban, a native of the island, whom he instructs in his own language and religion. After Caliban's attempted rape of Miranda, Prospero enslaves him, earning the rage and resentment of his erstwhile pupil. Modern scholars often note the echoes between this play and the realities of imperial conquest and settlement in Shakespeare's day. It is no accident, they argue, that the playwright portrayed Caliban as a monstrous dark-skinned island native who was best-suited for slavery. However, Shakespeare himself borrows words from Montaigne's essay "On Cannibals," suggesting that he may have intended to criticize, rather than endorse, racial intolerance.

Religious Conversion in the New World

Converting indigenous people to Christianity was a key ambition for all European powers in the New World. Galvanized by the desire to spread their religion and prevent any gains by Protestants, Catholic powers actively sponsored missionary efforts. Franciscans, Dominicans, Jesuits, and members of other religious orders who accompanied the conquistadors and subsequent settlers established Catholic missions throughout Spanish and Portuguese colonies. Later French explorers were also accompanied by missionaries who preached to the Native American tribes with whom they traded.

Rather than a straightforward imposition of Christianity, conversion entailed a complex process of cultural exchange. Catholic friars were among the first Europeans to seek understanding of native cultures and languages as part of their effort to render Christianity comprehensible to indigenous people. In addition to spreading Christianity, missionaries taught indigenous peoples European methods of agriculture and instilled loyalty to colonial masters. In turn, Christian ideas and practices in the New World took on a distinctive character. For example, a sixteenth-century apparition of the Virgin Mary in Mexico City, known as the Virgin of Guadalupe, became a central icon of Spanish-American Catholicism.

Missionaries' success in the New World varied over time and space. In Central and South America large-scale conversion forged enduring Catholic cultures in Portuguese and Spanish colonies. Conversion efforts in seventeenth-century North America were less effective due to the scattered nature of settlement and the lesser integration of native people into the colonial community. On the whole, Protestants were less active than Catholics as missionaries, although some dissenters like Quakers and Methodists did seek converts among native people. Efforts to Christianize indigenous peoples in the New World were paralleled by missionary work by the Jesuits and other orders in the Far East.

Quick Review
How did the discovery and colonization of the New World change Europeans' sense of themselves and their place in the world?

Connections

JUST THREE YEARS separated Martin Luther's attack on the Catholic Church in 1517 and Ferdinand Magellan's discovery of the Pacific Ocean in 1520. Within a few short years western Europeans' religious unity and notions of terrestrial geography were shattered. Old medieval certainties about Heaven and earth collapsed. In the ensuing decades Europeans struggled to come to terms with religious differences among Protestants and Catholics at home and with the multitudes of new peoples and places they encountered abroad. While some Europeans were fascinated and inspired by this new diversity, too often the result was violence. Europeans endured decades of religious civil war, and indigenous peoples overseas suffered massive population losses as a result of European warfare, disease, and exploitation. Tragically, both Catholic and Protestant religious leaders condoned the trade in slaves that was to bring suffering and death to millions of Africans.

Even as the voyages of discovery contributed to the fragmentation of European culture, they also factored into state centralization and consolidation in the longer term. Henceforth, competition to gain overseas colonies became an integral part of European politics. Spain's investment in conquest proved spectacularly profitable, and yet, the ultimate result was a weakening of its power. Over time the Netherlands, England, and France also reaped tremendous profits from colonial trade, which helped them build modernized, centralized states.

The most important consequence of the European voyages of discovery was the creation of enduring contacts among five of the seven continents of the globe—Europe, Asia, Africa, North America, and South America. From the sixteenth century onward, the peoples of the world were increasingly entwined in divergent forms of economic, social, and cultural exchange. Our modern era of globalization had begun.

- **For a list of suggested readings for this chapter, visit** *bedfordstmartins.com/mckayworldunderstanding*.
- **For primary sources from this period, see** *Sources of World Societies*, Second Edition.
- **For Web sites, images, and documents related to topics in this chapter, see Make History at** *bedfordstmartins.com/mckayworldunderstanding*.

Chapter 16 Study Guide

To do these exercises online, go to bedfordstmartins.com/mckayworldunderstanding.

Step 1 GETTING STARTED

Below are basic terms about this period in global history. Can you identify each term below and explain why it matters?

TERMS	WHO (OR WHAT) AND WHEN	WHY IT MATTERS
bride wealth, p. 409		
caravel, p. 414		
Ptolemy's *Geography*, p. 414		
Treaty of Tordesillas, p. 418		
conquistador, p. 420		
Mexica Empire, p. 420		
Inca Empire, p. 422		
viceroyalties, p. 423		
encomienda system, p. 423		
Columbian exchange, p. 424		

Step 2 MOVING BEYOND THE BASICS

The exercise below requires a more advanced understanding of the chapter material. Examine the nature and impact of Spanish exploration and conquest in the Americas by filling in the chart below with descriptions of the motives behind Spanish expansion across the Atlantic. Next, identify key Spanish conquests and discoveries and the institutions of Spanish rule in the Americas. Finally, describe the impact of Spanish conquest in the New World and Europe. When you are finished, consider the following questions: How do the motives you listed help explain the course of Spanish expansion in the New World? Were the ambitions of the men who carried out Spain's conquests always consistent with those of the crown? What intended and unintended consequences resulted from Spanish expansion?

MOTIVES	CONQUESTS AND DISCOVERIES	INSTITUTIONS OF SPANISH RULE	IMPACT IN THE NEW WORLD AND EUROPE

Step 3

PUTTING IT ALL TOGETHER

Now that you've reviewed key elements of the chapter, take a step back and try to see the big picture. Remember to use specific examples from the chapter in your answers.

THE AFROEURASIAN TRADE WORLD BEFORE COLUMBUS

- Which states were at the center of global trade prior to 1492? Why?
- Why were Europeans at a trading disadvantage prior to 1492? How did geography limit European participation in world trade? What role did Europe's economy and material culture play in this context?

DISCOVERY AND CONQUEST

- In your opinion, what was the most important motive behind European expansion? What evidence can you provide to support your position?

- What was the Columbian exchange? How did it transform both Europe and the Americas?

CHANGING VALUES AND BELIEFS

- How did European expansion give rise to new ideas about race?
- How did expansion complicate Europeans' understanding of themselves and their place in the world?

LOOKING BACK, LOOKING AHEAD

- If Europe was at the periphery of the global trading system prior to 1492, where was it situated by the middle of the sixteenth century? What had changed? What had not?
- What connections can you make between our own experience of globalization in the twenty-first century and the experience of globalization in the sixteenth century? In what ways are the experiences similar? In what ways do they differ?

In Your Own Words Imagine that you must explain Chapter 16 to someone who hasn't read it. What would be the most important points to include and why?

Chapter Endnotes

Chapter 2

1. J. B. Pritchard, ed., *Ancient Near Eastern Texts Relating to the Old Testament*, 3d ed. with Supplement, p. 372. © 1950, 1955, 1969, renewed 1978 by Princeton University Press. Reprinted by permission of Princeton University Press.

Chapter 3

1. Ainslie T. Embree, trans., *Sources of Indian Tradition*, 2d ed. Vol. 1: *From the Beginning to 1800*, p. 148. Copyright © 1988 by Columbia University Press. Reprinted with permission of the publisher.

Chapter 4

1. Patricia Buckley Ebrey, *Chinese Civilization: A Sourcebook,* 2d ed., revised and expanded (New York: Free Press/Macmillan, 1993), p. 11. All quotations from this work reprinted and edited with the permission of The Free Press, a Division of Simon & Schuster Adult Publishing Group. Copyright © 1993 by Patricia Buckley Ebrey. All rights reserved.
2. Edward Shaughnessy, "Western Zhou History," in *The Cambridge History of Ancient China*, ed. M. Loewe and E. Shaughnessy (New York: Cambridge University Press, 1999), p. 336. Reprinted with the permission of Cambridge University Press and Edward L. Shaughnessy.
3. Patricia Buckley Ebrey, *The Cambridge Illustrated History of China* (Cambridge: Cambridge University Press, 1996), p. 34. Reprinted with permission of Cambridge University Press.
4. Victor H. Mair, Nancy S. Steinhardt, and Paul Goldin, ed., *Hawai'i Reader in Traditional Chinese Culture* (Honolulu: University of Hawai'i Press, 2005), p. 117. Copyright © 2005 by University of Hawaii Press. Reprinted with permission of the publisher.
5. Ebrey, *Chinese Civilization,* p. 21.
6. Ibid.
7. *Analects* 7.19, 15.30. Translated by Patricia Ebrey.
8. Ebrey, *Chinese Civilization,* p. 26.
9. Ibid., p. 27.
10. Ibid., p. 28, modified.
11. Ibid., p. 28.
12. Ibid.
13. Ibid., p. 33.
14. Ibid., p. 35.

Chapter 5

1. Ahmad Hasan Dani et al., *History of Civilizations of Central Asia* (Paris: UNESCO, 1992), p. 107.

Chapter 8

1. Quoted in E. Patlagean, "Byzantium in the Tenth and Eleventh Centuries," in *A History of Private Life*. Vol. 1: *From Pagan Rome to Byzantium*, ed. P. Ariès and G. Duby (Cambridge, Mass.: Harvard University Press, 1987), p. 573.

Chapter 9

1. See B. F. Stowasser, *Women in the Qur'an, Traditions, and Interpretation* (New York: Oxford University Press, 1994), pp. 94–118.
2. Quoted in B. F. Stowasser, "The Status of Women in Early Islam," in *Muslim Women,* ed. F. Hussain (New York: St. Martin's Press, 1984), p. 25.
3. Quoted ibid., pp. 25–26.
4. F. E. Peters, *A Reader on Classical Islam* (Princeton: Princeton University Press, 1994), p. 250.

Chapter 10

1. T. Spear, "Bantu Migrations," in *Problems in African History: The Precolonial Centuries,* p. 98.
2. J. S. Trimingham, *Islam in West Africa* (Oxford: Oxford University Press, 1959), pp. 6–9.
3. R. A. Austen, "The Trans-Saharan Slave Trade: A Tentative Census," in *The Uncommon Market: Essays in the Economic History of the Atlantic Slave Trade,* ed. H. A. Gemery and J. S. Hogendorn (New York: Academic Press, 1979), pp. 1–71, esp. p. 66. Used by permission of R. A. Austen.
4. Quoted in A. A. Boahen, "Kingdoms of West Africa, c. A.D. 500–1600," in *The Horizon History of Africa* (New York: American Heritage, 1971), p. 183.
5. This quotation and the one in the next paragraph ("the king of Ghana . . .") appear in E. J. Murphy, *History of African Civilization* (New York: Delta, 1972), pp. 109, 111.
6. Pekka Masonen and Humphrey J. Fisher, "Not Quite Venus from the Waves: The Almoravid Conquest of Ghana in the Modern Historiography of Western Africa," *History in Africa* 23 (1996): 197–232.
7. Austen, "The Trans-Saharan Slave Trade," p. 65; J. H. Harris, *The African Presence in Asia* (Evanston, Ill.: Northwestern University Press, 1971), pp. 3–6, 27–30; P. Wheatley, "Analecta Sino-Africana Recensa," in Neville Chittick and Robert Rotberg, *East Africa and the Orient,* (New York: Africana Publishing, 1975), p. 109.
8. I. Hrbek, ed., *General History of Africa,* vol. 3, *Africa from the Seventh to the Eleventh Century* (Berkeley: University of California Press; New York: UNESCO, 1991), pp. 294–295, 346–347.

Chapter 12

1. Trans. in Denis Sinor, "The Establishment and Dissolution of the Türk Empire," in *The Cambridge History of Early Inner Asia,* ed. Denis Sinor (Cambridge: Cambridge University Press, 1990), p. 307.

Chapter 14

1. Fulcher of Chartres, *A History of the Expedition to Jerusalem,* 1095–1127, trans. Frances Rita Ryan, ed. Harold S. Fink (Knoxville: University of Tennessee Press, 1969), pp. 121–123.
2. Edwin Panofsky, trans. and ed., *Abbot Suger on the Abbey Church of St. Denis and Its Art Treasures* (Princeton, N.J.: Princeton University Press, 1946), p. 101.

Chapter 15

1. Niccolò Machiavelli, *The Prince*, trans. Leo Paul S. de Alvarez (Prospect Heights, Ill.: Waveland Press, 1980), p. 101.

2. Quoted in E. H. Harbison, *The Age of Reformation* (Ithaca, N.Y.: Cornell University Press, 1963), p. 284.
3. Ibid., p. 137.

Chapter 16

1. Quoted in C. M. Cipolla, *Guns, Sails, and Empires: Technological Innovation and the Early Phases of European Expansion, 1400–1700* (New York: Minerva Press, 1965), p. 132.
2. Thomas Benjamin, *The Atlantic World: Europeans, Africans, Indians and Their Shared History, 1400–1900* (Cambridge, U.K.: Cambridge University Press, 2009), pp. 35–59.
3. Quoted in C. Gibson, ed., *The Black Legend: Anti-Spanish Attitudes in the Old World and the New* (New York: Knopf, 1971), pp. 74–75.
4. Herbert S. Klein, "Profits and the Causes of Mortality," in *The Atlantic Slave Trade*, ed. David Northrup (Lexington, Mass.: D. C. Heath and Co., 1994), p. 116.
5. C. Cotton, trans., *The Essays of Michel de Montaigne* (New York: A. L. Burt, 1893), pp. 207, 210.
6. Ibid., p. 523.

Index

A Note About the Index: Key terms and the pages where they are defined appear in boldface. Letters in parentheses following page numbers refer to:

(i) illustrations, including photographs and artifacts
(f) figures, including charts, graphs, and tables
(m) maps
(b) boxed features

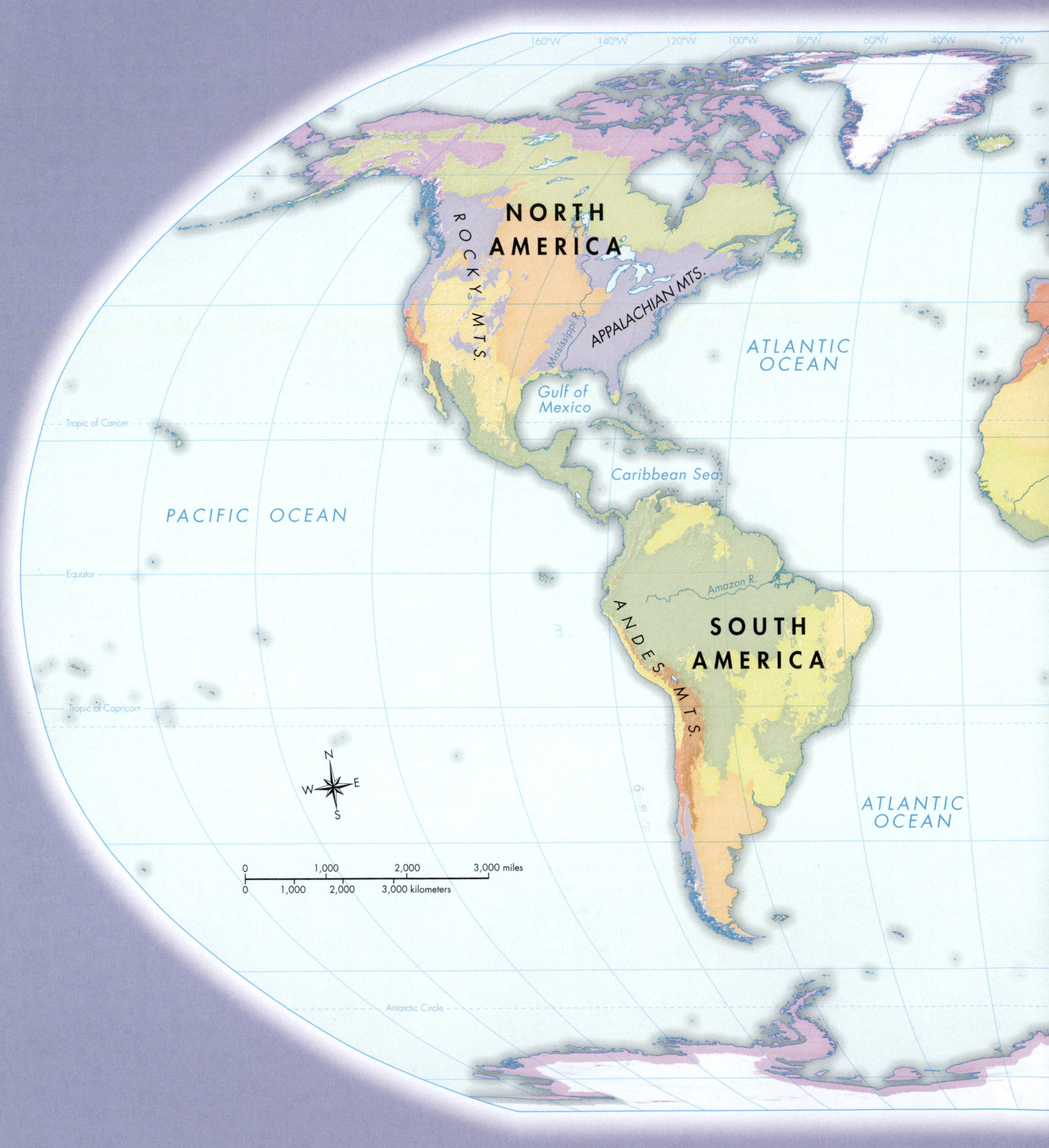
160°W
140°W
120°W
100°W
80°W
60°W
40°W
20°W
Arctic Circle
NORTH AMERICA
ROCKY MTS.
APPALACHIAN MTS.
Mississippi R.
ATLANTIC OCEAN
Gulf of Mexico
Tropic of Cancer
Caribbean Sea
PACIFIC OCEAN
Equator
Amazon R.
ANDES MTS.
SOUTH AMERICA
Tropic of Capricorn
N
W
E
S
ATLANTIC OCEAN
0
1,000
2,000
3,000 miles
0
1,000
2,000
3,000 kilometers
Antarctic Circle

EUROPE
ALPS
URAL MTS.
Volga R.
Ob R.
ASIA
GOBI
Yellow R. (Huang He)
Yangzi R.
HIMALAYA MTS.
Ganges R.
Mediterranean Sea
SAHARA
ARABIAN DESERT
Nile R.
AFRICA
Congo R.
Zambezi R.
KALAHARI DESERT
Arabian Sea
Bay of Bengal
South China Sea
PACIFIC OCEAN
INDIAN OCEAN
AUSTRALIA
Arctic Circle
Tropic of Cancer
Equator
Tropic of Capricorn
Antarctic Circle
20°E
40°E
60°E
80°E
100°E
120°E
140°E
160°E
80°N
60°N
40°N
20°N
0°
20°S
40°S
60°S
80°S
Vegetation zones
Tundra
Northern forest
Temperate forest
Temperate grassland
Desert and dry shrub
Mediterranean shrub
Mountain grassland
Tropical grassland and savanna
Tropical forest
Permanent ice cover

THE CONTEMPORARY WORLD
80°N
60°N
40°N
20°N
0°
Equator
20°S
40°S
60°S
80°S
160°W
140°W
120°W
100°W
80°W
60°W
40°W
20°W
Greenland
(Den.)
ICELAND
Alaska
(U.S.)
CANADA
UNITED STATES
UNITED KINGDOM
IRELAND
FRANCE
SPAIN
PORTUGAL
ATLANTIC OCEAN
Azores
(Port.)
Bermuda (U.K.)
MOROCCO
Canary Is.
(Sp.)
Western Sahara
(Mor.)
MEXICO
BAHAMAS
DOMINICAN REPUBLIC
HAITI
CUBA
JAMAICA
BELIZE
Puerto Rico (U.S.)
ST. KITTS AND NEVIS
ANTIGUA AND BARBUDA
Guadeloupe (Fr.)
DOMINICA
Martinique (Fr.)
ST. VINCENT AND THE GRENADINES
ST. LUCIA
BARBADOS
GRENADA
TRINIDAD AND TOBAGO
GUYANA
SURINAME
French Guiana (Fr.)
GUATEMALA
HONDURAS
EL SALVADOR
NICARAGUA
COSTA RICA
PANAMA
VENEZUELA
COLOMBIA
ECUADOR
CAPE VERDE
MAURITANIA
SENEGAL
GAMBIA
MALI
GUINEA-BISSAU
GUINEA
SIERRA LEONE
LIBERIA
CÔTE D'IVOIRE
BURKINA FASO
Hawaii (U.S.)
PACIFIC OCEAN
Galápagos Is.
(Ec.)
BRAZIL
PERU
BOLIVIA
SAMOA
TONGA
PARAGUAY
CHILE
Easter I.
(Chile)
N
E
W
S
URUGUAY
ATLANTIC OCEAN
ARGENTINA
0
1,500
3,000 miles
0
1,500
3,000 kilometers
Falkland Is.
(U.K.)

ARCTIC OCEAN
RUSSIAN FEDERATION
NORWAY
SWEDEN
FINLAND
ESTONIA
LATVIA
LITHUANIA
DEN.
NETH.
GERMANY
POLAND
BELARUS
LUX.
CZ.
SLK.
UKRAINE
AUS.
HUNG.
MOLDOVA
SLN.
ROMANIA
SWITZ.
CR.
SE.
ITALY
B.H.
BULGARIA
MO.
KO.
ALB.
MAC.
GREECE
GEORGIA
ARMENIA
TURKEY
AZERBAIJAN
KAZAKHSTAN
UZBEKISTAN
KYRGYZSTAN
TURKMENISTAN
TAJIKISTAN
MONGOLIA
N. KOREA
S. KOREA
JAPAN
CHINA
MALTA
TUNISIA
CYPRUS
SYRIA
LEBANON
ISRAEL
IRAQ
IRAN
AFGHANISTAN
PAKISTAN
Gaza Strip
West Bank
JORDAN
KUWAIT
BAHRAIN
BHUTAN
NEPAL
ALGERIA
LIBYA
EGYPT
SAUDI ARABIA
QATAR
UNITED ARAB EMIRATES
OMAN
BANGLADESH
INDIA
MYANMAR (BURMA)
LAOS
VIETNAM
Taiwan
PACIFIC OCEAN
NIGER
CHAD
SUDAN
YEMEN
ERITREA
DJIBOUTI
THAILAND
CAMBODIA
PHILIPPINES
Mariana Is. (U.S.)
Guam (U.S.)
MARSHALL IS.
NIGERIA
BENIN
TOGO
CENTRAL AFRICAN REP.
SOUTH SUDAN
ETHIOPIA
MALDIVES
SRI LANKA
BRUNEI
MALAYSIA
PALAU
FEDERATED STATES OF MICRONESIA
CAMEROON
SOMALIA
EQ. GUINEA
GABON
CONGO
UGANDA
RWANDA
KENYA
SINGAPORE
NAURU
KIRIBATI
SÃO TOMÉ PRÍNCIPE
DEM. REP. OF THE CONGO
BURUNDI
TANZANIA
COMOROS
SEYCHELLES
INDIAN OCEAN
INDONESIA
PAPUA NEW GUINEA
TUVALU
SOLOMON IS.
ANGOLA
ZAMBIA
MALAWI
TIMOR LESTE
VANUATU
FIJI
ZIMBABWE
MADAGASCAR
NAMIBIA
BOTSWANA
MAURITIUS
New Caledonia (Fr.)
AUSTRALIA
MOZAMBIQUE
SOUTH AFRICA
SWAZILAND
LESOTHO
NEW ZEALAND
Tasmania (Aust.)
ABBREVIATIONS
ALB. ALBANIA
AUS. AUSTRIA
BEL. BELGIUM
B.H. BOSNIA AND HERZEGOVINA
CR. CROATIA
CZ. CZECH REPUBLIC
DEN. DENMARK
HUNG. HUNGARY
KO. KOSOVO
LUX. LUXEMBOURG
MAC. MACEDONIA
MO. MONTENEGRO
NETH. NETHERLANDS
SE. SERBIA
SLK. SLOVAKIA
SLN. SLOVENIA
SWITZ. SWITZERLAND
ANTARCTICA
20°E
40°E
60°E
80°E
100°E
120°E
140°E
160°E

About the Authors

John P. McKay (Ph.D., University of California, Berkeley) is professor emeritus at the University of Illinois. He has written or edited numerous works, including the Herbert Baxter Adams Prize–winning book *Pioneers for Profit: Foreign Entrepreneurship and Russian Industrialization, 1885–1913*.

Bennett D. Hill (Ph.D., Princeton University), late of Georgetown University, published *Church and State in the Middle Ages* and numerous articles and reviews, and was one of the contributing editors to *The Encyclopedia of World History*. He was also a Benedictine monk of St. Anselm's Abbey in Washington, D.C.

John Buckler (Ph.D., Harvard University), late of the University of Illinois, published numerous works, including *Theban Hegemony, 371–362 B.C.*; *Philip II and the Sacred War*; and *Aegean Greece in the Fourth Century B.C.* With Hans Beck, he most recently published *Central Greece and the Politics of Power in the Fourth Century*.

Patricia Buckley Ebrey (Ph.D., Columbia University), professor of history at the University of Washington in Seattle, specializes in China. She has published many journal articles and *The Cambridge Illustrated History of China* as well as numerous monographs. In 2010 she won the Shimada Prize for outstanding work of East Asian Art History for *Accumulating Culture: The Collections of Emperor Huizong*.

Roger B. Beck (Ph.D., Indiana University) is Distinguished Professor of African and twentieth-century world history at Eastern Illinois University. His publications include *The History of South Africa*, a translation of P. J. van der Merwe's *The Migrant Farmer in the History of the Cape Colony, 1657–1842*, and more than a hundred articles, book chapters, and reviews. He is a former treasurer and Executive Council member of the World History Association.

Clare Haru Crowston (Ph.D., Cornell University) teaches at the University of Illinois, where she is currently associate professor of history. She is the author of *Fabricating Women: The Seamstresses of Old Regime France, 1675–1791*, which won the Berkshire and Hagley Prizes. She edited two special issues of the *Journal of Women's History*, has published numerous journal articles and reviews, and is a past president of the Society for French Historical Studies.

Merry E. Wiesner-Hanks (Ph.D., University of Wisconsin–Madison) is a UWM Distinguished Professor and chair in the Department of History at the University of Wisconsin–Milwaukee. She is the senior editor of the *Sixteenth Century Journal* and the author or editor of more than twenty books, most recently *The Marvelous Hairy Girls: The Gonzales Sisters and Their Worlds* and *Gender in History*. She is the former Chief Reader for Advanced Placement World History.

About the Cover Art

Serving Boy from a Fresco at Chihil Soutoun

The Safavid dynasty in Persia flourished under Shah Abbas II (r. 1642–1666). In the capital, Isfahan, he built a new audience hall, or Chihil Soutoun, and had its walls covered with murals. The outer rooms where foreign ambassadors were received were painted in an up-to-date European style, but the smaller, more private rooms were painted in a traditional style. This picture of a serving boy is from one of the private rooms.